Picture credits:
Front cover photograph: La Maison Aux Volets Bleus, Venasque, Vaucluse,
Provence
All other photographs were taken from the AA's picture library
(©AA photo library)
All other photos were supplied by the proprietors and managers of the
establishments featured in this guide

Editorial contributions from:
Jim Barker, Christopher Blackford and Sarah Catliff

French regional maps are based on maps supplied by the French Tourist
Office and reproduced with their kind permission.

Typeset and colour repro by Microset Graphics Ltd, Basingstoke
Printed and bound by Gráficas Estella, SA, Navarra, Spain

Advertisement Sales:
Head of Advertisement Sales: Christopher Heard, direct line 01256 491544
Advertisement Production: Karen Weeks, direct line 01256 491545

A CIP catalogue record for this book is available from the British Library

ISBN: 0 7495 17565

AA ref no: 10057

Published by AA Publishing, a trading name of Automobile Association
Developments Limited, whose registered office is Norfolk House, Priestley
Road, Basingstoke, Hampshire, RG24 9NY. Registered number 1878835

▐▐ Contents ▐▐

"Regions & *Départements***"**

In this book France has been divided into 21 regions as numbered and colour-coded on the map opposite. Individual maps of these regions appear at the beginning of each section. The map also shows the *départements* into which France is divided. Each *département* has a standard number, as shown on the map and in the key, which for postal purposes replaces its name. These numbers also form part of the registration number of French cars, thus indicating the *département* in which the car was registered. The *départements* are listed alphabetically within their regions.

BRITTANY	
Côtes d'Armor	22
Finistère	29
Ille-et-Vilaine	35
Morbihan	56

NORMANDY	
Calvados	14
Eure	27
Manche	50
Orne	61
Seine-Maritime	76

NORD/PAS-DE-CALAIS	
Nord	59
Pas-de-Calais	62

PICARDY	
Aisne	02
Oise	60
Somme	80

CHAMPAGNE-ARDENNE	
Ardennes	08
Aube	10
Haute-Marne	51
Marne	52

LORRAINE VOSGES	
Meurthe-et-Moselle	54
Meuse	55
Moselle	57
Vosges	88

ALSACE	
Bas-Rhin	67
Haut-Rhin	68

WESTERN LOIRE	
Loire-Atlantique	44
Maine-et-Loire	49
Mayenne	53
Sarthe	72
Vendeé	85

VAL DE LOIRE	
Cher	18
Eure-et-Loir	28
Indre	36
Indre-et-Loir	37
Loir-et-Cher	41
Loiret	45

PARIS & ILE DE FRANCE	
Essonne	91
Hauts-de-Seine	92
Paris	75
Seine-et-Marne	77
Seine-St-Denis	93
Val-de-Marne	94
Val-d'Oise	95
Yvelines	78

BURGUNDY	
Côte-d'Or	21
Nièvre	58
Saône-et-Loire	71
Yonne	89

FRANCHE-COMTE	
Doubs	25
Haute-Saône	70
Jura	39
Territoire-de-Belfort	90

POITOU-CHARENTES	
Charente	16
Charente-Maritime	17
Deux Sèvres	79
Vienne	86

LIMOUSIN	
Corrèze	23
Creuse	19
Haute-Vienne	87

AUVERGNE	
Allier	03
Cantal	15
Haute-Loire	43
Puy-de-Dôme	63

RHONE ALPES	
Ain	01
Ardèche	07
Drôme	26
Haute-Savoie	74
Isère	38
Loire	42
Rhône	69
Savoie	73

AQUITAINE	
Dordogne	24
Gironde	33
Landes	40
Lot-et-Garonne	47
Pyrénées-Atlantiques	64

MIDI-PYRENEES

Ariège	09
Aveyron	12
Gers	32
Haute-Garonne	31
Hautes-Pyrénées	65
Lot	46
Tarn	81
Tarn-et-Garonne	82

LANGUEDOC-ROUSSILLON

Aude	11
Gard	30
Hérault	34
Lozère	48
Pyrénées-Roussillon	66

PROVENCE

Alpes-de-Haute-Provence	04
Bouches-du-Rhône	13
Hautes-Alpes	05
Var	83
Vaucluse	84

COTE D'AZUR

| Alpes Maritimes | 06 |

5

■ Introduction ■

Welcome to the AA's second edition of **Bed & Breakfast in France**, a guide to the wealth of farmhouses, inns, chambres d'hôtes, small hotels and pensions available to holidaymakers.

To make the selection of B&Bs in this guide we have worked in close collaboration with the French Tourist Office in London and its regional departments throughout France to bring you more than 1,500 recommended places to stay stretching the length and breadth of the country.

In the directory, establishments are listed under the village, town or city closest to them, which in turn are listed alphabetically under the appropriate region. Paris is divided into arrondissements (postal districts) and to help you find your way around Paris we have included a map of the Périphérique and central Paris on pages 24/5.

France is divided into twenty one regions (see the map on pages 4/5 showing all regions with their corresponding départements), each with its own character, tradition and cuisine. Each region in the directory begins with an **Essential Facts** introduction, giving information and insight into the history, attractions, a diary of events and festivals, (dates given were correct when we went to press but should be checked on arrival - see below) plus the gastronomic delights of the area. Although we have also given the addresses and phone numbers of the major tourist offices for each region, on arrival at your holiday destination you should always find the local one, which will give you detailed information on the dates and venues of any events and festivals taking place during your stay.

To help you book your stay at a hotel, we have drawn up a standard booking letter and helpful phrases you may wish to use if booking by phone. To help you further we have included a **'France At A Glance'** section - see page 10 - which gives the addresses and phone numbers of all the major ferry companies which sail to the French ports. Also **'Motoring in France'** - see page 13 - which gives advice on motoring abroad, should be read before you set off on your trip.

Once you reach France and find you are spoilt for choice by the vast and varied array of food on offer, we hope our **What's On The Menu?** section will help you. See page 30. Equally, we hope our **Useful French Phrases** section, page 26, will come to your aid at the hotel, in the supermarket, or if your car breaks down.

At the back of the guide you will find an index of location names, with page numbers of where the town or village is listed in the guide.

We have tried to provide as much information as possible about the B&Bs in our directory, but please note that if you wish to have dinner, you may have to order it well in advance, e.g. at breakfast time. Meals are often taken with the family. Unlike hotels, non-residents cannot just drop in for a meal, as French law requires these establishments to provide meals only for residents. If you write to an establishment for further information, do remember to enclose an international reply coupon, and please quote this publication in any enquiry. Although we try to publish accurate and up-to-date information, please remember that any details, and particularly prices, are subject to change without notice. If you have a complaint we strongly advise you to take the matter up with the management there and then, but we should be grateful if you let us know of any dissatisfaction. Please note that all the establishments listed have been classified and inspected by the French Tourist Board and not by the AA Hotel & Restaurant Inspectorate.

"Using the Guide"

ANYTOWN Département Name

Any B&B (Proprietor's name)
3 rue General de Gaulle *29270*
☎123456789. FAX 12345678
From the motorway, follow signs to the centre of town.
Converted from an old watermill, the pension is situated on
the river in the centre of town.
All bedrooms are furnished in traditional rustic style and
many retain the mill's original features of wooden beams and
stone floors. The restaurant specialises in local seafood and
rustic dishes.
In wooded area Near motorway
8 rms (3 bth/shr), (1 with balcony). CTV in lounge. Child
discount available 10 yrs Last d 20.00. Free parking. ROOMS
s55-75FF d90-110FF
MEALS Breakfast 15FF dinner fixed price 35-45FF
CARDS ▨ ▨ ▨ Travellers cheques

1) **TOWN NAME FOLLOWED BY DEPARTMENT NAME**

2) **B&B NAME**

3) **PHONE NUMBER**

4) **ACCOMMODATION DESCRIPTION AND LOCATION DETAILS**

5) **HOTEL FACILITIES**

6) **MEALS & ROOMS**

7) **PAYMENT DETAILS**

1. TOWN NAME

Listed in the directory in alphabetical order by region: Brittany, Normandy, Nord/Pas de Calais, Picardy, Champagne-Ardenne, Lorraine Vosges, Alsace, Western Loire, Val de Loire, Paris and the Ile de France, Burgundy, Franche-Comté, Poitou-Charentes, Limousin, Auvergne, Rhône Alpes, Aquitaine, Midi-Pyrénées, Languedoc-Rousillon, Provence, Côte d'Azur.

After the town name comes the département name. At the back of the book is an index of locations with page numbers of where the town or village is listed in the guide. We have provided simple maps at the beginning of each regional section, so that you can see where in the region a town is, but for driving and precise orientation you will need a large-scale road atlas.

2. ESTABLISHMENT NAME

All the establishments listed in the directory are approved by the French Tourist Office, but there are no official grades as there are for hotels. The proprietor's name follows in brackets. Some of the places listed, particularly farmhouses and private residences, have not given us the name of the establishment, but simply their own name and address. If this is the case, the establishment is referred to as 'B&B'.

The postal address and telephone number follow the hotel name.

3 ADDRESS & TELEPHONE NUMBER

Please see the notes on page 11 about using the telephone in France. The postal code which appears in italics should be used in front of the town name for address purposes eg *29270* ANYTOWN.

4. DESCRIPTION & LOCATION

Descriptions and a summary of the location (e.g. Forest area Near motorway), have been provided by the establishments themselves. We believe the details to be accurate and we have published them in good faith. Where a place has stated that it is 'In town centre' and 'Near Motorway', remember that 'Near Motorway' may refer to the town/village itself, and not to the B&B directly. Similarly, 'In Forest area' may refer to the town or village, not to the grounds of the establishment.

4. ACCOMMODATION DETAILS

The first figure shows the number of letting bedrooms, followed by the numbers of rooms that have en suite bath or shower and WC.

5. CHAMBRE D'HOTE FACILITIES

fmly family bedrooms
CTV/TV colour/black & white television in lounge or in bedrooms. Check when booking
STV satellite TV channels at no extra cost, but check details when booking.
Last d indicates the latest time at which dinner may be ordered

6. ROOMS & MEALS

Prices are provided by proprietors in good faith and are indications not firm quotations. They have also informed us of reductions for stays of more than one night, or special break offers. However, you must check when booking. In some hotels children can sleep in the parents' room at no extra cost. Please check when booking.

Details of the style of food and price range are given. If there is a fixed-price menu(s), this is the price range quoted. If the words '**& alc**' follow, it means an à la carte menu is available and its prices may be much higher than those on the table d'hôte menus.
V meals a choice of vegetarian dishes is normally available, but check first.

7. CREDIT & CHARGE CARDS

- Mastercard
- American Express
- Visa
- Diners
- Travellers cheques

Check the position on credit cards when booking. They may be subject to a surcharge. See the note on Payment.

Useful Information

BOOKING

Book as early as possible, particularly during the peak holiday periods from the beginning of June to the end of September, at public holiday weekends and, in some parts of France, during the skiing season. Some establishments ask for a deposit, or even full payment in advance, especially for one-night bookings from chance callers. Not all, however, will take advance bookings for bed and breakfast for overnight or short stays. Some may not take reservations from mid week in high season.

CANCELLATION

Once the booking has been confirmed, notify the hotel immediately if you are in any doubt as to whether you can keep to your reservation. If your accommodation cannot be re-let you may be liable to pay about two-thirds of the price you would have paid if you had stayed there. A deposit will count towards this payment. Illness is not usually accepted as a release from this contract. You are advised to effect insurance cover, for example, AA Travelsure, against possible cancellation.

LICENCE TO SELL ALCOHOL

Unless otherwise stated, all establishments listed are licensed and resident guests should have no problem in obtaining drinks either with a meal or from the bar.

PAYMENT

Most establishments will only accept Eurocheques in payment of accounts if notice is given and identification (e.g., a cheque card) produced. Not all take Eurocheques or travellers cheques, even from leading banks and agencies. If credit cards are accepted, the information is shown at the end of the entry.

PRICES

Throughout all prices are given in French francs and so will fluctuate with the exchange rate.

Prices given usually refer to the cost of a room per night rather than per person per night. Most include the cost of breakfast in their room rates. If it is not, and we have been able to obtain a price for breakfast, it is shown.

An asterisk (*) against prices indicates 1997 prices have been given by the proprietor.

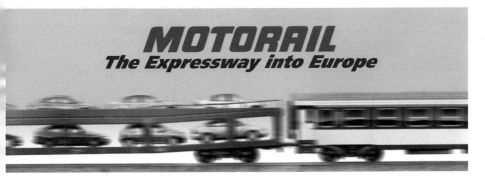

"France at a Glance"

W hat is it about France that draws millions of francophiles back year after year for a taste of la vie française? Is it the chic boulevards of Paris, the sparkling ski slopes of the Alps, sunlit vineyards and sun-baked beaches, coffee and croissants in an undiscovered village or a relaxing picnic in Provence, where the air is fragrant with wild herbs and lavender? France is a land of great contrasts, catering for all tastes and offering an endless choice of enticing destinations, a rich diversity of landscape, cuisine, climate and people, and an exceptional cultural heritage.

Next time you hop across the Channel, consider your destination with care. Before you head off yet again for your annual fix of Mediterranean sunshine, or to the alluring Dordogne, consider the delights of other little-known regions such as Franche-Comté, Gascony or Berry, whose sleepy villages offer visitors a chance to sample the true douceur de vivre of provincial France.

Whichever destination you choose, you won't be disappointed. Each region offers its own character, charm and attractions, and you will soon discover why the French stay at home for their holidays.

AT-A-GLANCE FACTS AND FIGURES

Capital: Paris
IDD code: 33. To call the UK dial 00 44
Currency: Franc (Fr1 = 100 centimes).
At the time of going to press £1 =Frs9.7
Local time: GMT + 1 (summer GMT + 2)
Emergency numbers: Police 17; Fire 18;
Ambulance - dial number given in callbox, or,
if no number given, the police
Business hours: Banks: Mon-Fri 09.00-12.00 &
14.00-16.00
Shops: Mon-Sat 09.00-18.00 (times may vary for
food shops)
Average daily temperature:

Paris	Jan 3° C	May 13°C	Sep 15°C
	Mar 6°C	Jul 18°C	Nov 6°C

TOURIST INFO:

French Tourist Office
178 Piccadilly, London W1V 0AL Tel: 0891 244123
(premium rate information line; 08.30-21.30 weekdays,
09.00-1700 Saturdays)
Monaco Government Tourist and
Convention Office
3-18 Chelsea Garden Market Chelsea Harbour
London SW10 0XE
British Embassy
75383 Paris, Cedex 08, 35 rue de Faubourg St-Honoré
Tel: 0144513100
Consular section
75008 Paris, 16 rue d'Anjou Tel: 0142663810
There are British Consulates in Bordeaux, Lille, Lyon and
Marseille; there are British Consulates with Honorary
Consuls in Biarritz, Boulogne-sur-Mer, Calais, Cherbourg,
Dunkerque (Dunkirk), Le Havre, Nantes, Nice, St Malo-
Dinard and Toulouse

USING THE PHONE IN FRANCE

For all calls inside France dial 0 before the 9-digit
number eg Paris 01 .. .. .., Marseille 04 .. .. ..
To call abroad from France dial 00 and country code.
To call the UK dial 00 44 followed by the UK number
ignoring the first digit (0).
For information and directory assistance dial 12

To use your mobile phone abroad:
● contact your service provider before you leave to
arrange international access

● take your mobile phone handbook with you to ensure
you know how to manually roam onto a foreign
network
● to call the UK dial 00 44 (or use the + key on the
keypad - see your handbook) followed by the UK
number ignoring the first digit (0)

HOW TO GET THERE

Apart from the direct crossing by the Channel Tunnel
(Folkestone-Calais, 35 mins, see French ABC, page 00), the
following ferry services are available:

Short ferry crossings
From Dover to Calais takes 75-90 mins or 45 mins by Lynx
Catamaran

Longer ferry crossings
From Ramsgate to Dunkirk takes 2 hrs 30 mins
From Newhaven to Dieppe takes 4 hrs or 2 hrs 15 mins by
Lynx Catamaran
From Portsmouth to Le Havre takes 5 hrs 30 mins (day); 7
hrs 30 mins / 8 hrs (night)
Caen takes 6 hrs
Cherbourg takes 5 hrs (day); 7 hrs / 8 hrs 15 mins (night)
St Malo takes 8 hrs 45 mins (day); 11 hrs 30 mins (night)
From Poole to Cherbourg takes 4 hrs 15 mins
From Poole to St Malo takes 8 hrs (summer service only)
From Plymouth to Roscoff takes 6 hrs
From Southampton to Cherbourg takes 5 hrs

FERRY COMPANIES

Brittany Ferries
Millbay Docks, Plymouth PL1 3EW
Tel: 01752 221321
The Brittany Centre, Wharf Road, Portsmouth
Tel: 01705 827701
Caen Tel: 31 96 88 80   Cherbourg Tel: 33 43 43 68
Roscoff Tel: 98 29 28 28   St-Malo Tel: 99 40 64 41

Hoverspeed Ltd
International Hoverport, Western Docks, Dover,
Kent CT17 9TG Tel: 01304 240241
Boulogne Tel: 21 30 27 26   Calais Tel: 21 46 14 14

P&O European Ferries
Channel House, Channel View Road, Dover CT17 9TJ
Tel: 01304 203388   Calais Tel: 21 46 04 40
Le Havre Tel: 35 19 78 50   Cherbourg Tel: 33 88 65 70

Sally Ferries

Sally Line Ltd, Argyle Centre, York Street, Ramsgate, Kent CT11 9DS Tel: 01843 595522 0181 858 1127
Dunkirk Tel: 28 21 43 44

Stena Sealink

Charter House, Ashford, Kent Tel: 01233 647047
Calais Tel: 21 46 80 00   Cherbourg Tel: 33 20 43 38
Dieppe Tel: 35 06 39 00

Fast Hoverspeed services

Hoverspeed/Hovercraft from Dover to Calais takes 35 mins. Hoverspeed/Seacat catamaran from Folkestone to Boulogne takes 55 mins.

Car sleeper trains

A daily service operates from Calais to the south of the country

For details of the AA European Routes Service see page 35.

For details of the AA European Routes Service see page 35.

ON THE ROAD

Please refer to Motoring in France on page 13. Remember that during peak holiday times traffic will be very heavy and delays are likely in some places. Remember too that during the month of August most Parisians leave the city for the coast, so all roads leading out of Paris will be packed. In general, times to avoid travelling are at weekends, at the beginning and end of school holidays, before and after public holidays and religious feasts and festival days at religious centres (see list below). Contact local tourist boards for information on road congestion.

Public Holidays

New Year's Day	January 1
Easter Sunday	April 12
Easter Monday	April 13
Labour Day	May 1
V.E Day	May 8
Ascension Day	May 31 - June 1
Bastille Day	July 14
Assumption Day	August 15
All Saints' Day	November 1
Remembrance Day	November 11
Christmas Day	December 25

French School Holidays for 1998

(staggered throughout France)

Winter half-term	February 6th - March 9th
Easter/Spring holiday	April 2 - April 27
Summer	June 30 - September 2
Autumn half-term	October 23 - November 3
Christmas	December 19 - January 4

Garages and service stations

In France garages are generally open from 08.00 to 18.00 (sometimes with a break at midday, 12.00 to 15.00), Monday to Saturday. On Sunday and public holidays fuel and service are often unobtainable, and in some rural areas of France it may be difficult to get repairs done in August, when many firms close for the annual holidays. Ask your local dealer for a list of franchised repairers in Europe before you leave.

Always ask for an estimate before you have your repairs done; it can save disputes later. Always settle any dispute with a garage before you leave; subsequent negotiations by post are usually lengthy and unsatisfactory.

Road signs

Although most road signs are the same and therefore easily identifiable throughout the Continent, below are explanations of specifically French ones:

Allumez vos phares - Switch on your headlights
Attention travaux - Road works ahead
Chaussée déformée - Uneven road surface
Fin d'interdiction de stationner - End of restricted parking
Gravillons - Loose chippings
Haute tension - Electrified lines
Interdit aux piétons - No pedestrians
Nids de poules - Potholes
Priorité à droite - Give way to traffic on the right (see Priority including roundabouts on page 18)
Passage protégé - Your right of way
Rappel 50 - Remember 50 kph (or whatever speed is relevant)
Route barrée - Road closed

And finally, remember always when driving through France, **drive on the right** and **overtake carefully on the left**.

Safe motoring - and enjoy your holiday!

❚❚Motoring in France❚❚
General Information

Motoring in France should cause little difficulty to British motorists, but remember to drive on the right-hand side of the road, and take particular care when approaching junctions, traffic lights, roundabouts, etc. Also ensure that you comply with signs showing speed limits.

Ensure that your vehicle is in good order mechanically. We recommend a full service by a franchised dealer. AA members can arrange a thorough check of their car by an experienced AA engineer. Any AA shop can organise this, given a few days' notice. There is a fee for this service, and for more information or, if you wish to book an inspection, please telephone 0345 500610.

❚❚A❚❚

ACCIDENTS AND EMERGENCIES ❚

In the event of an accident, you must stop. In the event of injury or damage, you should inform the police, and notify your insurers by letter if possible within 24 hours. If a third party is injured your insurers will advise you, or, if you have a Green Card (see Motor Insurance below), contact the company or bureau given on the back of the card for advice over claims for compensation

❚❚B❚❚

BANKING HOURS ❚

Banks close at midday on the day prior to a national holiday, and all day on Monday if the holiday falls on a Tuesday. Otherwise hours are similar to those in Britain. Most French banks will no longer cash Eurocheques, but if you have a Eurocheque or credit card with a PIN you can withdraw cash from a network of around 15,000 cash dispensers. Eurocheques are quite widely accepted in shops in large towns. See also Fuel/Petrol and Money.

BBC WORLD SERVICE ❚

The BBC World Service broadcasts globally in 45 languages, including a 24 hour-a-day English service. If your are travelling in north-west Europe, you can listen on medium wave and long wave at these times:

kHz	Metres	Summer broadcasting times GMT
198	151	52345-0500
648	463	0000-0800;
		0830-1200; 1215-1530;
		1600-1730; 1800-2400

BBC World Service also transmits on short wave, and comprehensive details of all frequencies are available in a free programme guide from BBC World Service, PO Box 76, Bush House, London WC2B 4PH. A digitally tuned radio makes it easier to find frequencies than the traditional 'dial and pointer' set. A monthly magazine, BBC On Air, provides details of all World Service programmes. It costs £2 per issue, or £18.00 (US $30) for an annual subscription. For information, telephone 0171 557 2211.

BRITISH EMBASSY/CONSULATE ❚

The British Embassy is at 75383 Paris Cedex 08, 35 rue du Faubourg St Honoré, telephone 144513100; consular section 16 rue d'Anjou, telephone 142663810. There are British Consulates in Bordeaux, Lille, Lyon and Marseille; there are British Consulates with Honorary Consuls in Biarritz, Boulogne-sur-Mer, Calais, Cherbourg, Dunkerque (Dunkirk), Le Havre, Nantes, Nice, St Malo-Dinard and Toulouse.

"C"

CHILDREN IN CARS

A child under 10 years old may not travel as a front-seat passenger. A baby of up to 9 months and weighing less than 9kg may travel in the front of the car in a rear-facing seat. Children under 10 years old in rear seats must use a restraint system appropriate to their age and weight.

Note: in no circumstances should a rear-facing restraint be used in a front seat with an airbag.

CUSTOMS AND EXCISE

When you enter the UK from another EC country without having travelled to or through a non-EC country you do not need to go through the red or green channels. Look for the blue channel or blue exit reserved for EC travellers. But please remember that, although the limits on duty and tax paid goods bought within the EC ended on 31 December 1992, EC law sets out limits on purchases from duty-free and tax-free shops. It also establishes guidence levels for tobacco goods and wines and spirits bought elsewhere within the EC. Additionally the importation of certain goods into the UK is prohibited or restricted.

The quantities shown below may be bought from duty-free and tax-free shops for personal use. This is your entitlement each time you travel to and from another EC country.

Tobacco goods: 200 cigarettes; or 100 cigarillos; or 50 cigars; or 250gms of tobacco

Wines & Spirits: 2 litres of still table wine and 1 litre of spirits or strong liqueurs over 22% volume; or 2 litres of fortified wine, sparkling wine or other liqueurs

Perfume: 60cc/ml of perfume and 250cc/ml of toilet water

Other Goods: £75 worth of all other goods, including gifts and souvenirs

Note: Under 17s cannot have tobacco or alcohol allowance

The guidence levels, which include any duty-free purchases, are the amounts you may bring in for your personal use. If you bring in more, and cannot prove that the goods are for your personal use, they may be seized. The levels for tobacco goods are 800 cigarettes, 400 cigarillos, 200 cigars and 1kg smoking tobacco; for wines and spirits 10 litres of spirits, 20 litres of fortified wine (such as port and sherry), 90 litres of wine (of which not more than 60 litres are sparkling) and 110 litres of beer. Prohibited or restricted goods include drugs, firearms, ammunition, offensive weapons (such as flick knives), explosives, obscene material, indecent and obscene material featuring children, unlicensed animals that could be carrying rabies (such as cats, dogs and mice).

When you enter the UK from a non-EC country or an EC country having travelled to or through a non-EC country, you must go through Customs. If you have more than the customs allowances or any prohibited, restricted or commercial goods, go through the red channel. Only go through the green channel if you are sure that you have "nothing to declare".

For customs allowances see above, but for "other goods" read £145 not £75.

Prohibited goods include unlicensed drugs; offensive weapons; obscene material; counterfeit and copied goods.

Restricted goods include firearms, explosives and ammunition; dogs, cats and other animals; live birds; endangered species; meat and poultry; certain plants; radio transmitters.

Don't be tempted to hide anything or to mislead the Customs. Penalties are severe and articles not properly declared may be forfeit. If articles are hidden in a vehicle that too becomes liable to forfeiture. Customs officers are legally entitled to examine your luggage. You are responsible for opening, unpacking and repacking it. If you require more information, obtain a copy of Customs Notice 1, available at UK points of entry and exit, or telephone an Excise and Inland Customs Advice Centre (see Customs and Excise in the telephone directory).

"D"

DIESEL

See Fuel/Petrol

DOCUMENTS

A tourist driving abroad should always carry a current passport, and a full, valid national driving licence, even if an International Driving Permit (IDP) is also held, the vehicle registration document and certificate of motor insurance. (See Motor Insurance below). Any AA shop will advise you of the procedure for personal or postal applications for an IDP, for which a statutory charge is made. If you have no registration document, apply to a Vehicle Registration Office (in Northern Ireland a Local Vehicle Licensing Office) for a temporary certificate of registration (V379) to cover the period abroad. Consult the local telephone directory for addresses, or leaflet V100, available from post offices. Apply well in advance of your journey.

The proper International Distinguishing Sign should be displayed on the rear of the vehicle and any trailer.

Remember that foreign vehicles are often subject to spot checks, so to avoid delay or a possible police fine, ensure that your papers are in order and that your International Distinguishing Sign is of the approved standard design (oval with black letters - GB for UK residents - on a white background at least 6.9 in by 4.5 in and affixed to the rear of the vehicle). If you are carrying skis, ensure that their tips point to the rear. If you have cycle rack, ensure that it does not obscure the number plate or IDS.

"E"

EMERGENCY MESSAGES

In emergencies the AA will help in the passing on of messages to tourists wherever possible. Members wishing to use this service should telephone the AA Information Centre on 0990 500600. The AA can arrange for messages to be published in the overseas editions of the Daily Mail, and in the case of extreme emergency (death or serious illness) undertake to pass on messages to the appropriate authorities so they can be broadcast. The AA cannot guarantee that messages will be broadcast, nor can the AA or Daily Mail accept any responsibility for the authenticity of messages.

EUROCHEQUES

Most French banks will no longer cash Eurocheques, but they are widely accepted in shops. See also Banking Hours and Money.

EUROTUNNEL

Eurotunnel's Le Shuttle car passenger service provides up to four departures per hour at peak times from Folkestone to Calais. Services operate 24 hours a day with up to four departures an hour at peak times. The journey takes only 35 minutes from platform to platform (45 minutes at night), and just over an hour from the M20 in Kent to the A16 at Calais.

Motorists leave the M20 at Exit 11a (clearly signposted to the Channel Tunnel) and buy a ticket on arrival at the tollbooths by cash, check or payment card (charge/credit/debit) or in advance from the Le Shuttle Customer Service Centre, travel agents or any AA shop. For more information telephone Le Shuttle Customer Service Centre on 0990 353535 or write to PO Box 300, Folkestone, Kent CT19 4QW. Remember, vehicles with LPG or duel fuel systems or petrol cans cannot be carried aboard Le Shuttle.

The Eurostar passenger service to Paris leaves from Waterloo Station in London and may also be boarded at Ashford in Kent.

▮▮F▮▮

FUEL/PETROL ▮

Motorists will find comparable grades of petrol and familiar brand names along main routes. You will normally have to buy a minimum of 5 litres (just over a gallon), but it is wise to keep the tank topped up, especially in rural areas, and on Sundays and National Holidays when many local service stations may close. Fuel is generally available with 24-hr service on motorways, but on other roads, some service stations may close between 12 noon and 15.00 hours. Do not assume that service stations will accept credit cards. See also Money. Leaded, unleaded, diesel fuel are all available. Unleaded (sans plomb) and leaded are both available as 'normal' and 'super'. You may also find unleaded 98 octane instead of or as well as 95 octane. It may also be described as 'super plus' or 'premium'. Take care to use the recommended fuel, especially if your car is fitted with a catalytic converter. The octane grade should be the same or higher. If you accidentally fill the tank of a catalyst-equipped car with leaded fuel the best course is to have the tank drained and refilled with unleaded.

Diesel fuel is generally known as diesel or gas oil. It is normally available, but do ensure that you keep the tank topped up. If you accidentally put more than about a gallon of petrol into a diesel car (or vice versa), you must drain the tank and refill with the correct fuel before starting the engine.

Note: ferry operators and motorail forbid the carriage of fuel in spare cans, though empty cans may be carried.

▮▮L▮▮

LIGHTS ▮

Headlights should be altered so that the dipped beam does not dazzle other drivers. Easily fitted headlamp beam converter kits are on sale at AA shops, but remember to remove them as soon as you return to the UK.

Dipped headlights should be used in tunnels, irrespective of length and lighting. Police may wait at the end of a tunnel to check vehicles. In the dark or in poor visibility, you must use headlights, as driving on side lights only is not permitted. Yellow-tinted headlights, however, are no longer necessary. In fog or mist, two dipped headlights or two fog lights must be switched on. Headlight flashing is used only to signal approach or when overtaking at night. If used at other times, it could be taken as a sign of irritation and lead to misunderstandings. *See also Spares.*

▮▮M▮▮

MEDICAL TREATMENT ▮

Travellers who normally take certain medicines should ensure they have a sufficient supply as they may be difficult to obtain abroad. Those with certain medical conditions (diabetes, coronary artery diseases) should get a letter from their doctor giving treatment details and obtain a translation. The AA cannot make translations.

Travellers who, for legitimate health reasons, carry drugs (see also Customs regulations for the United Kingdom) or appliances (e.g., a hypodermic syringe), may have difficulty with Customs or other authorities. They should carry translations which describe their special condition and appropriate treatment in the language of the country they intend to visit to present to

Customs. Similarly, people with special dietary requirements may find translations helpful in hotels and restaurants.

The National Health Service is available in the UK only, and medical expenses incurred overseas cannot generally be reimbursed by the UK Government. There is a reciprocal health agreement with France, but you should not rely exclusively on this arrangement, as the cover provided may not be comprehensive. (For instance, the cost of bringing a person back to the UK in the event of illness or death is not covered). You are strongly advised to take out adequate insurance before leaving the UK, such as the AA's Personal Travel Insurance.

Urgent medical treatment in the event of an accident or unforeseen illness is available for most visitors at reduced costs, from the health care schemes of those countries with whom the UK has health-care arrangements. Details are in the Department of Health booklet T5 which also gives advice about health precautions and vaccinations. Free copies are available from main post offices or by ringing the Health Literature Line on 0800 555 777 any time, free of charge. In some of these countries, visitors can obtain urgently needed treatment by showing their UK passport, but in some an NHS medical card must be produced, and in most European Economic Area countries a certificate of entitlement (E111) is necessary. The E111 can be obtained over the counter of the post office on completion of the forms incorporated in booklet T5. However, the E111 must be stamped and signed by the post office clerk to be valid. Residents of the Republic of Ireland must apply to their Regional Health Board for an E111.

MONEY

You should carry enough local currency notes for immediate needs and also local currency travellers cheques which can often be used like cash. Sterling travellers cheques can be cashed at banks, and you will need your passport with you. Credit cards are widely accepted, and there are about 15,000 automatic cash dispense machines which you can use to obtain cash. See also Eurocheques.

MOTORING CLUB

The AA is affiliated to the Automobile Club National (ACN) whose office is at 75009 Paris, 5 rue Auber. Telephone 144515399.

MOTOR INSURANCE

When driving abroad you must carry your certificate of motor insurance with you at all times. Third-party is the minimum legal requirement in most countries. Before taking your vehicle abroad, contact your insurer or broker to ask for advice. Some insurers will extend your UK or Republic of Ireland motor policy to apply in the countries you intend visiting free of charge; others may charge an additional premium. It is most important to know the level of cover you will actually have, and what documents you will need to prove it.

A Green Card is not essential in France. This document issued by your motor insurer provides internationally recognised proof of insurance. It must be signed on receipt as it will not be accepted without the signature of the insured person. Motorists can obtain expert advice through AA Insurance Services for all types of insurance. Ask at your local AA shop or contact AA Insurance Services Ltd, PO Box 2AA Newcastle upon Tyne NE99 2AA. Do also check that you are insured for damage in transit other than when the vehicle is being driven (e.g. on the ferry).

❚❚P❚❚

PARKING

As a general rule, park on the right hand side of the road so as not to obstruct traffic or a cycle lane, etc., but better still, park in an authorised place as regulations are stringent, especially in large towns and cities and fines are heavy. In Paris it is absolutely forbidden to stop or park on a red route. The east-west route includes the left bank of the Seine and the Quai de la Megisserie; the north-south route includes the Avenue du Général Leclerc, part of the Boulevard St Michel, the Rue de Rivoli, the Boulevards Sébastopol, Strasbourg, Barbès and Ornano, the Rue Lafayette and the Avenue Jean Jaurès. Parking is also absolutely forbidden in some parts of the green zone.

PASSPORTS

Each person must hold, or be named on, a valid passport and should carry it with them at all times. For security, keep a separate note of the number, date and place of issue. If it is lost, report the matter to the police. There is now only one type of passport, the standard 10 year passport. Full information and application forms are available from main Post Offices, branches of Lloyds Bank, Artac World Choice travel agents or from one of the passport offices in Belfast, Douglas (Isle of Man), Glasgow, Liverpool, London, Newport (Gwent), Peterborough, St Helier (Jersey), St Peter Port (Guernsey). Allow at least 15 working days at peak periods.

PETROL

See Fuel/Petrol

POLICE FINES

In France, the police may impose an immediate deposit for a traffic infringement and subsequently may levy a fine which must normally be paid in cash in French francs either to the police or at a post office against a ticket issued by the police. The amount can, for serious offences, exceed the equivalent of £1000. A receipt should be obtained, but motorists should be aware that disputing a fine usually leads to a court appearance with all the extra costs and delays that may entail.

PRIORITÉ À DROITE

Probably the most unfamiliar aspect of driving in France to British motorists is the rule giving priority to traffic coming from the right - priorité à droite - and unless this priority is varied by signs, it must be strictly observed. In built-up areas (including small villages) you must give way to traffic coming from the right. Also remember that farm vehicles and buses may expect to be given priority. At roundabouts, priority is generally given to vehicles entering the roundabout (the opposite of the rule in Britain). However, at roundabouts bearing the words 'Vous n'avez pas la priorité' or 'Cédez le passage', traffic on the roundabout has the priority.

Outside built up areas, all main roads of any importance have right of way. This is indicated by one of three signs: a red-bordered triangle showing a black cross on a white background with the words 'Passage Protégé' underneath; a red-bordered triangle showing a pointed black upright with horizontal bar on a white background; or a yellow square within a white square with points vertical.

"R"

ROADS

Roads in France are generally very good, but the camber is often severe and edges can be rough. In July and August, especially at weekends, traffic is likely to be very heavy. Special signs are erected to indicate alternative routes and it is usually advantageous to follow them, though they are not guaranteed to save time. A free road map showing marked alternative routes is available from service stations display the 'Bison Futé' poster (a Red Indian chief in full war bonnet). These maps are also available from Syndicats d'Initiative and Information Offices.

"S"

SPARES

Motorists are recommended to carry a set of replacement bulbs. If you are able to replace a faulty bulb when asked to do so by the police, you may still have to pay a fine but you may avoid the cost and inconvenience of a garage call out. Other useful items are windscreen wiper blades, a length of electrical cable and a torch. Remember when ordering spare parts for dispatch abroad you must be able to identify them clearly - by the manufacturer's part numbers if known. Always quote your engine and vehicle identification number (VIN).

SPEED LIMITS

On normal roads - Built up areas: 50kph (31mph) **Outside built up areas**: 90kph (55mph). **Dual Carriage-ways with central reservation:**110kph (69mph) **On motorways-** 130kph (80mph)

Note: minimum speed in the fast lane on a level stretch of motorway in good daytime visibility is 80kph (49mph).

Maximum speed on the Paris Périphérique is 80kph (49mph); on other urban stretches of motorway, 1109kph (69mph).

In fog, when visibility is reduced to 50 metres, the speed limit on all roads is 50kph (31mph) and in wet weather speed limits outside built-up areas are reduced to 80kph (49mph), 100kph (62mph) on dual carriageways and 110kph (69mph) on other motoways.

Drivers who have held a licence for less than two years must at all times observe these reduced speed limits.

"T"

TAX DISC

See Vehicle Excise Licence

TOLL ROADS (PÉAGE)

Tolls are payable on most motorways in France, and over long distances charges can be considerable. Motorists collect a ticket on entering the motorway and pay at the exit. You must have local currency or a credit card. Travellers' cheques and Eurocheques are not accepted. Please note that (for a UK driver) booths are virtually always on the passenger side of the car).

TRAFFIC LIGHTS

Traffic lights are similar to those in the UK, except that they turn directly from red to green, but from green through amber to red. The intensity of the light is poor, and they could be easily missed, especially those overhead. There is usually only one set by the right-hand side of the road, at some distance before the junction and if you stop too close to the corner, you may not be able to see them change. Watch for 'filter' lights enabling you to turn right and enter the appropriate lane.

TRAMS

Trams have priority over other vehicles. Never obstruct the passage of a tram. Always give way to passengers boarding and alighting. Trams must be overtaken on the right except in one-way streets.

"V"

VEHICLE EXCISE LICENCE

Remember that your tax disc needs to be valid on your return from abroad, so if it is due to expire while you are away, you can apply by post to a Head Post Office up to 42 days in advance of the expiry date. You should explain why you need it and ask for it to be posted either to your home address or your address abroad. The application form must be completed with your UK address, however.

Residents of the Republic of Ireland should contact their local Vehicle Registration Office.

Residents of Northern Ireland should apply to the Driver and Vehicle Licensing Northern Ireland, Vehicle licensing Division, County Hall, Coleraine BT51 3HS.

WARNING TRIANGLE

If you should break down or be involved in an accident, the use of a warning triangle or hazard warning lights is compulsory. As hazard warning lights may be damaged, we recommend that you carry a warning triangle, which should be placed 30 metres behind the vehicle (100 metres on motorways), about 60 cm from the edge of the road, but not in such a position as to present a danger to oncoming traffic, and be clearly visible from 100 metres, by day and night.

WEATHER INFORMATION

UK Regional weather reports are provided direct from the Met. Office by the AA Weatherwatch recorded information service.

National Forecast*	0336 401 130
London & SE England	0336 401 131
West Country	0336 401 132
Wales	0336 401 133
Midlands	0336 401 134
East Anglia	0336 401 135
NW England	0336 401 136
NE England	0336 401 137
Scotland	0336 401 138
Northern Ireland	0336 401 139

For weather reports for crossing the Channel and northern France, call 0336 401 361, whilst Continental Roadwatch on 0336 401 904 provides information on traffic conditions to and from ferry ports, ferry news and details of major European events. A world-wide, city-by-city six-day weather forecast is also available on 0336 411 212.

For other weather information for the UK and the Continent (but not road conditions) please contact:

The Met Office
Enquiries Officer, London Road
Bracknell, Berkshire RG12 2SZ
or telephone 01344 854455 during normal office hours.

* Calls are charged at 50p per minute at all times.

AA Hotel Booking Service

The AA Hotel Booking Service - Now AA Members have a free, simple way to find a place to stay for a week, weekend, or a one-night stopover.

Are you looking for somewhere in the Lake District that will take pets; a city-centre hotel in Glasgow with parking facilities, or do you need a B & B near Dover which is handy for the Eurotunnel?
The AA Booking Service can not only take the hassle out of finding the right place for you, but could even get you a discount on a leisure break or business booking.

And if you are touring round the UK or Ireland, simply give the AA Hotel Booking Service your list of overnight stops, and from one phone call all your accommodation can be booked for you.

Telephone
0990 050505

to make a booking.
Office hours 8.30am - 7.30pm
Monday - Saturday.

Full listings of the 7,920 hotels and B & Bs available through the Hotel Booking Service can be found and booked at the AA's Internet Site:

http://www.theaa.co.uk/hotels

"Booking Accommodation"

Below is a standard letter which can be sent out to the place you're planning to stay. Do remember to enclose an international reply coupon with your letter. These are available from all post offices and at the time of going to press cost 60p. In Britain, a room with bath/shower automatically includes a WC. In France you need to ask. **Please do not send an SAE with your letter, as English stamps are invalid in France**.

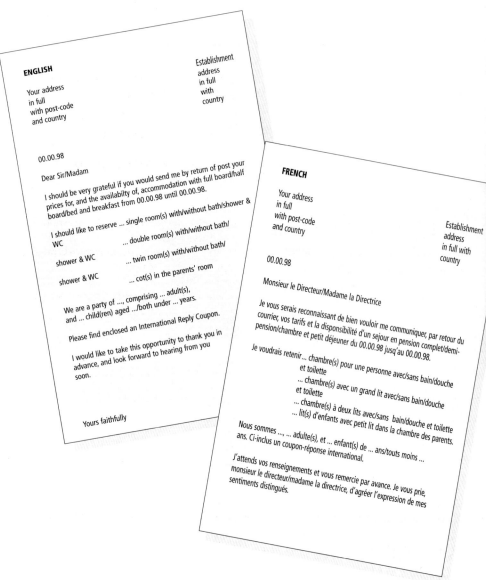

ENGLISH

Your address
in full
with post-code
and country

Establishment
address
in full
with
country

00.00.98

Dear Sir/Madam

I should be very grateful if you would send me by return of post your prices for, and the availabilty of, accommodation with full board/half board/bed and breakfast from 00.00.98 until 00.00.98.

I should like to reserve ... single room(s) with/without bath/shower & WC

... double room(s) with/without bath/shower & WC

shower & WC ... twin room(s) with/without bath/shower & WC

shower & WC ... cot(s) in the parents' room

We are a party of ..., comprising ... adult(s), and ... child(ren) aged .../both under ... years.

Please find enclosed an International Reply Coupon.

I would like to take this opportunity to thank you in advance, and look forward to hearing from you soon.

Yours faithfully

FRENCH

Your address
in full
with post-code
and country

Establishment
address
in full with
country

00.00.98

Monsieur le Directeur/Madame la Directrice

Je vous serais reconnaissant de bien vouloir me communiquer, par retour du courrier, vos tarifs et la disponibilité d'un séjour en pension complet/demi-pension/chambre et petit déjeuner du 00.00.98 jusq'au 00.00.98.

Je voudrais retenir... chambre(s) pour une personne avec/sans bain/douche et toilette

... chambre(s) avec un grand lit avec/sans bain/douche et toilette

... chambre(s) à deux lits avec/sans bain/douche et toilette

... lit(s) d'enfants avec petit lit dans la chambre des parents.

Nous sommes ..., ... adulte(s), et ... enfant(s) de ... ans/touts moins ... ans. Ci-inclus un coupon-réponse international.

J'attends vos renseignements et vous remercie par avance. Je vous prie, monsieur le directeur/madame la directrice, d'agréer l'expression de mes sentiments distingués.

❚❚ Booking by Telephone ❚❚

Remember, even if you make a reservation by telephone, it is always advisable to then write to the establishment confirming your booking arrangements. The French for numbers, days of the week, months and telling the time can be found on pages 26.

ENGLISH	FRENCH
Hello, I'd like to make a reservation please_____	Bonjour, je voudrais faire une réservation
We shall need xx rooms with bath/shower and WC for__	Il nous faut xx chambre(s) avec bain/douche et toilette pour
xx nights from (10 July to 13 July):_____	xx nuits, du (dix juillet jusqu'au treize juillet):
xx single rooms_____	xx chambres pour une personne
xx twin-bedded rooms_____	xx chambres à deux lits
xx double rooms _____	xx chambres à grand lit
There are (four) people with a baby and a child of_____	Nous sommes (quatre) personne(s) accompagnés d'un bébé et
(10) years	d'un enfant âgé de (dix) ans
Reply a) - I'm sorry, we are fully booked _____	Reply a) - Je suis désolé, mais l'hôtel est complet
Reply b) - Of course; we have rooms available _____	Reply b) - Bien sûr; nous avons des chambres
I'll arrive about midday/4 pm on 10 July _____	J'arriverai vers midi/quatres heures de l'après midi le
	dix juillet
How long will you be staying? _____	Pour combien de temps voulez-vous rester?
For ... nights, please _____	Pour ... nuits
Would you like full board, half-board, or bed and _____	Voulez-vous rester avec pension complet, demi pension, ou
breakfast?	chambre avec petit déjeuner?
How much does full board/half-board/bed and_____	C'est combien pour rester avec pension complet /demi-pen-
breakfast cost?	sion/ chambre avec petit déjeuner?
It costs ... francs_____	ça coute ... franc
I'd like full board,/half-board,/bed and breakfast _____	Je voudrais rester avec pension complet/demi pension/chambre
please	avec petit déjeuner, s'il vous plaît
a) - Certainly sir/madam; your name, address and_____	a) - Bien sûr, monsieur/ madame; votre nom, adresse et nom-
telephone number?	bre de téléphone?
b) - How many are there in your party? _____	b) - Vous êtes combien?
There are ... of us; ... adult(s) and ... child(ren)_____	Nous sommes ..., ... adulte(s) et ... enfant(s)
How old is/are your child(ren) _____	Quel age a/ont l'(les) enfant(s)?
a) - ...and ... years old_____ _____	a) - Ils ont ... ans et ... ans
b) - The girl/boy is ... years old _____	b) - La fille/le garçon a xx ans
I'd like a double room and a twin-bedded room _____	J'aimerais une chambre à grand lit, et une chambre
	à deux lits
I'm sorry but we only have two double rooms - _____	Je suis désolé, mais nous n'avons que deux chambres à grand
will that be alright?	lit – ça va bien?
With shower or bath?_____	Avec bain ou douche?
Could you put a cot in the parents' room? _____	Pouvez-vous mettre un petit lit dans la chambre des parents?
Certainly sir/madam, thank you_____	Bien sûr monsieur/madame, merci.

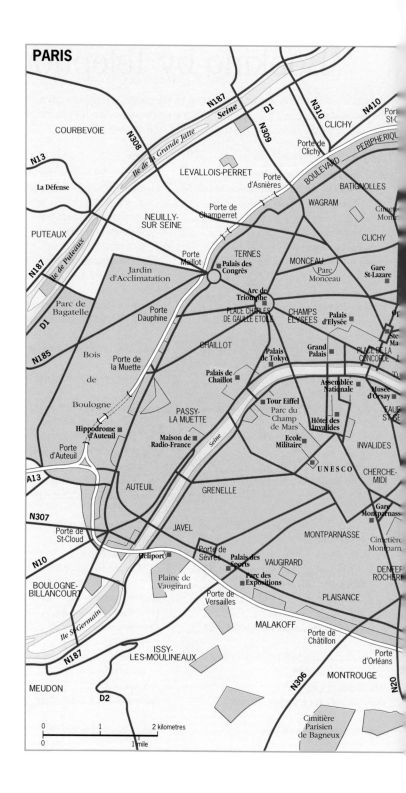

PARIS

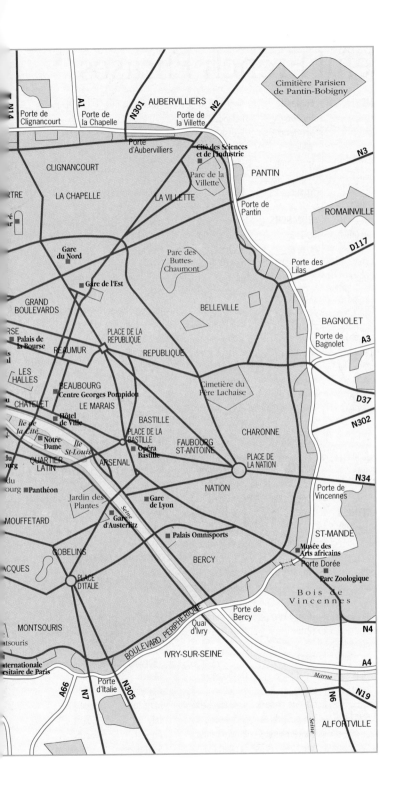

"Useful French Phrases"

GENERAL EXPRESSIONS

Hello _____ Bonjour
Goodbye _____ Au revoir
Good morning _ Bonjour
Good evening _ Bonsoir
Good night ____ Bonne nuit
See you later __ A bientôt
Please/ _____ S'il vous plaît/
thankyou   merci
You're _____ Je vous en prie
welcome
Yes/no _____ Oui/non
Excuse me ____ Excusez-moi
I'm sorry _____ Pardon
How are you? _ Comment allez-
               vous?
I'm fine, thanks Très bien merci
My name is ___ Je m'appelle
Mr/Mrs/Miss   Monsieur/
               Madame/
               Mademoiselle
I like/don't____ J'aime/je n'aime
like ...   pas ...
That's fine/OK _ Ça va
What time ____ A quelle heure
do you open/   vous ouvrez/
close?   fermez?

LANGUAGES AND COUNTRIES

I am English ___ Je suis Anglais(e)
Scottish   Ecossais(e)
Welsh / Irish ... Gallois(e) /
                Irlandais(e) ...
Do you speak _ Parlez-vous
English?   anglais?
I don't speak __ Je ne parle pas
French   français
I don't_____ Je ne comprends
understand   pas
Could you_____ Pourriez-vous
speak more   parler plus
slowly please? lentement,
                s'il vous plaît?

England _____ Angleterre
Ireland _____ Irelande
Scotland _____ Écosse
Wales_____ Pays de Galles
Germany _____ Allemagne
Italy _____ Italie
Spain _____ Espagne

NUMBERS

1, 2, 3 _____ un, deux, trois
4, 5, 6 _____ quatre, cinq, six
7, 8, 9, 10 _____ sept, huit, neuf,
                dix
11, 12, 13 _____ onze, douze,
                treize
14, 15, 16 _____ quatorze, quinze,
                seize
17, 18, 19 _____ dix-sept, dix-huit,
                dix-neuf
20, 21, 22 _____ vingt, vingt-et -un,
                vingt-deux
30, 40, 50 _____ trente, quarante,
                cinquante
60, 70, 80 _____ soixante, soixante-
                dix, quatre-vingts
90, 100, 101 __ quatre-vingts-dix,
                cent, cent-et-un
1000, 2000 ___ mille, deux milles
1st, 2nd, 3rd__ premier, deuxième,
                troisième
4th, 5th, 6th __ quatrième,
                cinquième, sixième
7th, 8th, 9th __ septième,
                huitième,
                neuvième
10th, 11th,____ dixième, onzième,
12th   douzième

TIME

What time ____ Quelle heure
is it?   est-il?
It's one o'clock Il est une heure
Ten past three_ Trois heures dix
Quarter past__ Quatre heures
four   et quart

Half past five__ Cinq heure set
                demi
Twenty to six__ Six heures moins
                vingt
Quarter to ____ Sept heures moins
seven   le quart
This morning/ _ Ce matin/soir
evening
Now _____ Maintenant
At once _____ Tout de suite
It's late/early __ Il est tard/tôt
Sorry I'm late _ Je suis désolé
                d'être en retard
second, _____ seconde,
minute, hour   minute, heure
yesterday,____ hier,
today,   aujourd'hui,
tomorrow   demain
midday _____ midi
midnight_____ minuit
day, night_____ le jour, la nuit

DAYS OF THE WEEK

Monday _____ lundi
Tuesday _____ mardi
Wednesday ___ mercredi
Thursday_____ jeudi
Friday _____ vendredi
Saturday _____ samedi
Sunday _____ dimanche

MONTHS AND DATES

What's the ____ Quelle est la
date?   date?
It's the first____ Nous sommes le
of July /   premier juillet / le
2nd August   deux août
January_____ janvier
February _____ février
March _____ mars
April_____ avril
May, June _____ mai, juin
July _____ juillet
August _____ août
September____ septembre

October _____ octobre
November _____ novembre
December_____ décembre

SHOPPING
How much? ____ Combien?
I'm just_____ Je regarde
looking seulement
That's enough, _ Ça suffit, merci
thank you
May I have a __ Puis-je avoir un
bag please? sac, s'il vous plaît?
Have you got...? Est-ce que vous
avez ... ?
I'd like ..._____ Je voudrai ...
Could you_____ Pouvez-vous me
show me ... ? montrer
supermarket___ supermarché
newsagent_____ marchand de
journaux
newspaper_____ journal
bookshop _____ librairie
writing paper _ papier à lettres
envelopes_____ envelopes
a map _____ une carte
(of the area) (de la région)
town plan_____ plan de la ville
a colour/black _ une pellicule
and white film couleur/noir et
blanc
tights_____ un collant
a guide book __ un guide
an umbrella ___ un parapluie
coins_____ des pièces
change _____ la monnaie

CHEMIST _____ LA PHARMACIE
I've got a _____ J'ai mal à
headache la tête
stomach ache _ mal au ventre
I've got a cold _ Je suis enrhumé
aspirin_____ de l'aspirine
antiseptic _____ antiseptique
cotton wool ___ du coton
disposable ____ couches en
nappies cellulose
paper tissues__ Kleenex

sanitary towels couches
périodiques
tampons _____ tampons
périodiques
suntan oil_____ huile solaire
toilet paper___ papier hygiénique
razor blades ___ lames de rasoir
plasters _____ pansements
adhésifs
soap _____ savon
toothpaste_____ dentifrice

POST OFFICE __ LA POSTE
How much is __ Combien coûte un
a stamp for timbre pour
England? l'Angleterre?
Where can I____ Où puis-je
telephone? téléphoner?
letter _____ lettre
postcard _____ carte postale
parcel _____ paquet
post box _____ boîte aux lettres
phone box _____ cabinet
téléphonique
tobacconist___ bureau de tabac
A packet of ..._ Un paquet de ...
please s'il vous plaît
cigarettes_____ cigarettes
cigars_____ cigares
tobacco _____ tabac
matches_____ allumettes
lighter_____ briquet

FOOD SHOPPING
BAKER/CAKE___ BOULANGERIE/
SHOP PÂTISSERIE
pastries _____ pâtisseries
bread_____ pain
French stick ___ baguette
cake _____ gâteau
rolls_____ petits pains
butcher/_____ boucherie/
delicatessen charcuterie
one/two_____ une/deux
slice(s) of ... tranche(s) de ...
half a kilo of ... un demi-kilo de ...
a pound_____ une livre
(weight)

250 grams of ... deux cent
cinquante
grammes de
fresh, raw, ____ frais, cru, cuit,
cooked, fumé
smoked
cheese_____ fromage
ham _____ jambon
kidneys_____ rognons
liver _____ foie
mince_____ viande hachée
pâté _____ pâté
sausage _____ saucisse

FISHMONGER__ POISSONNERIE
anchovies _____ anchois
mussels _____ moules
oysters _____ huîtres
prawns _____ crevettes roses
sardines_____ sardines
crab _____ crabe
lobster _____ homard
squid _____ calmar
octopus _____ poulpe
GREENGROCER_ MARCHAND DE
FRUITS ET
LÉGUMES
apples_____ pommes
bananas_____ bananes
grapefruit_____ pamplemousse
grapes_____ raisins
melon _____ melon
oranges _____ oranges
peaches _____ pêches
raspberries ___ framboises
strawberries___ fraises
carrots _____ carottes
cucumber _____ concombre
garlic_____ ail
green beans ___ haricots verts
lettuce _____ laitue
mushrooms ___ champignons
onions_____ oignons
peas _____ petit pois
potatoes _____ pommes de terre
tomatoes _____ tomates

DIRECTIONS

Where is/are ... Où se trouve/
trouvent ...
Turn left / right Tournez à gauche
/à droite
Go straight on Continuez tout
droit
Take the first Prenez la première
left/right à gauche / droite

AT THE HOTEL

I have a J'ai une
booking, my réservation, je
name is ... m'appelle
What floor is À quel étage se
the room on? trouve la
chambre?
Is there a lift? Y a-t-il un
ascenseur?
Could I see Pourrais-je voir la
the room? chambre?
Does the price Est-ce que le prix
include ...? comprend?
The key for La clef pour
room ... chambre s'il vous
please plaît
Please call S'il vous plaît,
me at ... réveillez-moi à ...
Where can Où puis-je garer la
I park? voiture?
Are there any Y a-t-il des lettres
letters for me? pour moi?
The bill please? La note, s'il vous
plaît?
guesthouse pension
inn auberge
single room chambre à un lit
twin bedded chambre à deux
room lits
double room chambre à grand
lit

blanket couverture
coat hanger cintre
chambermaid femme de
chambre
manager directeur
porter concierge
pillow oreiller
room service service d'étage
sheets draps
towel serviette de
toilette

TRAVEL
(See also Directions)
ON THE ROAD SUR LA ROUTE
Fill it up Faites le plein,
please s'il vous plaît
(10) litres of (10) litres de
4 star, please super, s'il vous
plaît
unleaded sans plomb
diesel diesel / gas oil
LPG gaz de pétrole
liquéfié (GPL)
Please check Veuillez vérifier
water level niveau d'eaul
antifreeze l'antigel
battery la batterie
brake fluid le liquide des
freins
oil huile
oil filter le filtre à huile
My car.... Ma voiture ...ne
won't start démarre pas
has broken est en panne
down
I've lost my J'ai perdu ma clef
car key de contact
It won't go Il ne marche pas
I have no Je n'ai plus
petrol d'essence
to hire a car louer une voiture
the bill? la facture?

broken cassé
engine le moteur
exhaust l'échappement
handbrake frein à main
horn klaxon
ignition l'allumage
puncture crevaisson
tow remorquer
windscreen pare-brise

AT THE STATION À LA GARE
[Note: at railway stations, when
you have purchased your ticket,
you must validate it (i.e. get it
date-stamped) in one of the
machines you will find on your
way to the platform. If you forget
to do this, you may incur a fine.]

by rail/bus par train /autobus
railway/bus gare / gare
station routière
a single to un billet simple
pour
a return un aller-et-retour
pour
When is the A quelle heure
next bus/train part le prochain
to ...? autobus/train
pour?
Is this the Est-ce bien le train
train/bus for...? / le bus pour?...
Do I have to Faut-il changer?
change?
platform quai
bus stop arrêt d'autobus
entry/exit entrée/sortie
seat la place
Is this seat Est-ce que cette
taken? place est occupée?
ticket collector le contrôleur
ticket office le guichet
timetable horaire

Welcome to the GREAT NAUSICAÄ from 30ᵗʰ May1998

NAUSICAÄ will be twice as big and invite you to live the Sea

Dive in an unbelievable Sub-Marine observatory and come nose to nose with the Sea-Lions

Come and discover the blue lagoon village and its superb coral reef

Open every day, minimum from 9.30 am to 6.30 pm
Rates from 30ᵗʰ May 1998 : Adults : 65 FF - Children (3 to 12 years) : 45 FF
NAUSICAÄ, Boulevard Sainte-Beuve 62200 BOULOGNE sur MER France
Tél. 00 33 3 21 30 98 98
http : // www. NAUSICAÄ-SEA-CENTRES.COM

NAUSICAÄ
Centre National de la Mer

Boulogne/Mer FRANCE

"What's on the Menu"

A holiday in France can be the gastronome's idea of heaven. Each region has a different specialty or drink associated with it, but wherever you are, always look out for the set menu (menu à prix fixé), which will give you the best value for money.

Below is a list of phrases which should be useful when ordering a meal in a restaurant, and the list also includes words for the types of foods and dishes you will come across on the menu. Each section lists some traditional dishes, as well as ordinary menu terms.

recommend? recommandez?
I'd like ... please_____ Je voudrais ... s'il vous plaît
Do you have ...?_____ Avez-vous ...?
tourist menu_____ menu touristique
knife, fork_____ couteau, fourchette
spoon_____ cuillière
cup, saucer_____ tasse, soucoupe
plate, dish_____ assiette, plat
napkin _____ serviette
pepper/salt_____ poivre/sel

PROBLEMS

Where are our drinks? Où sont nos boissons?
The food is cold _____ Le plat est froid
It is not properly _____ Ce n'est pas bien cuit
cooked

BOOKING AND ARRIVING

I'd like to book a_____ Je voudrais réserver une table
table for two at pour deux à huit heures
eight o'clock
I've booked a table __ J'ai reservé une table
A table for ... please_ Une table pour ... s'il vous plaît
Is this table taken? __ Cette table est-elle libre?
May we have an _____ Pouvons-nous avoir un cendrier,
ashtray please? s'il vous plaît?
Where is the _____ Où se trouvent les toilettes?
cloakroom?
self service café _____ libre-service
bar _____ bar
take-away_____ mets à emporter

ORDERING

Is there a set menu?_ Y a-t-il un menu à prix fixe?
Do you serve _____ Servez-vous des portions
children's portions? d'enfant?
What is the regional_ Quelle est la spécialité du pays?
speciality?
What is the dish of___ Quel est le plat du jour?
the day?
What do you_____ Qu'est-ce que vous

PAYING

May I have the bill? _ L'addition s'il vous plaît?
Is service included? __ Le service, est-il compris?
Do you take credit_____ Acceptez-vous les cartes de
cards/traveller's crédit/ les chèques de voyage?
cheques?
Thank you, the meal_ Merci, c'était très bon
was wonderful

THE MENU

starter _____ hors d'oeuvres
main course_____ entrée
dessert _____ dessert
meat _____ viande
chop, cutlet _____ côtelette
escalope_____ escalope
grilled, fried _____ grillé(e), frit(e)
rare, medium,_____ saignant, à point,
well done bien cuit
roast, boiled _____ rôti(e), bouilli(e)
stewed, baked_____ à l'étouffée, au four

beef _____ boeuf
chicken _____ poulet
ham _____ jambon
lamb _____ agneau
pork _____ porc
steak _____ bifteck
veal _____ veau

andouille _____ smoky flavoured sausage
boeuf bourguignon ___ rich beef stew made with red wine, mushrooms and onions
boudin blanc _____ white sausage made with a variety of meats
carbonnade de boeuf_ a beef and beer stew
carré d'agneau _____ loin of lamb, cooked with herbs
Châteaubriand _____ a thick fillet steak
cochon de lait _____ sucking pig
crépinettes _____ small sausages enriched with herbs and brandy
jambon persillé _____ a Burgundy speciality of jellied ham and parsley
potée auvergnate _____ a salt pork and vegetable stew from the Auvergne and Languedoc
tripes à la mode _____ traditional Norman dish of tripe,
de Caen with onions and carrots

FISH/SHELLFISH _____ POISSON/FRUITS DE MER
fish _____ poisson
carp _____ carpe
clams _____ palourdes
cod _____ morue
crab _____ crabe
Dublin Bay prawns/ ___ langoustines
scampi
freshwater crayfish ___ écrevisses
lobster _____ homard
mackerel _____ maquereau
monkfish _____ lotte
mussels _____ moules
octopus _____ poulpe
oysters _____ huîtres
rock lobster _____ langouste
salmon _____ saumon
sardines _____ sardines
sea bass _____ loup de mer

sea urchin _____ oursin
shellfish _____ fruits de mer
shrimps/prawns ___ crevettes
skate _____ raie
sole _____ sole
squid _____ calmar
trout _____ truite
tuna _____ thon
turbot _____ turbot
whiting _____ merlan

assiettes de fruit ___ a mixed platter of cooked
de mer seafood and assorted shellfish
bisque de homard ___ lobster soup
bouillabaisse _____ a Mediterranean fish stew
moules marinières ___ mussels in a white wine sauce
quenelles de brochet _ a classic dish of pike rissoles
salade Niçoise _____ tuna salad, from Provence
sole Véronique _____ sole garnished with grapes

POULTRY/GAME _____ VOLAILLE/GIBIER
wing _____ aile
breast _____ blanc/suprême
chicken _____ poulet
duck _____ canard
goose _____ oie
partridge _____ perdreau
quail _____ caille
rabbit _____ lapin
spring chicken _____ poussin
turkey _____ dinde
venison _____ chevreuil
wild boar _____ sanglier

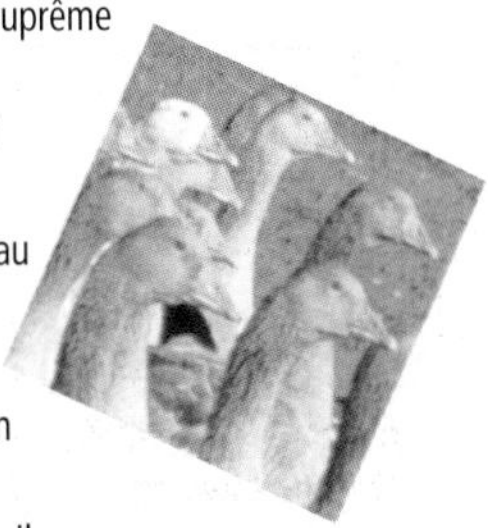

canard à l'orange ___ duck in orange sauce
caneton à la _____ pink-fleshed duck
Rouennais
civet de lièvre _____ jugged hare
confit de canard/ ___ wings or legs of duck or goose,
d'oie preserved in their own fat, found especially in the Perigord and Quercy areas
coq au vin _____ chicken in red wine, onions, bacon and mushrooms
foie gras _____ goose liver, often made into a very rich pâté

31

EGGS_____	ŒUFS
boiled, fried, _____	à la coq, sur le plat, brouillés,
scrambled, poached	pochés
savoury omelette ____	omlette aux fines herbes
soufflé_____	soufflé

œufs à la mayonnaise	egg mayonnaise
pipérade_____	scrambled eggs prepared with peppers and tomatoes
Quiche Lorraine _____	an open savoury tart filled with a rich egg custard filling with bacon and onion

VEGETABLES/ _____	LÉGUMES/
SIDE DISHES	GARNITURES
artichoke hearts_____	fonds d'artichauts
chips _____	frites
French dressing _____	vinaigrette
green salad _____	salade verte
mixed salad_____	salade panachée
oil _____	huile
pasta_____	pâtes
pepper_____	poivre
rice_____	riz
vinegar _____	vinaigre

aioli _____	garlic mayonnaise
choucroute_____	sauerkraut
cousinat _____	chestnut, cream and fruit stew
galettes _____	buckwheat pancakes
mojettes_____	kidney beans in butter made from pasteurised cream, west coast speciality
truffes _____	truffles
pissaladière_____	onion tart
potage julienne _____	vegetable soup
ratatouille_____	tomato, aubergine, onion and pepper stew
vichyssoise_____	creamy leek and potato soup

FRUIT AND NUTS ____	FRUITS ET NOIX
(See also Food Shopping)	
cherry_____	cerise
chestnut_____	marron
fig_____	figue
hazelnut_____	noisette
lemon_____	citron
pineapple _____	ananas
plum _____	prune
raisin_____	raisin sec
raspberry_____	framboise
walnut_____	noix
water melon _____	pastèque
wild strawberries ____	fraises des bois

DESSERT_____	DESSERT
cake_____	gâteau
cheese _____	fromage
fritters_____	beignets
fruit salad_____	salade de fruits
ice cream_____	glace
pancakes _____	crêpes
(strawberry) tart ____	tarte (aux fraises)

DRINKS_____	BOISSONS
black/white coffee ___	café noir/au lait
fruit juice_____	jus de fruit
beer_____	bière
lemonade _____	limonade
mineral water _____	eau minérale
fizzy_____	gazeuse
orangeade _____	orangeade

tea with milk/lemon __ thé au lait/avec citron
red/white/rosé wine __ vin rouge/blanc/rosé
dry/sweet _____ sec/doux
sparkling _____ pétillant/mousseux
glass _____ verre
half bottle/bottle_____ demi bouteille/bouteille

SOME TRADITIONAL DRINKS

Bénédictine _____ liqueur made from aromatic
                     herbs by the monks of Fécamp
Calvados _____ apple brandy from Normandy
                     and Brittany
cassis _____ either a sweet blackcurrant
                     liqueur or a provençal wine
                     traditionally drunk with
                     bouillabaisse
Champagne _____ champagne
cidre _____ cider
cognac_____ brandy fom Bordeaux
pastis _____ an aniseed aperitif
vin de Xérès _____ sherry

CHEESE

France is justly famous for its many different
cheeses. Here are just a few to look out for

Boursin _____ Garlic and herb cheese
Brie _____ Originally from the Ile de France
                     region but widely available,
                     combining a creamy texture
                     with a full taste
Camembert _____ A creamy cheese from
                     Normandy
Cantal _____ hard and yellow, with a 2000
                     year-old tradition, from
                     Auvergne
Epoisses _____ a ripe Burgundian speciality
Gruyère_____ a hard, full-fat cheese with a
                     nutty taste
Livarot_____ a Normandy speciality, with a
                     strong taste
Munster _____ highly aromatic, with a sharp
                     taste, developed in the Alsace
                     region by monks during the 7th
                     century
Reblochon_____ a soft, fruity Alpine cheese

▌▐"World Cup"▌▐
Tourist Offices and Fixtures

WORLD CUP CONTACTS

French tourist office contacts for the towns and cities that are hosting the various rounds for the World Cup:

BORDEUX
Jean-Daniel Terrassin, Office de Tourisme, 19 Cours du 30 Juillet, 333080 Bordeaux.
Tel 0033 556442841 Fax 0033 556818921

LENS
Yves Silvain, Office de Tourisme, 26 rue de la Paix, 63200 Lens.
Tel 0033 321676666 Fax 0033 321676566

LYONS
Eriv Ballarin, Office de Tourisme, Place Bellecour, BP 2254, 69214 Lyon.
Tel 0033 472777230 Fax 0033 178370206

MARSEILLES
Maxime Tissot, Office de Tourisme 4 La Canabiere, 13000 Marseille
Tel 0033 491138900 Fax 0033491138920

MONTPELLIER
Helene Schneider, Office de Tourisme 78 Avenue du Piree, 34000 Montpellier
Tel 0033 467606060 Fax 0033 467606061

NANTES
Michele Guillossiou, Office de Tourisme 7 rue Valmy, 44041 Nantes Cedex 01
Tel 0033 251882020 Fax 0033 240891199

PARIS
Stephanie Bertrand, Office de Tourisme 127 avenue des Champs Elysees. 75008 Paris
Tel 0033 149525381 Fax 0033 149525310

SAINT-DENIS
Theodoulitsa Kouloumbri,
Office de Tourisme, 1 rue de la Republique, 93200 Saint-Denis
Tel 0033 155870870 Fax 0033 148202411

SAINT ETIENNE
Dominique Vettier, 3 place Roannelle, 42029 Saint Etienne, Cedex 1
Tel 0033 477251214 Fax 0033 477322728

TOULOUSE
Marc Julia, Office de Tourisme, Donjon du Capitol 31080 Toulouse
Tel 0033 561110222 Fax 0033 561220303

FIXTURES CALENDAR

A useful guide for both those who wish to attend the 1998 World Cup football events and for those who would prefer to avoid them.

FIRST ROUND

MONTPELLIER
Stade de la Mosson
Wed 10/6 Fri 12/6 Wed 17/6
Mon 22/6 Thur 25/6 Mon 29/6

SAINT-DENIS
Stade de France
Wed 10/6 Sat 13/6 Thur 18/6
Tue 23/6 Fri 26/6 28/6

BORDEAUX
Stade Lescure
Thur 11/6 Tue 16/6 Sat 20/6 Wed 24/6
Fri 26/6 Tues 30/6

TOULOUSE
Stadium Municipal
Thur 11/6 Sun 14/6 Thur 18/6
Mon 22/6 Wed 24/6 Mon 29/6

LENS
Stade Felix-Bollaert
Fri 12/6 Sun 14/6 Sun 21/6 Wed 24/6
Fri 26/6 Sun 28/6

LYONS
Stade de Gerland
Sat 13/6 Mon 15/6 Sun 21/6
Wed 24/6 Fri 26/6

MARSEILLES
Stade Municipal
Sat 13/6 Mon 15/6 Sat 20/6 Tues 23/6
Sat 27/6

NANTES
Stade de la Beaujoire
Sat 13/6 Tues 16/6 Sat 20/6 Tues 23/6
Thur 25/6

SAINT-ETIENNE

Stade Geoffroy-Guihard
Sun 14/6 Wed 17/6 Fri 19/6 Tue 23/6
Fri 26/6 Tues 30/6

PARIS
Parc des Princes
Mon 15/6 Fri19/6 Sun 21/6
Thur 25/6 Sat 27/6

QUARTER FINALS

NANTES
Stade de la Beaujoire
Fri 3/7

SAINT-DENIS
Stade de France
Fri 3/7

LYONS
Stade de Gerland
Sat 4/7

MARSEILLES
Stade Municipal
Sat 4/7

SEMI FINALS

MARSEILLES
Stade Municipal
Tues 7/7

SAINT-DENIS
Stade de France
Wed 8/7

FINALS

PARIS
Parc des Princes
Sat 11/7

SAINT-DENIS
Stade de France
Sun 12/7

Driving to Europe for your holiday this year

YOU NEED A ROUTE FROM European Routes Service

Brittany

Of all France, Brittany most preserves an individuality and character of its own. Partly attributable to the religious heritage of its inhabitants, but also to its geographical location as the most westerly region; once it was almost inaccessible to the rest of the country. Early Christians of the 5th and 6th centuries arrived and built monasteries here. Breton, its native language, similar to old Cornish and Welsh, is still spoken; traditional costumes still worn; old Celtic customs and pilgrimage-processions adhered to. Away from the mystical aura, one finds countless little coves and miles of glorious, sandy beaches around its rocky coastline.

(Top): Trecesson is one of the many châteaux in a region which often needed to protect itself from its worst enemy of the middle ages, - France!

(Bottom): Seafood platter is on the menu at this Cancale restaurant. The town is best known for its oysters.

ESSENTIAL FACTS

DÉPARTEMENTS:	Côtes d'Armor, Finistère, Ille-et-Vilaine, Morbihan
PRINCIPAL TOWNS	Rennes, Fougères, St Brieuc, Brest, Quimper, Lorient,Vannes, St Malo
PLACES TO VISIT:	The standing stones at Carnac; the castles and fortresses of inland Brittany: Josselin, Vitré, Fourgères and Combourg; the medieval town of Dinan; the pilgrimage procession at Carantec on the first Sunday after 15 August
REGIONAL TOURIST OFFICE	74B r de Paris, 35069 Rennes Tel: 99 28 44 40
LOCAL GASTRONOMIC DELIGHTS	Assiette de fruits de mer, a seafood platter which may include lobster, langoustines, crab, mussels, sea perch, oyster and other seafood; cotriade, a seafood stew; coquilles-St-Jacques; the classic homard à l'armoricaine; far, a local pudding; galettes, savoury pancakes made with buckwheat flour; crêpes, sweet pancakes
DRINKS	Heady Breton cider, strong local beer, poiré, pear cider and lambig, fiery cider brandy
LOCAL CRAFTS WHAT TO BUY	Pottery and textiles from Quimper, numerous traditional craftsmen including woodcarvers, glass-blowers, weavers, engravers and turners are resident in Dinan

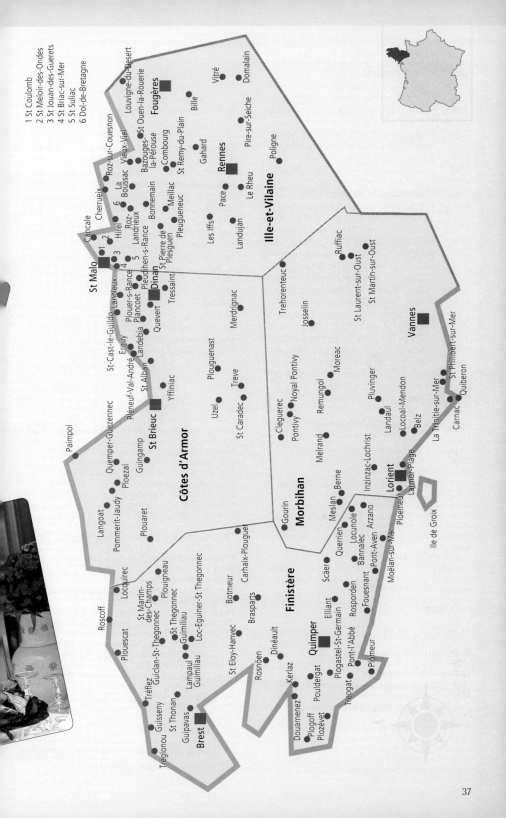

1 St Coulomb
2 St Meloir-des-Ondes
3 St Jouan-des-Guerets
4 St Briac-sur-Mer
5 St Suliac
6 Dol-de-Bretagne

Fougères
Vitré
Louvigne-du-Desert
Bille
St Ouen-la-Rouerie
Bazouges-la-Pérouse
Combourg
St Remy-du-Plain
Pire-sur-Seiche
Gahard
Roz-sur-Couesnon
Vieux-Viel
Rennes
Poligne
Vitré
Domalain

Cherrueix
Hirel
6 La Boussac
Roz-Landrieux
Bonnemain
Meillac
Pace
Le Rheu
Ille-et-Vilaine
Cancale
Les Iffs
Landujan

St Malo
1 2
3
4 5
Pleugueneuc
Pleudihen-s-Rance
St Pierre de Plesguen
Ruffiac

Dinan
Tressaint
St Laurent-sur-Oust
St Martin-sur-Oust
Plancoet
Langueux
Plouer-s-Rance
Erquy
Quevert
Merdignac
Josselin
Vannes
St-Cast-le-Guildo
St Alban
Trehorenteuc
Landebia
St Philibert-sur-Mer
Plérneuf-Val-André
Yffiniac
Plouguenast
Noyal Pontivy
Quiberon
St Brieuc
Uzel
Treve
Pontivy
Moreac
Pluvinger
La Trinité-sur-Mer
Carnac
Côtes d'Armor
St Caradec
Cleguerec
Remungol
Landaul
Locoal-Mendon
Belz
Quemper-Guezennec
Paimpol
Melrand
Berne
Ploezal
Gourin
Morbihan
Inzinzac-Lochrist
Lorient
Guingamp
Meslan
Larmor-Plage
Langoat
Querrien
Ploemeur
Pommerit-Jaudy
Locunole
Arzano
Ile de Groix
Plouaret
Bannalec
Pont-Aven
Moëlan-sur-Mer
Locquirec
Carhaix-Plougue
Fouesnant
Roscoff
St Martin-des-Champs
Plouigneau
Scäer
Plouescat
Botmeur
Elliant
Rosporden
Brasparts
Finistère
St Thegonnec
Loc-Eguiner-St Thegonnec
Treflez
Guiclan-St-Thegonnec
St Eloy-Hanvec
Quimper
Pont-l'Abbé
Guisseny
Guimiliau
Rosnöen
Plogastel-St-Germain
St Thonan
Lampaul Guimiliau
Dinéault
Treogat
Guipavas
Kerlaz
Pouldergat
Plomeur
Treglonou
Brest
Douarnenez
Plogoff
Plozévet

EVENTS & FESTIVALS

Mar Rennes International Fair
Apr St-Quay-Portrieux Festival of The Scallop
May St-Malo Festival of Travel Writers, Tréguier
St-Yves'Pardon (patron saint of lawyers)
Jun Rumengol, le Faou Pardon of Our Lady of
Rumengol; La Faouet, Pardon of Sainte
Barbe;
Jul La Pauline Festival (old sailing ships) at
Pléneuf-Val-André; Pont-l'Abbé Embroider
Festival; Josselin Medieval Festival; Gourin
Pancake Fête; Quiberon Festival of Sea-
Shanties; Fouesnant Apple-Tree Festival;
Quimper Festival of Celtic Music; Vannes Jazz
Festival; Concarneau Maritime Book Festival;
Paimpol Festival of Newfoundland & Iceland
Fishermen; Pontivy Musical Summer;
Guingamp Folk Dancing Festival for Children;
Camaret Musical Mondays; Auray Music &
Folklore Festival; Plozevet Folklore Festival;
Auray Pardon of Sainte-Anne Procession;
Aug Lorient Interceltic Festival; Concarneau Fête
Les Filets Bleus; Guingamp Dance Festival &
Fête de St Loup; Étel Tuna Fair; Plomodiern
Folklore Menez-Hom Festival; Arvor Folklore
Festival; Vannes Arvor Folklore Festival;
Perrros-Guirec Pardon of Notre Dame de la
Clarté; Lamballe Fête des battages St-Aaron

Sep Free concerts (classical, jazz, rock) on Brest
waterfront; Plouha Pardon of Kermaria-en
Isquit
Oct St-Brieuc Art Rock Festival
Dec Les Transmusicales (rock) at Rennes

Saints and Remedies

Saints are an integral part of Britanny's rich
traditional culture. No other part of France venerates
as many, as you'll discover from their statues in the
numerous, fascinating chapels which are well worth
visiting. Quimper diocese claims around 7,500 alone,
yet only three of them get the Vatican's seal of
approval. Bretons seem to have a saint to call on for
every ailment and problem. Saint Livertin, whose
statue is outside the chapel of Notre-Dame-du-Haut
in Trédaniel, is the headache specialist; Saint
Mammert takes care of stomach aches. Saints
Nicodemus and Tugen are invoked at times of
epidemics and rabies respectively; you can visit the
former's holy well at Saint-Nicolas-des-Eaux.
Women saints like Nonna, Ivy and Derrien are said to
help with childhood illnesses. There's even a saint
(Agatha) who helps mothers' problems with babies.

ARZANO Finistère

Château de Kerlarec (Prop: Michel Bellin)
29300
☎ 298717506 FAX 298717455
(from Quimperle take D22 towards Arzano, then left for
Kerlarec.)
In the heart of the Scorff Valley and only two steps from the
ocean, tucked away in green fields, the Château de Kerlarec is
waiting to welcome you to its individual rooms and gourmet
breakfasts. Monique and Michel Bellin are the hosts. English
spoken.
Near river Forest area
6 en suite (bth/shr) (1 fmly) (5 with balcony) TV available
Full central heating Open parking available Supervised
Languages spoken: English & Italian
ROOMS: d 450-380FF *
CARDS: 💳 💳

BANNALEC Finistère

Stang Huel (Prop: Jaouen family)
29380
☎ 298394396 FAX 298395023
(leave N165 at "Kerandreo-Bannalec" exit in the direction of
Scaer (D4). In Bannalec on traffic circle follow Scaer, 500m
from traffic circle turn left & follow signs "Gites du France-
Stang-Huel")
In the heart of the Pays des Portes de Cornouaille (land of the
door to Cornwall), the Jaouen family offer you all the
hospitality of a Breton country home. All rooms have an
independent entrance. A small living room with TV is
reserved for guests. Traditional Breton breakfast is made with

home-grown products. A wooded park is nearby, Pont-Aven is
a ten minute drive away,Concarneau and Quimper are all
within a twenty minute drive. Sporting activities include
tennis, fishing and horse-riding. English spoken.
Near river Forest area
Jun-Sep & long wknds
2 en suite (bth/shr) No smoking on premises TV in all
bedrooms Full central heating Open parking available
Languages spoken: English

BAZOUGES-LA-PÉROUSE Ille-et-Vilaine

Château de la Ballue (Prop: Alain Schrotter)
35560
☎ 299974786 FAX 299974786
(from Rennes or Mont-Saint-Michel follow the N175 then
signposts to the Château)
Five large bedrooms, with canopy bed. Each room has been
decorated in a different but sober and sophisticated style,
Near river Near lake Near sea Forest area Near motorway
5 en suite (bth/shr) (5 fmly) No smoking on premises Full
central heating Open parking available No children 5yrs
Child discount available 12yrs Tennis Fishing Riding V
meals Last d 10.30pm Languages spoken: English & Italian
ROOMS: d 650-850FF Reductions over 1 night
MEALS: Dinner fr 190FF*
CARDS: Travellers cheques

Taking your mobile phone to France?
See page 11

BELZ Morbihan

Kercadoret (Prop: Jean-François Rolland)
56550
☎ 297554401
(from Auray take D22 towards Belz. Before village take right
to Ninezure. After 0.5 miles take right to the farm)
Old Breton farm situated in the calm of the countryside. To
help you unwind, your hosts offer a living room with TV,
eating area in the garden, cooking area (at small extra cost)
and a barbecue area. The beach is three kilometres away.
Open all year round. English spoken.
Near river Near sea Near beach
5 en suite (shr) (1 fmly) No smoking on premises TV
available Full central heating Open parking available
Covered parking available Table tennis Languages spoken:
English
ROOMS: s 190FF; d 240FF Reductions over 1 night
CARDS: Travellers cheques

BERNÉ Morbihan

Marta (Prop: Isabelle Bregardis)
56240
☎ 297342858
This accommodation lies on the edge of the Pont-Calleck
forest, two kilometres from the Scorff Valley. A lovely home-
made breakfast is available in the mornings. Barbecue,
patio,TV and boules are all at the disposal of guests. A little
English spoken.
Near river Near lake Forest area Near motorway
6 en suite (shr) (2 fmly) Full central heating Open parking
available Child discount available Languages spoken: English
CARDS: Travellers cheques

BIEUZY-LES-EAUX Morbihan

Lezerhy (Prop: Martine Maignan)
56310
☎ 297277459
(from Pontivy take D768 towards Lorient.At Port Arthur turn R
onto D1 to St Nicholas-d-Eaux.R after bridge,follow signs for
'Chambre d'Hote/Poterie')
Mme. Maignan welcomes you to her rural home, situated in
the valley of Blavet. Two guest rooms are available on the first
floor, with independent access. A living room, lounge and
garden room are all available to guests. Mountain bikes also
available free of charge. Barbecue and swings on-site.
Children under three years are free. Restaurants within three
kilometres. A little English spoken.
Near river Forest area
Closed Nov-Mar
2 en suite (shr) Full central heating Open parking available
Child discount available Bicycle rental
ROOMS: s 180FF; d 220FF

BILLÉ Ille-et-Vilaine

Mesauboin (Prop: J Roussel)
35133
☎ 299976157 FAX 299975076
Near river
6 en suite (bth/shr) (4 fmly) Full central heating Open
parking available Child discount available 10yrs
MEALS: Dinner fr 81FF*
CARDS: ●● ▆ Travellers cheques

BONNEMAIN Ille-et-Vilaine

Mont Servin (Prop: Mme B M Froud)
35270
☎ 299737062 FAX 299737062
(from St Malo take N137 towards Rennes. turn left to Miniac
Morvan & onto Lanhelin. At x-rds turn left onto D10. 2nd left
into Montservin, house 1st left)

Two of the bedrooms in this family home are suitable for
disabled guests. Continental breakfast served or English
breakfast by request. Two golf courses within close proximity.
English hosts.
Near lake Near sea Near beach Forest area Near motorway
2 rms No smoking on premises Open parking available
Child discount available Languages spoken: English
ROOMS: d 250FF *

Le Rocher-Cordier (Prop: Colin et Brigitte Adams)
☎ 299734545 FAX 299734545
Near river Near lake Forest area
3 en suite (bth/shr) (1 fmly) Radio in rooms Full central
heating Open parking available Child discount available
Languages spoken: English & Italian

BOTMEUR Finistère

Kreisker (Prop: M-T Solliec)
29690
☎ 298996302 FAX 298996302
(leave Morlaix/Quimper road D785 and take D42 in the
direction of Botmeur)
Situated in the heart of the Armorique Park, three kilometres
from the Lac Saint Michel, this converted eighteenth-century
workers' cottage is a relaxing place in which to unwind. Direct
access to many walks, an old monastery, museums and local
sights. Garden and library available to guests. Also on offer is
a separate renovated stone house. English spoken.
Near river Near lake Forest area
1 en suite (bth) Full central heating Open parking available
Child discount available 3yrs Languages spoken: English
ROOMS: d 210FF

BOUSSAC, LA Ille-et-Vilaine

Moulin du Brégan (Prop: Mary-Anne Briand)
35120
☎ 299800529 FAX 299800622
This old mill is situated in a thirteen hectare park, with lake
and woods. Accommodation is available for up to eleven
persons. Continental breakfast served. Dinner at a fixed price
cont'd

of 80 francs, by reservation. Fishing, pedaloes and boats are available, together with plenty of walks. Children under three years can stay free. English spoken.
Near river Near lake Forest area
4 en suite (bth/shr) Full central heating Child discount available 3yrs Last d 20.00hrs Languages spoken: English German Italian Spanish
MEALS: Dinner 80FF*
CARDS: Travellers cheques

BRASPARTS Finistère

Garz Ar Bik (Prop: Marie Chaussy)
29190
☎ 298814714 FAX 298814799
Set between Morlaix and Quimper in the heart of the Arée Mountains, this farmhouse has been completely renovated. The ground floor has a reception room with a large fireplace, which is for the guests' use. Being near a park, this property is ideally situated for country walks and horse-riding. English spoken.
Near river Near sea Forest area
4 en suite (bth/shr) (2 fmly) No smoking on premises Radio in rooms Full central heating Open parking available Covered parking available Child discount available TV room Languages spoken: English
ROOMS: s fr 200FF; d fr 250FF
CARDS: Travellers cheques

CANCALE Ille-et-Vilaine

La Gaudichais (Prop: M & Mme Loisel)
Les Oyats *35260*
☎ 299897361
(from Cancale proceed in direction of St Malo on the D201, 2km before Pointe du Grouin turn right Chambre d'Hote signposted) Situated ten minutes by foot from the beach, not far from St Malo and Mont St Michel, this old, renovated farm has a garden with activities for children. Separate dining room for breakfast. Out of season reductions available. Various sports available within close proximity. English spoken.
Near sea Near beach
4 en suite (shr) (4 fmly) No smoking on premises Full central heating Open parking available Reading room Languages spoken: English & German

La Ville et Gris (Prop: Marie-Christine Masson)
35260
☎ 299896727
Close to the port de Cancale, which is famous for its oysters, this house stands in its own gardens. The proprietor, Marie-Christine Masson, is happy to welcome you at her table for breakfast. and will advise you of the best walks in the area.
Near sea Near beach
5 en suite (bth/shr) (3 fmly) Full central heating
CARDS: Travellers cheques

CARHAIX-PLOUGUER Finistère

Manoir de Prévasy (Prop: M & Mme Novak)
29270
☎ 298932436
(take the bypass to the south of Carhaix (RN164) turn between Distri Center and Hotel des Impots in 800m turn right follow signs to Prevasy)
Forest area
Closed 8 Dec-19 Mar

4 en suite (bth/shr) (1 fmly) Full central heating Open parking available Boule Open terrace Covered terrace Languages spoken: English & Spanish

CARNAC Morbihan

L'Alcyone (Prop: M & Mme Balsan)
Impasse de Beaumer, Carnac Plage *56340*
☎ 297527811 FAX 297521302
Set in a recently converted Breton house, calm and comfort are guaranteed. Friendly welcome, breakfast offered, home cooking available. Saltwater swimming pool, tennis, horse-riding, golf, all available nearby. Beach clubs for children. Spa at Carnac, five kilometres.
Near sea
5 en suite (shr) TV available Direct-dial available Full central heating Open parking available

Kerguéarec (Prop: Mme Brient)
56340
☎ 297568116
(off D186 equidistance between Kergroix/la Trinite-sur-Mer) Mme. Brient offers you comfortable rooms plus a veranda and cooking area. Close to sandy beaches , a spa, island visits, golf at Morbihan, tennis, horse-riding, eighteen hole golf, bowling and many aquatic sports. This is also an ideal place for fishing enthusiasts.
Forest area
Closed Dec
5 en suite (bth/shr) Full central heating Open parking available Child discount available

CHERRUEIX Ille-et-Vilaine

La Croix Gaillot (Prop: Michel Taillebois)
35120
☎ 299489044
Near sea
5 en suite (shr) (2 fmly) No smoking on premises Full central heating Open parking available Child discount available Languages spoken: English
CARDS: ▦ Travellers cheques

CLÉGUÉREC Morbihan

Kerantourner (Prop: A & P Jouan)
56480
☎ 297380614
(from Cleguerec, take D18 towards Guemene sur Scorff. After 2kms turn left. Parking on left after 80 metres)
Guests' rooms are situated in an eighteenth century building constructed of blue stone. Four rooms available, one of which is a family room. This is a working dairy farm and you are welcome to have a look around. Situated ten kilometres from Guerledan Lake and the forest of Quenecan. Dinner available. English spoken.
Near river Near lake Forest area
4 en suite (shr) (1 fmly) TV available Full central heating Open parking available Child discount available 10yrs Boule Languages spoken: English & German
ROOMS: (incl. dinner) s fr 160FF; d 210-300FF
MEALS: Lunch 80-140FF Dinner 80-140FF

DINAN Côtes-D'Armor

Moulin de la Fontaine (Prop: M Garside)
Vallee de la Fontaine des Eaux *22100*
☎ 296879209 FAX 296879209
(from Dinan town centre drive past Château towards Port of Dinan. Down hill & turn right before viaduct. Along river through Port, 1st left at blue Chambre d'Hotes sign. Moulin 100m on right after Youth Hostel)

This eighteenth-century water mill makes an ideal base for a holiday exploring the historic beauty of Brittany. It is situated in the heart of magnificent countryside, with its own gardens and lake, in which otters can often be spotted and is within easy walking distance of the famous medieval town of Dinan and the port. From here a daily ferry trip can be taken to St Malo and Dinard. Comfortable, modern en-suite facilities are available. Dinners are available on request. Your British hosts, Marjorie and Harry Garside, are on hand to give advice on local places of interest.
Near river Near lake Forest area In town centre Near motorway
Closed closed in winter at certain times
5 en suite (shr) (3 fmly) No smoking on premises Full central heating Open parking available Covered parking available Child discount available 12yrs Last d 21.00hrs Languages spoken: English & Welsh
ROOMS: s 220FF; d 300FF Reductions over 1 night Special breaks
MEALS: Dinner 90FF

La Rénardais (Prop: John & Susanne Robinson)
Le Répos *22490*
☎ 296868981 FAX 296869922
(From N176, take Ploüer exit and turn towards Ploüer. Driving along D12, do not enter village, stay on road for 3km and the house is on right hand side.)
Just a short distance from Dinan lies the old village of Ploüer. La Rénardais, an elegant 19-th century stone-built country house is situated on the outskirts of the village. It has recently been restored by its British owners both to preserve its original charm, and to offer modern-day comforts to the guests. Enjoy summer meals on a private terrace set in a lovely floral garden; in winter you have the warmth of full central heating, plus a traditional open fireplace in the spacious lounge. There is a fine watercolour collection for art lovers, and the area offers river/countryside walks, excellent restaurants or simple bistros. The beach is 15 mins. away; Mont St. Michel 45 mins. English spoken.
Near river Near lake Near sea Near beach Forest area Near motorway
Closed Feb

5 en suite (bth/shr) (3 fmly) No smoking on premises Full central heating Open parking available Open terrace Last d 20.00hrs Languages spoken: English & German
ROOMS: s 250FF; d 280-300FF
MEALS: Full breakfast 30FF Dinner 90FF
CARDS: ● ■ Travellers cheques

DINÉAULT Finistère

Rolzac'h (Prop: Anne-Marie L'Haridon)
29150
☎ 298862209
Restored farmhouse just three kilometres from Châteaulin offering comfortable rooms in a peaceful setting close to a forest. This charming property is within twelve kilometres of the beach.
Near river Forest area
4 en suite (shr) No smoking in all bedrooms TV in 2 bedrooms Full central heating Open parking available Supervised

DOL-DE-BRETAGNE Ille-et-Vilaine

La Crochardière (Prop: Janine Lebret)
35120
☎ 299480066
The rooms are situated in an old seventeenth century château in the countryside, just one kilometre from the town centre. There is a garden for the guests to relax in and facilities include table-tennis and children's games. English spoken.
RS Etr-Jun & Sep-Oct
5 en suite (shr) Full central heating Open parking available Supervised Table tennis Languages spoken: English
CARDS: Travellers cheques

Manoir de Launay Blot (Prop: M Bernard Mabile)
Baguer Morvan *35120*
☎ 299480748
(from Dol-de-Bretagne take N176 to Dinan. At last set of lights take D119 to Bagner-Morvan. Follow signs for Manoir de Launay-Blot')
A magnificent seventeenth-century manor house, situated near woods, fields and a lake. Nearby is the famous Mont-St-Michel, the beach and the pretty seaside town of Dinard. All bedrooms are en suite, and have been tastefully renovated. Dinner is available on request. Guests are invited to make use of the dayroom. The beach is within a short distance of the property. English spoken.
Near lake Forest area

cont'd

3 en suite (bth) No smoking in 1 bedroom Full central heating Open parking available Supervised Fishing
Languages spoken: English
ROOMS: (room only) d 300-360FF
MEALS: Dinner 100FF
CARDS: Travellers cheques

DOMALAIN Ille-et-Vilaine

Les Hairies (Prop: Mauries Templon)
05680
☎ 99763629
Maurice and Marcel welcome you to their rural home, situated on a farm. Two guest rooms are available, one on the first floor and one on the ground floor, which includes one family room. A living room is available for guests and a regional breakfast is available. There is a no smoking policy in the house. Swimming, tennis, horse-riding and fishing within close proximity.
Forest area Near motorway
2 en suite (shr) (1 fmly) (1 with balcony) No smoking on premises Full central heating Open parking available No children 6yrs

DOUARNENEZ Finistère

Kerléguer (Prop: Jean Larour)
29100
☎ 298923464
Kerléguer is an old farm close to the sea which offers two rooms in the family home and three rooms in a separate ivy-covered stone cottage. Close to the local village and within easy distance of the beach and its various water activities.
Near sea Near beach Near motorway
2 en suite (bth/shr) Full central heating Open parking available

Manoir de Kervent (Prop: Marie-Paule Lefloch)
Pouldavid *29100*
☎ 298920490 FAX 296920490
A warm welcome awaits you at this residence. Especially pretty is the pink room, which has been furnished in Art Deco style. The beach is close at hand.
Near sea Near beach Forest area
(1 fmly) Full central heating Open parking available Child discount available 5yrs
CARDS: Travellers cheques

ELLIANT Finistère

Ferme de Quelennec (Prop: M & Mme Le Berre)
Quelennec *29370*
☎ 298591043
A traditional country welcome will be found at this peaceful and comfortable guest house. The property is situated just twenty minutes from the beaches of Sud-Finistère. Fishing available on-site (River Odet). You can enjoy a traditional Breton breakfast of pancakes and other specialities. Children free up to three years old.
Near river Forest area
4 en suite (bth/shr) No smoking on premises TV available Full central heating Open parking available Child discount available
CARDS: Travellers cheques

ERQUY Côtes-D'Armor

Les Ruaux Les Bruyères (Prop: M & Mme Dutemple)
22430
☎ 493723159 FAX 296720468
Your hosts welcome you to their typical Breton home and would like to introduce you to the traditions and specialities of this region. Quiet and comfort await you, in a family atmosphere, where six guest rooms are available, and a kitchen and dining room at guests disposal. There is also a gite, with half-board available for four persons. Plenty of restaurants nearby. Erquy has a pretty fishing harbour and is within fifteen kilometres of the Fort La Latte, which is well worth a visit. The beaches are of fine sand.
Near sea Near beach
6 en suite (shr) (2 fmly) (1 with balcony) No smoking on premises Child discount available
CARDS: ▨

FOUGÈRES Ille-et-Vilaine

Bed & Breakfast (Prop: M & Mme Juban)
5 chemin du Patis *35300*
☎ 299990052
The family Juban are pleased to welcome you to their guesthouse, where small details will make your visit an extremely pleasant one. The breakfast is substantial and a large garden is available for guests to use, and where games can be played by children.
Near river Forest area
Closed Dec-Feb
4 rms (2 bth/shr) No smoking on premises Full central heating Open parking available Supervised

GAHARD Ille-et-Vilaine

Les Viviers (Prop: Mr Dugueperoux)
35490
☎ 299395019
(from Rennes take N175 north, through St Aubin and turn right to Gahard)
This stone and granite house in the countryside awaits your visit. Your hosts, Anne-Marie, Victor and their children, welcome you to a warm and friendly family atmosphere, which is extended to their evening table. All meals are cooked from fresh farm produce. Large, open fire. Plenty of interesting walks. Climbing, riding, fishing, canoeing, sailing and swimming are within ten kilometres.
Near river Forest area Near motorway
4 en suite (bth/shr) (2 fmly) Full central heating Open parking available Supervised Child discount available
ROOMS: s 165FF; d 185-240FF *

GUICLAN-ST-THEGONNEC Finistère

Moulin de Kerlaviou (Prop: Mme Therese Cornily)
29410
☎ 298796057
Near river Forest area Near motorway
Closed Etr-Oct
2 en suite (bth/shr) No smoking on premises Full central heating Open parking available Supervised Fishing

Taking your mobile phone to France?
See page 11

GUIMILIAU Finistère

Croas Avel (Prop: Christine Croguennec)
29400
☎ 298687072
Pleasant surroundings and its own large garden are a feature of this attractive property.
3 en suite (bth/shr) No smoking on premises TV available Full central heating Open parking available

GUIPAVAS Finistère

La Chataigneraie Keraveloc (Prop: Michelle Morvan)
29490
☎ 298415268
(From Guipavas take D712 towards Brest for 3.5km, then left at traffic lights towards Keraveloc and follow signs)
The house stands on high ground amidst its own pleasant gardens. From the terrace there are panoramic sea views and it is close to 'the vallon du Stangalard' and its botanic gardens.
Near sea Near beach Forest area
3 en suite (bth/shr) (1 fmly) No smoking on premises TV in all bedrooms Full central heating Open parking available Child discount available 6yrs Indoor swimming pool (heated) Boule Languages spoken: English & Spanish
ROOMS: s fr 220FF; d fr 250FF Reductions over 1 night
CARDS: Travellers cheques

GUISSENY Finistère

Keraloret (Prop: M Pierre Le Gall)
29880
☎ 298256037 FAX 298256988
(from Roscoff take D10(right off D58) towards Brest. At Goulven take D10 to Guissény)
Near river Near lake Near sea Near beach
6 en suite (bth/shr) (3 fmly) No smoking in 2 bedrooms Full central heating Open parking available Covered parking available Supervised Child discount available 12yrs Last d 21.00hrs Languages spoken: English, German & Spanish
ROOMS: d 275FF
MEALS: Full breakfast 35FF Dinner 100FF
CARDS: ●● 💳 Travellers cheques

HIREL Ille-et-Vilaine

La Maison de Quokelunde (Prop: M Jean Paul Raux)
41 rue Bord-de-Mer *35120*
☎ 299488012 FAX 299488012
Four of the rooms in La Maison de Quokelunde look directly out onto the bay of Mont St Michel - a more exquisite location is hard to imagine. Communal living room for breakfast. The awning of the house faces south, making a real sun trap. Picnic tables outside. Special offers out of season, discounts for children. Traditional Breton breakfast served. Your hosts' ten years of experience will guarantee a peaceful and relaxing holiday. A little English spoken.
Near sea
5 en suite (shr) (2 fmly) No smoking in 2 bedrooms TV available Full central heating Open parking available Child discount available
ROOMS: s 170FF; d 200FF
CARDS: Travellers cheques

IFFS, LES Ille-et-Vilaine

Château de Montmuran (Prop: Herne de la Villeon)
35630
☎ 299458888 FAX 299458490
(autoroute Rennes-St Malo exit Tinteniac/Becherel then follow signs)
The château is filled with history. Bertrand de Guesclin was knighted here in 1354 and married Jeanne de Laval in 1373. It is a protected building. Two rooms are available, both furnished with antiques. Billiards available. Good walks in the park. English spoken.
Forest area Near motorway
Closed Nov-Apr
2 en suite (bth/shr) Full central heating Open parking available Languages spoken: English

ILE-DE-GROIX Morbihan

Les Cornorans (Prop: Jacques & Catherine Hardy)
rue du Chalutier les Deux Ange *56590*
☎ 297865767
Les Cormorans is a windswept isolated house, just two paces away from the sea, on an island. If you are looking for fresh air and a break from the city, then this is the place to blow the cobwebs away. Comfortable rooms, living room, kitchen, gardens with attractive flowers. Watch the sun setting over the harbour and return home relaxed and happy again.
Near sea
3 en suite (shr) (1 fmly) No smoking on premises Full central heating Open parking available Supervised

La Grek (Prop: Sol Guilloux)
3 pl du Leurhé *56590*
☎ 297868985
Charming old restored house, furnished with antiques, near to a wood. Set on Groix island, guests may enjoy the pleasures of solitude; sea breeze, fresh air and a sense of escape. Take advantage of these pleasures from the garden or stroll around the island. Continental breakfast served. Reductions for children under six years.
Near sea
Closed Oct-Mar
5 en suite (bth/shr) (2 fmly) No smoking on premises Full central heating Open parking available Child discount available 6yrs

INZINZAC-LOCHRIST Morbihan

Tymat-Penquesten (Prop: Catherine Spence)
56650
☎ 297368926
(From Lochrist towards Penquesten establishment 3.5kms on left)
Tymat is a charming eighteenth and nineteenth century manor. Ideally located in the peaceful countryside, the guesthouse is only twenty kilometres from the sea. Many activities nearby: tennis, riding, canoeing. The peaceful haven offers you comfortable rooms, farmland and forest. There is a large lounge, with television, and a dining room. English spoken.
Near river Forest area
4 en suite (bth) No smoking on premises Full central heating Open parking available Supervised Languages spoken: English
ROOMS: d 280FF Reductions over 1 night
CARDS: Travellers cheques

43

JOSSELIN Morbihan

Bed & Breakfast (Prop: M & Mme Jean & Marie Guyot)
Butte St-Laurent *56120*
☎ 297222209 FAX 297339010
The Guyot family house is set on the edge of the Oust Valley, overlooking the Château of Josselin. The family truly enjoy receiving visitors to their home, and hearty breakfasts are served.
Near river Forest area Near motorway
Closed 21 Sep-Mar
4 en suite (bth/shr) (1 fmly) No smoking on premises Full central heating Open parking available Covered parking available Child discount available 15yrs

Bed & Breakfast (Prop: M & Mmme Elsden)
13 r St Jacques *56120*
☎ 297756606
(from N24 Rennes/Lorient take La Trinite Parhoet/Les Forges exit, follow sign for centre of village, house is 650m along the road on the right before fountain)
Situated in medieval Josselin, with its château, river, shops, bars, restaurant and museum. The Elsden family welcome you to their home, which is comfortably furnished. A sitting room, dining room and garden are available to guests.
Near river Near lake Near sea Forest area In town centre Near motorway
3 rms (1 fmly) Open parking available Child discount available Languages spoken: English
CARDS: Travellers cheques

La Carrière (Prop: M et Mme Bignon)
8 rue de la Carrière *56120*
☎ 297222262 FAX 297222262
(just over midway between Rennes and Lorient off the N24)
Just outside the town of Josselin. The chambre d'hôte is in attractive gardens, bedrooms are bright and furnished with antiques.
Near river Forest area In town centre Near motorway
7 rms (2 bth 4 shr) Full central heating Open parking available Languages spoken: English & German
ROOMS: s 250-350FF; d 300-400FF
CARDS: ●● ▆▆ Travellers cheques

KERLAZ Finistère

Bed & Breakfast (Prop: M & Mme H Gonidec)
Lanevry *29100*
☎ 298921912
A statue of St Anne marks the entrance to this attractive farm, which is only five minutes from the beach. M and Mme Gonidec have recently retired from running the farm and offer both bed and breakfast accommodation and three gites on-site. Guests have use of a lounge with television. Madame makes a fabulous Breton breakfast with crêpes and Breton cake. The beach is just five minutes away.
Near river Near sea Forest area
Full central heating Open parking available Covered parking available Supervised
CARDS: Travellers cheques

LAMPAUL-GUIMILIAU Finistère

Pen Ar Yed (Prop: Claude Gaschet)
29400
☎ 298686105
Near river Forest area Near motorway

Closed mid Oct-mid Nov
2 en suite (shr) Full central heating Open parking available Supervised Languages spoken: English
CARDS: Travellers cheques

LANCIEUX Côtes-D'Armor

Les Hortensias (Prop: Cosson)
40 rue du Moulin *22770*
☎ 296863115
(between Ploubalay and Lancieux)
Near sea Near beach Forest area
4 en suite (shr) (2 fmly) No smoking on premises Full central heating Open parking available Languages spoken: English
ROOMS: s fr 230FF; d fr 300FF Reductions over 1 night
CARDS: Travellers cheques

LANDAUL Morbihan

Bed & Breakfast (Prop: Mme Odile Plunian)
27 rue de Kermabergal *56690*
☎ 297246110
Near river Near sea Forest area Near motorway
Closed mid Sep-Etr
3 en suite (bth/shr) No smoking on premises Full central heating Open parking available Child discount available

LANDÉBIA Côtes-D'Armor

Le Pont a l'Ane (Prop: Nichole Robert)
22130
☎ 296844752
(Rennes-Dinan-Plancoet)
Near river Forest area
Closed Dec-Feb
5 en suite (shr) No smoking on premises Full central heating Open parking available Languages spoken: English

LANDUJAN Ille-et-Vilaine

Château-de-Leauville
35360
☎ 299072114 FAX 299072180
An elegant château set in lovely countryside, built in the sixteenth century on the remains of an eleventh century manor and restored by the present owners. A warm and personal welcome awaits you. The romantic setting will make you lose your heart to this place. Swimming pool on-site. Meals may be taken with hosts by prior arrangement. Tennis, riding and fitness centre ten kilometres away. English spoken.
Near sea Forest area Near motorway
Closed 16 Oct-Mar open Etr
8 en suite (bth/shr) (4 fmly) Radio in rooms Full central heating Open parking available No children 6yrs Child discount available 12yrs Outdoor swimming pool (heated) Open terrace Languages spoken: English
MEALS: Continental breakfast 56FF Dinner fr 185FF*
CARDS: ●● ▆▆ Travellers cheques

LANGOAT Côtes-D'Armor

Bed & Breakfast (Prop: Marie Francoise Bouget)
9 rue du Fort Castel *22450*
☎ 296913212
Near river Near sea
1 rms (1 fmly) No smoking on premises Radio in rooms Full central heating

LARMOR-PLAGE Morbihan

Les Camelias (Prop: Paulette Allamo)
9 rue des Roseaux *56520*
☎ 297655067
(exit N165 signposted Lorient Larmor Plage and in town
centre take direction for Kerpape Lomener for 100mtrs, house
by traffic lights)
Near sea Near beach
5 en suite (shr) No smoking on premises Full central heating
CARDS: Travellers cheques

LOC-EGUINER-ST-THÉGONNEC Finistère

Ty Dreux (Prop: Anne Martin)
29410
☎ 298780821
Jean and Annie will be happy to welcome you to their home,
set in a weavers' village dating back to the seventeenth
century, where two charming guest rooms are available on the
second floor on this milking farm. Costumes and photographs
of your hosts' ancestors are displayed on the first floor. Ample
breakfasts are served in a rustic environment. Cider tasting
available on the farm. Breton evenings available, by
reservation. Three gites also available in the grounds.
Restaurant within four kilometres. Tennis, swimming, sailing,
fishing and horse-riding in close proximity.
Near river Forest area
2 en suite (bth/shr) No smoking on premises TV available
Full central heating Open parking available Supervised

LOCOAL-MENDON Morbihan

Kervihern (Prop: Gabriel Maho)
56550
☎ 297246409
Twelve kilometres from Carnac, on a working farm dating
back to the seventeenth century. Living room on the ground
floor, furnished in typical regional style. Six rooms are
available with one family room. Dinner is available in the
evening. Understanding of English.
Near river Near sea
6 en suite (1 fmly) Full central heating Open parking
available Languages spoken: English
ROOMS: s 200FF; d 230-250FF
MEALS: Dinner 80FF
CARDS: Travellers cheques

LOCQUIREC Finistère

Bed & Breakfast (Prop: Comte/Comtesse Hubert
Germiny)
11 rue de Kerael *29241*
☎ 298674711
This property is owned by the Count and Countess Hubert Le
Bègue de Germiny and is situated on the edge of a protected
village. Elegant décor, with antique furniture. Comfortable and
spacious rooms. Absolute tranquillity. Pretty garden with view
of the sea and the coast. Your Franco-American hosts speak
perfect English - he is an ex-diplomat and both are well
travelled . Excellent breakfasts and dinners by arrangement.
Near river Near sea
Closed 15 Oct-14 Apr
4 rms (3 bth/shr) (1 fmly) No smoking on premises Full
central heating Open parking available No children 1yr TV
room

LOCUNOLÉ Finistère

La Biquerie (Prop: C Guimard)
29310
☎ 298713226
A convivial welcome awaits you at La Biquerie, where
comfortable guest rooms are offered, as well as a pretty
garden to relax in and a warm fireplace for the colder evenings.
A lounge with satellite television, plus a library and video
library is offered for guests' use. Dinner with your hosts by
reservation, with regional specialities available. English spoken.
Near river Near lake Near motorway
6 en suite (shr) Open parking available Languages spoken:
English
MEALS: Dinner 100-200FF*

LOUVIGNÉ-DU-DÉSERT Ille-et-Vilaine

La Basse Grezilière (Prop: M & Mme R K Tubbs)
St-Georges-de-Réintembault *35420*
☎ 299971019
(St James is on the D998 & is equidistant from Avranches &
Fougeres. St Georges de Reintembault is well signposted from
St James off the D30, approx 6kms)

Large stone farmhouse dating back to the late 1600's, which
has been beautifully restored whilst maintaining its original
oak beams, open fireplace and bread oven. Two double
bedrooms are on offer, sharing a large bathroom/WC. Guests
are completely separate from their English hosts. Situated just
over a mile from the Normandy/Brittany border, in an idyllic
setting, surrounded by fields and orchards. Guests may
telephone from the main square of St Georges, where they
will be met, while those booking in advance will be provided
with a map as well as being met. Many restaurants in close
proximity.
Near river Near lake Near sea Near beach Forest area Near
motorway
2 rms No smoking on premises Full central heating Open
parking available Supervised No children 5yrs Languages
spoken: English & German
ROOMS: d 250FF

MEILLAC Ille-et-Vilaine

Bed & Breakfast (Prop: Nelly & Christian Dragon)
La Ville Guimon *35270*
☎ 299731717
Christian and Nelly Dragon welcome you to their farm where
peace and quiet are assured. Two guest rooms are offered. The
garden provides games for children. Situated near an aquatic

cont'd

45

park and just six kilometres from Combourg, famous for its château, park and waters.
Forest area
Closed Nov-Feb
2 en suite (shr) Full central heating Open parking available

MELRAND Morbihan

La Mijotiere (Prop: M & Mme Chavel)
Quenetevel *56310*
☎ 297277282
M and Mme Chavel own several rooms which are comfortable and quiet. The rooms form part of the restaurant which the Chavels run, so you're in an ideal spot to discover the delights of Breton cuisine.
Near river Forest area
Closed Jan-Feb & 8 days Oct
4 en suite (bth/shr) Full central heating Open parking available Supervised Child discount available Last d 21.00hrs
CARDS: ●● ▨

MERDRIGNAC Côtes-D'Armor

Manoir de la Peignie (Prop: Jacques Douin)
rue du Mène *22230*
☎ 296284286
Warm welcome offered in this renovated thirteenth century manor. Six large rooms are available. Breakfast is served in the medieval dining room. The large park is a haven of tranquillity.
Near river Near lake Forest area In town centre
6 en suite (bth/shr) (2 fmly) No smoking in 3 bedrooms TV available Radio in rooms Full central heating Open parking available Covered parking available

MESLAN Morbihan

Bed & Breakfast (Prop: Mme Jambou)
Roscalet *56320*
☎ 297342413 FAX 297342413

You will be welcomed by Mme. Marie-France Jambou to this old stone house with living room, private garden, kitchen and library for guests use. The sea is thirty kilometres away. Various sporting pursuits to be found locally. Free for children up to two years. A little English spoken.
Near river Forest area
Closed Nov-Mar
5 en suite (shr) No smoking on premises Full central heating Open parking available Covered parking available Supervised Languages spoken: English
ROOMS: s 210FF; d 260FF

MOËLAN-SUR-MER Finistère

Trenogoat (Prop: M & Mme Williams)
29350
☎ 298396282 FAX 298397809
(from centre of Moelan-sur-Mer, take D24 signposted Clohars/Carnoet/Lorient and at roundabout turn right. After 50mtrs turn left signposted Merrien-le-Port. Follow road for 2.5kms)
An English family-run, restored Breton farmhouse situated two minutes from the sea in the midst of quiet, unspoilt countryside. Five en suite bedrooms, licensed dining room, large comfortable sitting rooms, games room, laundry. Two and half acres of grounds, including orchard, farmyard with small animals, barbecue, boules. Good food using fresh local produce.
Near river Near sea Near beach Forest area
Closed Sept-June
6 en suite (shr) (1 fmly) No smoking in all bedrooms Licensed Full central heating Open parking available Supervised Boule Bicycle rental Open terrace Billiard table Last d 19.30 Languages spoken: English
ROOMS: s 210FF; d 260FF
CARDS: ●● ▨ Travellers cheques

MORÉAC Morbihan

Kerivin (Prop: M & Mme Sergent)
56500
☎ 297601888
Two houses, independent of the main residence, are on offer at this dairy farm. Four rooms in the main house are also available. Living room plus games for the children in the garden. Private lake.
Forest area Near motorway
4 en suite (shr) No smoking in 2 bedrooms Full central heating Open parking available

NOYAL PONTIVY Morbihan

Pennerest (Prop: P Roberts)
56920
☎ 297383576 FAX 297382380
(on arrival in Pontivy follow direction to Vannes/Josselin, fork left on D764 to Josselin, after 4km there is crossroads take the next turn on right 'Pennerest')
A friendly welcome awaits guests at this attractively decorated, inexpensive accommodation. There are grounds of 3 acres with lawns, orchard and garden furniture, amenities include a swimming pool, table tennis and pool table.
Near river Near lake Forest area In town centre
2 en suite (shr) (1 fmly) No smoking in all bedrooms Full central heating Open parking available Outdoor swimming pool Tennis Boule Croquet Badminton Table tennis Languages spoken: English
ROOMS: (room only) s 160-200FF; d 160-200FF
MEALS: Continental breakfast 20FF

PACÉ Ille-et-Vilaine

Manoir de Méhault (Prop: Herve Barre)
35740
☎ 299606288
(6km from Rennes in direction St Brieuc)
This restored seventeenth century manor, near Rennes, is surrounded by a park of trees and flowers. Guests may use the barbecue in the garden. Golf, riding, tennis, swimming, lakes

and forests nearby. Thirty-five minutes from St.Malo. English spoken.
Near river Forest area Near motorway
Closed 1 Nov-31 Mar

5 rms (4 bth/shr) (2 fmly) Full central heating Open parking available Supervised Languages spoken: English
ROOMS: d 215FF

PIRÉ-SUR-SEICHE Ille-et-Vilaine

Les Épinays (Prop: M & Mme Colleu)
35150
☎ 299000116
A farmhouse on the borders of Brittany. You are invited to explore the farm or take pony rides. Games are provided for the children. Guests are also welcome to join the family for dinner. Walks, fishing and bathing nearby. English spoken.
Near river Near motorway
4 en suite (1 fmly) No smoking on premises TV available Full central heating Open parking available Supervised Languages spoken: English
MEALS: Dinner 85-100FF*

PLANCOËT Côtes-D'Armor

La Pastourelle (Prop: E Ledé)
St-Lormel *22130*
☎ 296840377 FAX 296840377
Evelyne Ledé has six guest rooms in this old, country home, furnished with antiques. Living room and dining room available to guests. Garden with summer house, garden furniture and games. The sea and beaches are only ten kilometres away. Special offers for visitors staying five days or more. English spoken.
Near river
6 en suite (bth/shr) (1 fmly) (5 with balcony) Full central heating Child discount available 9yrs Boule Open terrace Languages spoken: English
ROOMS: s 235-245FF; d 235-255FF Reductions over 1 night
MEALS: Dinner fr 85FF*
CARDS: ▨ Travellers cheques

PLEUDIHEN-SUR-RANCE Côtes-D'Armor

La Cour aux Meuniers (Prop: Mme Therese Tartar-Hue)
rue des Camèlias *22690*
☎ 296833423 FAX 296832051
(on dual carriageway between St Malo & Rennes, take the Chateauneuf/Pleudihen exit, then follow directions for Pleudihen. Chambre d'hôte is behind church towards the 'Maine'.)

Located on the Rance estuary, between Dinan and St.Malo. This stone built house in the village centre has bedrooms with panoramic views of the fields and river. Tailor-made breakfasts on offer in the typically Breton living room. Tennis available nearby; golf, ten kilometres. English spoken.
Near river In town centre
4 rms (1 bth 2 shr) (1 fmly) (1 with balcony) TV available Radio in rooms Full central heating Open parking available Supervised Child discount available 5yrs Tennis nearby Table tennis Languages spoken: English
ROOMS: s 170FF; d 220-240FF Reductions over 1 night

Le Vau Nogues (Prop: Simone Mousson)
22690
☎ 296832294 FAX 296832294
Simone and François Mousson welcome you to their modern farmhouse. Meals may be taken with your hosts. Families are invited to look around the farm and try fresh, warm milk. St Malo and Mont St Michel nearby. English spoken.
Near river Near sea Forest area Near motorway
3 en suite (shr) (2 fmly) No smoking on premises Full central heating Open parking available Supervised Child discount available Last d 18.00hrs Languages spoken: English & German
MEALS: Dinner fr 75FF*
CARDS: Travellers cheques

PLEUGUENEUC Ille-et-Vilaine

Les Bruyères (Prop: J Parker)
35720
☎ 299694775 FAX 299694775
(D974 between Dinan & Combourg)
Your English hosts, Janet and David, fell in love with this house the minute they saw it and they hope you will too. The only complaint they ever had from their guests is that the breakfasts are too large! A beautiful dining room and lounge with open fire, plus French and satellite Sky TV in English available for guests.
Near lake Forest area Near motorway
Closed 15 Dec-1 Feb
3 en suite (bth/shr) No smoking on premises Radio in rooms Full central heating Open parking available Supervised Child discount available 8yrs Languages spoken: English
MEALS: Dinner 85FF*

PLOEMEUR Morbihan

Le Petit Hanvot (Prop: M Georges Mestric)
56270
☎ 297862234
(from Vannes to Quimper road exit Ploemeur Airport)
3 en suite (shr) Full central heating Open parking available Child discount available

PLOËZAL Côtes-D'Armor

Ferme de Kerléo (Prop: Mr and Mrs Jean Louis Herve)
22260
☎ 296956578
This farm is situated next to a château. Well placed for visitors to explore the ever-changing coastline of Paimpol, Bréhat, Tréguier and its cathedral. The "Pink Granite" coast is only twenty minutes away. Ten percent reduction after two nights. Reductions for children under twelve.
Near river Forest area

cont'd

4 rms (2 shr) No smoking on premises Full central heating Open parking available Supervised Child discount available 12yrs
CARDS: Travellers cheques

PLOGASTEL-ST-GERMAIN Finistère

Kerguérnou (Prop: M & Mme le Henaff)
29710
☎ 98545630
Old, stone Breton cottage which has been lovingly restored by your hosts, the Le Henaff family. The setting is a dairy farm in the middle of the countryside. The beach is only ten to fifteen kilometres away.
6 en suite (bth/shr) Full central heating Open parking available

PLOGOFF Finistère

Ferme de Kerguidy Izella (Prop: Jean Noel Le Bars)
29770
☎ 298703560
(exit Quimper Sud road in the direction Audierne Points du Raz take D765 then D784)
Old, renovated farm dating back to 1832, near to Pointe du Raz. Leisure activities available on the Cap Sizun include walks, a bird reserve, snail farming at Goulien, visits to a bee-keeper, guided tours of local chapels, riding centre, bike hire, diving centre and tennis. A little English spoken.
Forest area
6 en suite (shr) (1 fmly) TV available Full central heating Open parking available Child discount available 7yrs
ROOMS: d 250FF
MEALS: Continental breakfast 25FF Dinner 80FF

PLOMEUR Finistère

Keraluic (Prop: Irene et Luis Gomez-Centurion)
29120
☎ 298821022 FAX 298821022
(20 km South from Quimper (D-785). Road from Pont L'Abbé to St Jean Trolimon. Signposted.)

Old, Breton style stone farm and thatched cottage. Guests may dine with their hosts - seaweed a speciality and organic produce guaranteed. English spoken.
Near sea Near beach Forest area
5 en suite (bth/shr) (2 with balcony) No smoking on premises Full central heating Open parking available Child discount available 3yrs Boule Bicycle rental Table tennis Volleyball Languages spoken: English, German & Spanish

ROOMS: d 330-380FF
MEALS: Dinner fr 110FF
CARDS: Travellers cheques

PLONÉVEZ-PORZAY Finistère

Bed & Breakfast (Prop: Claude Revel)
Crec'h Levern, St Anne-le-Palud *29550*
☎ 298925098
(from Quimper direction to Plnevez-Porzay the St Anne-la-Palud, 2nd street on left marked with blue sign)
Closed mid Nov-mid Mar
2 en suite (bth/shr) TV in all bedrooms Full central heating Open parking available
ROOMS: (room only) s 350FF; d 380FF
CARDS: ●●

PLOUARET Côtes-D'Armor

Le Presbytère (Prop: Nicole de Morchoven)
Trégrom *22420*
☎ 296479415
(from the N12 exit at Louargat for Tregrom)
This is an old presbytery in the centre of a small, peaceful village. Built in the seventeenth century, the place is enclosed by high walls bedecked with violets and roses. This is a place to find serenity and peace. Ideal spot from which to explore Western Brittany. English spoken.
Near river Forest area
3 en suite (bth/shr) No smoking on premises Full central heating Open parking available Languages spoken: English
ROOMS: s 250FF; d 300FF
MEALS: Dinner fr 125FF

PLOUESCAT Finistère

Penkear (Prop: Marie & Raymond Duff)
29430
☎ 298696287 FAX 298696733
(situated between Plouescat and the sea)
Marie-Thérèse and Raymond Le Duff offer a warm welcome to their rustic home. Two rooms available in the house plus one cottage. Large breakfast. Restaurants within one kilometre. Casino and beaches, two kilometres. Health spa nearby where you can try seawater therapy.
Near sea Near beach
2 en suite (bth/shr) TV in all bedrooms Radio in rooms Full central heating Open parking available Supervised Bicycle rental Baby-Foot
ROOMS: s 300FF; d 360FF
CARDS: Travellers cheques

PLOUGUENAST Côtes-D'Armor

Garmorin (Prop: Bernard & Madeleine Lucas)
22150
☎ 296287061 FAX 296268500
Located in the heart of Brittany, this guesthouse offers a pleasant atmosphere. Three rooms are available, one of these being a family room. Many activities available nearby. Self-catering cottage also available. Restaurants within one and a half kilometres. Reductions for children may be available. Notional English.
Near river
4 rms (3 shr) (1 fmly) Full central heating Open parking available
ROOMS: s fr 180FF; d fr 200FF

St-Theo (Prop: Eliane Collet)
22150
☎ 296287001
Your hostess, Eliane Collet, welcomes you to her large, stone house in the heart of the French countryside. The garden enjoys splendid views. The summer room may be enjoyed when it is too cold to sit outside and the living room has a television and open fire. Large French breakfast.
Near river Near lake Forest area
3 rms (2 bth/shr) No smoking on premises Full central heating Open parking available Supervised

PLOUIGNEAU Finistère

Manoir de Lanleya (Prop: André Marrec)
29610
☎ 298799415
André, your host, having run a book shop for many years, gave it up to renovate this small, sixteenth century manor house. Now he has four rooms on offer which are reached via a staircase in the tower. Three cottages are also available. André is happy to show you around the charming chapel which belonged to the manor. English spoken.
Near river Near sea Forest area
3 en suite (shr) (1 fmly) No smoking on premises Full central heating Open parking available Languages spoken: English
ROOMS: d 320FF

PLOZEVET Finistère

Kerongard Divisquin (Prop: M & Mme Trepos)
29710
☎ 298543109
Near sea
3 en suite (shr) No smoking on premises Full central heating Boule
ROOMS: d 250FF

PLUVIGNER Morbihan

Chaumière de Kerréo (Prop: M Gerard Greves)
56330
☎ 297509048 FAX 297509069
(from N24, leave motorway in Baud, head towards Auray, then leaving Baud, turn right to Landevant, after 10km turn right again following signs for Chambre d'Hôtes)
The Greves family welcome you to their eighteenth century thatched cottage. Here you can enjoy the peace and quiet of the countryside. Delicious meals feature traditional Breton fare. English spoken.
Forest area
5 rms (1 bth 3 shr) Full central heating Open parking available Child discount available 7yrs Languages spoken: English
ROOMS: s 190-210FF; d 260-310FF
MEALS: Dinner fr 95FF
CARDS: Travellers cheques

Kerdavid-Duchentil (Prop: M & Mme Collet)
56330
☎ 297560059
An old house set in a wooded park in the heart of the countryside. Fully equipped kitchen, living room and television room available to guests. This is a place which allows you to discover the charms of the countryside. Add to this the pleasure of the sea and beaches at the nearby Golfe

du Morbihan and you will have a delightful holiday. English spoken.
Near river Near lake Near sea Forest area
5 en suite (bth/shr) Radio in rooms Open parking available

Kermec (Prop: Noemi Lorgeoux)
56330
☎ 297249297
(Motorway Rennes-Lorient, exit at Baud, follow the direction to Auray and at Pluvigner, towards Sainte Anne d'Auray, Kermec is a hamlet on the right, halfway between Pluvigner and Sainte Anne.)
This cottage has a kitchen area, living room with open fire and laundry facilities. For guests' use there is a garden, summer house, barbecue, table-tennis. Reductions off-season. The sea is within twenty kilometres; fishing close by. English spoken.
Near river Forest area
2 en suite (bth/shr) TV available Radio in rooms Full central heating Open parking available Languages spoken: English
CARDS: Travellers cheques

POLIGNE Ille-et-Vilaine

Château du Bois Glaume
35320
☎ 299438305 FAX 299437940
The residence dates back to the beginning of the 18th century, and is together with its chapel, classified as an historic monument. Situated in an extensive park with mature oak trees and a lake, it features an elegant interior with cosy public areas and excellent bedrooms with modern facilities. It has an extraordinary roof where the tiles are laid like fish scales and which is the only one of its kind in France.
Near river Near lake Forest area Near motorway
4 en suite (bth/shr) (2 fmly) (1 with balcony) TV available Radio in rooms Full central heating Open parking available Child discount available 12yrs Last d 19.00hrs Languages spoken: Spanish
MEALS: Lunch fr 150FF Dinner fr 150FF*

POMMERIT-JAUDY Côtes-D'Armor

Château de Kermézen (Prop: Comte and Comtesse de Kermel)
22450
☎ 296913575 FAX 296913575
(take motorway 12 as far as Guingamp, then follow signs to Treguier, for 23km, at traffic lights in Pomerit, turn left- Kermezen is 2km further on)
The Count and Countess de Kermel invite you to their seventeenth century château, which is situated in a quiet rural valley. The family de Kermel has owned the château for more than 500 years. Top class restaurants nearby, although guests are invited to dine with the Count and Countess, by reservation. English spoken.
Near river Near sea Near beach Forest area
5 en suite (bth/shr) (2 fmly) Full central heating Open parking available Child discount available 12yrs Fishing Riding Boule Open terrace Languages spoken: English
ROOMS: s 420FF; d 460-520FF
CARDS: ▦ Travellers cheques

Quillevez Vraz (Prop: Georges Beauverger)
22450
☎ 296913574
The bedrooms are located in the courtyard of the main residence. Access for the disabled. Large living room. Cooking facilities (twenty franc supplement). Sporting pursuits within ten kilometres.
Closed Oct-Etr
3 en suite (bth) No smoking on premises Full central heating Open parking available

PONT-AVEN Finistère

Kermentec (Prop: Alain Larour)
29930
☎ 298060760
(from the centre of the village take direction of Quimper/Rosporden D24 then right turn for La Chapelle de Tremalo in 200m house on the right)
Located in the hills of Pont Aven, this stone house offers a large living room with dining area and kitchenette. Breakfasts may be taken outside in the fresh air, or inside by the fire. Swimming, beaches, golf, all nearby. English spoken.
Near river Forest area In town centre
3 en suite (shr) (1 fmly) Full central heating Open parking available Languages spoken: English
ROOMS: d fr 250FF
CARDS: Travellers cheques

PONTIVY-NEUILLAC Morbihan

La Bretonnière Bel Air (Prop: Adele Miloux)
56300
☎ 297396248 FAX 297396248
Adèle Miloux welcomes you to her home, situated in the heart of Brittany. Garden with boules and children's games, leading into a huge park. Thé Guerlédan Lake is only fifteen kilometres away. Many sporting activities available. English spoken.
Near river Near lake Forest area
4 en suite (bth/shr) (1 fmly) (1 with balcony) No smoking on premises TV available Full central heating Open parking available Boule Languages spoken: English

POULDERGAT Finistère

Listi Vras (Prop: Louis et Angele Kervares)
29100
☎ 298524800
Situated at the crossroads of the Glazik, Bigouden and Capiste regions, Louis and Angèle welcome you to their guest house and cottage, where guests can enjoy the flowers and peaceful surroundings. Sea and beach, seven kilometres away, and there are many walks nearby.
3 en suite (shr) (3 fmly) Full central heating Open parking available Supervised
CARDS: Travellers cheques

QUEMPER-GUÉZENNEC Côtes-D'Armor

Kergocq (Prop: Marie Clair Thomas)
22260
☎ 296956272 296956398
2 en suite (bth/shr) No smoking on premises Full central heating Open parking available Covered parking available

QUERRIEN Finistère

Kerfaro (Prop: Yves Le Gallic)
29310
☎ 298713002
The guest rooms are situated in a quiet, relaxing environment, overlooking a valley and lake. The bedrooms have sloping wooden ceilings and wood-block floors. The lawns of the property slope down through a belt of trees onto a lake where fishing and boats are available. Table-tennis and swings in the garden.
Forest area
2 en suite (shr) No smoking on premises Full central heating Open parking available Supervised Child discount available
ROOMS: s 200FF; d 230FF *
CARDS: ▓ Travellers cheques

QUÉVERT Côtes-D'Armor

Le Chêne Pichard (Prop: M & Mme Boullier)
22100
☎ 296850921
(from Dinan take the N176 in the direction of St Brieuc establishment in 2km on the right)
4 rms (1 bth 2 shr) (1 with balcony) TV available Full central heating Open parking available

REMUNGOL Morbihan

La Villeneuve (Prop: Jean an Solanges Le Texier)
Le Texier, La Villeneuve *56500*
☎ 297609835
M. and Mme. Le Texier welcome you to their farmhouse, which is an old stone building with arched windows and doors and many of the original beams still in place inside. Comfortable living and dining rooms. There are many activities available: swimming pool, tennis court, farm visits, walks. Guests are invited to dine with their hosts.
Forest area
4 en suite (bth/shr) (1 fmly) Full central heating Child discount available

RHEU, LE Ille-et-Vilaine

Domaine de la Freslonniere (Prop: Mme C D'Alincourt)
35650
☎ 299148409
Guest rooms, cottages and fully-furnished apartments, either in or near the Château de la Freslonnière, a seventeenth century building set in the heart of a wooded parkland near an eighteen-hole golf course and a lake. On site: tennis, swimming pool, fishing and restaurant. Three kilometres from town centre. English spoken.
Near lake Forest area
2 en suite (bth/shr) (1 fmly) TV available Full central heating Open parking available Outdoor swimming pool Golf 18 Tennis Fishing Table tennis Languages spoken: English & Spanish
CARDS: Travellers cheques

Taking your mobile phone to France?
See page 11

ROSNOËN Finistère

Ferme Auberge du Seillou (Prop: M Herve le Pape)
29590
☎ 298819221 FAX 298810714
(on the N165 Brest/Quimper exit Le Faou take D791 direction
Crozon for 6km signposted)
The family Le Pape offer you a holiday on a farm. Three totally
independent rooms are available in a peaceful atmosphere.
Farm produce, such as chicken, beef and pork, are used in the
preparation of meals. Crêpes also served. English spoken.
Near river Near sea Near beach Forest area Near motorway
6 en suite (bth/shr) (2 fmly) Full central heating Open
parking available Child discount available Last d 21.00hrs
Languages spoken: English
ROOMS: s 260FF; d 260FF
MEALS: Lunch 82-110FF Dinner 82-110FF
CARDS: ● █ ▬

ROSPORDEN Finistère

Kerantou (Prop: M Bernard)
29140
☎ 298592779
Rooms available in an old farm close to the proprietor's house.
One of the rooms is a family room. Kitchen area and living
room available to guests. Babysitting by arrangement.
Barbecue in garden. The beach is fifteen minutes away.
English spoken.
Near river Near lake Forest area
6 en suite (bth/shr) (1 with balcony) Full central heating
Open parking available Child discount available Table tennis
Languages spoken: English
CARDS: █

ROZ-LANDRIEUX Ille-et-Vilaine

Manoir de la Méttrie (Prop: Mr Claude Jourdan)
35120
☎ 299482921
Near sea Near beach Forest area Near motorway
5 en suite (shr) (2 fmly) No smoking on premises Full central
heating Open parking available Child discount available
10yrs V meals Last d 21.00hrs
MEALS: Dinner fr 82FF*
CARDS: █ Travellers cheques

ROZ-SUR-COUESNON Ille-et-Vilaine

Bed & Breakfast (Prop: Helene Gillet)
Le Val St-Révert *35610*
☎ 299802785
Eighteenth century house with fantastic view of the Mont
St Michel and the bay. Living room with television. Beach is
within ten kilometres. Fishing, walking, tennis and riding all
within a short distance. A little English spoken.
Near sea Near beach Near motorway
5 en suite (bth/shr) (1 fmly) (3 with balcony) No smoking on
premises TV available Open parking available Child discount
available
CARDS: Travellers cheques

La Bergerie (Prop: M Jacky Piel)
35610
☎ 299802968 FAX 299802968
Situated on the bay of Mont St Michel, this is a seventeenth
century stone farmhouse. A kitchen area, bar and library are

available for guests' use. Cottage also for hire. Tourist sites of
the Emerald Coast within close proximity. Attractive gardens.
English spoken.

Near lake Near sea
6 en suite (bth/shr) (4 fmly) Full central heating Open
parking available Covered parking available Boule
Languages spoken: English
ROOMS: s 190-230FF; d 210-250FF
CARDS: Travellers cheques

RUFFIAC Morbihan

Ferme de Rangera (Prop: Germaine and Gilbert
Couedelo)
56140
☎ 297937218
5 en suite (shr) (1 fmly) No smoking on premises Full central
heating Open parking available Child discount available
10yrs

ST-ALBAN Côtes-D'Armor

Ferme de Malido (Prop: M Legrand)
22400
☎ 296329474 FAX 296329267
Houguette and Robert Legrand and their children welcome
guests to a peaceful stay in their country farm, which is
situated near beaches and the sea. Living room, television,
games area, table-tennis, children's billiard table and barbecue
available to guests. Sailing, riding, swimming pool, golf and
walks all within four kilometres. English spoken.
Near motorway
6 en suite (shr) (2 fmly) (1 with balcony) Full central heating
Open parking available Languages spoken: English
CARDS: █ Travellers cheques

ST-BRIAC-SUR-MER Ille-et-Vilaine

The Laurel Tree (Prop: Oliver & Helen Martin)
41 blvd de la Houle *35800*
☎ 299880193
A 300 year old traditional French stone building with a large
garden, a tasteful combination of old and new. Breakfast is
taken in a lovely stone and beamed dining room with large
open fireplace.
Near sea Near beach
5 en suite (shr) (3 fmly) No smoking on premises TV in 4
bedrooms Full central heating Open parking available Child
discount available 4yrs Languages spoken: English & German
cont'd

ROOMS: s 245-290FF; d 245-360FF
MEALS: Dinner fr 85FF*
CARDS: Travellers cheques

Manoir de la Duchée (Prop: M S F Stenou)
35800
☎ 299880002
You will find this small seventeenth century Breton manor house situated in open countryside, offering five comfortable bed & breakfast rooms, furnished with pieces from the nineteenth century, with floral motifs. Dining room featuring exposed beams and decorative objects. Open March to December.
Near river Near sea Near beach Forest area
Closed Jan & Feb
5 en suite (bth/shr) (1 fmly) (1 with balcony) TV available
Full central heating Open parking available
CARDS: Travellers cheques

ST-CARADEC Côtes-D'Armor

Ferme de L'Hilvern (Prop: Collette Nagat)
22600
☎ 296250266
(N164 between Rennes and Brest to St Caradec, on leaving village, first turning on right)
Bedrooms include a family room with a kitchen area in this dark stone house. Many interesting walks in the area and on the farm. Evening entertainment at nearby Thère. Your hosts are very welcoming. English spoken.
Near river Near lake Near sea Near beach Forest area In town centre Near motorway
4 en suite (bth/shr) (1 fmly) No smoking on premises Full central heating Open parking available Covered parking available Supervised Languages spoken: English German & Spanish
CARDS: Travellers cheques

ST-CAST-LE-GUILDO Côtes-D'Armor

Château du Val d'Arguenon
Notre-Dame du Guildo *22380*
☎ 296410703 FAX 296410267
(25km west of St Malo in the direction St Cast)
Le Château du Val is a private house, some parts of which date back as far as the 16th century, and has been in the hands of the same family for 200 years. It stands in the middle of a large park near the sea and thus combines the charm of the countryside with the splendour of the Emerald Coast. The furnishings are in harmony with the architecture of the building and complemented by modern facilities.
Near river Near sea Near beach Forest area

Closed Oct-Mar
6 en suite (bth/shr) Open parking available Tennis
Languages spoken: English
ROOMS: d 450-610FF

Villa Griselidis
r des Hauts de Plume *22380*
☎ 296419522
(on left side of the 'Mairie' town hall, take the 'rue Tourneuf' which links with the 'rue de la Fosserolle' and on the right side is 'rue des Hauts de Plume'. It takes 30mins to get to the house)
A pleasant, stone villa on a hill with views of sea and country, very quiet, attractively furnished, well located and surrounded by a flowered park. A small path followed by steps leads to the centre of the town and the beach. The two en-suite bedrooms are furnished in the style of Louis XV1, the remaining rooms being in a modern style.
Near sea Near beach
2 en suite (shr) Radio in rooms Full central heating Open parking available No children 2yrs Languages spoken: English
ROOMS: d 245-285FF
CARDS: Travellers cheques

ST-COULOMB Ille-et-Vilaine

La Ville Jaquin (Prop: Mme Dominque Lesne)
35350
☎ 299890562
In a country setting, near to the sea, the Lesné family welcomes you to their stone farmhouse. Garden with barbecue and swings for children. 800 metres from the shops, ten kilometres from St Malo. Bedrooms are situated on the first floor. Ground floor room also available, with facilities for the disabled. English spoken.
Near sea Near beach
3 en suite (shr) (2 fmly) Open parking available Supervised Child discount available Languages spoken: English & Spanish

ST-ÉLOY-HANVEC Finistère

Kerivoal (Prop: Mme N le Lann)
29460
☎ 298258614 FAX 298258614
Rustic farmhouse, where the Le Lann family look forward to meeting you. Reservation is available but reservations must be made and your hosts will dine with you; breakfast is served by the open fire. Reductions are available for children under ten years old and there are swings in the garden. English spoken.
Near river Forest area
2 en suite (shr) No smoking on premises Full central heating Open parking available Child discount available 10yrs Bicycle rental Languages spoken: English & Italian
ROOMS: s fr 200FF; d fr 250FF
MEALS: Dinner 80FF

ST-JOUAN-DES-GUÉRETS Ille-et-Vilaine

Manoir de Blanche-Roche (Prop: M Pilorget)
35430
☎ 299824747
English-style nineteenth century house situated in the heart of a wooded park. The rooms are comfortable. Breakfast is large and is different every day. Magali, your host, will help you find the best tourist attractions on offer in the area. The sea, tennis,

sailing, riding, all at five kilometres. Golf, ten kilometres.
English spoken.
Near motorway
Closed 16 Nov-Dec
5 en suite (bth/shr) (1 fmly) Open parking available Boule
Languages spoken: English

ST-LAURENT-SUR-OUST Morbihan

Evas (Prop: Jean & Madeleine Gru)
56140
☎ 297750262
The bedrooms face south west with a view over countryside.
Conservatory with barbecue available to guests. French
breakfast served, featuring home-made crêpes. Breakfast
reductions for children under five years. The house is
decorated with colourful window boxes.
Near river Forest area
1 en suite (bth) TV in all bedrooms Full central heating

ST-MALO Ille-et-Vilaine

La Goelettrie (Prop: M Henri Trevilly)
35400
☎ 299819264
Stone-built residence close to the sea. Two rooms have a sea
view. Evening meal available by reservation. On Monday,
Wednesday and Friday nights Breton specialities are served.
Regional breakfast served. Children under two years go free.
Near sea
5 en suite (shr) (1 fmly) Full central heating Open parking
available Child discount available
MEALS: Dinner 70-90FF*

Ville Auray (Prop: Josette Feret)
35400
☎ 299816437 FAX 299822327
(travel towards St Malo centre, over rdbts, at last rdbt, travel
towards St Michel, take 2nd road on left after campsite, house
is along road)
Near sea Near beach Forest area
4 en suite (bth/shr) (1 fmly) TV in all bedrooms Full central
heating Open parking available Covered parking available
Table tennis, Baby foot, Billiards Languages spoken: English
& Spanish
ROOMS: s 200FF; d 260FF
CARDS: Travellers cheques

ST-MARTIN-DES-CHAMPS Finistère

Kereliza (Prop: N Abiven-Gueguen)
29600
☎ 298882718
A restored, handsome nineteenth century house surrounded
by a large flower garden, with living room, library, piano and
television available for guests' enjoyment. The proprietors
grow strawberries and shallots. Restaurants and shops within
one kilometre. English spoken.
Near motorway
6 en suite (bth/shr) Full central heating Open parking
available Supervised Languages spoken: English
ROOMS: s 150FF; d 220FF
CARDS: Travellers cheques

ST-MARTIN-SUR-OUST Morbihan

Le Château de Castellan (Prop: P et M Cosse)
56200
☎ 299945169 FAX 299915741
Splendid large château, looking out onto a circular lawn. All
bedrooms are comfortably furnished in a stylish way. Two
rooms are family rooms. All overlook the garden at the rear of
the château. English spoken.
Near river Forest area
7 rms (5 bth/shr) (2 fmly) No smoking on premises Radio in
rooms Full central heating Open parking available Child
discount available 10yrs V meals Languages spoken: English
ROOMS: s fr 250FF; d 450-600FF
MEALS: Continental breakfast 50FF Lunch 100-150FF Dinner
100-150FF
CARDS: ●● ▩ ▨ ▣ Travellers cheques

ST-MÉLOIR-DES-ONDES Ille-et-Vilaine

Les Croix Gibouins (Prop: Denise Basle)
35350
☎ 299821197 FAX 299821197
Situated two kilometres from Bourg, the property is part of a
farm by the same name and features two ancient crosses in its
grounds. English spoken by your hostess, who will be
delighted to tell you the history of the property.
Near sea Near beach
2 en suite (bth/shr) (1 fmly) Full central heating Open
parking available Supervised Child discount available 2yrs
Languages spoken: English

Langa Van (Prop: M Loic Collin)
35350
☎ 299892292
Guest rooms, including one family room, situated on a
restored farm. Some rooms have views over the Bay of Mont
St.Michel. Evening meal available for a fixed price by
arrangement. French breakfast served. Reductions for
children under ten years. English spoken.
Near sea Near motorway
Closed 30 Sep-Mar
5 en suite (shr) (3 fmly) Full central heating Open parking
available Child discount available 10 yrs Open terrace Last d
19.30hrs Languages spoken: English
MEALS: Dinner fr 60FF*
CARDS: ▩ Travellers cheques

ST-OUEN-LA-ROUÊRIE Ille-et-Vilaine

La Morissais (Prop: Francois Legros)
35460
☎ 299983880
All bedrooms have exposed beams and wood block floors, and
are tastefully furnished, overlooking the lawn. Lounge
available for guests' use, with television. French breakfast can
be eaten in the garden. Peace and comfort assured.
Near river Forest area Near motorway
4 en suite (shr) (2 fmly) No smoking on premises Full central
heating Open parking available Supervised Child discount
available 4yrs
ROOMS: s 180FF; d 200-230FF

ST-PÈRE-MARC-EN-POULET Ille-et-Vilaine

La Ville Hermessan (Prop: Marcel Lebihan)
35430
☎ 299582202 FAX 299582202
(from Saint-Malo take D4 in direction of Gouesniere)
Marie-Claude and Marcel welcome you to their eighteenth
century property situated in a large park. Continental
breakfast served. Dinner by reservation only. Farm animals
on-site. Picnic table and barbecue in garden. English spoken.
Near sea Forest area
Closed 16 Nov-14 Mar
4 en suite (shr) (2 fmly) No smoking on premises Full central
heating Open parking available Child discount available
12yrs Tennis Boule Bicycle rental Pitching green
Languages spoken: English
ROOMS: s 210FF; d 240-260FF
MEALS: Dinner 100FF

ST-PHILIBERT-SUR-MER Morbihan

Cuzon du Rest
Lann Kermane, 13 rue des Peupliers *56470*
☎ 297550375 FAX 297300279
Set in a sunny area in a peaceful and green area of the
countryside, close to the beaches and yachting harbour of La
Trinité. Near to tennis courts and three beautiful golf links, in
the heart of Carnac country. A very warm welcome awaits
you. Many restaurants in the area. Cars to rent nearby.
English spoken.
Near river Near sea Near beach
2 en suite (bth/shr) No smoking on premises Full central
heating Open parking available Languages spoken: English
ROOMS: s fr 350FF; d fr 400FF
CARDS: Travellers cheques

ST-PIERRE-DE-PLESGUEN Ille-et-Vilaine

Le Clos du Rouvre (Prop: M & Mme Harrison)
35720
☎ 299737272
(follow the N137 from St Malo to St Pierre de Plesguen, then
take D794 for 1km in direction of Combourg take left turn
signposted Lanhelin Clos de Rouve is 2km on the left)
This property is set in the Breton countryside, within easy
reach of St Malo, Dinan, Dinard and Mont St Michel. The
owners are English and pride themselves on giving a
traditional family holiday, with great food and comfortable
surroundings. The house, which dates back over two hundred
years, has many of the original beams. Dinner available.
Near river Near lake Near sea Forest area Near motorway
6 en suite (bth/shr) (2 fmly) Full central heating Open
parking available Child discount available Boule Languages
spoken: English
ROOMS: s 200-250FF; d 275-350FF
CARDS: Travellers cheques

Le Petit Moulin du Rouvre (Prop: Mme Annie Michel-
Quebriac)
35720
☎ 299738584 FAX 299737106
(situated between Rennes and St Malo, St Pierre de Plesguen
is on N137, from here take D10 in the direction Lanhelin)
Old watermill dating back to the seventeenth century.
Bedrooms are in the restored part of the mill. Near to Mont St
Michel, the medieval town of Dinan and the beaches of the
Emerald Coast. Many restaurants serving all types of food

within three to twelve kilometres.
Near river Forest area
4 en suite (bth/shr) (2 fmly) No smoking on premises Full
central heating Open parking available No children 5yrs
Child discount available
CARDS: Travellers cheques

Le Pont Ricoul
35720
☎ 299739265 FAX 299739417
This property is a renovated bakery. On the ground floor is a
living room overlooking the lake, while a spiral staircase leads
to the guest room on the first floor. During the summer a
barbecue is available in the garden. Dinner by reservation.
English spoken.
Near lake Forest area Near motorway
1 en suite (shr) (1 fmly) Full central heating Open parking
available Covered parking available Child discount available
Bicycle rental Languages spoken: English
MEALS: Dinner fr 80FF*
CARDS: ▣ Travellers cheques

ST-RÉMY-DU-PLAIN Ille-et-Vilaine

La Haye d'Irée (Prop: Leschevin de Prevoisin)
35560
☎ 299736207 FAX 344490999
(in Saint Rémy du Plain, take the D90, after 1.5km, take 2nd
road on right onto D12, the château is 300m on right after
crossrds.)

This property was built in the eighteenth century on an old
Gallic-Roman site on the borders of Normandy and Brittany.
Set in the heart of the main tourist centre, it is situated in an
elevated position with a charming view over the surrounding
countryside. A feature of the property is the border of yew
trees which were planted at the beginning of the seventeenth
century. Bedrooms are furnished in period style. Heated
swimming pool, table-tennis, bicycles and lake fishing
available. Possible babysitting service.
Near lake Forest area
Closed Oct-Apr
5 en suite (bth/shr) TV in 1 bedroom Full central heating
Open parking available Supervised Child discount available
4yrs Outdoor swimming pool (heated) Fishing Table tennis
Languages spoken: English, Italian & Spanish
ROOMS: d 500-700FF Reductions over 1 night
CARDS: Travellers cheques

ST-SULIAC Ille-et-Vilaine

Les Mouettes (Prop: Isabelle Rouvrais)
35430
☎ 299583041 FAX 299583941
(3km from Chateauneuf off the St Malo/Rennes road)
Rooms painted in light colours have cotton curtains and
wooden floors with rugs, giving a simple and comfortable
atmosphere.
Near river Near sea Near beach Forest area
5 en suite (bth/shr) Full central heating Languages spoken:
English
ROOMS: s 220-260FF; d 250-290FF
CARDS: ▭ Travellers cheques

ST-THÉGONNEC Finistère

AR Prospital Coz (Prop: Mme Catherine Caroff)
18 rue Lividic *29140*
☎ 298794562 FAX 298794847
Near river Near motorway
6 en suite (bth/shr) Full central heating Open parking
available
CARDS: Travellers cheques

ST-THONAN Finistère

Bed & Breakfast (Prop: Marie Jo Edern)
29800
☎ 298202699 FAX 298202713
Ten minutes from Brest. Marie-Jo Edern, your hostess, offers
you three rooms, one of which is a family room. Each room
has a kitchenette and its own entrance, separate from the
main house. The churches of Saint Herbot de Botiguéry are
200 metres away. Rural cottage also available . Some
reductions available.
Forest area Near motorway
3 en suite (shr) (1 fmly) TV available Full central heating
Open parking available
CARDS: Travellers cheques

SCAER Finistère

Kerloai (Prop: M & Mme Penn)
29390
☎ 298594260
(from Scaer take D50 towards Quimper turn left Cafe Ty Ru,
Kerloal on left fork)
Thérèse and Louis Penn run a farm as well as their guesthouse
and they welcome you to their home. Beautifully quiet and
green, visitors may relax on the farm or the nearby beaches.
Many walks possible in the area. English spoken.
Near river
4 en suite (shr) Open parking available Languages spoken:
English & German

TRÉFLEZ Finistère

Pen Ar Roz (Prop: Yvette Roue)
29430
☎ 298614284
Near sea In town centre
2 en suite (bth/shr) No smoking on premises Full central
heating Open parking available
CARDS: Travellers cheques

TRÉGLONOU Finistère

Keredern (Prop: Viviane Le Gall)
29870
☎ 298040260
Old, detached waterside residence. The region of Abers is not
too far away from the town or beaches, but does not suffer
from an invasion of tourists. Your hostess, Viviane Le Gall,
enjoys an exchange of conversation with her guests and
speaks English fluently.
Near river Near sea Forest area
3 en suite (bth/shr) No smoking on premises TV available
Full central heating Open parking available Supervised
Child discount available 4yrs Languages spoken: English &
German
CARDS: Travellers cheques

Manoir de Trouzilit (Prop: M. Stephan)
29870
☎ 298040120 FAX 298041714
Rooms available in this farm and crêperie, which looks out
onto a courtyard and is surrounded by fields. All rooms are
furnished in typical rustic Breton style. Riding centre,
miniature golf, tennis courts, bridle ways, bar and crêperie all
available to guests. Dinner also available. English spoken.
Near river Near sea Near beach Forest area Near motorway
5 en suite (bth) Full central heating Open parking available
Tennis Fishing Riding Mini-golf Languages spoken: English
& German
ROOMS: s 140-160FF; d fr 240FF
CARDS: ●● ▭ Travellers cheques

TRÉHORENTEUC Morbihan

Belle-Vue (Prop: Mme Jagoudel)
56430
☎ 297930280
Mme Jagoudel welcomes you to her house situated in the
heart of the forest of Brocéliande. She has one room available
on the ground floor, one on the first floor. Continental
breakfast served in the dining room. English spoken.
Near river Near lake Forest area Near motorway
2 en suite (shr) No smoking on premises Full central heating
Open parking available Supervised Child discount available
2yrs Languages spoken: English

TRÉOGAT Finistère

Keramoine (Prop: M & Mme Faou)
29720
☎ 298876398
Hélène and Michel welcome you to their home, in the midst of
lakes in the Bigouden region, a stone's throw from a beach of
white sand. Three rooms are available on the first floor of this
property and there is a terrace, with garden furniture and
barbecue. A little English spoken.
Near river Near lake Near sea
2 en suite (shr) (1 fmly) No smoking on premises Full central
heating
CARDS: Travellers cheques

Taking your mobile phone to France?
See page 11

55

TRESSAINT Côtes-D'Armor

La Ville Améline (Prop: Huguette Lemarchand)
22100
☎ 296393369
Ancient farmhouse situated three kilometres from Dinan. Dining room, garden room and games area for the use of guests. Evening meal available, on request.
Near river Forest area
4 en suite (bth/shr) (3 fmly) No smoking on premises Full central heating Open parking available Covered parking available Child discount available 10yrs
CARDS: Travellers cheques

TRÉVÉ Côtes-D'Armor

Ferme Sejour (Prop: Paulette et Jean Donnio)
22600
☎ 296254453
Enjoy the family atmosphere on this traditional farm close to Loudéac. Comfortable rooms are equipped with kitchenette. Join your hosts for a meal prepared with farm produce. Camping also available. Sun-loungers. Nearby you will find swimming, riding, tennis, fishing and canoeing. English spoken.
Near lake
4 en suite (bth/shr) Full central heating Open parking available Child discount available 8yrs Bicycle rental Table tennis Barbecue Languages spoken: English
ROOMS: s fr 140FF; d 200-220FF
MEALS: Dinner 70FF
CARDS: Travellers cheques

La Ville aux Véneurs (Prop: Marie Chauvel)
22600
☎ 296250202
Situated in the centre of Brittany, this typical Breton house offers traditional French breakfast, and lunch can be taken at the family table. The property is close to a lake and forest. Canoeing possible at the nearby river. A little English spoken.
Near river Forest area
2 en suite (bth/shr) No smoking on premises Full central heating Open parking available Supervised Child discount available 10yrs

TRINITÉ-SUR-MER, LA Morbihan

La Maison du Latz (Prop: Le Rouzic)
Le Latz *56470*
☎ 297558091 FAX 297301410
Near river Forest area
4 en suite (bth) No smoking on premises TV in 1 bedroom Full central heating Open parking available Supervised Fishing Open terrace
CARDS: Travellers cheques

UZEL Côtes-D'Armor

Bizoin (Prop: Marie Cadoret)
22460
☎ 296288124 FAX 296262842
Working farm, with milking cows and fowl, situated in the heart of Brittany. French breakfast served. Children will enjoy a stay on a farm, where they can visit the animals and play in the fields. River and lake fishing available on-site. English spoken.
Near river Forest area
4 en suite (shr) (2 fmly) Full central heating Open parking available Child discount available 12 yrs Open terrace
MEALS: Lunch fr 70FF*
CARDS: Travellers cheques

VIEUX-VIEL Ille-et-Vilaine

Le Veux Presbytère (Prop: Madeline Stracquadanio)
35610
☎ 299486529 FAX 299486529
Madeleine Stracquadanio and her family welcome you to their old presbytery in a country village. Breakfast and dinner are served in the living room around a large wooden table. Just four kilometres from the Forest of Villecartier, with its lake offering relaxing walks, fishing and pedaloes. English spoken.
Near river Near lake Forest area
5 rms (3 shr) (3 fmly) No smoking on premises Full central heating Open parking available Covered parking available Supervised Child discount available 12yrs Boule V meals Languages spoken: English
MEALS: Dinner fr 80FF*

YFFINIAC Côtes-D'Armor

Le Grenier (Prop: Marie-Reine Loquin)
rte de Plédran *22120*
☎ 296726455 FAX 296729874
This country house is part of a working farm and three rooms are offered. Living room, television room with video, lawn games, barbecue. Cooking is possible for guests. The beach is six kilometres away, with fishing, riding, walks and sailing all possible. Bikes for hire. Comfort assured. Babysitting facilities. English spoken.
Near sea Near beach Forest area
3 en suite (bth/shr) (1 fmly) No smoking on premises Full central heating Open parking available Supervised Boule Bicycle rental Languages spoken: English German & Spanish
ROOMS: s fr 190FF; d fr 210FF
CARDS: ▓ Travellers cheques

ASPECTS OF BRITTANY

Dinan
You can't leave Brittany without visiting the medieval town of Dinan. Its half-timbered houses are the finest example of the local architecture, but don't forget to investigate the beauty of its old mansions, Romanesque and Gothic churches, convents and chapels. Traditional craftsmen such as woodcarvers, glass-blowers, weavers, engravers and turners, at work in the Rue de Jerzual, evoke the atmosphere of an industrious medieval town. Since the mid-1980s, a major restoration programme has seen the town's massive gateways

and fortifications returned to their former imposing glory. However, Dinan is a town as much concerned with the present and the future as the past. It is home to an army base, hospitals and many shops.

The bridge at Dinan spans the River Rance

Beachcombing
Gathering a tasty snack of seafood at low tide is within anyone's grasp in Brittany. Popular sites are the bays between Cancale and Mont-St-Michel, or Quiberon and the Gulf of Morbihan. You only need a pair of Wellington boots, a coat with enough pockets to hold a pen-knife and a few plastic bags to sort out the catch, plus a shrimping-net to comb the weeds. Limpets, mussels and wild oysters can be prised off the rocks; leave the oyster beds and commercial piles to the professionals. You can collect cockles, clams and winkles easily enough by hand. Shrimps like the sandy bottoms of pools left by the tide, while prawns can be found amongst the seaweed under rocks. An ideal project for all the family.

Normandy

Normandy is without doubt a most beautiful area and much seems to be untouched by the twentieth century. Just a hop across the Channel, Normandy is close enough for a weekend break and full of interest for a longer visit. A vast region, full of variety which stretches from the majestic Mont-Saint-Michel in the west to almost the outer reaches of Paris, but far removed from Parisienne chic. Much of the region's economy is derived from the rich harvests from both the sea and the land and there are many gastronomic delights to sample and savour.

(Top): The Allied invasion of occupied France in 1941 is commemorated by this beautiful stained glass window at Sainte-Mère-Église

(Bottom): The high chalk cliffs at Étretat have been worn into strange shapes by the constant action of the sea.

ESSENTIAL FACTS

DÉPARTEMENTS:	Calvados, Eure, Manche, Orne, Seine-Maritime
PRINCIPAL TOWNS	Bayeux, Caen, Alençon, Rouen, Le Havre, Cherbourg, Lisieux, Dieppe, Evreux.
PLACES TO VISIT:	The famous Bayeux Tapestry at Bayeux; the D-Day beaches; Chateau Gaillard; Monet's garden at Giverny; Mont-St-Michel
REGIONAL TOURIST OFFICE	30 Le Doyenné, 14 rue Charles-Corbeau, 27000 Evreux Tel 32 33 79 00
LOCAL GASTRONOMIC DELIGHTS	Chicken or pork with apples, cream and cider; creamy cheese such as Pont l'Evêque, Livarot and Camembert; duckling à la Rouenais (a pink fleshed duck); tripes à la mode de Caen (traditional dish featuring tripe); sole Dieppoise, a seafood speciality from Dieppe.
DRINKS	Calvados (apple-flavoured brandy); doux (sweet), sec (dry) and bouché (sparkling) cider; Pommeau, a local apple liqueur; Benedictine, a liqueur made by the monks of Fécamp from the aromatic herbs of the Pays de Ceux; poire pear cider
LOCAL CRAFTS WHAT TO BUY	Lace from Alençon and Bayeux; copper-ware and pewter from Villedieu-les-Poeles; stone-carving from the areas of Avrancles and Mortain; cloth and textiles from Louviers; linen from Orbec

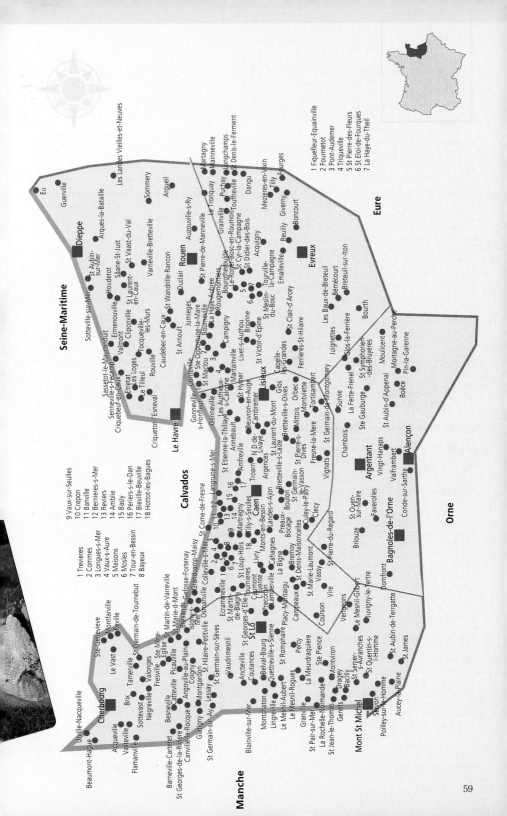

EVENTS & FESTIVALS

Mar Lisieux Tree Fair; Mortagne Pudding Fair; Rouen Scandinavian Film Festival; Caen Contemporary Music; Rouen International Fair

Apr Deauville 'Scales of Deauville'; Rouen Water Motor Sports

May Mortrée Vintage and Collectors Car Meeting; Mont-St-Michel Spring Festival; Coutances 'Jazz Under the Apple Trees' Festival; Cambremer AOC Festival; Argentan Antiques Show; Eure Département King Richard Calvalcade; Honfleur Seafarers' Pilgrimage; Rouen Joan of Arc Festival;

Jun Lisieux Son et Lumière 'From the Vikings to Thérèse'; Trouville Folklore Festival; Luneray Jazz Festival; Le Havre Blessing of the Sea Festival; Cabourg Romantic Film Festival; Flers Vibrations Festival; Blainville-Crévon Archeojazz; Le Pin-au-Haras 'Thursdays at The Stud du Pin' stallion musical show

Jul Bayeux Medieval Festival, La Haye de Routot Feast of St Clair; Forges les Eaux Horse Festival; Dives sur Mer Puppet Festival; Trouville 'Terrasses Musicales' Festival (*concerts on the pavements & beaches*); Sées Cathedral Son et Lumière; Deauville Bridge Festival; Le Pin-au-Haras 'Thursdays at The Stud du Pin' stallion musical show 3pm Thurs;

Trouville Festival of The Sea & The Mackerel; La Hay de Routot, Feast of St Clair; Mont-St Michel Pilgrimage across the beaches;

Aug Dieppe Ancient Music Festival; Bagnoles-de l'Orne Fireworks and Musical Show on the Lake; Livarot Cheese Fair; Ile de Tatihou 'Les Traversées' (*traditional dancing*); Le Pin-au Haras 'Thursdays at The Stud du Pin' stallion musical show 3pm Thurs; Deauville Thoroughbred Yearling Auction; Domfront Medieval Market; Lisieux Turkey Market; Saint-Lô 'Thursdays at the National Stud';

Sep Belleme International Mushroom Fair; Caen International Fair; Deauville American Film Festival; Lessay Ancient St Croix Fair; Le Neubourg Horse Show at Champ de Bataille Castle; Le Pin-au-Haras 'Thursdays at The Stud du Pin' stallion musical show 3pm Thurs; Le Havre Celebration of the sea; Lisieux Grand Feast of Ste Theresa; Le Pin-au-Haras horse racing & parade;

Oct Beuvron-en-Auge Grand Cider Market & Festival; Lisieux International Flower Festival; Honfleur Shrimp Festival; Rouen National Antique Fair; October in Normandy at Rouen, Dieppe, Le Havre; Lisieux Blues Festival; Calvados Equi'days (*horse riding competition & sale*); Vimoutiers Apple Festival;

ACQUEVILLE Manche

La Belangerie (Prop: M & Mme Geoffroy)
50440
☎ 233945949
A sixteenth century manor house, recently renovated. The dining area has an unusual chimney breast which has been recognised by the Department of Fine Arts. The bedrooms are on the first floor and all have beamed ceilings. Meals are mainly prepared form local farm products, including beef, pork, lamb and chicken. English is spoken.
Near river Near lake Near sea Near beach Near motorway
3 rms (1 shr) (1 fmly) Radio in rooms Full central heating Open parking available Child discount available 6yrs TV room V meals Last d 20.30hrs Languages spoken: English
ROOMS: s fr 180FF; d fr 230FF *
MEALS: Dinner fr 80FF*

ACQUIGNY Eure

Bed & Breakfast (Prop: C & M Heullant)
Quartier St-Mauxé *27400*
☎ 232502010
(off N154, 15km from Evreux, 5km from Louviers)
The owners of La Roseraie welcome guests into their home and also into a separate building opposite the main house. Facilities include a living room with billiard table. There are three restaurants in the village, offering good quality food at reasonable prices. English spoken.
Near river Near lake Near motorway
3 en suite (bth/shr) (1 fmly) Open parking available Child discount available Languages spoken: English
CARDS: Travellers cheques

AMBLIE Calvados

Hameau de Pierrepont (Prop: Elaine Ringoot Fiquet)
14480
☎ 231801004 FAX 231081759
(from Caen Memorial take D22 to Pierrepont, approx 12km)
Near river Forest area
2 en suite (shr) Full central heating Open parking available
CARDS: Travellers cheques

AMFREVILLE Calvados

L'Écarde (Prop: M & Mme Enguerrand)
10 rte de Cabourg *14860*
☎ 231724765
(off the Caen/Ouistreham autoroute towards Franceville/Cabourg)
Simple lodgings which are situated in a charming, clean environment. On the last Friday of the month you can sample a speciality of the house, a ragoût of fish and shellfish in typical Catalan style.
Near river Near sea Near motorway
Closed mid Sep-mid Oct
2 rms No smoking on premises Full central heating Open parking available Child discount available
MEALS: Dinner 85-145FF*
CARDS: ●● ▪

Taking your mobile phone to France?
See page 11

ANCTEVILLE Manche

Manoir de la Foulerie (Prop: Michel & Sylvie Enouf)
50200
☎ 233452764 FAX 233457369
(from Coutances take D2 towards Lessay. Follow signs for
Ancteville on the right)
Simple yet comfortable rooms are available in this eighteenth
century manor house. Come and enjoy a sporting holiday -
horse-riding, tennis and golf is available locally, or simply
come and eat the crêpes! English spoken.
Near river Near lake Near sea
5 en suite (bth/shr) (3 fmly) TV in all bedrooms Open parking
available Tennis Riding Boule Mini-golf Bicycle rental
Languages spoken: English & German
ROOMS: s fr 140FF; d fr 190FF
MEALS: Dinner fr 85FF*
CARDS: ☰ Travellers cheques

ANGOVILLE-AU-PLAIN Manche

Ferme d'Allain (Prop: Jeanne Flambard)
12 rue de l'Eglise *50480*
☎ 233421130
(from Cherbourg take N13 south,on through Valognes.
Angoville-au-Plain is on left off D913)
Spend your holiday on this relaxing farm, where peace and
tranquillity await you. The two guest rooms are furnished in
traditional style. The nearby beautiful Marais regional park
offers special discounts to guests who wish to visit off-season.
Near river Near sea Near beach Near motorway
2 en suite (shr) (1 fmly) Full central heating Open parking
available
ROOMS: s fr 160FF; d 185-200FF

La Guidonnerie (Prop: M & Mme Leonard)
50480
☎ 233423351
(from N13 at St Come du Mont take D913 towards Utah beach,
turn right for Angoville-au-Plain)
Near sea Forest area Near motorway
Closed Oct-mid Mar
2 en suite (bth) Full central heating Open parking available
Languages spoken: English
CARDS: Travellers cheques

ANNEBAULT Calvados

Bed & Breakfast (Prop: M & Mme Leroy)
rte de Rouen, La Basse Cour *14430*
☎ 231648086 FAX 231648086
(from A13 exit at la Haie-Tondue. Take N175 towards Caen for
4kms. 3rd house after crossroards in Annebault)
Forest area Near motorway
4 rms (3 bth/shr) (2 fmly) Radio in rooms Full central heating
Open parking available
ROOMS: s fr 170FF; d fr 200FF Reductions over 1 night
Special breaks

ARGENCES Calvados

Bed & Breakfast (Prop: M & Mme G & A Jautee)
28 rue Maréchal-Joffre *14370*
☎ 231236482
(south east of Caen off N13)
Situated at the foot of the Pays d'Auge hills and near the D-
Day landing beaches, this house is surrounded by numerous

fruit trees. The owners look forward to sharing their
considerable geographical and historical knowledge of the
area with you.
Near river
3 rms (2 bth) (1 fmly) No smoking on premises TV available
Full central heating Open parking available

ARGUEIL Seine-Maritime

Les Quatre Oiseaux (Prop: Jeanette & Keith Mills)
St-Lucien *76780*
☎ 235905195
(from Dieppe take D915 to Forges-les-Eaux. In market square
turn right onto D921 to Argueil, then onto Nolleval. Turn right
to St Lucien)
Accommodation is in a traditional 200 year old cottage run by
your hosts, Jeanette and Keith Mills. The four charming
bedrooms are all unique, with exposed beams, shower and
washbasin. There is a visitors' sitting room with television. An
enclosed garden offers a good place to relax during the day.
Dinners available.
Forest area Near motorway
4 rms (1 fmly) No smoking in all bedrooms Full central
heating Open parking available Boule Languages spoken:
English
ROOMS: s 160FF; d 210FF
MEALS: Dinner 80FF
CARDS: Travellers cheques

ARQUES-LA-BATAILLE Seine-Maritime

Villa del Kantara (Prop: Daniele Lasgouses)
2 rue de la Petite Chaussée *76800*
☎ 235855885
Near river Near lake Near sea Forest area Near motorway
3 en suite (bth) No smoking on premises TV in all bedrooms
Radio in rooms Full central heating Open parking available
Child discount available Languages spoken: English
MEALS: Full breakfast 25FF Lunch fr 100FF*

AUCEY-LA-PLAINE Manche

La Provostière (Prop: René & Maryconne Feuvrier)
50170
☎ 233603367
René and Maryconne Feuvrier welcome you to their farm,
which dates back to the eighteenth century. The two
bedrooms are simple but peaceful. The hosts enjoy sharing
the history of the region with their guests. English spoken.
Forest area
2 en suite (shr) No smoking on premises TV available Full
central heating Open parking available Child discount
available Languages spoken: English

AUTHIEUX-SUR-CALONNE, LES Calvados

Bed & Breakfast (Prop: M & Mme Leroux)
rte de Blangy-le-Château *14130*
☎ 231646728
Large modern house with wooden beams. Five rooms
available, with four situated on the first floor and one on the
ground floor. All rooms are prettily decorated. There are
garden toys for the children and garden furniture for adults to
relax in. There are reductions for children sharing their
parents' room.

cont'd

Near river Near lake Near sea Forest area
5 rms (1 bth 2 shr) No smoking on premises Radio in rooms
Full central heating Open parking available Child discount
available

AUZOUVILLE-SUR-RY Seine-Maritime

Gentilhommière (Prop: Paul & Ginette Cousin)
76766
☎ 235234074
Guest rooms are all on one floor of this landowner's house,
which dates back to 1680. Family atmosphere where guests
can try cider and calvados made on the farm. Reductions for
children under twelve years old. Special rates for stays of
more than three nights. Attractive wooded setting.
Near river Forest area Near motorway
2 en suite (bth/shr) TV available Full central heating Open
parking available Supervised Child discount available 12yrs
V meals
CARDS: ▨

BACILLY Manche

Le Grand Moulin Lecomte (Prop: Alan Harvey)
50530
☎ 233709208
(from channel ports follow signs for Mont St Michel and
Avranches, before reaching Avranches take D41 into village of
Bacilly then D231 in the direction of Genets)

A restored 18th-century farmhouse where two rooms have
private entrances on ground level while, of the three rooms on
first floor, one has an extension. Large dining room with
original Norman granite fireplace and lounge with TV,
reserved for guests,(English & French channels available). 3
kilometres from the town of Genêts which faces Mont St
Michel; an area of beautiful sandy beaches. English owners.
Near river Near sea
5 en suite (bth/shr) (3 fmly) Full central heating Open
parking available Covered parking available Languages
spoken: English, German & Welsh
ROOMS: s 150FF; d 180FF
CARDS: Travellers cheques

BANVILLE Calvados

Ferme le Petit Val (Prop: Gerard Lesage)
24 r du Camp Romain *14480*
☎ 231379218 FAX 231379218
Five rooms have been completely renovated in an eighteenth
century farm. The rooms are decorated in traditional style
with stone floors and a view of the park. There is also a

separate building with its own entrance. Traditional rustic
meals are served by request. English spoken.
Near river Near sea Forest area
5 en suite (bth/shr) (1 fmly) Full central heating Open
parking available Covered parking available Supervised
Child discount available 7yrs V meals Last d 17.00hrs
Languages spoken: English & Spanish
MEALS: Dinner 85FF*
CARDS: Travellers cheques

BARNEVILLE-CARTERET Manche

Bed & Breakfast (Prop: M G Lebourgeois)
5 rue du Pic-Mallet *50270*
☎ 233049022 FAX 233045461
(centre of Barneville-Carteret, near the church)
In the market town of Barneville, Gérard Lebourgeois
welcomes you to his sixteenth century home. Gérard is
passionate about the region and will give you plenty of ideas
for wonderful walks. Dayroom available for the use of guests.
Riding, swimming, tennis and golf within two kilometres.
Near sea Near beach In town centre Near motorway
Closed 12 Nov-Etr
3 en suite (bth/shr) (2 fmly) Full central heating Open
parking available Child discount available Bicycle rental
ROOMS: s 200FF; d 230FF
CARDS: Travellers cheques

Ti Gwenn (Prop: Marc & Yvette Cesne)
74-76 rte du Cap Barneville *50270*
☎ 233046284
This property is situated in the hills of the Carteret, with
superb views of the sea and countryside. The Anglo-Norman
islands are half-an-hour away, with shops and beach 800
metres away. Boules can be played in the garden. Within easy
distance you will find facilities for tennis, horse-riding and
golf.
Near sea Near beach
3 en suite (shr) (2 fmly) No smoking in all bedrooms Full
central heating Open parking available Supervised Boule
CARDS: Travellers cheques

BASLY Calvados

Bed & Breakfast (Prop: M C Desperques)
14 rte de Douvres *14610*
☎ 231809415
Near sea Forest area
6 rms (1 shr) (1 fmly) TV available Full central heating Open
parking available
CARDS: Travellers cheques

BAUX-DE-BRETEUIL, LES Eure

La Bourganière (Prop: Mme M Noël)
27160
☎ 232306818 FAX 232301993
(from Breteuil take D833)
Old farm-style house which your hostess, Marie Noël, gladly
welcomes you to. Living/dining room is traditionally
furnished, with original wooden beams. Two spacious, light
rooms, one of which is a family room. Reductions offered for
children under eight years.
Forest area
2 en suite (bth) (1 fmly) (1 with balcony) Full central heating
Open parking available Child discount available 10yrs
ROOMS: s fr 230FF; d fr 230FF

BAYEUX Calvados

Manoir du Carel (Prop: M et Mme Aumond)
Maisons *14400*
☎ 231223700 FAX 231215700
(leave N13 onto D6 in direction of Port-de-Bessin, after 4.5km
turn left, manor 1km on right)
M and Mme Aumond welcome you to this historic manor
house. The interior has recently been renovated and a small,
independent house in the grounds is also available for guests.
Numerous excellent restaurants nearby. English spoken.
Near beach Forest area Near motorway
2 en suite (bth/shr) TV in all bedrooms Full central heating
Open parking available Covered parking available Tennis
Riding Languages spoken: English & German
CARDS: ● ▅

River Cottage (Prop: Soria Pirot)
3 Impasse Moulin de la Riviere *14400*
☎ 231923123
(situated 5mins drive from the centre of Bayeaux)
An old renovated cottage where the en suite bedrooms are
decorated in English style with matching duvet and curtains
and Edwardian furniture. The garden extends to the river.
Near river Near sea Near beach Forest area
3 en suite (shr) No smoking on premises Full central heating
Open parking available Fishing Languages spoken: English
ROOMS: s 210FF; d 240FF Reductions over 1 night
MEALS: Dinner fr 65FF
CARDS: ● ▅ ▆ ▣

BEAUMONT-HAGUE Manche

Le Closet (Prop: M & Mme Dalmont)
2 allée des Jardins *50440*
☎ 233527246
Near sea
4 rms (2 fmly) Full central heating Open parking available
Languages spoken: English
CARDS: ▅ Travellers cheques

BELVAL-BOURG Manche

La Guerandiere (Prop: M Paul Trout)
50210
☎ 233452103 FAX 233452103
This property is situated in the small village of Belval, about
five minutes outside the town of Coutances, within easy reach
of the beaches of the Carentan peninsula. The village offers
beautiful views in a country setting, offering excellent walks.
Meals available by request. English hosts.
Near river Near lake Near sea Forest area
Closed Oct-Mar
5 rms (2 shr) (4 fmly) No smoking on premises Full central
heating Open parking available Supervised Child discount
available 7yrs Languages spoken: English
MEALS: Dinner 70FF*

BÉMÉCOURT Eure

Le Vieux Château (Prop: Maryvonne Lallemand-Legras)
27160
☎ 232299047
(from Breteuil take D141 towards Rugles,through forest. At
Bémécourt turn left 300m after traffic lights)
Built on the site of a fortified castle, this half-timbered manor
house is flanked by two 15th-century towers and encircled by

a moat. The garden is a haven of peace. Breakfast can be
described as 'more of a brunch', with homemade bread and
jams.
Forest area Near motorway
Closed Jan-Feb
3 rms Full central heating Open parking available No
children 8yrs Child discount available 12yrs Fishing Boule
Open terrace Languages spoken: English & German
ROOMS: s 280FF; d 350FF Reductions over 1 night
MEALS: Dinner fr 100FF*
CARDS: Travellers cheques

BERNIÈRES-SUR-MER Calvados

Bed & Breakfast (Prop: M Michel Lambard)
31 rue Montauban, "La Louveraie" *14990*
☎ 231965312 FAX 231965312
Lovely renovated house which retains its original atmosphere
and details. Small but charming rooms. This bed & breakfast
is situated near the D-Day landing beaches which are there to
be explored. Tennis courts, equestrian centre, sea-water
therapy centre, sailing school and bike rental all available
nearby. English spoken.
Near sea In town centre
1 en suite (shr) TV available Radio in rooms Full central
heating Open parking available Boule Mini-golf Bicycle
rental Languages spoken: English & Spanish

BESNEVILLE Manche

Hotel Danois (Prop: Michel Lamy)
50390
☎ 233416263
This old stone farmhouse has rooms with independent access
by an external stairway. Comfortable reception area for the
use of guests. Situated is a quiet, peaceful environment, the
property is open from April to September. French breakfast is
served.
Forest area
Closed Oct-14 Apr
2 rms Open parking available

BEUVRON-EN-AUGE Calvados

Manoir de Sens (Prop: Philippe David)
14430
☎ 231792305 FAX 231794520
Situated at the heart of a working stud-farm and located just
one kilometre from the protected village of Beuvron-en-Auge,
reputed to be one of the most beautiful in France. Ten
kilometres from the sea. Peace and tranquillity assured.
English spoken.
Near river Forest area
6 en suite (bth/shr) (1 fmly) (3 with balcony) Full central
heating Open parking available Supervised
CARDS: Travellers cheques

BIÉVILLE-BEUVILLE Calvados

Bed & Breakfast (Prop: J M & A Bartassot)
4 rue Haute *14112*
☎ 231443499 FAX 231439415
Five rooms are available in this nineteenth century farm,
located five kilometres from the D-Day landing beaches and
cont'd

Caen. Furnished apartments are also on offer which can be rented for a week or a month. English spoken.
Near motorway
5 en suite (shr) Full central heating Open parking available
Child discount available

Le Londel (Prop: Jean-Claude & Danielle Bruand)
14112
☎ 231445174 FAX 231445174
The proprietors welcome you to their modern house, situated fifteen kilometres from the beach near Caen. Set in a hectare of land in the middle of Bieville-Beuville, your hosts value peace and quiet and enjoy chatting with their guests. Guests are welcome to walk in the garden.
Near sea Near motorway
3 en suite (bth/shr) Full central heating Open parking available Covered parking available Child discount available
CARDS: Travellers cheques

La Petite Londe (Prop: Françoise Lance)
14112
☎ 231445203 FAX 231445203
(leave the Northern peripheric at the way out: Cote de Nacre D7, 3km further at La Bijude turn right in direction of Le Londel, 700m further at first farm on right take gravel lane)
Easily accessible from the D7, this establishment is a modern house with a large garden. There are two double bedrooms and a single on the first floor.
Near motorway
2 en suite (bth/shr) (2 fmly) TV available Full central heating Open parking available Languages spoken: English
ROOMS: s 150-160FF; d 200-220FF *
CARDS: Travellers cheques

BIGNE, LA Calvados

Le Quettevillière (Prop: Andre & Elizabeth Bamford)
14260
☎ 231774594 FAX 231775927
Near river Near lake Forest area Near motorway
7 en suite (bth/shr) (5 fmly) (2 with balcony) No smoking in 3 bedrooms Radio in rooms Full central heating Open parking available Child discount available V meals Languages spoken: English

BLAINVILLE-SUR-MER Manche

Bed & Breakfast (Prop: M Jean Bouton)
Villa "Alice", 21 rte de la Louverie *50560*
☎ 233472839 & 145223923 FAX 233472839 & 145223923
(from Coutance take D44 to Tourville and Courtainville, then D651 to Blainville-sur-Mer)
Set in the heart of preserved woodland and farmland, this house offers peace, tranquillity and comfort, surrounded as it is by a large garden. There are two sitting rooms for guests' use, which have a Steinway piano and a Pianola-Steck. A beautiful sandy beach is only one kilometre away. Golf (18-hole course), tennis, horse-riding and a casino are all nearby. English spoken.
Near sea
Closed Oct-14 May(except by arrangement)
3 rms Full central heating Open parking available No children 6yrs Child discount available 10yrs Languages spoken: English,German & Spanish
ROOMS: s fr 180FF; d fr 200FF
CARDS: Travellers cheques

BOËCÉ Orne

La Fosse
61560
☎ 233254179
Two guest rooms and one suite are available, all with independent access, in this country house, which will accommodate up to twelve people. Lounge and dining room available for the use of guests. Covered, heated swimming pool and table-tennis on-site. Continental breakfast served. Dinner available at a fixed price. Barbecue facilities. Reductions for children under ten years. English spoken.
Forest area Near motorway
3 en suite (bth/shr) (1 fmly) No smoking on premises Full central heating Open parking available Child discount available Outdoor swimming pool (heated) Last d 20.00hrs Languages spoken: English
MEALS: Dinner fr 80FF*

BONCOURT Eure

Les Ormes (Prop: Mme Beghini)
5 rue Divette *27120*
☎ 232369244 & 232367301 FAX 232263911
(take D534 to Boncourt from N13 between Pacy-sur-Eure/d'Evreux)
Brigitte Beghini welcomes you to an area of peace and quiet. This eighteenth century grange is typical of the Vallée d'Eure and offers an attractive dining room with open fire. Bicycles can be rented from the owner. Various gastronomic restaurants are close to the property. English spoken.
Forest area Near motorway
5 en suite (bth/shr) No smoking in all bedrooms TV available Open parking available Open terrace Languages spoken: English

BOSC-ROGER-EN-ROUMOIS, LE Eure

Bed & Breakfast (Prop: Nicole & Pierre Fontaine)
1034 ch du Bas-Boscherville, La Queue Bourguignon *27670*
☎ 235877516
(from Bourgtheroulde take D313 towards Elbeuf.500m after Lampes Berger follow sign for 'Chambres d'Hôte 1ere à droite. Establishment in 1km.)

Attractive house set in the middle of an orchard. The surrounding countryside is extremely beautiful, being close to the Parc Naturel de Bretonne. Facilities nearby include tennis, horse-riding, swimming and fishing . English spoken.
Near river Near lake Forest area Near motorway
4 rms (3 shr) No smoking on premises Radio in rooms Full

central heating Open parking available Child discount
available 2yrs Boule Languages spoken: English
ROOMS: s 200-220FF; d 270FF
MEALS: Dinner fr 90FF*
CARDS: ▨ Travellers cheques

BOULON Calvados

Bed & Breakfast (Prop: Mme Duchemin)
789 rue de la République *14220*
☎ 231392386
(from Caen take D562 in the direction of Thury-Harcourt. Take
left turn for Boulon)

Mme. Duchemin welcomes you to her home in Boulon, where
two rooms are on offer. The rooms are comfortable and your
hostess makes every effort to ensure you enjoy your stay in
this undiscovered part of France. Garden for the use of guests.
English spoken.
Forest area
2 en suite (bth/shr) (2 fmly) No smoking on premises Full
central heating Air conditioning in bedrooms Open parking
available Languages spoken: English
ROOMS: s 150-170FF; d 210-230FF *

BOURGTHEROULDE Eure

Château de Boscherville (Prop: Mme du Plouy)
27520
☎ 235876212 & 235876141 FAX 235876212
(from A13 exit Maison Brulée)
Mme. Henry du Plouy welcomes you to her eighteenth
century château in a park. Breakfast available. Picnic baskets
on request. Open all year round, offering peace and
tranquillity in this comfortable and attractive residence.
English spoken.
Forest area Near motorway
5 en suite (bth/shr) (1 fmly) Full central heating Open
parking available Croquet Bridge tables Languages spoken:
English
CARDS: Travellers cheques

BOURNEVILLE Eure

La Grange (Prop: C & J Brown)
rte d'Aizier *27500*
☎ 232571143
(from A13 Paris to Caen exit 26 westbound then D89
Bourneville)
Surrounded by beautiful lawn, flowers and a patio facing

south, this old red-brick building dates back to 1827.
Converted in 1993, two rooms are now offered to guests.
Breakfast is served in a magnificent dining room, paved in
terracotta and with a large Normandy fireplace. English
spoken.
Near river Forest area Near motorway
Closed 20 Dec-Feb
2 en suite (shr) No smoking on premises Full central heating
Open parking available Languages spoken: English
ROOMS: s 200FF; d 230FF Reductions over 1 night

BOURTH Eure

Bed & Breakfast (Prop: M & G Brugger)
21 av de Kronstorf *27580*
☎ 232327029
(from Verneuil-sur-Avre take N26 in the direction of l'Aigle
after 6km turn right to Bourth)
This large turn-of-the-century house is the home of Anglo-
Canadian hosts, M. and Mme. Brugger-Wright. The interior is
elegant yet intimate. The dining room, patio and pretty garden
are all open to guests. Shops and restaurants are nearby. Local
facilities include tennis, riding, swimming, golf and fishing .
Near river Forest area In town centre Near motorway
4 en suite (bth/shr) (2 with balcony) Full central heating
Open parking available Child discount available 18yrs TV
room Languages spoken: English
CARDS: Travellers cheques

BRÉMOY Calvados

Carrefour des Fosses (Prop: Jacqueline et Gilbert
Lalleman)
14260
☎ 231778322
2 en suite (shr) No smoking on premises Full central heating
Open parking available Table tennis
MEALS: Dinner 75FF*

BRETEUIL-SUR-ITON Eure

Bed & Breakfast (Prop: P & R Mieuset)
79 rue J-Girard *27160*
☎ 232297047
Large eighteenth century house with shaded gardens.
Spacious rooms. French breakfast available. Shops and
restaurants nearby. No animals allowed.
Near river Forest area In town centre
1 en suite (shr) Full central heating Open parking available
Covered parking available Supervised

BRETTEVILLE-SUR-DIVES Calvados

Le Pressoir de Glatigny
14170
☎ 231206893
Stone built house, dating back to the nineteenth century, in an
environment full of flowers in the summer, in the heat of the
Auge region. Three rustic-style bedrooms available on the first
floor. No smoking policy in the house. Continental breakfast
served. Reductions for children up to eight years. Sandpit,
table-tennis, barbecue, picnic table and sun-loungers in
garden.
3 rms (1 bth 1 shr) No smoking on premises Full central
heating Open parking available Child discount available 8yrs
Table tennis
CARDS: Travellers cheques

BRETTEVILLE-SUR-LAIZE Calvados

Château des Riffets
14680
☎ 231235321 FAX 231237514
Forest area
4 en suite (bth/shr) (2 fmly) (1 with balcony) Licensed Open
parking available Supervised Child discount available
Outdoor swimming pool (heated) Open terrace Last d
17.00hrs Languages spoken: English,German

BRÉVANDS Manche

La Capitainerie (Prop: Jaqueline Feron)
50500
☎ 233423309
This unusual accommodation is set against a backdrop of
greenery and calm. The sea is three kilometres away and the
canal flows into the sea at the Port de la Rentan is only
200 metres away. Watching the boats sail past is a very
relaxing pastime!
Near river Near sea Near motorway
2 rms Full central heating Open parking available
Supervised Barbecue
CARDS: Travellers cheques

BRIONNE Eure

Le Coeur de Lion (Prop: P & H Baker)
14 bd de la Reépublique *27800*
☎ 232434035 FAX 232469531
(from Brionne follow directions for 'Base de Loisirs' this will
bring you to blvd de la Republique 150 yds turn right into
'Impass du Lac'-ignore no entry sign)
This large detached house, with enclosed garden terrace and
stream, is just five minutes walk from the historic town of
Brionne in the Risle Valley. Situated next to a lake, with leisure
area. Excellent base from which to explore the Normandy
countryside. Market twice weekly at Brionne. English spoken.
Near river Near lake Near sea Forest area Near motorway
Closed end Nov-14 Jan
5 rms (4 shr) (2 fmly) Full central heating Open parking
available Outdoor swimming pool Riding Boule Mini-golf
Bicycle rental V meals Languages spoken: English
ROOMS: d 205-250FF
MEALS: Dinner 90FF
CARDS: ☯ ▆ Travellers cheques

BRIOUZE Orne

Bed & Breakfast (Prop: M & Mme Pierrot)
rte de Bellou *61220*
☎ 233660798
(from Argentan take D924 towards Flers. At the church in
Briouze take D21 to Bellou)
The accommodation, situated in a large landscaped garden, is
in a small, traditionally-built cottage that is separate from the
proprietor's house.
Closed Aug
1 en suite (shr) Full central heating Open parking available
Table tennis
ROOMS: s 170FF; d 200FF
CARDS: Travellers cheques

BRIX Manche

Château Mont Eqinguet (Prop: M Berridge)
50700
☎ 233419631 FAX 233419877
(from Cherbourg take N13 towards Valognes. After 11kms
turn right onto D119 for Ruffosses (not Brix), cross motorway
& follow blue and white signs to the château approx 2kms)
Informal eighteenth century château guest house. Your
English hosts, Mark and Fiona Berridge, hope you enjoy the
peaceful, relaxed rural surroundings as much as they do.
Plenty of faded splendour and friendly atmosphere. Close to
good restaurants and thirty kilometres from superb beaches.
Riding and bicycle hire on site. Golf within five kilometres.
Closed 3 Jan-15 Feb
4 rms (2 bth) (1 fmly) (1 with balcony) Open parking
available Child discount available 14yrs Languages spoken:
English
ROOMS: s 140-160FF; d 200-240FF * Reductions over 1 night
CARDS: Travellers cheques

CAHAGNES Calvados

Bed & Breakfast (Prop: M & Mme Joseph Guilbert)
Benneville *14240*
☎ 231775805 FAX 231773784
(7km from Villers Bocage and 4km from Cahagnes)
This creeper-clad house is typical of the area. It is set on a
farm with chickens and cows. Children, in particular, will love
discovering life on the farm. Walks, fishing, golf, swimming
and riding all available within close proximity. Basic English
spoken.
Near river Near lake Forest area Near motorway
5 en suite (bth/shr) 2 rooms in annexe (3 fmly) Open parking
available Child discount available Boule Open terrace Table
tennis, Volley ball Languages spoken: English
MEALS: Dinner fr 70FF*
CARDS: Travellers cheques

CAMBREMER Calvados

Bed & Breakfast (Prop: M & Mme Bernard)
Le Clos de St-Laurent, St-Laurent-du-Mont *14340*
☎ 231634704 FAX 231634692
(on the D50 between Lisieux and Carrefour Saint-Jean)
This charming, nineteenth century style house with garden
and park enjoys pleasant views over the Dive Valley. Come
and enjoy the cider road or the springs of St Laurent. Thirty-
five minutes to the American landing beaches. Enjoy meals
cooked by the proprietor, with regional dishes a speciality. A
warm welcome is offered. A little English spoken.
Forest area Near motorway
6 en suite (bth/shr) (2 fmly) TV available Radio in rooms Full
central heating Air conditioning in bedrooms Open parking
available Child discount available 5yrs
ROOMS: s 230FF; d 280FF * Reductions over 1 night
MEALS: Dinner fr 90FF*
CARDS: ▆ Travellers cheques

CAMPEAUX Calvados

Le Champ Touillon
14350
☎ 231686686
Near lake Forest area Near motorway
5 en suite (shr) (4 fmly) Full central heating Open parking

available Child discount available V meals Languages
spoken: English
MEALS: Lunch 75-95FFalc Dinner 75-95FFalc*
CARDS: ▄▄

CAMPIGNY Eure

Le Clos Mahiet (Prop: Alain Vauquelin)
27500
☎ 232411320
Forest area
Closed 22 Dec-3 Jan
3 en suite (shr) Full central heating Open parking available
Child discount available 10yrs
MEALS: Dinner fr 80FF*
CARDS: Travellers cheques

CANVILLE-LA-ROCQUE Manche

La Rue (Prop: Gisele Frugier)
50580
☎ 233530306
This engaging seventeenth century farm is furnished with
traditional Normandy furniture. Two large windows open onto
a glorious courtyard, full of flowers. Children welcome - small
beds can be provided for them. The Frugier family look
forward to meeting you. English spoken.
1 en suite (shr) No smoking in all bedrooms Full central
heating Open parking available

CAPELLE-LES-GRANDS Eure

Val Perrier (Prop: P et M Beaudry)
27270
☎ 232447633
(from Bernay take Orbec D131, from Broglie take N138 then
follow arrows to establishment)
A large house situated in the heart of the peaceful Normandy
countryside, surrounded by fields and with a pleasant garden
to relax in.The bedrooms are large and comfortable, each with
a kitchen and lounge. Guests can enjoy large gastronomic
meals that include many well-known French specialities.
Near river Forest area Near motorway
2 en suite (shr) (1 fmly) (1 with balcony) No smoking on
premises Full central heating Open parking available
Covered parking available Supervised Child discount
available 12yrs Bicycle rental Table tennis Exercise
equipment Last d 20.00hrs Languages spoken: English
ROOMS: s 160FF; d 200-220FF *
MEALS: Dinner 80-100FF*

CATTEVILLE Manche

Le Haul (Prop: Gerard Langlois)
50390
☎ 233416469 FAX 233416469
(on the D900 Saint-Sauveu-le-Vincente/la Haye-du Puits, take
D215)
A 19th century farm in the heart of a National Park where the
interior is furnished with antiques from Normandy. There is a
large living room with television and an open fire. Two
cottages also available. The observation hut by the lake may
be used by guests. Racehorses are bred here. Tennis, cycling,
kayaking and mountaineering are available nearby and it is an
ideal area for walkers.

Near river Near sea Near beach Forest area
5 en suite (bth/shr) (1 fmly) Full central heating Open
parking available Covered parking available Child discount
available 5yrs Table tennis, Games room V meals
ROOMS: s fr 180FF; d 220-260FF
CARDS: Travellers cheques

CAUDEBEC-EN-CAUX Seine-Maritime

No 1 Cavée St-Léger (Prop: Christiane Villamaux)
68 rue République *76490*
☎ 235961015 FAX 235967525
(in village at the tourist office take the direction of Yvetot,
chambres d'hôtes 500m on the right, D131)
In an area known as the 'Parc Naturel de Brotonne' this house
is only 500 metres from the Seine, the forest, the restaurants
and the shops along the Route of the Abbeys. There is a large
garden with a summer room, which guests may use in the
good weather. You are assured of a warm welcome and this
establishment is ideally situated as a stopover from the ferries
to the South of France or as a base for visiting Normandy.
English spoken.
Near river Forest area
4 en suite (shr) (2 fmly) No smoking on premises TV in all
bedrooms Full central heating Open parking available
Bicycle rental Languages spoken: English
ROOMS: s 180-225FF; d 225-265FF

CAUMONT-L'ÉVENTÉ Calvados

Bed & Breakfast (Prop: C et J-P Boullot)
19 rue Thiers *14240*
☎ 231774785
(from Caen take N175 towards Avranches, then at Villers take
D71 to Caumont-l'Eventé)

Claude and Jeanne-Paule Boullot welcome you to their home
where a relaxing atmosphere is created by the presence of a
garden filled with trees and flowers. Guests are invited to try
their hand at sculpture on-site. Swimming pool, table-tennis.
5 en suite (bth/shr) (2 fmly) (2 with balcony) No smoking on
premises Full central heating Open parking available No
children 3yrs Outdoor swimming pool Open terrace Table
tennis
ROOMS: d 320FF *
MEALS: Dinner fr 140FF*
CARDS: ▄▄▄ Travellers cheques

CHAMBOIS Orne

Le Château (Prop: Mme Clapeau)
rte de Vimoutiers *61160*
☎ 233367134
This recently restored building in the heart of the village of Chambois, is situated in the middle of a wooded park and in the shadow of a twelfth century keep. A warm welcome awaits you and bedrooms are comfortable and quiet. Fishing, swimming, riding and walks all available locally. English spoken.
Near river Near lake Forest area In town centre Near motorway
5 en suite (bth/shr) (2 fmly) TV available Full central heating Open parking available Child discount available Boule Table tennis Languages spoken: English
CARDS: Travellers cheques

CLÉCY Calvados

La Loterie (Prop: R Aubry)
14570
☎ 231697438
(Leave Clécy for Pont le Vey, continue south of river on D133 for 1m. House is on left with Gite sign)
Old restored house, with antique furniture and exposed beams. Ample French breakfasts served. Large enclosed garden, with flowers and apple trees. Reduced rates for children up to two years.
Near river Forest area
3 en suite (bth/shr) Open parking available Child discount available
ROOMS: s 150FF; d 200-300FF *

CLIPONVILLE Seine-Maritime

Hameau de Rucquemare (Prop: Beatrice & J-Pierre Leveque)
76640
☎ 235967221
Enjoy a holiday on a farm at this typical Normandy house, built in the 17th century. Situated just ten kilometres from Yvetot, surrounded by beech groves and a large lake. A kitchen and living room, with open fireplace, are available for guests' use. Table tennis and bikes available. A little English spoken.
4 en suite (shr) (3 fmly) Full central heating Open parking available Languages spoken: English

COIGNY Manche

Château de Coigny (Prop: Odette Ionckheere)
50250
☎ 233421079
This sixteenth century château offers two en suite guest rooms. The birthplace of the Dukes of Coigny, Marshals of France in the reign of Louis XIV and Louis XV. Each room is decorated in the style of each of these. Dinner available by arrangement.
Closed All Saints Day-Etr
2 en suite (bth/shr) No smoking on premises Full central heating Open parking available Supervised No children 3yrs Child discount available 12yrs

COLLEVILLE-SUR-MER Calvados

Ferme du Clos Tassin (Prop: Daniel Picquenard)
14710
☎ 231224151 FAX 231222946
A relaxing atmosphere, in comfortable rooms is on offer at this working farm, where milk is produced alongside cider, Pommeau and Calvados. Breakfast is served at the family table. Numerous walks available.
Near sea Near beach
5 rms (2 bth 1 shr) (1 fmly) No smoking on premises Open parking available

COMMES Calvados

Bed & Breakfast (Prop: M & L Cairon)
L'Eglise *14520*
☎ 231217108
Near sea
4 en suite (bth/shr) Full central heating Open parking available

CONDÉ-SUR-SARTHE Orne

Le Clos des Roses (Prop: M et Mme P Pellegrini)
10 rue de la Jardinière *61250*
☎ 233277068
(travelling in the direction of Rennes/St Malo exit at Alencon on D112 and proceed to Boissiere take the r du Chateau d'Eau on the left turn right Conde-sur-Sarthe)
Near river Near motorway
3 en suite (bth/shr) No smoking on premises Radio in rooms Full central heating Open parking available
ROOMS: s fr 150FF; d fr 200FF *

CONTEVILLE Eure

Ferme du Pressoir
Le Clos Potier *27210*
☎ 232576079
This Normandy farmhouse is charmingly furnished, with antiques and displays of dried flowers. English spoken. Bikes for hire.
Forest area
No smoking on premises Full central heating Open parking available Languages spoken: English

COURSON Calvados

La Brandonnière (Prop: Maurice Perrard)
14380
☎ 231688571
(100mtrs from church on left in direction of Sept Freres)
Situated 100 metres from the Church of Courson, this house has a large courtyard for parking and offers a calm atmosphere. Fixed price dinner possible, by reservation. Lake and forest close by.
Closed Nov-27 Mar
2 en suite (bth) Open parking available Child discount available

CRÉPON Calvados

Le Haras de Crépon (Prop: Pascale Landeau)
Le Clos Mondeville *14480*
☎ 231213737 FAX 231211212
(coming from Caen in the direction of Cherbourg, exit D158B

signed Creully then Brecy St Gabriel to Arromanches. At
Villiers Le Sec passing the church, continue for 2 kms)
This restored sixteenth century manor house offers
comfortable and clean rooms. Mme. Landeau welcomes you
to the family table and will serve you fresh garden and sea
produce. Table-tennis and bikes available. English spoken.
Near lake Near sea Near beach
5 en suite (bth/shr) (1 fmly) Full central heating Open
parking available Child discount available 11yrs Table tennis
Last d 20.50 Languages spoken: English
MEALS: Full breakfast 35FF Continental breakfast 35FF
Dinner 150-290FF*
CARDS: ● ▆

Manoir de Crépon (Prop: Anne-Marie Poisson)
rte d'Arromanches *14480*
☎ 231222127 FAX 231228880
(exit A13 at Creully and take D22 and then D65 in direction of
Arromanches. On reaching Crépon, house is on left in
direction of Ver-sur-Mer as you leave village)
The first-floor guest rooms are large, with views over the park
and rear garden. All are furnished in the style of the manor
and some have stone fireplaces. Peaceful walks in the park.
Continental breakfast served. The beach is within four
kilometres. A little English spoken.
RS winter
3 en suite (bth/shr) (1 fmly) TV in 2 bedrooms Full central
heating Open parking available Child discount available
15yrs Languages spoken: English
ROOMS: s 330FF; d 400FF Special breaks
CARDS: ● ▆ Y

CRIQUEBEUF-EN-CAUX Seine-Maritime

Ferme Auberge de la Cote (Prop: Michel Basille)
190 Le Bout de la Ville *76111*
☎ 235280132 FAX 235280132
(from Le Havre take D489 to Fécamp, then D940. Turn right
onto D211 towards Yport)
Situated on a farm, in a house built of brick and flint, rooms
are available, one of which is a family room. Calm
atmosphere. Meals by reservation.
Near sea Near beach
2 en suite (shr) (1 fmly) Full central heating Open parking
available Child discount available 12yrs
ROOMS: d 245FF *
MEALS: Lunch 112-165FF Dinner 112-165FF*
CARDS: ● ▆ ▆

CRIQUETOT-L'ESNEVAL Seine-Maritime

Bed & Breakfast (Prop: G et D Paumelle)
rte de Gonneville *76280*
☎ 235272847
This establishment is situated in a peaceful area and five non-
smoking rustic guest rooms are offered on the ground floor of
this farmhouse, with French windows opening onto the flower
garden. Exposed beams are a feature of this property. English
spoken.
Near sea Near beach Forest area
Closed Nov-Mar
5 rms (4 bth/shr) (3 fmly) No smoking on premises Open
parking available Supervised
ROOMS: d 210FF *

CULEY-LE-PATRY Calvados

Bed & Breakfast (Prop: Mme C Ballanger)
allée des Chânes *14220*
☎ 231796000
The main guest room is linked with a second room for friends
or children. These rooms are well furnished and comfortable
and are situated on the ground floor, with a panoramic view of
the woods. A third guest room is on the first floor and is
equipped with a television. Golf, canoeing, pedaloes, kayaking,
and tennis within six kilometres. English spoken.
Near river Forest area
3 rms (2 shr) (1 with balcony) No smoking on premises
Radio in rooms Full central heating Open parking available
Child discount available 2yrs Languages spoken: English

DANGU Eure

Les Ombelles (Prop: Poulain de Saint-Pere)
4 rue du Gué *27720*
☎ 232550495 FAX 232555987
Restored eighteenth century country house. Madame de
Saint-Père, the owner, is happy to advise guests on places of
interest, golf, fishing, visits to local farms and, if you would
like painting lessons during your visit, she will be pleased to
help you. Facilities available in the village include fishing
(river and pond), hiking, tennis, horse-trekking and
sailboarding. English spoken.
Near river Near lake Forest area
Closed 16 Dec-14 Mar
3 en suite (bth/shr) No smoking on premises Full central
heating Open parking available No children 5yrs Child
discount available Fishing Open terrace Languages spoken:
English
CARDS: Travellers cheques

DOMFRONT Orne

La Demeure d'Olwen (Prop: Sylvia Tailhandier-Jacobson)
1 rue de Godras *61700*
☎ 233371003 FAX 233371003
(follow signs for Centre Ancien on reaching Domfront. House
in immediate vicinity of Court of Justice, in front of the Post
Office)
In the medieval town of Domfront, you will be welcomed to a
residence full of charm and surprises. Beautifully decorated,
with paintings and period furniture, this property is set in
pretty gardens. Relax there in a sun-lounger with a book and
drink. English spoken.
Near river Forest area In town centre
3 en suite (shr) (2 fmly) No smoking in 1 bedroom Full
central heating Open parking available Supervised
Languages spoken: English & Italian
ROOMS: s 280FF; d 280FF
CARDS: Travellers cheques

DRAGEY Manche

Belleville (Prop: O et F Brasme)
l'Église *50530*
☎ 233489396 FAX 233485975
Dating from the seventeenth century Belleville is situated in
the bay of Mount Saint Michel, which can be seen from the
bedrooms when the weather is clear. The house is surrounded
by fields and the garden is a haven of peace and tranquility.
cont'd

69

The beach is just a 10 minute drive away and there are many historical sites to visit.
Near sea Near beach
2 en suite (bth) No smoking on premises Full central heating
Open parking available Languages spoken: English
ROOMS: s 280FF; d 320FF

DUCLAIR Seine-Maritime

Bed & Breakfast (Prop: M & Mme B Lemercier)
282 chemin du Panorama *76480*
☎ 235376884
Your hosts welcome you to their house with panoramic views over the Seine. Nearby, lakes are open all year round for fishing enthusiasts. Tennis is also within one kilometre, with golf and canoeing just eight kilometres away. Bikes available. Several restaurants to choose from in the town of Duclair.
Near river Near lake Forest area Near motorway
5 en suite (bth/shr) No smoking on premises Full central heating Open parking available Cycling
CARDS: ▨ Travellers cheques

ECRAMMEVILLE Calvados

Ferme de l'Abbaye (Prop: A Fauvel)
14710
☎ 231225232
(from Bayeaux take N13 west. After 14kms take D30 to Ecrammeville. Farm is near church)
In the fifteenth century this farmhouse was a monks' dormitory, and still looks out onto the Abbey church which is floodlit at night. Situated in a peaceful area, close to the landing beaches of World War Two, the house has a fine stone staircase and stone columns, a large fireplace, and exposed beams. Trotting horses and cattle are bred, and cider is made on the farm. Madame Fauvel, a grandmother of nine, has plenty of time for her guests. All rooms have independent access. Dinner is available at a fixed price.
Near river Near sea Near beach
5 en suite (bth/shr) (2 fmly) No smoking on premises Full central heating Child discount available 9yrs
ROOMS: s 160FF; d 220FF * Reductions over 1 night

ÉMALLEVILLE Eure

Château d'Émalleville (Prop: M & Mme C Thieblot)
17 rue de l'Église *27930*
☎ 232340187 FAX 232343027
(from Louviers, south of Rouen, take D155 towards Evreux. Through Le Boulay Morin & 500m after leaving village turn left to Emalleville. Château on right in village)
This charming 18th-century Normandy château is surrounded by parkland. Large breakfast of ham, eggs, cheese, home-made jam and coffee served. Private tennis court and horse-riding facilities within one kilometre. Dinner available on request for a minimum of six people. English spoken.
Near river Forest area
5 en suite (bth/shr) (2 fmly) No smoking in 1 bedroom Full central heating Open parking available Covered parking available Tennis
ROOMS: s fr 450FF; d 450-650FF Reductions over 1 night
CARDS: ●● ▨ ▨ ▣ Travellers cheques

ERMENOUVILLE Seine-Maritime

Château de Mesnil-Geoffroy (Prop: Docteur et Madame Kayali)
76740
☎ 235571277 FAX 235571024
(Leave A13 at exit 25 to Yvetot. In Yvetot take direction for St Valery-en-Caux. 1 mile after Ste Colombe, to the right the château is signed as an historic monument)
Surrounded by French-style gardens with a maze and exotic birds, this imposing house was once the residence of the Princes of Montmorency Luxembourg and is classified as an 18th-century historic monument. The guest rooms are furnished with pieces of antique furniture which have been in the family for generations. The lounges have superbly carved wood panelling which act as a reminder of bygone days. Guests are served an excellent breakfast prepared with home-made produce, and dinner can be enjoyed by candlelight in an 18th-century atmosphere.
Near sea Near beach
6 en suite (bth/shr) Open parking available Supervised Boule Bicycle rental Open terrace
ROOMS: d 380-650FF
MEALS: Continental breakfast 50FF Dinner fr 230FF
CARDS: ●● ▨ Travellers cheques

ÉTRETAT Seine-Maritime

Villa St-Sauveur (Prop: Yanick & Anne-Marie)
Chemin d'Anilaville *76790*
Rooms available in this old house, built at the end of the last century. The house is situated in the middle of a large garden surrounded by walls, six or seven minutes from the centre of Etretat by foot. Beaches, tennis, sailing club, riding centre and many walks are within close proximity to the property. Reductions for children under ten years. English spoken.
Near sea Near beach Forest area
2 rms No smoking on premises Full central heating Open parking available Supervised No children 5yrs Child discount available 10yrs Languages spoken: English

EU Seine-Maritime

Manoir de Beaumont (Prop: Catherine Demarquet)
76260
☎ 235509191
(from D49 on entering Eu, turn left in the direction of the Forest of Eu and Beaumont - 2kms)
An old Normandy house set in a park and situated in countryside on a hilltop with wonderful views, only four kilometres from the beach. The forest begins where the garden ends. The manor house and bedrooms are furnished with antiques. An ideal location for visiting the castle, churches, and 17th-century hospital in the ancient town of Eu. Tennis and riding (on the beach) are available nearby. Continental breakfast served. English spoken.
Near river Near sea Near beach Forest area
3 en suite (shr) (2 fmly) No smoking in 1 bedroom Full central heating Open parking available Supervised Child discount available 2yrs Languages spoken: English
ROOMS: s 200FF; d 250FF
CARDS: Travellers cheques

FAVEROLLES Orne

Le Mont Roti (Prop: Bernard Fortin)
61600
☎ 233373472
(on D19)

All the rooms are set apart from the main residence, which is a farm where peace and quiet reign. Breakfasts served - you'll love the home-made jam. Evening meal with hosts by request. Half-price rooms for children. Fishing, swimming, tennis and golf within easy access. English spoken.
Near river Near lake Forest area
2 en suite (shr) No smoking on premises Full central heating Air conditioning in bedrooms Child discount available Boule Languages spoken: English
ROOMS: s 160FF; d 200FF
MEALS: Dinner 75FF

FERRIÈRES-ST-HILAIRE Eure

La Fosse Nardière (Prop: Madeline Drouin)
27270
☎ 232432667 FAX 231323116
Madéleine Drouin looks forward to welcoming guests to Ferrières-St-Hilaire all year round. The guesthouse is situated near a forest so great walks are assured. The Château Vainheure is within easy access. Fishing available for enthusiasts. Dinner and breakfast available.
Near river Forest area Near motorway
4 rms (2 bth/shr) (1 fmly) (1 with balcony) Full central heating Open parking available No children Last d 19.00hrs
MEALS: Dinner 80FF*

FERTÉ-FRÊNEL, LA Orne

Le Château (Prop: M & Mme Sodechaff)
61550
☎ 233242323 FAX 233245019
Nineteenth century Norman castle, situated in a twenty hectare park, amidst fifty hectares of private property. Just fifty metres from the village, where you will find a good restaurant and shops. Each room has a private kitchenette. Monumental entrance of marble. The château looks down onto a huge lawn, surrounded by trees, close to a lake, where guests may fish. Eighteen guests rooms are available, three of which are family rooms. Swings in garden for children. Reductions for children under twelve years.
Near river Forest area Near motorway

18 rms (12 bth) (3 fmly) Full central heating Open parking available Supervised Child discount available 12yrs Languages spoken: English German & Spanish
CARDS: ●● 🖾 🗖 ●

FIQUEFLEUR-ÉQUAINVILLE Eure

Bed & Breakfast (Prop: M & Mme J Delanney)
27210
☎ 232576646
Situated between Honfleur, Beuzeville and Pont l'Evêque , this guesthouse is modern but beautifully appointed, with well-manicured gardens. Living room available for guests with open fireplace. Patio access. The sea, tennis, swimming pool, riding and sailing are close by. Forest within two or three paces of the house.
Forest area
2 en suite (bth/shr) (1 fmly) Full central heating Open parking available

FLAMANVILLE Manche

Hameau Cavelier (Prop: Nicole Travers)
50340
☎ 233524283
Nicole Travers welcomes guests to her modern farm, set against a backdrop of peace and quiet. Swimming available close by and summer activities to be enjoyed at the Château de Flamanville. Forest trips can be undertaken either by foot, by horse or by moped. Your hosts can organise these activities on your behalf. Trips to Guernsey possible.
Near sea Near beach Forest area
2 en suite (shr) No smoking on premises Full central heating

FOURGES Eure.

Bed & Breakfast (Prop: M & Mme P Stekelorum)
24 rue du Moulin *27630*
☎ 232521251 FAX 232521312
Country lovers will appreciate the Fourges area and the hospitality of the owners. Many leisure opportunities are available within easy distance: golf, riding, fishing, gliding, windsurfing, tennis, a swimming pool and leisure centre. There are also plenty of restaurants nearby.
Near river Forest area
3 en suite (shr) No smoking on premises Full central heating Open parking available Covered parking available

FOURMETOT Eure

L'Aufragere (Prop: N Dussartre)
La Croisée *27500*
☎ 232569192 FAX 232577534
(from Pont Audemer take the direction towards Le Havre on N182 and fork right towards Fourmetot on D139. In town turn right before the church and house is 1km on your left through 2 brick pillars)
Forest area
5 en suite (bth/shr) (2 fmly) No smoking in all bedrooms Licensed Full central heating Open parking available Covered parking available Riding Boule Open terrace Last d 19.30hrs Languages spoken: English
MEALS: Dinner 100FF*

FRESNÉ-LA-MÈRE Calvados

La Vieille Ferme (Prop: M & Mme Bass)
Le Bourg *14700*
☎ 231903498 FAX 231903498
(from Falaise take route to Trun and after 6kms turn to the left immediately after the automatic barrier at Fresne-La-Mere. After 500mtrs turn right by the side of the bakery)
An eighteenth-century stone-built farmhouse set in five acres of tranquil,rural France and within easy reach of Falaise. 45 years of experience ensures that the farmhouse meals are interesting, delicious and of the highest quality. English spoken.
Near river Near lake Near sea Near beach Forest area Near motorway
4 en suite (bth/shr) (1 fmly) No smoking in all bedrooms Full central heating Open parking available Covered parking available Supervised Child discount available 12yrs Boule Enclosed children's play area Last d 10.00hrs Languages spoken: English
ROOMS: s 200FF; d 250FF
MEALS: Dinner 85FF

FRESVILLE Manche

Grainville (Prop: B Brecy)
50310
☎ 233411049 FAX 233210757
Your hosts have been welcoming guests to their home for more than fifteen years and find visitors are astonished by the charm and beauty of the location. This impressive château is situated in open countryside and is built in the style of the eighteenth century, with large, spacious rooms throughout. Three rooms available, two of which are family rooms. Each guest room is comfortable and furnished in the style of the era, with canopied beds. A quiet and peaceful setting, where the song of the birds will awaken you each morning. Large swimming pool in parkland surrounding the château. English spoken.
Near river Near lake Near sea Near beach In town centre Near motorway
3 en suite (bth/shr) (2 fmly) Full central heating Open parking available Supervised Languages spoken: English & Spanish
CARDS: Travellers cheques

GÉFOSSE-FONTENAY Calvados

L'Hermerel (Prop: Francois & Agnes Le Marie)
14230
☎ 231226412 FAX 231226412
Near sea Near beach
4 en suite (shr) (2 fmly) No smoking on premises Full central heating Open parking available Supervised Child discount available Languages spoken: English
CARDS: Travellers cheques

GENÊTS Manche

Le Moulin (Prop: M L Daniel)
50530
☎ 233708378
(from Arranches take the coast road "eglise de Genets", pass Vains and entering the town, take second turning on right)
Near river Near lake Near sea Near beach

4 en suite (shr) No smoking on premises Full central heating Open parking available Supervised Child discount available 12yrs Languages spoken: English
CARDS: Travellers cheques

GENNEVILLE Calvados

Bed & Breakfast (Prop: M & Mme Crenin)
Le Bourg *14600*
☎ 231987563
Bernadette and Daniel Crenin extend a warm welcome to their bed & breakfast accommodation, situated in a small, rural village, six kilometres from Honfleur. Five comfortable rooms are available. This typical Norman half-timbered house dates back to the eighteenth and nineteenth centuries. Breakfast served in the attractive dining room. Gite accommodation also available in the grounds.
5 en suite (shr) Full central heating Open parking available

GLATIGNY Manche

Le Manoir (Prop: M Duvernois)
50250
☎ 233070833
Near river Forest area
4 en suite (bth/shr) (1 fmly) Full central heating Open parking available

GLOS Calvados

La Haute-Follie (Prop: Mme Roue)
14100
☎ 231627128
Yvette Roue welcomes you to her country home, surrounded by a large garden. The bedrooms are individually decorated in a rustic style. Living room for the use of guests with open fireplace, television and mini-library. French or full English breakfast. A little English spoken.
Forest area
4 rms Full central heating Open parking available

GLOS-LA-FERRIÈRE Orne

Haras-du-Boile (Prop: Catherine Dussaut)
61550
☎ 233348759 FAX 233240326
(In l'Aile take direction of Lisieux and after 10km come to village. Farm at end of village on right)
Forest area Near motorway
5 en suite (bth/shr) TV available Full central heating Open parking available Supervised Child discount available Outdoor swimming pool Tennis Riding Languages spoken: English
CARDS: Travellers cheques

GONNEVILLE-SUR-HONFLEUR Calvados

La Ferme de Beauchamp (Prop: Daniel Andre Michel)
14600
☎ 231891993
Near river Near lake
Closed Xmas & family holidays
2 en suite (shr) No smoking on premises TV available Full central heating Open parking available Covered parking available

GRAINVILLE Eure

Ferme du Château (Prop: M Ammeux)
2 r Grand-Mare *27380*
☎ 232490953
Near river Forest area Near motorway
2 rms (1 fmly) No smoking on premises Full central heating
Open parking available Supervised Child discount available

GRANDCAMP-MAISY Calvados

Ferme du Colombier (Prop: M Legrand)
14450
☎ 231226846 FAX 231221433
Near sea Near beach In town centre
5 en suite (shr) (1 fmly) Full central heating Open parking
available Supervised Child discount available V meals Last
d 21.00hrs Languages spoken: English
MEALS: Full breakfast 60FF Lunch 69-280FF Dinner 69-
280FF*
CARDS: Travellers cheques

Vaumanoir (Prop: M & Mme Maudelonde)
11 r du chateau-d'Eau *14450*
☎ 231219541 FAX 232172205
Near sea Near beach Near motorway
Closed Oct-May
2 en suite (shr) (1 fmly) Full central heating Open parking
available Supervised Child discount available 8yrs

GUERVILLE Seine-Maritime

Ferme de la Haye (Prop: Jean and Dominique Mairesse)
76340
☎ 322261426
Forest area
1 en suite (shr) Full central heating Open parking available
Child discount available 5yrs Languages spoken: English &
Spanish
ROOMS: s 170FF; d 230FF
MEALS: Dinner fr 75FF

HAYE-AUBRÉE, LA Eure

Bed & Breakfast (Prop: M & Mme Verhaeghe)
rue du Bois *27350*
☎ 232573109
One family room is offered in this very pretty house
overlooking a small valley. The rooms is situated on the first
floor and has independent access. Charming garden, with
swings, bikes and table-tennis. Restaurant in nearby village.
Set at the entrance to the Brotonne forest, you have an
opportunity to see the forest ponies. Open all year round.
Forest area
1 en suite (bth/shr) Radio in rooms Full central heating Open
parking available Supervised Child discount available

HAYE-DU-THEIL, LA Eure

Domaine de la Coudraye (Prop: L Demaegdt)
27370
☎ 232355207 FAX 232351721
(Autoroute de Normandie exit 24 (Maison Brulée)
establishment on the D26)
Two large rooms on one floor of this rural property. Television
room available plus tennis courts. This property is a working

farm; guests may buy the farm products including foie gras
and picnic foodstuffs. English spoken.
Near river Forest area Near motorway
2 en suite (bth/shr) Full central heating Open parking
available Languages spoken: English
ROOMS: s fr 195FF; d fr 230FF

HOTTOT-LES-BAGUES Calvados

Le Vallon (Prop: Cecile Grenier)
14250
☎ 231081185 FAX 231081185
(from the west of Caen take D9 at Carpiquet towards
Fontenay, and on to Hottot-les-Bagues. Follow signs for Le
Vallon from village centre)

A convivial and quiet ivy-clad house, situated ten miles south
of Bayeux in six hectares of garden. Close to the sea.
Vegetarian meals are available on requst in the evening.
Attractive rustic style dining room, with open fireplace.
Spacious rooms. A little English spoken.
Forest area
5 en suite (shr) (1 fmly) (2 with balcony) No smoking on
premises Full central heating Open parking available
Covered parking available Supervised Fishing Boule V
meals
ROOMS: s 140FF; d 220FF
MEALS: Dinner fr 70FF
CARDS: Travellers cheques

HOUDETOT Seine-Maritime

Bed & Breakfast (Prop: M J F Bocquet)
76740
☎ 235790873 FAX 235971921
Attractive half-timbered house set in a pretty garden. Your
host, Jean-François Bocquet invites you to dine with him at
very reasonable rates (only available from October to April).
Guests may use the garden. A warm welcome assured.
3 rms (2 shr) Full central heating Open parking available
Supervised

ISIGNY-SUR-MER Calvados

Bed & Breakfast (Prop: M R le Devin)
7 rue du Docteur Boutrois *14230*
☎ 231211233 FAX 231211875
This is a beautifully appointed, beamed building. The room
has its own entrance, which leads into the garden where the
sun can be enjoyed on the patio. A kitchen areas is provided

cont'd

for guests and this is where your breakfast will be served to you. Reductions for children. A little English spoken.
Near river In town centre Near motorway
1 en suite (bth/shr) TV available Full central heating Open parking available Child discount available

La Rivière (Prop: M & Mme Marie)
St-Germain-du-Pert *14230*
☎ 231227292 FAX 231220163
(from Bayeux take N13 to Carentan, then D113 south. After 1km take D124 towards St-Germain-du-Pert)
This fortified sixteenth century farmhouse rests on the edge of the Aure Valley, which is part of the Parc Naturel des Marais du Colentin et du Bessin. Farm produce served. Only ten kilometres from the beaches and 25 kilometres from Bayeux. Slightly closer to home, there are many chateaux and churches in the region.
Near river Near sea Near motorway
Closed Nov-Mar
3 en suite (bth/shr) (1 fmly) Full central heating Open parking available Supervised Child discount available 8yrs Open terrace
ROOMS: d 220FF *
MEALS: Dinner fr 85FF
CARDS: Travellers cheques

Ferme Auberge de la Pommeraie (Prop: M & Mme Vaudron)
27250
☎ 233349184
(7km from Rugles in the direction of Lisieux)
This comfortable farmhouse is typical of the Normandy region. Home-made cider, made from both apples and pears in the traditional manner, is available. Traditional meals are served. English spoken.
Near motorway
3 en suite (bth/shr) No smoking on premises Full central heating Open parking available Child discount available 10yrs Boule V meals Last d 20.30hrs
ROOMS: s fr 180FF; d fr 210FF Special breaks
MEALS: Dinner 90-110FF*
CARDS: Travellers cheques

Le Relais de l'Abbaye (Prop: M Patrick Chatel)
798 rue du Quesney *76480*
☎ 235372498
(25kms from Rouen)
Brigitte and Patrick Chatel welcome you to their attractive Normandy home which offers an independent entrance for guest rooms. The house is situated behind the Abbey. Rooms are quiet and comfortable. To add to this peaceful atmosphere, a wooded park stands behind the house. Tourist office on-site. Restaurant and shops are 600 metres away and swimming, fishing, tennis and horse-riding are all nearby.
Near lake Forest area
4 en suite (shr) Full central heating Open parking available

Bed & Breakfast (Prop: Marylene Fillatre)
Le Logis *50520*
☎ 233593820 FAX 233593820
(In Twigny, go towards St Hilaire (D55) for 1km, turn left

towards 'Le Logis' for less than 1km. The manor-house 'Le Logis' is on the left).
Bedrooms are found in a converted dovecot but there is a pleasant reception room which guests may use in the main residence. Tennis on-site. Home-made produce includes cider, jam and paté. Meals served. Reductions for three days stay. English spoken.
Near river Near lake Forest area
3 en suite (shr) (2 fmly) Radio in rooms Full central heating Open parking available Supervised Child discount available 12yrs Fishing Bicycle rental V meals Languages spoken: English
ROOMS: s 190FF; d 230FF Reductions over 1 night
MEALS: Dinner fr 70FF*
CARDS: Travellers cheques

Le Château (Prop: Francoise de Brunville)
50160
☎ 233561570 FAX 233563526
Near lake Forest area
Closed 16 Dec-14 Feb
3 en suite (bth/shr) (1 fmly) TV available Full central heating Open parking available Child discount available

Le Château (Prop: Therese Vauquelin)
14310
☎ 231770888
Bed & breakfast accommodation available in this residence dating back to the seventeenth century, set on a farm, near to the church of a small village. Your hosts offer you three rooms, with English or French breakfast. Dinner is available at a fixed price, by arrangement. Reductions for children under ten or for families with more than two children.
Near river
1 en suite (bth/shr) Full central heating Open parking available Supervised Child discount available 10yrs

Château des Landes (Prop: Jacqueline Simon-Lemettre)
76390
☎ 235940379 FAX 235940373
(leave the N29 between Neufchâtel/Aumale, take D16 in direction of Caulé then St-Beuvé, then D7 towards St-Leége in 2km find Les Landes)
A pretty brick-built,19th-century château, close to the Eu forest, stands in 2.5 acres of tree-lined parkland. The bedrooms, 4 large rooms and one suite, have been individually decorated in pastel colours and are appointed with family heirlooms. In spring and summer guests may enjoy eating breakfast on the veranda. Shops and sporting facilities nearby. English spoken.
Forest area Near motorway
5 en suite (shr) Full central heating Open parking available Child discount available 3yrs Languages spoken: English
ROOMS: d 300-350FF
MEALS: Dinner fr 110FF
CARDS: Travellers cheques

LANGRUNE-SUR-MER Calvados

Bed & Breakfast (Prop: A & A Jeanne)
5 av de la Libération *14830*
☎ 231972449
Near sea
Closed 12 Nov-7 Apr
2 en suite (bth/shr) (1 fmly) No smoking on premises Full
central heating Open parking available Languages spoken:
English
CARDS: Travellers cheques

LESSAY Manche

Bed & Breakfast (Prop: M & Mme Boulland)
15 r Geslonde *50430*
☎ 233460484
In town centre
2 en suite (shr) Full central heating Open parking available
Supervised

LINGREVILLE Manche

Blanche Pré (Prop: M Mme Gautier)
Village Hue *50660*
☎ 233079124
This quiet house stands by the sea and overlooks parkland.
Bed & breakfast available in pretty, well furnished rooms.
Garden, with use of barbecue. English spoken.
Near sea Near beach
2 en suite (bth) (1 fmly) Full central heating Open parking
available Languages spoken: English & German
CARDS: Travellers cheques

LIVET-SUR-AUTHOU Eure

Château de Livet sur Authou (Prop: Gerard Angar)
27800
☎ 232459426 FAX 232459411
(from Paris: freeway A13 - exit 25 to Maison Brulée -
Bourgtheroulde - Brionne -Authou - Livet sur Authou)
Impressive château, offering five rooms and one suite, which
are all decorated in an individual style. Situated in seven and a
half hectares of grounds, featuring a trout river. Indoor and
outdoor swimming pool, exercise room, tennis, and table-
tennis available. Well-behaved dogs admitted. English spoken.
Near river Near lake Forest area Near motorway
Closed 16 Oct-14 Apr
5 en suite (bth/shr) No smoking on premises TV available
STV Full central heating Open parking available Outdoor
swimming pool Tennis Languages spoken: English
CARDS: Travellers cheques

LIVRY Calvados

La Suhardière (Prop: Alain Petitoy)
14240
☎ 231775102
Three rooms available on this family farm, overlooking fields
and close to a lake in the Calvados region of France. Meals by
request.
Near lake Near sea Forest area
3 en suite (shr) Full central heating Open parking available
Child discount available

LOGES, LES Seine-Maritime

Ferme du Jardinet (Prop: Beatrice Vasse)
76790
☎ 235270407
Near sea Near beach Forest area
7 rms (2 shr) (1 fmly) Radio in rooms Full central heating
Open parking available

LONGCHAMPS Eure

Bed & Breakfast (Prop: Mme Reine Thibert)
67 rue du Bourgerue *27150*
☎ 232555439
Charming house surrounded by countryside. Comfortable
rooms, in typical rustic style. Garden full of flowers. A tranquil
stay awaits you.
Forest area Near motorway
4 en suite (shr) Full central heating Open parking available
CARDS: Travellers cheques

LONGUES-SUR-MER Calvados

Ferme de la Tourelle (Prop: Le Carpentier)
Hameau de Fontenoille *14400*
☎ 231217847 FAX 231218484
Constructed in the seventeenth century, this farm overlooks a
well tended lawn. Full breakfast can be taken with the hosts in
their kitchen. Close to the landing beaches of World War II.
Golf is seven kilometres. Bicycles available.
Near sea Near beach Forest area
5 en suite (shr) (3 fmly) Full central heating Open parking
available Child discount available Outdoor swimming pool
Golf Tennis
ROOMS: s fr 200FF; d fr 250FF

Hameau de Fontenailles (Prop: Jean Chatel)
14400
☎ 231217849
Rooms available at a renovated farmhouse. All are situated on
the first floor and have independent access. Living room with
television and kitchen area for guests' use. Close to the
landing beaches. Restaurant within one and a half kilometres.
Near sea Near beach
4 rms (3 shr) (2 fmly) Full central heating Open parking
available Supervised
CARDS: ● ▦ Travellers cheques

LONGVILLERS Calvados

La Nouvelle France (Prop: Anne-Marie Godey)
14310
☎ 231776336
(autoroute Caen/Rennes exit D6 Aunay sur Odon take D216 to
Longuillers, 1st house on the left)
Constructed of typical country stone, this old grange is
decorated in Normandy style with three rooms available for
bed & breakfast. Traditional French breakfast served. Parking
at the back of the house, with large, shaded lawn. A little
English is spoken.
Forest area
3 en suite (shr) Full central heating Open parking available
Child discount available 10 yrs Languages spoken: English
ROOMS: s 160FF; d 200FF
CARDS: ▣

MAINNEVILLE Eure

Ferme Ste-Genévieve (Prop: Jean-Claude & Jeannine Marc)
27150
☎ 232555126 FAX 232275089
(leave Paris from porte St Ouen, on porte de Clignancourt in direction of Pontoise. Go towards Gisors until Eragny-sur-Epte, turn left just before rail bridge, go along for 13km to arrive in Mainneville)
This farm is situated in a verdant environment, offering four guest rooms, including one family room, with sloping roofs. The property benefits from exposed beams. A living room is available on the ground floor, with television. Peace and tranquillity assured. Many sports and leisure facilities close by. English spoken.
Near river Forest area
4 en suite (shr) (3 fmly) No smoking on premises Full central heating Open parking available Table tennis Badminton
Languages spoken: English
ROOMS: s fr 190FF; d 220FF
CARDS: Travellers cheques

MAISONS Calvados

Moulin Gerard (Prop: Bernard Pierre)
14400
☎ 231214416
(N13 Bayeux direction Port en Besson 5km -D6)
Pierre and Christiane Bernard welcome you to their renovated mill. Three rooms for four people and a cottage for six to eight people are available. Good breakfasts served. Some reductions for children.
Near river Near sea
3 en suite (bth/shr) TV available Full central heating Open parking available Child discount available Boule Bicycle rental
ROOMS: s 225FF; d 355FF

MARTAGNY Eure

Ferme des Simons (Prop: Jacques Laine)
21 r de la Chasse *27150*
☎ 232555722 FAX 232551401
Traditional Normandy building. Three rooms are available together with a fully equipped kitchen plus living room. Breakfast is served using products from local farms, except for the jam and cakes which are home-made. A special welcome is provided for honeymooners. English spoken.
Near river Forest area
3 en suite (shr) (1 fmly) Open parking available Child discount available 12yrs Languages spoken: English

MARTAINVILLE Eure

Bed & Breakfast (Prop: J & O Bouteiller)
27210
☎ 232578223
Jacques and Odette Bouteiller offer you two rooms in their property, which is furnished with Normandy antiques. Living room and living area plus gardens at your disposal. Dinner may be taken with your hosts. Reductions for children up to ten years. Tennis, swimming and horse-riding are all close by.
Forest area Near motorway

2 en suite (bth/shr) (1 fmly) No smoking on premises Full central heating Open parking available Child discount available 10yrs
ROOMS: d fr 210FF
MEALS: Dinner fr 80FF*

MARTRAGNY Calvados

Manoir de l'Abbaye (Prop: M & Y Godfroy)
15 rue de Creully *14740*
☎ 231802595
(from Caen take N13 direction of Cherbourg exit Martragny take direction of Creully)

The manor dates back to the seventeenth century and comprises ten main rooms plus outhouses and a large park. The residence is located in a village in the middle of the popular Bayeux-Caen area. Sea and landing beaches nearby. The region is rich in magnificent châteaux, cathedrals and churches dating back many centuries. English spoken.
Near sea Near beach Near motorway
5 rms (3 shr) (1 fmly) TV in 4 bedrooms Full central heating Open parking available Covered parking available Supervised Child discount available 10yrs Riding Boule Bicycle rental Languages spoken: English
ROOMS: s 180-200FF; d 200-250FF Reductions over 1 night
CARDS: ▄▄

MESNIL-AUBERT, LE Manche

Ferme de le Peurie (Prop: Antoinette Davenel)
50510
☎ 233519631
The Davenel family has been living on this farm for 300 years. Successive generations have added to and improved the buildings. Three guest rooms are available, one with views over the countryside, the other two looking out over a huge courtyard. Breakfast is served in a rustic dining room, furnished with Normandy antiques.
Near river Near sea Forest area
3 en suite (shr) No smoking on premises Full central heating Open parking available

MESNIL-GILBERT, LE Manche

La Motte (Prop: Marcel Le Marchant)
50670
☎ 233598309 FAX 233694546
(from Brecey take D911 for approx 8km in direction of Mortain Sourdeval)

cont'd

Deep in the Vallomme countryside, on the banks of the Sec, Agnes and Marcel welcome guests to their farm, where peace and quiet are assured. The old house is exclusively for the guests. Three rooms available with fireplace and kitchen area. Farm produce served. The area is perfect for those who enjoy walking.
Near river Forest area
3 en suite (shr) (1 fmly) No smoking on premises Full central heating Open parking available Child discount available Boule
CARDS: Travellers cheques

MESNIL-ROGUES, LE Manche

La Pinotière (Prop: Etiennette Legallais)
50450
☎ 233613898
Near river Forest area
4 en suite (bth/shr) (1 fmly) Full central heating Open parking available Supervised
CARDS: ▨ Travellers cheques

Le Verger (Prop: Gordon Bennett)
Le Hameau de la Ville *50450*
☎ 233901920 FAX 233917359
(from Gavray take D7 south for 8kms, le Mesnil-Rogues signed on left, follow signs to establishment or from Villedieu-le-Poeles take D924 west then D7 for 3kms. Singposted on right)

Gordon and Dee Bennett welcome you to their eighteenth-century farmhouse, set in an area of outstanding natural beauty and only three minutes walk from the village centre. Four en-suite bedrooms available. Beautiful gardens. Ideally placed for Granville, with boats to Jersey (one every hour). Mont St Michel, Bayeux, St Malo all within easy reach. English hosts.
Near river Near sea Near beach Forest area Near motorway
Closed Xmas
4 en suite (bth/shr) No smoking on premises Full central heating Open parking available Riding Bicycle rental Languages spoken: English
ROOMS: s fr 170FF; d fr 240FF
CARDS: Travellers cheques

MEURDRAQUIÈRE, LA Manche

La Butte (Prop: Marie-Therese)
50510
☎ 233613152
(between Gavray and La Haye-Pesnel on the D7)
Near river Forest area
3 en suite (shr) Full central heating Open parking available

MÉZIÈRES-EN-VEXIN Eure

Hameau de Surcy (Prop: Simone Vard)
29 rue de l'Huis *27510*
☎ 232523004 FAX 232522877
You will appreciate the calm of this farmhouse, situated on the Vexin Plateau. All rooms face south. The breakfast room is reserved for the use of guests. Piano available. The Claude Monet Museum is within close proximity, as is the Château Gaillard.
Closed 1 Nov-31 Mar
4 en suite (bth/shr) No smoking on premises
ROOMS: s 160-190FF; d 200-250FF

MITTOIS Calvados

Le Vieux Château (Prop: Piérre Pflieger)
14170
☎ 231207394 FAX 231207350
(off the D4 between St-Pierre-sur-Dives and Boissey)
Anne and Pierre Pflieger offer you one family room, totally separate from the rest of the old, beamed house, which is surrounded by trees. Breakfast is tailor-made to suit individual tastes. English spoken.
Forest area
1 en suite (shr) (1 fmly) No smoking on premises TV in all bedrooms Full central heating Open parking available Languages spoken: English
ROOMS: s fr 200FF; d fr 250FF

MONTCHATON Manche

Le Quesnot (Prop: André Palla)
50660
☎ 233450588 FAX 233450588
(from Coutances to Montmartin-sur-mer, and from Cherbourg to le port de la Rofue, 1200m by D72 to Montchaton)
This restored eighteenth century residence made from local stone is halfway between Mont St Michel and the Cap de la Hague. The cosy, comfortable bedrooms are located in a separate building and boast fireplaces and rustic-style furniture. Beaches, fishing and trips to the Channel Islands are all close by. English spoken.
Near river Near motorway
3 en suite (shr) No smoking on premises Full central heating Open parking available Open terrace Languages spoken: English
ROOMS: s 200FF; d 230FF Reductions over 1 night
CARDS: Travellers cheques

MONTFARVILLE Manche

Le Manoir (Prop: Claudette Gabroy)
50760
☎ 233231421
(from Cherbourg to Barfleur on D901 and then D1 towards St Waast La Hougue. Take second turning on right after leaving Barfleur and then first left - chambre d'hôte signposted)
This family house was built between the fifteenth and sixteenth centuries and is situated on the top of a hill on the remains of a château. Panoramic view over the sea, which is a mere 300 metres away. Tennis, sailing and riding within close proximity.
Near sea Near beach

2 en suite (shr) (1 fmly) No smoking on premises Full central heating Open parking available Supervised No children 6 yrs
MEALS: Dinner 230-330FF
CARDS: Travellers cheques

MONTGARDON Manche

Le Mont-Scolan (Prop: Yves Seguineau)
50250
☎ 233461127
Yves and Nicole Seguineau welcome you to their farmhouse which has a rustic dining room with open fire,a living room, patio and childrens' play area. Evening meals served by request. Reductions offered for children up to twelve. This is a good spot between the sea and the countryside, where you can relax and enjoy life.
4 en suite (shr) (1 fmly) (1 with balcony) No smoking on premises Open parking available Supervised Child discount available 12yrs V meals Last d 17.00hrs
MEALS: Dinner fr 80FF*

MONTS-EN-BESSIN Calvados

La Varinière (Prop: P L Edney)
La Vallée *14310*
☎ 231774473
(from Caen take N175 towards Rennes/Mont-St-Michel and exit at Monts-en-Bessin on D92, turn right and right at cross-roads, turning right again just before the château. House second on left)
La Varinière is a pleasant stone building, located in a picturesque and peaceful valley by the village of Monts-en-Bessin. This area is Calvados country, renowned for its cider, seafood, dairy products and, of course, Calvados brandy. Guests may dine at La Varinière but reservations are needed. Walks, bike rides, beaches nearby. English spoken.
Near motorway
5 en suite (bth/shr) (2 fmly) No smoking in all bedrooms Full central heating Open parking available Supervised Last d 19.30hrs Languages spoken: English
MEALS: Dinner fr 120FF*
CARDS: Travellers cheques

MONTVIETTE Calvados

Le Manoir d'Annique (Prop: Anni Wiltshire)
La Gravelle *14140*
☎ 231202098 FAX 231207436
(from Livarot take D4 towards St Pierre sur Dives. After 4km, turn left D2739 towards Tortisambert. Annique is 1st house on right after 2km)
Sixteenth century accommodation specialising in holiday courses, run by an English couple. Subjects include a "Taste of .... Calvados Country Cooking; Golf; French Conversation; German; Spanish; Photography; or Painting". All courses are held in English. Good home cooking.
Near river Near lake Forest area In town centre
7 rms (1 bth 4 shr) (2 fmly) No smoking in all bedrooms Full central heating Open parking available Supervised Child discount available 10yrs Indoor swimming pool (heated) Riding Boule Mini-golf Bicycle rental Last d 8PM
Languages spoken: English
ROOMS: s fr 200FF; d fr 260FF Reductions over 1 night
MEALS: Lunch fr 100FF Dinner fr 100FF
CARDS: Travellers cheques

MONTVIRON Manche

La Turinière (Prop: M & Mme Leroy)
50530
☎ 233488837
Jacqueline and Emile Leroy welcome you to their spacious two rooms in their home. They will gladly help you plan day trips to surrounding attractions, or you can walk to the the beaches of Sablonne nearby. Many museums, abbeys and châteaux to visit. English spoken.
Near river Forest area Near motorway
7 rms (2 shr) Full central heating Open parking available Child discount available 4yrs Languages spoken: English
ROOMS: s 160FF; d 200FF Reductions over 1 night

MOSLES Calvados

Quartier d'Argouges (Prop: Anne Marie Lefevre)
14400
☎ 231924340
(leaving Bayeaux in the direction of Cherbourg, take D37 in direction of Ste-Honorine-des-Pertes, house first on right)
Sixteenth century farmhouse with stone staircase leading to guest rooms. Cots available for babies. Bike hire available. Restaurants within walking distance. English spoken.
Near river Near sea Near beach Forest area Near motorway
Closed Nov-Apr
2 en suite (shr) (1 fmly) No smoking in all bedrooms Full central heating Open parking available Supervised Languages spoken: English

MOULICENT Orne

La Grande Noe (Prop: M & Mme de Longcamp)
61290
☎ 233736330 FAX 233836292
(on N12, at the Sainte Anne xroads and Montagne, head for Longny-au-perche, then left for Moulicent)
Set in a beautiful thirty acre park ninety miles from Paris, this house has belonged to the same family since 1393. The owners will share their evening meal with you in the warmth of the eighteenth-century oak panelled dining room. Reservations are needed.
Forest area
Closed Dec-Feb RS winter
3 en suite (bth/shr) Full central heating Open parking available Covered parking available Supervised Child discount available 2yr-FREE Bicycle rental horse riding
ROOMS: s 450-550FF; d 500-600FF Reductions over 1 night Special breaks
MEALS: Dinner 100-200FF
CARDS: Travellers cheques

NÉGREVILLE Manche

La Vignonnerie (Prop: Jules Rose)
50260
☎ 233400258
Eighteenth century farmhouse in the middle of Normandy. Two rooms are offered by your host, Jules Rose. Living room and kitchen can be used by guests whose rooms enjoy private access. Restaurants are only 800 metres away. Children up to the age of two go free.
Near river Near motorway
2 en suite (shr) No smoking in all bedrooms Full central heating Open parking available Child discount available 2yrs

NOTRE-DAME-DE-LIVAYE Calvados

Les Pommiers de Livaye (Prop: Lambert-Dutrait)
14340
☎ 231630128 FAX 231637363
(N13 between Caen and Lisieux)
Forest area Near motorway
Closed 2 Dec-28 Feb
5 en suite (bth/shr) (4 fmly) Licensed Full central heating
Open parking available Supervised Child discount available
5yrs Boule Bicycle rental Open terrace V meals Last d
20.00hrs Languages spoken: English,Dutch
ROOMS: s 360FF; d 350-450FF * Reductions over 1 night
MEALS: Dinner fr 100FF&alc*
CARDS: Eurocheques Travellers cheques

ORBEC Calvados

Le Manoir de l'Engagisté (Prop: M Dubois)
14 rue de Géolé *14290*
☎ 231325722 FAX 231325558
A recently restored sixteenth century manor house. The
bedrooms are comfortable. Hosts Christian and Annick will be
happy to advise you on the best tours and walks in the area.
Table-tennis, billiards and bikes available. English spoken.
Near river In town centre Near motorway
5 en suite (bth/shr) (1 fmly) No smoking in 2 bedrooms TV in
all bedrooms Full central heating Open parking available
Child discount available 8yrs Table tennis Languages spoken:
English & Spanish
ROOMS: s 310FF; d 375FF

OSMANVILLE Calvados

Le Champ Manlay (Prop: M Guy Manlay)
14230
☎ 231220291 FAX 231220291
Modern house with large heated swimming pool. The rooms
face south, looking out over the garden and pool. Guests are
invited to relax in the garden or cook on the barbecue. A small
farm is run from here and guests may find themselves sharing
the garden with ducks and sheep! English spoken.
Forest area Near motorway
Closed mid Sep-Etr
2 en suite (shr) Full central heating Open parking available
Supervised Outdoor swimming pool (heated) Languages
spoken: English
ROOMS: d fr 220FF *
CARDS: Travellers cheques

PERCY Manche

La Voisinnière (Prop: Mary Duchemin)
50140
☎ 233611847 609382183 FAX 233614347
David and Mary-Claude Duchemin welcome you to their
country cottage. So fond are the Duchemins of all things
floral, that they've named the guest bedrooms after the
flowers in their garden. Luckily, they speak English so garden-
lovers will be able to converse freely with them. Restaurants
nearby.
Near river
5 en suite (shr) (2 fmly) Full central heating Open parking
available Child discount available Fishing Languages
spoken: English
ROOMS: s 200-240FF; d 210-250FF

PÉRIERS-SUR-LE-DAN Calvados

Le Clos Fleuri du Dan (Prop: Marie Carmen)
11 rue du Bont-Perdu *14112*
☎ 231441152
One comfortable bedroom here has a balcony and a charming
view over the flower garden. Veranda and pavilion available,
where guests may take their breakfast.
Near sea Near beach Near motorway
1 May-30 Sept
3 en suite (bth/shr) (1 with balcony) No smoking in all
bedrooms Radio in rooms Full central heating Open parking
available
ROOMS: s 180FF; d 240FF

PICAUVILLE Manche

Château de l'Isle-Marie (Prop: Dorothea de La
Houssaye)
50360
☎ 233213725 FAX 233214222
(close to Ste-Mère-Église and the N13 between Caen and
Cherbourg, located on the D67 between Chef-du-Pont and
Picauville)
On the site of a former Viking fortress, the castle of L'Isle-
Marie is surrounded by water in winter. In summer, the visitor
can see endless blooms and woodland. The same family has
lived here for centuries . English spoken.
Near river Near sea Near beach Forest area Near motorway
Closed Oct-Etr
5 rms (4 bth/shr) No smoking on premises Full central
heating Open parking available Supervised Tennis Riding
Bicycle rental Tennis Bicycles Languages spoken: English,
Dutch & German
ROOMS: d 550-650FF
CARDS: Travellers cheques

Manoir de Founecroup (Prop: Mr Ben Trumble)
50360
☎ 233213663
A fifteenth century manor house with a tower, set within
national parkland. A boules court and shooting range are
available for guests to use and within easy reach you will find
the D-Day beaches. Bayeux, Mont St Michel and the natural
beauty of the Cotentin are all popular tourist spots. English
spoken.
Near river Near sea Forest area Near motorway
Closed Dec-Mar
(1 fmly) No smoking in 3 bedrooms Full central heating
Open parking available Supervised Open terrace Languages
spoken: English
CARDS: Travellers cheques

PIN-LA-GARENNE Orne

La Miotère
61400
☎ 233838401
Near river Forest area Near motorway
7 en suite (bth/shr) (7 fmly) Full central heating Open
parking available

Taking your mobile phone to France?
See page 11

79

PLACY-MONTAIGU Manche

Arpents Verts (Prop: Philip Voisin)
50160
☎ 233575376
M. Philippe Voisin welcomes guests to this old, beamed country house. Comfortable rooms and kitchen area available, plus living room. Independent access to rooms. A comfortable rural setting, near Mont St Michel. English spoken.
Forest area Near motorway
2 en suite (bth/shr) (1 fmly) (1 with balcony) TV available Open parking available Supervised Languages spoken: English

POILLEY-SUR-LE-HOLME Manche

Le Logis (Prop: M Lambert)
50220
☎ 233583590 FAX 233583590
Renovated sixteenth century building set in a large park which boasts century-old trees and a small lake. Mont St Michel is only fifteen kilometres away. Children up to eight years old half price . English spoken.
Near river Forest area Near motorway
3 en suite (bth) (1 fmly) No smoking in 2 bedrooms Full central heating Open parking available Covered parking available Child discount available 8yrs Outdoor swimming pool Boule Bicycle rental Languages spoken: English & German
ROOMS: s fr 260FF; d fr 300FF Special breaks
CARDS: Travellers cheques

PONT-AUDEMER Eure

La Ricardière (Prop: Mme Carel)
Tourville *27500*
☎ 232410914 FAX 232425828
This is an old house set at the foot of a hill which looks out over a park with trees and a trout river. Originally constructed in the Middle Ages, it was destroyed during the Revolution and was only rebuilt in the last century. English spoken.
Near river Forest area
4 en suite (bth/shr) No smoking on premises Full central heating Open parking available No children Open terrace Languages spoken: English
ROOMS: d 340FF
CARDS: Travellers cheques

St-Germain-Village (Prop: Mme Roux)
94 rue Jules-Ferry *27500*
☎ 232412532
Mme Roux welcomes you to her small, modern house, situated near the town centre, where plenty of restaurants and shops will be found. You will enjoy the peace and tranquillity of her large garden. Tennis, swimming, horse-riding, golf and fishing within close proximity.
Forest area In town centre Near motorway
3 en suite (bth/shr) (1 fmly) No smoking in 1 bedroom Radio in rooms Full central heating Open parking available Supervised
CARDS: Travellers cheques

Taking your mobile phone to France?
See page 11

PONT-L'ÉVÊQUE Calvados

Manoir du Poirier de Chio (Prop: Mme Piat)
40 av Liberation *14130*
☎ 231641178 FAX 231641178
(Going to Pont L'Eveque take the road direction "Centre de Loisirs", front of the "Palace du Tribunal". at the end of this road is the Manoir du Poirier de Chio.)
Small charming 17th century completely renovated manor, surrounded by garden. The property is not far from the sea or sports facilities and Paris is only an hour and a half hours away.
4 en suite (bth/shr) (2 fmly) No smoking on premises Leisure centre within 1km Languages spoken: English & Spanish
ROOMS: s fr 280FF; d 300-400FF * Reductions over 1 night
MEALS: Dinner 100-150FF*
CARDS: ●● ▨▨

PRÉAUX-BOCAGE Calvados

La Crête aux Oiseaux (Prop: M Claude Chesnel)
14210
☎ 231796352
Your hosts, Claude and Monique Chesnel, offer you independent rooms situated next to their main residence. Many tourist attractions on offer: walks through the large forest of Grimbosq and journeys along the "Cider Route" and the "Cheese Route". English spoken.
Near river Forest area
No smoking on premises Radio in rooms Full central heating Open parking available Languages spoken: English

PRÉCORBIN Manche

Le Manoir (Prop: Simone Octave Feret)
Le Bourg *50810*
☎ 233561681
A renovated farm in lush surroundings where your hosts hope you will try their Normandy produce, particularly some extremely good Calvados. The whole house is furnished with Normandy antiques. English spoken.
Near river Forest area
5 rms (2 fmly) No smoking on premises Full central heating Open parking available Supervised Child discount available V meals Languages spoken: English & German

PUCHAY Eure

Bed & Breakfast (Prop: M & Mme Deceunink)
14 rue Gossé *27150*
☎ 232557355
M and Mme Deceuninck speak only a few words of English but they are willing to try. Two rooms available, plus living room with television and open fire. Relatively new house (built in 1990), the interior of which is mainly of wood. Guests are invited to dine with their hosts.
Forest area
2 en suite (bth/shr) No smoking in all bedrooms TV available Full central heating Open parking available Covered parking available Supervised

QUETTREVILLE-SUR-SIENNE Manche

La Lande (Prop: Francoise Martin)
50660
☎ 233074829
Guest rooms available, including one family rooms and one

80

with wheelchair access, situated on the ground floor of this family home. Camping, mobile homes and caravans also available. Beach and horse-riding within six kilometres; river fishing within 200 metres. No smoking policy. English spoken.
Near river Near sea Near beach Near motorway
2 en suite (shr) No smoking on premises Full central heating Open parking available

REUILLY Eure

Ferme de Reuilly (Prop: Lucien Nuttens)
20 rue de l'Église *27930*
☎ 232347065
This cereal farm is set in two hundred hectares in the Evreux region. The farm is an old seventeenth century priory. Bikes can be hired from the owners. Swings and a barbecue available in the garden. Tennis is within 500 metres. Dinner available. Reductions for children under five.
Near river Forest area
5 en suite (bth/shr) Full central heating Open parking available Covered parking available Child discount available Last d 18.00hrs
MEALS: Dinner fr 80FF*

REVIERS Calvados

Bed & Breakfast (Prop: L Fras-Julien)
6 rue des Moulins *14470*
☎ 231378562 FAX 231374628
(3km south of Courseulles-sur-Mer)
Three rooms are available, two of which are family rooms, decorated and furnished in an individual style. Situated on a farm three kilometres from Courselles-sur-Mer. Sun beds and a hammock are available in the garden, plus swings for the children. English spoken.
Near river Near sea Near beach Near motorway
3 rms (2 bth/shr) (3 fmly) Full central heating Open parking available Boule Languages spoken: English
ROOMS: s 190FF; d 250FF Special breaks: for 6 nights, 1 is free
CARDS: Travellers cheques

RÉVILLE Manche

La Gervaiserie (Prop: Travert)
50760
☎ 233545464
The guest cottage is located 200 metres from the beach, near the owners' farmhouse. Facilities include two double bedrooms, lounge, dining room with fireplace, and a kitchen with dishwasher, fridge, oven and a washing machine. Rooms also available at the farmhouse. Ponies and horses can be hired from the owners. Games room. Good, local walks. English spoken.
Near river Near sea Near beach
2 en suite (bth/shr) Full central heating Open parking available Riding Mini-golf Languages spoken: English
ROOMS: s fr 225FF; d fr 280FF
CARDS: Travellers cheques

ROCHELLE-NORMANDE, LA Manche

La Bellangerie (Prop: J & M Mesenge)
50530
☎ 233609040
Your hosts, Jean and Marie-Jo Mésange offer you a warm welcome to their working dairy farm. A stone staircase gives access to the guest rooms, which have use of a kitchen area.

Babysitting service available. Bicycles, table-tennis, swings and games area for guests' use..
Near sea Forest area
4 rms (3 shr) (2 fmly) Full central heating Open parking available Supervised Child discount available 10yrs

ROUGEMONTIERS Eure

Bed & Breakfast (Prop: M & F Letellier)
27350
☎ 232568480 FAX 232568480
(on the RN175)
Françoise and Michel welcome you to their house filled with antique furniture. The lounge is at your disposal with television, books and hi-fi. Situated on the edge of the forest of Brotonne, where you can go riding or visit the various abbeys in the region. Fishing available within three kilometres. English spoken.
Forest area Near motorway
2 en suite (bth/shr) (2 fmly) Full central heating Open parking available Child discount available Languages spoken: English
ROOMS: d 260-300FF Reductions over 1 night
MEALS: Dinner fr 100FF
CARDS: Travellers cheques

ROUVILLE Seine-Maritime

Ferme du Château (Prop: M & Mme Hervieux)
76210
☎ 235311398 FAX 235390077
Suites available are in this attractive red-brick house of character, set outside the village and 20 minutes from Honfleur. The house looks out on to flower beds. All bedrooms are prettily decorated Dinner is available and the dining room features an open fireplace.
Forest area Near motorway
3 en suite (shr) No smoking on premises Full central heating Open parking available Child discount available 10yrs Open terrace

SAÂNE-ST-JUST Seine-Maritime

Bed & Breakfast (Prop: D & J Fauvel)
rte de la Mer *76730*
☎ 235832437
This old farm has been restored in typical Norman style, with exposed beams, wooden floors and brick exterior. Cosy communal lounge available, with kitchen area where guests can prepare meals. French breakfast served. Two rural gites also available in an enclosed garden.
Near river Forest area
5 en suite (bth/shr) (2 fmly) No smoking on premises Open parking available
CARDS: Travellers cheques

ST-ARNOULT Seine-Maritime

Le Bergerie (Prop: C et L Lefrancois)
rte de la Bergerie *76490*
☎ 235567584 FAX 235567584
Two spacious and comfortable rooms are on offer in a rustic farmhouse dating back to the nineteenth century. The farm is set in twenty hectares of land. A friendly welcome awaits you and calm is assured. Each bedroom is furnished in a rustic style. Traditional food served using local product. Garden swing. English spoken.

cont'd

Forest area
4 rms (1 shr) (5 fmly) Full central heating Open parking available Last d 20.00hrs Languages spoken: English
MEALS: Lunch 80-140FF Dinner 80-140FF*
CARDS: ●● ▦ ▆ Travellers cheques

ST-AUBIN-D'APPENAI Orne

Le Gueé-Falot (Prop: M & Mme Flochlay)
61170
☎ 233286812
(from le Mele/Sarthe take D4 to Courtomer. 3km after le Mele take on left D214 to Boitron, there are two 'pubs' to drive by, at 2nd pub turn left, this road leads to farm.)
In the heart of a preservation area, in a traditionally restored house, two self-contained rooms are available. You are invited to join your hosts for dinner, but make a reservation first. Tennis and fishing are available locally.
Near river Near lake Forest area
3 en suite (shr) (2 fmly) No smoking on premises Full central heating Open parking available Supervised Child discount available 18months Table tennis Languages spoken: English German
ROOMS: s 160FF; d 220FF
MEALS: Lunch 95FF Dinner 95FF
CARDS: Travellers cheques

ST-AUBIN-DE-TERREGATTE Manche

Ferme de la Patrais (Prop: Jean Pierre et Helene Carvet)
50240
☎ 233484313 FAX 233485903
(take D178 SW from Ducey and turn left at St-Aubin-de-Terregatte in direction of St-Laurent-de-Terregatte for 2kms)
Comfortable rooms are available at this old restored farm which is situated on the borders of Normandy and Brittany. French breakfast served. English spoken.
Near lake
Closed Feb
4 en suite (shr) (2 fmly) No smoking on premises TV available Full central heating Open parking available Supervised Languages spoken: English & German
CARDS: Travellers cheques

ST-AUBIN-SUR-MER Seine-Maritime

La Fermette de Ramouville (Prop: Serge et Gisele Genty)
rte de Quiberville *76740*
☎ 235834705
This old, restored farm house is situated 700 metres from the sea. Rooms are available to guests, decorated and furnished in a style typical of the region. Evening meals available by reservation.
Near river Near sea Near beach
5 en suite (bth/shr) (3 fmly) No smoking on premises Full central heating Open parking available Supervised Child discount available
CARDS: Travellers cheques

ST-CLAIR-D'ARCEY Eure

Domaine du Plessis (Prop: M & Mme Gouffier)
27300
☎ 232466000
Beautifully located on the edge of a lake, this eighteenth century manor-house offers comfortable rooms, dining room

and living room with open fire. The surrounding park is five hectares. Open all year round, this is an ideal site to relax in. Many walks available nearby. English spoken.
Forest area
3 en suite (bth/shr) Full central heating Languages spoken: English Italian & Spanish
CARDS: ▆

ST-CÔME-DE-FRESNÉ Calvados

La Poterie (Prop: Catherine Le Petit)
5 rte de Bayeux *14960*
☎ 231929578 FAX 231518969
Creeper-clad building, separate from the main house. The proprietors also run a pottery and guests may take pottery classes if they wish. Open all year round, M and Mme Le Petit look forward to welcoming you to their interesting home. English spoken.
Near sea Near beach Forest area
TV in 1 bedroom Radio in rooms Full central heating Open parking available Supervised Languages spoken: English
ROOMS: d 230FF
CARDS: ●● ▦ ▆ ▣ Travellers cheques

ST-CYR-LA-CAMPAGNE Eure

Bed & Breakfast (Prop: M Meslin)
27370
☎ 235819098 FAX 23581097
An ideal overnight stopping place in the centre of town. Rooms are situated on the first and second floors of the Town Hall, a brick building constructed in 1882 but which has recently been renovated. Living room on the ground floor, with veranda and a dining room on the first floor. English spoken.
Near river Forest area
4 en suite (bth/shr) No smoking on premises Full central heating Open parking available Covered parking available Child discount available Tennis
ROOMS: s fr 180FF; d fr 210FF Reductions over 1 night
CARDS: Travellers cheques

ST-DENIS-LE-FERMENT Eure

Bed & Breakfast (Prop: M & Mme Bourillon-Vlieghe)
29 rue de St-Paer *27140*
☎ 232552786
(on D17)

Guest rooms in a wooded, rural setting. The rooms are spacious and a living room with open fire and kitchen area is provided for guests. There is a restaurant five hundred metres

away. The guesthouse is near many tourist sites. English spoken.
Near river Near lake Forest area
4 en suite (shr) No smoking on premises Radio in rooms Full central heating Open parking available
ROOMS: d 200FF

ST-DENIS-MAISONCELLES Calvados

La Valette (Prop: Alain & Odile Gravey)
14350
☎ 231687431
Alain and Odile welcome you to their guest house. They are dairy farmers and offer you a delicious breakfast, with evening meals available. Reductions for children under fifteen. Guest rooms are located on the eastern side of the house and are completely separate from the rest of the property. English spoken.
Near river Forest area
2 rms (1 shr) (3 fmly) Full central heating Open parking available Supervised Languages spoken: English & German

ST-DIDIER-DES-BOIS Eure

Au Vieux Logis (Prop: Annick Auzoux)
1 pl de l'Église *27370*
☎ 232506093
Half-timbered seventeenth century house, with sloping floors and a brick courtyard. Annick, a former antiques dealer, now sculptor, lives in a separate house at the foot of the garden. She has been restoring the house, a job to which she has to devote all her energies. Dinner is available . English spoken.
Near river Near lake Forest area
4 en suite (shr) (2 fmly) Full central heating Open parking available Supervised Languages spoken: English

ST-ÉLOI-DE-FOURQUES Eure

Manoir d'Hermos (Prop: P & B Noel-Windsor)
27800
☎ 232355132 FAX 232355132
(exit A13 at Maison Brulée in the direction of Alençon onto N138 & 5km after Bourgtheroulde turn left onto D83 then 5km on right take D92, then 3rd entrance on right)
Constructed in the sixteenth century, this property has belonged to the same English family since 1836. Situated in magnificent grounds, with lime trees and a large lake, breakfast may be served either by the open fire or in the shade of the trees. Dinner by arrangement. English spoken.
Near lake Forest area Near motorway
2 en suite (bth/shr) (1 fmly) Full central heating Open parking available Supervised Fishing Bicycle rental
Languages spoken: English
ROOMS: s 220-270FF; d 250-300FF
MEALS: Full breakfast 40FF Dinner fr 90FF*

ST-ÉTIENNE-LA-THILLAYE Calvados

Bed & Breakfast (Prop: M & Mme P Champion)
Chemin de la Barberie *14950*
☎ 231652197 FAX 231651831
Comfortable bedrooms are on offer in this house, set in a well laid out garden. Tennis, riding, swimming pool, fishing and walking on offer nearby. Good breakfast available. Reductions for children. The Champion family are looking forward to meeting you. A little English spoken.
Near river Near motorway

3 rms (2 bth/shr) (1 fmly) Full central heating Open parking available Child discount available Outdoor swimming pool Tennis Fishing Riding
CARDS: Travellers cheques

Le Friche Saint-Vincent (Prop: Monique & Guy Baratte)
14950
☎ 231652204 FAX 231651016
Accommodation in a family home. French breakfast is served with homemade jams and honey. Close by, you can enjoy golf, tennis, horse riding and the lake.
Near lake Near sea Near beach Forest area Near motorway
4 en suite (shr) (3 fmly) (1 with balcony) Full central heating Open parking available Supervised
ROOMS: s 180FF; d 240FF

ST-GEORGES-DE-LA-RIVIÈRE Manche

Manoir de Caillemont (Prop: Michel et Elaine Coupechoux)
50270
☎ 233538116 FAX 233532566
(from Barneville Carteret, take the D903 towards Coutances. At the cross 'St Georges de la Riviere' turn left towards St Maurice en Cotentin. The manor house is the first building on the left.)
This old Normandy manor offers one studio and two suites with lounge and fireplace. Rooms are comfortable and quietly situated, with the suites being decorated in country or classic style. Continental breakfast served in the dining room. Heated swimming pool during the summer months. Table-tennis. English spoken.
Near sea Near beach
RS Oct-Mar
3 en suite (bth/shr) (1 fmly) Full central heating Open parking available Outdoor swimming pool (heated) Billiards
Languages spoken: English
ROOMS: d 340-560FF

ST-GEORGES-D'ELLE Manche

Bed & Breakfast (Prop: Jocelyne Heurtevent)
Le Muthier *50680*
☎ 233058147 FAX 233571417
This old, family home, built in local stone, looks out onto lawns and pretty flowers beds. Situated in the heart of the countryside, surrounded by fields, this is a peaceful setting. Barbecue. Evening meals by arrangement. Fishing and tennis nearby. Ideal for families, as it is close to beaches and a pretty forest.
Near river Forest area
4 rms (1 shr) (1 fmly) Full central heating Open parking available Child discount available 10yrs Boule V meals
CARDS: Travellers cheques

ST-GERMAIN-DE-MONTGOMERY Calvados

Le Vaucery (Prop: M F Catel)
14140
☎ 233390391
(from Vimoutiers or Livarot, take the road to 'St Germain de Montgommery' and follow the 'Chambre d'hote/Gite de France' signs.)
A traditional Norman welcome awaits you with home-made cider at this eighteenth century half-timbered farm. Pretty rooms available, decorated and furnished with taste. Copious
cont'd

continental breakfast served. A fully furnished cottage is also available on a weekly basis (no breakfast), suitable for four adults and two children. Horse-riding and pond onsite. Leisure centre with swimming and tennis within two miles. Restaurant nearby. No smoking policy. English spoken.
Near lake Forest area
Closed Nov-Mar
3 rms (2 shr) (1 fmly) Open parking available Child discount available 14yrs Languages spoken: English
ROOMS: s fr 150FF; d fr 220FF Reductions over 1 night
CARDS: Travellers cheques

ST-GERMAIN-DE-TOURNBUT Manche

Château de la Brisette (Prop: De La Hautiere)
50700
☎ 233411178 FAX 233412232

This magnificent castle, looking out onto a lake, is surrounded by woodland. It has been owned by the same family for more than 200 years. The chapel and outbuildings are particularly delightful. The bedrooms are decorated in different styles: Gothic, Empire and Louis XVI. The castle is full of stunning historical features and furniture. Continental breakfast.
Near lake Forest area
Closed Nov-Apr
3 en suite (bth/shr) No smoking on premises TV in all bedrooms STV Full central heating Open parking available
ROOMS: d 400-500FF Special breaks: (more than 5 nights)
CARDS: ●● 🎫 🖭 American Express

ST-GERMAIN-LE-VASSON Calvados

Le Broguette (Prop: M & Mme Giard)
14190
☎ 231905175
(from Caen, head towards Falaise for abut 15km. Then head towards St-Germain-le-asson, then follow signs 'Chambre d'Hôtes.)
Although the accommodation is located in a new building, the annexe is part of an old farm which is presently being restored by your hosts. Golf, riding and tennis in close proximity. Bikes, table-tennis and billiards on-site. English spoken.
Near river Forest area Near motorway
2 en suite (shr) (2 fmly) (2 with balcony) Full central heating Air conditioning in bedrooms Open parking available Billiards Pool Table tennis Languages spoken: English
ROOMS: d 200FF Reductions over 1 night
CARDS: Travellers cheques

ST-GERMAIN-SUR-AY Manche

Bed & Breakfast (Prop: M & Mme Moisan)
26 rue de l'Anjou *50430*
☎ 233463249
Near sea Near beach Forest area Near motorway
4 rms (3 bth/shr) (2 fmly) TV available Open parking available Supervised Open terrace
CARDS: ●● Travellers cheques

ST-GERMAIN-SUR-SÈVES Manche

Les Tilluels
r de Remeurge *50190*
☎ 233466434 FAX 233466434
(autoroute Paris-Cherbourg exit Carentan onto D971 towards Periers after 15km take D301 & follow signs)
Eat a hearty Normandy breakfast in front of the fireplace of this family home set in the countryside. Bedrooms are furnished with antiques, but include modern comforts
Near river
5 en suite (bth/shr) (2 fmly) Open parking available Child discount available 2yrs
ROOMS: s fr 120FF; d 180-195FF Reductions over 1 night

ST-HILAIRE-PETITVILLE Manche

Ferme de Marigny (Prop: M & Mme D & R Picquenot)
50500
☎ 232420440
Farm situated between Bayeux and St.Mère Eglise. Bedrooms, with two family rooms, are situated on the first floor. Small kitchen exclusively for the use of guests. The children of the house speak English.
Near motorway
4 rms (2 fmly) Full central heating Open parking available

ST-HYMER Calvados

Le Moulin (Prop: M et Mme Valle)
14130
☎ 231642351 FAX 231643972
(At Deauville, go towards the A13, then take the N117 as far as Pont L'Évèque. Turn right on to N175 towards Caen. After 'Le Preui de St Hymen' sign turn left and go down to the watermill - Signposted)
Genuine thirteenth century mill, set in a hectare of parkland, which has a river running through it. Very close to golf course, which is open all year round. Horse-riding on-site. Many attractive rides through the wood possible. Cooler evenings can be spent in front of the fire.
Near river Near lake Near sea Near beach Forest area Near motorway
5 rms (4 bth/shr) (2 fmly) No smoking on premises TV in 1 bedroom Full central heating Open parking available Supervised All listed activities are nearby.
ROOMS: s fr 280FF; d 300-400FF Special breaks
CARDS: 🎫

ST-JAMES Manche

Le Ferme de L'Étang (Prop: Brigitte Gavard)
"Bouceel", Vergoncey *50240*
☎ 233483468 FAX 233484853
(from Avranches, go towards Rennes. After 12km turn right to Rennes the Mont St Michel, just after turn left to Rennes D40,

then the D308, turn left, there is a sign just before B&B which is the 2nd house)
This large family house faces a lake and is close to woods where walks may be taken. Games, billiards and table-tennis are available for guests. English spoken.
Near lake Forest area Near motorway
5 rms (4 bth/shr) (2 fmly) No smoking on premises Full central heating Open parking available Covered parking available Child discount available 12yrs Pool table Boule Last d 19.00hrs Languages spoken: English
ROOMS: s fr 185FF; d 210-225FF
MEALS: Full breakfast 20FF Dinner fr 80FF
CARDS: Travellers cheques

La Gautrais
50240
☎ 233483186 FAX 233485817
(A84 exit St James in direction of Autrain on D12)
Ideal for stopovers en route or longer stays, a pleasant farmhouse in calm, green surroundings. Local produce is used in the evening meal.
Near river
4 en suite (bth/shr) (2 fmly) (1 with balcony) Radio in rooms Full central heating Open parking available Supervised Child discount available 12yrs Languages spoken: English
ROOMS: s fr 160FF; d 200-220FF Reductions over 1 night
MEALS: Dinner fr 83FF*

ST-JEAN-LE-THOMAS Manche

Bed & Breakfast (Prop: M & Mme Malle)
7 bd Stanislas *50530*
☎ 233681037 FAX 233683100
Your hosts offer individually decorated and furnished rooms. They hope that you will join them in enjoying a simple, relaxed way of life. Barbecue, living room with library and kitchen area available to guests. English spoken.
Near sea Near beach Forest area
3 en suite (shr) (2 fmly) No smoking on premises TV in 1 bedroom Full central heating Child discount available Tennis Fishing Riding Boule Mini-golf Bicycle rental
ROOMS: s 180FF; d 200FF

ST-LAURENT-DU-MONT Calvados

La Vignerie (Prop: Marie-France Huet)
14340
☎ 231630865 FAX 231630865
(from Lisieux take the N13 to La Boissiere, then onto the D50. Pass the village, after approx 700m, there is a sign for 'La Vignerie', take the small road, the house is 500m along.)
Guest rooms situated in a seventeenth century building independent of the main house, in the middle of one hectare of lawn and parkland. Quiet, green environment.
5 en suite (bth/shr) (4 fmly) (1 with balcony) Full central heating Open parking available Child discount available 4yrs Bicycle rental Languages spoken: English
ROOMS: s 190FF; d 230FF Reductions over 1 night
CARDS: Travellers cheques

ST-LAURENT-EN-CAUX Seine-Maritime

Hameau de Caltot (Prop: M & Mme Mayeu)
76560
☎ 235966526
2 en suite (bth/shr) Full central heating Open parking available
CARDS: Travellers cheques

ST-LOUP-HORS Calvados

Bed & Breakfast (Prop: M & Mme Jeanette)
Chemin des Marettes *14400*
☎ 231922468
Modern house with a sun-lounge looking out onto the garden. Restaurants nearby. Ten kilometres from the landing beaches at Normandy. Your hosts are learning English at the moment.
Near sea Near beach Forest area In town centre Near motorway
1 en suite (shr) TV in all bedrooms Radio in rooms Full central heating Child discount available 12yrs
ROOMS: d 200FF

Manoir du Pont Rouge (Prop: Lt Col M J P Chilcott)
14400
☎ 231223909 FAX 232219784
(take D572 towards St Lo from the Southern Peripherique of Bayeux. Then 2nd right at chambre d'hote sign continue for approx 1km)
Four guest rooms are offered in this largely seventeenth century stone manor house, which stands in five acres of land, with two orchards. Swings and boules in the garden, with sheep, goats, chickens, rabbits, guinea-pigs, ducks, geese and turkeys, which the children will love! They can help let them out and put them to bed. English hosts.
Near river Near sea Near beach Forest area Near motorway
4 en suite (bth/shr) No smoking on premises Full central heating Open parking available Child discount available 14yrs Boule Table tennis, Table football Languages spoken: English German Italian & Russian
ROOMS: s 170FF; d 200FF Special breaks

ST-MACLOU Eure

La Brière (Prop: M Gilbert Aube)
27210
☎ 232566335 FAX 232569562
(exit Beuzeville off A13)
Accommodation available in this attractive, half-timbered house set in farmland. Open all year round.
Forest area Near motorway
2 en suite (shr) Open parking available Supervised Child discount available 10yrs
ROOMS: d fr 200FF
CARDS: Travellers cheques

ST-MARTIN-DE-BLAGNY Calvados

Le Coquerie (Prop: Genevieve & Alain Pasquet)
14710
☎ 231225089
Large en-suite rooms are available in the home of Geneviève and Alain Pasquet, which is close to Bayeux. The traditional game of pétanque can by played in the garden, as well as volleyball and table-tennis.
2 en suite (shr) No smoking on premises Open parking available Child discount available 6yrs Petanque pin-pong volley ball

ST-MARTIN-DE-VARREVILLE Manche

Les Mézières (Prop: Leone Dessoliers)
50790
☎ 233413502
Two rooms available in this family manor house. Museum and
cont'd

restaurants three kilometres away. Landing beaches close by.
Near sea Near beach
Closed Oct-Mar
2 en suite (bth/shr) (1 fmly) Full central heating Supervised

ST-MESLIN-DU-BOSC Eure

Le Bourg (Prop: Michel Chalumel)
33 rue de l'Église *27370*
☎ 232355453
Situated in the heart of Normandy, this charmingly decorated residence offers three rooms, one of which is a family room. French breakfast served. English spoken.
Forest area
2 en suite (bth/shr) (1 fmly) TV available Full central heating Open parking available Supervised Languages spoken: English

ST-OUEN-SUR-MAIRE Orne

La Cour (Prop: Mme Roma Smith)
61150
☎ 233367483
(from Argentan, N158 take D924 west towards Flers for 11km, then take 1st road on left after the rdbt beyond Ecouche signposted St Ouen-sur-Maire & follow "chambre d'hotes" signs)
English hosts George and Roma Smith invite you to their restored seventeenth century farmhouse, set in lovely walled gardens. Quiet country area. Double room on ground floor; two further rooms on the first floor, sharing a bathroom. Ideal for a family of up to six. Continental breakfast served.
Near river Forest area
3 en suite (bth/shr) Radio in rooms Full central heating Open parking available Supervised Child discount available 4yrs
Languages spoken: English
ROOMS: s 180FF; d 250FF
CARDS: Travellers cheques

ST-PAIR-SUR-MER Manche

Bed & Breakfast (Prop: M & Mme Elie)
152 rue de la Hogue *50380*
☎ 233505842
Forest area In town centre Near motorway
Closed Nov-Apr
3 rms (1 bth 1 shr) No smoking on premises TV available Full central heating Open parking available Table tennis

ST-PIERRE-DE-MANNEVILLE Seine-Maritime

Bed & Breakfast (Prop: M & Mme Bernard)
78 rue de Bas *76113*
☎ 235320713
Half-timbered house with exposed beams inside. All rooms are individually decorated and are comfortable. Very pretty garden with flowers. Peaceful, relaxing location. Several restaurants nearby. English spoken.
Near river Forest area
4 en suite (bth/shr) (2 fmly) No smoking on premises Full central heating Open parking available Languages spoken: English
CARDS: ● ▆ Travellers cheques

ST-PIERRE-DES-FLEURS Eure

Bed & Breakfast (Prop: M & Mme Bonvoisin)
rte de Thuit Signol *27370*
☎ 235878191
An attractive old house, dating back two hundred years. There are well-kept garden with old trees, flowers, a greenhouse, and ornamental ponds, with ducks. The calm atmosphere, and country location are very relaxing. Bicycles can be hired. English spoken.
Near river Forest area Near motorway
3 rms (1 bth/shr) Full central heating Open parking available
Languages spoken: English

ST-PIERRE-DU-REGARD Orne

Manoir de Moissy (Prop: M & Mme Prevot)
61790
☎ 231690149
Eighteenth century manor, which was formerly the meeting place for the De Coeur Doux family when they took part in the hunt. A Normandy cottage, with rooms looking out over the flower-filled garden. A theatre, piano and library are for the use of guests. In August, a music festival is held at the house.
Near river Near lake Near sea Forest area Near motorway
Closed Oct-Mar
3 en suite (bth) Radio in rooms Full central heating Open parking available Covered parking available Child discount available Fishing Bicycle rental

ST-PIERRE-SUR-DIVES Calvados

Le Pressoir (Prop: Annick Duhamel)
Berville *14170*
☎ 231205126 FAX 231200303
Bedrooms are situated in a renovated building, dating from 1462. The property is set in a wooded park which is a haven of peace and quiet and where guests are welcome to walk. A barbecue is available in the garden and there is carp fishing. English spoken.
Forest area
4 en suite (bth/shr) (2 fmly) Air conditioning in bedrooms Fishing Open terrace Languages spoken: English & German
CARDS: Travellers cheques

ST-QUENTIN-SUR-LE-HOMME Manche

Les Vallées (Prop: Jean Louis Beaucoup)
50220
☎ 233606151
Near river Near motorway
4 en suite (shr) (1 fmly) No smoking on premises Full central heating Open parking available Child discount available
MEALS: Dinner fr 75FF*

ST-ROMPHAIRE Manche

Le Mariage (Prop: Renee Letellier)
50860
☎ 233558006
Your hosts, Renée and René, have retired from raising milking cows and now offer bed & breakfast accommodation to guests. Two comfortable rooms are available. Breakfast served using farm produce. Restaurant within one kilometre of the property.
Near motorway
2 en suite (shr) No smoking in all bedrooms Full central heating Open parking available

St-Senier-Sous-Avranches Manche

Le Champs du Genêt (Prop: M & Mme Jouvin)
rte de Mortain *50300*
☎ 233605267 FAX 233605267
Near river Forest area
4 en suite (bth/shr) Full central heating Open parking
available Languages spoken: English
CARDS: Travellers cheques

St-Symphorien-Des-Bruyères Orne

La Fransonniere
61300
☎ 233240458
Seventeenth century renovated farm, on the edge of the Saint
Evroult forest. Independent access to the guest rooms, one of
which has a kitchenette and dining area. Mini-golf, tennis,
fishing, riding and table-tennis. English spoken.
Near lake Forest area Near motorway
2 en suite (shr) (1 fmly) TV available Full central heating
Open parking available Boule Table tennis Languages
spoken: English & Italian

St-Vaast-Du-Val Seine-Maritime

Parc du May (Prop: M & Mme Pascal Vandenbulcke)
Hameau de Glatigny *76890*
☎ 235346191
An eighteenth century white house set in the middle of a
country park. Children and babies can easily be
accommodated. French breakfast served. A little English
spoken.
Near river Forest area Near motorway
1 en suite (bth/shr) Full central heating Open parking
available Child discount available

St-Victor-D'épine Eure

Le Clos St-François (Prop: M Jacques Canse-
Grandhomme)
27800
☎ 232459890 FAX 232464309
Near river Near lake Forest area
1 en suite (shr) TV available Radio in rooms Full central
heating Open parking available No children 10yrs Boule
Languages spoken: English

St-Wandrille-Rançon Seine-Maritime

Manoir d'Abbeville (Prop: Mme Sautreuil)
76490
☎ 235962089
Bedrooms on the first floor of this old house covered in
Virginia Creeper. Outlook over the countryside and forest
begins two hundred metres from the house. Peaceful area.
Restaurants two kilometres away. Open all year. Some
reductions for children.
Near river Forest area
1 en suite (shr) (4 fmly) Full central heating Open parking
available Child discount available 12yrs

Ste-Gauburge Orne

La Bussiere (Prop: Mr & Mme Le Brethon)
61370
☎ 233340523 FAX 233347147
This large, ivy-covered family house is close to the Ouche and
Le Perche country. A warm welcome is guaranteed by your
hosts, M. and Mme. Le Brethon, who offer two cosy
bedrooms with period furniture. Fishing and hiking on-site.
Swimming pool, fifteen kilometres. Other sporting activities
close by. English spoken.
Near river Forest area Near motorway
2 en suite (bth/shr) (1 fmly) Full central heating Open
parking available Child discount available 12yrs Languages
spoken: English & German
MEALS: Dinner fr 145FF*
CARDS: Travellers cheques

Ste-Geneviève Manche

La Fèvrerie (Prop: Marie Caillet)
50760
☎ 233543353
16th-century manor house, just two kilometres from the sea,
offers attractive rooms and a comfortable lounge with open
fireplace. Your hostess, Madame Caillet, would be happy to
cook a lobster for you, a speciality of the region, or offer you
home-made pastries. English spoken.
Near sea Near beach
3 en suite (bth/shr) Full central heating Open parking
available
CARDS: Travellers cheques

Ste-Marie-Du-Mont Manche

Bed & Breakfast (Prop: M & Mme Nauleau)
pl de l'Église *50480*
☎ 233719106 FAX 233719106
(take N13 Cherbourg to Caen road exit onto D913 in the
direction of Ste-Marie-du-Mont)
Nathalie and Philippe welcome you to their large house, set in
the heart of an historic town. The house is located between a
fifteenth century château and a church which boasts a twelfth
century nave. Reductions for children less than four years old
and for visitors staying more than one night. English spoken.
Near sea Near beach
2 en suite (bth/shr) Child discount available 4yrs Languages
spoken: English
ROOMS: s 180FF; d 200FF Reductions over 1 night
CARDS: Travellers cheques

Bed & Breakfast (Prop: M S Busquet)
Le Hameau Hubert *50480*
☎ 233424349
19th century house situated in the heart of the Parc Régional
des Marais, close to the landing beaches. Two guest rooms are
available and a French breakfast is served. There is a pleasant
flower garden, with conservatory and swings; possibility of
horse-riding and canoeing close by. English spoken.
Near river Near sea Near beach Near motorway
2 en suite (bth) (2 fmly) Radio in rooms Full central heating
Open parking available Supervised Languages spoken:
English

La Chausee (Prop: Clifford John Longlands)
50480
☎ 233424659 FAX 233424659
A traditional stone farmhouse, on a working beef and stud farm, 3km from Utah beach. Bedrooms are comfortably furnished and guests have the freedom to come and go as they please and use the garden. Evening meals are available by reservation, alternatively local restaurants and cafe's serve superb food at reasonable prices.
Near river Near sea Near beach Forest area Near motorway
3 en suite (bth/shr) No smoking in all bedrooms Full central heating Open parking available Child discount available
12yrs Languages spoken: English
ROOMS: s fr 220FF; d fr 250FF
MEALS: Dinner 75FF

STE-MARIE-LAUMONT Calvados

Le Picard (Prop: Nelly Guillaumin)
14350
☎ 231684321
Nelly and Marc Guillaumin would like you to visit their home, set in a green and pleasant area. One guest room is available and there is a large dining room, where meals may be taken with your hosts. Attractive gardens add to the harmony of the surroundings. Peace and tranquillity are assured here. Children under two stay free of charge.
Near river Forest area
1 en suite (shr) No smoking on premises Full central heating Open parking available Supervised Child discount available 2yrs
MEALS: Dinner 60FF*

STE-MÈRE-ÉGLISE Manche

Ferme Riou (Prop: Victor Destres)
50480
☎ 233416340
Madeleine and Victor Destres welcome you to their working farm. Independent access to rented rooms. Picnics a possibility. Tennis nearby. The sea is ten kilometres away.
3 en suite (shr) Open parking available Supervised

La Fière (Le Pont du Merdéret) (Prop: Chantal et Yves Poisson)
50480
☎ 233413177
Your hosts welcome you to their home, situated in the Parc Naturel Régional of Marais. The guesthouse is a separate building, with two rooms on the ground floor, one of which has a kitchenette and the other has a mezzanine. Independent access. River fishing nearby. English spoken.
Near river
2 en suite (shr) Full central heating Open parking available Supervised Child discount available Languages spoken: English
CARDS: Travellers cheques

Musée de la Ferme
50480
☎ 233413025 FAX 233453474
Traditional seventeenth century farmhouse, featuring rural displays. Items from farm activities have been preserved, such as the old dairy, with its milk and butter churns and the bakehouse where the weekly bread was cooked. Surrounded by broad pasture land and paddocks, in a region of large

farms. Bedrooms all have a peaceful outlook onto the orchard of the walled garden. English spoken.
Near river Near motorway
Closed Dec
4 en suite (bth/shr) Open parking available

Village de Beauvais (Prop: Emile et Marie Viel)
50480
☎ 233414171
This farm in Sainte-Mère-Église offers three guest rooms on the first floor. Living room with fireplace. Kitchen area. Picnics on-site. Continental breakfast available.
Near motorway
3 en suite (bth/shr) No smoking on premises Child discount available 10yrs
CARDS: ▩ Travellers cheques

STE-OPPORTUNE-LA-MARE Eure

La Vallée (Prop: Etienne Blondel)
Quai de la Forge *27680*
☎ 232421252
One floor of this Normandy house is reserved for guests. Living room with open fire. Exceptional surroundings in the Marais-Vernier region. There is a huge lake. Guests may dine with the Blondel family. Reductions for children and visitors who extend their stay more than one night. English spoken.
Near river Near lake Forest area
2 en suite (bth/shr) No smoking on premises Supervised Child discount available V meals Languages spoken: English & German
MEALS: Dinner 125FF*

STE-PIENCE Manche

Manoir de la Porte (Prop: M Lagadec)
50870
☎ 233681361 FAX 233682954
(From N175 take D39 and at 'Le Parc' follow signs to the manor on D175)
An attractive, turreted, sixteenth century manor house, in the calm setting of a park, thirty kilometres south of Mont St Michel. Guests are invited to dine with their hosts. Walks, rides and tennis offered. Special discounts may be available. Children under two stay free. Your hosts look forward to welcoming you either for one night or for several days. English spoken.
Near river Near sea Forest area Near motorway
Closed Nov-Mar
5 rms (2 bth 1 shr) (5 fmly) No smoking on premises Radio in rooms Full central heating Open parking available Child discount available 6yrs Fishing Bicycle rental V meals Last d 20.00hrs Languages spoken: English & German
ROOMS: s 200FF; d 230FF
MEALS: Dinner 80FF

SASSETOT LE MAUCONDUIT Seine-Maritime

Ferme du Manege (Prop: M & Mme M Soudry)
Hameau de Criquemauville *76540*
☎ 235274564
Danièle and Michel Soudry invite you to their half-timbered home set in a country garden. Four rooms are available, one of which has a balcony overlooking the garden. Attractive rooms, with modern furniture and exposed beams. French breakfast served. Three kilometres from the beach.
Forest area Near motorway

4 en suite (shr) (1 with balcony) Full central heating Open parking available

SENNEVILLE-SUR-FÉCAMP Seine-Maritime

Val de la Mer (Prop: Mme Mireille Lethuillier)
76400
☎ 235284193
Situated in an extremely attractive half-timbered house, traditionally furnished, comfortable guest rooms are available, all with exposed beams. French breakfast served. Terrace available on which to have breakfast.
Near sea Near beach
Closed holidays & end of year
3 en suite (bth/shr) No smoking on premises Full central heating Open parking available
ROOMS: s fr 250FF; d fr 300FF

SERVON Manche

Le Petit Manoir (Prop: Annick Gedouin)
50170
☎ 233600344 FAX 233601779
(from Mont St Michel, take the D225, after 5km on right take D107, Servon is along this road.)
Eighteenth century farm just nine kilometres from Mont St Michel. Restaurants, tennis and swimming pool all close by. Riding school five kilometres away. English spoken.
Near sea Forest area Near motorway
2 en suite (bth) Full central heating Open parking available Supervised Child discount available 2yrs Languages spoken: English & Italian
ROOMS: d 210FF
CARDS: Travellers cheques

SOMMERY Seine-Maritime

Ferme de Bray (Prop: Liliana et Patrice Perrier)
76440
☎ 235905727
These totally renovated rooms are situated in a seventeenth century farm. Also on-site are a watermill and cider press from the eighteenth century. Available on the farm: fishing in the lakes and many walks. English spoken. Restaurants close by.
Near river Near lake Forest area
5 en suite (bth/shr) (2 fmly) Full central heating Open parking available Supervised
CARDS: Travellers cheques

SOTTEVAST Manche

Hameau Ès Adam (Prop: Francoise Lebarillier)
50260
☎ 233419835
(from Cherbourg N13 South, exit to Brix and the D50 to Sottevast in village, D62 towards Rauville la Biget. 2nd right towards Hameau es Adam, then 1st left.)
François Lebarillier invites you to enjoy a relaxing experience in simple and comfortable surroundings in his eighteenth century manor house. Games room with table-tennis and boules available in the garden. English spoken. Reductions for children under two years.
3 en suite (bth/shr) (2 fmly) Full central heating Open parking available Supervised Child discount available 2yrs Boule Languages spoken: English
ROOMS: s 210FF; d 250FF
CARDS: Travellers cheques

SOTTEVILLE-SUR-MER Seine-Maritime

Bed & Breakfast (Prop: M & Mme Lefebvre)
rue du Bout du Haut *76740*
☎ 235976105
(from Dieppe, take D925 in direction of Fecamp-Le Haire after the exit for La Chapelle-sur-Dun 1st right)
Situated on a farm just 600 metres from the sea, in one of the oldest villages between Dieppe and Fécamp. Evening meals, by arrangement, at the hosts' table. Fixed price menu with drinks included. English spoken.
Near sea Near beach Forest area
3 en suite (shr) (1 fmly) (1 with balcony) Full central heating Open parking available Covered parking available Supervised Child discount available 1yr Farm visits.
ROOMS: s 220FF; d 220FF
MEALS: Dinner 80FF
CARDS: Travellers cheques

SURVIE Orne

Les Gains (Prop: M & Mme Wordsworth)
61310
☎ 233360556 FAX 233360556
(from Liseux & Vimoutiers on D579 take the Argentan road through Vimoutier. On leaving Vimoutier take the road signed Exmes. Follow signs for Exmes on the D26. Les Gains is signed on the left of the road. Turn right opposite after church & house.)
"Les Gains" is an English-owned eighteenth century dairy, sheep and cider apple farm set amongst meadows in the beautiful Pays d'Auge area of Normandy. The bedrooms are situated in an old building overlooking a small stream. The emphasis is on a warm welcome, peaceful surrounds and fresh farm food.
Near river Near lake Near sea Near beach Forest area Near motorway
3 en suite (bth/shr) (1 fmly) No smoking on premises Full central heating Open parking available Child discount available 12yrs V meals Last d am Languages spoken: English
ROOMS: d 250-280FF Reductions over 1 night
MEALS: Dinner 120FF*

TAMERVILLE Manche

Manoir de Belaunay (Prop: Jacques Allix Desfauteaux)
50700
☎ 233101062
Set in a manor built between the 15th and 16th centuries on the ruins of a monastery, the charming and traditional guest rooms open out onto the park. One room is on the ground floor, with exposed beams; the other two are on the first floor, one with a large stone fireplace and the second in Louis XV style. French breakfast served. English spoken.
Near sea Forest area Near motorway
Closed 15 Nov-15 Mar
3 en suite (bth/shr) Some rooms in annexe Radio in rooms Open parking available Covered parking available Supervised Languages spoken: English
ROOMS: s 200-250FF; d 250-300FF
CARDS: Travellers cheques

Taking your mobile phone to France?
See page 11

89

TILLEUL, LE Seine-Maritime

Bed & Breakfast (Prop: M & Mme Delahais)
pl General-de-Gaulle *76790*
☎ 235271639
Old house with garden, independent of proprietors' home. Six rooms available, all with access to the garden. Restaurants in the village. The Delahais family look forward to meeting you and to introducing you to this delightful area of France.
Near sea Forest area Near motorway
6 rms (4 shr) (2 fmly) Full central heating Open parking available

TILLY Eure

Bed & Breakfast (Prop: M & Mme Lefebvre)
1 rue Grande *27510*
☎ 232535617 FAX 232529211
Bedrooms are spacious and located on the first floor of this house, connected by a corridor to the bathroom. Traditional French breakfast served.
Forest area Near motorway
2 en suite (bth) No smoking on premises TV available Full central heating Open parking available Covered parking available
CARDS: Travellers cheques

TILLY-SUR-SEULLES Calvados

Bed & Breakfast (Prop: M & Mme S Brilhault)
7 rue de la Varènde *14250*
☎ 231082573
(from Caen: ring road around Caen towards Cherbourg, come off at Carpiquet / D9 Tilly-sur-Seulles. From Bayeux: D6 to Tilly sur Seulles)
This splendid house was constructed of stone in 1898, and is situated between Caen and Bayeux. A rounded, turret-style room at the back of the house, overlooks the garden, and has stained glass windows. Each guest room is individually and stylishly furnished. Within close proximity you will find tennis, lake fishing, riding, swimming, forest, the sea and golf. Restaurants in the village. English spoken.
Near river Near sea Forest area
2 en suite (bth/shr) (2 fmly) No smoking on premises Full central heating Open parking Covered parking available Child discount available Languages spoken: English
ROOMS: s 170-190FF; d 190-210FF
CARDS: Travellers cheques

TOCQUEVILLE-LES-MURS Seine-Maritime

Ferme du Rome (Prop: M Antoine Daubeuf)
79110
☎ 235277084
Near river Near sea Near beach Forest area
2 en suite (shr) No smoking on premises Full central heating Open parking available Child discount available 10yrs
Languages spoken: English
ROOMS: d 220FF Reductions over 1 night
MEALS: Dinner 75FF
CARDS: Travellers cheques

Taking your mobile phone to France?
See page 11

90

TORTISAMBERT Calvados

La Boursaie (Prop: Peter et Anja Davies)
14140
☎ 231631420 FAX 231631428
(in Livarot take D4 for 500m, then turn right onto D38, the village is 600m along road, turn left and follow signs.)
La Boursaie is an ancient cider farm, dating back to the sixteenth century, situated in the heart of the beautiful region of Auge. With a superb outlook over meadowland and woods, in a quiet valley, this farm has been well restored and provides an ideal base to explore this region. Self-catering cottages are available to rent. Rooms are spacious and comfortable. Nearby are games for the children. Dinner available. English spoken.
Near river Near sea Forest area
2 en suite (shr) No smoking on premises Full central heating Open parking available Supervised Child discount available 10yrs Tennis Fishing Riding Bicycle rental Languages spoken: English & German
ROOMS: d 260-360FF Reductions over 1 night Special breaks
MEALS: Continental breakfast 30FF Dinner 98-120FF
CARDS: Travellers cheques

TOUFFRÉVILLE Eure

Bed & Breakfast (Prop: Daniel & Therese Herman)
27440
☎ 232491737
A fine property with a river running through the garden. Lyon Forest within eight kilometres. A little English spoken.
Near river Forest area
1 en suite (shr) (1 fmly) Full central heating Open parking available Child discount available 4yrs Open terrace

TOUR-EN-BESSIN Calvados

La Vignette (Prop: M & Mme Girard)
rte de Crouay *14400*
☎ 231215283
(from Bayeux N13 towards Cherbourg, through Tour-en-Bessin, then left towards Route de Crouay for about 1km. House is on right with cartwheel)
Comfortable, Bessin-style farmhouse, built in 1801, close to beaches and forests. Tastefully furnished bedrooms. Generous breakfasts. Family atmosphere. Games available in the garden. Plenty of walks in the area; close to the landing beaches. English spoken.
Near river Near sea Near beach Forest area Near motorway
4 rms (3 bth/shr) (1 fmly) No smoking on premises TV in 2 bedrooms Full central heating Open parking available Covered parking available Supervised Child discount available 10yrs Bicycle rental Stables are 1km away Last d 18.00hrs Languages spoken: English
ROOMS: s fr 190FF; d fr 240FF
MEALS: Dinner 100FF
CARDS: ▆ Travellers cheques

TOURNIÈRES Calvados

Ferme du Marcelet (Prop: M & Mme Isidor)
14330
☎ 231229086
Family residence situated fifteen kilometres from the sea and four kilometres from the forest. French breakfast served. Evening meals available by reservation. English spoken.
Near river Near sea Forest area

5 en suite (shr) (3 fmly) No smoking in 2 bedrooms Open parking available Supervised Child discount available 2yrs Last d 17.00hrs Languages spoken: English
MEALS: Lunch 70FF Dinner 70FF*

TOURVILLE-LA-CAMPAGNE Eure

Le Michaumière (Prop: M Paris)
72 rue des Canadiens *27370*
☎ 232353128
A warm Normandy welcome awaits you in the quiet of the countryside. Breakfast includes home-made yoghurt, brioche and cake with home-made jam. Golf with five kilometres and tennis at eight kilometres. Restaurants close by. A little English spoken.
Forest area
3 en suite (bth/shr) Full central heating Open parking available

TREVIERES Calvados

Château de Colombieres (Prop: Comte Etienne de Maupeou)
14710
☎ 231225165 FAX 231922492
(7kms from Bayeux. From Bayeux N13 towards Cherbourg, turn left D29 Trevieres then D5 to Colombieres. From Cherbourg take N13 to Isigny-sur-Mer turn right onto D5 to Colombieres)
A private château where guests are welcomed in a personal way. The comfortable rooms are furnished with antiques. The castle, different parts of which date from 14th-18th century, is located in a peaceful and romantic private park close to Bayeux.
Near river Near sea Near beach Forest area Near motorway
Closed Oct-May
3 en suite (bth/shr) Open parking available No children 12yrs Tennis Fishing Bicycle rental Languages spoken: English
ROOMS: d 800-100FF
CARDS: 💳 Travellers cheques

TRIQUEVILLE Eure

La Clé des Champs (Prop: Mme Michelle Le Pleux)
27500
☎ 232413799
This eighteenth century distillery offers bedrooms for non-smokers on the first floor in what was originally an apple storage area. Pretty garden with sun loungers and umbrellas. Breakfast served outside in good weather. Situated twenty kilometres from Honfleur. Bikes for guests' use. Children over eight years accepted.
Near river Near lake Near sea Forest area Near motorway
2 en suite (shr) No smoking on premises Full central heating Open parking available Covered parking available No children 8yrs Bicycle rental

Ferme du Ponctey (Prop: M. Jaouen)
27500
☎ 232421037 FAX 232575453
Large country house, situated in the middle of fields on the edge of a plateau. Super view over the valley. Set in 20 hectares, with forest 100 metres away, making this an ideal location for long walks. Garden games include pétanque, table-tennis and croquet. Tennis, fishing and riding nearby. Dinner available. English spoken.
Near river Forest area Near motorway

2 en suite (bth/shr) Full central heating Open parking available Covered parking available Croquet Table tennis V meals Last d 20.00hrs Languages spoken: English & German
MEALS: Dinner 80-150FF*
CARDS: Travellers cheques

TROARN Calvados

Manoir des Tourpes (Prop: Landon-Cassady)
Bures-sur-Dives *14670*
☎ 231236247 FAX 231238610
Perched on the west bank of the Dives River, this manor dates back to the seventeenth century but offers twentieth century comforts and decor. Sun-loungers and picnic table in garden. Close to the D-Day beaches, Bayeux, Deauville, Swiss Normandy and Honfleur. English spoken.
Near river Near sea Near motorway
4 en suite (bth/shr) (1 fmly) (1 with balcony) No smoking on premises Full central heating Open parking available Child discount available 4yrs . Languages spoken: English
ROOMS: s fr 250FF; d 280-360FF
CARDS: Travellers cheques

TRONQUAY, LE Eure

La Grand Fray (Prop: M Gerard Monnier)
1 rue des Angles *27480*
☎ 232495338
(from Rouen towards Lyons la Furet, then onto le Tronquay)
Nineteenth century half-timbered house with thatched roof. The guest rooms have their own bathroom facilities. Kitchenette reserved for guests' use. Breakfasts are served in the summer house. Beautiful garden. Shops and restaurants within three kilometres. Open all year round. English spoken.
Forest area
1 en suite (shr) TV available Full central heating Open parking available Bicycle rental Languages spoken: English
ROOMS: s 200FF; d 230FF
CARDS: 💳

URVILLE-NACQUEVILLE Manche

La Blanche Maison (Prop: Michael Potel)
874 rue St-Laurent *50460*
☎ 233034879
Old farm with views over the sea. The guest room, together with kitchen and dining area, is located in an annexe to the side of the property. Evening meals with hosts by arrangement. Beach, with sailing facilities, at 500 metres. English spoken.
Near sea Forest area
1 en suite (shr) Full central heating Open parking available Covered parking available Supervised Languages spoken: English & German

VALFRAMBERT Orne

Haras du Bois Beulant (Prop: M Siri)
61250
☎ 233286233
Set in the heart of the countryside, this Normandy manor-house is now a stud-farm, which is situated in a six hectare park. Sit beneath the creeper decorating the exterior of the house and enjoy the peace and quiet. Horse-riding is available close by, whilst tennis, golf, swimming and a forest are all within five kilometres. English spoken.

cont'd

Forest area In town centre Near motorway
2 en suite (shr) Full central heating Open parking available
Supervised Languages spoken: English, German, Italian &
Spanish
ROOMS: s fr 200FF; d fr 260FF Reductions over 1 night

VALMONT Seine-Maritime

Le Clos du Vivier (Prop: Mme Dominque Cachera)
4 chemin du Vivier *76540*
☎ 235299095 FAX 235274449
Thatched cottage set in well-kept gardens. This long, low
building offers a rustic setting for visitors coming to the Seine
Maritime region of France. Peace and calm can be found here,
as well as a warm welcome from your hostess, Mme.
Dominique Cachera. Children over eleven years only please.
English spoken.
Near river Near lake Near sea Near beach Forest area
3 en suite (bth/shr) (1 fmly) TV in 2 bedrooms Radio in
rooms Full central heating Open parking available No
children 10yrs Languages spoken: English & Spanish
ROOMS: d 380-430FF

VARNÉVILLE-BRETTEVILLE Seine-Maritime

Bed & Breakfast (Prop: M & Mme Auberville)
Les Vernelles *76890*
☎ 235340804
The guest house is an individual cottage situated near the
main house in the middle of a wooded area, surrounded by
apple trees. Here you will find peace and quiet in the heart of
the Normandy countryside. There is a dining room, a small
lounge, plus an open fire. The bedrooms feature beams.
Breakfast is served at the cottage. English spoken.
Near motorway
1 en suite (shr) (1 fmly) Full central heating Open parking
available Covered parking available Tennis Riding Bicycle
rental Open terrace Languages spoken: English
ROOMS: d 280-510FF

VASSY Calvados

La Calbrasserie (Prop: M & Mme De Saint-Leger)
La Calbrasserie *14410*
☎ 231685153
In a farm in the heart of the countryside, this house offers
rooms on the ground floor and the first floor. A cordial
welcome awaits you from the De Saint Leger family, whose
children speak English. The house is typical of the Bocage
area. Picnics provided on request. Bike hire possible. Shops
and restaurants within two kilometres. Well-equipped kitchen
available. Farm nearby that may be visited.
Forest area
2 en suite (shr) (2 fmly) Radio in rooms Full central heating
Open parking available Covered parking available
Supervised Child discount available 2yrs Bicycle rental Table
Tennis
CARDS: Travellers cheques

VAST, LE Manche

La Dannevillerie (Prop: Francoise & Benoit Passenaud)
50630
☎ 233445045
Situated in the heart of the Saire Valley, this seventeenth
century farm offers two renovated rooms with independent
entrance, overlooking fields with sheep and donkeys. Fresh

bread from the bakers is collected each morning for
traditional French breakfast. The sea is six kilometres away.
English spoken.
Near river Near sea Forest area
2 en suite (shr) (2 fmly) No smoking on premises TV in all
bedrooms Full central heating Open parking available Child
discount available -2 Free Languages spoken: English
ROOMS: s 160FF; d 195FF

VASTEVILLE Manche

Le Manoir (Prop: M Hubert Damourette)
50440
☎ 233527608 FAX 322935988
Situated in a modern house, clean and comfortable guest
rooms are available on the first floor. Extra childrens' beds are
available for a small supplement. There is a restaurant 200
metres from the property. Tennis, riding, fishing and walks are
available within five kilometres.
Near sea Forest area
2 rms Full central heating Open parking available Child
discount available
CARDS: Travellers cheques

VAUDRIMESNIL Manche

La Rochelle (Prop: Alain & Olga Berthou)
50490
☎ 233467495
Creeper-covered farmhouse situated ten kilometres from
Coutances, in a calm, peaceful environment. A large dovecote
dating back to the Middle Ages is now used for games and
relaxation. Table-tennis and billiards on-site.
Near sea Forest area
2 en suite (shr) No smoking on premises Full central heating
Open parking available Supervised Table tennis

VAUX-SUR-AURE Calvados

Hammeau du Quesnay (Prop: M Louis Roulland)
14400
☎ 231921126
Recently-built house with all rooms having their own
entrance. Large lawn and garden with garden furniture. The
house is near the museums and the beaches of Normandy.
Near river Near motorway
1 en suite (bth) Radio in rooms Open parking available
CARDS: ●■ Travellers cheques

VAUX-SUR-SEULLES Calvados

Ferme du Clos Mayas (Prop: Marie-Helene Bastard)
☎ 231223271 FAX 231223350
This property is open all year round. Prices include breakfast.
Dinner available, by early reservation, at a fixed price. English
spoken.
Near river Near sea Near motorway
4 en suite (bth/shr) (1 fmly) Full central heating Open
parking available Child discount available
MEALS: Dinner fr 85FF*
CARDS: Travellers cheques

Taking your mobile phone to France?
See page 11

92

VENGEONS Manche

Le Val (Prop: Jeanne Desdoits)
50150
☎ 233596416
Situated on the borders of the regions of Calvados and Orne, this stone farm offers four rooms, one of which is a family room with independent access. Views over the surrounding countryside. French breakfast served. Boules, swings and sandpit available. English spoken.
Near lake Near motorway
4 rms (1 bth 1 shr) (1 fmly) No smoking on premises Full central heating Open parking available Covered parking available Supervised Boule Languages spoken: English
CARDS: ▆ Travellers cheques

VIGNATS Calvados

Bed & Breakfast (Prop: M & Mme Brunton)
La rue d'Avé *14700*
☎ 231408323 FAX 231408323
The proprietors of this restored house have maintained the original flavour of the place, keeping the exposed beams and the open fireplace in the lounge. Two bedrooms are available. The owners ask that you make yourselves totally at home. Evening meals are provided with prior notice. Reductions for children up to twelve. Library, living room and games room. English spoken.
Forest area
2 rms No smoking on premises Full central heating Open parking available Supervised Child discount available 12yrs Languages spoken: English & Spanish
MEALS: Dinner 70FF*
CARDS: Travellers cheques

VINGT-HANAPS Orne

Les Quatre Saisons (Prop: M Claude Ivaldi)
Les Chauvières *61250*
☎ 233288292
Near lake Forest area Near motorway
4 en suite (bth/shr) (4 fmly) (2 with balcony) TV available Full central heating Air conditioning in bedrooms Open parking available Supervised V meals Languages spoken: English
MEALS: Full breakfast 25FF Lunch 90-175FF Dinner 90-175FF*

Nord/Pas de Calais

An underestimated tourist area as French regions go, the Nord/Pas de Calais has much to reward the inquisitive visitor. Distinctive bell towers, prominent in each town, were formerly watch towers erected by the towns' burgomasters as a symbol of State power to rival the Church's spires, which are dominant features of the flat countryside. Locals call their sandy, grassy coastline — the northernmost in France — the Opal Coast because of its mysterious, bluish-purple light. Inland, rivers and canals are dotted with windmills, and picturesque villages spring to life in uproarious festivals celebrating the myths and legends of the past.

(Top): Cheese and wine from the village of Maroilles. The cheese is rinsed in beer to make a richly flavoured cheese tart.

(Bottom): Rodin's famous statue is a tribute to the 'Burghers of Calais', who risked their lives to save the town from destruction in 1347.

ESSENTIAL FACTS

DÉPARTEMENTS:	Nord, Pas-de-Calais
PRINCIPAL TOWNS	Calais, Lille, Arras, Boulogne-sur-Mer, Cambrai, Dunkerque, Valenciennes
PLACES TO VISIT:	The medieval Château Comtal at Boulogne-sur-Mer; the important Musée des Beaux-Arts at Lille; Vaucelles Abbey, founded by the Cisterian order in 1132 at Les Rues des Vignes; family amusement park in the Parc de Bagatelle at Merlimont
REGIONAL TOURIST OFFICE	6 place Mendès France, 59800 Lille. Tel: 20 14 57 57
LOCAL GASTRONOMIC DELIGHTS	Favourite regional dishes include flambee coffee and chicory Charlotte with caramel gin sauce and brown sugar; licques chicken and waterzoï; crab Charlotte from the Opal Coast; fish (cod and turbot) carbonade with beer
DRINKS	Many breweries produce lager as well as top-fermented ale like beers in the Belgian style. Houlle and Wambrechies are well known for their gin, while mead is brewed in Bavay and Bouin-Plumoison.
LOCAL CRAFTS WHAT TO BUY	Glass engraving from Bellignies, puppets from Camphin-en-Carembault, wood sculpture from Cassel, pottery and ceramics from Desvres, miniature paintings from Masny, silk painting from St-Laurent-Blangy

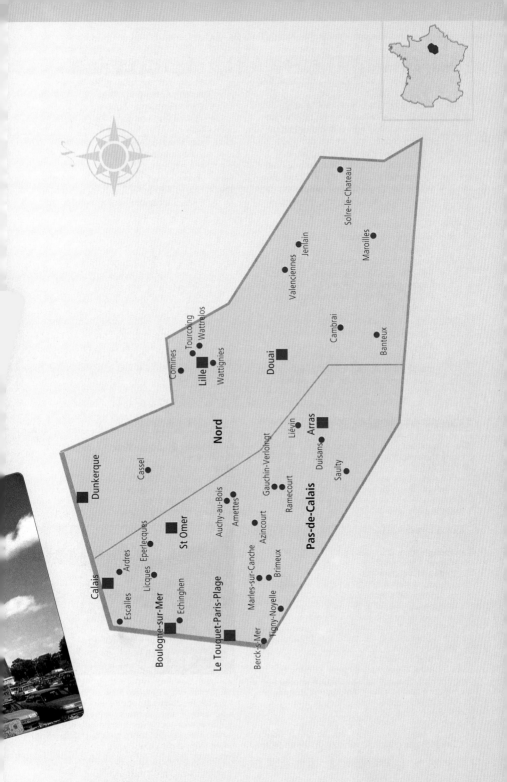

Dunkerque

Cassel

Calais

Escalles

Ardres

Licques Éperlecques

Echinghen

Boulogne-sur-Mer

St Omer

Auchy-au-Bois

Amettes

Azincourt

Gauchin-Verloingt

Ramecourt

Marles-sur-Canche

Brimeux

Le Touquet-Paris-Plage

Tigny-Noyelle

Berck-s-Mer

Comines

Tourcoing

Wattrelos

Lille

Wattignies

Nord

Douai

Valenciennes

Jenlain

Solre-le-Chateau

Maroilles

Cambrai

Banteux

Arras

Liévin

Duisans

Saulty

Pas-de-Calais

EVENTS & FESTIVALS

Feb Lille Mozart Festival; Carnivals at Dunkirk & Equihen-plage

Mar Carnivals at Cassel and Dunkerque; Berck Kite Festival; Valenciennes Cultural Spring Festival; Cassel Carnival & Parade of giant effigies; Aire-sur-la-Lys Carnival Parade

Apr Avesnes-sur-Helpe Fly Fair (*traditional celebration*); Roost Warendin Fête du Pureux - traditional feast & parade with giant effigy; Walled City Day: 14 walled cities have historical pageants, concerts, bell-ringing, theatre etc

May Tourcoing Medieval Festival

Jun Maroilles Flea market; Samer Strawberry Festival; Lille Festival

Jul Douai Gayant Procession & Festival; Boulogne-sur-Mer Napoleon Festival; Opal Coast Contemporary Music Festival; Neuville en-Ferrin Carnival & Festival; Wimereux Mussel Festival

Aug Hardelot Music Festival; Les Quesnoy Carnival with giant Pierre Bimberlot; Maroilles Fête de la Flamiche (a local delicacy); Cambrai Historical Parade with giant figures; Arras Carnival & Festival with giant figures; Le Touquet Music Festival

Sep Lille Giant Street market; Wattrelos Berlouffes Festival (commemorating the Beggars' Revolt); Arleux Garlic Fair; Aire-sur-la-Lys Andouille Festival; Armentieres Nieulles Festival (small cakes thrown down from town hall)

Oct Lille Festival; Comines Carnival Parade with giant figures; Bailleul Monts des Cats St Hubert Festival

Nov Tourcoing Jazz Festival

Dec Licques Turkey Festival; Boulogne-sur-Mer Guénels (hollowed-out beetroot) Festival

---

AMETTES Pas-de-Calais

Bed & Breakfast (Prop: M & Mme Gevas)
2 rue de l'Église *62260*
☎ 321271502
Near river Near motorway
3 en suite (shr) No smoking on premises TV in 2 bedrooms
Full central heating Open parking available Supervised
Languages spoken: English

ARDRES Pas-de-Calais

La Chesnaie (Prop: B & G Leturgie)
N43 Bois-en-Ardres *62610*
☎ 321354398 FAX 321364870
(from Calais take N43 towards St Omer.On entering Bois-en-Ardres 'La Chesnaie' is 2nd on right)
This manor house is nestled in the middle of wooded parkland. Four rooms are available - extra beds can be provided for children. French billiards is on offer and games for both children and adults are available in the park. There are 10 restaurants within a three mile radius.
Near lake Near motorway
6 rms (4 bth/shr) (3 fmly) No smoking on premises Full central heating Open parking available Child discount available 3yrs Pool table Boule Languages spoken: English
ROOMS: s 200FF; d 220FF
CARDS: Travellers cheques

Taking your mobile phone to France?
See page 11

AUCHY-AU-BOIS Pas-de-Calais

Les Cohettes (Prop: Jean-Michel & Gina Bulot)
28 r de Pernes
☎ 321020947 FAX 321028168
(45 mins from Calais. Take A26 to exit 4, onto D341 towards Arras. Approx 12 minutes after Therouanne is Auchy-au-Bois. At x-rds "Vert Dragon" turn right & follow green & white "chambre d'hôtes" sign, 2nd house after church)

Five guest rooms, in a restored old stone farmhouse, all of which are very comfortable. A quiet place ideal for walkers and children. A large garden has been laid to lawn and there is a garden room with table-tennis, javelot (a local game with javelins) and pétanque. Situated near church in the village, between Vimy and the Côte d'Opale.
Forest area

5 en suite (bth/shr) (2 fmly) Radio in rooms Open parking available Supervised Child discount available 10yrs Boule Last d 17.00hrs Languages spoken: English & German
ROOMS: s 190FF; d 220-280FF
MEALS: Dinner 95-120FF
CARDS: Travellers cheques

AZINCOURT Pas-de-Calais

La Gacogne (Prop: M-J & P Fenet)
62310
☎ 321044561 FAX 321044561
(from A26 S of Calais take D928 towards Hesdin. After Fruges take L turn in Ruisseauville for Azincourt)
Near the woods of Agincourt near the pretty village of Artois, visitors will find an old converted schoolhouse built from white stones. Peaceful setting, English spoken.
Near river Forest area
4 en suite (shr) No smoking on premises Open parking available Languages spoken: English
ROOMS: d 250FF

BANTEUX Nord

Ferme de Bonavis (Prop: M Delcambre)
rte Nationale *59266*
☎ 327785508
(off N44, 10km from Cambrai, 25km from St Quentin)
The Delcambres give a warm welcom to all those who stay on their working farm, where rooms are available in the farmhouse or in separate gites. This is an ideal venue for ramblers walking through the Haut Escaut valley to the Abbaye de Vaucelle. Boat rides and pony-treks are available in the nearby leisure park. Some access for handicapped people. English spoken.
Near river Forest area Near motorway
6 en suite (shr) (3 fmly) (1 with balcony) TV available Full central heating Open parking available Covered parking available (charged) Open terrace

BRIMEUX Pas-de-Calais

Ferme du Saule (Prop: M et Mme G Trunnet)
20 rue de l'Eglise *62170*
☎ 321060128 FAX 321814014
(6km from Monreuil Sur Mer on the N39)
Near river Near lake
3 en suite (shr) (3 fmly) TV available Full central heating Open parking available Covered parking available Child discount available 3yrs Tennis Fishing Boule Languages spoken: English
ROOMS: s 190FF; d 250FF

CAMBRAI Nord

La Chope (Prop: M & Mme Roussel)
17 rue des Docks *59400*
☎ 327813678 FAX 327839760
Near river Near lake Forest area In town centre Near motorway
10 en suite (shr) (3 fmly) TV in all bedrooms Direct dial from all bedrooms Licensed Full central heating Open parking available Covered parking available Child discount available 12yrs V meals Last d 21.30hrs
ROOMS: (room only) d 220-245FF *
CARDS: ●● 🈺 💳 Travellers cheques

DUISANS Pas-de-Calais

Le Clos Grincourt (Prop: Annie Senlis)
18 rue du Chaâteau *62161*
☎ 321486833 FAX 321486833
(first house on left on entering village from direction of Arras on D56)
Attractive seventeenth century manor-house, surrounded by a private park filled with flowers. The hospitality, interior decoration and family photos make you feel immediately at home. A room is reserved for guests to enjoy their breakfast in each morning and where they can discuss with their hosts their itinery for the day. Mature, sheltered garden. The beach is close by. English spoken.
Near river Forest area Near motorway
3 en suite (bth/shr) No smoking on premises Full central heating Open parking available Covered parking available Supervised Child discount available
ROOMS: s 170FF; d 240FF

ECHINGHEN Pas-de-Calais

Le Clos d'Ecsh (Prop: Mme J Boussemaere)
rue de l'Église *62360*
☎ 321911434 FAX 321311505
Located in the heart of a small village, this renovated farm offers four rooms, each with its own independent entrance. Quiet guaranteed. Comfortable spacious accommodation, living and dining rooms, courtyard and stables are available to guests. Traditional French breakfast served. English spoken.
Near river
4 en suite (shr) Languages spoken: English

ÉPERLECQUES Pas-de-Calais

Château du Ganspette (Prop: M & Mme Pauwels)
133 rue du Ganspette *62910*
☎ 321934393 FAX 321957498
Situated in Audomarois in eight hectares of wooded park, this 19th century castle gives you comfort and relaxation with bedrooms opening onto the park. A restaurant and swimming pool are open from May to September. The castle was occupied by the Germans during World War II, and is located close to a former V2 base. English spoken.
Near river Forest area Near motorway
4 rms (3 shr) Full central heating Open parking available Supervised Outdoor swimming pool Tennis Boule Languages spoken: English

ESCALLES Pas-de-Calais

Le Grand'Maison (Prop: M & Mme Boutnoy)
Hameau de La Haute Escalles *62179*
☎ 321852775 FAX 321852775
(take A16 from Channel Tunnel and take exit 10/11, passing the village of Peuplingués, then after 2kms turn into first house on left)
Peace and tranquillity are the order of the day at this farmhouse. The scenery in this region is magnificent, ideal for rambles through the countryside and strolls along the coast. Jacqueline and Marc Boutroy invite you to join them for meals.
Near sea Near beach
6 en suite (bth/shr) (1 fmly) No smoking in all bedrooms TV in 3 bedrooms Full central heating Open parking available Supervised Child discount available Boule
MEALS: Dinner 90FF*
CARDS: Travellers cheques

GAUCHIN-VERLOINGT Pas-de-Calais

Le Loubarre (Prop: M C Vion)
550 rue des Montifaux *62130*
☎ 321030505
(at Saint Pol sur Ternoise take D343 towards Anvin and after 1km turn right following "chambre d'hote" sign before entering village)

A lovely 19th century manor furnished with antiques and a dining room with an open fireplace. The bedrooms are located in a converted dovecot with original beams. Croix-en-Ternois racing track is two kilometres away. Restaurants are within a short distance and tennis, golf and riding facilities are all close by. Alternatively, you can enjoy country walks which start right outside the front door!
Near river Forest area
(2 fmly) TV in 2 bedrooms Full central heating Open parking available Supervised Child discount available 5yrs Bicycle rental Open terrace Languages spoken: English,German & Spanish
ROOMS: s 200FF; d 240FF Special breaks

JENLAIN Nord

Château d'en Haut (Prop: M & Mme Demarcq)
59144
☎ 327497180 FAX 327497180
(from A21 exit at junction 22 towards Le Quesnoy)
Set in a small village, near the Belgian border, Michel and Marie-Hélène welcome you to their small eighteenth century château, which they have been restoring since 1982. The rooms have been decorated with great care and attention to detail. Ten percent reduction for people staying three nights or more.
Forest area Near motorway
6 en suite (bth/shr) (2 fmly) No smoking on premises TV in 2 bedrooms Full central heating Open parking available Covered parking available Supervised
ROOMS: s 240-280FF; d 280-370FF Reductions over 1 night
CARDS: Travellers cheques

LILLE Nord

Bed & Breakfast (Prop: Mme Jeannine Hulin)
28 rue de Hannetons *59000*
☎ 320534612
(S of Lille near Ronchin. From A25 exit Porte de Postes, on the roundabout take Blvd de Strasbourg then Blvd d'Alsace. Turn right into rue Armand Carrel, follow rue du Faubourg de Douai. Turn right rue L Senault then 1st right into rue de Hannetons)

In a quiet street near tube station. The house has a garden, cosy rooms decorated with a personal touch and is furnished with antique pieces.
In town centre Near motorway
1 en suite (bth) Full central heating Child discount available 14yrs
ROOMS: s 140FF; d 190FF Reductions over 1 night

MARLES-SUR-CANCHE Pas-de-Calais

Manoir Francis (Prop: M & Mme Leroy)
1 rue de l'Église *62170*
☎ 321813880 FAX 321813856
(from Calais take motorway to Boulogne, then the N10 to Montreuil/Mer, then go towards Neuville and take the D113 to Marles/Canche)
Set in a seventeenth century manor house, situated in a small village four kilometres from Montreuil-sur-Mer. Living room with vaulted ceiling. Courtyard and private lake. Open fire. Set in beautiful surroundings, in a peaceful and calm atmosphere. English spoken.
Near river Forest area
3 en suite (bth) (1 fmly) Full central heating Open parking available Supervised Open terrace Languages spoken: English
ROOMS: s 230FF; d 280FF

RAMECOURT Pas-de-Calais

La Ferme du Bois Quesnoy (Prop: M Deleau)
62130
☎ 321416660
François Deleau welcomes you to his farm, which offers rooms in a quiet and relaxing setting. English spoken.
Forest area
4 en suite (bth/shr) Radio in rooms Full central heating Open parking available Covered parking available Child discount available Languages spoken: English & German

SAULTY Pas-de-Calais

Bed & Breakfast (Prop: Françoise & Pierre Dalle)
82 r de la Gare *62158*
☎ 321482476 FAX 321481832
(from N25 go into l'Arbret, take third turning on right, Saulty is approx 800m along road. Chambre d'hôte is the first big house on the right)

Magnificent eighteenth century château set in a lawned park, where guests are treated as friends and can enjoy the quiet, the gardens and the library. Living room available for guests' use. Fifteen minutes from the historic towns of Arras and

Doullens. Guests will find plenty on offer to visit in this area. Restaurants within six kilometres. Reductions for stays of more than three nights. English spoken.
Forest area Near motorway
Closed Jan
5 en suite (bth/shr) (2 fmly) No smoking on premises Full central heating Open parking available Child discount available Languages spoken: English
ROOMS: s 190FF; d 260FF Reductions over 1 night

SOLRE-LE-CHÂTEAU Nord

Bed & Breakfast (Prop: Patrick & Pierrette Mariani)
5 Grand'Place *59740*
☎ 327616530 FAX 327616371
This attractive nineteenth century residence, built on the ruins of an ancient château-fort, offers spacious, comfortable bedrooms, each decorated in pretty, matching fabrics. Lounge with television. Dinner available at a fixed price. Restaurants within three kilometres. English spoken.
Near lake Forest area In town centre Near motorway
6 rms (2 bth 2 shr) (2 fmly) Full central heating Open parking available Child discount available 4yrs Languages spoken: English & Italian
MEALS: Dinner 0.80FF*

TIGNY-NOYELLE Pas-de-Calais

Le Prieure Impasse de L'Église
(Prop: Mr Roger Delbecque)
62180
☎ 321860438 FAX 321813995
Old rectory surrounded by greenery, stylishly furnished with antiques. The residence is situated next to a church, in the middle of a nature preserve, a very peaceful setting. Dinner by reservation. Golf two kilometres away. Beaches and the Bay of Somme are within close proximity.
5 en suite (bth/shr) (2 fmly) (1 with balcony) TV in all bedrooms Open parking available Supervised Child discount available 5yrs Boule Open terrace Languages spoken: English
ROOMS: s 250FF; d 310FF
MEALS: Dinner 120-140FF
CARDS: ● ▨ Travellers cheques

WATTIGNIES Nord

Le Bot (Prop: Chantel Le Bot)
59 rue Faidherbe *59139*
☎ 320602451
(from A1 exit 19 on D549 to Wattignies. At Pharmacy bear left to village centre, house on left just before the church on right) The house is approx 6kms from Lille. Breakfast is served in the living room with views onto the garden.
3 rms (1 shr) TV in all bedrooms Full central heating Open parking available Child discount available 14yrs Bicycle rental Languages spoken: English
ROOMS: s fr 200FF; d 235-255FF
MEALS: Dinner 100FF*

Picardy

France was said to have been born in Picardy. The region has been a crossroads of history and there is much to discover here, from ancient times through to the present day. The easily accessible capital, Amiens, is an action-packed city which has successfully married a rich heritage and impressive buildings with 20th-century innovations: elegant modern architecture and a lively contemporary arts scene have been sensitively integrated with the past. Take time to leave the motorways, you will be surprised and rewarded, not to mention seduced by the Picardy cuisine.

(Top): This quaint doorway is in the village of Gerberoy which was restored by a community of artists in the 19th century.

(Bottom): The waterfront at Amiens, the capital of Picardy, built on the banks of the Somme.

ESSENTIAL FACTS

DÉPARTEMENTS:	Aisne, Oise, Somme
PRINCIPAL TOWNS	Amiens, Beauvais, Abbeville, Noyon, Compiègne, St-Quentin, Soissons, Château-Thierry.
PLACES TO VISIT:	The cathedrals of Amiens and Beauvais; the battlefields and millitary cemeteries of the Somme; the sandy beaches and conservation areas in the Somme estuary.
REGIONAL TOURIST OFFICE	12, rue Chapeau de Violettes, Amiens Tel: 22 91 79 28 1, place de l'Admiral Courbet, 80100 AbbevilleTel: 22 24 27 92
LOCAL GASTRONOMIC DELIGHTS	Eels in a variety of guises: beer, smoked and as a pâté; duck pâté; delicious melting macaroons from Amiens; sauterelles, grey shrimps caught off the Picardy coast; savoury stuffed pancakes; gateau battu; mussels reared on farms in Marquenterre; lamb with a distinctive flavour due to salt marsh grazing methods
DRINKS	Locally produced cider; red berry spirits; top-fermented ales and of course, champagne.
LOCAL CRAFTS WHAT TO BUY	Pottery from the Pays de Bray; lace and tapestries are on sale throughout the region, huge selection of pastel paintings locally produced.

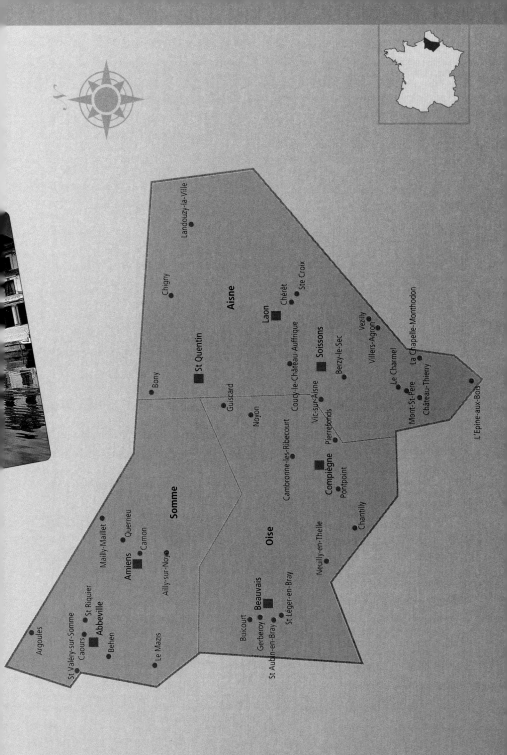

N

Aisne

Landouzy-la-Ville

Chigny

Chérêt
Laon
Ste Croix
La Chapelle-Monthodon

St Quentin
Vezilly
Soissons
Villers-Agron
Coucy-le-Château-Auffrique
Berzy-le-Sec
Bony
Le Charmel

Guiscard
Vic-sur-Aisne
Mont-St-Père
Château-Thierry

Noyon
Pierrefonds
L'Epine-aux-Bois

Cambronne-les-Ribecourt
Compiègne
Pontpoint

Somme
Chantilly

Mailly-Maillet
Querrieu
Neuilly-en-Thelle
Camon
Amiens
Oise
Ailly-sur-Noye

St Riquier
Caours
Beauvais
Abbeville
Buicourt
St Léger-en-Bray
Behen
Gerberoy
Argoules
St Valéry-sur-Somme
St Aubin-en-Bray
Le Mazis

101

EVENTS & FESTIVALS:

Mar St-Quentin Comic Book Festival; Beauvais Festival of Wildlife Films; Laon International Children's Film Festival

Apr Abbeville Bird Film Festival; St Aubin en Bray Dance Festival; Compiègne Lily of the Valley Festival

May Compiègne Joan of Arc Festival; Amiens Jazz Festival; Amiens Carnival; Chaumont-en Vexin Music Festival; Camon Festival of the Moors; Compiègne International Horse Show; St-Quentin Jesters' Festival

Jun Verneuil-en-Halatte Rock Festival; Doullens Gardening Days in the Citadelle; Amiens Town Festival; Château-Thierry 'Jean de la Fontaine' Festival (entertainment based on the fables, procession, fireworks); Coucy-le-Château Medieval Festival; Chantilly Horse Racing; St-Valéry sur Somme William the Conqueror Festival; Gerberoy Rose Festival; Beauvais 'Jeanne Hachette' Festival (commemorating the town's resistance in 1472)

Jul Guiscard, Noyonnais Son et Lumière Festival; Pierrefonds Festival; St-Michel-en-Tiérache, Holy, Ancient & Baroque Music Festival; Noyon Red Fruits Festival; Laon 'Promenades au crepuscule' (visits & entertainment); St Riquier Classical Music Festival

Aug Laon Music and Monuments; Ailly sur Noye Son et Lumière

Sep Amiens Water Festival; La Capelle International Cheese Festival; Ailly sur Noye Son et Lumière; Guise Festival at the Castle; throughout Picardy 'Festival of the Cathedrals' (classical & choral music); Pontpoint Jazz in Moncel Abbey; Laon French Music Festival

Oct Oise Classical Music Festival; Versigny Plant Fair

Nov Amiens International Film Festival

Dec Chantilly, 'Christmas, the horse and the child' (riding show in costume at the Living Museum of the Horse)

Home of the Impressionist Movement
The visual intensity of Picardy's scenery has inspired many artists; particularly those of the Impressionist movement, which has its roots here. The light Claude Monet discovered in Giverny so impressed him that he lived there for most of his life. You can enjoy the collection of Japanese prints exhibited in his house, then stroll in the sun-filled gardens which inspired so many of his pictures. Walk across the Japanese-style wooden bridge and you can almost imagine yourself in one of his famous water lily paintings.

ABBEVILLE Somme

La Maison Carrée-Bonance (Prop: J et M Maillard)
Port-Le-Grand 80132
☎ 322241197 FAX 322316377
Near sea Near beach Forest area
Closed mid Dec-mid Feb
6 en suite (bth/shr) Full central heating Open parking available Supervised Child discount available 2yrs Outdoor swimming pool (heated) Languages spoken: English & German
ROOMS: s 300FF; d 380FF *
CARDS: ▒ Travellers cheques

ARGOULES Somme

Abbaye de Valloires
80120
☎ 322296233 FAX 322296224
Cistercian monastery on the Picardy coast, built in the twelfth century and then restored in the eighteenth century. Spacious rooms are offered,furnished with antiques and beautiful paintings. Visit the chapel with its ornate gates or the sixteenth century dovecote situated in gardens with over 4000 varieties of plants and bushes. English spoken.
Near river Forest area
Full central heating Open parking available Languages spoken: English
CARDS: ▒ ▒ Travellers cheques

BEHEN Somme

Château des Alleux (Prop: Réne-François de Fontange)
Les Alleux 80870
☎ 322316488
(from Abbeville take A28 towards Rouen, exit at Monts-Caubert, at the stop turn right, then at Les Croisettes turn right & follow signs 'Les Alleux')
In an old family castle with a big garden, set in woodland, guests can enjoy a quiet and comfortable stay. Meals are prepared using fresh fruit and vegetables from the garden.
Near sea Near beach Forest area Near motorway
4 en suite (bth/shr) TV available Full central heating Open parking available Child discount available Languages spoken: English
ROOMS: s 250FF; d 300FF Reductions over 1 night
MEALS: Dinner 130FF

BERZY-LE-SEC Aisne

Ferme Lechelle (Prop: Mme N Maurice)
02200
☎ 323748329 FAX 323748247
This old Picardian farm offers great comfort and space. The large living room has a fireplace which is constantly lit in winter. The garden is peaceful and green. Dinners can be taken with your hosts by request. All food is prepared with local farm produce. English spoken.
Forest area Near motorway
5 rms (1 bth 1 shr) (1 fmly) No smoking on premises TV in 1 bedroom Full central heating Open parking available Covered parking available Child discount available 6yrs

Boule Open terrace V meals Languages spoken: English
MEALS: Dinner fr 100FF*
CARDS: Travellers cheques

BONY Aisne

Ferme-Auberge du Vieux Puits (Prop: M & Mme
Gyselinck)
5 rue de l'Abbaye *02420*
☎ 323662233 FAX 323662527
(25km from Cambrai in the direction of St Quentin)
All bedrooms in this property have kept their original
character. Your hosts are happy to help you discover the local
tourist attractions on offer in this region. Meals available if
requested in advance. Living room with kitchen and
independent access available to guests. Swimming pool in
grounds.
Near motorway
6 en suite (bth/shr) (2 fmly) TV available STV Full central
heating Open parking available Child discount available 8yrs
Outdoor swimming pool Table tennis Last d 21.00hrs
MEALS: Lunch 98-150FF Dinner fr 98FF*
CARDS: ●● ▆

BUICOURT Oise

Bed & Breakfast (Prop: M & Mme Verhoeven)
3 rue de la Mare *60380*
☎ 344823115
(from Gournay-en-Bray take D930. Turn left for Buicourt.
Guest house is in village centre)
Eddy and Jacqueline Verhoeven welcome you to their home in
the countryside, surrounded by forests, flowers and
tranquillity. A choice of restaurants in nearby Gerbury, just
two kilometres away.
Forest area In town centre
2 en suite (bth/shr) Full central heating Open parking
available Child discount available
ROOMS: s 180FF; d 230-250FF Reductions over 1 night

CAMBRONNE-LES-RIBECOURT Oise

Chambres d'Hote Bellerive (Prop: Pauline Brugher)
492 rue de Bellerive *60170*
☎ 344750213
(from A1 junct 12 follow direction Noyon then Compiegne N31
then D66)

Situated in an 'Ancien Corps de Ferme' alongside the canal
L'oise next to the forest of Compiegne. Shops are close by and
Eurodisney, Paris and the champagne area are in about 1hr
travelling time.

Near river Near lake Forest area
5 en suite (bth/shr) Full central heating Open parking
available Child discount available 10yrs Outdoor swimming
pool (heated) Tennis Fishing Riding Boule Bicycle rental
Languages spoken: English
ROOMS: s 190FF; d 275FF Reductions over 1 night Special
breaks
CARDS: Travellers cheques

CAOURS Somme

La Rivierette (Prop: M & Mme de Lamarliere)
2 rue de la Ferme *80132*
☎ 322247749 FAX 322247697
Marc and Hélène, (a former English teacher), and their young
children have six rooms to offer to guests. One room has its
own entrance. The bed & breakfast is situated on the banks of
the Rivièrette. A super restaurant is open nearby but guests
may also cook for themselves in the kitchen provided.
Near river Forest area Near motorway
6 en suite (bth/shr) 1 rooms in annexe (5 fmly) Full central
heating Open parking available Open terrace Languages
spoken: English & German
CARDS: Travellers cheques

CHAPELLE-MONTHODON, LA Aisne

Bed & Breakfast (Prop: M & Mme Christian Douard)
Hameau de Chezy *02330*
☎ 323824766 FAX 323727296
Forest area
(1 fmly) No smoking on premises Child discount available
12yrs Languages spoken: English
CARDS: Travellers cheques

CHARMEL, LE Aisne

Bed & Breakfast (Prop: M & Mme Gaston Assailly)
6 rue du Moulin *02850*
☎ 323703127 FAX 323703127
(A4, exit at Chateau-Thierry, then take D34 towards Dormans.
Follow road through Jaulgonne and onto le Charmel)

This house is located in a quiet village near the Champagne
tourist route. A modern home, set in a large, well-manicured
garden, full of fruit trees and flowers. There are four spacious
and comfortable double rooms. Guests are invited to dine with
their hosts, the Assailly family. Meals are served in the dining
room or on the patio.

cont'd

Near river Near lake Forest area Near motorway
4 en suite (bth/shr) (1 with balcony) No smoking on premises
TV in 40 bedrooms STV Full central heating Open parking
available Child discount available Last d 20.00hrs
ROOMS: s 200FF; d 250FF
MEALS: Dinner fr 130FF
CARDS: ▨

CHÉRÊT Aisne

Le Clos (Prop: Michel Monnot)
02860
☎ 323248064
Five rooms are available on this old farm, dating back to the
eighteenth century. All rooms are spacious and are named
after flowers. A warm welcome awaits you in a relaxing
atmosphere. Dinner available by arrangement and served in
the family dining room (fixed price with wine included). You
will find golf, tennis and beaches all within six kilometres. A
little English spoken.
Near lake Forest area
Closed 15 Oct-15 May
5 rms (3 bth/shr) (1 fmly) Full central heating Open parking
available Child discount available Languages spoken: English
MEALS: Dinner fr 90FF*
CARDS: Travellers cheques

CHIGNY Aisne

Melle Piette
(Prop: Françoise & Bernadette Piett)
6 et 7 pl des Maronniers *02120*
☎ 323602204
(from St Quentin take N29 through Guise towards la Capelle.
Right for Chigny)

Your hosts welcome you to their eighteenth century home
surrounded by a flower garden. Evening meals including wine
are available on request. A very relaxing time will be enjoyed
here.
Near river Near lake Forest area Near motorway
7 rms (2 bth/shr) (2 fmly) Full central heating Open parking
available Covered parking available Supervised Child
discount available V meals
ROOMS: s 180-190FF; d 250-270FF Reductions over 1 night
MEALS: Dinner fr 90FF
CARDS: ▨ Travellers cheques

CROTOY, LE Somme

Villa "La Mouclade" (Prop: M & Mme C Weyl)
Quai Jules Noiret, plage Promenades *80550*
☎ 322270944 FAX 322278829
(from Calais to Abbeville, D40 to Le Crotoy, in town go right
towards "La Plage" along rue Desjardins, Victor Pelletier,
Gourlain, Victor Petit; house on sea front)

The owners of this house combine their enthusiasm for
French cuisine and good wines. Guests are welcomed to a
comfortable home with an upper-floor dining room terrace
looking over the beautiful Bay of Somme.
Near sea Near beach Near motorway
5 en suite (bth) (1 with balcony) TV in all bedrooms Full
central heating Languages spoken: English German & Italian
ROOMS: (room only) s 320FF; d 380FF
MEALS: Dinner 160-210FF

ÉPINE-AUX-BOIS, L' Aisne

Les Patrus (Prop: Mary-Ann Royal)
02540
☎ 323698585 FAX 323699849
Stone-built farmhouse dating back to the sixteenth century,
situated in seven hectares of land and with a lake for fishing
enthusiasts. A peaceful holiday is assured in the heart of this
pretty countryside. Traditional fresh food served in generous
proportions. Two pianos and television available. Special rates
for families and friends booking together. Ideal for cycle rides
or those who enjoy walking. Good English spoken.
Near river Forest area
6 en suite (bth/shr) (2 fmly) Full central heating Open
parking available Child discount available Languages
spoken: English & German
CARDS: ▨

LANDOUZY-LA-VILLE Aisne

Bed & Breakfast (Prop: M Jean Tirtiaux)
02140
☎ 323984344 FAX 323984499
Near river Near lake Forest area Near motorway
3 en suite (bth/shr) TV in all bedrooms Full central heating
Open parking available Supervised
ROOMS: s 220FF; d 260FF
CARDS: Travellers cheques

MAILLY-MAILLET Somme

Les Bieffes (Prop: M Harle d'Hermonville)
27 rue Pierre Lefebvre *80560*
☎ 322762144
(A1 exit Albert, Mailly-Maillet is on the D919)
Situated at the end of the village , next to the 1916 Somme-Battlefield. During the first World War the house was used as a first-aid hospital.
Near river Forest area
3 en suite (bth/shr) No smoking on premises TV in all bedrooms Full central heating Open parking available Child discount available 10yrs Languages spoken: English
ROOMS: d 180-250FF
MEALS: Dinner fr 120FF*

MAZIS, LE Somme

Bed & Breakfast (Prop: Onder Delinden)
80430
☎ 322259010 322259088 FAX 322257604
Guest rooms and an apartment, which has a kitchen and accommodates up to six people, are available in this large house. There are beautiful views from the house, with sloping fields leading to wooded hills. The apartment has a kitchen. Large breakfast provided by your Dutch hosts.
Near river Forest area
4 en suite (shr) Full central heating Open parking available Languages spoken: Dutch

MONT-ST-PÈRE Aisne

Bed & Breakfast (Prop: M & Mme Comyn)
7 bis rue Fontaine Ste-Foy *02400*
☎ 323702879 FAX 323703644
Your proprietors, Jean and Marie-Claire Comyn are winemakers and welcome you to their traditional home, nine kilometres from Château-Thierry. The wine grown is from the Champenois, a Mont Saint Père grape. The rooms are welcoming and have separate entrances plus communal living room, which opens out onto a flower-filled patio. A little English spoken.
Near river Forest area Near motorway
Closed Jan
2 en suite (bth/shr) Open parking available Supervised Covered terrace
CARDS: 💳 📧

NEUILLY-EN-THELLE Oise

Les Relais du Thelle
16 Hameau Belle *60530*
☎ 344267112 FAX 344749129
(leave Beauvais in direction of Paris N1 at Ste Genevieve turn left in direction Neuilly en Thelle, through Neuilly turn right for le Belle)
Le Relais du Thelle enjoys an exceptional position and is surrounded by magnificent forests criss-crossed by many bridle paths, and is the ideal venue for those who would like an equestrian holiday. It has about 10 horses for hacking and six more are used for trotting, whilst the proprietor Jean-François Favier is a qualified riding instructor. The rooms are functional with private facilities, and a variety of leisure options are on offer.

Forest area Near motorway
4 en suite (shr) Full central heating Open parking available Riding
ROOMS: s 185FF; d 250FF Reductions over 1 night

QUERRIEU Somme

Château de Querrieu (Prop: Yves D'Alcantara)
11 rue du Bois Galhaut *80115*
☎ 322401555 322401342 FAX 322401753
(8km from Amiens on the D929)
Situated on an old farm looking out onto a central courtyard. All rooms have exposed beams and are comfortable and well-furnished. Continental breakfast served. Children up to five years go free. English spoken.
Near river Near lake Forest area
5 en suite (bth/shr) (1 fmly) TV available Full central heating Open parking available Covered parking available Supervised Child discount available Languages spoken: English

ST-LÉGER-EN-BRAY Oise

Domiane du Colombier (Prop: M Menard)
1 Grande rue *60155*
☎ 344476716 FAX 344477263
(from Rouen take main route to N31 turn left at Rainvillers in direction of St Léger-en-Bray)
A property of charm and harmony, dating from the 18th century, in four hectares of park.
Near river Near lake Forest area Near motorway
3 en suite (shr) Full central heating Open parking available Child discount available 12yrs Fishing Languages spoken: English
ROOMS: s 240FF; d 350FF Reductions over 1 night
MEALS: Continental breakfast 30FF Lunch 65FF

STE-CROIX Aisne

La Besace (Prop: Jean Lecat)
21 rue Haute *02820*
☎ 323224874 FAX 323224874
(off N44 Laon-Reims road)

Five guests rooms available in a pretty village fifteen kilometres from Laon. Meals available by reservation. Table-tennis, volley ball and bikes available on-site.
Near lake Forest area Near motorway
RS 1 Oct-31 Mar, by reservation

cont'd

5 en suite (shr) (1 fmly) Full central heating Open parking available Covered parking available Supervised Child discount available 10yrs Boule V meals
ROOMS: s 185FF; d 220FF
MEALS: Lunch fr 90FF
CARDS: ▩ Travellers cheques

VÉZILLY Aisne

Bed & Breakfast (Prop: M & Mme Noel)
6 rte de Fisnes *02130*
☎ 323692411 FAX 323692411
Rooms available in the pretty village of Tardenois, in a lovely house built in local style. Tennis, golf and riding close by. Mountain bikes and table-tennis available on site.
Forest area Near motorway
2 en suite (bth) (1 fmly) TV available Full central heating Open parking available Covered parking available Supervised Open terrace Table tennis
CARDS: Travellers cheques

VIC-SUR-AISNE Aisne

Domaine des Jeanne (Prop: M & Mme Martner)
r Dubarle *02290*
☎ 323555733 FAX 323555733

Constructed in 1611, this house was once the property of Napoleon's finance minister and sits in a 2.5 hectare park which leads down to the river. All the bedrooms open out onto the park and guests may use the swimming pool and tennis court. The house is sometimes used for conferences and social gatherings. Shops nearby. English spoken.
Near river Forest area In town centre Near motorway
5 en suite (shr) (3 fmly) TV in all bedrooms Radio in rooms Full central heating Open parking available Child discount available 8yrs Outdoor swimming pool (heated) Tennis Fishing Boule Mini-golf Bicycle rental Open terrace Table tennis Last d 20.00hrs Languages spoken: English
ROOMS: d 320-370FF Special breaks
MEALS: Dinner fr 95FF
CARDS: ⊕ ▩ Travellers cheques

L'Orchidee (Prop: M & Mme Henry)
2 bis Av de la Gare *02290*
☎ 323553276 FAX 323559398
(from A1, exit for Compiegne and onto Vic-sur Aisne)
Situated one hour's drive from Paris in an old, half-timbered country house, three spacious family rooms are available which will sleep up to five persons. Ample French breakfast served. Gastronomic meals are offered, with regional specialities, by reservation only. Children's games and barbecue on-site. English spoken.
Near river Forest area In town centre
5 en suite (shr) (2 fmly) Full central heating Open parking available Supervised Child discount available 12 yrs Barbecue Languages spoken: English, German & Spanish
ROOMS: s 180FF; d 210FF Special breaks: (discount for more than 3 nights)
MEALS: Dinner 75-75FF*
CARDS: Travellers cheques

VILLERS-AGRON Aisne

Ferme du Château (Prop: Xavier et Christine Ferry)
02130
☎ 323716067 FAX 323693654
(On A4 between Paris and Reims, take exit 21 then take road on right towards Villers Agron)
This fifteenth century restored house, is set on a farm on the borders of Champagne and Picardy. Ideal location for visits to Reims and Epernay. Guest are invited to dine with the family. Reductions for stays of one week. English spoken.
Near river Near lake Forest area Near motorway
4 en suite (bth/shr) (1 fmly) TV in all bedrooms Full central heating Open parking available Covered parking available Child discount available 12 yrs Tennis Fishing Bicycle rental Last d 18.00hrs Languages spoken: English German
ROOMS: s 320-410FF; d 350-410FF Reductions over 1 night Special breaks: (7 nights for price of 6)
MEALS: Dinner 170FF
CARDS: Travellers cheques

VILLERS-SUR-AUTHIE Somme

La Bergerie (Prop: M et Mme P Singer de Wazières)
80120
☎ 322292174
Near river Near sea Near beach Forest area Near motorway
2 en suite (bth/shr) No smoking on premises TV in 1 bedroom Full central heating Open parking available Languages spoken: English
ROOMS: d 320FF Reductions over 1 night

HISTORY ON THE SOMME

Battle fields of the Somme

The Somme is a calm and winding river, it brings life to a myriad of lakes, joining a thousand streams which refresh lush woods and deep valleys. In this tranquil landscape it is difficult to imagine the destruction that this region faced in 1916. The war graves, cemeteries and impressive monuments recall the most terrible battles fought during the First World War. A visit to the fascinating and unique Historial de la Grand Guerre at Péronne offers a global view of the conflict. The museum gives an insight into a situation which undoubtedly involved the largest number of armies of different nationalities. Portrayals of life at the front and behind the lines are exhibited and the importance of the civilian population during the war is explored.

Gargoyles on the church at St Valery. It was from this town that William the Conqueror set off with a fleet of 400 ships to invade England.

A short distance away, the Grottes de Naours is a most interesting place. Burrowed into a wooded hillside above the village are 30 tunnels and 300 separate rooms including chapels and stables, used as hide-outs in times of danger and invasion from the Gallo-Roman era to the 18th century. They were also adopted by salt smugglers and used as stores for the British Army in wartime.

The Somme is a place of exchange, where armies, battle fronts and frontiers have come and gone, but where peace and co-operation treaties have been agreed. Monuments, cathedrals, châteaux and churches have been created over history bearing witness today to the strong Picardy identity.

Champagne-Ardenne

The region of Champagne-Ardenne is world famous for its wine and it is worth taking the opportunity to visit one of the many vineyards to gain an insight into how the emperor of celebratory wines is made. Champagne-Ardenne offers a huge variety of sights and attractions that a short break or longer holiday can be enjoyed at any time of year. Stretching from the Belgian border, and not an onerous drive from Calais, this region has all the assets for an ideal family destination: active holidays amidst protected countryside with wonderful food and traditions rooted in a landscape steeped in history. Champagne-Ardenne is a region of variety and many pleasures, but beware, the sampling the rich history of gastronomy could put pressure on your waistline after a visit here.

(Top): The impressive interior of a church at St-Amand-sur-Fion.

(Bottom): An atmospheric scene from the Mercier Champagne catacombs in Épernay.

ESSENTIAL FACTS

DÉPARTEMENTS:	Ardennes, Aube, Haute-Marne, Marne
PRINCIPAL TOWNS	Troyes, Charleville-Mézière, Reims, Chaumont, Chalons-Sur-Marne, Langres
PLACES TO VISIT:	Reims cathedral; Montmort-Lucy castle; the Saturday market at Charleville-Mézière and see their animated clock come alive on the hour; the viaduct at Chaumont and the lapidary exhibits in the Museum of Archeology
REGIONAL TOURIST OFFICE	16 boulevard Carnot, 10000 Troyes. Tel: 25 82 62 70 3 quai des Arts, 51000 Chalons-Sur-Marne. Tel: 26 65 17 89
LOCAL GASTRONOMIC DELIGHTS	Wild boar; boudin blanc - a white pudding from Rethel; smoked Ardennes ham; folies Troyennes - praline pastry puffs; local cheeses such as brie de Meaux and chaource
DRINKS	Casibel - cider with cassis and lemon; ratafia - a champagne liqueur; and that most famous of drinks: champagne
LOCAL CRAFTS WHAT TO BUY	Crystal glass from Bayel; cutlery from Nogent; basket work and willow weaving from Fayl-Billot; puppets from Charleville-Mézières

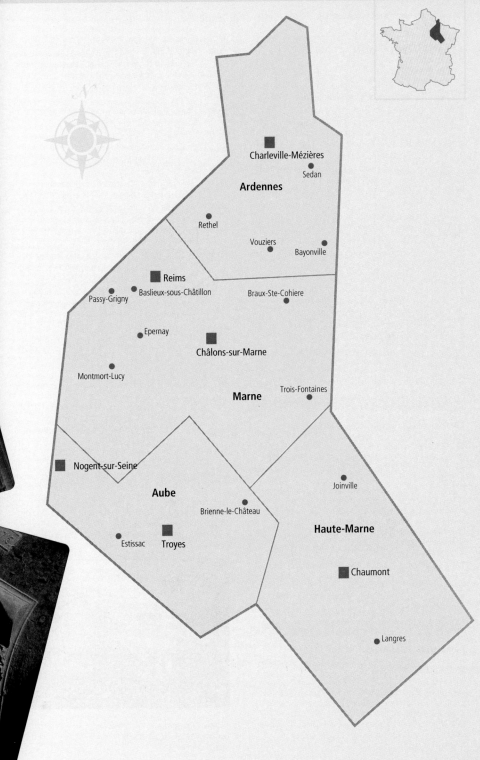

Charleville-Mézières

Sedan

Ardennes

Rethel

Vouziers

Bayonville

Reims

Passy-Grigny Baslieux-sous-Châtillon

Braux-Ste-Cohiere

Epernay

Châlons-sur-Marne

Montmort-Lucy

Trois-Fontaines

Marne

Nogent-sur-Seine

Joinville

Aube

Brienne-le-Château

Haute-Marne

Estissac Troyes

Chaumont

Langres

EVENTS & FESTIVALS:

Jan Joinville Winter Festival

Mar Poucy La Nuit de la Chouette; Tintamars (March Madness) - music & comedy in numerous villages in southern Haute-Marne;

Apr Sedan Arts Festival & Craft Market;

May Sedan European Rally Jamboree; Revin Bread Festival; Troyes Champagne Fair;

Jun Sedan Medieval Fair; Reims Folklore Festival Celebration of St Joan; Trois-Fontaines Horse & Carriage Festival; Chaumont International Graphic Art Fair; Châlons-Sur-Marne Furies Festival (street theatre & circus artists); Launois-sur- Vence Art & Creative Crafts Festival; Braux Ste-Cohière Festival at the Castle (chamber music & exhibitions) (till early Sept); Reims Summer Music Festival (150 free concerts until mid-Aug)

Jul Aube Wine Festival; Bastieux-sur-Châtillon Champagne Festival Tourist Route; Langres July Festival (Sats & Suns); Vendresse Light & Sound Show at Cassina Castle; Joinville "Grand Jardin" concert in the castle & all over the department (till Aug); Chaumont L'Eté en Fête (till mid-Aug);

Aug Estissac Local Food Fair; Aube Wine Festival; Langres Halbardiers' Round - spectators mix with the cast & become actors for an evening (Fris & Sats); Aube (Othe & Amance) Festival - theatre, jazz, rock;

Sep Brienne-le-Château Choucroute Festival; Montier-en-Der Thursdays at The Stud (Haras) - horses & carriages in ceremonial dress at 3pm; Brienne-le-Château Sauerkraut Fair; Charleville-Mézières World Puppet heatre Festival

Oct Sedan Model Collectors Fair; Reims Marathon; Montier-en-Der Thursdays at The Stud (Haras) - horses & carriages in ceremonial dress at 3pm; Reims Marathon; Reims Octob'rock festival; Troyes Nights of Champagne (voice festival)

Nov Montier-en-Der Thursdays at The Stud Farm - horses & carriages in ceremonial dress at 3pm

Dec Braux-Ste-Cohière Shepherds' Christmas - traditional gathering of shepherds in the Castle on Christmas Eve, with music followed by midnight mass.

BAYONVILLE Ardennes

Château de Landreville (Prop: D Meixmoron)
08240
☎ 324300439 FAX 324300439
(from Reims take (RD380) D980 to Mazagran,then D947 to Buzancy. Take D12 to Bayonville,then Landreville.Signposted from Buzancy)
Guests are received at this twelfth century château and its neighbouring lodge. In addition to a warm welcome, your hosts are very knowledgeable about the region and will be happy to help you arrange your holiday itinerary. Children under five stay free. A little English spoken.
Near river Near lake Forest area
Closed Dec-Mar
4 en suite (bth/shr) (3 fmly) Full central heating Open parking available Child discount available 5yrs Languages spoken: English
ROOMS: s 380FF; d 420-470FF * Reductions over 1 night
CARDS: Travellers cheques

ESTISSAC Aube

Domaine du Moulin (Prop: Edouard Mesley)
10190
☎ 325404218 FAX 325404092
Built in 1255 and set in a leafy, flower-filled garden beside a clear running river, this guesthouse is part of an old flour mill which has been superbly renovated. Restaurant available, which seats eighty people, or guests are invited to eat with their hosts. Specialities include trout and salmon (both fresh and smoked). An exquisite setting. English spoken.
Near river Forest area

5 en suite (bth/shr) (1 fmly) No smoking on premises TV available Full central heating Open parking available Supervised Child discount available V meals Languages spoken: English, German & Spanish
MEALS: Dinner 98FF*
CARDS: Travellers cheques

MATOUGUES Marne

La Grosse Haie
chemin de St Pierre *51510*
☎ 326709712 FAX 326701242
(A26 exit St Gibrien onto N27 after toll on to D3 in direction of Epernay)

3 en suite (bth/shr)
ROOMS: s 195FF; d 255-265FF *
MEALS: Dinner 90FF*

MONTMORT-LUCY Marne

Ferme de Bannay (Prop: M & Mme Curf)
51270
☎ 326528049 FAX 326594778
The Curf family is happy to welcome you to Brie
Champenoise, and to share their evening meal where
specialities could include guinea-fowl served with apples and
cabbage, hot beef, farm cheeses and home-made jam.
Relaxation is the order of the day here. English spoken by
some members of the family.
Forest area
3 en suite (bth) TV in 1 bedroom Licensed Child discount
available V meals Languages spoken: English
CARDS: Travellers cheques

PASSY-GRIGNY Marne

Le Temple (Prop: Michel and Chantal Le Varlet)
51700
☎ 326529001 FAX 326521886
A working farm in the heart of the country. Close by are the
champagne vineyards of Reims and Epernay. Dinner is taken
with your hosts. Some English spoken.
Forest area Near motorway
9 rms (4 shr) Full central heating Open parking available
Supervised Child discount available -2 yrs Last d 19.30hrs
Languages spoken: English
ROOMS: s 280FF; d 300FF
MEALS: Dinner fr 120FF*
CARDS: Travellers cheques

VOUZIERS Ardennes

Le Pied des Monts
Grivy-Loisy *08400*
☎ 324719238 FAX 324719621
Le Pied des Monts offers two guest rooms, the larger one is an
apartment accommodating four people with sitting room, TV,
phone and private bathroom on the ground floor and sleeping
accommodation on a mezzanine-floor. The other bedroom is
laid out in a traditional way with double bed as well as private
facilities.
Near river Near lake Forest area
6 en suite (bth/shr) (4 fmly) TV in 5 bedrooms Full central
heating Open parking available Child discount available
10yrs
ROOMS: (room only) s 200FF; d fr 200FF * Special breaks
MEALS: Continental breakfast 25FF Lunch 65-110FF Dinner
65-110FF*
CARDS: ● ▄

Lorraine Vosges

This northern region is best known for its spa towns, lakes, winter sports resorts and eclectic architectural heritage, which includes Gothic cathedrals in Metz and Toul, Gallo-Roman remains in Bliesbruck, and ravishing Art Nouveau in Nancy. It also possesses the largest area of woodland in France, notably the Haye Forest, Charlemagne's former hunting ground. Even a high-tech industrial city like Nancy is not without a natural charm, being completely surrounded by a network of delightful waterways. Lorraine's social calendar is impressively wide-ranging. Events range from medieval fairs and avant-garde music, to the curious Trout and Ice Cream Festival.

(Top): These elegant gates in Nancy are a fine example of the largely intact 18th-century planning which makes the heart of the town so attractive.

(Bottom): Unusual monument to the children of Hattonchâtel killed in WWI.

ESSENTIAL FACTS

DÉPARTEMENTS:	Moselle, Meuse, Meurthe-en-Moselle, Vosges
PRINCIPAL TOWNS	Bar-Le-Duc, Briey, Metz, Nancy, Epinal, Verdun
PLACES TO VISIT:	The many vineyards of the Vosges; the splendid red sandstone church of Marmoutier; Notre-Dame Cathedral at Verdun; the 16th Century Château de la Varenne at Haironville; Nancy School Museum at Nancy
REGIONAL TOURIST OFFICE	1 place Gabriel Hocquard, BP 81004, 57036 Metz. Tel: 87 37 02 16
LOCAL GASTRONOMIC DELIGHTS	Rabbit in Mirabelle Jelly; Quiche Lorraine; Carp with Glasswort; vol-au-vents; frogs legs pie; choux puff buns filled with Mirabelle plums; walnut and Vosges honey cake
DRINKS	White wines such as Riesling, Muscat, Sylvaner, Tokay, Pinot Blanc and Pinot Noir. Beer is brewed at the famous Tourtel Brewery in Tantonville. Mineral water from Vittel and Contrexéville
LOCAL CRAFTS WHAT TO BUY	Glassware from Baccarat, Daum, Hartzviller, Portieux, Meisenthal, St-Louis and Vannes-le-Châtel; pottery, enamelware and "Chinese ware" from Lunéville, St-Clement and Longwy

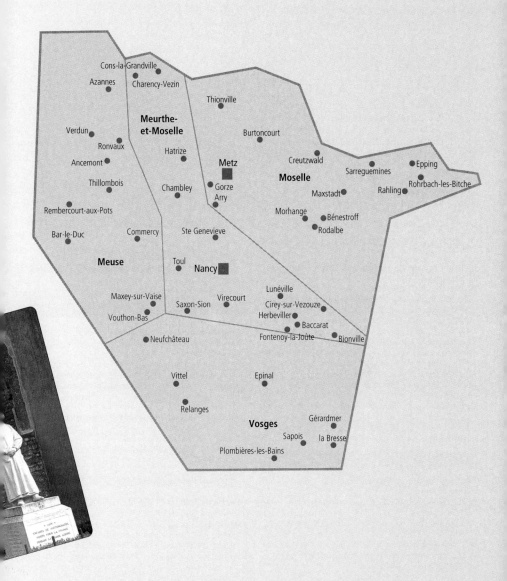

Cons-la-Grandville

Azannes

Charency-Vezin

Thionville

**Meurthe-
et-Moselle**

Verdun

Ronvaux

Burtoncourt

Hatrize

Ancemont

Metz

Creutzwald

Epping

Moselle

Sarreguemines

Rohrbach-les-Bitche

Thillombois

Chambley

Gorze

Maxstadt

Rahling

Arry

Rembercourt-aux-Pots

Morhange

Bénestroff

Bar-le-Duc

Commercy

Ste Genevieve

Rodalbe

Meuse

Toul

Nancy

Maxey-sur-Vaise

Virecourt

Lunéville

Saxon-Sion

Cirey-sur-Vezouze

Vouthon-Bas

Herbeviller

Baccarat

Fontenoy-la-Joûte

Bionville

Neufchâteau

Vittel

Epinal

Relanges

Gérardmer

Vosges

Sapois

la Bresse

Plombières-les-Bains

113

EVENTS & FESTIVALS

Jan Gérardmer Adventure Film Festival; Nancy Photographic Exhibition

Feb Epinal Paper Boat Festival; Nancy Strip Cartoon Festival; Sarreguemines Carnival

Mar Commercy Jazz Festival; Creutzwald Carnival & Pageants; Epinal Classical Music Festival

Apr Toul French Wine Fair; Sarrebourg Ancient Music Festival

May Azannes Romagnes Crafts Festival each Sunday; La Bresse Woodcarving Festival; Domrémy Joan of Arc Festival; Vandoeuvre lès-Nancy Avant-garde Music Festival; Epinal Caricature Festival; Gorze Medieval Fair; Nancy Choral Song Festival; Montmedy City Walls Festival

Jun Lunéville Tableware Festival; Metz Summer Book Festival; Meuse Festival of Organ Music; Nancy Masquerade Puppet Event; Epinal Street Entertainment Festival

Jul La Bresse Forest Festival; Threshing Festival at Maxstadt; Plombières-les-Bains Trout and Ice Festival; St-Dié des Vosges Freedom Week - traditional entertainment & games; Contrexéville Old Crafts & Scenes from 19th century life

Aug Bénéstroff Harvest Festival; Cons-la Grandville Medieval Festival; Contrexéville Fireworks Display; Metz Mirabelle Plum estival; Sapois Loggers Sledging Festival; Madine Lake Festival - concert & fireworks; Jaulny Medieval entertainment plus fireworks; Gérardmer Lights on the Lake - show & fireworks

Sep Baccarat Lorraine Pâté Festival; Lunéville Pumpkin Festival; Vittel International Horse Show

Oct Epinal Theatrical Farce Festival; Nancy International Jazz Festival; Vandoeuvre-lès Nancy Mushers' Race (sledge dog racing); Metz International Fair

Nov Lachaussée Fish Festival; Lindre Basse Grand Fishing Festival; Metz Sacred Songs Festival

Dec St Nicholas Festivals at St-Nicholas-de-Port, Epinal, Metz & Nancy; Christmas markets at Metz & Nancy

ANCEMONT Meuse

Château de Labessière (Prop: M & Mme Eichenauer) *55320*
☎ 329857021 FAX 329876160
Small, eighteenth century château near Verdun. The bedrooms are traditionally furnished and there is a Louis XV bedroom with fireplace available to guests. The quality of the welcome is second to none and guests are assured of delicious home-made meals in the beautiful Louis XVI dining room. A small garden containing a swimming pool can be enjoyed by guests. Nearly covered parking is available. Tandem bikes can be hired. Full breakfast available. English spoken.
Near river Near lake Forest area In town centre Near motorway
11 rms (1 bth 3 shr) (1 fmly) TV available Full central heating Open parking available Child discount available 12yrs Outdoor swimming pool Languages spoken: English & German

ARRY Moselle

Les Fougeres (Prop: Francois Mangin)
25 Grande Rue *57680*
☎ 387528297 FAX 387528297
(off N57)
Situated in the Metz Valley, this house offers all modern comforts but is furnished with antiques. Accommodation can be provided for up to four people. Various sporting pursuits, such as tennis, fishing, horse-riding and swimming are within in short distance. English spoken.

Near river Near lake Forest area Near motorway
3 en suite (bth/shr) Radio in rooms Full central heating Open parking available Child discount available 12yrs Languages spoken: English
CARDS: Travellers cheques

AZANNES Meuse

Chambres d'Hôtes (Prop: Francois Fazzari)
9 route de Mangiennes *55150*
☎ 329856188
An extremely quiet, lush area in pleasant surroundings near the vineyards of Moselle and Meurthe Moselle. Many tourist sites to explore in the area. Children up to six years go free.
Near river Near lake Forest area Near motorway
3 en suite (bth/shr) (1 fmly) (1 with balcony) TV available Radio in rooms Full central heating Open parking available Covered parking available Supervised Child discount available Languages spoken: Italian
ROOMS: s 190-240FF; d 350FF *
CARDS: ▨ ▩

BIONVILLE Meurthe-et-Moselle

Ferme du P'tit (Prop: M & Mme Hoblingre)
Les Noires Colas *54540*
☎ 329411217
Modern, spacious bed & breakfast, with two rooms with balcony. This property is situated in the middle of a beautiful area of the Massif Vosgien, offering fabulous views of the mountains. Only five kilometres from a stunning lake. Enjoy the gastronomic delights of Alsace in the local restaurants. English spoken.

Near river Near lake Forest area
3 en suite (shr) (1 fmly) (2 with balcony) Full central heating
Open parking available Supervised Child discount available
12yrs Last d 20.00hrs Languages spoken: English

BURTONCOURT Moselle

Bed & Breakfast (Prop: Alina Cahen)
51 rue Lorraine 57220
☎ 387357265 FAX 387690790
(from Metz take D3 towards Bouzonville.Approx 20kms turn
right for Burtoncourt)
This old house in Lorraine is found in the heart of a small
village surrounded by forests. This peaceful site has direct
access to a small lake. Just sixty kilometres from Luxembourg
and close to Germany, this is a good base from which to plan
your visits to places of interest. Swimming, tennis and fishing
are available on site. Organic food served. Vegetarian meals
on request. English spoken.
Near lake Forest area
No smoking on premises TV in 1 bedroom Radio in rooms
Full central heating Open parking available Languages
spoken: English & Polish
ROOMS: d 250FF
MEALS: Dinner 70-95FF

CHARENCY-VEZIN Meurthe-et-Moselle

L'An X12 (Prop: Viviane Jakircevic)
4 rue Coquibut 54260
☎ 382266626 FAX 382266626
Nineteenth century building with guest rooms situated on one
floor. Each room has its own kitchen and living room, with
stone fireplaces. Oak doors and beams all lend character to
this home. Large garden. Situated in the centre of a small
village, which sits on the borders of Belgium and
Luxembourg. English spoken.
Near river Near lake Forest area Near motorway
5 rms (1 bth 2 shr) (2 fmly) No smoking on premises TV
available STV Radio in rooms Full central heating Open
parking available Child discount available Open terrace
Languages spoken: English & German
MEALS: Dinner fr 65FF*

CIREY-SUR-VEZOUZE Meurthe-et-Moselle

Bed & Breakfast (Prop: Monique Bouvery)
18 rue du Val 54480
☎ 383425838 FAX 383425150
Bedrooms are situated on the first floor. Lounge with
fireplace; billiards room. Surrounded by a large park, this area
is suitable for walking, or there are bicycles for hire. You are
invited to join your hosts for dinner. A little English spoken.
Near river Forest area
5 en suite (bth/shr) Full central heating Open parking
available Child discount available Last d 18.00hrs Languages
spoken: English
MEALS: Dinner 70-100FF*

EPPING Moselle

Bed & Breakfast (Prop: M & Mme R Faber)
34a rue de Rimling 57720
☎ 387967612
(from A4 exit south of Saarbrucken and take N61 to
Sarreguemines. From there take N62 towards Bitche. Turn L
onto D34 to Epping)

The village in which the property is situated forms part of the
Parc Naturel Régional des Vosges du Nord. The region is a
paradise for hikers and full of historical interest- the Maginot
Line Park, Franc-Roman archaeological sites, châteaux, etc.
There are several restaurants available in the village. Leisure
pursuits include swimming, riding, fishing and golf.
Near river Near lake Near beach Forest area
2 en suite (shr) (2 fmly) No smoking on premises TV in 1
bedroom STV Radio in rooms Full central heating Open
parking available Covered parking available Child discount
available 5yrs Languages spoken: German
ROOMS: d fr 180FF Reductions over 1 night

HATRIZE Meurthe-et-Moselle

La Trembloisière (Prop: M Arizzi)
54800
☎ 382331430 FAX 382201555
(from A4 exit Jarny and take N103)
La Trembloisière is a modern farmhouse set in the heart of the
Lorraine countryside. Breakfast is served either in the dining
room or on the terrace. The champagne region and the
comfort of the house will bring you peace and relaxation. The
rooms are comfortable and well appointed. The gardens are
neatly kept. Office with phone and photocopier are available.
Parking is enclosed within the grounds. English spoken.
Near river Near lake Forest area Near motorway
5 en suite (bth/shr) No smoking on premises Radio in rooms
Full central heating Open parking available Languages
spoken: English
CARDS: Travellers cheques

HERBEVILLER Meurthe-et-Moselle

Bed & Breakfast (Prop: M & Mme Bregeard)
7 r Nationale 54450
☎ 383722473 FAX 383722473
(from Nancy or Luneville take the direction of Strasbourg)
Your young hosts, Gilbert and Brigitte, will give you a warm
welcome to their old Lorraine farm. Living room, television,
open-fireplace, garden with patio and games area are all
available for your use. You are invited to dine with your hosts.
Near river Forest area Near motorway
2 en suite (bth/shr) (1 fmly) Full central heating Open
parking available Child discount available
ROOMS: s 160FF; d 230FF
CARDS: Travellers cheques

MAXEY-SUR-VAISE Meuse

Bed & Breakfast (Prop: Daniella Cardot)
55140
☎ 329908519 FAX 329908288
(in centre of village)
Near river Forest area Near motorway
2 en suite (shr) Full central heating Open parking available
Languages spoken: English & German
CARDS: Travellers cheques

MORHANGE Moselle

La Musardière Lidrezing (Prop: M & Mme Mathis)
Lidrezing 57340
☎ 387261405 FAX 387864016
Cécile, René and their children are pleased to welcome you to
their home. They will prepare evening meals using local fresh
cont'd

115

farm produce and traditional recipes. Fireplace in living room. Playground for children. English spoken.
Near lake Forest area
Closed Nov-Mar
3 en suite (bth/shr) (1 fmly) No smoking on premises TV available Radio in rooms Full central heating Open parking available Covered parking available Child discount available 8 yrs Fishing Boule V meals Languages spoken: English & German
ROOMS: s 250FF; d 310FF
MEALS: Dinner 110-150FF
CARDS: 👄 🎫

RAHLING Moselle

Bed & Breakfast (Prop: M & Mme Bach)
2 r du Vieux Moulin *57410*
☎ 387098685
An old, renovated mill in the Mosel in the heart of the Northern Vosges. Communal kitchen and living room. Your hosts, M. and Mme. Bach, look forward to welcoming you to this attractive part of France. English spoken.
Forest area Near motorway
3 en suite (shr) (1 fmly) No smoking on premises TV available Radio in rooms Full central heating Open parking available Languages spoken: English & German

RELANGES Vosges

Chateau de Lichécourt (Prop: Elisabeth Labat)
88260
☎ 329093530 FAX 329098534
17th century house offering two suites, one with a canopied bed and a child's bed; the other on the first floor, with a mezzanine floor. Continental breakfast. Bikes are available and there are walks in the forest. English spoken.
Near river Near lake Forest area Near motorway
Closed Oct-Apr
2 en suite (bth/shr) (1 with balcony) TV available Full central heating Open parking available Supervised Child discount available 5yrs Languages spoken: English & Spanish
CARDS: Travellers cheques

REMBERCOURT-AUX-POTS Meuse

Bed & Breakfast (Prop: Marie-Christine Oury)
24 r des Cordeliers *55250*
☎ 387606810 329706263
An imposing house set in an enclosed garden and surrounded by parkland. There is a sitting room available for guests' use. Near to the forest of Argonne.
Near river Forest area
1 en suite (bth/shr) No smoking on premises Radio in rooms Full central heating Open parking available Child discount available

RODALBE Moselle

Bed & Breakfast (Prop: Robert Schmitt)
26 r Principale *57340*
☎ 387015670 387015665 FAX 387015019
Situated within six kilometres from Morhange, in a tranquil atmosphere close to forests and lakes. This farm, which produces foie gras, offers five very pretty rooms, with canopied beds, mini-bar and telephone. Fishing available in

private lake. Mountain bikes available free-of-charge. Dinner available; local produce used.
Near lake Forest area
5 en suite (bth/shr) (1 fmly) TV available Full central heating Open parking available Child discount available Languages spoken: German
CARDS: 🎫 Travellers cheques

ROHRBACH-LÈS-BITCHE Moselle

Bed & Breakfast (Prop: Marlyse & Rene Neu)
40 r des Verges *57410*
☎ 387027123
Accommodation is available on the first floor of this family home which looks out onto a pretty park. The rooms are comfortable and clean. Breakfasts are ample. Dinner by arrangement. English spoken.
Near river Forest area Near motorway
3 en suite (shr) (1 fmly) (2 with balcony) No smoking in all bedrooms TV available Radio in rooms Full central heating Open parking available Child discount available Table tennis Barbecue Languages spoken: English & German
CARDS: Travellers cheques

RONVAUX Meuse

Le Logis des Côtes (Prop: Mme Marie Jose Wurtz)
4 rue Basse *55160*
☎ 329873221
(A4 exit Ville en Woevre-direction Fresnes en Woevre D908, then direction Verdun D903 after Manheulles take D24 for Ronvaux)
Situated in a small country village at the foot of the Côtes de Meuse, near to Verdun. Communal rustic living room with fireplace. Dinner available at a fixed price, including wine. Garden games and bikes available. A little English spoken.
Near river Near lake Near sea Forest area Near motorway
Closed Nov-Mar
2 en suite (bth/shr) (1 fmly) (1 with balcony) No smoking on premises Full central heating Open parking available Covered parking available Child discount available 8yrs Bicycle rental Languages spoken: English & German
ROOMS: s 190FF; d 230FF Reductions over 1 night Special breaks: 10% off if stay is longer than 3 nights
MEALS: Dinner 80FF
CARDS: Travellers cheques

STE-GENEVIÈVE Meurthe-et-Moselle

Ferme Auberge St Genevieve (Prop: Marc Gigleux)
4 rte de Bezaumont *54700*
☎ 383822555 FAX 383822555
(A31 enter Nancy et Matz exit 27 (Atton-Nomeny) in direction Nomany)
Accommodation offered on a working farm. Two rooms overlook the Moselle Valley. Possibility of dining with your hosts, where regional specialities will be served. English spoken.
Near river Forest area Near motorway
3 en suite (bth/shr) (1 fmly) No smoking on premises TV available Radio in rooms Full central heating Child discount available 10yrs Last d 20.30hrs Languages spoken: English & German
MEALS: Dinner 60-80FF*
CARDS: Travellers cheques

SAXON-SION Meurthe-et-Moselle

Les Grands Champs (Prop: M T Leclerc)
54330
☎ 383251033 FAX 383251024
Country home in an exceptional setting with breathtaking hilltop views offers self-catering flat and bed & breakfast accommodation. The flat caters for six people and has a fully equipped kitchen. Guest rooms are available, with private bathroom and lounge with television. Super hiking country. Region rich in history. English spoken.
Forest area
2 en suite (bth/shr) Full central heating Open parking available Supervised Child discount available Languages spoken: English

THILLOMBOIS Meuse

Le Clos du Pausa (Prop: Mme Lise Dufour-Tanchon)
r du Château
☎ 329750785 FAX 329750072
All the bedrooms are named after flowers, and include three family rooms, with views overlooking parkland. There is a large lounge with open fire and dinner available by arrangement.Table tennis is available. English spoken.
Near river Near lake Forest area
4 en suite (bth/shr) (3 fmly) No smoking on premises Radio in rooms Full central heating Open parking available Covered parking available Child discount available 8yrs Boule Last d 21.00hrs Languages spoken: English
ROOMS: s 250-300FF; d 300-400FF Reductions over 1 night Special breaks
MEALS: Dinner 130-150FF
CARDS: Travellers cheques

VIRECOURT Meurthe-et-Moselle

Bed & Breakfast (Prop: M & F Beyel)
14 r de la Republique *54290*
☎ 383725420 FAX 383725420
At the foot of the Vosges mountains, three spacious rooms are offered in a renovated country house of character. Small kitchen for guests' use. Communal use of dining room, games area and barbecue. Reductions for stays of more than three nights.
Near river Near lake Forest area Near motorway
3 en suite (shr) (2 fmly) No smoking on premises TV available Full central heating Open parking available Supervised Child discount available Languages spoken: Portuguese
CARDS: Travellers cheques

VOUTHON-BAS Meuse

Bed & Breakfast (Prop: Simone Robert)
55130
☎ 329897400 FAX 329897442
Two comfortable guest rooms, furnished in Lorraine style, are available in this country house. One room will take up to four people. The other accommodates three. Dining room and terrace available to guests, where breakfast is often served.
Near river Forest area Near motorway
2 en suite (shr) TV available Radio in rooms Full central heating Open parking available Covered parking available Supervised

Alsace

Alsace prides itself on being the smallest region in France and with its unique blend of German and French influences, distilled over a thousand years, makes this tiny province a popular tourist destination. Enjoying its own special identity, which is not quite German nor wholly French, the local customs, folklore, dances and dialects are fervently preserved.

(Top): The black grapes of the Rhein Valley.

(Bottom): The château and church at Eguisheim, home of the 11th-century Pope Léon IX. Much of the town is built on a plan of concentric circles which was used for 1200 years.

ESSENTIAL FACTS

DÉPARTEMENTS:	Bas-Rhin, Haut-Rhin
PRINCIPAL TOWNS	Strasbourg, Colmar, Mulhouse, Haguenau
PLACES TO VISIT:	Petite France area of Strasbourg; the Krutenau district of Colmar, Castle of Haut-Koenigsbourg; old St Bartélemy mine at Ste-Marie-aux-Mines; Mont Ste-Odile pilgrimage centre plus the opportunity to walk some of the old pilgrim paths in the area; the Éco-musée de Haut Alsace near Guebwiller, reconstruction of traditional homes, farms and workshops showing the domestic life of past generations
REGIONAL TOURIST OFFICE	26 avenue de la Paix, 67080 Strasbourg Tel 88 25 01 66
LOCAL GASTRONOMIC DELIGHTS	Munster cheese, choucroute/sauerkraut (cabbage) cooked in Riesling or Kirsch, perhaps with Strasbourg sausage or pork chops; turkey cooked with chestnuts; fricassée of chicken with cream; pâté de foie gras with trufffles; kougelhopf, Alsatian cake; baeckoffe, stew; trout; venison; snails; blueberries; cherries; gingerbread
DRINKS	Famed white wines such as Riesling, Sylvaner, Gewürztraminer, Tokay; Crémant is a sparkling Alsace wine made using the Champagne method; German-sounding beers brewed in the region; eaux de vies of Kirsch (cherry), Mirabelle (plum) or Framboise (raspberry).

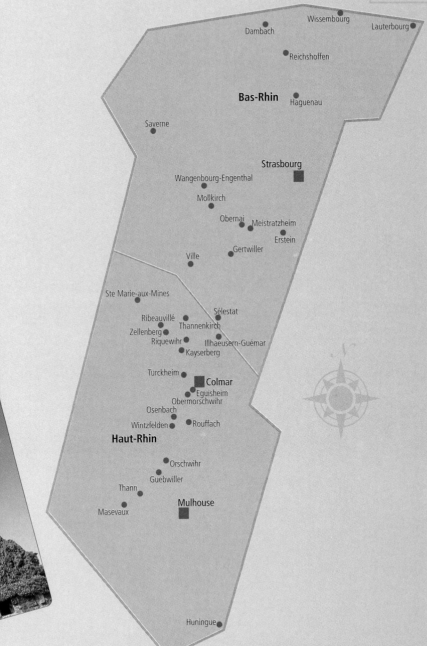

Wissembourg

Dambach

Lauterbourg

Reichshoffen

Bas-Rhin Haguenau

Saverne

Strasbourg

Wangenbourg-Engenthal

Mollkirch

Obernai
Meistratzheim

Erstein

Gertwiller

Ville

Ste Marie-aux-Mines

Sélestat

Ribeauvillé
Thannenkirch

Zellenberg

Riquewihr

Illhaeusern-Guémar

Kayserberg

Turckheim

Colmar

Eguisheim

Obermorschwihr

Osenbach

Wintzfelden
Rouffach

Haut-Rhin

Orschwihr

Guebwiller

Thann

Mulhouse

Masevaux

Huningue

EVENTS & FESTIVALS

Mar Masevaux Passion Play; Strasbourg Carnival and International Calvacade;

Apr Kayserberg Painted Easter Egg Market; Osenbach Snail Festival; Strasbourg Light & Sound Show at the Cathedral;

May Haguenau Humorous Notes Festival; Mulhouse Bach Festival; Strasbourg Light & Sound Show at the Cathedral; Guebwiller Wines Fair; Mulhouse International Exhibition and Fair

Jun Riebauville Kougelhopf Festival; Mulhouse Bach Festival; Strasbourg Music Festival; Turckheim Round of the Night Watch; Colmar Folk Art Performances; Saverne Rose Fair; Ste-Marie-aux-Mines International Mineral Market;

Jul Colmar Classical Music Festival; Strasbourg Music Festival; St-Pierre-Bois Light & Sound Show; Strasbourg Light & Sound Show at the Cathedral; Colmar Folk Art Performances; Zellenberg 'S'Wielada" (*Alsatian wine-making traditions*); Orschwihr Grand Crémant Night; Illhaeusern Boatmen's Fair; Thannenkirch Cherry Festival; Mutzig Parade of the 'Sans-Culottes'; Rouffach Witch Festival; Husseren-les-Châteaux Open-Air Café Festival; Dambach Blueberry Festival; Hunawihr Ami

Fritz Folklore Festival; Stotzheim Harvest Festival

Aug Lauterbourg Rock Festival; Thann Classical Music Festival; Mulhouse Jazz Festival; Strasbourg Romanesque Festival (*medieval music in the churches along the Romanesque route*); Strasbourg Light & Sound Show at the Cathedral; Turckheim Round of the Night Watch; Zellenberg 'S'Wielada" (*Alsatian wine-making traditions*); Guebwiller Open Air Folk Festival; Colmar Wines Fair; Rosheim Munster Cheese & Folk Festival; Gertwiller Gingerbread & Wine Festival

Sep Sélestat Gregorian Music Festival in Ste-Foix Church; Ribeauvillé Ancient Music Festival; Strasbourg Musica (contemporary music); Strasbourg European Fair; Riquewihr Wine Festival; Meistratzheim Sauerkraut Festival; Wuenheim New Wine Festival & Procession

Oct Strasbourg Light & Sound Show at the Cathedral; Turckheim Round of the Night Watch; Grape Harvest Festivals at Barr & Obernai;

Nov Mulhouse Antiques Fair; Christmas Markets at Strasbourg and Kaysersberg

Dec Christmas Markets at Strasbourg and Kaysersberg; Huningue Feast of St Nicholas; Riquewihr Christmas Market

---

MOLLKIRCH Bas-Rhin

Fischutte (Prop: Schahl)
rte de Grendelbruch *67190*
☎ 388974203 FAX 388975185
Near river Forest area
Closed 16 Feb-14 Mar
17 rms (5 bth 10 shr) (2 fmly) (6 with balcony) TV in all bedrooms STV Full central heating Open parking available Supervised Child discount available 10yrs Last d 21.00hrs
Languages spoken: English & German
CARDS: ☎ 🎫 ✖ 💳 Travellers cheques

VILLE Bas-Rhin

La Maison Fleurie (Prop: Mme Doris Engel-Geiger)
19 route de Neuve Eglise, Dieffenbach-au-Val *67220*
☎ 388856048 FAX 388856048
Set into the hillside in a small, village, this typical Alsacienne house has a profusion of flowers spilling from window boxes in the garden and the house. Large, peaceful garden. All rooms are pleasant and have their own bathroom facilities. Home-made Kougelhopfs (a type of bun) feature in the large, traditional breakfast. English spoken.
Forest area
(1 fmly) No smoking on premises Full central heating Open parking available Child discount available Childs play area
Languages spoken: English & German
ROOMS: s 220FF; d 240-260FF

ALSACE

The Rich Heritage of Colmar

At the heart of the Route du Vin lies the small but influential town of Colmar. The largely unspoilt centre with its pattern of winding streets and half-timbered houses (many of which are colourfully painted) is ideal for an afternoon stroll or an exploration of historical architecture. Also ideal for exploration

Colmar by night.

is the Musée Unterlinden which is second only to the Louvre in the number of visitors it attracts. One of its most famous exhibits is Matthias Grünewald's 'Issenheim Altarpiece'. Another artistic

Colmar's town hall is topped by glorious polychrome roof tiling.

element of the town's heritage is provided by Colmar-born sculptor Auguste Bartholdi, who often visited the Unterlinden in search of inspiration. His most famous work is New York's 'Statue of Liberty' which was unveiled in 1886. The town has a museum devoted to his life and work. The town is also blessed with many other beguiling features such as 'La Petite Venise' along the Lauch, the church of St-Martin (which is notable for its 14th-century Crucifixion), the refurbished Quartier des Tanneurs, and the 15th-century Koïfhus, which is now the town hall.

Western Loire

The Atlantic coast is a serious rival to the Riviera. There are 140 km of fine, white sandy beaches which stretch out to the horizon; rocky creeks wait to surprise and delight and with 210 days of sunshine each year, this must be a perfect holiday destination. The coastline is splashed with charming fishing villages and sophisticated resorts offering extensive sports and leisure facilities. The invigorating sea air and famously clear waters should give you an appetite for sampling some of the delicious seafood and regional wines.

(Top): Wherever you go in France it's certain that a wide selection of fresh vegetables will await you at market.

(Bottom): A bizarre inhabitant of the Magic Museum at Saumur.

ESSENTIAL FACTS

DÉPARTEMENTS:	Loire-Atlantique, Maine-et-Loire, Mayenne, Sarthe, Vendée
PRINCIPAL TOWNS	La Roche-sur-Yon, Nantes, Angers, Fontenay-le-Compte; Chateaubriant, les Sables-d'Olonne, Saumur, Le Mans, Laval, Cholet
PLACES TO VISIT:	Visit the Troglodyte caves near Saumur; the Cadre Noir (High School Riding) at Saumur; the historic theme park of the Puy du Fou, the brilliant crescent-shaped beach of les Sables-de-Olonne; the notable châteaux of Brissac, le Plessis-Bourre. le Lude, and Montreuil-Bellay
REGIONAL TOURIST OFFICE	2 rue de la Loire, 44204 Nantes Tel: 40 48 24 20
LOCAL GASTRONOMIC DELIGHTS	Beurre-blanc, a butter sauce usually served with shad or pike; matelote d'anguille, eels stewed in wine; noisette de porc aux pruneaux, fillet of pork in a cream and prune sauce; citrouillat, pumpkin pie; cotignac, delicate apple and almond paste; Petit Lu, these crisp butter biscuits from Nantes have been part of the tradition since the Middle Ages when they were the staple diet of sailors; charcuterie of rillettes, terrines and pâtés of game and foie gras.
DRINKS	Cider and Saumar-Champigny, a light and fruity red wine.
LOCAL CRAFTS WHAT TO BUY	Cloth from Clisson and Cholet famous for their textile industry; traditional wooden crafts from Jupilles; pottery from le Fuilet; fine china from the workshops in Malicorne; silk from the farms in Montreuil-Bellay

Mamers
Champfleur
Monhoudou   la Ferte-Bernard

Sarthe

Montreuil-Poulay   St Calais
Mayenne   **Le Mans**
        Mezangers   Lavenay
Mayenne   Poncé-sur-le-Loir
                            Asnieres-sur-Vegre   Chateau-du-Loir
Laval   Oize Dissay-sous-Courcillon
                    Sablé-sur-Sarthe   la Flèche Mareil-sur-Loir
            St Denis-d'Anjou
Château-Gontier   Durtal
        Ménil
Renazé   la Jaille-Yvon   le Vieil-Bauge
        le Lion-d'Angers   Montreuil-sur-Loir
Chazé-sur-Argos   St Mathurin-sur-Loire   Allonnes
            Grez-Neuville   Fontevraud-
Châteaubriant   **Angers** St Lambert-des-Levees   l'Abbaye
                                            Chemellier   **Saumur**
            St Georges-sur-Loire   Brissac-Quince
                                        Montreuil-Bellay
                        Doué-la-Fontaine
Nozay   le Puy-Notre-Dame
            Ancenis   St Florent-le-Vieil

Loire-Atlantique   **Maine-et-Loire**

Missillac   Cholet
        Besné   **Nantes**
Herbignac
    St Lyphard   Clisson
St Molf   St Malo-de-Guersac   St Lumine-de-Clisson   la Flocellière
St Nazaire
la Turballe   St Michel-Mont-Mercure
    la Baule

                                    St Martin-des-Fontaines
            Challans   la Roche-sur-Yon
Noirmoutier-en-l'Ile   le Perrier   **Fontenay-le-Comte**
        St Jean-de-Monts

                Vendée

            les Sables-d'Olonne

EVENTS & FESTIVALS

Mar Nantes Children's Carnival & Parade; Fontevraud, Holy Week in the Royal Abbey Church (*holy music & medieval games*); Sablé sur-Sarthe Carnival; Champagné 'Lances' Festival (*historical pageant*); St-Etienne de Montluc Daffodil Carnival;

Apr Cholet Harlequin Festival, & Carnival; International Fairs at Nantes & Angers; Le Mans 24-hours of Motorcycling; Nantes Grand Night Parade; Saumur International Horse Show; St Nazaire 'Theatre at Play' Festival; Saumur, Cadre Noir Riding School Displays

May Saumur, Loire Festival & Wine Fair; Nantes Spring Arts Festival; St Gilles-Croix-de-Vie Jazz Festival; Le Mans Festival of Epau Abbey; Saumur International Horse Show;

Jun Anjou Festival, throughout Maine-et-Loire; St Florent-le-Vieil, Asia-West Festival (*music & dance*); Gala evenings at the Cadre Noir Riding School, Saumur;

Jul Doué-la-Fontaine Rose Days (*rose & flower shows*); Challans Historic Fair; Clisson Music Festival; Nantes Summer Festival; Mayenne Nights: concerts in castles & churches throughout Mayenne; La Flèche, Street Theatre Festival; Saumur, Gala evenings at the Cadre Noir Riding School; Le Mans 'Les Cénomanies' (*historical celebrations*); La Ménitré Headwear Festival; Sablé-sur-Sarthe Rockissimo (*children's rock festival*); Clisson Medieval & Classical Music Festival; La Baule International Dance Encounters; Saumur Military Tattoo

Aug Sablé-sur-Sarthe Ancient Dance & Music Festival, & Baroque Festival; St Nazaire Chamber Music 'Consonances' Festival; Angrie Harvest & Old Crafts Festival; Challans Historic Fair; Noirmoutier Vintage Sailing Ship Regatta; Le Perrier Village Fête (*unusual & traditional event*); La Baule Elegance Automobile; Noirmoutier Island Festival (*theatre in castle courtyard*)

Sep Nantes Les Rendez-vous de l'Edre, Saumur International Horse Show; Cadre Noir Riding School Displays, Saumur

Oct Le Mans 24-hours Book Fair; Durtal Curiosity and Bric-à-Brac Fair; Le Mans 24-hours Truck Race; Angers International Horse Show; Angers Antiques Show; Saumur, Cadre Noir Riding School Displays

Nov Nantes Antiques Show; Nantes Three Continents Festival

Dec Brissac Carols & Christmas Market at Castel Festival

ALLONNES Maine-et-Loire

Château "Le Courbet" (Prop: Mme Canivet-Golfar)
49650
☎ 241528365 FAX 241387934
This château dates back to the seventeenth century and is surrounded by orchards and forests, close to La Loire. It has a swimming pool and is close to a wide range of sporting facilities. There is plenty to visit in the region, including local châteaux, caves, abbeys, vineyards, museums and the famous "School of Equestry" and the "Cadre Noir" of Saumur. English spoken.
Near river Near lake Forest area Near motorway
3 en suite (bth/shr) No smoking on premises Full central heating Open parking available No children 14yrs
Languages spoken: English & German
CARDS: Travellers cheques

Manoir de Beauséjour (Prop: Colette Thimoleon)
49650
☎ 241528668 FAX 241388558
Family mansion dating from the seventeenth century, recently restored and decorated. Beauséjour offers you calm and rest against a background of green countryside. The bedrooms are huge, comfortable and luxurious. Your hosts extend a warm welcome to you and will help you to discover the marvels of the Anjou and the Touraine. Facilities include a private heated swimming pool with jacuzzi, games room with billiards, table tennis and library. Bicycles are available for the guests. A good choice of restaurants is available in the vicinity. English spoken.

Near river Forest area Near motorway
3 en suite (bth/shr) No smoking on premises Full central heating Open parking available Child discount available 6yrs
Outdoor swimming pool (heated) Bicycle rental Pool, Table tennis Languages spoken: English
ROOMS: (room only) d 550-750FF Special breaks: (4 nights for the price of 3)
CARDS: Travellers cheques

ASNIÈRES-SUR-VÈGRE Sarthe

Manoir des Claies (Prop: Jean Anneron)
72430
☎ 243924050 FAX 243926572
(from Paris A11 then A81 and D22 towards Sable-sur-Sarthe)
Near river Forest area
4 en suite (bth/shr) (2 fmly) (1 with balcony) Full central heating Open parking available Child discount available

10yrs Fishing Open terrace Last d 22.30hrs Languages
spoken: English
ROOMS: s fr 385FF; d fr 420FF
MEALS: Dinner fr 130FF
CARDS: Travellers cheques

BEAULIEU-SUR-LAYON Maine-et-Loire

Bed & Breakfast (Prop: Mme June Friess)
35 rue St Vincent *49750*
☎ 241786082 FAX 241786082
(from Angers follow direction of Cholet on the N160. Turn left
at crossroads Beaulieu/Layon, the property is situated in the
centre of the village beside the church)
This house dates back to the early 18th century and was once
known as the Old Post Office Inn of the village. All the rooms
are comfortable and nicely decorated.
Near river Forest area Near motorway
4 en suite (shr) (1 fmly) (1 with balcony) No smoking on
premises Full central heating Open parking available
Covered parking available Child discount available 12yrs
Languages spoken: English
ROOMS: s 180FF; d 220FF Reductions over 1 night
CARDS: Travellers cheques

BESNÉ Loire-Atlantique

Les Pierres Blanches
44160
☎ 240013251 FAX 240013818
Near sea Near beach Forest area Near motorway
2 en suite (bth/shr) No smoking on premises TV available
Full central heating Open parking available Supervised
CARDS: Travellers cheques

BRISSAC-QUINCÉ Maine-et-Loire

Bed & Breakfast (Prop: Mme Monique Deforge)
Ste-Anne *49320*
☎ 241912217
(from Angers take D748 towards Poitiers. Exit to Brissac.
House on left, immediately after Domaine Sainte Anne)
Ideally situated for a stopover in the Loire Valley on the 'Route
des Chateaux de le Loire'and 'Route des Vins'. Built by a wine
grower this large house is surrounded by vineyards and has
two guest rooms available.
Near motorway
Closed 1 Nov-30 Apr
2 en suite (bth/shr) (1 fmly) Radio in rooms Full central
heating Open parking available Languages spoken: English
ROOMS: s fr 200FF; d fr 250FF Reductions over 1 night
Special breaks: 10% reduction after 3 nights
CARDS: Travellers cheques

CHAMPFLEUR Sarthe

Garenciere (Prop: Denis & Christine Langlais)
72610
☎ 33317584
Situated in the heart of the rural countryside, this handsome
18th-century farmhouse has individually furnished bedrooms
with private facilities. Meals are taken at the hosts' table and
are prepared with fresh farm produce. The specialities of the
house are poulet aux cidre, canard au vin and tarte du
camembert .
Forest area

5 en suite (shr) Full central heating Open parking available
Covered parking available Boule V meals Last d 8.30pm
Languages spoken: English
ROOMS: s fr 180FF; d 250FF * Reductions over 1 night
MEALS: Dinner fr 100FFalc*
CARDS: Travellers cheques

CHÂTEAU-DU-LOIR Sarthe

Bed & Breakfast (Prop: Mme Le Goff)
22 rue de l'Hôtel de Ville *72500*
☎ 243440338
(at Le Mans take N138 towards Tours. In Chateau du Loir, the
B & B is on the main square behind the bandstand.)
This house was built in 1850 and is situated at the heart of the
of the Loire Valley. Also ideally located for travellers coming
from the car-ferries to the South of France. One of the rooms
has fine views over the oldest parts of the town. The rooms
are comfortable and furnished with antiques. Bikes can be
hired. English spoken.
Near river Near lake Forest area In town centre Near
motorway
Closed Oct-Mar
4 rms (3 shr) (2 fmly) Full central heating Open parking
available Covered parking available Supervised Languages
spoken: English
ROOMS: s 215FF; d 260FF
CARDS: Travellers cheques

CHÂTEAU-GONTIER Mayenne

Château de Mirvault-Azé (Prop: Françoise d'Ambrières)
53200
☎ 243071082 FAX 243071082
(Mirvault is 1km north of the centre of Château-Gontier,
entrance is on the N162 which links Laval/Angers)

A warm welcome awaits you at this chateau, which has been
in the same family since 1573, and was restored in the 19th
century. Situated on the Mayenne River guests enjoy the
beauty and the tranquility of its setting. The elegant rooms
have period furniture and overlook the river. In the evening a
free boat trip can be taken to a small restaurant located on the
opposite bank of the river.
Near river Forest area Near motorway
5 rms (2 bth) TV available Open parking available Covered
parking available Child discount available 5yrs Fishing Open
terrace Languages spoken: English
ROOMS: s 300FF; d 350-400FF Reductions over 1 night
Special breaks: 10% discount for 3 night break
CARDS: Travellers cheques

CHAZE-SUR-ARGOS Maine-et-Loire

La Chaufournaie (Prop: Susan & Peter Scarboro)
49500
☎ 241614905 FAX 241614905
(ignore signs to Chaze-sur-Argos and travel along the D770, situated between the villages of Vern D'Anjou and Angrie)

This 1850's farmhouse standing in its own 44 acres is an ideal base for exploring this area, renowned for the Chateaux, waterways and wine. The south facing garden with sun loungers, giant chess and petanque court are availble to guests. Meals are taken communally, breakfast round the large kitchen table or in the garden, and evening meals can be booked in advance.
Near river Near lake Forest area Near motorway
5 en suite (shr) No smoking in all bedrooms Full central heating Open parking available Child discount available 13yrs Indoor swimming pool (heated) Outdoor swimming pool (heated) Golf Fishing Riding Boule Mini-golf Bicycle rental Games room Languages spoken: English
Rooms: s 200FF; d 230FF Reductions over 1 night Special breaks: Golfing breaks
MEALS: Dinner fr 90FF*

CHEMELLIER Maine-et-Loire

La Poirère (Prop: Eliette Edon)
Maunit *49320*
☎ 241455950
(from D761 south of Angers take D90 on left at les Alleuds.Take 6th exit left, 'la Poirière' on right)
The bedrooms are situated on the first floor and are peaceful and quiet. This is a super environment for relaxing and getting away from it all. Visit the tapestries of the châteaux at Angers. Meals served in the evenings.
Forest area
3 en suite (shr) (1 fmly) Full central heating Open parking available Child discount available 10yrs Pool table Table tennis V meals

DISSAY-SOUS-COURCILLON Sarthe

La Chataigneraie (Prop: Mme M Letanneux)
72500
☎ 243794530
(from N138 just south of Dissay, take left turn onto small road on a bend and follow signs for Chambre d'Hotes. Establishment in 1km)
This establishment has been described 'a fairy tale cottage', built of mellow, old stone, with white shutters and covered in green ivy. Set in the heart of the Loire Valley, in a quiet

location, the rooms overlook fields of sunflowers or the large garden. Guests can use a separate entrance and so can be as independent as they wish. Meals by prior arrangement. Nearby is a 12th-century château. The proprietors will be happy to help organise your visits to local places of interest.
Near river Near lake Forest area Near motorway
Closed Oct-Apr
3 rms No smoking on premises Full central heating Open parking available Supervised Child discount available Tennis
Languages spoken: English & Spanish
ROOMS: s 190FF; d 250FF * Special breaks
MEALS: Dinner 80-90FF*

DURTAL Maine-et-Loire

Château de Gouis (Prop: Mme Linossier)
Grande Rue *49430*
☎ 241760340
This splendid château in the heart of the Anjou region offers you a restful holiday or, if preferred, a sporting holiday. Each room is decorated differently. Breakfasts and home made cakes and jams are served in the house, or on the terrace. Your hosts are pleased to help you discover the region. English spoken.
Near river Near lake Near beach Forest area Near motorway
8 rms (6 bth/shr) (4 fmly) (1 with balcony) Radio in rooms Night porter Full central heating Open parking available Supervised Child discount available 4yrs Fishing Open terrace

Château de la Motte (Prop: Michel Francois)
Baracé *49430*
☎ 241769375
(A11 exit at Durtal, take D859 towards Châteauneuf for 2km, then to the left D68 to Baracé via Huillé)
Near river Near lake Forest area
5 en suite (bth/shr) (1 with balcony) Open parking available (charged) Child discount available Fishing Boule Languages spoken: English & Spanish
ROOMS: (room only) s 350-400FF; d 400-500FF
MEALS: Continental breakfast 25FF Dinner 135FF
CARDS: Travellers cheques

FLOCELLIÈRE, LA Vendée

Château de la Flocellière (Prop: Erika & Sandrine Vignial)
85700
☎ 251572203 FAX 251577521
(from Cholet take N160 towards La Roche. At Les Herbiers take D755 towards Pouzauges.In St Michael-Mont-Mercure take D64 to La Flocellière and follow signs for the Château)
Built beside a 900-year-old castle, located in the heart of the Vendee, which was both a fortress in times of war and the home of poets and famous men in more peaceful times, the chateau's spacious rooms and suites offer guests authentic style with modern comfort. Set in a 15 hectare park, with exotic trees including a gigantic Thuya. Luncheons and dinners are served daily. There is a large outdoor pool, table tennis, billiards and a private library with various games and TV. English spoken.
Near lake Forest area
8 en suite (bth/shr) (1 fmly) TV in 3 bedrooms Full central heating Open parking available Child discount available 12yrs Outdoor swimming pool (heated) Boule Table tennis Billiards Languages spoken: English, German & Italian

ROOMS: (room only) d fr 570FF Reductions over 1 night
MEALS: Continental breakfast 40FF Dinner fr 200FF
CARDS: Travellers cheques

FONTEVRAUD-L'ABBAYE Maine-et-Loire

Le Domaine de Mestre
49590
☎ 241517587 & 241417232 FAX 241517190
This is an immensely attractive house. The oldest part dates
back to the thirteenth century - the stones are traditional
White Loire stone. Originally used as a farmhouse, the same
family has occupied this residence since the eighteenth
century and have recently renovated it. Your hosts look
forward to your visit to this elegant residence and, as an
added bonus, they will provide you with superb food.
Near river Forest area Near motorway
12 en suite (bth/shr)

GREZ-NEUVILLE Maine-et-Loire

La Croix d'Étain (Prop: Auguste Bahuaud)
2 r de l'Ecluse *49220*
☎ 241956849
In town centre Near motorway
4 en suite (bth/shr) Full central heating Open parking
available Child discount available 16yrs Languages spoken:
English
MEALS: Dinner 130FF*
CARDS: Travellers cheques

HERBIGNAC Loire-Atlantique

Château de Coetcaret (Prop: M & Mme de la Monneraye)
44410
☎ 240914120 FAX 240913746
(from Nantes take N165 direction of Vannes before La Roche
Bernard take D774 direction La Baule at Herbignac take D47
for 4kms Coetcaret on left)
This small nineteenth century château is the home of M and
Mme de la Monneraye. Set in 100 hectares, with horse-riding
on site. The bedrooms include two family rooms and are
welcoming and comfortable. Your hostess is a teacher of floral
art and her skills are evident throughout the house. Dinner by
candlelight is offered at your host's table, by prior
arrangement. English spoken.
Forest area
4 en suite (bth/shr) (2 fmly) Full central heating Open
parking available Child discount available Riding Pool table
Boule Bicycle rental Table tennis Languages spoken: English
& Spanish

JAILLE-YVON, LA Maine-et-Loire

Château-du-Plessis-Anjou
49220
☎ 241951275 FAX 241951441
This sixteenth century château combines modern comfort with
romantic, old-world style. Antique furniture and wood
panelling offer a pleasant and comfortable atmosphere.
Continental or English breakfast served. Dinner is served with
your hosts. Tennis, clay pigeon shooting, fishing and walks
available. English spoken.
Near river Forest area Near motorway
Closed Nov-Mar

8 en suite (bth/shr) (3 with balcony) Full central heating
Open parking available Child discount available Solarium
Boule Languages spoken: English & Spanish
CARDS: ●● ▨ ▨ ● Travellers cheques

LAVAL Mayenne

Le Bas du Gast (Prop: François-Charles Williot)
6 r de la Halle aux Toiles *53000*
☎ 243492279 FAX 243564471
(on the south bank of the River Mayenne joining the town hall
square - follow signs - the château is close to the cathedral)

A lovely château in private parkland, yet uniquely situtaed in
the lovely old city of Laval. The building is listed as 17th-18th
century, each room has been carefully retained in its former
magnificence with delicately tinted carved wooden wall
panelling, crested marble fireplaces and furniture of the
period.
In town centre Near motorway
Closed Dec-Jan
5 en suite (bth/shr) (3 fmly) (5 with balcony) Full central
heating Open parking available Child discount available
10yrs Boule Open terrace Special arrangements for AA
guide users Languages spoken: English
ROOMS: (room only) d 550-650FF *
CARDS: ▨

LAVENAY Sarthe

Les Patis du Vergas (Prop: M & Mme J Deage)
72310
☎ 243352818 FAX 243353818

Ideal for those who wish to relax in a peaceful park close to
nature. For anglers there is a 1.2 hectare pond, storage is
cont'd

available for fishing equipment and a fridge for keeping fish fresh. Walking in the nearby Vallee du Loir is popular. Near river Near lake Near sea Forest area
Closed 4 Nov-Feb
5 en suite (shr) TV in 1 bedroom Full central heating Open parking available Child discount available 10yrs Fishing Boule Bicycle rental Croquet Table tennis Sauna Volley ball Last d 8pm Languages spoken: English
ROOMS: s 250-300FF; d 270-330FF Reductions over 1 night
MEALS: Dinner 90FF
CARDS: Travellers cheques

LION-D'ANGERS, LE Maine-et-Loire

Le Petit Carqueron (Prop: M & Mme Carcaillet)
49220
☎ 241856265
(from Le Lion D'Angers take D770 in approx 1.5km Le Petit Carqueron)
This renovated farm dates back 200 years and is situated in the heart of the countryside. Visitors have said that they love the tranquillity of the area. Private swimming pool. The guests' living room has an open fire, and they are invited to take their evening meal with the Carcaillet family, which is served outside, weather permitting. English spoken.
Forest area
Closed Nov-29 Mar
4 rms (1 fmly) (2 with balcony) Open parking available Outdoor swimming pool Fishing Riding Open terrace Languages spoken: English

MAREIL-SUR-LOIR Sarthe

Ferme de Semur
72200
☎ 243454424
(8km NE of the Flèch along N23 towards Le Mans, at Clermont-Créans take D13 towrads Mareil-sur-Loir. The farm is 1km from the village - signposted)
The owners of this 14th century farmhouse are artists, a talent that is evident in the profusion of colours. One kilometre from the village in the heart of the countryside, each of the cosy rooms has its own terraced area. Art classes are available.
Near river Forest area
6 rms (5 bth/shr) No smoking in 1 bedroom Full central heating Open parking available Covered parking available Child discount available 3yrs Fishing Riding Boule Languages spoken: English
ROOMS: s 200-320FF; d 320-350FF Reductions over 1 night

MENIL Mayenne

Les Boisards (Prop: Mme May)
53200
☎ 243702738
(N162 (Laval-Angers). 7km south of Château Gontier turn right towards Molierès (C2) at crossroads Menil/Molierès, farm is 300m on left)
An 18th century farmhouse in classic Mayenne style, with high beamed rooms and metre thick stone walls, set in extensive gardens. Convenient to the N162.
Near river Forest area Near motorway
3 en suite (bth/shr) No smoking on premises Full central heating Open parking available Child discount available 14yrs Fishing Boule V meals Last d 8pm Languages spoken: English & Spanish

ROOMS: s 160FF; d 220FF Reductions over 1 night
MEALS: Dinner 60-80FF
CARDS: Travellers cheques

MÉZANGERS Mayenne

Le Cruchet (Prop: Leopold Nay)
53600
☎ 243906555
(from Laval N157 towards Le Mans at Soulge-sur-Ouette D20 left to Evron then D7 towards Mayenne, in Mezangers signposted)
Marie-Thérèse and Léopold Nay welcome you to their 15th-century house, where two rooms are available for guests, with a garden and parking to the rear of the house. Mme Nay is happy to serve you food. Indoor heated and outdoor swimming pools within five kilometres. Fishing, golf, riding and tennis court within one kilometre. English spoken.
Near lake Forest area
2 en suite (bth/shr) (1 fmly) Full central heating Open parking available Supervised Languages spoken: English
CARDS: ▓ Travellers cheques

MISSILLAC Loire-Atlantique

La Ferme de Morican (Prop: Oliver & Brigitte Cojean)
Morican *44780*
☎ 240883882 FAX 240883882
(From Missillac D2 to St Gildas des Bois, in Perny turn left. From Redion way to Portchateau, in St Gildas des bois D2 to Missillac, in Perny turn right)
A truly different but relaxing holiday can be had at this forty acre stud farm. Horse-and-cart trips available, and guests can learn how to harness a horse (120 francs/hour). Golf is available at nearby Bretesche. English spoken.
Near lake Forest area
5 en suite (bth/shr) (2 fmly) Full central heating Open parking available Fishing Languages spoken: English & Spanish
ROOMS: s 210-240FF; d 250-280FF
MEALS: Dinner fr 140FF
CARDS: Travellers cheques

MONHOUDOU Sarthe

Chateau de Monhoudou (Prop: Michel de Monhoudou)
72260
☎ 243974005 FAX 243331158
(from Paris: exit La Fertie-Bernard" onto D2, after St Cosmen-Vairais go left towards Moncé & Monhoudou: from Alençon: N138 towards Le Mans to Le Hutte then D310, drive 10km & turn right, at Courgains head towards Monhoudou)

Forest area
4 en suite (bth/shr) (4 fmly) Licensed Full central heating
Open parking available Supervised Child discount available
12yrs Outdoor swimming pool (heated) Fishing Bicycle
rental Languages spoken: English
ROOMS: d 450-550FF Reductions over 1 night Special breaks
MEALS: Dinner fr 195FF

MONTREUIL-BELLAY Maine-et-Loire

Démeure des Petits Augustins (Prop: M & Mme
Guezenec)
pl des Augustins *49260*
☎ 241523388 FAX 241523388
(take D147 S from Saumur towards Poitiers for 1.6km. In
Montreuil Bellay, Place des Augustins is parallel to, and on the
left of 'Rue Nationale'- near the church 'Eglise des Grands
Augustins'- and chapelle 'des Petits Augustins')
Attractive seventeenth century building, which belonged
originally to the Champrobert family. All rooms have an open
fireplace and the original beams plus antiques. The
atmosphere is pleasant and calm. The château is situated near
to the town centre. Reductions available for week-long stays.
English spoken.
Near river Forest area In town centre Near motorway
Closed Dec-Mar
3 en suite (bth/shr) (1 fmly) Open parking available
Languages spoken: English
ROOMS: s 200FF; d 290FF
CARDS: ● ▥ ▭ Travellers cheques

MONTREUIL-POULAY Mayenne

Le Vieux Presbytère (Prop: Legras-Wood)
53640
☎ 243008632 FAX 243008142
Two rooms in a wing of an eighteenth century presbytery,
built in the middle of fields. The original beams can still be
seen and the rooms are furnished with antiques. TV plus
satellite available. A large garden with a stream surrounds the
building. Sailing, tennis and riding are close by. English
spoken.
Near river Near lake Forest area Near motorway
2 en suite (bth/shr) Radio in rooms Full central heating Open
parking available Covered parking available Supervised
Open terrace Languages spoken: English, German, Spanish &
Russian
MEALS: Dinner fr 110FF*
CARDS: Travellers cheques

MONTREUIL-SUR-LOIR Maine-et-Loire

Château de Montreuil (Prop: M Balliou)
49140
☎ 241762103
(on the right on leaving the village)
Château constructed in the middle of the nineteenth century
by the Angevin architect, Hodé, following the neo-gothic
"Troubadour" style. Beautiful location overlooking the Loire
Valley. Large wooded park with direct access to the river. One
floor is set aside for guests and a cottage also available. A little
English spoken.
Near river Forest area
Closed 16 Nov-14 Mar
6 rms (2 bth 2 shr) (2 fmly) Open parking available Child
discount available 10yrs Open terrace Boating Last d noon
ROOMS: s 200-300FF; d 350FF Special breaks
MEALS: Dinner fr 120FF
CARDS: Travellers cheques

OIZÉ Sarthe

Château de Montaupin (Prop: M David)
72330
☎ 243878170 FAX 243872625
Located in a small country village, Nicole and Alain welcome
you to their seventeenth century property. Guests may dine
with the family. Private swimming pool, fishing.
Near river Near lake Forest area Near motorway
8 rms (3 bth 3 shr) (3 fmly) Full central heating Open parking
available Supervised Child discount available 10yrs Outdoor
swimming pool (heated) Fishing Covered terrace Last d
20.00hrs Languages spoken: English
ROOMS: d 260-320FF Reductions over 1 night
CARDS: Travellers cheques

PONCÉ-SUR-LE-LOIR Sarthe

Château de La Volonière (Prop: Mme B Becquelin)
72340
☎ 243796816 FAX 243796818
(from Paris on A11 exit La Ferte-Bernard to St Calais and then
in direction of La Charte-sur-Loir to Poncé)
This is an ideal spot to tour the châteaux of the Loire. Your
hosts, Brigitte and Claude Becquelin, have been restoring this
charming old château. They will be happy to pass on their
knowledge of the area to guests. English spoken.
Near river Near lake Forest area In town centre
Closed Dec-Feb
6 rms (5 bth/shr) (1 fmly) Radio in rooms Full central heating
Open parking available Child discount available 12yrs

LA POSSONNIÈRE Maine-et-Loire

La Rousselière (Prop: Mme J Charpentière)
49170
☎ 241391321 FAX 241391321
(at Angers take N20 towards Nantes, in St Georges-sur-Loire
turn left on D961 towards Challonnes for 3km; just before
railway bridge turn left on D111 towards La Possonnière,
continue for 1.5km & turn left)
This beautiful 18th century residence on the slopes of the
Loire has kept its old world charm. Enjoy breakfast and dinner
on the terrace. A good location with atmosphere and a warm
welcome.

cont'd

Near river
Closed mid Nov-mid Dec
6 en suite (bth/shr) (6 fmly) (1 with balcony) TV in 3
bedrooms Full central heating Open parking available Child
discount available 10yrs Outdoor swimming pool Fishing
Boule Bicycle rental Trampoline, ping-pong Languages
spoken: English
ROOMS: d 300-400FF Reductions over 1 night
MEALS: Dinner 90-150FF

PUY-NOTRE-DAME, LE Maine-et-Loire

Le Moulin de Couché (Prop: Jean Francois Berville)
49260
☎ 241388711 FAX 241388699
Near river Near lake Near sea Forest area
9 en suite (bth/shr) (3 fmly) No smoking in all bedrooms TV
available Open parking available Supervised Child discount
available Last d 22.00hrs Languages spoken: English
CARDS: ⊕ ▥ ⧈ Travellers cheques

RENAZÉ Mayenne

Le Petit Bois Gleu (Prop: M & Mme Goodman)
53800
☎ 243068386 FAX 243068386
This old farmhouse, nestles in an unspoilt corner of the Loire.
A paradise for painters, birdwatchers and ramblers. Fresh,
local, home-grown produce prepared and served by Paul,
either in the vaulted dining room or under the shade of the
trees. Your hostess is an artist and offers special painting
holidays to budding artists.
Near river Near lake Near sea Forest area Near motorway
5 en suite (shr) (1 fmly) No smoking on premises Open
parking available Child discount available Boule Open
terrace Painting courses V meals Last d 21.00hrs Languages
spoken: English
ROOMS: s fr 200FF; d fr 300FF Special breaks
MEALS: Dinner 75-95FF
CARDS: Travellers cheques

ST-CALAIS Sarthe

Le Boulay (Prop: Mme Guillon)
Conflans sur Anille *72120*
☎ 243350741
(D98 towards Semur and 3kms after Conflans-sur-Anille
passing the church, take left turning 20mtrs after cross-roads)
Edwige Guillon, your hostess, is an artist. Her home is
charming and is situated in the heart of the country by a large
forest. Here you will find a calm and relaxing atmosphere.
Tennis available. Large continental breakfast served. English
spoken.
Forest area Near motorway
Closed 16 Nov-Mar
2 en suite (bth/shr) No smoking on premises Full central
heating Open parking available Languages spoken: English
& Spanish

ST-DENIS-D'ANJOU Mayenne

Le Logis du Ray (Prop: M & Mme Lefebure)
53290
☎ 243706410 FAX 243706553
(at 9km SW de Sable-sur-Sarthe take D309 then D27 in
direction of Angers)

Martine and Jacques welcome you to their old home, built in
1830. The substantial breakfast is served in the cosy dining
room in winter, and in the garden in summer. Your host offers
you a horse and cart ride through the medieval village of St.
Denis. English spoken.
Near lake
Closed Jan
3 en suite (shr) (2 fmly) No smoking on premises TV
available Full central heating Open parking available Child
discount available 12yrs Bicycle rental Last d prev day
Languages spoken: English
MEALS: Dinner 130FF*
CARDS: ⊕ ▥ Travellers cheques

ST-GEORGES-SUR-LOIRE Maine-et-Loire

Prieure de L'Épinay (Prop: Mme Genevieve Gaultier)
49170
☎ 241391444 FAX 241391444
(from St Georges-sur-Loire take N23 for 1 km in direction of
Nantes then turn left for Prieure de l'Epinay)
Situated in charming countryside, with the Loire, vineyards
and the châteaux all at hand. The history of the old priory
combined with the comfort of the large rooms and home
made food mixed with the pleasure of the outdoor pool, all
readily awaiting visitors.
Near river
Closed 1 Nov-31 Mar
3 en suite (bth/shr) (3 fmly) TV in all bedrooms STV Full
central heating Open parking available Child discount
available 4 yrs Outdoor swimming pool Fishing Bicycle
rental Last d 19.00hrs Languages spoken: English
ROOMS: s 350FF; d 400FF
MEALS: Dinner 120FF
CARDS: Travellers cheques

ST-LAMBERT-DES-LEVEES Maine-et-Loire

La Croix de la Voulte (Prop: Jean Pierre & Helga
Minder)
rte de Boumois *49400*
☎ 241384666 FAX 241384666
(from the train station of Saumur follow the D229 in direction
of St Lambert-des-Levees. After leaving village continue on
D229 for 1500m - property signed)
La Croix de la Voulte has a very long history dating from
between the 15th and the end of the 17th century. Throughout
time buildings were added around the grand courtyard
including the manor house with its low-arch windows, carved
oak panelling and Louis XIV fireplace. The guest rooms have
been renovated in traditional style and are equipped with all
modern comforts.
Near river
Closed 2 Oct-Apr
4 en suite (bth/shr) Open parking available Outdoor
swimming pool Languages spoken: English & German
ROOMS: (room only) s 330-430FF; d 330-430FF
MEALS: Full breakfast 35FF
CARDS: Travellers cheques

ST-LUMINE-DE-CLISSON Loire-Atlantique

Le Tremblay (Prop: Mme Jacqueline Bossis)
44190
☎ 240547111
Set in a wine-growing region, this modern solar-powered
house has two guest rooms with independent access. There is

a quiet garden, full of flowers, to relax in. French breakfast is served and dinner can be eaten with the hosts by arrangement. Nearby you will find canoeing and kayaking. English spoken.
Near river Forest area
2 en suite (shr) Full central heating Open parking available Child discount available 2yrs Languages spoken: English

ST-LYPHARD Loire-Atlantique

Le Pavillon de la Brierie (Prop: Mme Anny Hulcoq)
23 rue des Aubrépines *44410*
☎ 240914471 FAX 240913468
Near river Near lake
4 en suite (bth/shr) No smoking on premises TV available Full central heating Supervised

ST-MALO-DE-GUERSAC Loire-Atlantique

25 Errand Ty Gween (Prop: M & Mme Collard/Lecarrer)
44550
☎ 240911504
(from St Nazaire to Nantes road take D50 Montoir de Bretagne)
Situated by the National Brière Park, on the Ile d'Errand, this thatched cottage offers a romantic and peaceful stopover. Dinners may be taken with your hosts. Barge rides, fishing, swimming and golf on offer nearby.
Near river
Closed Oct-Feb
4 en suite (shr) No smoking on premises TV in all bedrooms Full central heating Open parking available Child discount available 2yrs
MEALS: Dinner 90FF
CARDS: Travellers cheques

ST-MARTIN-DES-FONTAINES Vendée

Roselyne Garreau (Prop: Mme Porcher)
85570
☎ 251001262 FAX 251877974
(turn right off the N148 just north of Fontenay-le-Comte, take D30/D99 or D14 all these roads lead to St Martin-des Fontaines)

Built in 1930, the gîtes are situated in a working farm in the south of the Vend region, close to the Marais Poitevin. Tastefully restored in 1993, the interiors have been given a face-lift and visitors are welcomed by a roaring log-fire. As well as the normal private facilities, there is a swimming pool, a terrace with barbecue and a sauna for every gîte. For those who like a more energetic holiday, mountain-bikes are for hire, and there is a track in the immediate vicinity.

Near river Forest area Near motorway
5 en suite (shr) Covered parking available Child discount available 5yrs Outdoor swimming pool (heated) Tennis Fishing Riding Mini-golf Bicycle rental
ROOMS: s 200FF; d 400FF Reductions over 1 night Special breaks
MEALS: Dinner 100FF*

ST-MATHURIN-SUR-LOIRE Maine-et-Loire

Verger de la Bouguetterie (Prop: Mme C Pinier)
118 rue du Roi Rene *49250*
☎ 241570200 FAX 241573190
Claudine Pinier looks forward to welcoming guests to her home, built in the nineteenth century. Rooms are spacious and well-lit , overlooking the garden and the Loire. Two new rooms have been built in converted outbuildings, decorated in a rustic manner, with kitchenette and independent entrance. Summer house in garden, with games for the children. English spoken.
Near river Forest area
6 en suite (shr) (3 fmly) No smoking in 3 bedrooms Full central heating Open parking available Child discount available 7-15yrs Outdoor swimming pool (heated)
Languages spoken: English
ROOMS: s 215-275FF; d 290-340FF Reductions over 1 night Special breaks
MEALS: Dinner 110FF&alc
CARDS: ●● ▬ Travellers cheques

ST-MOLF Loire-Atlantique

Kervenel (Prop: J Brasselet)
44350
☎ 240425038
Individually-styled spacious rooms available in this old stone house, built in 1869, and now entirely restored. One room is in rustic style, one in Louis-Philippe style and the third is contemporary. Living room with television and library. Quiet is assured in this country location, just three kilometres from the sea. English spoken.
Near sea Near beach Forest area
Closed Apr-Oct
6 rms (3 shr) No smoking on premises Full central heating Open parking available Supervised Child discount available 3yrs Languages spoken: English & German
CARDS: Travellers cheques

SAUMUR Maine-et-Loire

La Bouère Salée (Prop: E Bastid)
rue Grange Couronne, des Levées *49400*
☎ 241673885
(from A85 head into Saumur centre, do not cross the Loire, at the Renault garage, turn right, the rue Grange Couronne is the first right and the house entrance is the first gate on the right)
Restored by a young couple and their four children, this house is prettily decorated and furnished. Your hosts have a shop selling natural produce in the town and they serve delicious organic produce for breakfast at the family table, or in fine weather, in the shaded park. Ideal base from which to visit the châteaux of the Loire. English spoken.
Near river Forest area Near motorway

cont'd

4 rms (3 bth/shr) (1 fmly) (1 with balcony) TV in 1 bedroom
Full central heating Open parking available Child discount
available 12yrs Languages spoken: English
ROOMS: s 200FF; d 250-350FF
CARDS: Travellers cheques

Château de Beaulieu (Prop: Andre Michaut)
rte de Montsoreau *49400*
☎ 249676951 FAX 249504268
(in Saumur, head towards Chinon (D947), house is next to the
caves 'Gratien and Meyer', on the border of the Loire)
Small, attractive, 18th-century château surrounded by a large
park. The rooms are comfortable, with antique furniture and
canopied beds. Heated swimming pool, billiards and park at
the disposal of guests. Evening meals by reservation. Golf,
tennis and riding nearby. English spoken.
Near river Forest area Near motorway
Closed Dec & Jan
6 en suite (bth/shr) (1 fmly) Full central heating Open
parking available Child discount available 4yrs Outdoor
swimming pool (heated) Languages spoken: English &
German
ROOMS: s 250-400FF; d 300-450FF Reductions over 1 night
MEALS: Dinner 120-200FF
CARDS: ● ▆

TURBALLE, LA Loire-Atlantique

Ker Kayenne
744 Bd de Lauvergnac *44420*
☎ 240627430 FAX 240628338
Near sea Near beach Forest area
Closed 16 Nov-14 Mar
8 en suite (shr) (2 fmly) Full central heating Open parking
available Outdoor swimming pool (heated)

VIEIL-BAUGÉ, LE Maine-et-Loire

La Chalopinière (Prop: M & Mme Kitchen)
49150
☎ 241890438 FAX 241890438
(from Le Mans follow road for Saumur, pass through Fleche to
Baugé, at traffic lights on Baugé by-pass turn right to Vieil
Baugé, through village approx 2km from church)
John and Vanessa Kitchen welcome you to their home which
is an ideal base for touring the area. Guests live and eat with
the family. Table-tennis, garden room and barbecue available.
Reductions for children. English spoken.
Forest area
3 en suite (bth/shr) (3 fmly) Full central heating Open
parking available Child discount available 12yrs Outdoor
swimming pool Tennis Riding Bicycle rental Table tennis
Last d 1800hrs Languages spoken: English
ROOMS: d 250FF
MEALS: Dinner 85FF
CARDS: Travellers cheques

MEDIEVAL LIFE IN WESTERN LOIRE

A Summer Day Out in a Recreated Medieval Village

South of the Loire river, amidst unspoilt countryside, lies the theme park at Puy de Fou. From June to September, for a fascinating and unusual family day out, this reconstructed and animated medieval village should give plenty of enjoyment. Set amidst 30 hectares of meadows and woods you can discover a delightful water theatre, hear traditional musicians play, and watch a show of stunt riding and horsemanship staged close to a Renaissance château. See a collection of ancient animal breeds and an awesome display of falconry. In the centre of the park, flanked by towers, a feudal enclosure recreates a bustling Medieval market place. A different world and constantly

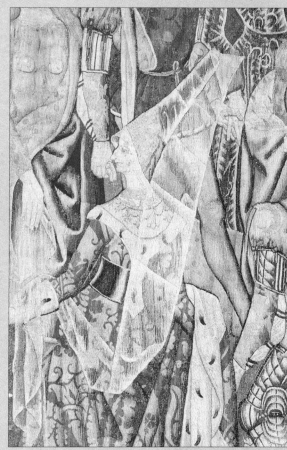

changing scene lies just across the draw-bridge, where you can experience the smell of freshly baked bread and hear the gossip as it echoes round the narrow alleys. A herbalist, glassblower, stone carver and manuscript illuminator display their wares and entertain. Minstrels draw you deeper into this clever illusion until you are part of the dream. An evening at the Cinescenie will draw the day to an unforgettable finale with an impressive display of fireworks, lasers, music and fountains.

The splendour of medieval life: A detail from the 15th-century tapestry 'Les Bals des Sauvages'

Val de Loire

Described as the "historic cradle of the kingdom of France", the gentle climate of the Loire Valley nurtures some truly beautiful sights. Chief among them are the seemingly limitless number of majestic castles, cathedrals and châteaux: awesome "cathedral of cathedrals" at Chartres, pinnacle of medieval Christian art and architecture; the gothic splendour of St-Etienne Cathedral at Bourges. Vast, sun-drenched vineyards yield characterful wines from Sancerre, Menetou-Salon and Touraine, while famous Orléans, capital city of the old kingdom during the 10th and 11th centuries, basks under the spiritual protection of Joan of Arc.

Two fine examples of the many châteaux that are scattered throughout the region. Azay-le-Rideau (top), erected between 1518 and 1527, and Sully-sur-Loire (bottom), which is a medieval fortress with extensive 17th-century additions.

ESSENTIAL FACTS

DÉPARTEMENTS:	Eure-et-Loire, Loiret, Loir-et-Cher, Indre, Indre-et-Loire, Cher
PRINCIPAL TOWNS	Chartres, Orléans, Blois, Tours, Bourges, Châteauroux
PLACES TO VISIT:	The milky-white Renaissance châteaux of the Loire - there are over 150 in the area so it pays to be selective. The more notable ones include Amboise, Beauregard, Blois, Chambord, Cheverny, Chenonceau and Villesavin. Visit also Sologne - a region of wild forest and heath broken by streams and innumerable lakes.
REGIONAL TOURIST OFFICE	Conseil Regional, 9 r St-Pierre-Lentin, 45041 Orléans. Tel: 38 54 95 42
LOCAL GASTRONOMIC DELIGHTS	Fresh fish: brochet (pike), carpe (carp) and saumon (salmon), cooked with sorrel or butter, vinegar and shallot sauce; asparagus; mushrooms; rillettes, cold potted pork; pork with prunes (a specialty of Tours); tarte Tatin, a caramelized upside-down apple pie.
DRINKS	There are many distinctive wines of the Loire region: dry whites and reds from Touraine, the richer reds from Bourgueil and the flinty-tasting white from Sancerre.
LOCAL CRAFTS WHAT TO BUY	Goat's cheese from Berry; spicy partridge and duck pâté from Chartres; and "cotignac", a delicately coloured quince jelly from Orléans.

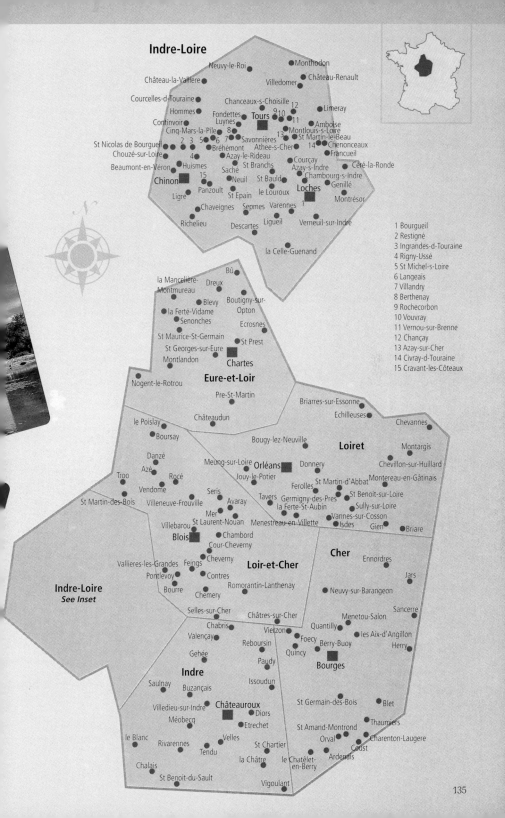

Indre-Loire

Neuvy-le-Roi • Monthodon
Château-la-Vallière • Château-Renault
Villedomer •

Courcelles-d-Touraine •
Chanceaux-s-Choisille 12
Hommes • Fondettes 9 10 • Limeray
Continvoir • Luynes 11 Amboise
Cinq-Mars-la-Pile 8 Montlouis-s-Loire
2 3 5 6 7 Savonnières 13 St Martin-le-Beau
St Nicolas de Bourgueil Bréhémont Athee-s-Cher 14 Chenonceaux
Chouzé-sur-Loire 4 Azay-le-Rideau Courçay Francueil
Beaumont-en-Véron Huismes St Branchs Céré-la-Ronde
Chinon 15 Saché Neuil St Bauld Azay-s-Indre Chambourg-s-Indre
Ligre Panzoult St Epain le Louroux Loches Genillé
Chaveignes Sepmes Varennes Montrésor
Richelieu Descartes Ligueil Verneuil-sur-Indre

la Celle-Guenand

Tours

Loches

Chinon

1 Bourgueil
2 Restigné
3 Ingrandes-d-Touraine
4 Rigny-Ussé
5 St Michel-s-Loire
6 Langeais
7 Villandry
8 Berthenay
9 Rochecorbon
10 Vouvray
11 Vernou-sur-Brenne
12 Chançay
13 Azay-sur-Cher
14 Civray-d-Touraine
15 Cravant-les-Côteaux

Bû •
la Mancelière- Dreux •
Montmureau • Boutigny-sur-
Blevy • Opton
la Ferté-Vidame • Senonches Ecrosnes •
St Maurice-St-Germain • St Prest •
St Georges-sur-Eure •
Montlandon • Chartres

Eure-et-Loir

Nogent-le-Rotrou •
Pre-St-Martin •
Briarres-sur-Essonne •
le Poislay • Châteaudun Echilleuses •
Boursay • Chevannes •
Bougy-lez-Neuville •
Danzé • Montargis •
Azé • Meung-sur-Loire Orléans Donnery Chevillon-sur-Huillard •
Troo • Rocé • Jouy-le-Potier Montereau-en-Gâtinais •
Vendome Seris Ferolles St Martin-d'Abbat St Benoit-sur-Loire
St Martin-des-Bois • Villeneuve-Frouville Avaray Tavers Germigny-des-Pres Sully-sur-Loire
Mer la Ferte-St-Aubin Vannes-sur-Cosson
Villebarou • St Laurent-Nouan Menestreau-en-Villette Isdes Gien Briare
Blois Chambord
Cour-Cheverny

Loiret

Orléans

Vallieres-les-Grandes Feings Cheverny Ennordres •
Pontlevoy Contres Loir-et-Cher Jars •
Indre-Loire Bourre Chemery Romorantin-Lanthenay Neuvy-sur-Barangeon
See Inset Selles-sur-Cher Châtres-sur-Cher Sancerre •
Chabris Menetou-Salon
Valençay Vietzon Quantilly les Aix-d'Angillon
Reborsin Foecy Berry-Buoy Herry
Gehée Quincy
Paudy Bourges

Blois

Cher

Bourges

Indre

Saulnay Issoudun
Buzançais
Villedieu-sur-Indre Châteauroux St Germain-des-Bois Blet •
Méobecq Diors
Etrechet Thaumiers •
le Blanc Velles St Amand-Montrond
Rivarennes St Chartier Orval Charenton-Laugere
Tendu la Châtre le Chatelet- Coust
Chalais en-Berry Ardenais
St Benoit-du-Sault Vigoulant

Châteauroux

Loir-et-Cher

135

EVENTS & FESTIVALS

Mar Beauregard Plant Festival; Donjon des Aigles Birds of Prey at Montrichard; St-Cosme Spring Music Festival

Apr La Bourdaisiere Plant & Garden Festival; Bourges Spring Music Festival

May Orléans Joan of Arc Festival; La Ferté-St-Aubin Plant & Garden Festival; Perche Music Festival; Tours Vocal Music Festival

May-Sep Chambord"The Horse King" equestrian art performances

Jun Chaumont-Sur-Loire International Garden Show; Sully-Sur-Loire Festival; Orléans Jazz Festival; Chambord Game Fair; Chartres Summer Festival; Nohant Romantic Festival

Jul Loches Musical Theatre Festival; Tours Music Festival; Chartres International Organ Festival; La Chatre Chopin Festival;

Aug Chinon Rabelais Market; Berry Jazz Festival; Bué-en-Sancerre Sorcerers' Festival; Chinon Old-fashioned Market;

Sep Tours Jazz Festival; Orléans Horse Festival; Chartres Lyrical Festival; Valençay Music Festival SON ET LUMIÈRES (*Light & Sound Shows*)

May-Sep Azay-le-Rideau - imaginary voyage to the Renaissance by night; Blois Castle "Tale of Blois";

Jun-Aug Villeprevost - a stroll through the park to poetry & music; Semblancay - the history and legend of the Château de la Source; Amboise: Royal Château - a nocturnal renaissance extravaganza featuring 450 characters in period costume each Wed & Sat;

Jun-Jul Beaugency - town centre

Jul Ste-Maure de Touraine in the Château, Cléry St-André outside the Basilica ;

Jul-Aug Chenonceau Château - "In the days of the Ladies of Chenonceau"; Loches "The Knight & The Wolf" - combines history with the fantastic; Valencay Château every Fri & Sat; Argenton-sur-Creuse - based on a play

Sologne

Escape the urban pressure to the rural simplicity of Sologne, an area of the Loire Valley with some 3,000 lakes, deep forests and wild fern moors. The waterways of the Cosson, Beuvron and Sauldre provide excellent angling country; consequently, the local restaurants feature the best in fresh carp, pike, eel, trout and zander dishes. Sologne is also long-established hunting territory, where partridge, duck, hare, wild boar and venison further enhance the region's gourmet cuisine. With all this fresh air and fine food, it's not surprising that Sologne has become popular for hiking holidays.

AIX-D'ANGILLON, LES Cher

La Chaume (Prop: Yves Proffit)
Rians *18220*
☎ 248644158 FAX 248642971
(from Bourges take D955 to les Aix-d'Angillon. 2nd right (Route Ste Salagne).Follow signs 'Chambres d'hôtes'. 4kms)
Odile and Yves Proffit are happy to welcome you to their guest house. They hope you enjoy their beautiful region, Le Berry, as much as they do. Located twenty kilometres from Bourges and thirty kilometres from the wine-producing town of Sancerre. Guest rooms enjoy their own access, independent of the rest of the house. Dinner by reservation only.
Near river Forest area Near motorway
Closed Xmas
3 en suite (shr) No smoking on premises Full central heating Open parking available Child discount available Fishing Bicycle rental
ROOMS: d 210-230FF Reductions over 1 night Special breaks
MEALS: Dinner 60-90FF*

AMBOISE Indre-et-Loire

Bed & Breakfast (Prop: Mme Lucette Jolivard)
2 clos de la Gabilière *37400*
☎ 247572190
(off D751)
Near river Forest area
Closed 11 Jan-14 May
6 en suite (bth/shr) (1 fmly) No smoking on premises TV available STV Full central heating Open parking available Languages spoken: English
CARDS: Travellers cheques

Château de la Barre (Prop: M & Mme Marliere)
Mosnes *37530*
☎ 247573340
(8km from Amboise in the direction of Blois)
The building dates from the seventeenth century and is situated in the middle of the Loire Valley, between Blois and Amboise. One room is in the main house and the other two in outbuildings close by. You will be welcomed into a friendly atmosphere, with authentic regional cooking available on request. English spoken.
Near river Forest area
5 rms (4 bth/shr) Full central heating Open parking available Child discount available 10yrs Languages spoken: English & German
MEALS: Dinner fr 150FF*
CARDS: ●● ▩ Travellers cheques

Le Petit Manoir (Prop: Mme Hélène Party)
rte de Chenonceaux *37400*
☎ 247305950
(on outskirts of Amboise, 2 miles from centre)
Rooms are situated in the outbuildings of this charming eighteenth century house. All rooms are furnished with antique furniture. The charming host, Madame Hélène Party, will happily provide guests with picnic provisions on request. Special rates are available off-season for weekend stays. English spoken.
Near river Forest area Near motorway
2 en suite (bth/shr) (1 fmly) Full central heating Open parking available Child discount available Languages spoken: English & Italian
CARDS: Travellers cheques

ARDENAIS Cher

La Folie (Prop: Mme Jacquet)
18170
☎ 248961759
(from A71-E11 exit at J8.Take D925 towards Lignieres.Take left to Orcenais, then Marcais.In Marcias turn left onto D38 towards Calau.Left to Ardenais.)
Annick Jacquet and her children will be happy to welcome you to their eighteenth century farm. Large garden and library, with plenty of information concerning the area, and Annick, who organises an annual tourist car rally and knows the region well, will be pleased to inform you further. Evening meals on request. English spoken.
Near river Forest area
Closed Nov-Mar
2 en suite (bth/shr) (2 fmly) Full central heating Open parking available Supervised Child discount available 3yrs Boule Bicycle rental
ROOMS: d 240-260FF Reductions over 1 night
CARDS: Travellers cheques

Vilotte (Prop: Jacques Champenier)
18170
☎ 248960496 FAX 248960496
(from the A71 exit St-Amand Montrond, then take D951 to Ardenais, then D38 in the direction of Reigny)

Your hosts at this former Roman site will welcome you to their home where you may enjoy the peace and tranquility of Vilotte, and where it is said 'time stands still'. Guests can relax in the rose garden and by the lake.
Near river Near lake Forest area
Closed Jan
6 rms (5 bth/shr) (1 fmly) No smoking in 3 bedrooms Full central heating Open parking available Child discount available Fishing Boule Bicycle rental 3 hectare gardens Table tennis Languages spoken: English
ROOMS: s 330-350FF; d 350-410FF Reductions over 1 night
MEALS: Dinner 140-150FFalc*

ATHÉE-SUR-CHER Indre-et-Loire

Le Pavillon de Vallet (Prop: Mme Fort)
37270
☎ 247506783 FAX 247506831
(turn off N76 before Blere and head for Vallet and the banks of the Cher, 25KM east of Tours)
A former 18th century priory situated in over seven acres on the banks of the river Cher, furnished with a comfortable mix of American and European antiques, paintings and personal memorabilia. Bedrooms feature queen-size beds and absolute

peace and quiet is assured here. Considered by some to be the Loire Valley's most unusual bed & breakfast. American host.
Near river Forest area Near motorway
4 en suite (bth/shr) (1 fmly) No smoking on premises Full central heating Open parking available Supervised No children 8yrs Languages spoken: English, German & Spanish

AUBIGNY-SUR-NÈRE Cher

Bien Dormir
12 av Paris *18700*
☎ 248810404 FAX 248580087
(off D940)
Near river
5 rms (4 bth/shr) (2 fmly) (1 with balcony) Full central heating Open parking available Covered parking available Child discount available Languages spoken: English
ROOMS: s 270FF; d 250-300FF Reductions over 1 night
CARDS: ▆

AVARAY Loir-et-Cher

Bed & Breakfast (Prop: Mireille & Didier Sauvage)
2 r de la Place *41500*
☎ 254813322
Near river Forest area Near motorway
2 en suite (shr) Some rooms in annexe Full central heating Open parking available Covered parking available Languages spoken: English
CARDS: Travellers cheques

AZAY-LE-RIDEAU Indre-et-Loire

Le Clos Philippa (Prop: A de Dreziglie)
10,12 r de Pineau *37190*
☎ 247452649
(22km from Tours, take N751 in direction of Chinon, turn off in Azay le Rideau)
All rooms are furnished with antiques in this house dating from the 18th century. A huge living room is available to guests, as well as a library and TV room. In the summer all meals are served in the garden. The house is situated next to the park of the Château d'Azay le Rideau.
Near river Forest area In town centre Near motorway
(2 fmly) Full central heating Open parking available Boule Bicycle rental
ROOMS: s 250FF; d 300-360FF Reductions over 1 night
MEALS: Dinner 150FF
CARDS: ▆▆ ▆▆ ▆ Travellers cheques

Manoir de la Remoniere
Cheille *37190*
☎ 247452488 FAX 247454569
(from D151 Tours-Chinon take D17 to Azay-le-Rideau and la Remoniere)
Located in a unique position facing the Alzay-le-Rideau Château, this fifteenth century manor house was built on the site of a Franco-Roman villa. Set in eighty-two acres of parkland and meadows, it has its very own bird reserve. The Indre river is only one kilometre away. The manor, looks particularly spectacular at night. English spoken.
Near river Forest area
6 en suite (bth/shr) (2 fmly) Full central heating Open parking available Outdoor swimming pool Fishing Boule Open terrace Languages spoken: English
CARDS: Travellers cheques

Le Vaujoint (Prop: Bertrand Jolit)
Cheille *37190*
☎ 247454889 FAX 247586811
(from centre of Azay-le-Rideau towards Chinon, after 700m
into village La Chapelle St Blaise turn right opposite the
"maine" turn right in direction of Usse Castle, turn left at Le
Vaujoint sign & follow signs for Chambre d'Hote)
Rooms available in the outbuildings of this nineteenth century
property, set in a small hamlet four kilometres from Azay-le-
Rideau. This residence is beautifully renovated, with exposed
beams and stone floors. A lounge is reserved for guests, with
television, fireplace and antique furniture. Large, shady
garden with barbecue and conservatory. Within twenty
kilometres you will find at least a dozen châteaux, golf
courses, canoeing, sailing, tennis and horse-riding centres.
English spoken.
Near river Forest area
3 en suite (shr) Full central heating Open parking available
Languages spoken: English & Italian

AZAY-SUR-CHER Indre-et-Loire

La Patouillard (Prop: Mme Moreau)
37270
☎ 247504132 FAX 247504765
3 en suite (bth/shr) No smoking on premises Full central
heating Open parking available
CARDS: Travellers cheques

AZAY-SUR-INDRE Indre-et-Loire

Le Prieure (Prop: Danielle Papot)
37310
☎ 247922529
Danielle Papot, the owner of this romantic property built in
1856, has been much praised for her cooking. As you can
imagine, therefore, excellent meals are available for guests.
This old house borders on the canal and has a well-kept
garden.
Near river Forest area
3 rms (2 bth) TV available Radio in rooms Full central
heating Open parking available Supervised Child discount
available
CARDS: Travellers cheques

AZÉ Loir-et-Cher

Bed & Breakfast (Prop: M & Mme Boulai)
Gorgeat Azé *41100*
☎ 254720416 FAX 254720494
The rooms of the Boulai family are situated on one floor of an
old farmhouse. Living and dining room available for guests, as
well as kitchen. Brochures provided giving information about
the surrounding area. Bike-rides and walks possible. Farm
goat's cheese and eggs may be bought. English spoken.
Forest area
6 en suite (shr) (3 fmly) No smoking on premises Full central
heating Open parking available Supervised Child discount
available 8yrs Languages spoken: English

Bed & Breakfast (Prop: M & Mme Guellier)
Ferme de Crisliane *41100*
☎ 254721409 FAX 254721803
A charming farmhouse covered in Virginia Creeper. It is a
working farm with sixty-five milking cows. There is a
swimming pool in the orchard. A garden patio is for the use of
guests. The bedrooms are located on the first floor, with a

kitchen area reserved for guests. Ideal locations for ramblers
or those who enjoy bike-riding.
Forest area
5 en suite (shr) Full central heating Open parking available
Covered parking available Child discount available 11yrs
Outdoor swimming pool Table tennis

BEAUMONT-EN-VÉRON Indre-et-Loire

La Balastière (Prop: Antoinette Degremont)
Grézille *37420*
☎ 247588793 FAX 247588241
One of the rooms is situated in the loft and has a kitchen and
dining area. There is also a separate fishing lodge. The
buildings are very old but have been recently renovated. A
garden is available for the guests. La Balastière is situated
between the Loire and the Vieuve, in the heart of vineyard
country. Two separate gites are also available. English spoken.
Near river Forest area
2 en suite (bth/shr) (1 fmly) Radio in rooms Full central
heating Open parking available Languages spoken: English,
German & Spanish

Château de Coulaine (Prop: M & Mme Bonnaventure)
37420
☎ 247930127
The comfortable rooms are situated on the first floor of the
château. This family home belongs to the Bonnaventures,
direct descendants of Johan de Guarguesalle, who built it at
the end of the fifteenth century. A relaxing holiday is assured
in this wonderful building.
Forest area
Etr-mid Nov
5 en suite (bth/shr) Full central heating Open parking
available
CARDS: Travellers cheques

BERRY-BUOY Cher

L'Ermitage (Prop: Mme de la Forge)
18500
☎ 248268746 FAX 248260328
Your hosts welcome you to their farm where three charming
rooms are available in the attractive main house and a further
three are available in an old mill in the grounds. Guests may
use the garden. English spoken.
Near river Near motorway
6 en suite (bth/shr) (2 fmly) TV available Full central heating
Open parking available Languages spoken: English

BERTHENAY Indre-et-Loire

La Grange Aux Monies (Prop: J Millet)
37510
☎ 247500691
Restored 18th century farmhouse, situated in a leafy park.
There is a private swimming pool and bicycles are available
for hire. Dinner available on request. English spoken.
Near river Forest area
Closed 12 Nov-14 Mar
6 en suite (bth/shr) (3 fmly) Full central heating Open
parking available Child discount available Outdoor
swimming pool Bicycle rental
ROOMS: s fr 290FF; d 340-390FF *
MEALS: Dinner fr 120FF*
CARDS: Travellers cheques

BLANC, LE Indre

Les Chezeaux (Prop: A & A Jubard)
36300
☎ 254373217 254374021
Near river
Closed mid Oct-mid Mar
2 en suite (bth/shr) Open parking available Supervised
ROOMS: s 240-260FF; d 260-280FF *

BLET Cher

Château de Blet
18350
☎ 248747202 & 248747666
(after the Bourges exit take the N76 towards Moulins, Blet is 35km south-east of Bourges on this road)
Built in the fifteenth century on the site of an old château and extended in the nineteenth century, Château de Blet is a local landmark. On site facilities include billiards, a large park and a collection of vintage cars. Tennis, golf and a swimming pool are nearby.
Forest area Near motorway
3 en suite (bth) (2 fmly) TV available Full central heating
Open parking available Pool table
CARDS: Travellers cheques

BLÉVY Eure-et-Loir

Bed & Breakfast (Prop: Daguy & Roger Parmentier)
2 rue des Champarts *28170*
☎ 237480121 FAX 237480121
(leave N12 at Dreux and take D20 to Blevy)

A warm welcome, and peace and quiet, await at the 200-year-old home of Daguy and Roger Parmentier. Roger is a retired chef and delicious meals are guaranteed. Both the comfortable bedrooms are en suite, are beautifully furnished and have a TV and a fridge.
Near river Forest area Near motorway
Closed Feb
2 en suite (bth/shr) (2 fmly) TV in all bedrooms Radio in rooms Full central heating Open parking available Child discount available 10yrs Languages spoken: English & German
ROOMS: s 220-270FF; d 250-300FF
MEALS: Dinner fr 100FF

Taking your mobile phone to France? See page 11

BLOIS Loir-et-Cher

Le Vieux Cognet (Prop: Francoise Cosson)
4 Levée des Grouets *41000*
☎ 254560534 FAX 254748082
(in the centre of the village, on N152 towards Tours)

Unusual house which looks out over the Loire. Home-made breakfasts on offer. Direct access to the Loire or visit the romantic châteaux between Blois and Angers. English spoken.
Near river Forest area Near motorway
6 en suite (bth/shr) (4 fmly) Full central heating Open parking available Languages spoken: English
ROOMS: s 250-300FF; d 320-450FF
CARDS: Travellers cheques

BOUGY-LEZ-NEUVILLE Loiret

Le Climat des Quatre Coins (Prop: Mme Glotin)
45170
☎ 238918089
(leave the D97 north of Orleans and take D297 to Bougy-lez-Neuville)
Quiet and spacious rooms are available on this small goat farm, where guest rooms are in a building separate to the family home. The ground floor overlooks parkland and a kitchen is provided for guests' use, as is a barbecue. Bicycles are available. English spoken.
Near lake Forest area
2 en suite (bth/shr) (1 fmly) TV available Full central heating Open parking available Languages spoken: English & German

BOURGUEIL Indre-et-Loire

Château des Reaux (Prop: Florence Goupil de Bouille)
Chouzé-sur-Loire *37140*
☎ 247951440 FAX 247951834
(from A85 towards Chinon/ Bargueil leave at exit towards Chinon & at traffic lights turn right onto N152 take 1st road on right, Château signed)
This château is an historic monument which is considered to be one of the prettiest in the Loire Valley. The property is family-owned and the hosts welcome guests as friends. Dine with them at their table and discuss the local attractions of the area.
Near river Forest area Near motorway
18 en suite (bth/shr) 5 rooms in annexe (3 fmly) Full central heating Open parking available Child discount available 12yrs Tennis Bicycle rental

cont'd

ROOMS: (room only) s fr 250FF; d fr 450FF Reductions over 1 night
MEALS: Full breakfast 55FF Lunch 180-250FFalc Dinner fr 230FF
CARDS: ●● ▦ �; ▣ Travellers cheques

BOURRÉ Loir-et-Cher

Manoir de la Salle (Prop: Jean Boussard)
69 rte de Vierzon *41400*
☎ 254327354 FAX 254324709
(leave A10 at Blois Sud and proceed to bourre via D764)
This elegant fifteenth century residence is located in an enchanting position, towering high above the Cher Valley. You will find tennis courts, rose gardens, an orangery, greenhouse, solarium, ponds, flower-beds and a bowling green. Special weekend rates include tennis, fishing and hunting. All bedrooms have fireplaces. Grilled meals are a speciality. English spoken.
Near river Forest area Near motorway
5 en suite (bth/shr) TV available Full central heating Open parking available Open terrace Covered terrace Languages spoken: English
CARDS: ●● ▩ ▣ Travellers cheques

BOURSAY Loir-et-Cher

La Madeleinière (Prop: Colette le Guay)
21 rue des Écoles *41270*
☎ 254809261
(from A11 at Chartres take N10 and turn right for Boursay)
The owner of this residence will delight you with her excellent French cuisine. The accommodation is near Saint Peter's Church, a historic twelfth century monument. Stroll down Boursay's Path, a botanical walk which takes in fifty-four species of tree and one hundred and eight types of plant.
Near river Forest area Near motorway
3 en suite (shr) (2 fmly) Radio in rooms Full central heating Open parking available Child discount available 10yrs
CARDS: Travellers cheques

BOUTIGNY-SUR-OPTON Eure-et-Loir

Bed & Breakfast (Prop: Serge & Jeanne-Marie Maréchal)
11 rue des Tourelles, La Musse *28410*
☎ 237651874
(leave the N12 at the village of Houdan and proceed to La Musse via Boutigny)
Jeanne-Marie and Serge Maréchal welcome you to their farm. They offer a cottage which can accommodate up to fifteen people or be let as individual rooms. Guests are invited to dine with them, sampling home-cooked food using their farm's

produce. Traditional French breakfasts served. A little English spoken.
Forest area Near motorway
4 en suite (bth/shr) (2 fmly) No smoking on premises Full central heating Open parking available Child discount available Languages spoken: English
MEALS: Dinner fr 70FFalc*

BRÉHÉMONT Indre-et-Loire

Les Brunets (Prop: Carolyn Smith)
37130
☎ 247965581
(situated in the village of Langeais, route D57 to Azay le Rideau cross Langeais bridge then take D16 establishment on the right in 2kms)
Angela and Derek, an English couple, welcome you to their Tourangelle style house, situated on the banks of the Loire. Covered parking and tranquil garden with patio and barbecue. Beamed lounge with open fireplace. Guests may eat with the hosts by prior reservation.
Near river Near lake Forest area
3 en suite (shr) (1 fmly) No smoking on premises TV available Full central heating Open parking available Child discount available 8yrs Open terrace V meals Languages spoken: English
MEALS: Dinner fr 120FFalc*
CARDS: Travellers cheques

BRIARE Loiret

Domaine de la Thiau (Prop: Francois Ducluzeau)
45250
☎ 238382092 & 238370417 FAX 238674050
(midway between Gien and Briare on D952, close to nurseries)
This imposing eighteenth century building is the home of Mme. François-Ducluzeau. Set in a large estate by the Loire, there is a choice of two residences. Swimming, fishing and cycling all nearby. Shops are within four kilometres. Private access to Loire. English spoken.
Near river Forest area Near motorway
4 en suite (bth/shr) (2 fmly) No smoking in all bedrooms TV in 3 bedrooms Radio in rooms Full central heating Open parking available Covered parking available Supervised Child discount available 2yrs Tennis Fishing Pool table Boule Bicycle rental Open terrace Table tennis, Children's playground Languages spoken: English, German & Spanish
ROOMS: s 215-280FF; d 250-320FF Special breaks: 10% reduction for 3 nights

BRIARRES-SUR-ESSONNE Loiret

Moulin de Francorville (Prop: Bernard Coulon)
45390
☎ 328391359
(from Malesherbes take D25 to Briarres-sur-Essonne, on towards Villereau.Take left turn towards Chatillon.)
Situated on the River Essonne in a peaceful setting, this old mill has two double rooms with en suite facilities, one having an additional single bed. There is a small lounge with TV on the first floor.
Near river Forest area
2 en suite (bth/shr) Full central heating Open parking available Fishing
ROOMS: s 180FF; d 220FF * Reductions over 1 night
CARDS: Travellers cheques

BU Eure-et-Loir

Auberge de l'Avloir (Prop: Christian Borbot)
8 rue St-Antoine *28410*
☎ 237821385 FAX 237821682
(3 kms from Dreux on D21 to Bû)
Christian and Anne-Marie Barbot offer to look after you in the traditional way. They breed horses so why not hire a pony and cart to explore the local countryside? All rooms are on the first floor, with independent access. Evening meals by arrangement. English spoken.
Forest area
3 en suite (shr) No smoking on premises Full central heating
Open parking available Covered parking available
Supervised Child discount available 3yrs Riding V meals
Last d 21.00 hr Languages spoken: English & German
ROOMS: s fr 170FF; d fr 200FF Special breaks
MEALS: Continental breakfast 20FF Lunch 62-92FFalc Dinner
62-92FFalc

BUZANÇAIS Indre

Château de Boisrenault (Prop: Yves du Manoir)
36500
☎ 554840301 FAX 554841057
(A20/E9 Paris/Limoges after Vierzon take exit 11 Levroux then
D926 to Buzançais)

This impressive nineteenth century château is steeped in history. The mysterious initials "HB" are engraved on the living room mantelpiece - are they those of Huard du Boisrenault, who built the château for his daughter? Private swimming pool. Acres of woodland and park. Eighteen-hole golf course just eight kilometres away. Tennis court and riding school within easy reach. English spoken.
Forest area Near motorway
Closed 16 Dec-Feb
7 en suite (bth/shr) Full central heating Open parking
available Child discount available Outdoor swimming pool
(heated) Open terrace Covered terrace Library TV Table
tennis Languages spoken: English
ROOMS: s 355-470FF; d 395-510FF
CARDS: ●● ▦ ▭ Travellers cheques

CELLE-GUENAND, LA Indre-et-Loire

Château de la Guénand (Prop: Jane de l'Aigle)
37350
☎ 247949449 (after 19.30Hrs)
Forest area In town centre
7 en suite (bth/shr) Full central heating Open parking
available

CÉRÉ-LA-RONDE Indre-et-Loire

Bed & Breakfast (Prop: Mme Martine Laizé)
Le Petit Biard *37460*
☎ 247595118
(from Bloise take D764 to Montrichard and then on towards Genillé. After 5kms take left onto D281 to Céré-la-Ronde)
This character residence is situated in the quiet of the countryside, fifteen kilometres south of Chenonceau, in the centre of the Châteaux of the Loire. Three bed & breakfast rooms are available, on the first floor, one of which is a family room, furnished with antiques. Living room, with fireplace, for guests' use. Breakfasts served all morning! Possibility of picnics. Reductions of ten percent for stays of more than three nights. Restaurant within two kilometres. A little English spoken.
Near river Forest area Near motorway
4 en suite (shr) (1 fmly) Full central heating Open parking
available Languages spoken: English & German
ROOMS: s fr 160FF; d 195-215FF Reductions over 1 night
CARDS: Travellers cheques

CHABRIS Indre

Les Bizeaux (Prop: Bernadette Planques)
36210
☎ 254401451
(Chabris is south of N76(Tours/Vierzon).On D35 follow signs
'Gites de France')

Les Bizeaux is a small farm, which stretches over two hectares, in the Loire Valley. The farm is one mile outside the town of Chabris, beside the River Cher. All the bedrooms have pleasant views over the fields, the woods and the farms in the distance. Breakfast is served on the terrace. English hosts.
Near river Near sea Forest area
3 en suite (shr) (1 fmly) Full central heating Open parking
available Child discount available 10yrs Languages spoken:
English
ROOMS: s 220FF; d 280FF Reductions over 1 night
CARDS: Travellers cheques

CHALAIS Indre

Le Grand Ajoux (Prop: A de la Jonquiere-Aymé)
36370
☎ 254377292 FAX 254377292
(from A20 take N151 towards Poitiers. At Ciron take D44, then
turn right onto D927 towards Bélâbre. Establishment is 5kms
before Bélâbre)

cont'd

Located in the 'Parc Naturel Regional de la Brenne', this elegant 17th-century manor house is set in a 150-acre estate, which is well known for its 'one thousand ponds'. There is fine decor and period furniture throughout the manor making the accommodation extremely comfortable. Guests are invited to dine at their hosts' table. This is an ideal place to find peace and tranquility and is an especially good area for bird-watching, and hiking. English spoken.
Near river Near lake Forest area
Closed Nov-Mar
4 en suite (bth/shr) (2 fmly) TV in all bedrooms Open parking available Child discount available 4yrs Outdoor swimming pool (heated) Fishing Riding Boule Bicycle rental Table tennis Last d 18.00hrs Languages spoken: English & Spanish
ROOMS: s 250FF; d 280FF * Reductions over 1 night Special breaks
MEALS: Dinner fr 90FF

CHAMBOURG-SUR-INDRE Indre-et-Loire

Le Petit Marray (Prop: M Mesure)
37310
☎ 247925058 FAX 247925067
(A10 exit 23 in direction Loches/Chateauroux, N143 1.5km after Chambourg turn right)

Large, comfortable rooms situated on an old farm, dating from the nineteenth century. Plenty of superb walks around the chateaux. Reductions for children up to ten years old. English spoken.
Near river Forest area
4 en suite (bth/shr) (2 fmly) TV in all bedrooms Full central heating Open parking available Child discount available 10yrs Boule Table tennis Languages spoken: English
ROOMS: s 290FF; d 290-360FF * Reductions over 1 night
MEALS: Dinner 120FF

CHANCAY Indre-et-Loire

Ferme de Launay (Prop: B et J-P Schweizer)
37210
☎ 27522821 FAX 27522821
(15km NE of Tours via N152, north bank of Loire, direction Amboise. In Vouvray take D46 direction Vernou-sur-Brenne, then Chançay - signs before Chançay)
Eighteenth century farmhouse, lovingly restored. Set in the heart of the Vouvray wine region, between Tours and Amboise. Luxurious, comfortable en suite bedrooms. Large salon with fireplace. Gourmet meals served at the family table. English breakfasts available. Walking, fishing and riding nearby. Bicycle rentals and wine-tastings arranged. Fluent English spoken.
Near river Forest area Near motorway
3 en suite (bth/shr) No smoking on premises Full central heating Open parking available Covered parking available No children 15yrs Languages spoken: English, German & Italian
ROOMS: s 350-450FF; d 400-500FF
MEALS: Full breakfast 50FF Dinner fr 115FF
CARDS: Travellers cheques

CHANCEAUX-SUR-CHOISILLE Indre-et-Loire

Le Moulin de la Planche (Prop: Jacqueline Chauveau)
Langennerie *37390*
☎ 247551196 FAX 247562434
(just north of Tours in the direction of Beaumont la Ronce)
An old watermill, dating back to the 15th century, which now houses a restaurant with guest rooms and a picture gallery. Set in a park, surrounded by woods with a river running close by, ensures a peaceful, relaxing environment. An 18-hole golf course is nearby, and it is conveniently situated for visiting the chateaux of the Loire.
Near river Forest area
3 en suite (shr) (1 fmly) (2 with balcony) No smoking in 2 bedrooms TV in all bedrooms Full central heating Open parking available Child discount available Fishing Boule Bicycle rental Last d 21.00hrs
ROOMS: s fr 235FF; d fr 270FF Reductions over 1 night
MEALS: Full breakfast 35FF Continental breakfast 35FF Lunch fr 70FF Dinner fr 70FF
CARDS: ●● 〓

CHARENTON-LAUGERE Cher

La Serre (Prop: M & Mme Moreau)
18210
☎ 248607582
(either A71 exit St-Amand Montrond direction Sancoins Nevers: Bourges directon Moulins then right Dun/Auron, Ainay-le-Château)
Large building, surrounded by four hectares of parkland. The house is near the Tronais Forest, the châteaux of the Jacques Coeur route and the beautiful village of Bourges. Fixed price dinner with traditional, regional food served. English spoken.
Near river Near lake Forest area Near motorway
Closed Oct-Mar
3 en suite (bth/shr) (1 fmly) (1 with balcony) Full central heating Open parking available Covered parking available Child discount available 12yrs Fishing Riding Boule Bicycle rental Open terrace Covered terrace Languages spoken: English
CARDS: Travellers cheques

CHÂTEAUDUN Eure-et-Loir

Bed & Breakfast (Prop: Monique Allezy)
Crépainville, 8 rue de l'Étoile *28200*
☎ 237453744
(from Châteaudun take D955 towards Alençon. After 3kms turn left onto D23 to Crépainville. In village take 3rd road on right)
Located on a cereal farm, accommodation is in a separate house next to the owner's home. As well as the three bedrooms there is also a kitchen for the guests' use.
Near river Forest area
3 rms (2 shr) No smoking on premises Radio in rooms Full central heating Open parking available Covered parking available Child discount available Boule Table tennis Swing Last d 19.00hrs Languages spoken: English
ROOMS: s 130-150FF; d 160-180FF Reductions over 1 night
MEALS: Dinner 50-55FF
CARDS: Travellers cheques

CHÂTEAU-LA-VALLIÈRE Indre-et-Loire

Vaujours (Prop: Gerard & Martine Ribert)
37330
☎ 247240855
(on the D959, Le Lude 17km, Tours 33km)
Three independent guest rooms, situated on the ground floor of a farm which produces goat's cheese. Guests are invited to dine with their hosts, the Ribert family. Reductions for children up to four years old. English spoken.
Near river Near lake Forest area Near motorway
4 en suite (shr) (1 fmly) TV available Open parking available Child discount available 4yrs Outdoor swimming pool Barbecue Languages spoken: English
MEALS: Dinner fr 75FF*

CHÂTELET-EN-BERRY, LE Cher

Estiveaux (Prop: Mme Faverges)
rte de La Chatre *18170*
☎ 248562264
(off the D951)
Bedrooms at this manor house are spacious and comfortable. A shaded park to the rear of the house is very pleasant. Children's games and bicycles available. This beautiful area is little known, so come and discover what it has to offer. Golf nearby. Many châteaux to visit in close proximity.
Near river Near lake Forest area
5 rms (3 bth) (4 fmly) (1 with balcony) No smoking in 1 bedroom TV available Full central heating Open parking available Child discount available

CHÂTRES-SUR-CHER Loir-et-Cher

Bed & Breakfast (Prop: M & Mme Laclautre)
19 rue Jean Segrétin *41320*
☎ 254981024
(N76 Tours/Vierzon, 20km from Vierzon)
The bedrooms available in this old market town house have private access to rooms . Close to both the Canal and the Cher River. Sailing available on-site. Fishing also on-site, as are cycling and walking. Riding, three kilometres, swimming pool, three kilometres. Tennis court on-site.
Near river Forest area Near motorway
3 en suite (shr) (2 fmly) Full central heating Open parking available Child discount available 5yrs Open terrace
MEALS: Dinner 50-90FF*

CHAVEIGNES Indre-et-Loire

La Varenne (Prop: Joelle Dru-Sauer)
37120
☎ 247582631 FAX 247582747
This seventeenth century house in the middle of the country is near to the châteaux of the Loire and Futuroscope. La Varenne is a farm which produces honey and grows nuts. English spoken.
Forest area
3 en suite (bth) (1 with balcony) Full central heating Open parking available Child discount available Outdoor swimming pool Languages spoken: English

CHÉMERY Loir-et-Cher

Château de Chémery (Prop: M & Mme Fontaine)
41700
☎ 254718277 FAX 254717134
(on the road from Contres to Selles-sur-Cher, between Chambord and Valencay.)
Thirty kilometres south of Blois, near the border of Sologne, you will find this fifteenth century château which is currently undergoing restoration. It was converted to a farm in 1729. Surrounded by a moat, the buildings enclose a courtyard with the château forming one side and the outbuildings the other. Access is via an old drawbridge. Breakfast and evening meal available by arrangement. Theatre shows in the summer. Boats available. English spoken.
Near lake Forest area
5 rms (4 bth) (2 fmly) (1 with balcony) Open parking available Child discount available 14yrs Fishing Boule Bicycle rental Stables 3km away. Last d 20hrs Languages spoken: English
ROOMS: s 250FF; d 250-450FF Reductions over 1 night Special breaks
MEALS: Dinner 120FF&alc
CARDS: Travellers cheques

CHEVANNES Loiret

Bed & Breakfast (Prop: Olivier Tant)
Le Village *45210*
☎ 238909223
Mireille and Olivier offer you a relaxing holiday within one hour of Paris. This restored farm is in the heart of the village of Gatinais and there is an independent house available for guests, with three bedrooms, lounge and kitchen area. Evening meals by reservation; home-grown produce is used. Possible activities within close proximity include canoeing, kayaking, swimming, fishing and tennis. English spoken.
Near river Forest area
3 en suite (shr) (3 fmly) No smoking on premises Radio in rooms Open parking available Child discount available Languages spoken: English

CHEVERNY Loir-et-Cher

Le Clos Bigot
rte le Buchet *41700*
☎ 254792638 FAX 254792638
(17km S of Blois off the D765)
Bed and breakfast available in this eighteenth century building surrounded by parkland. Private swimming pool. Golf and forest within five minutes walk. English spoken.
Forest area

cont'd

4 en suite (bth/shr) (2 fmly) No smoking on premises Full central heating Open parking available No children 10yrs Child discount available Outdoor swimming pool Languages spoken: English, Spanish

CHEVILLON-SUR-HUILLARD Loiret

Bed & Breakfast (Prop: Gerard Granddenis)
Le Grande Casseau 45700
☎ 238978045
Calm and comfort assured in this house of character, situated on the edge of a forest. Three rooms available on the ground floor. Communal living room. Possibilities of picnics. Golf, horse-riding, sailing, fishing and swimming all within close proximity. English spoken.
Near river Forest area Near motorway
Closed Nov-Mar
3 rms (1 shr) No smoking on premises Full central heating Open parking available Languages spoken: English

CHINON Indre-et-Loire

Moulin de la Voie (Prop: Mme Cottereau)
Cinais 37500
☎ 247958290 FAX 247959116
(in Chinon cross bridge over River Vienne towards Saumur. At 1st & 2nd roundabouts follow signs for Saumur. 'Moulin de Ca Voie' 150m on left)
Close to Chinon, on the road to Saumur, the sixteenth century Moulin de la Voie has been restored and now offers four guest rooms, all of which are charming and spacious. A river runs through the garden. Ideal spot from which to visit the attractions of the region. Many leisure activities within close proximity. A little English spoken.
Near river Forest area
4 en suite (bth/shr) Full central heating Open parking available Supervised Fishing Languages spoken: English & Italian
ROOMS: d 300FF Reductions over 1 night

CHOUZE-SUR-LOIRE Indre-et-Loire

Montachamps (Prop: M & Mme Plassais)
37140
☎ 247951073
A warm welcome awaits you at the Ferme de Montachamps, where you will enjoy the calm of the countryside. Four rooms available, including one family room. Dinner is served with fresh farm produce. English spoken.
Near river Near sea Forest area
5 en suite (bth/shr) (1 fmly) No smoking in all bedrooms Full central heating Open parking available Languages spoken: English & Spanish

CINQ-MARS-LA-PILE Indre-et-Loire

La Meulière
10 rue de la Gare 37130
☎ 247965363
Set in an enclosed garden, this attractive town house has five guest rooms situated on the first floor. Breakfast is included. Fishing, walking, golf, swimming and sailing all within close proximity.
Closed 15 Sep-15 Oct & 15 Nov-1 Jan
6 en suite (bth/shr) (1 fmly) (1 with balcony) Full central heating Air conditioning in bedrooms Open parking available

CIVRAY-DE-TOURAINE Indre-et-Loire

Les Cartes (Prop: M & Mme Pinquet)
37150
☎ 247579494 FAX 247578933
(in Amboise on D31, southwards, take D81 towards Civray-de-Touraine for 3kms. Take lane on right, follow signs on right,then left & left again)
House on the edge of woodland with heated and covered swimming pool, and guests can use the sauna at a small extra charge. Breakfast is served either in the lounge or in the garden in summer months.
Near river Forest area
2 en suite (bth/shr) TV in all bedrooms Full central heating Open parking available Child discount available Indoor swimming pool (heated) Table tennis Languages spoken: English
ROOMS: d 380-480FF Reductions over 1 night
CARDS: Travellers cheques

CONTINVOIR Indre-et-Loire

La Butte de l'Épine (Prop: Michel Bodet)
37340
☎ 247966225 FAX 247966225
(from Tours take N152 towards Saumur-Langrais. At St Patrice take D35 to Bourguiel. Then take D749 to Gizeux & onto Continvoir. In village, turn left, follow signpost)

Built in the 17th century, this character house offers comfortable rooms on the first floor with an independent access. Breakfast is served in the large dining room. Set in a wooded area, close to the vineyards of Bourgueil, a relaxing atmosphere prevails. Restaurants close by. A little English spoken.
Near lake Forest area
2 en suite (shr) No smoking on premises Full central heating Open parking available No children 10yrs Open terrace Covered terrace
ROOMS: s 290FF; d 320FF
CARDS: Travellers cheques

CONTRES Loir-et-Cher

Bed & Breakfast (Prop: M & Mme Bonnet)
r de Stade 41700
☎ 254795278
(from Blois take D956 to Contres, then on towards Saint-Aignan. Take 1st right to Oisly on D21. Establishment is last on right, before stadium and after church)
Bedrooms on this wine producing farm have a kitchen and TV. There is a shaded courtyard with a small pond and a garage

games room for guests' use. A swimming pool, tennis courts and shops are all within 5 kilometres.
3 en suite (shr) TV in 2 bedrooms Full central heating Open parking available
ROOMS: s 150FF; d 190-210FF

La Rabouillere (Prop: M & Mme Thimonnier)
chemin de Marcon *41700*
☎ 254790514 FAX 254795939
Forest area
7 en suite (bth) TV in all bedrooms Full central heating Child discount available Languages spoken: English
CARDS: ●● ☲ Travellers cheques

COURCAY Indre-et-Loire

Manoir de Chemalle (Prop: Anne-Marie-Valiere)
37310
☎ 247941048 FAX 247941048
(from Tours take N143 towards Loches. At Comery take D17 to Courcay.After Courcay take 2nd right & Manor is on right)

Guest rooms, with direct access onto a courtyard, are available in a 12th century grange set in the grounds of an ancient manor house. The lounge is decorated in a rustic manner and a kitchen is available. Tennis and mini-golf are available close by. Dinner by arrangement. English spoken.
Near river Forest area
17 en suite (shr) Full central heating Open parking available
V meals Languages spoken: English, German & Italian

COURCELLES-DE-TOURAINE Indre-et-Loire

La Gallechere (Prop: Mme P Bontemps-Wallez)
3 la Frande Gallechère *37330*
☎ 247249077
(exit A10 at Chateau Renault ou Tours and take direction for Château Lavalliere, then direction for Angers)
Near river Near lake Near sea Near beach Forest area
5 en suite (bth/shr) (2 fmly) Full central heating Open parking available Supervised Child discount available 12yrs Fishing Boule Table tennis Billiards
MEALS: Dinner 100FF*
CARDS: Travellers cheques

COUR-CHEVERNY Loir-et-Cher

Le Beguinage (Prop: M & Mme Deloison)
41700
☎ 254792992 FAX 254799459
(exit A10 at Blois and take direction for Vierzon, Cour-Cheverny)

This house, close to the Château de Cheverny, is situated in the centre of Châteaux country and set in an extensive landscaped park. River fishing available, as is petanque and basketball. Fixed price dinner menu. English spoken.
Near river Forest area
4 en suite (shr) (2 fmly) TV available Full central heating Open parking available Covered parking available Supervised Child discount available 12yrs Fishing Boule Languages spoken: English & Spanish
CARDS: Travellers cheques

COUST Cher

Changy (Prop: M Maurice Luc)
18210
☎ 248635403
Old, renovated house set in a large shaded garden with a sun terrace. The sitting room has a fireplace and a TV for guests' use. The forest of Tronçais, horse-riding,fishing, bathing and karting are all nearby. There are many restaurants in the area.
Near motorway
3 en suite (shr) No smoking on premises TV available Full central heating Open parking available Supervised Child discount available 5yrs Languages spoken: Spanish

CRAVANT-LES-COTEAUX Indre-et-Loire

La Gabelle (Prop: Vincent Hearne)
Briancon *37500*
☎ 247932297 FAX 247932297
(take the D8 from Chinon towards L'ile Bouchard follow the signs 4km from Chinon)
A sensitively restored 16th century farm on the banks of the river Vienne, which has three cottages and two studio apartments set in pretty gardens. Breakfast is served on the riverside terrace. English spoken.
Near river Near beach Forest area Near motorway
Closed Nov-Etr
8 en suite (bth/shr) Open parking available Child discount available 12yrs Tennis Fishing Riding Boule Bicycle rental Riverside terrace Languages spoken: English
ROOMS: (room only) s 300-400FF; d 300-400FF
MEALS: Continental breakfast 50FF
CARDS: ●● ☲ Travellers cheques

DANZÉ Loir-et-Cher

La Borde (Prop: N Kamette)
41160
☎ 254806842 FAX 254806368
(from Vendome take D36 to Danze, then D24 for Ville-aux-Clercs)
This family-run guesthouse is situated in a manor overlooking a lovely park. There is a large indoor swimming pool, which can be opened up in fine weather. Tennis facilities are available within two miles and horse-riding within ten miles. English spoken.
Near river Forest area Near motorway
5 en suite (shr) (2 fmly) (2 with balcony) Full central heating Open parking available Supervised Indoor swimming pool Languages spoken: English, Spanish & German
ROOMS: s 190-250FF; d 240-300FF * Reductions over 1 night
CARDS: ▨

DESCARTES Indre-et-Loire

Villouette (Prop: M & Mme Delaunay)
37160
☎ 247598007
Children are welcome to this property, which has a large garden with children's games. In the winter, you can sit by a cosy open-fire and enjoy the relaxing atmosphere.
Near river Forest area
3 rms (2 with balcony) Full central heating Open parking available Covered parking available Supervised Child discount available V meals
CARDS: Travellers cheques

DIORS Indre

Le Parc (Prop: Astrid Gaignault)
36130
☎ 254260443 FAX 254261332
The rooms are situated in a lodge dating back to the eighteenth century, which is surrounded by parkland and bordered by a very pretty garden. Some English spoken.
Forest area
6 rms (3 bth) Full central heating Open parking available
Child discount available

DONNERY Loiret

Cornella (Prop: Jacques Avril)
27 rue de Vennecy *45450*
☎ 238592674 FAX 238592674
(take rue A Bolland to the right of the church and Mayor's office and after 600mtrs r du Vennecy is on right)
Jacques and Marie-Pierre Avril genuinely welcome guests to their home. Meals with the family available on request, served in the garden on fine evenings, or by an open fire in the winter. Games are provided for children. Some English spoken.
Near lake Forest area
2 en suite (bth/shr) TV available Full central heating Open parking available Child discount available 10yrs Languages spoken: English

La Poterie (Prop: M & Mme C Charles)
45450
☎ 238592003 FAX 238570447
(from A10 exit at Orleans Nord & take N60 towards Chateauneuf. Take left to Fay-aux-Croix. With church on your right take 1st left and take D709 to Donnery. Farm 2.5kms on right)
Quietly situated on a working farm that grows cereal products, just outside the village. Meals available by arrangement, served at the family table. Simple, traditional French food. Your hosts have booklets available for guests, giving details of places of interest in the region. Walk along the canal, visit Orleans, Orleans Forest or the Loire River. Golf is one kilometre away. Some English spoken.
Near river Forest area Near motorway
3 en suite (shr) No smoking on premises Open parking available
ROOMS: d 240FF
MEALS: Dinner fr 85FF
CARDS: Travellers cheques

ÉCHILLEUSES Loiret

Bed & Breakfast (Prop: Mme F Hyais)
3 Cour du Château *45390*
☎ 238336016
(autoroute du Sud A6 exit at Ury and take direction for La Chapelle la Reine)
Françine Hyais has two rooms to offer to guests coming to Echilleuses. Each room is well equipped and the garden is accessible to guests for sunbathing. Guests are invited to eat with their hostess. Typical French breakfast is served.
Near motorway
Closed 15 Nov-15 Dec
2 en suite (shr) (1 fmly) Open parking available Supervised
Last d 18.00hrs
MEALS: Dinner 70FF*

ÉCROSNES Eure-et-Loir

Château de Jonvilliers (Prop: M & Mme Thompson)
17 rue d'Epernon, Hameau de Jonvilliers *28320*
☎ 237314126 FAX 237315674
(from A1 exit at J1(Ablis) & take N10 towards Rombouillet.Take left onto D176 & at Orphin take D32 to Ecrosnes. In Ecrosnes take 2nd right towards Jonvilliers)

This eighteenth century residence is situated in the middle of a private park and is bordered by a large wood. The impressive house overlooks an enormous lawn. Guests are invited to dine with the proprietors but meals must be booked in advance. Continental breakfast served. English spoken.
Near river Forest area Near motorway
5 en suite (shr) (1 fmly) No smoking on premises TV available Full central heating Open parking available Supervised Languages spoken: English
ROOMS: s 250-280FF; d 280-330FF Reductions over 1 night
CARDS: Travellers cheques

ENNORDRES Cher

Moulin Laurent (Prop: Lahalle Daniel)
Le Gué de la Pierre *18380*
☎ 248580470 FAX 248584545
Bedrooms look out onto an attractive garden which guests may relax in. The Cher area belongs to the province of Berry, home to historical castles and Romanesque churches. Breakfast served in a huge living room. Fishing golf, archery and bike-hire are available on site. A little English spoken.
Near river Near lake Forest area
3 rms (2 bth/shr) (2 fmly) No smoking on premises TV available Full central heating Open parking available No children 4yrs Child discount available 8yrs

ÉTRECHET Indre

Manoir en Berry (Prop: Mme N Lyster)
Les Ménas *36120*
☎ 254226385 FAX 254226385
(A20 exit at Châteauroux onto D67, between N20 & D943, Les Ménas signposted)

Historic Tudor site, which belonged to Mary Stuart, Queen of Scots. Splendid 18th century family mansion, set in three acres of grounds, where one bedroom has a fireplace and guests have the use of a private lounge with library. Evening meal with wine available on request and special diets can be catered for. Fishing in the Indre at 300 metres. Swimming pool. Childrens' swings. Tennis, bathing and windsurfing are all within easy reach. English spoken.
Near river Near lake Near beach Forest area Near motorway
5 en suite (bth/shr) (2 fmly) No smoking on premises TV in 3 bedrooms Full central heating Open parking available Child discount available 11yrs Bicycle rental Open terrace Languages spoken: English & Spanish
ROOMS: s 180-220FF; d 270-300FF Reductions over 1 night
MEALS: Continental breakfast 30FF Dinner 65-85FF
CARDS: ●● ▓ Travellers cheques

FEINGS Loir-et-Cher

Le Petit Bois Martin (Prop: M & Mme Papineau)
41120
☎ 254202731
Delightful eighteenth century house set beneath the old trees. M. and Mme. Papineau welcome you to their peaceful residence. Situated in the heart of the Loire, this residence offers walks through the forest and by the lake, breakfast in the attractive dining room and comfortable, spacious rooms.
Forest area
Closed 15 Mar-15 Oct
3 en suite (bth/shr) (2 fmly) (1 with balcony) No smoking on premises TV available Full central heating Open parking available Supervised

FEROLLES Loiret

Susan De Smet (Prop: Mme S de Smet)
8 Route de Martroi La Breteche *45150*
☎ 238597953
(from Orléans take N460 to Jargeau, then D921 to Ferolles - Chambres d'Hôtes is signposted)
The proprietor, Susan de Smet, has her own self-imposed B&B code. The rooms should be clean and comfortable, the host should be welcoming and available. This guesthouse certainly

conforms to those criteria. In addition, guests can enjoy a continental breakfast and meals in the evening (reservations needed). The garden offers a sandpit and swings so children are not forgotten! English spoken.
Near river Forest area
3 en suite (shr) (2 fmly) No smoking on premises Full central heating Open parking available Languages spoken: English
ROOMS: s 170FF; d 210FF
MEALS: Dinner fr 70FF

FERTÉ-ST-AUBIN, LA Loiret

Ravenel
rte de Jouy le Potier *45240*
☎ 238765720
(A71 exit at Orleans and take RN20 towards La ferte St Aubin, then D18 towards Jouy-le-Poitier for 5km turn right for La Vielle Foret)
Forest area Near motorway
3 en suite (bth) (1 fmly) Full central heating Open parking available Languages spoken: English, German & Spanish
CARDS: Travellers cheques

FERTÉ-VIDAME, LA Eure-et-Loir

Manoir de la Motte
28340
☎ 237375169 FAX 237375156
Come and enjoy this nineteenth century manor situated on the borders of Normandy and the Perche. This elegant guesthouse is surrounded by a three hectare park. The proprietors assure you of a warm and traditional welcome. Golf on site (three holes for training) and jogging path available in the park. Open all year round. English spoken.
Forest area
4 rms (2 bth) (2 fmly) No smoking on premises Full central heating Open parking available Supervised Child discount available 10yrs Languages spoken: English
CARDS: Travellers cheques

FOËCY Cher

Le Petit Prieure (Prop: Claude et Chantal Alard)
7 rue l'Église *18500*
☎ 248510176
(from Bourges take N76 to Mehun-sur-Yèvre, then D60 to Foëcy)
This small, delightful Priory is positioned against a backdrop of forests between the Loire châteaux and the Jacques Coeur Highway. The warmth of the welcome, the peace and quiet - and a superb breakfast - may tempt you to stay more than just one night.
Near river Forest area
3 en suite (bth/shr) (3 fmly) No smoking on premises TV in 2 bedrooms Full central heating Open parking available Supervised Child discount available 14yrs
ROOMS: d 250-300FF *

FONDETTES Indre-et-Loire

Manoir du Grand Martigny (Prop: Henri Desmarais)
Vallières *37230*
☎ 247422987 FAX 247422444
(3m W of Tours on N152, signposted 600yds after petrol station)

cont'd

At the heart of the Loire Valley, the Manoir du Grand Martigny is a perfect base for touring the châteaux country. It offers comfort, charm and a warm welcome and is only three miles downriver from Tours. Attractively decorated rooms. Situated in a six hectare park, this ivy-clad château is truly spectacular.
Near river Near motorway
Closed 13 Nov-Mar
5 en suite (bth/shr) (1 fmly) No smoking on premises Full central heating Open parking available Supervised No children 12yrs Languages spoken: English
ROOMS: s 430FF; d 460-700FF
CARDS: Travellers cheques

FRANCUEIL Indre-et-Loire

Le Moulin Neuf (Prop: M & Mme Sansonetti)
28 rue du Moulin Neuf *37150*
☎ 247239344 FAX 247239467

Roses adorn the length of the garden and fill the air with perfume. Each guest room looks out onto the park and a large entrance hall, music room and veranda all contribute to an enjoyable stay. A swimming pool is available for guests' use.
Near river Forest area Near motorway
3 en suite (bth) No smoking on premises TV available Full central heating Open parking available Covered parking available Outdoor swimming pool Fishing Languages spoken: English Spanish
ROOMS: s 390FF; d 450-500FF
CARDS: Travellers cheques

GEHÉE Indre

Château de Touchenoire (Prop: De Clerck)
36240
☎ 254408734 FAX 254408551
Near river Near lake Near beach Forest area
Closed Oct-Apr
6 en suite (bth/shr) (2 fmly) No smoking on premises Full central heating Open parking available Supervised Child discount available 5yrs Last d 20.30hrs Languages spoken: English, Dutch & Italian
MEALS: Dinner fr 85FF*

GENILLÉ Indre-et-Loire

Le Moulin de la Roche (Prop: Josette & Clive Miéville)
37460
☎ 247595658 FAX 247595962
(from A10 exit at Chateau Renault-Amboise,left onto A10 to Genille. Mill 1km before Genille)
The mill, dating back to the fifteenth century, is surrounded by

cool and lush vegetation. From the bedrooms, decorated in colourful fabrics and stencil designs, you can hear the soft and relaxing sounds of the river. All bedrooms have tea and coffee making facilties. Your hosts are a Franco-British couple.
Near river Near lake Forest area
Closed 21Dec-3 Jan
4 en suite (bth/shr) (1 fmly) No smoking on premises Full central heating Open parking available Supervised Fishing Table tennis BBQ Languages spoken: English & Spanish
MEALS: Dinner 130FF

GERMIGNY-DES-PRÉS Loiret

Bed & Breakfast (Prop: M & Mme J Jarsale)
28 rte de Chateauneuf *45110*
☎ 238582115 FAX 238582115
(from Chateauneuf-sur-Loire take D952 towards Vien, then D60 to Germigny-des-Prés)
Near river Near lake Forest area
5 en suite (shr) No smoking on premises Full central heating Open parking available Supervised Child discount available 5yrs Table tennis
ROOMS: s 200FF; d 270-320FF * Special breaks

HERRY Cher

Bed & Breakfast (Prop: M Genoud)
10 pl du Champ de Foire *18140*
☎ 248795902
Enjoy your stay in this comfortable and colourful nineteenth century house, set in a rural and peaceful part of the Loire Valley. Fishing is possible either in the canal or in the Loire. Beaches close by. The house is situated in the village and is easy to find. Home-made breakfast is available. Special discounts for a three-night stay. English spoken.
Near river Forest area
3 en suite (shr) (2 fmly) TV available Full central heating Open parking available Languages spoken: English

HOMMES Indre-et-Loire

Le Vieux Château d'Hommes
37340
☎ 247249513 FAX 247246867
In the heart of the Loire Valley, with its vineyards and châteaux, stands this fifteenth century medieval château. The comfortable guest rooms are situated in the authentic tithe barn. Meals are served in the restaurant, which is in the original Knight's Hall room. Swimming pool available to guests. English spoken.
Near river Near lake Forest area
5 en suite (bth/shr) (1 fmly) TV available Full central heating Open parking available Covered parking available Child discount available Outdoor swimming pool V meals Last d 21.00hrs Languages spoken: English & Italian
MEALS: Full breakfast 40FF Lunch 135-150FF Dinner 135-150FF*

HUISMES Indre-et-Loire

Le Clos de l'Ormeau
37420
☎ 247954154 FAX 247954154
(at side of the church pass under arch then 1st left, 2nd house on right)
Near river Near lake Forest area
2 rms (1 bth/shr) No smoking on premises Full central

heating Open parking available Child discount available 2yrs
Outdoor swimming pool
ROOMS: s 240-260FF; d 240-260FF Special breaks

La Pilleterie (Prop: Mme Prunier-Guilletat)
37420
☎ 247955807
Peace and quiet assured is assured in the three appealing
guest rooms set in a converted barn. A living room with
fireplace and colour TV, a kitchen and a large garden are all
available for guests' use. Parking. Swimming, tennis, fishing
and horse-riding available nearby.
Near river Forest area
4 en suite (bth/shr) No smoking on premises Full central
heating Open parking available

INGRANDES-DE-TOURAINE Indre-et-Loire

Le Clos St-André (Prop: M Pincon)
37140
☎ 247969081 FAX 247969081
(in Ingrandes on the main road from Bourgueil to Langeais
D35, look for telephone box turn into street opposite, then
right into second street follow signs)

Clos Saint André is a small working vineyard with very
comfortable, quiet accommodation in the eighteenth century
extension to the sixteenth century farmhouse. Your hostess,
Mme Pinçon, is a splendid cook. Half board is compulsory
Apr-Oct. She offers guests a traditional evening meal,
accompanied by the estate Bourgueil wine. You will be joined
by your hosts, who both speak excellent English. Children's
games, pétanque and table-tennis available.
Near river Near lake Forest area
Closed 16 Nov-14 Mar
6 en suite (bth/shr) (4 fmly) Full central heating Open
parking available Child discount available 12yrs Boule
Bicycle rental Table tennis Languages spoken: English
ROOMS: s 250-300FF; d 280-330FF
MEALS: Dinner 105-150FF
CARDS: ●● ▬ Travellers cheques

ISDES Loiret

Bed & Breakfast (Prop: Mme Renée Hatte)
30 r de Clemont *45620*
☎ 238291089
(A71 exit Lamotte/Beuvron in direction Sully sur Loire)
A charming house set in a quiet village location with four
guest rooms available, one of which is a suite with French
doors that open onto a vast garden. Parking. Some English
spoken.

Near river Near lake Near beach Forest area In town centre
Near motorway
2 en suite (bth) No smoking in 1 bedroom Radio in rooms
Full central heating Open parking available Languages
spoken: English & Spanish
ROOMS: s 200-230FF; d 220-250FF *

Bed & Breakfast (Prop: Mme Bernard)
4 rte de Clemont *45620*
☎ 238291089
(A71 exit Lamotte/Beuvron direction Sully sur Loire)
There are two guest rooms here, one is in the annexe of the
house, charmingly called The Dolls House, and opens directly
onto the well-stocked walled garden; the other is located in
the proprietors' home. On sunny days a delicious breakfast is
served outside. Close to the Loire and Orléans. English spoken.
Near river Near beach Forest area In town centre Near
motorway
2 en suite (bth/shr) No smoking on premises Radio in rooms
Full central heating Open parking available Languages
spoken: English & Spanish

JARS Cher

La Brissauderie (Prop: M Philippe Jay)
18260
☎ 248587089 FAX 248587176
A warm welcome is assured at this renovated family
farmhouse. The Jay family raise goats and Philippe Jay is a
cheese-tasting expert.
Forest area
1 en suite (shr) Full central heating Open parking available
ROOMS: d fr 190FF
CARDS: Travellers cheques

JOUY-LE-POTIER Loiret

Bed & Breakfast (Prop: Jacques & Christiane Becchi)
778 r de Chevenelles *45370*
☎ 238458307
(12km from A71 exit2)
The house has been constructed in the traditional Solognet
style. One bedroom has a library, with television, which leads
off from the room. Large, wooded garden, with patio. The
hosts make sure that visitors know the best places to visit in
the area. Near to the Châteaux of Chambord, Cheverny and
Blois.
Forest area Near motorway
2 rms (1 shr) Radio in rooms Full central heating Open
parking available Supervised Child discount available 9yrs
ROOMS: s fr 200FF; d fr 250FF
MEALS: Dinner fr 90FF
CARDS: Travellers cheques

LANGEAIS Indre-et-Loire

Château de Cinq-Mars (Prop: M & Mme Untersteller)
37130
☎ 247964049
(from Tours take N152 follow river Loire towards Saumur at
Cinq Mars la Pile the chateau is on right, follow signposts)
Near river Near lake Near sea Forest area Near motorway
3 en suite (bth/shr) (1 fmly) Full central heating Open
parking available Child discount available Languages
spoken: English & German
ROOMS: s 380FF; d 340-440FF Reductions over 1 night
CARDS: Travellers cheques

LIGRÉ Indre-et-Loire

Bed & Breakfast (Prop: M & Mme Boucher-Marolleau)
5 rue Saint-Martin *37500*
☎ 247933753 FAX 247933753
The hosts extend a warm welcome to those who stay in one of the three spacious and individually decorated guest rooms in their home. Garden available for guests' use. English spoken.
Near river Forest area
3 en suite (bth/shr) (1 fmly) No smoking on premises Full central heating Open parking available Child discount available Languages spoken: English & Spanish
CARDS: Travellers cheques

LIGUEIL Indre-et-Loire

Moulin de la Touche (Prop: Michael Rees)
37240
☎ 247920684 FAX 247920684
(A10 to St Maure, D59 to Ligueil, chambre d'hôte is 2km out of Ligueil on the right of the D31 Ligueil to Loches road).

This is an eighteenth century watermill, attached to a large, comfortable miller's house. Bedrooms are spacious and prettily furnished. The guest lounge and dining room have open fireplaces. The watermill and house are surrounded by thirty acres of land and two rivers run through the grounds. Discounts available for stays in excess of five nights. Fishing available on site. Camping facilities also available at this location. English hosts.
Near river Near lake Forest area In town centre Near motorway
Closed Xmas
5 en suite (shr) (2 fmly) (1 with balcony) No smoking on premises Full central heating Open parking available Child discount available 12yrs Fishing Last d 18.00hrs Languages spoken: English
ROOMS: s fr 260FF; d 270-350FF Reductions over 1 night
MEALS: Dinner fr 120FF
CARDS: ●● ▄▄ Travellers cheques

LIMERAY Indre-et-Loire

Les Grillons (Prop: M & Mme Guichard)
37530
☎ 247301176
Nicole, Gilbert and their children offer a traditional welcome and invite guests to enjoy with them the regional cuisine, based on fresh products of the season, by reservation. Situated in the Loire Valley on a working farm, with poultry, growing cereals and vines. English spoken.
Near river Near motorway

Closed 15 Dec-5 Jan
5 en suite (bth) (3 fmly) (1 with balcony) TV available Open parking available Child discount available 10yrs Boule Last d 20.00hrs Languages spoken: English & German
MEALS: Dinner 100-130FF*
CARDS: ●● ▄▄ Travellers cheques

LOCHES Indre-et-Loire

Les Jolletières (Prop: Elisabeth Douard)
37600
☎ 247590661 FAX 247590661
Four bed & breakfast rooms available on this farm in a rural setting between the river and the forest. Meals in the evening by arrangement, residents only, aperitif and wine included. Panoramic view over the Château de Loches. English spoken.
Near river Near lake Forest area
Closed Jan
4 en suite (bth/shr) (1 fmly) No smoking on premises Full central heating Open parking available Child discount available 10 yrs Bicycle rental Last d 18.00hrs Languages spoken: English
ROOMS: d 220FF Reductions over 1 night
MEALS: Dinner fr 90FF

Le Moulin
St Jean St Germain *37600*
☎ 247947012 FAX 247947798
(take N143 from Loches direction of Chateauroux, go through Perusson turn left over the bridge on left)
Situated on its own private island in the middle of the River Indre, this lovely property features a garden with lawns sloping down to the water's edge. All rooms are well-furnished and meals are provided from local produce. Within easy reach of most major châteaux and many vineyards where you can sample and buy the wine. Private small sandy beach plus 300 metres of private fishing with a small boat available for messing about on the river. Not suitable for young children. English hosts.
Near river Near beach Forest area Near motorway
Closed Dec-Feb
6 en suite (bth/shr) (1 fmly) (2 with balcony) No smoking in all bedrooms Full central heating Open parking available Child discount available -7yrs Fishing Boule Open terrace 2 rowing boats V meals Last d 8.30pm Languages spoken: English
ROOMS: s 260-300FF; d 300-350FF Reductions over 1 night
MEALS: Dinner fr 150FF
CARDS: Travellers cheques

LOUROUX, LE Indre-et-Loire

La Chaumine (Prop: M & Mme Baudoin)
37240
☎ 247928209
The old farmhouse at Chaumine offers one room on the ground floor which can accommodate up to six people. Static caravans also available. Home-made bread and jam available at breakfast. Meals served on request in the evenings. English spoken.
Near river Near lake Forest area
4 rms (2 bth/shr) (2 fmly) TV available Full central heating Open parking available Child discount available Last d 18.30hrs Languages spoken: English & Spanish
MEALS: Dinner fr 85FF*
CARDS: Travellers cheques

LUYNES Indre-et-Loire

Moulin Hodoux (Prop: Jocelyne Vacher)
37230
☎ 247557627 FAX 247557627
(A10 exit Ste Radegande, direction of Sayour on N152. 12km after Tours is Luynes centre and D76 for St Ettienne de Chigny for 1.25km to Le Pont de Grenouille, then right for 1.25km) In the heart of the Loire countryside, this comfortable accommodation lives up to the expectations of this region. The property is an eighteenth century mill and has been extensively restored. Situated in an attractive spot, with garden for use of guests, featuring a swimming pool. Calm, peaceful atmosphere. Evening meals available. A little English spoken.
Near river Forest area
4 en suite (shr) (3 fmly) Full central heating Open parking available Child discount available 2 yrs Outdoor swimming pool Fishing Boule Bicycle rental Open terrace Covered terrace Languages spoken: English & German
ROOMS: s fr 290FF; d fr 330FF Reductions over 1 night
CARDS: Travellers cheques

MANCELIÈRE-MONTMUREAU, LA Eure-et-Loir

La Musardière (Prop: M & Mme Schaffner)
28270
☎ 237483909 FAX 237483909
(on the D4 8km from Brezolles, 8km from La Ferte Vidame) Set in an attractive one-hectare park. Property owned by the Schaffner family, offering three rooms independent of the rest of the house. Living room, colour television and kitchen available for guests' use. Table-tennis. Ideal location for weekends away, holidays and special occasions.
Near river Near lake Forest area
Closed Nov-Mar
3 en suite (bth/shr) (1 fmly) TV in 1 bedroom Full central heating Open parking available Supervised Child discount available Indoor swimming pool (heated) Outdoor swimming pool (heated) Table tennis Languages spoken: English & German
ROOMS: s fr 300FF; d fr 360FF Reductions over 1 night

MÉNESTREAU-EN-VILLETTE Loiret

Bed & Breakfast (Prop: Oliver Cadel)
115 Chemin de Bethleem *45240*
☎ 238769070
(turn of N20 at La Ferte St Aubin in direction Menestreau en Villette)
Forest area
4 rms (1 bth) (2 fmly) No smoking on premises Full central heating Open parking available Child discount available Languages spoken: English & German

Ferme des Foucault (Prop: Rosemary Beau)
45240
☎ 238769441
(6km after Marcilly en Villette on the D64 (route to Sennely) on the right small sign Les Foucault, then turn left at mailboxes) Rosemary Beau offers you a ground floor room with lounge, which has a private entrance. A second room under the eaves has a super view of the surroundings. The rooms are located in an old brick farmhouse in the forest of Sologne. Perhaps the best feature is the peace and quiet of the area. Both rooms have a mixture of American and French antiques. English spoken.

Near river Forest area
RS Nov-Apr
2 en suite (bth/shr) No smoking on premises TV available Full central heating Open parking available Bicycle rental Languages spoken: English & German
ROOMS: s 220FF; d 280FF Reductions over 1 night Special breaks: (4 nights or more)
CARDS: Travellers cheques

MENETOU-SALON Cher

Bed & Breakfast (Prop: Mme Marguerite Jouannin)
17 r Franche *18510*
☎ 248648085
Mme Marguerite Jouannin offers nine rooms in this large, old house, set back from a quiet street. A courtyard and gardens are there to encourage the weary traveller to relax. This house is situated near many châteaux.
Forest area
7 rms (4 shr) No smoking on premises Full central heating Open parking available No children

MÉOBECQ Indre

Le Bourg (Prop: Cecile Benhamou)
1 rue de Neuillay *36500*
☎ 254394436
Fifteenth century monastery located between Châteauroux and Le Blanc, which provides a good stopover on the motorway to the south. Alternatively, lovers of the Brenne area are welcome to stay longer. Two spacious rooms available. Many châteaux and restaurants in the area. English spoken.
Near river Near lake Forest area Near motorway
Closed Nov-Mar
2 rms Full central heating Open parking available No children Languages spoken: English

MER Loir-et-Cher

Bed & Breakfast (Prop: Claude & Joelle Mormiche)
Le Clos, 9 r Dutems *41500*
☎ 54811736 FAX 54817019
A10, exit 16, Paris-Bordeaux 2km, near church, town centre.

Claude and Joelle Mormiche welcome you to their sixteenth century house. Guests are urged to take a walk through the gardens to appreciate fully the splendour of its location. Five guest rooms on offer. Bikes for hire. A good area to relax in. English spoken.

cont'd

Near river Forest area In town centre Near motorway
5 en suite (bth/shr) (1 fmly) No smoking on premises Full
central heating Open parking available Covered parking
available Bicycle rental Billiards Languages spoken: English
ROOMS: d 280-350FF
CARDS: ●● ▆▆ Eurocard Travellers cheques

MEUNG-SUR-LOIRE Loiret

Bed & Breakfast (Prop: Raymonde Bechu)
30 rte de la Batissiere *45130*
☎ 238443438 FAX 238443438
Guests are welcomed as friends in this quiet and peaceful
house set in open countryside and surrounded by a tree-laden
garden, home to many types of birds. One room on the
ground floor, with a wheelchair ramp, is suitable for disabled
guests. Flowers placed in each bedroom add to the charm and
home-made jam is served at breakfast. Table tennis, children's
games and a garden room are available. Reductions for
children.
Near river Forest area Near motorway
4 en suite (bth/shr) (1 fmly) No smoking on premises Full
central heating Open parking available Supervised Child
discount available Table tennis

MONTEREAU-EN-GATINAIS Loiret

Hostellerie Rurale de Courpale (Prop: Michel Hamelin)
Courpalet *45260*
☎ 238877244
Situated on the edge of the Orléans Forest, this residence is
set in four hectares of grounds and offers pretty, newly
decorated double guest rooms on the ground floor.
Independent access to terrace and swimming pool. Lounge
and dining room, furnished in Louis XIII style, are availabe to
guests. Dinner available by request at a fixed price.
Reductions available for children under ten years.
Near river Forest area Near motorway
3 rms Full central heating Open parking available Child
discount available 10yrs Outdoor swimming pool Last d
21.00hs
MEALS: Lunch fr 90FF Dinner fr 90FF*

MONTHODON Indre-et-Loire

La Marechalerie (Prop: Niedbalski)
6 r des Rosiers, Le Sentier, France *37110*
☎ 247296166
(at Château Renault, head in the direction of Angers for 2km,
turn right onto D54 towards le Boulay - le Senter is 3km after
leaving le Boulay)

Located close to the châteaux of this region, in the heart of the
countryside. Six rooms are offered in this eighteenth century
blacksmith's forge. The rooms have a private entrance
separate from the main house. Bike hire, tackle hire and
games available from your hosts. English spoken.
Near river Near lake Forest area
6 en suite (bth/shr) (2 fmly) Open parking available Covered
parking available Child discount available 12yrs Fishing
Bicycle rental Last d 19.00hrs Languages spoken: English &
German
ROOMS: d 200FF
MEALS: Dinner 75FF
CARDS: Travellers cheques

MONTILOUIS-SUR-LOIRE Indre-et-Loire

Le Colombier (Prop: M A Moreau Recoing)
4 Grande Rue *37270*
☎ 247508524
Near river Forest area Near motorway
3 en suite (bth/shr) (2 fmly) (2 with balcony) Full central
heating Open parking available Pool table Boule Table
tennis Languages spoken: English,German & Italian
CARDS: Travellers cheques

MONTLANDON Eure-et-Loir

Bed & Breakfast (Prop: M & Mme Gallet)
7 r de la Tour *28240*
☎ 237498106
In this modern house situated between Chartres and Nagent-
le-Rotrou, Gérard and Suzanne Gallet look forward to meeting
you. Calm surroundings, attractive view of the forest and large
garden. Two rooms available. Meals are served, although
reservations are required. Reductions for children up to ten.
Forest area Near motorway
2 en suite (bth/shr) No smoking on premises Full central
heating Open parking available Supervised Child discount
available 10yrs Last d 20.00hrs
MEALS: Dinner fr 70FF*
CARDS: Travellers cheques

MONTRÉSOR Indre-et-Loire

Le Moulin (Prop: Willem de Laddersous)
8 impasse de la Mécorique *37460*
☎ 247926820 FAX 247927461
(17km from Loches and 25km from Valencoup, take direction
of Chemillé-sur-Indrois & then follow signs to bed &
breakfast)
On the River Montrésor and in one of France's most attractive
villages, the mill is at the crossroads of a popular tourist
region.
Near river
4 en suite (bth/shr) (2 fmly) Full central heating Open
parking available Child discount available 12yrs Fishing
Boule Languages spoken: English, German & Polish
ROOMS: s 250-300FF; d 280-330FF Reductions over 1 night

NEUIL Indre-et-Loire

Les Hautes Mougonnières (Prop: Jean Mestivier)
37190
☎ 247268771
Soline and Jean-Pierre are your hosts at their farm where they
raise chickens and grow raspberries. Reductions for children

up to ten years old. Dinner, including wine, served in the evenings. English spoken.
Forest area
5 en suite (bth/shr) (2 fmly) No smoking on premises Full central heating Open parking available Child discount available 10yrs V meals Languages spoken: English
CARDS: ▩ Travellers cheques

NEUVY-LE-ROI Indre-et-Loire

Bed & Breakfast (Prop: Mme Ghislaine de Couesnongle)
20 rue Pilate *37370*
☎ 247244148
(from Tours/La Membrolle N138 towards Le Mans, at Neuillé-Pont-Pierre take D68 to Neuvy-le-Roi; house on road through village, oppposite turning to Loustault)
In the lovely Loire valley, a homely, quiet and welcoming house, which has been recently renovated.
Near lake Forest area Near motorway
1 en suite (bth/shr) Full central heating Open parking available Languages spoken: English
ROOMS: d 280FF
MEALS: Dinner fr 100FF

Ferme le Château-du-Bois
37370
☎ 247244476 FAX 247248658
Near river Forest area Near motorway
4 en suite (bth/shr) (2 fmly) TV available Open parking available Child discount available Fishing Riding Boule Open terrace V meals Languages spoken: English & Spanish
MEALS: Lunch fr 65FFalc Dinner fr 65FFalc*

NEUVY-SUR-BARANGEON Cher

Le Bas Guilly
18330
☎ 248516446
The Bas Guilly throws open its doors to all holiday makers. Large drawing room with open fires. All the following can be enjoyed either on-site or in close proximity: fishing in lakes, river fishing, walking, riding, motorbikes for hire, hunting, golf, tennis and châteaux visits. English spoken.
Near river Forest area Near motorway
6 en suite (shr) No smoking on premises Full central heating Open parking available Covered parking available Jacuzzi/spa Languages spoken: English & German
CARDS: ●● ▬ Travellers cheques

ORVAL Cher

La Trolière (Prop: M Dussert)
18200
☎ 248964745
A spacious eighteenth century house, set in a park, near Noirlac Abbey on the Jacques Coeur route and near to the Meillant Forest. Fishing, in the private lake. Swimming pool close by. Reductions for children under ten years. English spoken.
Near river Forest area Near motorway
3 en suite (bth/shr) No smoking on premises Full central heating Open parking available Supervised Child discount available 10yrs Fishing Languages spoken: English
CARDS: ●● Travellers cheques

PANZOULT Indre-et-Loire

Domaine de Beauséjour (Prop: Marie Chauveau)
37220
☎ 247586464 FAX 247952713
(Panzoult is located 12km east of Chinon, take D21 in the direction of L'île Bouchard through the village, 2km out of town signposted on the right)
Family home flanked on one side by forests and on the other by a splendid view over the vineyards. A large swimming pool is available in the garden. There are plenty of restaurants, châteaux and museums in this area. English spoken.
Near river Near lake Forest area
5 en suite (bth/shr) (1 fmly) Full central heating Open parking available Outdoor swimming pool Tennis Fishing Riding Mini-golf Bicycle rental Table tennis Languages spoken: English
ROOMS: s fr 350FF; d fr 450FF *

PAUDRY Indre

Château de Dangy (Prop: G M & Lucie Place)
36260
☎ 254494224 FAX 254494299
Near lake Forest area Near motorway
Closed Oct-Mar
17 rms (14 bth/shr) (3 fmly) No smoking on premises Night porter Open parking available Child discount available Languages spoken: English
CARDS: Travellers cheques

POISLAY, LE Loir-et-Cher

Les Coteaux (Prop: Gaec Coigneau)
41270
☎ 254805319 FAX 254801911
Guest rooms are in a farmhouse, typical of the region. Communal use of the facilities on the ground floor. Enjoy a game of pétanque in the garden or explore the countryside on bikes which can be borrowed from the hosts. Table-tennis. English spoken.
Near river Forest area
3 en suite (shr) (1 fmly) Full central heating Open parking available Child discount available 8yrs Boule Cycling Table tennis Last d 20.00hrs Languages spoken: English
MEALS: Dinner fr 80FF*
CARDS: Travellers cheques

PONTLEVOY Loir-et-Cher

Les Bordes (Prop: Josianne & François Galloux)
41400
☎ 254325108 FAX 254326443
Josianne and François Galloux welcome you to their restored home, situated on a working farm. The rooms are spacious and light. Breakfast and dinner served in the dining room. Walking, tennis, swimming, riding and fishing all within close proximity.
Forest area
6 en suite (bth/shr) (2 fmly) No smoking in all bedrooms Full central heating Open parking available Child discount available 10yrs

PRÉ-ST-MARTIN Eure-et-Loir

Le Carcotage Beauceron (Prop: M & Mme Violette)
8 rue St Martin *28800*
☎ 237472721 FAX 237473809
Guest bedrooms are in a restored part of this 18th century home, where the light and spacious rooms are furnished with antiques. Meals are available on request and are taken with the hosts. The garden has a children's swimming pool, swings, sandpit and views over wheat fields. Bicycles available for hire. English spoken.
4 en suite (shr) (2 fmly) No smoking on premises Full central heating Open parking available Covered parking available Languages spoken: English

QUANTILLY Cher

Château de Champgrand (Prop: M Alain Gazeali)
18110
☎ 248641215 FAX 248244100
(between St-Martin D'Auxigny and Menetou Salon)
Forest area Near motorway
4 en suite (bth/shr) TV available Full central heating Open parking available Languages spoken: English

QUINCY Cher

Domaine du Pressoir (Prop: M Claude Houssier)
18120
☎ 248513004
Near river Near lake Forest area Near motorway
Closed Jan & Feb
4 en suite (shr) (3 fmly) No smoking on premises Full central heating Open parking available

REBOURSIN Indre

Le Moulin (Prop: M Gerard Cheneau)
36150
☎ 254497205
Guest rooms are available in the small cottage and the 18th century house, both set in attractive grounds. A large park nearby and the museums and the old town of Levroux are within a 20 kilometre radius. Fishing is available in the lake at Reboursin and shops, tennis, horse-riding, golf are all quite close. English spoken.
Near river Near lake Forest area Near motorway
Closed Oct-14 May
4 en suite (shr) TV available Full central heating Open parking available Languages spoken: English, Spanish & Portuguese

RESTIGNÉ Indre-et-Loire

Château Louy (Prop: J S Luff)
37140
☎ 247969522
(off the E60 between Saumur and Restigne)
Very tranquil seventeenth century château with pretty garden - surrounded by vineyards. Self-contained studio. In easy reach of the Châteaux of the Loire Valley and the local markets. Recently restored. Reductions for children under fourteen. English owners.
Near river Near lake Forest area

1 en suite (bth/shr) Full central heating Open parking available Supervised Child discount available 14yrs Bicycle rental Languages spoken: English
ROOMS: s 240FF; d 290FF Reductions over 1 night Special breaks: 7 nights for price of 6.

RICHELIEU Indre-et-Loire

Bed & Breakfast (Prop: Mme Couvrat-Desvergnes)
6 rue Henri Proust *37120*
☎ 247582940
This grand mansion is elegantly furnished. The shady garden is quiet and peaceful. The visitor will feel very grand in these surroundings. Some English spoken.
Near river Near lake Forest area In town centre
Closed Nov-Etr
4 en suite (bth/shr) (2 with balcony) Night porter Open parking available Languages spoken: English & Italian
CARDS: Eurocheques

L'Escale (Prop: Marion & Tim Lawrence)
30 rue dela Galere *37120*
☎ 247582555
(A10 from Paris-St-Mauré direction Richelieu centre of town)
Traditional French house situated on the edge of a small village, set amidst cornfields, sunflowers, melons and vineyards. It offers hotel-type comforts in a more relaxed and informal atmosphere. English hosts, Marion and Tim Lawrence, extend a warm, friendly welcome. Tastefully furnished accommodation. Large lounge, leading to vine covered veranda. Plunge pool. Games room. Continental breakfasts and dinners with wine served in the evening. Splendid restaurants in locality.
Near river Near lake Forest area In town centre Near motorway
3 en suite (bth/shr) (2 fmly) Full central heating Child discount available 2yrs Languages spoken: English
ROOMS: s 270FF; d 290FF
CARDS: Travellers cheques

Les Religieuses (Prop: Mme Plâtre)
24 pl des Religieuses *37120*
☎ 247581042
(motorway Sainte-Maure exit (60km SW of Tours) then D760 to Noyant, then D757. At corner of Place des Religieuses and rue Jarry)
Mme Marie Josephe Le Plâtre welcomes you to her townhouse, which bears the marks of the Richelieu style. A charming hostess, who offers guests a traditional visit in comfortable well-furnished rooms. Breakfasts are hearty. Swimming pool, fishing, tennis and forest nearby.
Near river Near lake Forest area In town centre Near motorway
4 en suite (shr) TV available Full central heating

RIGNY-USSÉ Indre-et-Loire

Le Pin (Prop: M Porousset)
314320
☎ 247955299 FAX 247954321
(A10 exit Chamray-les-Tours direction Chinon)
Comfortable rooms are offered in this stone house, with swimming pool in the garden. Very calm surroundings. Bike rides and great walks through the forest which is right on the doorstep. Table-tennis, billiard table and sauna also on site.
Near river Forest area
4 en suite (bth/shr) Outdoor swimming pool Sauna Pool table Table tennis

RIVARENNES Indre

Château de la Tour (Prop: Mme de Clemont Tonnerre)
36800
☎ 254470612 FAX 254470608
Turreted château on the edge of the River Indre in a beautiful wooded park. Hundreds of small lakes in the area, which is renowned for hunting and fishing. There are many châteaux, forts, roman churches and medieval villages to visit in the area. English spoken.
Near river Forest area Near motorway
10 en suite (bth/shr) (3 fmly) Full central heating Open parking available Covered parking available Covered terrace
CARDS: Travellers cheques

ROCÉ Loir-et-Cher

La Touche - Rocé (Prop: Jean Louis Nouvellon)
41100
☎ 254771952 FAX 254770645
Anne-Marie and Jean-Louis Nouvellon welcome you to their restored farm in the country, where peace and relaxation await you. Six guest rooms are available, which are large and bright. A living room and kitchenette are available for the use of guests. Dinner served at a fixed price, with reduced price for children under ten years. Close to forests and paths. The nearby town of Vendôme is well worth a visit. English spoken.
Near river Near lake Forest area Near motorway
Closed 16 Sep-14 May
6 rms (4 shr) (1 fmly) Full central heating Child discount available Languages spoken: English
MEALS: Dinner fr 87FF*
CARDS: Travellers cheques

ROCHECORBON Indre-et-Loire

Château de Montgouverne
37210
☎ 247528459 FAX 247528461
(from A10 exit Tours Ste Radegonde, take N521 then N152 direction Vouvray then turn left to St Georges)
Located in listed parkland,this splendid 18th-century residence is surrounded by Vouvray vineyards and overlooks a lake. Both bedrooms and suites are beautifully furnished, all with en suite facilities and TV. Heated swimming pool, horse-riding and bicycles are available. Gourmet dinner by reservation.
Near river Forest area Near motorway
6 en suite (bth) (2 fmly) TV in all bedrooms Full central heating Open parking available No children 12yrs Outdoor swimming pool (heated) Bicycle rental Open terrace Languages spoken: English
ROOMS: d 590-1050FF
MEALS: Dinner 225-325FF*
CARDS: ●● ▦ ▨ Eurocard Travellers cheques

SACHÉ Indre-et-Loire

Les Tilleuls (Prop: Michelle Piller)
La Sablonniere *37190*
☎ 247268145 FAX 247268400
(coming from Tours, take direction for Chinon and turn off for Saché. In Saché follow signs for La Sablonniere where house is signposted)
Les Tilleuls dates back to the 19th century and stands in attractive gardens, thanks to the loving care of the host, Michelle Piller. The large breakfast served can be worked off via the many walks and cycle rides around. Children over ten years only. Some English.

Near river Forest area
Closed Dec-14 Mar
4 en suite (shr) No smoking on premises Full central heating Open parking available No children 10yrs Fishing Bicycle rental

ST-BAULD Indre-et-Loire

Le Moulin de Coudray (Prop: Sylvie Peria)
37310
☎ 247928264
Located between Cormery and Loches, this attractive 16th century residence, set within parkland of three hectares, has a shady terrace looking out the river and lake which are suitable for fishing. Independent access to the three guest rooms. Authentic regional cooking is served at a fixed price. Garden with table-tennis and bikes available. Some English spoken.
Near river Near lake Near beach Forest area
3 en suite (bth/shr) No smoking on premises Full central heating Open parking available Supervised Child discount available 10yrs Fishing Bicycle rental
MEALS: Dinner 110FF*

ST-BENOÎT-DU-SAULT Indre

Le Portail (Prop: Marie France Boyer Barral)
36170
☎ 254475720 FAX 254475720
(enter medieval city by the fortified gate in direction of priory and church)
Situated in the old medieval city of Saint Benoit du Sault, said to be one of the most beautiful villages in France, this 15th century house has an old fortified door, hence its name, and a belfry. English spoken.
Near river Forest area In town centre Near motorway
3 en suite (shr) (1 fmly) No smoking on premises TV in 2 bedrooms Full central heating Open parking available Supervised Child discount available 10yrs Languages spoken: English
ROOMS: s 200-250FF; d 250-350FF Reductions over 1 night

ST-BENOÎT-SUR-LOIRE Loiret

Bed & Breakfast (Prop: M & Mme Bouin)
6 Chemin de la Borde *45730*
☎ 238257053 FAX 238351006
Set in farmland, this relatively new house has a living room with kitchen area for guests to use. Children's games, table-tennis and bike hire are all available. Mireille and Dominique Bouin are pleased to show visitors round their farm and explain their farming techniques. English spoken.
Near river
5 en suite (shr) No smoking on premises Full central heating Open parking available Boule Bicycle rental V meals Languages spoken: English

ST-BRANCHS Indre-et-Loire

La Paqueraie (Prop: Monique Binet)
37320
☎ 247263151 FAX 247263915
(from Paris on the A10 exit Chambray and turn left onto N143 to Cormery, after railway crossing follow sign towards St-Branchs then sign Borne PR3, La Paqueraie is 4th house on the right)

cont'd

Surrounded by the castle of the Loire valley 'La Paqueraie' offers comfortable guest rooms, a garden with 100yr old oaks and a swimming pool. Meals are based on local produce accompanied by regional wine.
Near river Forest area
4 en suite (bth/shr) TV in all bedrooms Full central heating Open parking available Child discount available Outdoor swimming pool Fishing Boule V meals Last d 20.00hrs Languages spoken: English & Spanish
ROOMS: d 350FF
MEALS: Dinner fr 120FF
CARDS: Travellers cheques

ST-CHARTIER Indre

Château de Maitres Sonneurs (Prop: M Peubrier)
36400
☎ 254311017
This old château from the Plantagenet era is an historical monument. Large and comfortable guest rooms are available. The château is set in three hectares of parkland, with huge trees. Horse riding, golf and walks all within close proximity. English spoken.
Near river Forest area Near motorway
Closed 16 Nov-Apr
4 en suite (bth/shr) TV in 1 bedroom Open parking available Languages spoken: English

ST-ÉPAIN Indre-et-Loire

Château de Montgoger (Prop: Mireille & Paul Thilges)
37800
☎ 247655422 FAX 247658543
(A10 exit 25 Sainte-Maire-de-Touraine and take direction for Noyant-de-Touraine on D760, then Saint-Épain via D21)
This former residence of the Dukes of Choiseuil-Praslin is surrounded by a tree-filled seventeen hectare park. Set in the heart of the Loire Valley, near the main historical and cultural sites and offering many sporting activities, your hosts believe that this is an ideal place to stay. All rooms look out over the park. Rides are available as are many walks. English spoken.
Near river Forest area Near motorway
RS winter
4 en suite (bth) (4 with balcony) No smoking on premises TV in all bedrooms STV Full central heating Open parking available Supervised Child discount available 6-12yrs Languages spoken: English & German
ROOMS: s 400FF; d 450-500FF Special breaks: (10% discount)
CARDS: Travellers cheques

ST-GEORGES-SUR-EURE Eure-et-Loir

Hameau de Berneuse (Prop: Mme Marie-Laurence Varriale)
12 r Basse 28190
☎ 237268049
(autoroute Paris/Le Mans, exit Thivars, then in direction Fontenay-sur-Eure, then St-Georges-sur-Eure and Berneuse)
Set in large country garden, this modern house offers well furnished accommodation, with one room overlooking the terrace. French breakfast is served. Boules available and bikes for hire. Fishing close by. English spoken.
Near river Near lake Forest area Near motorway
Closed Aug

2 rms (1 bth) No smoking on premises Radio in rooms Full central heating Open parking available Supervised Child discount available 5yrs Fishing Boule Languages spoken: English, Italian & Spanish
ROOMS: s 220FF; d 250FF Special breaks: (3 or more nights, 10% off)
CARDS: Travellers cheques

ST-GERMAIN-DES-BOIS Cher

Bannay (Prop: M & Mme Chambrin)
18340
☎ 248253103
Three rooms available on a pretty creeper-covered farm set in the middle of fields. A living room with television and books are available for use by guests. Conservatory situated underneath a lime tree.
Forest area Near motorway
3 en suite (shr) Full central heating Open parking available Child discount available 10yrs
CARDS: 🔲

ST-LAURENT-NOUAN Loir-et-Cher

Bed & Breakfast (Prop: M & Mme Libeaut)
41220
☎ 254872472
Built in the 18th century and surrounded by three hectares of farmland, this family residence offers comfortable rooms in a quiet location. A swimming pool, a riding centre and golf are all close, while fishing is available in the nearby river and lakes. Some English spoken.
Forest area
3 en suite (shr) Open parking available Child discount available

ST-MARTIN-D'ABBAT Loiret

Bed & Breakfast (Prop: Chantel Pelletier)
Le Haut Des Bordes *45110*
☎ 238582209
Attractive, large house in a peaceful setting, bordered by a river and lake. Large, wooded garden. Suite available with two bedrooms. Open all year. English spoken.
Near river Near lake Forest area
1 en suite (bth) No smoking on premises Full central heating Open parking available Supervised Languages spoken: English

Bed & Breakfast (Prop: Françoise Vanalder)
La Polonerie, Les Places *45110*
☎ 238582151
(from Orleans, travel towards Montargis on the N60 for 35km. Exit at Chateauneuf-sur-dome, D952 towards Gien. Through St Martin d'Abbat, 3km on follow signs on left.)
Farmhouse, built at the beginning of the century, set in two hectares of garden, situated on the edge of the Orléans forest. You are warmly welcomed by Françoise and Thierry Vanalder and your hostess is happy to cook dinner for you. Both rooms are decorated in a charming fashion. English spoken.
Near river Forest area Near motorway
Closed 16 Feb-9 Mar & 18 Aug-8 Sep
No smoking in 2 bedrooms Full central heating Open parking available Supervised Child discount available Last d 20.00hrs Languages spoken: English, German & Italian
ROOMS: s 200FF; d 250FF Reductions over 1 night
MEALS: Dinner fr 100FF

VAL DE LOIRE

ST-MARTIN-DES-BOIS Loir-et-Cher

Les Pignons (Prop: Guy & Elisabeth Chevereau)
41800
☎ 254725743 FAX 254725739
A peaceful and relaxing atmosphere pervades this renovated
building where thehe ground floor has been made accessible
to guests with disabilities. The rustic reception room has a
fireplace and kitchen area. Peaceful and relaxing atmosphere.
Local information and brochures are available. Dinner is
available and is taken with the hosts. English spoken.
Forest area
4 en suite (shr) (2 fmly) Full central heating Open parking
available Supervised Child discount available Languages
spoken: English & German
ROOMS: s fr 180FF; d fr 220FF Reductions over 1 night
Special breaks
MEALS: Dinner 40-80FF
CARDS: Travellers cheques

ST-MARTIN-LE-BEAU Indre-et-Loire

Fombêche (Prop: M Jean Guestault)
37270
☎ 247502552 FAX 247502823
Six guest rooms available in the residence of wine-grower
Jean Guestault. Spacious, beautifully appointed rooms. Within
thirty metres of the residence you will find the wine-cellar
restaurant of the proprietor, called the Pigeonnier de
Fombêche. Here you will have the chance to sample some of
the local wines.
Near river Near lake Forest area Near motorway
6 en suite (bth/shr) Full central heating Open parking
available Riding V meals
ROOMS: d 250FF
CARDS: ● ▆ Travellers cheques

ST-MAURICE-ST-GERMAIN Eure-et-Loir

Le Clos Moussu (Prop: M et Mme J Thomas)
28240
☎ 237370446
(located on the D349, 7kms from La Loupe and 3km from
Pontgouin, close to the Châteaux-des-Vaux)
One hour from Paris, in the centre of the ancient forest of
Perche on the river Ure. Marie and Joseph Thomas welcome
you to stay in the warm friendly atmosphere of their 18th
century house.
Near river Near lake Forest area
3 en suite (bth/shr) (2 fmly) No smoking in 2 bedrooms TV in
2 bedrooms Full central heating Open parking available
Covered parking available Tennis Fishing Boule Table tennis
Last d 20.00hrs
ROOMS: s 200-250FF; d 250-300FF Reductions over 1 night
MEALS: Dinner 75-95FF
CARDS: Travellers cheques

Les Evesqueries (Prop: M F Goupil)
28240
☎ 237370047
Forest area Near motorway
2 en suite (bth/shr) (1 fmly) TV available Full central heating
Open parking available Covered parking available Child
discount available
ROOMS: s 180-200FF; d 180-200FF
CARDS: Travellers cheques

ST-MICHEL-SUR-LOIRE Indre-et-Loire

Château de Montbrun (Prop: Rita van Royen)
Langeais *37130*
☎ 247965713 FAX 247960128
(A10 Paris-Bordeaux exit Tours-Vouvray onto N152 in direction
of Saumur at Langeais follow signs)
Near river Near lake Forest area Near motorway
6 en suite (bth/shr) (2 fmly) (1 with balcony) TV in all
bedrooms Direct dial from all bedrooms Full central heating
Open parking available Supervised Outdoor swimming pool
(heated) Solarium Boule Bicycle rental Open terrace
Languages spoken: English German Dutch
ROOMS: d 470-695FF

ST-NICOLAS-DE-BOURGUEIL Indre-et-Loire

Manoir du Port Guyet (Prop: Mme Genevieve Valluet)
37140
☎ 247978220
Guests are welcomed as friends at the home of Mme
Genevieve Valluet, where the 16th century poet Ronsard wrote
some of his greatest love sonnets. Rooms are all
furnished with antiques and a Continental breakfast is served;
dinner is available if requested in advance. English spoken.
Near river Near lake Forest area Near motorway
Closed early Nov-Mar
3 en suite (bth/shr) Full central heating Child discount
available Languages spoken: English & Spanish
CARDS: Travellers cheques

ST-PREST Eure-et-Loir

Bed & Breakfast (Prop: Jacques & Ginette Ragu)
28 r de la Pierre Percee *28300*
☎ 237223038
Modern house in the Eure Valley, located between Chartres
and Maintenon. Large bedrooms, living room, open fire,
kitchenette. Reservations are required for dinner. Patio
available with sun loungers and garden furniture. Only
children over fifteen please. English spoken.
Near river Near lake Forest area Near motorway
1 en suite (shr) TV in all bedrooms Radio in rooms Full
central heating Open parking available No children 15yrs
Riding Boule Bicycle rental Languages spoken: English &
German
ROOMS: s 180FF; d 220FF Reductions over 1 night Special
breaks: (10% off)
MEALS: Lunch 70FF Dinner 70FF
CARDS: Travellers cheques

SANCERRE Cher

Bed & Breakfast (Prop: M & Mme Thibaudat)
31 r Saint-Andre *18300*
☎ 248780004
The beautiful restoration of this lovely Sancerre house gained
it second place in the best restored building of the region.
Good breakfasts are served here and there are numerous
restaurants nearby. The Loire is only one kilometre away and
there is a swimming pool nearby. Accompanied kayak trips
down the Loire. Some English.
Near river Forest area In town centre Near motorway
1 en suite (shr) TV available Full central heating Open
parking available Child discount available

157

Manoir de Vaudrédon (Prop: M Raymond Cirotte)
18300
☎ 248790029
Thirteenth century manor. There is also a separate cottage available. Located in calm surroundings near the vines of Sancerre. Nearest restaurant is only four kilometres away but some meals can be made on request. Many walks available in the areas, châteaux to visit, eighteen-hole golf course.
Forest area Near motorway
5 en suite (bth) TV available Full central heating Open parking available Child discount available Boule Open terrace
CARDS: ● ▨ ▨ Travellers cheques

SAULNAY Indre

La Marchandière (Prop: M & Mme Alain Renonlet)
36290
☎ 254384294
Alain and Jocelyne welcome you to their farm in the quiet of the countryside of Brennouse. Fully equipped kitchen for the use of guests. Table-tennis, mountain bikes and billiards on-site. A little English spoken.
Near river Forest area
2 en suite (shr) (1 fmly) Full central heating Open parking available

SAVONNIÈRES Indre-et-Loire

La Martinière
35 rte de la Martinière *37510*
☎ 247500446 FAX 247501157
(leave Tours on the D7 for approx 10km turn left into the village follow yellow sign "Relais de la Martinière", 2km form the village)

Closed Oct-Apr
10 rms (6 shr) Open parking available Outdoor swimming pool Golf Tennis Bicycle rental Languages spoken: English
ROOMS: s 240-340FF

Le Prieure des Granges (Prop: M Philippe Dufrense)
37510
☎ 247500967 FAX 247500643
(leave A10 at Saint-Avertin south of Tours and take direction Villandry)
This splendid château dominates the town of Savonnières. Built and added to between the 17th and 19th centuries, this house is hidden behind a belt of trees. The owner is an antique dealer so, as you may imagine, the interior is furnished accordingly. Large swimming pool. English spoken.

Near river Forest area Near motorway
Closed 2 Jan-14 Mar
8 en suite (bth/shr) Open parking available Supervised Outdoor swimming pool Open terrace Languages spoken: English
CARDS: Travellers cheques

SELLES-SUR-CHER Loir-et-Cher

Bed & Breakfast (Prop: M & Mme Lerate)
29 r des Rieux *41130*
☎ 254975135
Situated on the Berry Canal, this house has a garden with a swimming pool which guest are welcome to use. Fishing, cycling, walks, tennis and shops are within 100 metres. Other sporting facilities nearby.
Near river Forest area
2 en suite (bth/shr) Full central heating Open parking available Outdoor swimming pool
ROOMS: s 250FF; d 300FF
CARDS: ▨ Travellers cheques

Maison de la Rive Gauche (Prop: Mme Harvey Bacon)
15 r du four *41130*
☎ 254976385
This large three storey townhouse, located in the old town of Selles-sur-Cher, dates back to the sixteenth century. Spacious and comfortable rooms available, plus use of lounge, study and dining area. Two enclosed courtyards to front and rear of the house containing a variety of vines, fruit trees and roses. Separate cottage also available. Dinner available by reservation. English spoken.
Near river Forest area In town centre Near motorway
Closed Jan-Feb
6 rms (4 bth/shr) (2 fmly) Full central heating Open parking available Child discount available 6yrs Last d 20.30hrs Languages spoken: English & German
MEALS: Dinner 90FF*
CARDS: Travellers cheques

SENONCHES Eure-et-Loir

Bed & Breakfast (Prop: Aline Gerrer)
24 bis rue Louis Peuret *28250*
☎ 237379580 FAX 237379580
Situated in a small town, this establishment offers rooms with kitchen and dining room. Living room available with TV. Ideal base to visits places of interest, such as the Senonches Castle, with its museum of natural history, religious art, and local crafts & traditions. 4,000 hectare forest nearby, where long walks can be enjoyed. Swimming pool within six kilometres, open all year round. English spoken.
Near river Near lake Forest area In town centre
3 rms No smoking on premises

SEPMES Indre-et-Loire

La Ferme les Berthiers (Prop: Anne Vergnaud)
37800
☎ 247655061
(exit St Maure de Touraine from A10 onto N760 towards Loches, then take D59 towards Liguiel, from D59 the road for Sepmes is on the left)
This attractive house, built in 1856, is part of a working farm run by Joseph and Anne-Marie, who look forward to welcoming you. The rooms are situated in the main house and the annexe and are all individually decorated and furnished.

Evening meals are served in the rustic dining room, as are the country breakfasts which all the guests seem to enjoy. Basket ball area in garden. English spoken.
7 rms (1 bth 5 shr) (3 fmly) Full central heating Open parking available Child discount available Boule Open terrace Basketball Languages spoken: English
ROOMS: s 180-200FF; d 240-270FF
MEALS: Dinner 100FF
CARDS: Travellers cheques

SÉRIS Loir-et-Cher

Bed & Breakfast (Prop: Annie & Jean-Yves Peschard)
41500
☎ 254810783 FAX 254813988
Bed & breakfast is offered at this working farm, situated in the heart of the countryside, in a small village between Orléans and Blois. Dinner is available and includes local specialities, cheeses and wines. Breakfast includes Mme Peschard's home-made jams. All meals are served at your hosts table. Facilities include outdoor games, table-tennis and pétanque. English spoken.
Closed 1-14 Oct
5 en suite (bth/shr) (2 fmly) No smoking on premises TV available Full central heating Open parking available Child discount available 2yrs Languages spoken: English
MEALS: Dinner 0.90FF*

SULLY-SUR-LOIRE Loiret

Bed & Breakfast (Prop: M & Mme Meunier)
43-45 Ch de la Chevesserie *45600*
☎ 238365488
This pretty cottage, set in a peaceful location, surrounded by parkland offers accommodation with a real familly atmosphere, near the village centre. Large garden with terrace. English spoken.
Near river Forest area Near motorway
2 en suite (bth/shr) Full central heating Open parking available Supervised Languages spoken: English & Spanish
ROOMS: s 170FF; d 210FF

TAVERS Loiret

Le Clos de Pont-Pierre (Prop: Patricia Fournier)
115 r des eaux Bleues *45190*
☎ 238445685 FAX 238445894
(exit A10 at Meung-sur-Loire-on-Mer, Access N152 at 2km to Beaugency)

This old farmhouse, which has been renovated, looks out onto a large garden, with trees and flowers. A splendid terrace

surrounds the swimming pool. Dining room with antique furniture; lounge with fireplace. Tourist information available. Games available in the garden, with other sports nearby.
Forest area Near motorway
Closed Dec-Feb
4 en suite (shr) (2 fmly) No smoking on premises TV in all bedrooms Full central heating Open parking available Supervised Outdoor swimming pool Last d 19.30hrs
ROOMS: d 270FF Reductions over 1 night
MEALS: Dinner fr 90FF
CARDS: Travellers cheques

Les Gratte Lievres (Prop: Patrick Terlain)
74 bis r des Eaux Bleues *45190*
☎ 238449258
Quietly situated and surrounded by flowers this house has a tree-lined garden, with sun loungers, hammocks and swings. Living room with fireplace and television available to guests. Rooms are situated on the first floor. Dinner by reservation. English spoken.
Near river Forest area Near motorway
2 en suite (shr) (1 fmly) No smoking on premises Full central heating Open parking available Supervised Child discount available 7yrs Last d 18.00hrs Languages spoken: English
MEALS: Dinner fr 90FF*
CARDS: Travellers cheques

TENDU Indre

La Chasse (Prop: M & Mme Mitchell)
Prunget *36200*
☎ 254240776
(leave the A20 (N20) at Tendu, take D30 signposted to Chavin. Shortly after the turn behind Tendu Church signposts show direction to La Chasse)
Built at the end of the nineteenth century, this stone farmhouse has been tastefully modernised to a high standard. Situated on a 250 acre working farm, surrounded by 200 acres of woodland. The River Bouzanne adjoins the farm and offers carp fishing. Discount of seven percent for a stay of seven nights or more. All rooms are spacious and comfortable. Breakfast served in lounge with open fireplace. Evening meals by arrangement. Barbecue. Fishing nearby. English hosts.
Near river Near lake Forest area Near motorway
4 rms (1 shr) (1 fmly) No smoking on premises Full central heating Open parking available Supervised Child discount available 12yrs Languages spoken: English
CARDS: Travellers cheques

THAUMIERS Cher

Château de Thaumiers
18210
☎ 248618162 FAX 248618182
The handsome Château de Thaumiers features bedrooms and suites with private facilities, and because of its extensive corporate services it is a popular venue with business travellers and holiday makers alike. The dining-rooms are exclusively reserved for residents and cater for most tastes. The château offers a choice of varied entertainment and there is no shortage of leisure opportunities and cultural places of interest to visit in the region.
Near river Near lake Forest area
10 en suite (bth) (2 fmly) Full central heating Open parking available Outdoor swimming pool (heated) Fishing Boule Open terrace Languages spoken: English
CARDS: ●● ▥ Travellers cheques

TROO Loir-et-Cher

Château de la Vouté (Prop: M Jaques Clays)
41800
☎ 254725252 FAX 254725252
An impressive chateau with views over the river Loire and the valley beyond. The owners, Claude and Jacques, offer spacious guest rooms, each independently furnished and decorated with antiques. Large breakfast served on the terrace or in the bedrooms. Within walking distance of a good restaurant and the village.
Near river Forest area
5 en suite (bth/shr) Full central heating Open parking available Covered parking available Supervised No children 18yrs Fishing Languages spoken: English
ROOMS: d 480-580FF
CARDS: Travellers cheques

VALLIÈRES-LES-GRANDES Loir-et-Cher

La Ferme de la Quantinère (Prop: Andree Veys)
41400
☎ 254209953 FAX 254209953
Situated in an old winery, set in four hundred hectares. Ideal spot from which to tour the châteaux of the Loire. Your hosts will be happy to help you to plan your trip. Picnics, barbecues, walks, boules and a jacuzzi are available. English spoken.
Forest area
Closed 3 Dec-Mar
4 rms Full central heating Open parking available Supervised Child discount available 5 yrs Outdoor swimming pool (heated) Boule Jacuzzi/spa Bicycle rental Barbecue
ROOMS: s 250FF; d 250FF
CARDS: Travellers cheques

VANNES-SUR-COSSON Loiret

Bed & Breakfast (Prop: M & Mme Nicourt)
6 r de la Croix Ste Madeleine *45510*
☎ 238581543
18th-century renovated house situated in the heart of Solognot village, amidst a large garden. The hosts are a hunting family and game is often served as a speciality for dinner, but advance booking is necessary. Solognot is a small peaceful town. Definitely the place for a quiet holiday. English spoken.
Near river Forest area In town centre Near motorway
6 rms (2 bth 3 shr) Full central heating Open parking available Supervised Child discount available 12yrs Languages spoken: English
MEALS: Continental breakfast 80FF*

VARENNES Indre-et-Loire

Crene
37600
☎ 247590429
3 en suite (bth/shr) (2 fmly) No smoking in all bedrooms Full central heating Open parking available Child discount available 13yrs Last d 20.30hrs
MEALS: Dinner fr 80FF*

VELLES Indre

Manoir de Villedoin (Prop: M et Mme Limousin)
36330
☎ 254251206 FAX 254242829
A pretty manor house on the banks of a river. Attractive

interior with spacious rooms. Evening meals by reservation, or alternatively, why not try the regional dishes on offer at the restaurants nearby. Tennis, canoeing, fishing, table-tennis, boules and bicycles on-site. Riding centre, golf and swimming pool nearby.
Near river Near lake Forest area
Closed Jan
5 en suite (bth/shr) (1 fmly) TV available Full central heating Open parking available Supervised Child discount available
MEALS: Lunch 150-270FF Dinner 150-270FF*
CARDS: Travellers cheques

VERNEUIL-SUR-INDRE Indre-et-Loire

La Capitainerie (Prop: Malvina Masselot)
37600
☎ 247948815 FAX 247977075
(from Loches stay in lane for Châteauroux until traffic circle, look out for Lecclerc supermarket. Follow Châteauroux signs, cross Perrusson then turn right towards Verneuil. La Capitainerie 150mtrs before "leaving Verneuil" sign)
Right in the heart of the Loire valley castle and vineyards, the owner welcomes guests to her 18th century property, surrounded by 8 hectares of countryside. In the evening your hostess may, on reservation only, introduce guests to the gourmet pleasures of authentic Touraine cooking.
Near river Forest area
3 en suite (shr) (1 with balcony) No smoking on premises Full central heating Open parking available Outdoor swimming pool V meals Languages spoken: English
ROOMS: s 190-230FF; d 250-290FF
MEALS: Dinner fr 100FF

VERNOU-SUR-BRENNE Indre-et-Loire

Château de Jallanges (Prop: Stephane Ferry-Balin)
372110
☎ 247520171 FAX 247521118
(from Tours take N152 towards Blais. In Vouvray take D46 to Vernou-sur-Brenne & from there the D76 to Château)
Near river Forest area
7 en suite (bth/shr) (2 fmly) TV available Open parking available Covered parking available Supervised Child discount available Mini-golf Bicycle rental Languages spoken: English & Italian
MEALS: Full breakfast 50FF Continental breakfast 50FF Lunch fr 260FF*
CARDS: ● ▨ ▨ ▣ Travellers cheques

VIGOULANT Indre

Les Ferme des Vacances (Prop: M & Mme Hyzard)
Les Pouges *36160*
☎ 254306060
Located in the heart of the country, this is a typical old farm which has been completely restored. A living room, dining room and games room are open to guests. The house is located in the midst of beautiful countryside. Meals are made with fresh farm produce. This is an ideal spot for children to come and discover farm life. English spoken.
Near river Forest area
4 en suite (shr) (3 fmly) Open parking available Child discount available Boule Table tennis Play room Last d 21.00hrs Languages spoken: English
MEALS: Full breakfast 30FF Continental breakfast 20FF Dinner 60-80FF*
CARDS: ● ▨ Travellers cheques

VILLANDRY Indre-et-Loire

Manoir de Foncher (Prop: Michel et Francoise Salles)
37510
☎ 247500240 FAX 247500240
(from Tours D7 to Savonnieres, turn right across the bridge then immediately left. House is 3km along on right)
Listed as an historical monument, this fifteenth century manor has two guest rooms available, situated on the first floor. The family atmosphere, together with the quality of service offered will ensure that visitors feel welcome. Well placed to visit the châteaux of the Loire. English spoken.
Near river Forest area
Closed Oct-Mar
2 rms (1 bth/shr) (2 fmly) (2 with balcony) Open parking available Languages spoken: English
ROOMS: s 650FF; d 650FF
CARDS: Travellers cheques

VILLEBAROU Loir-et-Cher

Bed & Breakfast (Prop: Agnès & Jacques Masquilier)
Le Retour, 8 rte de la chaussée, St-Victor *41000*
☎ 254784024
(on D924 towards Chateauden-Chartres, at lights turn right to Villebrau. Alternatively from A10 take D50 towards Villerbou, in 300m turn first left)
Situated in a typical Beauceronne farm, these bedrooms all look out over the grassy courtyard. Your initial welcome and breakfast takes place in the main residence of the proprietors but guests have use of a kitchenette which has a wood oven, currently being restored. A park is adjacent to the property with games area and a small wood. English spoken.
Near river Near lake Forest area Near motorway
RS winter
3 en suite (shr) (3 fmly) No smoking on premises Radio in rooms Full central heating Open parking available Covered parking available (charged) Supervised Child discount available Bicycle rental Languages spoken: English
ROOMS: s 260FF; d 270FF Special breaks
CARDS: Travellers cheques

VILLEDIEU-SUR-INDRE Indre

La Bruère (Prop: M Stone)
36320
☎ 254261717
An old farm set in two hectares of ground situated in a small hamlet seven kilometres from Villedieu and four kilometres from Bazançais. Four guests rooms are available, one of which is a family room. Continental breakfast served. English hosts.
Near river Near lake Forest area Near motorway
4 rms (3 shr) (1 fmly) No smoking on premises Open parking available Covered parking available Languages spoken: English

VILLEDÔMER Indre-et-Loire

La Hémond (Prop: Gosseaume Gaetan)
37110
☎ 247550699 FAX 247550936
A warm welcome is offered on this farm in the heart of the Loire. Swings and pétanque area are available in the garden. Evening meal available by reservation. English spoken.
Forest area Near motorway
5 rms (1 bth 2 shr) (3 fmly) Open parking available Covered parking available Boule Languages spoken: English
ROOMS: s 100FF; d 190FF Reductions over 1 night
MEALS: Dinner fr 55FF*
CARDS: Travellers cheques

VILLENEUVE-FROUVILLE Loir-et-Cher

Bed & Breakfast (Prop: Bernard & Micheline Pohu)
5 place de l'eglise *41290*
☎ 254232206
This typically French village is situated between Blois and Vendôme and is the home of Bernard and Micheline Pohu. Easy access to the châteaux of the Loire. Leisure facilities within fifteen kilometres. Reductions for children under four.
Near motorway
3 en suite (shr) (1 fmly) (2 with balcony) No smoking on premises Full central heating Open parking available Covered parking available Child discount available
CARDS: Travellers cheques

VOUVRAY Indre-et-Loire

Le Chêne Morier
37210
☎ 247527883
Situated two kilometres from the centre of Vouvray and set in the middle of a large park, this property also has a swimming pool for guests'use. Vouvray offers a variety of restaurants, all specialising in regional cuisine. Golf is available three kilometres away.
Forest area Near motorway
5 rms (3 bth/shr) (1 fmly) TV available Radio in rooms Open parking available Outdoor swimming pool

Paris & Ile de France

There's a part of Paris to suit your every mood. History and culture from a host of wonderful galleries and museums, like the famous Louvre which houses important antiquities and many of the world's masterpieces from painting and sculpture. Visit Notre Dame Cathedral, that jewel of medieval architecture, or the Eiffel Tower and the Arc de Triomphe. Shop till you drop for fashionable haute couture, or hunt for bargains and curios among the flea markets. A bite to eat and drink at a street café or a chic bar; a night of revelry at the Pigalle or Moulin Rouge.

(top): The world-famous Notre Dame Cathedral, completed in 1330, and capable of holding nearly 10,000 people.

(bottom): Commissioned by Napoleon, the Arc de Triomphe is a tribute to the Unknown Soldier, and is the central hub of twelve avenues.

ESSENTIAL FACTS

DÉPARTEMENTS:	Paris, Essonne, Hauts de Seine, Seine-et-Marne, Seine-St-Denis, Val-d'Oise, Val-de-Marne, Yvelines
PRINCIPAL TOWNS	Paris, Mantes-la-Jolie, Pontoise, Creil, St Denis, Meaux, Melun, St-Germain
PLACES TO VISIT:	The sights, shops, museums, and boulevards of Paris, Auvers-sur-Oise, the village which inspired the Impressionists, Barbizon, which inspired Rousseau and Millet, the châteaux of Champs, Chantilly and Rambouillet, the Basilica of St-Denis, EuroDisney, and the palaces at Versailles, Vaux-le-Vicomte and Fontainebleau
REGIONAL TOURIST OFFICE	26 av de l'Opéra, 75001 Paris. Tel: 42 60 28 62
LOCAL GASTRONOMIC DELIGHTS	Paris is the place to come for chic food, gourmet food; in fact, every type of food. A la parisienne describes savoury dishes that are typical of Parisian cuisine: soup à la parisienne is made with leeks, potatoes, milk and chervil, while fish à la parisienne is served with heavy mayonnaise, artichoke hearts, hard-boiled eggs and aspic cubes. Other Parisian dishes include sole Dugléré, Anna potatoes, soufflé Rothschild, and Paris-Brest, a ring-shaped éclair filled with praline-flavoured cream.
LOCAL CRAFTS/WHAT TO BUY	Glassware at Soisy-sur-Ecole; the Arts Viaduct which showcases numerous creative and artistic trades, including artistic work in gold, wood, silver, brass, stone, porcelain, and wrought iron, as well as lace and tapestry.

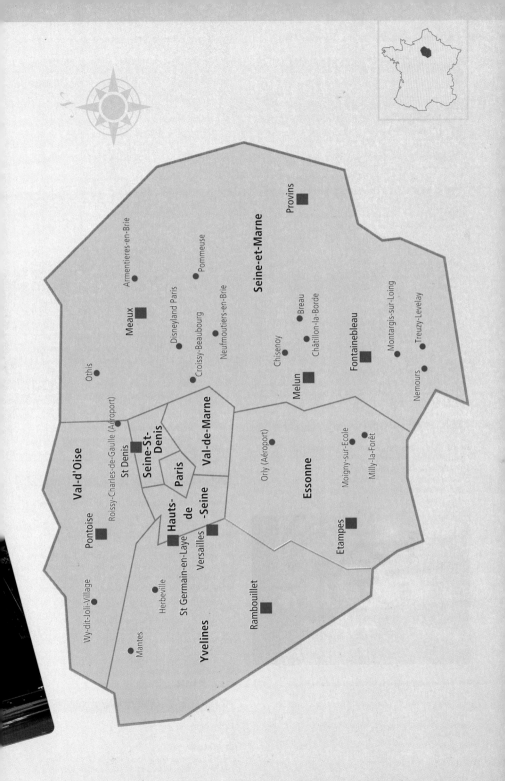

Provins

Seine-et-Marne

Armentieres-en-Brie

Pommeuse

Disneyland Paris

Meaux

Croissy-Beaubourg

Neufmoutiers-en-Brie

Breau

Châtillon-la-Borde

Montargis-sur-Loing

Treuzy-Levelay

Othis

Chisenoy

Fontainebleau

Melun

Nemours

Roissy-Charles-de-Gaulle (Aéroport)

St Denis

Seine-St-Denis

Val-de-Marne

Val-d'Oise

Paris

Orly (Aéroport)

Essonne

Moigny-sur-Ecole

Milly-la-Forêt

Pontoise

Hauts-de-Seine

St Germain-en-Laye

Versailles

Etampes

Wy-dit-Joli-Village

Herbeville

Rambouillet

Yvelines

Mantes

EVENTS & FESTIVALS

Jan Val-de-Marne Festival Sons d'Hiver de Fontainebleau (contemporary music and jazz)

Feb Paris Festival de Création Musical (*contemporary music*); Hauts-de-Seine Vocal Music Festival; Bois de Vicennes Bric-à-brac Fair

Mar Maisons-Lafitte Classical Music; Essonne Jazz Festival; Chatou Bric-a-Brac Fair; Coulommiers Wine & Cheese Fair

Mar-May Foire du Trône - fairground in Bois de Vincennes

Apr Hauts-de-Seine French Songs Festival; Seine et-Marne Dance Festival; Paris Parc de la Villette Classical Music Fair; Porte de Versailles Paris Fair

May Seine-et-Marne Music Festival de Meaux ; Essonne Festival d'Etampes (music & dance); Paris Jazz in Montmartre; Châteaufort Historical After-Dark Production; Ris-Orangis Traditional Music Festival; Champeaux Sacred Arts Festival; Conflans-Ste-Honorine Café Théâtre Festival

Jun Samois sur Seine Django Reinhardt Jazz Festival; Ville d'Avray Classical Music Festival; Seine St-Denis Music Festival d'Aubervilliers; aris St-Germain Festival & Fair; Parc de la Villette Jazz Festival; Paris Waiters' Race -

8.3km in uniform with tray on palm of hand; St-Denis Classical Music Festival; Provins Medieval Festival

Jun-Aug Provins Jousting Tournament each Saturday 4pm; St-Germain-en-Laye Fête des Loges (fairground)

Jun-Sep Meaux "On the Road to Europe" historical production after dark staged on one Friday and one Saturday each month;

Jul Hauts-de-Seine Classical Music Festival de l'Orangerie de Sceaux; Paris Tuilleries Gardens Festival

Aug Paris Rimes et Accords (*ancient and classical music*); Paris Sacred Music Festival en l'Ile; Provins Harvest Festival

Sep Paris Musique en Sorbonne ; Paris Autumn Music & Dance Festival; Pontoise Autumn Baroque Music Festival; Bagneux Grape Harvest Festival & Carnival; Arpajon Bean Festival; Blandy-les-Tours Château Traditional Fair

Oct Val-de-Marne French Song Festival; Yvelines Classical Music Festival de l'Abbaye des Vaux de Cernay; Montmartre Grape Harvest Festival; Boissy-St-Léger

Nov Paris Sacred Music Festival de la Ville de Paris; Val-de-Marne Dance Festival

---

ARMENTIÈRES-EN-BRIE Seine-et-Marne

Bed & Breakfast (Prop: Mme Denise Woehrle)
44 r du Chef de Ville *77440*
☎ 164355122 FAX 164354295
(from Meaux take N3 to Chalons-sur-Marnevia Trilport, turn left to Armentiéres through village. Pass church, house is one before last on right)

This house is conveniently situated only thirty kilometres from Roissy Airport and EuroDisney Paris. A warm and personal welcome is offered. Continental breakfasts are large and served with jam made by your hosts. Well situated in the country-side with attractive garden and views.
Near river Forest area
Closed Nov-Jan

4 en suite (bth/shr) (2 with balcony) Full central heating Open parking available Open terrace Languages spoken: English
ROOMS: s fr 180FF; d 280-340FF Reductions over 1 night

BREAU Seine-et-Marne

Ferme Relais du Couvent (Prop: M & Mme Le Grand)
77720
☎ 164387515 164387575
(leave A5 at exit 16, Chatillon La Borde, turn right in direction of Nangis then left to Breau)
Renovated farm situated about 55 kilometres from Paris. Peace and tranquillity is assured as the property is surrounded by six hectares of open land. Tennis-courts are available on site, as are hot-air balloon rides. All food is prepared from your hosts' own farm produce. The attractive golf course of Fontenaills is nearby.
Near river Forest area Near motorway
7 en suite (shr) (4 fmly) TV in 21 bedrooms Open parking available Child discount available 10yrs Tennis Open terrace V meals
ROOMS: s fr 215FF; d fr 245FF
MEALS: Dinner fr 100FF
CARDS: 💳 📰 💳 📱 Travellers cheques

CHÂTILLON-LA-BORDE Seine-et-Marne

Labordière (Prop: Yves Guerif)
16 Grande rue la Borde *77820*
☎ 160666054
(A5 to Châtillon-la-Borde, Honeur-de-la-Borde in 3km)
This large, old farm has a landscaped garden. Living room

and dining room may be used by guests, as may the TV. Warm welcome, especially at your hosts' table, where good food is served. Free bike hire. Reductions for children under twelve years old. Simple English spoken.
Forest area
3 rms (2 shr) Full central heating Open parking available Child discount available 12yrs Languages spoken: English
ROOMS: s 195-215FF; d 245-245FF * Reductions over 1 night
MEALS: Lunch fr 110FF Dinner fr 110FF
CARDS: Travellers cheques

CRISENOY Seine-et-Marne

Ferme de Vert Saint Pere (Prop: Philippe & Jeanne Mauban)
77390
☎ 164388351 FAX 164388352
(A5 to Troyes, 1st exit after toll (15) St Germain-Laxis. Take N36 to the right, then 1st right to Crisenoy at the entrance to Crisenoy 1st right (Stade,Tennis) straight ahead to Vert St Pere after tennis court)
A 17th-century stone farmhouse set in wide open fields, one hour from Paris by car. The accommodation consists one family room with a double and single bed and a family suite with four bedrooms and kitchenette.
Near motorway
2 en suite (shr) (1 fmly) TV in 1 bedroom Full central heating Open parking available Child discount available 5yrs
Languages spoken: Spanish
ROOMS: (room only) d fr 240FF * Reductions over 1 night

CROISSY-BEAUBOURG Seine-et-Marne

Bed & Breakfast (Prop: C &t J-L Pasquier)
allée de Clotomont *77183*
☎ 160064450 FAX 160050345
Just 25 kilometres east of Paris, a welcoming bed and breakfast with a French family who speak fluent English. The house dates from the 18th century and has comfortable rooms, while breakfast can be served on the south-facing veranda overlooking the private lake.
Near lake Forest area Near motorway
(1 fmly) No smoking on premises Full central heating Open parking available Boule Mini-golf Languages spoken: English
ROOMS: s 215FF; d 245FF Reductions over 1 night

HERBEVILLE Yvelines

Le Mont au Vent
2 r de Maule *78580*
☎ 130906522 FAX 134751254
Situated in ancient parkland on the outskirts of Paris, with comfortable rooms. Breakfast is served on the terrace, which has a charming view, or in the dining room. Magnificent oak panelled living room. Dinner can be eaten with your hosts by prior arrangement. Tennis, swimming pool, jacuzzi, volleyball and pond on-site. Versailles and Giverny nearby.
Forest area
2 en suite (bth/shr) (2 fmly) (1 with balcony) No smoking on premises TV available Full central heating Open parking available Covered parking available Child discount available
MEALS: Dinner fr 120FF*

MILLY-LA-FORÊT Essonne

Ferme de la Grange Rouge (Prop: Jean Charles Desforges)
91490
☎ 164989421 FAX 164989991
Renovated fifteenth century farm with five rooms on offer. Restaurants within four kilometres. Nearby tourist attractions include the Fontainebleau forest. Reductions for children up to six years.
Forest area
Closed January
5 en suite (shr) Open parking available Supervised Child discount available 6yrs
ROOMS: s 210FF; d 250FF
CARDS: Travellers cheques

MOIGNY-SUR-ÉCOLE Essonne

Clos de la Croix Blanche (Prop: M & Mme Lenoir)
9 r du Souvenir
☎ 164984784 & 164573353 FAX 164572250
The Lenoir family welcome you to their house, situated by a vineyard. Long, low building in the heart of the countryside. Summer house available, with bikes to rent. Meals served in the evening, including wine. English spoken.
Near river Forest area
3 en suite (bth/shr) (1 fmly) (1 with balcony) TV available Full central heating Open parking available Covered parking available Supervised Bicycle rental Languages spoken: English & Spanish
CARDS: Travellers cheques

MONTIGNY-SUR-LOING Seine-et-Marne

Bed & Breakfast (Prop: J-M Gicquel)
46 rue Renée Montgermont *77690*
☎ 164458792
(at Fontainebleau, at the crossroads 'The Obelisque', take the direction of Montigny/Loing, pass through the village of Bourron-Jarlotte then into Montigny/Loing)
Private bedrooms with en suite facilities are situated on the first floor of this old house in the centre of the village close to Fontainbleau.
Near river Forest area In town centre Near motorway
3 en suite (shr) (1 fmly) No smoking on premises TV in 2 bedrooms Full central heating Open parking available Child discount available 8yrs Languages spoken: English & German
ROOMS: d 240FF *
CARDS: Travellers cheques

NEUFMOUTIERS-EN-BRIE Seine-et-Marne

Bellevue (Prop: Mme Isabelle Galpin)
77610
☎ 164071105 FAX 164071927
(A4 exit 13 Villeneuve le Comte, then take direction Neufmontiers-en-Brie)
Isabelle and Patrick Galpin offer you refurbished guest rooms in the wing of their ancient farmhouse. Only ten minutes from Disneyland Paris. Five comfortable bedrooms available which overlook the garden, and one lodge in the garden. Your hosts will, on request, guide and chauffeur you to all the well-known sites of the region. Meals available in the evening upon reservation. English spoken.
Forest area Near motorway

cont'd

6 en suite (shr) (6 fmly) TV in all bedrooms Full central heating Open parking available Supervised Child discount available 12yrs Fishing Bicycle rental Table tennis Languages spoken: English
ROOMS: s 215-320FF; d 245-390FF
MEALS: Dinner 60-95FF

NEUILLY Hauts-de-Seine

Bed & Breakfast (Prop: Ruth Himmelfarb)
53 bd Victor-Hugo *92200*
☎ 146373728
Sunny, artistically furnished accommodation overlooking a pretty garden.
In town centre
1 en suite (bth/shr) Full central heating Child discount available Bicycle rental Languages spoken: English & German
ROOMS: (room only) d 200-260FF

OTHIS Seine-et-Marne

Plaisance (Prop: M & Mme Montrozier)
12 rue de Suisses, Beaumarchais *77280*
☎ 160033398 FAX 160035671
(from Charles de Gaulle airport take D401 to Dammartin-en-Goele then D64 to Othis, then follow signs to Beaumarchais. From Paris take A1, exit at Soisson onto N2 exit Othis then Beaumarchais)
In the main house there is an elegantly decorated large bedroom and a smaller room with wood panelling. Another room across the courtyard has all the standards of luxury and refinement.
Forest area
3 rms (2 bth) TV in 2 bedrooms Full central heating Open parking available Child discount available 8yrs Languages spoken: English
ROOMS: d 450-670FF
MEALS: Dinner 195FF

PARIS

1ST ARRONDISSEMENT

Bed & Breakfast (Prop: Mona Pierrot)
14 rue Bertin-Poirée *75001*
☎ 142365065
(from any motorway take direction of Paris Centre or paris Chôtelet. Once in Place du Chôtelet take beginning of Boulevard de Sebastopol, turn left in the rue de Rivoli and keep left, take 3rd street on left again, this is Bertin-Porée)
Cosy accommodation in the heart of Paris.
Near river
1 en suite (bth/shr) Full central heating Languages spoken: English & Spanish
ROOMS: s 290FF; d 350FF

2ND ARRONDISSEMENT

Boulevards (Prop: M Bonnet)
10 r de la Ville-Neuve *75002*
☎ 142360229 FAX 142361539
18 rms (14 bth/shr) TV available Full central heating

4TH ARRONDISSEMENT

Bed & Breakfast
7 rue Nicoles Flamel *75004*
☎ 148877015 FAX 148877015
2 en suite (bth/shr) Child discount available
ROOMS: (room only) d 420-460FF

5TH ARRONDISSEMENT

Grand Hotel de Progrés (Prop: Montana)*
50 r Gay Lussac *75005*
☎ 143545318
35 rms (6 shr) (12 with balcony) Lift Full central heating No children 4yrs Languages spoken: English, Italian & Portuguese
CARDS: Travellers cheques

12TH ARRONDISSEMENT

Luxor Hotel
22 r Moreau *75012*
☎ 143433482 FAX 143433482
Near motorway
30 rms (20 bth/shr) (5 fmly) TV available STV Full central heating Languages spoken: English

18TH ARRONDISSEMENT

Bed & Breakfast (Prop: Françoise Foret)
☎ 144850719
Stylish decoration in a property dating from the beginning of the century, ten minutes walk from Montmartre. The young hosts, who speak good English, are happy to share their passion for Paris with their guests. It is essential to phone for address details and accurate directions.
1 en suite (shr) (1 fmly) (1 with balcony) No smoking on premises TV in all bedrooms Full central heating Open parking available (charged) Languages spoken: English & Italian
ROOMS: s 300FF; d 300-350FF

Bed & Breakfast (Prop: Eliane Letellier)
☎ 142513735/142304947
(it is essential to phone for address details & directions - owner speaks good English)
2 en suite (bth/shr) No smoking on premises TV in 1 bedroom Full central heating V meals Languages spoken: English
ROOMS: s 180-220FF; d 280-320FF *
MEALS: Dinner 120-180FF*

Titania (Prop: Mr Yahia)
70 Bis Boulevard Ornano *75010*
☎ 146064322 FAX 146065254
Near motorway
103 rms (2 bth 13 shr) Full central heating Languages spoken: English

20TH ARRONDISSEMENT

Mary's Hotel (Prop: Mme Chettouh)
118 r Orfila *75020*
☎ 143615168 FAX 143611647
(A3 exit Bagnolet, to Gambetta then rue Orfila)
Near motorway

24 rms (18 bth/shr) (4 fmly) (4 with balcony) No smoking on premises TV available Full central heating Languages spoken: English
CARDS: ●● ▓▓ Travellers cheques

POMMEUSE Seine-et-Marne

Le Cottage du Martin Pêcheur (Prop: Annie and Jocky Thomas)
77515
☎ 164200098 FAX 164200098
The Thomas family offer you a relaxing holiday in their turn-of-the-19th-century house, which has been completely restored to give very comfortable accommodation throughout. The garden backs onto a river. Cultural and leisure pursuits are nearby in the village.
Near river Forest area
6 en suite (bth/shr) (2 fmly) No smoking on premises TV in all bedrooms Radio in rooms Full central heating Open parking available Supervised Child discount available Fishing Boule Table tennis Languages spoken: English
ROOMS: (room only) s fr 214FF; d fr 245FF
CARDS: Travellers cheques

TREUZY-LEVELAY Seine-et-Marne

Bed & Breakfast (Prop: M Gilles Caupin)
3 rue Creuse *77710*
☎ 164290747 FAX 164290521
Set in a rural village in the Lunain Valley, 20 kilometres from Fontainebleau, these guest rooms are situated in a recently refurbished barn independent of the main house. Continental breakfast, using local produce, is served in the room or at the family table. A garden is available for guests'use. Restaurants in the vicinity. Swimming pool, fishing and golf nearby. Climbing or walking in Fontainebleau Forest is slightly further away. English spoken.
Near river Near lake Forest area In town centre
2 en suite (bth/shr) (2 fmly) Full central heating Open parking available Supervised Child discount available 4yrs Languages spoken: English & Italian
CARDS: Travellers cheques

WY-DIT-JOLI-VILLAGE Val-D'Oise

Château d'Hazéville (Prop: M Deneck)
95420
☎ 134670617 FAX 134671782 & 145246260
A converted dovecote, in a typical farmhouse, where the main building is steeped in history and is a listed building. Your host, Guy Deneck, is a potter who fires and handpaints porcelain, which guests are invited to purchase. English spoken.
Forest area Near motorway
2 en suite (bth/shr) No smoking on premises TV in all bedrooms Full central heating Open parking available Covered parking available Supervised No children Open terrace Languages spoken: English & Spanish
ROOMS: d fr 620FF
CARDS: Travellers cheques

Taking your mobile phone to France?
See page 11

167

Burgundy

L ying between the wide open harvest plains of northern France and the industrialised Rhone Valley, Burgundy is a land on undulating hills, woods and unspoilt waterways flowing through a ragged mosaic of fields bordered by centuries-old hedges. Burgundy is a beautiful and fertile land whose wealth is nurtured by wine-growers, farmers and foresters, all applying skills passed down and refined over generations. Burgundians have transformed hospitality into an art form: simple, dignified and sincere. People here understand that the better things in life must be taken with time, naturally.

(Top): A moving memorial to the fallen of World War I at Nevers. The town is also the home of St Bernadette, who lies in a glass tomb at the Couvent St-Gildard.

(Bottom): The dramatic Roche de Solutré dominates the area, and is a popular spot for rock climbers and walkers.

ESSENTIAL FACTS

DÉPARTEMENTS:	Côte-d'Or, Nièvre, Saône-et-Loire, Yonne
PRINCIPAL TOWNS	Auxerre, Nevers, Dijon, Le Creusot, Monceau-les-Mines, Macon, Chalon-sur-Saône, Beaune
PLACES TO VISIT:	St Madeleine Basìlica in Vezelay; Fontenay Abbey; Semur-en-Auxois; Morvan Nature Park; Cluny; Dijon; Beaune - the centre of the wine industry and where there is a famous harvest festival and wine auction in November
REGIONAL TOURIST OFFICE	34 rue de Forges, 21022 Dijon Tel 80 44 11 44
LOCAL GASTRONOMIC DELIGHTS	Burgundy has been described as a gastronomic paradise. Among traditional favourites are boeuf bourguignon (beef casseroled in wine), jambon persillé (ham with parsley) and escargots (snails) in their shells. Dijon mustard is rightly famous and ripe cheeses such as Epoisses, Citeaux and Florentin are delicious
DRINKS	Burgundy produces some of the world's greatest wine, especially in the area around Beaune. Whites include Chablis, Mersault and Montrachet, whilst reds range from Chambertin to everyday Beaujolais. Dijon blackcurrant liqueur (cassis)
LOCAL CRAFTS WHAT TO BUY	Porcelain from Nevers; pottery form Puisaye; paintings on silk from Cluny; art books printed by Benedictine monks at La Pierre-qui-Vivre near St Leger Vauban; aniseed sweets and mustard from Dijon.

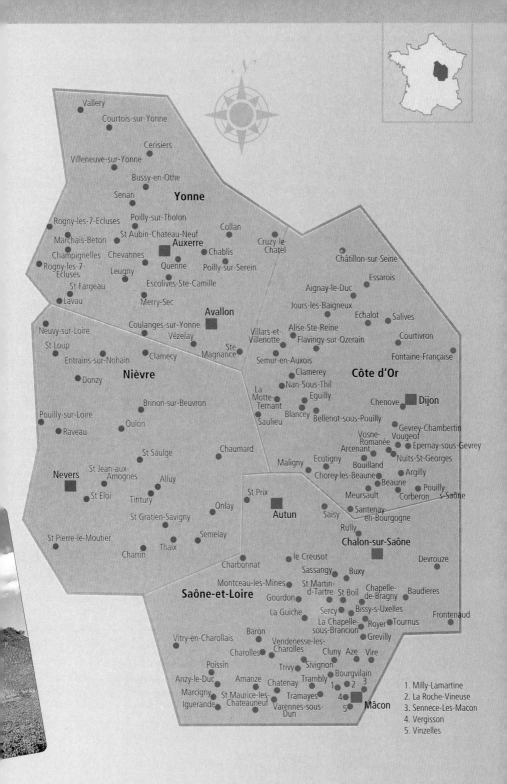

Vallery

Courtois-sur-Yonne

Cerisiers

Villeneuve-sur-Yonne

Bussy-en-Othe

Senan

Yonne

Rogny-les-7-Ecluses

Poilly-sur-Tholon

St Aubin-Chateau-Neuf

Collan

Marchais-Beton

Champignelles

Chevannes

Chablis

Cruzy-le-Chatel

Châtillon-sur-Seine

Auxerre

Rogny-les-7-Ecluses

Leugny

Quenne

Poilly-sur-Serein

Essarois

St Fargeau

Escolives-Ste-Camille

Aignay-le-Duc

Lavau

Merry-Sec

Jours-les-Baigneux

Echalot

Salives

Avallon

Coulanges-sur-Yonne

Vézelay

Villars-et-Villenotte

Alise-Ste-Reine

Flavigny-sur-Ozerain

Courtivron

Neuvy-sur-Loire

Ste Magnance

Fontaine-Française

St Loup

Clamecy

Entrains-sur-Nohain

Semur-en-Auxois

Côte d'Or

Nièvre

Clamerey

Donzy

Nan-Sous-Thil

Brinon-sur-Beuvron

La Motte-Ternant

Eguilly

Chenove

Dijon

Pouilly-sur-Loire

Oulon

Blancey

Bellenot-sous-Pouilly

Raveau

Saulieu

Gevrey-Chambertin

Vosne-Romanée

Vougeot

Epernay-sous-Gevrey

St Saulge

Chaumard

Arcenant

Bouilland

Nuits-St-Georges

Maligny

Ecutigny

Nevers

St Jean-aux-Amognes

Alluy

Chorey-les-Beaune

Argilly

Beaune

Pouilly-s-Saône

St Eloi

Tintury

St Prix

Meursault

Corberon

Onlay

Autun

Saisy

Santenay-en-Bourgogne

St Gratien-Savigny

Rully

St Pierre-le-Moutier

Semelay

Chalon-sur-Saône

Charrin

Thaix

Devrouze

Charbonnat

le Creusot

Sassangy

Buxy

Montceau-les-Mines

St Martin-d-Tartre

St Boil

Chapelle-de-Bragny

Baudieres

Saône-et-Loire

Gourdon

La Guiche

Sercy

Bissy-s-Uxelles

Frontenaud

La Chapelle-sous-Brancion

Royer

Tournus

Vitry-en-Charollais

Baron

Vendenesse-les-Charolles

Grevilly

Charolles

Cluny

Aze

Vire

Poissin

Trivy

Sivignon

Anzy-le-Duc

Amanze

Chatenay

Trambly

Bourgvilain

Marcigny

St Maurice-les-Châteauneuf

Tramayes

Iguerande

Varennes-sous-Dun

Mâcon

1. Milly-Lamartine
2. La Roche-Vineuse
3. Sennece-Les-Macon
4. Vergisson
5. Vinzelles

169

EVENTS & FESTIVALS

Jan Rully, Feast of St Vincent, Wine Grower Festival (procession, enthroning)

Mar Chalon-sur-Saône Carnival; Nuits-St-Georges Wine Sales of the Hospices;

May Dijon Antiques Fair; Chalons-sur-Saône 'Montgolfiades ' hot air ballooning event; Race of the Maidens & the Footloose Race of the Platter, Semur-en-Auxois; Magny Cours Historic Racing Vehicles;

Jun Donzy Classical Music Festival; St-Jean-de Losne Grand Pardon of the Bargemen (religious procession, blessing of river boats); Le Creusot National Blues Festival; Dijon Music Festival; Beaune Baroque Music Festival (each weekend until end July);

Jul Châtillon-sur-Seine Festival of north Burgundy (classical music & jazz); St Fargeau Castle Historical Show; Rogny-les-Sept Ecluses Fireworks on the Locks; Chalon-sur Saône European Street Theatre meeting; Pouilly-sur-Loire Fête des terroirs; Clamecy Water Jousting; Vézelay Madeleine's Pilgrimage;

Aug Coulanges-sur-Yonne Nautical Jousting; Saulieu Charolais Festival; Autun Augustodunum (Fris & Sats) gallo-roman show in Roman theatre;

Sep Dijon International Folkloriades & Grape Harvest Festival (folklore, dance & music); Alise-Ste-Reine The Mystery of St Reine (reconstruction in period costume of the martyrdom of Ste Reine); Chenove Pressée Festival (tasting & music around medieval wine presses)

Oct Saulieu - Grand Morvan Gourmand Days; Dijon Gastronomic Fair;

Nov International Jazz Festival, Nevers Wine Festival, Chablis Three Glorious Days Wine Festival at Vougeot, Meursault & Beaune; Nevers Jazz Festival; Chablis Wine Festival

Dec Dijon Gingerbread Fair; Dijon Contemporary Music Festival 'Why Note'

The first Burgundians.

In 422 AD, the Romans allowed a wandering tribe from an island off the Swedish coast (today the Danish island of Bornholm) to settle near Geneva. From there they expanded their kingdom across the Burgundy plateau and south to Provence and Marseille. These ' Burgundarholmers ' quickly adopted Roman manners and the Christian faith and gave their name to Burgundy.

AIGNAY-LE-DUC Côte-D'Or

Manoir de Tarperon (Prop: M de Champsavin)
Tarperon 21510
☎ 380938374
(30km south of Chatillion/Seine on the N71 towards Dijon, then D32 towards Aignay le Duc)
Situated by the banks of the Coquille river, this property blends both traditional and strikingly original styles. Gourmet breakfasts are served on the terrace and delicious rustic meals can be served. Special facilities available for fishermen, including private fly fishing. Plenty to see and do in the area. English spoken.
Near river Forest area Near motorway
Closed 2 Nov-Mar
5 en suite (bth/shr) (2 fmly) Full central heating Open parking available Child discount available Fishing Last d 20.00hrs Languages spoken: English & German
ROOMS: s 270FF; d 360FF Reductions over 1 night
MEALS: Dinner fr 150FF
CARDS: Travellers cheques

ALLUY Nièvre

Bouteville (Prop: M & Mme Le Jault)
58110
☎ 386840665 FAX 386840341
(halfway between Nevers & Chateau-Chinon. 1km from D978 and 5kms from Chatillon-en-Bezois)
Dating from the 18th century, this property forms part of an attractive collection of farm buildings offering views over fields and forests and within five kilometres of the beach. Private fishing facilities are available close by and swimming and tennis are within ten kilometres. A barbecue is situated in the gardens guests' use. The English-speaking proprietors will help you plan your days out in the Bazois region if required.
Near lake Forest area
4 en suite (bth/shr) (1 fmly) No smoking on premises TV in all bedrooms Full central heating Open parking available Covered parking available Supervised Child discount available Pool table Boule Bicycle rental Languages spoken: English
ROOMS: s 230-260FF; d 270-330FF Reductions over 1 night
CARDS: Travellers cheques

AMANZE Saône-et-Loire

Bed & Breakfast (Prop: Marie Christine Paperin)
Gaec des Collines 71800
☎ 385706634 FAX 385706381
Guest rooms are situated in the outbuildings of an old château, which was burnt down during the French Revolution but has since been restored. Ochre-coloured stone and wood set the style of the spacious guest rooms. The surrounding area is very peaceful. Guests can sample regional cooking using local farm produce. English spoken.
Forest area
4 en suite (shr) (1 fmly) TV in 1 bedroom Full central heating Open parking available Child discount available Languages spoken: English
ROOMS: s 210FF; d 265FF *
MEALS: Full breakfast 30FF Dinner 80FF
CARDS: Eurocheques

ANZY-LE-DUC Saône-et-Loire

Lamy Genevieve
Le Bourg *71110*
☎ 385251721
Near river Forest area In town centre Near motorway
Closed Nov-Etr
2 rms Full central heating Open parking available

ARCENANT Côte-D'Or

Bed & Breakfast (Prop: Nina Campo)
r de Bruant *21700*
☎ 380612893
(leave RN 74 at Nuits-St-Georges and head in the direction of
Meuilley and Arcenant)
Forest area
4 en suite (bth/shr) (1 fmly) (2 with balcony) Full central
heating Open parking available Child discount available 5yrs
Last d 20.00hrs Languages spoken: English
MEALS: Lunch fr 80FF Dinner fr 80FF*

ARGILLY Côte-D'Or

Bed & Breakfast
Jean Francois Bugnet *21700*
☎ 380625398 FAX 380625485
Three guest rooms are available in this 18th-century coaching
inn, offering old-style charm coupled with modern amenities;
one has a private garden. The living room has an open fire
and there is a well-equipped kitchen for guests' use. The
generous breakfasts can be served in the dining room or on
the terrace.
Near river Near lake Forest area
4 en suite (bth/shr) (1 fmly) No smoking on premises TV
available Full central heating Open parking available
CARDS: Travellers cheques

AZÉ Saône-et-Loire

Bed & Breakfast (Prop: Roger Barry)
en Rizerolles *71260*
☎ 385333326 FAX 385334013
(from Mâcon take N79 towards Cluny, then D17 exit at Roche
Vineuse, then onto Verze, Ige and Azé)
Comfortable rooms are available in this beautiful Mâconnaise
house. Balcony, terrace and garden are all there for the guests,
together with a communal room with dining area. Nearby
facilities include golf , swimming, horse riding, fishing and
tennis. There are many restaurants close to the property.
Near river Forest area
4 en suite (shr) (2 fmly) (2 with balcony) No smoking on
premises Full central heating Open parking available
Covered parking available Child discount available 14yrs
ROOMS: s 190FF; d 250FF
CARDS: Travellers cheques

BARON Saône-et-Loire

Bed & Breakfast (Prop: Jean Paul & Bernadette Larue)
Le Bourg *71120*
☎ 385240569
Forest area Near motorway
2 en suite (bth) TV available Radio in rooms Full central
heating Open parking available Covered parking available
Child discount available 12yrs
CARDS: Travellers cheques

BAUDRIÈRES Saône-et-Loire

Bed & Breakfast (Prop: Yvonne Perrusson)
Le Bourg *71370*
☎ 385473190
Forest area
2 rms (1 bth/shr) Full central heating Open parking available
Covered parking available

BELLENOT-SOUS-POUILLY Côte-D'Or

Bed & Breakfast (Prop: Martine Denis)
21320
☎ 380907182
Near river Forest area Near motorway
2 en suite (bth/shr) No smoking on premises Full central
heating Open parking available Child discount available
Languages spoken: English & German
MEALS: Dinner 70FF*

BISSY-SOUS-UXELLES Saône-et-Loire

La Ferme (Prop: P & D de la Bussiere)
Le Bourg *71460*
☎ 385501503 FAX 385501503
(from Tournus D14 towards Cluny, at Chapaize take D314
towards Bissy-sous-Uxelles. The house is next to church)
An old farmhouse with two suites converted for family use
overlooking pleasant countryside. Each room has personal
touches with attention to detail.
Forest area
6 rms (4 bth/shr) (2 fmly) Open parking available Child
discount available 2yrs
ROOMS: s 130-230FF; d 180-315FF

BLANCEY Côte-D'Or

Château-de-Blancey (Prop: Jean Yves Sevestre)
21320
☎ 380646680 FAX 380646680
Built between the 15th and 17th centuries, this restored
chateau is a historic monument and offers three comfortable
guest rooms, one of which is a family room, furnished with
antiques and decorated with character. Dinner is served in the
superb Guard Room complete with a Louis XIV fireplace. A
choice of family or gastronomic meals are available by
arrangement. Badminton and mountain bikes on-site.
Surrounded by parkland. English spoken.
Forest area Near motorway
3 en suite (bth/shr) (1 fmly) TV available Open parking
available Child discount available 11yrs Languages spoken:
English
MEALS: Lunch 150-230FF Dinner 150-230FF*

BOUILLAND Côte-D'Or

Bed & Breakfast (Prop: Bernard & Marie Russo)
21420
☎ 380215956 FAX 380261303
(turn off A6 at Beaune and head towards Dijon take D2 to
Savigny and then Bouilland)
Near river Forest area
2 en suite (shr) TV available Radio in rooms Full central
heating Open parking available Child discount available 5yrs
Languages spoken: English
CARDS: Travellers cheques

BOURGVILAIN Saône-et-Loire

Moulin des Arbillons (Prop: Dubois)
71520
☎ 385508283 FAX 385508632
(A6 exit Mâcon-Sud take N79 in direction of Moulin after 10km leave Cluny in the direction Tramayes and find the village of Bourgvilain)
The Moulin des Arbillons welcomes visitors with its large and comfortable lounge and offers spacious bedrooms furnished with period furniture and beautiful views over the area. The house is surrounded by a mill-dam and a park. Breakfast is served in the 'Orangerie', a very attractive room which is built on the foundations of the old mill.
Near river Near lake Forest area
Closed Nov-14 Apr
5 en suite (bth/shr) Full central heating Open parking available Child discount available 10yrs Fishing Boule
ROOMS: d 450FF
CARDS: Travellers cheques

BRINON-SUR-BEUVRON Nièvre

Château de Chanteloup (Prop: Pierre Maihcuet)
58420
☎ 386290208 & 38629012 FAX 386296771
(off D5, leave N7 at Nevers/La Charité)

Enjoy a peaceful rest in a castle surrounded by a fifteen hectare park.
Near river Near lake Forest area
Closed Jan
6 rms (2 bth/shr) TV available STV Radio in rooms Open parking available Riding Boule Bicycle rental Open terrace
Languages spoken: English & German
ROOMS: s 270FF; d 270-350FF *
CARDS: ▨ Travellers cheques

BUSSY-EN-OTHE Yonne

Bed & Breakfast (Prop: Maud Dufayet)
46/48 rue St-Julien *89400*
☎ 386919348
Old, attractive farmhouse, situated on the edge of a village, surrounded by forests and a large garden. Meals available by request, using local produce. Yoga, music and tennis available and there are sun loungers in the garden. Walks and horse-riding closeby with swimming six kilometres away. English spoken.
Near river Near lake Forest area
4 en suite (bth/shr) (1 fmly) No smoking on premises Full

central heating Open parking available Child discount available 5yrs V meals Languages spoken: English
MEALS: Dinner 110-150FFalc*
CARDS: Travellers cheques

BUXY Saône-et-Loire

Bed & Breakfast (Prop: Thierry Davanture)
Davenay *71390*
☎ 385920479
(from A6 exit south of Chalon-sur-Saone and take N80 le Creusot then left onto D977 to Buxy)
A large house built on a hillside in the traditional Devigneron style, surrrounded by two hectares of vineyards and close to many early Roman churches and on the Routes-des-Vins from Beaune to Cluny. Two rooms, on the first floor and each with shower and toilet, are completely private. There is a separate living room with billiard table, TV and a large outdoor terrace. Splendid views over the village and countryside. Regional cooking, available all year, is a speciality.
Near river Near lake Forest area Near motorway
2 en suite (shr) No smoking on premises Full central heating Open parking available Covered parking available Languages spoken: Spanish
ROOMS: s 250-300FF; d 300-350FF
MEALS: Dinner fr 150FF
CARDS: Travellers cheques

CERISIERS Yonne

La Montagne (Prop: Aubert Hodgendam)
89320
☎ 386962258
Set in an old house in the heart of cider country, two studios and a guest house with patio are available, each with cooking facilities. Typical French breakfast is served and dinner, if required, is taken with the hosts. Lake and forest walks nearby. Farm produce sold.
In town centre
3 en suite (shr) (3 fmly) Full central heating Open parking available Child discount available

CHAMPIGNELLES Yonne

Les Perriaux (Prop: M Noel Gillet)
☎ 386451322 FAX 386451614
Marie-France Gillet welcome you to her home. Dinner is served on request, with smaller portions being served for children. Families will enjoy the farm, where the atmosphere is very relaxing. Reductions in room prices for children up to ten years old. English spoken.
Near river Near lake Forest area
Closed Jan
1 en suite (shr) No smoking on premises TV available Full central heating Open parking available Child discount available 10yrs Languages spoken: English
CARDS: ● ▨ ▨

CHAPELLE-DE-BRAGNY Saône-et-Loire

L'Arcave (Prop: Jean-Pierre Jouvin)
71240
☎ 385922531
(from Chalon-sur-Saône on N6, take D6 at Varennes-le-Grand & continue to La Chapelle-de-Bragny. From Tournus, take D67 at Sennecey-le-Grand to Nanton, then D147 to La Chapelle-de-Bragny. B&B near church)

An old stone and oak house in the heart of Burgundy, boasting an entirely private apartment on the second floor. There is a kitchen and a mezzanine, and a big veranda is available, plus a large courtyard and garden. Bicycles and table-tennis on-site. Fluent English spoken.
Near river Near lake Forest area
1 en suite (shr) (1 fmly) No smoking in all bedrooms TV in all bedrooms Radio in rooms Full central heating Open parking available Covered parking available Child discount available 6yrs Bicycle rental Table tennis 3 Bikes Languages spoken: English, German & Spanish
ROOMS: s 200FF; d 250FF
MEALS: Dinner 90FF

CHAPELLE-SOUS-BRANCION, LA Saône-et-Loire

Château de Nobles (Prop: Bertrand de Cherisey)
71700
☎ 385510055
(14km west of Tournus on D14 exit Tournus from A6)
Two guests rooms, with a private entrance, are available in the wing of this 15th-century château, surrounded by vineyard. English spoken.
Near river Forest area Near motorway
Closed Nov-Mar
2 en suite (bth) (2 fmly) Full central heating Open parking available Bicycle rental Barbecue Languages spoken: English & Italian
ROOMS: s 340FF; d 390FF

CHARBONNAT Saône-et-Loire

Bed & Breakfast (Prop: Marie Urie-Bixel)
La Montagne 71320
☎ 385542647
(16km south of Autun, go through Etang-sur-Arroux, 9km further south turn right to St Nizier and follow to Charbonnat. La Montagne signposted from the church)
Individual suites in a separate cottage by the main residence are offered. The house is situated just outside of the village, in a pleasant setting, with magnificent panoramic views. Guests won't find a television here but you won't miss it! Your Franco-Australian hosts will help you discover the region. English spoken.
Near river Near lake Forest area
Closed 16 Oct- 30 Apr
2 en suite (shr) (2 fmly) Open parking available Languages spoken: English & German
ROOMS: s fr 180FF; d fr 200FF

CHAROLLES Saône-et-Loire

Bed & Breakfast (Prop: Mme Simone Laugerette)
3 rue de la Madelèine 71120
☎ 385883578
(in Charolles take street opposite church towards sous-Prefecture. Turn first right house a short distance)
Guest rooms are available in this renovated 18th-century house set in a peaceful location. The hosts collect antique furniture and paint in oils. Fishing, tennis, heated swimming pool, horse-riding, bikes to hire are all within close proximity, as are shops and restaurants.
Near river Forest area In town centre
3 en suite (bth/shr) No smoking on premises TV available Full central heating Open parking available Child discount available Open terrace Languages spoken: German

CHARRIN Nièvre

Bed & Breakfast (Prop: Oliver de Brem & Broll Patrick)
Château du Vernet 58300
☎ 386503687
(from Nevers N81 to Decize then D979 to Charrin)
Guest rooms are available in this 19th-century château, some 14 kilometres from Decize. A living room and library are available for guests' use while a park and garden with games are situated at the rear of the house. Mini-billiards, table-tennis, petanque and nine-hole golf (clubs provided) are also available. English spoken.
Near river Forest area
3 en suite (shr) (3 fmly) Radio in rooms Full central heating Open parking available Covered parking available Supervised Child discount available 10yrs Golf 9 Boule Table tennis Last d 21.00hrs Languages spoken: English & German
MEALS: Lunch 120FF Dinner 120FF*
CARDS: Travellers cheques

Bed & Breakfast (Prop: Francoise Aurosseau)
La Varenne 58300
☎ 386503014 FAX 386503856
Near river Forest area
2 en suite (shr) (1 fmly) (1 with balcony) TV in 1 bedroom Radio in rooms Full central heating Open parking available
ROOMS: d 220FF

CHÂTENAY Saône-et-Loire

Bed & Breakfast (Prop: Bernadette Jolivet)
Les Bassets 71800
☎ 385281951 FAX 385268310
Guest rooms are available on this restored farm. There is a living room and kitchen area for guests' use. English spoken.
Near river Forest area
4 en suite (shr) (2 fmly) Full central heating Open parking available

CHAUMARD Nièvre

Bed & Breakfast (Prop: M Vaissettes)
Le Château 58120
☎ 386780333 FAX 386780494
(north of Château-Chinon take D37 then D12. Establishment at entrance to village on left)
The bedrooms are found in a separate building at this chateau. The garden has a view of the lake and the property is set in two hectares of woods. Dinner can be taken with your hosts. English spoken.
Near river Near lake Forest area
Closed 1 Dec-1 Mar
6 rms (3 bth) (6 fmly) Full central heating Open parking available Child discount available 12yrs Fishing Boule Last d 20.00hrs Languages spoken: English
ROOMS: d 240-260FF
MEALS: Dinner 95-120FF
CARDS: Travellers cheques

Taking your mobile phone to France?
See page 11

173

CHEVANNES Yonne

Château de Riboudin (Prop: Claude Brodard)
89240
☎ 386412316 FAX 386412316
(leave A6/N6 at exit Auxere Nord in the direction St
Georges/Baulches then Chevannes)
Five guest rooms are available in the outbuildings of this 16th-
century château; one bedroom is suitable for guests with
disabilities. Each room is decorated individually and furnished
with antiques. Restaurants and shops close by. Well situated
for visits to regional vineyards and tourist attractions. English
spoken.
Near river Forest area Near motorway
5 en suite (bth/shr) (1 fmly) Full central heating Open
parking available Child discount available 5yrs Outdoor
swimming pool Bicycle rental Languages spoken: English
ROOMS: s fr 300FF; d 350-400FF

CHOREY-LES-BEAUNE Côte-D'Or

Le Château (Prop: Gernain)
21200
☎ 380220605 FAX 380240393
(on the Autoroute Beaune take the direction of Dijon N74, 3km
after Beaune 1st village on the right, Chateau on entry to
village)
Situated in the heart of Burgundy, this 17th-century château
offers spacious rooms comfortably furnished in period style.
Wines of the château can be sampled from the cellars.
Recommended restaurants close by. Swimming pool, tennis,
and golf near by. Possibility of hot-air ballooning. English
spoken.
Forest area
Closed Dec-Mar
5 en suite (bth) (4 fmly) (1 with balcony) Full central heating
Open parking available Languages spoken: English &
German
CARDS: ●● ▩ Travellers cheques

CLAMEREY Côte-D'Or

La Maison du Canal
21390
☎ 380646265 FAX 380646572
(from Paris exit A6 at Bierre-le-Semur, take D70 in the
direction of Vitteaux to just past Clamerey)

The light sunny rooms look out over the Burgundy Canal and
the Monts d'Auxois. All rooms have private facilities and are
furnished with fine Louis Philippe styled furniture.
Near lake Forest area Near motorway

Closed 16 Nov-14 Mar
6 en suite (shr) Full central heating Open parking available
Child discount available Languages spoken: English
ROOMS: s 210FF; d 260FF
CARDS: ●● ▩ Travellers cheques

CLUNY Saône-et-Loire

La Courtine (Prop: Noelle Donnadieu)
rue Pont de la Levée *71250*
☎ 385590510 FAX 385590510
(from A6 exit at Mâcon and take N79, then D980 to Cluny)

An old Burgundian farm, situated beside an old bridge, at the
river's edge. Large lounge available to guests. Breakfast
served in the garden. Five minutes by foot from the centre of
Cluny, and facilities such as the swimming pool and tennis
courts. English spoken.
Near river Forest area Near motorway
5 en suite (bth) (2 fmly) Full central heating Open parking
available Supervised Languages spoken: English & Italian
ROOMS: s 230FF; d 290FF
CARDS: Travellers cheques

COLLAN Yonne

Bed & Breakfast (Prop: M & Mme Lecolle)
2 r de L'Ecole la Marmotte *89700*
☎ 386552644
Three guest rooms, all with en suite facilities, are available in
this centrally located renovated renovated village house.
Meals are prepared using organic products and vegetables
from the garden. Regional cheese can be tasted including
Epoisses, Chaource and Soumaintrain. Plenty to see and do in
the area. Some English spoken.
Forest area
3 en suite (bth/shr) No smoking on premises Full central
heating Open parking available Child discount available
MEALS: Dinner fr 80FF*

CORBERON Côte-D'Or

Bed & Breakfast (Prop: Alain & Chantal Balmelle)
r des Ormes *21250*
☎ 380265319
Guest rooms are available in this 18th-century house set in a
small Burgundian village. Breakfast can be served in the
garden which leads into a field. English spoken.
Near river Forest area

4 en suite (bth/shr) (3 fmly) (1 with balcony) No smoking on premises Full central heating Open parking available Languages spoken: English
CARDS: Travellers cheques

COURTIVRON Côte-D'Or

Chalet de Genevroix (Prop: M & Mme J Huot)
21120
☎ 380751255 FAX 380751562
A chalet situated on a cereal farm. Living room, library, television, picnic area all available to guests. Restaurant in the village. Notional English.
Near river Forest area
2 rms No smoking on premises TV in all bedrooms Full central heating Open parking available Languages spoken: English & German
ROOMS: d 200-210FF * Reductions over 1 night
CARDS: Travellers cheques

COURTOIS-SUR-YONNE Yonne

Bed & Breakfast (Prop: D & H-F Lafolie)
3 rue des Champs Rouges *89100*
☎ 386970033 FAX 386970033
(from Sens take D58 through St Martin-du-Tertre and on to Courtois. In Courtois take 3rd right,establishment last house on left)
A comfortable country house, surrounded by a large garden, bordered by fields, in a small village. Evening meals served at the family table, in the living room with fireplace, or outside if the weather permits. Games available plus piano and library.
Near river Forest area Near motorway
4 rms (3 shr) (1 fmly) Full central heating Open parking available Covered parking available Table tennis
ROOMS: d 220-240FF
MEALS: Dinner fr 85FF
CARDS: Travellers cheques

CRUZY-LE-CHÂTEL Yonne

Bed & Breakfast (Prop: M & Mme Batreau)
Impasse du Presbytere *89740*
☎ 386752276
Near motorway
(1 fmly) Open parking available Supervised Child discount available Languages spoken: English
CARDS: Travellers cheques

DEVROUZE Saône-et-Loire

Domaine des Druides (Prop: A & J Hoehler)
71330
☎ 385724706 FAX 385724706
(from A6 exit at Tournas and take D971 to Louhans,then N78 north to crossroads at Quain.Turn right onto D24 towards St Germain-du-Bois, then right to establishment)
Set in a peaceful area, this is an ideal location for walks and bike rides. Bikes are available free of charge. The living room has a library for guests to use. There is a special area for children to play in the dining room. A swimming pool is situated within three kilometres, with fishing, golf and canoeing close by. Join your hosts for meals which include home-grown produce. Vegetarians are catered for. English spoken.
Near river Forest area Near motorway
Closed Jan-Feb

4 en suite (shr) (3 fmly) No smoking on premises Full central heating Open parking available Supervised Child discount available 16yrs Fishing Bicycle rental Canoeing, Donkey rides V meals Languages spoken: English,German & Italian
ROOMS: s 160FF; d 240FF Reductions over 1 night
MEALS: Dinner 80FF
CARDS: Travellers cheques

DONZY Nièvre

Jardins de Belle Rive Bagnaux (Prop: M & Mme Juste)
Bagnaux *58220*
☎ 386394218
Three beautiful guest rooms are situated in a house full of character next to the home of the proprietors. Large garden with swimming pool and sun loungers. Meals available by arrangement the previous day. Visitors can enjoy discovering the sights and gastronomic delights of this region. English spoken.
Near river Forest area
3 en suite (bth/shr) (2 fmly) (1 with balcony) No smoking on premises Open parking available Supervised Child discount available Outdoor swimming pool Languages spoken: English
MEALS: Dinner 90FF*
CARDS: Travellers cheques

ÉCHALOT Côte-D'Or

Bed & Breakfast (Prop: Mme R Bonnefoy)
rue du Centre *21510*
☎ 380938684
A restored house set in the centre of the village. Dinner available on request, inclusive of wine. A traditional Kir is served beforehand. Evening meals and breakfast are served in the lounge, which has an open fire.
Near river Forest area
2 en suite (shr) Full central heating Open parking available Supervised Child discount available Languages spoken: German
MEALS: Dinner 80FF*

ÉCUTIGNY Côte-D'Or

Château d'Ecutigny (Prop: M & Mme P Rochet)
21360
☎ 380201914 FAX 380201915
Furnished with antiques, this fifteenth century château has been completely renovated.
Near river Near lake Forest area
6 en suite (bth/shr) No smoking on premises TV available Radio in rooms Full central heating Open parking available Covered parking available Supervised Child discount available Last d am Languages spoken: English & Spanish
MEALS: Dinner 230FF*
CARDS: ● ▆ Travellers cheques

ÉGUILLY Côte-D'Or

Rente d'Eguilly (Prop: M & Mme Rance)
21320
☎ 380908348
Chantal and Michel Rance own this charming farm and extend a warm welcome. Guests may eat with the family, all food being prepared with local farm produce. Vegetarians are *cont'd*

175

catered for. Peace, tranquillity, and fresh air guaranteed. A little English spoken.
Near river Near lake Forest area Near motorway
5 rms (2 bth 1 shr) (1 fmly) No smoking on premises Full central heating Open parking available Covered parking available Supervised Child discount available 6yrs

ENTRAINS-SUR-NOHAIN Nièvre

Maison des Adirondacks (Prop: Noelle Weissberg)
pl Saint-Sulpice *58410*
☎ 386292323 FAX 247202159
Forest area In town centre
Closed 3 Nov-14 Apr
4 en suite (bth/shr) (2 fmly) STV Radio in rooms Child discount available Languages spoken: English & Italian

ÉPERNAY-SOUS-GEVREY Côte-D'Or

La Vieille Auberge (Prop: Jules Plimmer)
Grand Rue *21220*
☎ 380366176 FAX 380366468
(from A6 exit at Nuits St Georges.Take N74 in direction of Dijon and at large roundabout at Vougeot follow D25 for 6kms. House next to church)
Completely renovated by the new owners, this property was originally a farmhouse and then, until 1960, the village pub. Situated in a village, with a population of only 130, between Beaune and Dijon, the rooms look out onto the village square. Ideal location for exploring Burgundy, Beaujolais and Jura and for châteaux and monastery visits. All the major Burgundy vineyards are just a short drive away. The English hosts have two young children so their fully enclosed garden has swings etc.
Near lake Forest area Near motorway
Closed 16-31 Dec
6 rms (1 bth 4 shr) (2 fmly) (1 with balcony) No smoking on premises Full central heating Open parking available Supervised Child discount available 15yrs V meals Last d 20.00hrs Languages spoken: English
ROOMS: s 220-250FF; d 320-350FF
MEALS: Dinner fr 100FF
CARDS: Travellers cheques

ESCOLIVES-STE-CAMILLE Yonne

Bed & Breakfast (Prop: M & Mme Borgnat)
1 rue de l'Église *89290*
☎ 386533528 FAX 386536500
Set in the middle of a vineyard, this traditional house is attractive, with a square courtyard and an exquisite staircase, which is typical of the Bourguignon area. Large living room with billiard table. Kitchen area available to guests. English spoken.
Near river Near motorway
5 en suite (bth/shr) (1 fmly) TV in 2 bedrooms Full central heating Open parking available Supervised Child discount available Outdoor swimming pool Table tennis Last d 18.00hrs Languages spoken: English & German
MEALS: Dinner fr 120FF*
CARDS: ●● ▦

Taking your mobile phone to France?
See page 11

176

ESSAROIS Côte-D'Or

Abbaye du Val des Choues (Prop: M & Mme M Monot)
21290
☎ 380810109
(from Chatillon-sur-Seine take D928 and at Leuglay turn right onto D996 then right to Essarois)
Converted monastery steeped in history, set in the middle of the Val des Choues Abbey, which was founded in 1193 by Eudes III, Duke of Bourgogne. Families welcome. Quiet is guaranteed, with only the peacocks disturbing the peace in May and the bellowing deer in September. English spoken.
Near river Forest area
Closed Nov-Mar
6 rms (1 bth 1 shr) (1 fmly) Open parking available Supervised Languages spoken: English & Spanish
ROOMS: s 270-290FF; d 330-350FF Reductions over 1 night
CARDS: Travellers cheques

FLAVIGNY-SUR-OZERAIN Côte-D'Or

Couvent des Castafours (Prop: Judith Lemoine)
21150
☎ 380962492
(on reaching village from 'La Porte du Bourg' go to church, and house can be seen below in courtyard)
Set in the heart of a medieval city, this house has been restored from the remains of an old seventeenth century convent. The view over the Auxois is magnificent. Garden and parking available. Meals served with the hosts, although reservations are necessary. French breakfast served. Children up to ten years old receive special reductions. English spoken.
Near river Near beach Forest area
2 en suite (shr) No smoking on premises Full central heating Open parking available Child discount available 10yrs Last d 17.00hrs Languages spoken: English
ROOMS: s 185FF; d 250FF Reductions over 1 night Special breaks
MEALS: Dinner 100FF
CARDS: Travellers cheques

FONTAINE-FRANÇAISE Côte-D'Or

Le Vieux Moulin (Prop: Patrick Berger)
Le Vieux Moulin *21610*
☎ 380758216 FAX 380758216
(from A31 exit 5, take D961, then D960 to Bèze and on to Fontaine-Française)
The old mill was constructed in the seventeenth century and now offers flatlets, a living room and library for guests. Buffet suppers on request. Garden with private swimming pool and barbecue. Children's leisure activities available. Stores and services within walking distance. English spoken.
Near river Near lake Forest area In town centre
5 en suite (bth/shr) (2 fmly) (1 with balcony) No smoking on premises TV in 2 bedrooms Full central heating Open parking available Supervised Child discount available 12yrs Outdoor swimming pool Fishing Boule Languages spoken: English
ROOMS: s 240-290FF; d 290-330FF
MEALS: Lunch fr 90FF Dinner fr 90FF
CARDS: ●● ▦ Travellers cheques

FRONTENAUD Saône-et-Loire

Bed & Breakfast (Prop: Robert Guyot)
Le Venay *71580*
☎ 385748524
Near river Forest area Near motorway
Closed Nov-Mar
4 en suite (shr) (3 fmly) Full central heating Open parking
available Child discount available 10yrs Languages spoken:
English & German
MEALS: Dinner 100-130FF*

GEVREY-CHAMBERTIN Côte-D'Or

Bed & Breakfast (Prop: Mme G Sylvain)
14 r de l'Eglise *21220*
☎ 380518639
Forest area In town centre Near motorway
6 en suite (bth/shr) TV available Full central heating
CARDS: Travellers cheques

GOURDON Saône-et-Loire

Bed & Breakfast (Prop: Mme M Gibert)
Mont Bretange *71300*
☎ 385798078
Forest area
2 en suite (bth) No smoking on premises Full central heating
Open parking available Languages spoken: Italian
CARDS: Travellers cheques

GREVILLY Saône-et-Loire

Le Pre Menot (Prop: Claude Dépreay)
71700
☎ 385332992 FAX 385330279
(from Tournus take D14 towards Cormatin then left onto D163
towards Gratay. 1st right onto D356 to Grevilly)
Near river Forest area Near motorway
2 en suite (bth/shr) TV in all bedrooms Radio in rooms
Licensed Full central heating Open parking available Child
discount available 5yrs Boule Bicycle rental Open terrace
Languages spoken: English
ROOMS: d 270FF
CARDS: ●● ▥ ▣ Travellers cheques

GUICHE, LA Saône-et-Loire

La Roseraie (Prop: Rosslyn Binns)
71220
☎ 385246782 FAX 385246103
(exit Chalon Sud, D977 Buxy, D983 St Bonnet after Chevagny
right D303 La Guiche)
Near lake Forest area In town centre Near motorway
TV available Radio in rooms Full central heating Open
parking available Tennis Boule Bicycle rental Languages
spoken: English & Spanish
ROOMS: s 250FF; d 350FF

IGUERANDE Saône-et-Loire

Bed & Breakfast (Prop: M Martin)
Les Montees *71340*
☎ 385840969
(from D982 Roanne/Digoin turn off at Iguerande proceed to
Outre-Loire then Montees)
Set in a lovely leafy environment, near a river, this old house
enjoys spectacular panoramic views. Constructed of stone and
oak, which blends beautifully with the simple harmony of the
rustic decor, the house offers comfort and tranquillity. A living
area with open fire is set aside for guests and games are
provided for children. A warm welcome awaits you and a
place at the host's table is offered, by reservation. English
spoken.
Near river Near lake Forest area
4 en suite (bth/shr) (3 fmly) No smoking on premises Full
central heating Open parking available Supervised
Languages spoken: English & German

JOURS-LÈS-BAIGNEUX Côte-D'Or

Bed & Breakfast (Prop: Mme Juliette Descombes)
21450
☎ 380965222
A charming village house in a rural setting. A garden full of
trees surrounds the property. Breakfast is served in the garden
in summer. A little English spoken.
Forest area Near motorway
4 en suite (shr) No smoking on premises Full central heating
Open parking available
CARDS: Travellers cheques

LAVAU Yonne

La Chasseuserie (Prop: M & Mme Marty)
89170
☎ 386741609
Forest area
3 en suite (bth) (2 fmly) Full central heating Open parking
available Supervised Outdoor swimming pool Languages
spoken: English

LEUGNY Yonne

La Borde (Prop: M P Moreau)
89130
☎ 386476428 FAX 386476028
(from Toucy take D950 in the direction of Avallon)
Sixteenth century building set in the Bourgogne countryside.
The building surrounds a courtyard, and a seven hectare park
includes ponds, woods and orchards. The bedrooms are large
and comfortable, with the original beams still exposed. Meals
are generous and delicious. Your hostess is loyal to the local
cuisine but guests are free to improvise by choosing local
produce themselves. English spoken.
Near river Forest area
4 en suite (bth/shr) TV available Full central heating Open
parking available Child discount available Languages
spoken: English
CARDS: ●● ▥

MALIGNY Côte-D'Or

Bed & Breakfast (Prop: Mme Veronique Paillard)
21230
☎ 380842650 380842639
Well-restored old house which offers five rooms, one of which
leads out onto the well-kept garden. Living room with
television. Garden with games area for children and garage.
Reductions for children (no age limit), some reductions for
visits lasting more than one week. English breakfast served.
English spoken.

cont'd

Forest area
3 en suite (bth/shr) Full central heating Open parking
available Covered parking available Supervised Child
discount available

MARCHAIS-BETON Yonne

La Cour Alexandre (Prop: Mme Desvignes)
89120
☎ 386916433 FAX 386916992
As soon as you come down the long road of poplar trees that
lead to La Cour Alexandre, you will feel the peace and serenity
of this house. This 100 hectare residence is found on top of a
hill overlooking the village. English spoken.
6 en suite (bth/shr) (2 fmly) TV in 2 bedrooms Full central
heating Open parking available Covered parking available
Supervised Child discount available Outdoor swimming pool
Tennis Fishing Bicycle rental V meals Languages spoken:
English, German, Italian & Spanish
ROOMS: s fr 300FF; d fr 450FF Reductions over 1 night

MARCIGNY Saône-et-Loire

Les Récollets (Prop: Josette Badin)
71110
☎ 385250516 FAX 385250691
17th-century convent. The guest rooms are completely
separate from the hosts own home. It is situated at the edge of
a small village with a population of 2,500. Swimming
pool,tennis courts and shops all found in the village. Meals
may be taken with your hosts, if reservations are made.
English spoken.
Near river
9 en suite (bth/shr) (3 fmly) TV available STV Radio in rooms
Full central heating Open parking available Boule Open
terrace V meals Languages spoken: English
CARDS: ●● ▒▒ 🔲 Travellers cheques

MERRY-SEC Yonne

Bed & Breakfast (Prop: Pierre & Maryse Coevoet)
Pesteau *89560*
☎ 386416263 FAX 386416464
(signposted off N151 approx 17km from Auxerre in the
direction of Nevers)
Located at a stud, you will enjoy the peace and quiet on offer
here. Visitors are invited to sit out on the patio with its
panoramic views over the countryside. When you are not
relaxing there are plenty of sites to visit including the
vineyards of Chablis and various châteaux. English spoken.
Near river Forest area Near motorway
7 en suite (shr) (3 fmly) (1 with balcony) No smoking in 2
bedrooms Full central heating Open parking available Child
discount available 10yrs Riding Languages spoken: English &
German

MILLY-LAMARTINE Saône-et-Loire

Leif Nielsen (Prop: Leif Nielsen)
Les Echalys *71960*
☎ 385377978
In the heart of the Lamartinien Valley rooms are available on
the first floor of this modern building which looks out onto
rolling green hills. Communal living and dining rooms. Patio,
leading to vineyards. Fishing, swimming, tennis, and riding all
within close proximity. English spoken.
Near river Forest area Near motorway

1 en suite (shr) No smoking on premises Full central heating
Open parking available No children 6yrs Languages spoken:
English & German

MOTTE-TERNANT, LA Côte-D'Or

Le Presbytère
La Motte Ternant *21210*
☎ 380843485 FAX 380843532
(10km from Saulieu on the D26 at the side of the village
church)
This sixteenth century presbytery sits on the highest point of
the village of La Motte Ternant, adjacent to the eleventh
century church. Guests are invited to eat with their hosts,
Brian and Marjorie, who will introduce their own
interpretation of Burgundy cuisine.
Near river Near lake Forest area Near motorway
3 en suite (bth/shr) No smoking on premises Full central
heating Open parking available No children Languages
spoken: English
MEALS: Dinner 115-130FF*
CARDS: Travellers cheques

NAN-SOUS-THIL Côte-D'Or

Château de Beauregard
21390
☎ 380644108 FAX 380644728
(from A6 exit Bierre-les-Semur)
Renovated seventeenth century château built on the remains
of a thirteenth century castle. Situated in the heart of the hilly
landscapes of the Auxois. Three guest rooms and one suite
available.
Near river Near lake Forest area
Closed Dec-Etr
4 en suite (bth/shr) (1 fmly) Full central heating Open
parking available Languages spoken: English
CARDS: Travellers cheques

NEUVY-SUR-LOIRE Nièvre

Domaine de l'Étang (Prop: Bernard Pasquet)
L'etang *58450*
☎ 386392006 FAX 386392006
The Pasquet family welcome you to their large farmhouse and
stables. Guests may wander through the beautiful countryside
or hire bicycles. Play badminton or croquet on the large lawn.
Tennis courts and stables on site. This area of the Sologne is a
region that specialises in hunting and fishing. English spoken.
Near river Near lake Forest area
3 en suite (bth/shr) (4 fmly) TV available Radio in rooms Full
central heating Open parking available Covered parking
available Child discount available Tennis Fishing Boule
Open terrace Languages spoken: English, German & Italian

NUITS-ST-GEORGES Côte-D'Or

Domaine Comtesse Michel de Loisy
28 r de General de Gaulle *21700*
☎ 380610272 FAX 380613614
Family house situated in the heart of a typical Burgundian
village. The Countess Michel de Loisy will give you an
escorted tour of the wine cellars with tasting included. Golf
and air ballooning fifteen kilometres away. Swimming pool
and tennis within 300 metres. English spoken.
Forest area In town centre Near motorway
Closed 21 Nov-Mar

4 en suite (bth/shr) No smoking on premises Full central heating Open parking available Child discount available 4yrs Languages spoken: English & Italian

ONLAY Nièvre

Château de Lesvault
58370
☎ 386843291 FAX 386843578
(from Moulins-Engilbert take D18 toward Onlay and Park du Morvan, Chateau Lesvault is 5.5km from Moulins-Engilbert)

In the rolling green hills of the Sud-Morvan, bright rooms and exquisite food served at the hosts table offer a home-from-home for travellers. Midway between Sancerre and Beaune, the house is handy for the vineyards of the region, as well as its hiking routes. English spoken.
Near river Near lake Forest area
10 rms (8 bth/shr) Full central heating Open parking available Supervised Child discount available 12yrs Fishing Open terrace V meals Last d 17.00hrs Languages spoken: English, Danish, Dutch, German & Swedish
ROOMS: s 350FF; d 450FF
MEALS: Dinner 85-130FF
CARDS: ●● ▥ ▱ Eurocard Travellers cheques

OULON Nièvre

Ferme Auberge du Vieux Chateau (Prop: M & Mme Fayolle)
58700
☎ 386680677 FAX 386680677
A gourmet meal will be served to you by the roaring fire at this old château, or amongst the flowers on the patio in summer. Many leisure activities available in the château: swimming pool, swings, volleyball, table-tennis. Children will love the animals on the farm. Oak forests, châteaux, Roman churches, archaeology - something for everyone. English spoken.
Near lake Forest area
11 rms (1 bth 4 shr) (3 fmly) Open parking available Child discount available 10yrs Outdoor swimming pool Languages spoken: English
MEALS: Lunch 85-150FF Dinner 85-150FF*
CARDS: ●● ▱

POILLY-SUR-SEREIN Yonne

Le Moulin (Prop: M & Mme Moreau)
89310
☎ 386759246 FAX 386759521
Set in a two-hectare park, the Mill of Poilly-sur-Serein is a nineteenth century building, just on the edge of the village.

The area is well known for Chablis wine and potteries. River, swimming and canoeing plus riding within a three kilometre range. English spoken.
Near river Near lake Forest area Near motorway
Closed Oct-May
5 en suite (bth/shr) (2 fmly) TV available Open parking available Supervised Child discount available Languages spoken: English, German & Dutch
CARDS: Travellers cheques

POILLY-SUR-THOLON Yonne

Bed & Breakfast (Prop: Alain & Chantal Chevallier)
5 rte St Aubin Bleury *89110*
☎ 386635164 FAX 386915337
Chantal and Alain Chevallier welcome you to their farm. The rooms have a private entrance. The kitchen may be used, as may the library and billiard table. There are two restaurants within fifty metres. Golf, swimming pool and museum, are close by. English spoken.
Near river Forest area
3 en suite (shr) (1 fmly) (2 with balcony) Full central heating Open parking available Covered parking available Child discount available 10yrs Languages spoken: English & German
CARDS: Travellers cheques

POISSON Saône-et-Loire

Bed & Breakfast (Prop: Maguy & Paul Mathieu)
Sermaize *71600*
☎ 385810610 FAX 385810610
(from Paray-le-Monial head for Poisson on D34. In village turn left and head for Charolle, 2km further at the crossrds, go straight on for 2.5km, the house is on right after the river bridge)
The rooms at this property are found on the first-floor, which you access via an ancient staircase in the tower. Reductions for children under six years old. Dinner is served by the hosts. Children's games available in the garden, swings and table-tennis. Reductions available for visits lasting four days or more. Your hosts have a knowledge of English.
Near river Forest area
Closed 15 Nov-14 Mar
4 rms (3 shr) Full central heating Open parking available Child discount available 6yrs Boule Bicycle rental Table tennis Languages spoken: English
ROOMS: s 230-280FF; d 280-330FF Reductions over 1 night
MEALS: Dinner 80-100FF
CARDS: ▥ Travellers cheques

Château de Martigny (Prop: Edith Dor)
☎ 385815321 FAX 385815940
Edith Dor offers an unusual break - her ambition is to provide an environment where all types of creative expression can come together. The visitor may experience this through painting, sculpture, role playing, theatre, music, drawing or cooking. A theatre which seats 156 people may be used. Many other pursuits to be enjoyed, such as cycling or wine-tasting.
Near river Near lake Forest area
Closed 2 Nov-Mar
4 en suite (bth/shr) Full central heating Open parking available Supervised Child discount available 7yrs Outdoor swimming pool V meals Languages spoken: Portuguese

POUILLY-SUR-SAÔNE Côte-D'Or

Bed & Breakfast (Prop: Mme Angélique Délorme)
rte de Dinon *21250*
☎ 380210643 380211876
Country-style house with restored murals, decorative roof and
rustic furniture. Rooms are separate from the main residence.
Floral garden with barbecue and patio. Reductions on
childrens breakfasts. Certain reductions available for longer
stays. For very long stays, guests may make use of the kitchen.
Near river Near lake Forest area Near motorway
6 rms (5 bth) (2 fmly) (3 with balcony) No smoking on
premises TV in 3 bedrooms Radio in rooms Full central
heating Open parking available Supervised Child discount
available
ROOMS: d 220FF Reductions over 1 night

QUENNE Yonne

Les Granges (Prop: Eliane & Christian Dapoigny)
10 r de la Croix *89290*
☎ 386403118 FAX 386402845
(from Motorway A6 exit Auxerre Sud, head towards Auxerre,
take first road on the left to Quenne. From Auxerre, take N65
and the first road on right to Quenne)
In a small village between Auxerre and Chablis. Situated in
the areas vineyards. With five attractive cosy bedrooms, with
all modern conveniences in a 19th-century wine grower's
house. A terrace, overlooking the countryside, is available for
breakfast and evening picnics.
Closed Jan
5 en suite (bth/shr) Full central heating Open parking
available Child discount available 2yrs Covered terrace
Languages spoken: English
ROOMS: s 250-270FF; d 300-320FF
CARDS: Travellers cheques

RAVEAU Nièvre

Bed & Breakfast (Prop: D & J Mellet-Mandard)
Bois Dieu *58400*
☎ 386696002 FAX 386702391

(from La Charité-sur-Loire take direction of Clamecy-Auxerre
N151, then D179 to Raveau and D138 for 3km Le Bois Dieu is
250m after Peteloup on the right)
Close to La Charité-sur-Loire, Dominique and Jean Mellet-
Mandard welcome you to a guest house near their farm, on
the edge of the Bertranges Forest. The vineyards of the
Pouilly-sur-Loire and Sancerre are nearby. Meals are available.
Reductions for children sharing parent's room.
Near river Forest area Near motorway

4 en suite (bth/shr) No smoking in all bedrooms Full central
heating Open parking available Fishing Last d 16.00hrs
ROOMS: s 260FF; d 300FF
MEALS: Dinner fr 100FF
CARDS: Eurocheques

ROCHE-VINEUSE, LA Saône-et-Loire

Tinailler d'Aleane (Prop: Eliane Heinen)
Sommere *71960*
☎ 385378068
Forest area Near motorway
3 en suite (bth/shr) TV available Full central heating Open
parking available Supervised Child discount available
Languages spoken: English & German

ROGNY-LES-SEPT-ÉCLUSES Yonne

Bed & Breakfast (Prop: Paul & Mireille Lemaistre)
Les Gonneaux *89220*
☎ 386745189 FAX 386745634
Country cottage in an attractive part of the countryside, near
the Grand Rue Lake. Kitchen area with fridge. Swimming pool
and fishing on-site. Many walks available in the area. Library,
television, games area and sports equipment for guests' use.
Children under two stay free. Reductions for stays of more
than one night. English spoken.
Near river Near lake Forest area
1 en suite (bth/shr) TV available Radio in rooms Full central
heating Open parking available Outdoor swimming pool
Fishing Languages spoken: English

ROYER Saône-et-Loire

Bed & Breakfast (Prop: Thierry Meunier)
Le Bourg *71700*
☎ 385510342
Each room in this old winemakers house has its own
courtyard and entrance. Walks and fishing nearby.
Restaurants within two kilometres. Come and enjoy the wines
of the Mâconnais, the rivers and the chateaux of this fine area.
Forest area
3 en suite (shr) (3 fmly) (2 with balcony) No smoking on
premises Full central heating Open parking available
Languages spoken: English
ROOMS: s fr 180FF; d fr 230FF

ST-AUBIN-CHÂTEAU-NEUF Yonne

La Posterle (Prop: Daniel et Jeannette Chaumet)
2 pl Aristide Briand *89110*
☎ 386736409 FAX 386736409

Your hosts welcome their guests who are invited to dine with them (reservations needed). Living room with old bar, television and stereo. Calm surroundings. Plenty of walks. Tennis, boules, table-tennis, river fishing and hunting available on-site.
Near river Forest area Near motorway
4 en suite (bth/shr) (1 fmly) TV in 2 bedrooms Full central heating Open parking available Covered parking available Supervised Child discount available 10yrs Boule Bicycle rental Tennis nearby
ROOMS: s fr 300FF; d 350-400FF Reductions over 1 night

ST-BOIL Saône-et-Loire

Bed & Breakfast (Prop: Mme S Perraut)
Chaumois *71390*
☎ 385440796
(N 981 Buxy-Cluny road and at Saint-Boil leave village and take left turn to Chaumois, house signposted)
Near river Forest area
4 en suite (bth/shr) (1 fmly) (1 with balcony) No smoking on premises Full central heating Open parking available Supervised Riding Languages spoken: English
CARDS: Travellers cheques

ST-ÉLOI Nièvre

Domaine de Trangy
8 rte de Trangy *58000*
☎ 386371127 FAX 386371875
Close to the town, this eighteenth century house is situated within parkland, with swimming pool and well in the garden. English spoken.
Near river Forest area Near motorway
3 rms (2 shr) (1 fmly) Full central heating Open parking available Outdoor swimming pool Languages spoken: English & Spanish

ST-FARGEAU Yonne

Château-de-Dannery
89170
☎ 386740901
Charming manor house with moat and swimming pool, situated in a park of three hectares in the centre of the Puisaye region with its abbeys, châteaux and vineyards. Tranquillity is assured. Accommodation available for up to ten guests, with reductions on stays of more than three nights. Children over five years accepted. Large French breakfast served. English spoken.
Near lake Forest area Near motorway
TV in 1 bedroom Open parking available No children 5yrs Languages spoken: English

Famille Provot-Rolaz
10 rue Porte Marlotte *89170*
☎ 386740228
Situated near the town centre, this house has a private garden, with paved courtyard and children's play area. Reductions for children under ten. Shops and restaurants are close by. English spoken.
Near river Near lake Near beach Forest area In town centre Near motorway
2 en suite (shr) (2 fmly) Full central heating Open parking available Supervised Child discount available 10yrs Languages spoken: English

ST-GRATIEN-SAVIGNY Nièvre

la Marquise (Prop: Huguette et Noel Perreau)
La Forêt *58340*
☎ 386500677 FAX 386500714
Two rooms are available in this manor house owned by the Perreau family. Large living room. Swimming pool in garden. Riding possible. Meals provided.
Near river Forest area
3 en suite (bth/shr) (2 fmly) No smoking in 2 bedrooms TV available Radio in rooms Full central heating Open parking available Fishing Riding

ST-JEAN-AUX-AMOGNES Nièvre

Château-de-Sury (Prop: Hubert de Faverges)
58270
☎ 386586051 FAX 386689028
The bedrooms are situated on the first floor of this 17th-century château, that overlooks a lake and surrounding parkland. Family atmosphere. Riding is available on-site. River fishing nearby. English spoken.
Near river Forest area
3 en suite (bth/shr) TV available Full central heating Open parking available Child discount available 12yrs Fishing Covered terrace Languages spoken: English
MEALS: Dinner fr 150FF*
CARDS: ● ▩ ▭ ▣ Travellers cheques

ST-LOUP Nièvre

Elviré (Prop: M & Mme Duchet)
Chauffour *58200*
☎ 386262022
(take N7 in the direction of Cours-St-Loup then D114 & after St-Loup continue for 3km towards St-Verain)
Mme Elvire Duchet welcomes guests to her attractive nineteenth century farmhouse. Comfortable bedrooms, living room with library and games. You are invited to the family table for breakfast and dinner, by request.
Forest area
Closed early Nov-end Mar
2 en suite (shr) Open parking available Supervised Child discount available 12yrs Open terrace
CARDS: Travellers cheques

ST-MARTIN-DU-TARTRE Saône-et-Loire

Bed & Breakfast (Prop: Jacqueline Bergeret)
Maizeray *71460*
☎ 385492461
A typical Burgundy farmhouse, which has been entirely restored. Situated in a small village in the Charolais countryside the house has a balcony, with flower boxes, overlooking the terrace. Dinner available, by reservation. Your host is an excellent cook and prepares regional specialities. Quiet base from which to visit local Roman churches. English spoken.
Forest area
Closed mid Nov-mid Apr
2 en suite (bth/shr) (1 fmly) No smoking on premises Full central heating Open parking available Supervised Languages spoken: English
CARDS: Travellers cheques

ST-MAURICE-LES-CHATEAUNEUF Saône-et-Loire

Bed & Breakfast (Prop: Madeleine Chartier)
La Violetterie *71740*
☎ 385262660
Charming country house with attractive rooms, one with
sloping roof and exposed beams, situated on the first floor.
Open from April to November. Children's games, barbecue
and sun-loungers in garden. Ten percent reduction after the
fourth night. Children under two years go free. A little English
spoken.
Near river
Closed 15 Nov-14 Apr
3 en suite (bth/shr) (1 fmly) Full central heating Open
parking available Supervised Languages spoken: English
CARDS: Travellers cheques

ST-PIERRE-LE-MOUTIER Nièvre

Bed & Breakfast (Prop: Roselyne Lavasseur)
La Forêt de Cougny *58240*
☎ 386581201
(from D978 take D203 in direction of St Parize le Chatel to la
Foret de Cougny)
Each oak-floored room is named after one of the three
daughters of the proprietors: Anne, Thérèse and Noelle. Each
girl has chosen a theme for the decor: the sea for Noelle,
greenery for Anne and the Renaissance for Thérèse. Set near a
forest and lake. Ideal for nature lovers. Some English spoken.
Near lake Forest area Near motorway
3 en suite (shr) Full central heating Open parking available
Languages spoken: English

ST-PRIX Saône-et-Loire

L'Eau Vive (Prop: Catherine et Rene Denis)
Le Bourg *71990*
☎ 385825934
(from Autun take the rd to Moulins, 4km from Autun, turn
right to St-Leger-sous-Beuvray, cross La Grande Verriere, at
foot of St Leger, turn right to St Prix, following arrows 'Le
Haut Folin'-house is 200m after church)
On the edge of a village and the Morvan Parc, Catherine and
René offer bedrooms and a living room with open fire, which
is reserved for guests. Their property is in the mountains,
surrounded by forests, streams and wide open spaces. The
guest house has a private lake. Guests may take their evening
meal with the family. English spoken.
Near river Forest area
Closed 15 Nov-14 Mar
4 en suite (bth/shr) Full central heating Open parking
available Child discount available Fishing Boule Bicycle
rental Languages spoken: English & Spanish
ROOMS: s 230FF; d 265FF
MEALS: Dinner 100FF
CARDS: Travellers cheques

ST-SAULGE Nièvre

Les Beauvais (Prop: Mme M-F O'Leary)
58330
☎ 386582998 FAX 386582997
(in Nevers take D978 towards Autun-Dijon for 10kms, turn left
on to the D958 towards St Saulge and follow signs)
Marie Francis, who is a writer, welcomes guests to her
spacious country house, overlooking woodland gardens. Yoga
and relaxation classes are run by Marie.

Near lake Forest area In town centre
4 en suite (bth/shr) No smoking on premises Full central
heating Open parking available Child discount available
10yrs Last d 21.00hrs Languages spoken: English
ROOMS: (room only) s 200-300FF; d 350-500FF *
MEALS: Dinner 100FF

STE-MAGNANCE Yonne

Château Jacquot (Prop: Martine Costaille)
89420
☎ 386330022
Twelfth century residence offering one guest room with
canopied bed. The room features a fireplace and antique
furniture. Breakfast includes home-made pastries. Evening
meals served; medieval menu a speciality.
Forest area Near motorway
1 en suite (shr) Full central heating Open parking available
No children 8yrs V meals Languages spoken: English &
German
CARDS: Travellers cheques

SAISY Saône-et-Loire

Bed & Breakfast (Prop: Colette Comeaud)
Changey *71360*
☎ 385820755
Old house, set in a quiet, rural hamlet. Living room, veranda,
shaded garden, courtyard. Comfortable rooms. Walks,
swimming, tennis, bikes, lake, four kilometres away. Fishing
and riding, seven kilometres. Ten percent reduction for the
third night. Children over four only please.
Near lake Forest area Near motorway
2 en suite (shr) No smoking on premises Radio in rooms Full
central heating Open parking available No children 4yrs

SALIVES Côte-D'Or

Ferme de Larcon (Prop: Simone Ramaget)
21580
☎ 380756092 FAX 380756092
Tranquil hamlet where a country welcome awaits you. Simone
Ramaget invites you to take time to try her crêpes, omelettes,
or her hearty country meals. Reductions offered on stays of
three nights or more. Golf within 100 metres of the property.
Forest area
5 en suite (shr) No smoking on premises Full central heating
Open parking available Child discount available Open terrace

SANTENAY-EN-BOURGOGNE Côte-D'Or

Château de la Crée (Prop: Y E & R Remy-Thevenin)
Le Hauts-de Santenay *21590*
☎ 380206266 FAX 380206650
Eighteenth century manor which has been completely
renovated, in the heart of the vineyards of the Côte de Beaune.
Set in a wooded park, the wine from the château has a good
reputation. A warm welcome is extended to guests. Bar,
billiards table, library, period living room, reception room,
tennis court and private putting green. English spoken.
Forest area
4 en suite (bth/shr) (3 with balcony) No smoking in all
bedrooms TV in all bedrooms Radio in rooms Full central
heating Open parking available Covered parking available
Child discount available 10yrs Tennis Boule Mini-golf
Bicycle rental V meals Languages spoken: English, German
& Italian
ROOMS: s 600-800FF; d 650-850FF Reductions over 1 night
Special breaks
MEALS: Full breakfast 55FF Lunch 350-550FF Dinner 350-
750FF
CARDS: ●● ▇ Travellers cheques

SASSANGY Saône-et-Loire

Le Château (Prop: Andre & Ghyslaine Marceau)
71390
☎ 385961240 FAX 385961144
Accommodation is offered in this superb eighteenth century
château which has been fully restored and is set in peaceful
rural countryside, where guests are welcomed as friends.
Rooms are spacious and furnished with antiques. Attractive
dining room with domed ceiling, library, lounge and summer
terrace available to guests. Evening meals by prior
arrangement. Château produced and bottled Burgundy
available for sale. Reductions for three nights or more. English
spoken.
Forest area Near motorway
Closed mid Nov-mid Mar
6 en suite (bth/shr) No smoking on premises Full central
heating Open parking available Supervised No children 8
yrs Languages spoken: English
ROOMS: s 450-550FF; d 600-750FF *
CARDS: ●● ▇ Travellers cheques

SÉMELAY Nièvre

Domaine de la Chaume (Prop: Pierre & Valerie d'Été)
58360
☎ 386309123
Near river Forest area
Closed Oct-Apr
3 en suite (shr) (1 fmly) Open parking available Child
discount available Languages spoken: English
MEALS: Dinner fr 80FF*

SEMUR-EN-AUXOIS Côte-D'Or

Château de Flée (Prop: Marc Francis Bach)
21140
☎ 380971707 FAX 380973432
You are offered an unforgettable stay at this château, once the
home of the Treasurer of King Louis XV. Many pursuits are
available to you: relaxing in the ten hectare park, horse-riding,
strolls around the château and hot air ballooning. Dinner
available at a fixed price. Swimming pool. English spoken.

Near river Near lake Forest area Near motorway
2 en suite (bth/shr) TV available Radio in rooms Full central
heating Open parking available Child discount available
10yrs Languages spoken: English & German
CARDS: Travellers cheques

SENAN Yonne

Bed & Breakfast (Prop: Mme Paule Defrance)
4 pl de la Liberté *89710*
☎ 386915989
(from A6 exit Joigny take D89 towards Volgré & Senan)
Situated in a quiet position this is an ideal location for lovers
of authentic buildings and the simple things in life. Rooms are
spacious and well-lit. Situated just ten minutes from Joigny
and 25 minutes from Auxerre. Golf is at Roncenay, ten minutes
away.
Near motorway
3 en suite (bth/shr) Full central heating Open parking
available Covered parking available Bicycle rental Open
terrace
ROOMS: d 280-380FF Reductions over 1 night
MEALS: Dinner 100FF

SENNECÉ-LÈS-MÂCON Saône-et-Loire

Bed & Breakfast (Prop: Michel & Nadine Verjat)
483 rue Vremontoise *71000*
☎ 385360392 FAX 385360392
(exit Mâcon Nord from A6 in direction of Sennecé-Lè-Mâcon
after the pay booth)
Accommodation is in an annexe adjacent to the main house,
and one room has a kitchen. Each room, designed with a
rustic décor, has a television. Meals are available in the
restaurant on-site and there is a barbecue in the garden for
guests' use. Close to forest, with fishing available only two
kilometres away, and golf and riding within five kilometres.
Forest area Near motorway
3 en suite (shr) TV available Radio in rooms Full central
heating Open parking available Covered parking available
Supervised Child discount available Bicycle rental
ROOMS: s 180-200FF; d 230-250FF
CARDS: Travellers cheques

SERCY Saône-et-Loire

Bed & Breakfast (Prop: Josette Biwand)
Le Bourg *71460*
☎ 385926261 FAX 385925128
Hosts Josette and Pascal Biwand have taken care to provide
all comforts for visitors to their home. Direct access to an
enclosed tree-lined garden, full of flowers. Library, TV room.
Situated in a small village. Close to leisure facilities and shops.
English spoken.
Near river Forest area
2 en suite (bth/shr) TV available Open parking available
Child discount available Languages spoken: English &
German

SIVIGNON Saône-et-Loire

Bed & Breakfast (Prop: Jean Claude Geoffrey)
L'Écousserie du Bas *71220*
☎ 385596666
(between Cluny and Charolles, in South Burgundy)

cont'd

Comfortable rooms available in this typical Charolais farm, set in the Charolais Mountains. A number of leisure pursuits available within a short distance: châteaux visits, walks, riding, and art galleries. Large flower garden.
Forest area
3 en suite (shr) Full central heating Open parking available Supervised Child discount available 6yrs Languages spoken: German & Italian
ROOMS: d 280FF Reductions over 1 night
CARDS: Travellers cheques

THAIX Nièvre

L'Ombre Thaix (Prop: Mr Moulherat)
Château de l'Ombre *58250*
☎ 386502400
Renovated building in the heart of a park with a well stocked fishing lake. Many walks possible in the park. Children's games available. Evening meal available at a fixed rate.
Near lake Forest area
4 en suite (bth) (1 fmly) TV available Full central heating Open parking available Supervised Child discount available
MEALS: Lunch fr 85FF Dinner fr 85FF*
CARDS: Travellers cheques

TINTURY Nièvre

Fleury la Tour (Prop: Michel Gueny)
Fleury La Tour Tintury *58110*
☎ 386841242 FAX 386841242
Spacious, comfortable rooms are available in this country house, which looks out onto lush green lawns. Living room with fireplace, plus kitchen available for use of guests. Also in the grounds is a gite, with a view over the lake. A fifteenth century tower overhangs the water nearby. Ideal for fishing enthusiasts.
Near river Near lake Forest area
4 en suite (bth/shr) (2 fmly) Full central heating Open parking available Supervised Tennis Fishing Languages spoken: German
CARDS: Travellers cheques

TOURNUS Saône-et-Loire

En Chazot (Prop: Mme Lesley Cleaver)
La Croix Léonard *71700*
☎ 385511279
(from autoroute A6, take Tourus exit. follow N6 500m, then turn right onto D14 toward Mancey. Straight on for 1500m at brow of hill sign La Croix Leonard take lane to left, house is opppsite)
Owned by an English family, now resident in France, who welcomes visitors to their traditional stone-built home in a lovely Burgundy Valley. Recently restored, this bed & breakfast establishment has its own entrance for guests. There is a large garden with orchard, children's swing and deckchairs.
Near river Near lake Forest area Near motorway
1 en suite (bth/shr) (1 fmly) (1 with balcony) Radio in rooms Full central heating Open parking available Child discount available Orchard, deckchairs, swings, terrace Languages spoken: English
ROOMS: s 230FF; d 260FF Reductions over 1 night
CARDS: Travellers cheques

TRAMAYES Saône-et-Loire

Bed & Breakfast (Prop: George Moiroud)
rte de Pierreclos *71520*
☎ 385505644 FAX 385505682
Bed & breakfast available on the ground floor of this traditional Mâçonnaise house. Separate entrance. Breakfast can be served in the room, on the terrace, or in the dining room. You are welcome to lunch with your hosts. Tennis, trout fishing and numerous walks available. English spoken.
Near river Near lake Forest area
1 en suite (shr) (1 fmly) TV available Full central heating Open parking available Languages spoken: English

TRAMBLY Saône-et-Loire

Bed & Breakfast (Prop: Florence Gauthier)
Les Charrières *71520*
☎ 385504317
This large house of character, was built in 1830 and is situated in a village location. Comfortable, well-furnished rooms. English spoken.
Near river Forest area
2 en suite (bth/shr) (2 fmly) (1 with balcony) Full central heating Open parking available Supervised Child discount available 2yrs Languages spoken: English

TRIVY Saône-et-Loire

Bed & Breakfast (Prop: M & Mme Laronze)
Le Bourg *71520*
☎ 385502236
Bed & breakfast is available on this farm, situated in open countryside, in the region of Cluny. Your hosts raise cows, sheep, horses and chickens. The house overlooks the Mâçonnaise Mountains, creating a calm, relaxing atmosphere all year round. All meals are prepared with fresh farm produce.
Near lake Forest area Near motorway
(2 fmly) Full central heating Open parking available Supervised Child discount available hiking

VALLERY Yonne

La Margottière (Prop: M Deligand)
89150
☎ 386975797 FAX 386975380
An old restored building, where all rooms are totally independent. Your hosts love tradition and this is reflected in the way the house has been restored. There are beautiful, rural views. Within five kilometres the following can be found: eighteen-hole golf course, pony club, trout fishing and tennis. English spoken.
Near river Forest area
6 en suite (bth) TV available Full central heating Open parking available Supervised Child discount available Boule Table tennis Last d 19.00hrs Languages spoken: English
MEALS: Lunch fr 120FF Dinner fr 120FF*
CARDS: Travellers cheques

VARENNES-SOUS-DUN Saône-et-Loire

Bed & Breakfast (Prop: Alain & Michele Désmurs)
La Saigne *71800*
☎ 385281279 FAX 385281279
Small, restored old house run by Alain and Michèle, farmers in the Charollais-Brionnais area, and situated between

Beaujolais and Charollais. This is an area of many little valleys. Spacious living room with kitchen area. Benches and tables available in the flowered courtyard. Children's games. Meals will be served but reservations are required. English spoken.
Forest area
(1 fmly) Full central heating Open parking available Last d 20.30hrs Languages spoken: English
MEALS: Dinner fr 75FF*

VENDENESSE-LÈS-CHAROLLES Saône-et-Loire

Bed & Breakfast (Prop: Jean Marc & Chantal Dufour)
Virecache *71120*
☎ 385247160 FAX 385247815
In a calm little town situated one hour from Lyon, where fishing, sunbathing, walks and pony rides are available, Jean-Marc and Chantal Dufour will be happy to welcome you. One room plus a cottage available. Living room, veranda and summer house will help with your relaxation. A little English spoken.
Near river Near lake Forest area Near motorway
2 en suite (bth) (1 with balcony) Full central heating Open parking available Supervised Child discount available
CARDS: Travellers cheques

Bed & Breakfast (Prop: Jean & Anne Malacher)
Plainchassagne *71120*
☎ 385247022
Old, restored farm with panoramic views over the nearby park. Large living room with fireplace and a kitchen area available. The house is furnished with Burgundy antiques. Meals available in the evenings. Children's games available. Children under two are free and other reductions are available at certain times of year. English spoken.
Near river Near lake Forest area
4 en suite (bth/shr) (2 fmly) No smoking on premises Full central heating Open parking available Supervised Child discount available 2yrs V meals Languages spoken: English
MEALS: Full breakfast 50FF Continental breakfast 30FF Dinner fr 75FF*

VERGISSON Saône-et-Loire

Bed & Breakfast (Prop: Ineke & Jean-Claude Morlon)
Le Bourg *71960*
☎ 385358459 FAX 385381759
(from A6 exit Mâcon Sud, direction Vinzelles, Cluny, Soutre)
One room and a studio are available in this renovated stone house. One bedroom has an outlook over the rocks of Vergisson. Walking and climbing on-site. Other tourist attractions in the area include the museum at Solutré, wine-tasting, the abbey at Cluny and the lake at St.Point. Many wine routes taken in this area. Ineke and Jean-Morlon look forward to meeting you. English spoken.
Forest area Near motorway
2 en suite (shr) Radio in rooms Full central heating Open parking available Languages spoken: English, Dutch & German
ROOMS: s 180FF; d 240FF Reductions over 1 night

VÉZELAY Yonne

La Tour Gaillon (Prop: Mme Ginisty)
89450
☎ 386332574
(from A6 exit Avallon, go through to Vezelay. from N6 at Sermizelles, take road to Vézelay)

Situated in the centre in Vezelay, on the second floor of a fifteenth century house, the two guest rooms are reached by a spiral staircase. One room looks out onto a terrace, with views of the basilica. English spoken.
Near river Near lake Forest area Near motorway
Closed 24 Dec-3 Jan
2 rms (1 with balcony) No smoking on premises Child discount available Languages spoken: English
ROOMS: d 270FF Reductions over 1 night Special breaks: (10% off 3 or more nights)

VILLARS-ET-VILLENOTTE Côte-D'Or

Les Langrons (Prop: Mary & Roger Collins)
21140
☎ 380966511 FAX 380973228
(from Semur-en-Auxois take the D954 toward Venarey-les-Laumes for 2km to Villenotte, take 1st left in direction of Villars/Lantilly. Les Langrons is the last farm on right leaving Villars and is signposted)
Located in central Burgundy, this property offers spacious, well-appointed bedrooms in a large, attractive, nineteenth century farmhouse. All rooms command beautiful views over surrounding countryside. Quiet garden. Excellent walks and birdwatching. Bikes available. Only four kilometres to the medieval town of Semur en Auxois. English hosts.
Forest area
5 rms (4 shr) (2 fmly) No smoking on premises Full central heating Open parking available Covered parking available Supervised Child discount available 5 yrs Bicycle rental Last d 20.00hrs Languages spoken: English
ROOMS: s 200FF; d 250FF
MEALS: Dinner 120FF
CARDS: Travellers cheques

VILLENEUVE Yonne

Domaine Cochepie (Prop: Claire Strulik)
89500
☎ 386873976
(leave A6 at Courtenay exit onto D15 cross railway & river & turn in the direction of Sens cross the N6 & road for establishment left off the D15)
You will be welcomed as friends to this superb estate, located in the northern part of Burgundy. The non-smoking bedrooms are comfortable and have been recently renovated. The property is secluded in ten acres of woodland. Set amongst the trees you will find a large swimming pool and tennis court. English spoken.
Near river Forest area
2 en suite (bth/shr) (1 fmly) No smoking on premises Full central heating Open parking available Supervised Outdoor swimming pool Tennis Languages spoken: English German & Spanish
CARDS: ● ▄ Travellers cheques

VILLENEUVE-SUR-YONNE Yonne

La Lucarne Aux Chouettes (Prop: Leslie Caron)
Quai Bretoche *89500*
☎ 386871826 FAX 386872263
(take A6 to Lyon & exit at Courtenay/Sens. After the toll, in the direction of Sens (on right). At 1st crossroads, turn right to Villeneuve, once in Villeneuve, take direction of town centre cross the bridge & turn left)

cont'd

Four guest apartments, three of which overlook the river.
Elegant rustic accommodation recently renovated.
Near river Forest area In town centre Near motorway
Closed Sep-Jun Sun pm-Tue am
4 en suite (bth/shr) (1 fmly) TV in all bedrooms Full central
heating Open parking available Child discount available
ROOMS: (room only) d 490-830FF * Reductions over 1 night
MEALS: Full breakfast 85FF Continental breakfast 60FF
Dinner fr 178FFalc*
CARDS: 💳 🖼 🔁 📷

VINZELLES Saône-et-Loire

Bed & Breakfast (Prop: Dominique Mergey)
La Bruyère *71680*
☎ 385356657 FAX 385356225
Evelyne and Dominique Mergey extend a warm welcome to
their home, a modern house set in a wine-growers' village.
The guests may use a separate entrance but the veranda and
grounds are for communal use. Reductions for visits of three
nights or more. Large breakfasts are available.
Near motorway
1 en suite (shr) (1 fmly) Radio in rooms Full central heating
Open parking available Supervised

VIRÉ Saône-et-Loire

Bed & Breakfast (Prop: Jean-Noel & Josette Chaland)
Domaine des Chazelles *71260*
☎ 385331118 FAX 385331558
(Off A6)
Accommodation available in a wine-grower's house situated
amongst vineyards. You are invited to visit the cellars and
taste the wines. Your hosts can also organise receptions, with
traditional costumes and accordion music, by request. There is
also a small museum on site. Breakfast served on a large
veranda.
Near river Forest area Near motorway
1 en suite (bth) No smoking on premises Full central heating
Open parking available Supervised No children 2yrs
ROOMS: d 260FF
CARDS: Travellers cheques

VITRY-EN-CHAROLLAIS Saône-et-Loire

Bed & Breakfast (Prop: Guy Merle)
Les Bruyères *71600*
☎ 385811079 FAX 385811079
Six rooms on offer in this traditional Charollaise farm. Your
hosts, Guy and Michelle Merle are farmers, specialising in
organic produce. The house is situated amidst farmland and
hedgerows. There are numerous Roman churches in this area.
Rooms are simple but comfortable and quiet. Dinner available,
on request. Knowledge of English.
6 en suite (shr) (3 fmly) No smoking on premises Full central
heating Open parking available Bicycle rental V meals Last
d 17.00hrs Languages spoken: English (only little)
ROOMS: s fr 170FF; d fr 230FF
MEALS: Dinner fr 80FF

VOSNE-ROMANÉE Côte-D'Or

La Closerie des Ormes
21 rue de la Grand-Velle *21700*
☎ 380612024 FAX 380611963
((leave motorway at Nuits-St-Georges in the direction of Dijon
onto N74, then take the fourth turning on the left into Vosne-
Romanée, property 60 metres on right)
Near motorway
Closed 21 Oct-Mar
3 en suite (bth/shr) (1 fmly) No smoking on premises Full
central heating Open parking available No children 16yrs
Bicycle rental Languages spoken: English
ROOMS: d 450-550FF

BURGUNDY

Rivers, Streams and Canals

On the canals the pace is languid, the peace broken only by a heron's darting shadow or a kingfisher's call: these sleepy canals are now deserted by commercial traffic. Burgundy may be a drive from the sea, but it plays host to an incomparable network of clean canals and rivers. The Canal du Nivernais flows past the tree-lined boulevards of Auxerre, through green

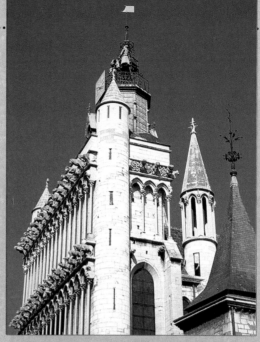

The church of Notre Dame in Dijon is an ideal site for gargoyle-spotters. It also has a Jacquemart clock tower.

pastures with bright wild flowers and pastel foxgloves that border the Morvan. Each canal route offers different aspects of Burgundy's rich past and present, from princely castles, ruminating charollais cattle, or a distant battlement carved against the sky line, to a friendly lock-keeper's wife offering delicious home-baked fare.

From Decorated Gothic to Rich Romanesque

Dijon is the capital of Burgundy and a town of outstanding artistic interest. As you stroll along the pedestrianised streets lined with private mansions, churches, parks and gardens you will discover an amazing historical heritage, witness to a prestigious past. The city is endowed with a great number of buildings centered around its Roman wall. There is a harmonious balance between the diversified styles and the architectural ornaments: half-timbered houses topped by coloured glazed tiles and the intricately carved stone of Gothic Churches. Cluny, Autun, Yonne and Beaune all show remarkable signs of their past - Roman remains mingling freely with historic buildings from the Middle Ages.

Decorations on Dijon's town gate include this winged Gorgon.

Franche-Comté

Franche-Comté is a region that invites you to experience the great outdoors, where you will find deep forests and a thousand lakes and rivers. Besançon, the fortified capital of the region, nestles inside a loop in the River Doubs and is a city of art and history, hosting prestigious international music festivals in the summer. This region is truly central to Europe, with a 143 mile/230km stretch of its eastern side bordering Switzerland and within reasonably easy reach of both Germany and Italy.

(Top): Salins-les-Bains is home to this stone wine-picker, although the town is chiefly known historically as a major salt producer.

(Bottom): The pretty village of Nans-sous-Ste-Anne, surrounded by greenery.

ESSENTIAL FACTS

DÉPARTEMENTS:	Doubs, Jura, Haute-Saône, Territoire-de-Belfort
PRINCIPAL TOWNS	Besançon, Montbeliard, Luxeuil-les-Bains, Dole,
PLACES TO VISIT:	The route-de-vin from Beaford to Arbois; the Herrisson Falls at the Sout de Doubs; Haut-Jura Nature Park; Cleron Castle; Ornans.
REGIONAL TOURIST OFFICE	9 rue de Pontarlier, 25044 Besançon Tel 81 83 50 47
LOCAL GASTRONOMIC DELIGHTS	Cheeses such as Comté, Morbier, Cancoillote, Bleu de Gex, Mont d'Or or Vacherin du Haut-Doubs; saucisse de Morteaux (smoked sausage); pognes; wild mushrooms; coq au vin jaune; tarts filled with fruit in summer and pumpkin in winter; regional fondu made with blue cheese
DRINKS	The AOC wine from Franche-Comté is Arbois. Three main districts, Arbois, Château-Chalon and L'Etoile, produce red, white or rosé. Château-Chalon also produces vin jaune (yellow wine) and vin de paille (straw wine). Vin jaune is aged in casks for at least six years, whilst vin de paille is made from grapes brought to maturity on beds of straw for three months. Vin fou (crazy or mad wine) is a locally produced sparkling wine. Macvin, a liqueur wine fortified with eau-de-vie, is served with melon, or as an apertif or with dessert.
LOCAL CRAFTS WHAT TO BUY	Watches and clocks from Besançon, lace from Montbéliard and Luxeuil-les-Bains, pottery and earthenware from Mathay and Salins-les-Bain, horn from Jeurre and Lizon, wood crafts and turned products from St Claude, Largillay and Mambelin.

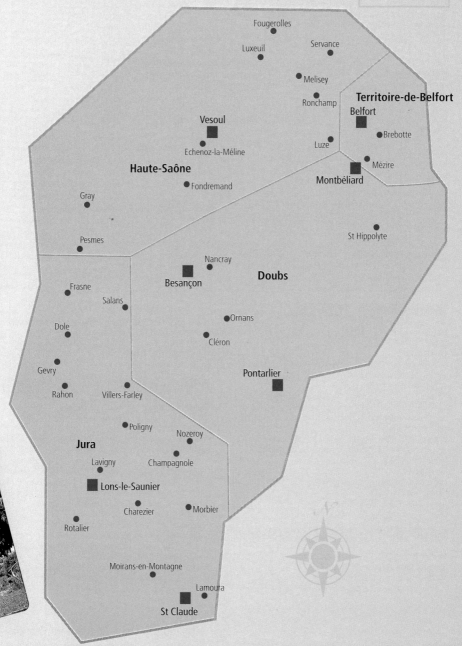

Fougerolles

Luxeuil

Servance

Melisey

Ronchamp

Territoire-de-Belfort

Belfort

Brebotte

Vesoul

Luze

Echenoz-la-Méline

Mézire

Montbéliard

Haute-Saône

Fondremand

Gray

St Hippolyte

Pesmes

Nancray

Doubs

Besançon

Frasne

Salans

Ornans

Dole

Cléron

Gevry

Pontarlier

Rahon

Villers-Farley

Poligny

Jura

Nozeroy

Lavigny

Champagnole

Lons-le-Saunier

Charezier

Morbier

Rotalier

Moirans-en-Montagne

Lamoura

St Claude

EVENTS AND FESTIVALS

Jan Aldenans Flea Market

Feb Morbier Cheese Festival

Mar Besançon Traditional Carnival; St-Valbert Brioche Festival; Pontarlier French Tarot Championship; Audincourt Carnival

Apr Mézire Snail Festival; Nancray Easter Flower Festival; Nancray Vegetable Fair; St-Claude Soufflaculs Festival; Melisey Carnival of the Haute Vallée de l'Ognon

May Sancey-le-Long Trout Festival; Belfort Flower Festival; Villersexel 'Le Triangle Vert' (*sport event*); Dole Festival of Tales & Legends; St Claude, Haut Jura Classical Music Festival; Besançon Comté Fair; Levier Fir Tree Festival

Jun Jazz Festival - St-Claude, Dole, Vesoul, Ornans, Pontarlier, Baume-les-Dames, Arc-et Senans; Nancray Haymaking; Lavigny Circus Festival; Belfort Cabaret & Theatre at the Castle

Jul Son et Lumière shows at St-Loup sur Semouse, Jougne, Fondremand, Rahon; Moirans-en-Montagne Children's Festival; Brebotte Historical Pageant; Fondremand Arts & Crafts Festival; Arbois Wine Fair; Nozeroy Medieval Fair

Aug Rahon Son et Lumière; Lamoura Local Craft Fair; Frasne Blueberry Festival; Pontarlier, Nights of Joux Festival; Morteau Sausage Festival

Sept Arbios Grape Harvest Ritual; Luxeuil les Bains Art Festival; Besançon Classical Music Festival; Luxeuil les-Bains Son et Lumière; Les Hôpitaux Neufs Descent of the herds from the Alps; Echenoz-la-Méline Honey Festival; MontbéliardVintage Car Rally; Ronchamp Veteran Cars & Motorbikes; Fougerolles Festival of Cherry Eau-de-Vie Tasters

Oct Luze Apple Fair; Montbéliard Model Building Sale; Audincourt Comic Book Festival

Nov Belfort Film Festival

Dec Audincourt Mechanical Figures Fair; Montbéliard Christmas Lights Festival

Route des Vins

If your interests lie in wine-tasting and you wish to increase your knowledge of the origins and making of French wines there are many wine routes suggested and organised by the French Tourist Board for you to explore. The Route des Vins du Jura, for example, provides an itinerary from Arbois (home town and work-place of Louis Pasteur), down to Bealfort with hotels located directly on the route for your gastronomic stopovers. You will be welcomed in these wine villages where gourmets will be able to admire the specialities of Franche-Comte, made of course with Jura wine.

CHAREZIER Jura

Chez Devanat (Prop: Mme Devenat)
39130
☎ 384483579
(A39 to Dole then Lons le Saunier, N78 direction Geneve for approx 22 km then left onto D27 towards lac de Chalain for 4km, look for Chambre d'Hote sign)
Charezier is a small village in the quiet countryside of central Jura near Lake Vouglans. The accomodation is in a spacious remodelled farmhouse, furnishings are simple and modest and a family atmosphere pervades as you share the living quarters of the Devenats and their two small children. Breakfast is an informal affair in the family kitchen.
Near river Near lake Near sea Forest area
5 en suite (shr) (5 fmly) No smoking in 2 bedrooms Open parking available Child discount available 10yrs Bicycle rental Last d 20.00hrs
ROOMS: s fr 140FF; d 190FF
MEALS: Dinner fr 60FF

GEVRY Jura

Bed & Breakfast (Prop: M & Mme R Picard)
3 rue du Puits *39100*
☎ 384710593 FAX 384710808
A renovated farm in the centre of a small village within an extensive park.
Near river Near beach Forest area In town centre Near motorway
Closed Jan-Feb

5 en suite (bth/shr) (2 with balcony) No smoking in 2 bedrooms Full central heating Open parking available Last d 18.00hrs Languages spoken: English & German
ROOMS: d 220FF
MEALS: Dinner fr 100FF*
CARDS: Travellers cheques

PESMES Haute-Saône

La Maison Royale (Prop: Mr Guy Hoyet)
70140
☎ 384312323
(from A36, take exit for 'Dole'. Join the D475 and turn right towards 'Gray')
Guests will receive a warm welcome at this 14th-century fort, which took five years to restore and is now considered an historic monument. Unusual decorations inside, both modern and old, and art exhibitions are shown here. English spoken.
Near river Forest area In town centre
Closed Oct-Mar
12 en suite (bth/shr) No smoking in 6 bedrooms Full central heating Open parking available No children 7yrs Fishing Bicycle rental Open terrace Billiards Languages spoken: English, German, Italian & Spanish
ROOMS: s 300-350FF; d 400-450FF Reductions over 1 night
MEALS: Dinner 120-150FF*
CARDS: Travellers cheques

Taking your mobile phone to France?
See page 11

190

ROTALIER Jura

Château Gréa (Prop: Benedicte & Pierre de Boissieu)
39190
☎ 384250507 FAX 384251424
(12km S of Lous-le-Saunier via H83, towards Bourg-en-Bresse
and Lyon for 10km. At railway Paisia, turn left towards
Rotalier, just before village on left)
The château is an 18th-century building set amongst the vines
of the Sud-Revermont. A huge park, with many trees,
surrounds the château and there are beautiful views of the
Bresse. Breakfasts are substantial. Riding is available.
Children are very welcome and those under four stay for free.
English spoken.
Near river Near lake Forest area
3 rms (2 bth/shr) (1 fmly) TV in 1 bedroom Full central
heating Open parking available Child discount available 3yrs
Languages spoken: English & Spanish
ROOMS: s 300FF; d 370-400FF Reductions over 1 night
Special breaks
CARDS: Travellers cheques

SALANS Jura

Château de Salans (Prop: M & Mme Oppelt)
39700
☎ 384711655 FAX 384813640
(turn off N73 (Dole to Besançon) at St-Vit and proceed to
Salans)

The Château still preserves some architectural features dating
back to its origins in the 17th century. It was sold shortly after
the Revolution when the last heir was executed. The
comfortable rooms overlook the park. Reductions for stays of
two or three days, depending on the season. English spoken.
Near river Forest area Near motorway
4 en suite (bth/shr) (1 fmly) TV available Full central heating
Open parking available Covered parking available Riding
Languages spoken: English & German
ROOMS: s 400FF; d 500FF
CARDS: Travellers cheques

SERVANCE Haute-Saône

Le Lodge du Monthury (Prop: Michele Chevillat)
70440
☎ 384204855
(take N19, then D486 until Servance then left onto D263)
Stone-built farmhouse, dating back to the 18th century, in a
rustic setting. Evening meals served, which feature regional
specialities. Ideal base for fishermen, in an area of a thousand
lakes, the house stands in 15 hectares and fishing is offered
on-site. English spoken.
Near river Near lake Forest area
6 en suite (shr) (1 fmly) TV available Full central heating
Supervised Child discount available 8yrs Last d 21.00hrs
Languages spoken: English & German
MEALS: Full breakfast 50FF Continental breakfast 35FF
Lunch 110-185FF&alc Dinner 110-185FF&alc*
CARDS: 💳 💳 💳 Travellers cheques

VESOUL Haute-Saône

Château d'Épenoux (Prop: Mme Germaine Gauthier)
rte de St-Loup, Pusy-et-Epenoux *70000*
☎ 384751960 FAX 384764505
This 18th-century château is surrounded by a pretty, five
hectare park full of flowers and trees. There is a small 12th-
century chapel in the grounds. This residence is just twenty
minutes from Vosges by car, where you can ski in winter time.
A warm welcome is offered. Dinner available by reservation
only. Ideal location for a relaxing holiday. English spoken.
Near lake Forest area Near motorway
6 en suite (bth/shr) (2 with balcony) TV available Full central
heating Open parking available Supervised Child discount
available V meals Languages spoken: English
MEALS: Dinner fr 200FF*
CARDS: Travellers cheques

VILLERS-FARLAY Jura

Château de Bel Air (Prop: M & Mme Dromard)
39600
☎ 384377337 FAX 384377337
The bedrooms here are large, as is the bathroom. A two
hectare park adjoins the château. The garden and flower beds
have been landscaped in the style of an eighteenth century
garden.
Near river Near sea Forest area
Closed Oct-Mar
2 en suite (bth/shr) (2 fmly) Full central heating Open
parking available Supervised

Poitou-Charentes

The sunniest region in the west of France with a mild climate even in the winter. Visit the old harbour at La Rochelle with its bustling quayside markets and fashionable bars, or stretch out and soak up the sun on the glorious beaches at the port des Minimes, Aytré and Angoulins. History-lovers should make for Chauvigny and its atmospheric remains of five castles. Royan caters for the sports-minded, offering tennis, squash, and an 18-hole golf course. Further north the villages around the Seudre rear the finest oysters, while in oak casks along the Charente Valley, the famous Cognac brandy matures.

(Top): These colourful puppets are the cast at the Theatre de Marionettes in the main square at Aubeterre-sur-Dronne.

(Bottom): Two 14th-century towers guard the harbour at La Rochelle, which has been called the French Geneva.

ESSENTIAL FACTS

DÉPARTEMENTS: Charente, Charente-Maritime, Deux Sèvres, Vienne

PRINCIPAL TOWNS Angoulême, La Rochelle, Niort, Poitiers, Royan

PLACES TO VISIT: Parc du Futuroscope; the old harbour at La Rochelle; Cognac and its distilleries, the ruins of five medieval castles at Chauvigny; 'Sleeping Beauty's Castle' at La Roche-Courbon

REGIONAL TOURIST OFFICE Comité Régional du Tourisme, BP 56, F-86002 Poitiers. Tel: 49 50 10 50

LOCAL GASTRONOMIC DELIGHTS Fruits de mer including mussels and oysters; entrecôte à la bordelaise; chaudrée, fish soup flavoured with white wine; eels and snails cooked in red wine; saddle of young goat with green garlic; mojettes, haricot beans cooked in butter

DRINKS Médoc, Sauternes, Graves, St-Emilion, Pomerol and Entre-deux-Mers are the main wine-producing areas, but the Charente Valley is famous for its brandy, produced at the distillery towns of Cognac and Jarnac

LOCAL CRAFTS WHAT TO BUY Glassware from Tusson, ceramics from Saintes and Thouars, pottery from Cognac

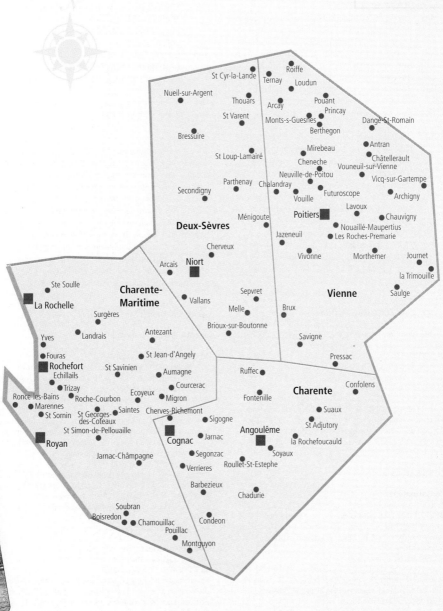

St Cyr-la-Lande
Roiffe
Ternay
Loudun
Nueil-sur-Argent
Thouars
Arcay
Pouant
Princay
St Varent
Monts-s-Guesnes
Dangé-St-Romain
Berthegon
Bressuire
Mirebeau
Antran
St Loup-Lamairé
Cheneche
Châtellerault
Vouneuil-sur-Vienne
Neuville-de-Poitou
Vicq-sur-Gartempe
Parthenay
Chalandray
Secondigny
Vouille
Futuroscope
Archigny
Lavoux
Ménigoute
Poitiers
Chauvigny
Deux-Sèvres
Nouaillé-Maupertius
Jazeneuil
Les Roches-Premarie
Cherveux
Vivonne
Morthemer
Journet
Arcais
Niort
la Trimouille
Ste Soulle
Charente-
Maritime
Sepvret
Vienne
Saulge
La Rochelle
Vallans
Surgères
Melle
Brux
Yves
Landrais
Antezant
Brioux-sur-Boutonne
Fouras
Savigne
Rochefort
St Jean-d'Angely
Pressac
Echillais
St Savinien
Aumagne
Ruffec
Confolens
Trizay
Courcerac
Charente
Ronce-les-Bains
Roche-Courbon
Ecoyeux
Migron
Fontenille
Marennes
Saintes
Cherves-Richemont
Suaux
St Sornin
St Georges-
des-Coteaux
Sigogne
St Adjutory
St Simon-de-Pellouaille
Angoulême
la Rochefoucauld
Royan
Cognac
Jarnac
Jarnac-Champagne
Segonzac
Soyaux
Roullet-St-Estephe
Verrieres
Barbezieux
Chadurie
Soubran
Boisredon
Chamouillac
Condeon
Pouillac
Montguyon

EVENTS & FESTIVALS

Jan Angoulême Comic Strip Festival

Apr Poitiers Spring Music Festival; Cognac International Police Film Festival; Royan Romanesque Festival

May Melle: St-Savinien Music Festival; Angoulême Multiracial Music Festival; La Rochelle International Sailing Week; Parthenay Meat Festival, Châtellerault Jazz Festival; Bressaire Circus Festival; Vivonne Song & Music Festival

Jun Nouaillé-Maupertius Medieval Spectacle; Creations en Val de Charente (*classical music festival*) at Cognac & Jarnac; Roquefort Celebrations

Jul La Rochelle International Film Festival; FLIP Games Festival at Parthenay; Saintes Folk Music & Dance Festival ; Parthenay Jazz Festival; La Rochelle French Language Music Festival; Montguyon World Folk Festival; Chauvigny Summer Festival in the medieval town; Ste-Maxime l'Ecole International Children's Folklore Encounters; Roquefort theatre, street entertainment & music; Thouars Arts Festival; Matha Folklore & Song Festival; Niort Street Art Festival; Son et Lumière at La Rochefoucauld Château & St

Brice Abbey; Château d'Oleron Story-telling Festival

Aug Chauvigny Summer Festival in the medieval town; Confolens International Festival of Folk Music & Dance; Parthenay-en-Gatine Traditional Music Festival; Vitrac St Vincent Music Festival; St-Palais sur Mer World Folklore Festival

Sep Cognac Festival of Street Arts; La Rochelle Boat Show; Angoulême Vintage Car Motor Racing; Fontaine-le-Comte Autumn Music Festival

Oct Ménigoute Ornithological Film Festival

Dec Poitiers Short Film Festival

Cognac

They say serendipity played a part in the creation of the smooth liqueur pineau. An absent-minded vintner accidentally mixed unfermented grape juice with cognac, and wine drinkers have been grateful ever since. But it's brandy that the Charente Valley is famous for, produced in the 20-mile "Golden Circle" region which includes the distillery towns of Cognac and Jarnac. One of the secrets of its luxurious savour is the chalky soil which nurtures a better quality grape juice. You can discover more about the production process by visiting the Cognac Museum or the distilleries which are open throughout the year.

ANTEZANT Charente-Maritime

Le Maurencon (Prop: P & M C Falleflour)
Les Moulins, 10 rue de Maurençon *17400*
☎ 546599452 FAX 546599452
(from St Jean d'Angely take D127 to Antezant)
Near river Forest area
Closed 25 Dec-2 Jan
2 rms (1 bth) (1 fmly) No smoking on premises Radio in rooms Full central heating Open parking available Child discount available 8yrs
ROOMS: d 230-280FF Reductions over 1 night
MEALS: Dinner 90FF
CARDS: Travellers cheques

ANTRAN Vienne

La Gatinalière
86100
☎ 549211502 FAX 549853965
Large white château built in 1763 and still owned by the same family. Situated in 400 hectares of parkland. Eighteen-hole golf course nearby.
Forest area Near motorway
Closed Nov-end Mar
2 en suite (bth/shr) No smoking on premises TV available Full central heating Open parking available Supervised Child discount available 10yrs

Taking your mobile phone to France?
See page 11

ARÇAIS Deux-Sèvres

Arçais (Prop: Jean Michel Deschamps)
10 chemin du Charret *79210*
☎ 59354334 FAX 59354335
(exit Niort of A10 Paris-Bordeaux in direction of Marais Poitevin & then in direction of Sansais-Le Vanneau & Arçais)
Spacious and well-lit family rooms are offered in this old renovated house. Situated in the heart of the Marais Poitevin region, which may be explored by canoe or boat on its pretty waterways. Special boating, canoeing or cycling holidays are offered. Quiet and comfort are assured. Picnic area in garden. The kitchen and dining is available for guests who wish to prepare their own meals. English spoken.
Closed Xmas RS Nov-Feb
3 en suite (shr) (3 fmly) No smoking on premises TV in 1 bedroom Full central heating Open parking available Supervised Boule Bicycle rental Languages spoken: English
ROOMS: s 200FF; d 250FF Reductions over 1 night Special breaks
CARDS: ▨ Travellers cheques

Bed & Breakfast (Prop: M & Mme Plat)
rue de l'Ouché *79210*
☎ 549354259 FAX 549359155
Elisabeth and Philippe welcome you to their home, situated on the water's edge, with a private swimming pool. The first floor bedrooms are reserved for non-smokers.Traditional French breakfast served. Covered parking available. Reductions available for children under two with cots provided. Restaurants and crêperie nearby. Facilities in area include boat rides, canoeing, bicycle rides, fishing and tennis.
Near river Forest area Near motorway

2 en suite (bth/shr) (1 fmly) No smoking on premises Full
central heating Open parking available Languages spoken:
English

ARÇAY Vienne

Château de Puy d'Arçay
86200
☎ 549982911
(from Paris in the direction of Bordeaux on A10, 30km after
Tours turn in direction of Richelieu/Loudun. Then after
Loudun in direction of Thouars, turn left for Arcay)
Ideally situated between Angers, Tours and Poitiers, only 45
kilometres from Futuroscope and near the romantic Loire
Châteaux. A warm welcome awaits you in this old, family
manor. Antique pictures and furniture adorn the house. Close
to picturesque parkland.
Near lake Forest area
Closed Oct-Mar
4 rms (2 bth/shr) (4 fmly) Full central heating Open parking
available Child discount available Languages spoken: English
ROOMS: d fr 220FF
MEALS: Lunch fr 90FF Dinner fr 90FF
CARDS: ▓ Travellers cheques

ARCHIGNY Vienne

La Talbardière (Prop: J Lonhienne)
86210
☎ 549853251 FAX 549856972
(south from Chatellerault take D9 towards Monthoiron. After
20kms turn left onto D3 towards la Roche-Posay. 2kms turn
left at sharp bend & continue for 1km to house)
A converted 16th-century dwelling, in a charming setting, is a
haven of peace and quiet. The downstairs bedroom has been
converted from the stables and still has the original hayrack.
Golf, tennis, Futuroscope and many historic buildings are
within easy access.
Near river Near lake Forest area Near motorway
3 en suite (bth/shr) (2 fmly) Full central heating Open
parking available Open terrace Table tennis Children's play
area Languages spoken: English, German,Italian & Russian
ROOMS: s 220FF; d 270FF Reductions over 1 night
CARDS: Travellers cheques

AUMAGNE Charente-Maritime

Le Treuil d'Aumagne (Prop: Eliane Dechamps)
17770
☎ 546582380
(leave A10 at St-Jean-d'Angely and take the D939 in the
direction of Matha, in the village of Reignier turn right to le
Treuil)
This farm is near the medieval town Saint Jean d'Angély. Your
hosts will introduce you to the joys of the countryside. You can
eat with them and spend your days relaxing or enjoy the local
sports, such as boules. Bikes are available for the use of
guests. Some English spoken.
Near river Near sea Forest area Near motorway
Closed Dec-Mar
5 en suite (bth/shr) Open parking available Child discount
available 3yrs

BERTHEGON Vienne

La Chaume (Prop: M & Mme Kosyk)
86420
☎ 549228669
Situated between the Loire châteaux and Futuroscope.
Beautiful 19th-century building with square courtyard and
leafy park and stone walls in the bedrooms. Living room and
library are available to guests. Numerous home-cooked
specialities are on offer at dinner. Bikes can be hired. English
spoken.
Forest area
Closed Nov-Mar
5 en suite (shr) (3 fmly) Full central heating Open parking
available Covered parking available Supervised Child
discount available 12yrs Boule Badminton table tennis Last d
20.00hrs

BOISREDON Charente-Maritime

La Chapelle (Prop: M & Mme Brunet)
17150
☎ 546493405 FAX 546493405
Set in the heart of the countryside on the banks of the
Gironde, this relatively new property offers a communal living
room with TV, bedrooms with direct access to a private
garden, car park and games for the children. Fifteen minutes
away is Lake Montendre which offers swimming, fishing and
other watersports. Nearby pine forests have excellent walks.
Good restaurants can be found within easy walking distance.
Near river Near lake In town centre Near motorway
(2 fmly) TV available STV Radio in rooms Full central
heating Open parking available Child discount available

BRIOUX-SUR-BOUTONNE Deux-Sèvres

La Rolanderie (Prop: Francois Riedel)
32 rue de la Gare *79170*
☎ 549072210
Pretty stone house, built in 1905, situated in an enclosed large
garden, with more than fifty trees, some fruit and ornamental,
surrounded by parkland. Your hosts offer four comfortable
bed & breakfast rooms. Ground floor rooms have direct access
into the garden. The house is 400 metres from the town of
Brioux sur Boutonne, with its shops, open-air swimming pool,
football pitch and several tennis courts. Bikes for hire on-site.
Two forests close by, with facilities for the children. English
spoken.
Near river Forest area
Closed Nov-30 Apr
4 rms (1 bth/shr) (2 with balcony) Full central heating Open
parking available Child discount available Bicycle rental
Languages spoken: English & German
ROOMS: s 180-200FF; d 200-250FF
CARDS: Travellers cheques

BRUX Vienne

Le Bourg (Prop: M & Mme Groller)
86510
☎ 549592310 FAX 549581803
The lakes near this accommodation provide a fisherman's
paradise and for ramblers there is a wealth of country walks to
be had. Your hosts can provide you with picnics in the shaded
garden. Parking is available in the courtyard. There is a leisure
park within fifteen kilometres and a choice of restaurants nearby.

cont'd

POITOU-CHARENTES

Near motorway
3 rms (2 shr) (1 fmly) Full central heating Open parking
available Child discount available
CARDS: Travellers cheques

CHADURIE Charente

Le Logis du Puy Fort-Haut (Prop: Marie Claude
Bergero)
16250
☎ 545248074 FAX 545240826
(from Angoulême D674 then D5 Chadurie, from Barbezieux
D5 Chadurie)
Set in the middle of the Charantaise countryside, this house
has a large swimming pool, and is an ideal spot for walking,
or as a central point from which to tour the area. Your hostess,
Marie-Claude, devotes herself to her guests and will organise
shopping trips, jazz or theatre evenings. Meals may be taken
with the family.
Forest area
4 en suite (shr) (3 fmly) Radio in rooms Full central heating
Open parking available Child discount available Outdoor
swimming pool Boule Volley ball, Table tennis

CHALANDRAY Vienne

Château de Trequel (Prop: Laurence Sarazin)
86190
☎ 549601895 FAX 549601895
(from Poitiers head towards Parthenay pass Ayron to
Chalandray)
Charming château, set in an enchanting 25 hectare park. The
rooms are furnished with antiques. Breakfast is served in the
dining room, as are evening meals. A personal welcome
awaits you. English spoken.
Near river Near lake Forest area Near motorway
8 en suite (bth) (2 fmly) No smoking on premises Full central
heating Open parking available Boule Table tennis Pony
Last d 22.00hrs Languages spoken: English
MEALS: Dinner fr 90FF*

CHAMOUILLAC Charente-Maritime

La Coussaie (Prop: Robert & Nichole Daviaud)
17130
☎ 546494101
(from A10 exit 37 Mirambeau in the direction of Montendre)
A house set in the middle of vineyards, where the proprietors
make Pineau and Cognac. The house is modern inside but is
actually quite old, with the exterior being typical of the
Charantaise region. A kitchen and living room may be used by
guests. Fluent English spoken.
Near lake Forest area Near motorway
2 en suite (bth/shr) (1 fmly) No smoking in all bedrooms TV
available Full central heating Open parking available
Covered parking available Languages spoken: English
CARDS: Travellers cheques

CHAUVIGNY Vienne

La Veaudepierre (Prop: M et Mme Jacques de Giafferri)
8 rue du Berry *86300*
☎ 549463081 549414176 FAX 549476412
This large, eighteenth century house has a lovely garden with
superb views over the medieval city. Guests can join their
hosts for dinner. Swings, table-tennis and boules available.
English spoken.

Near river Forest area In town centre Near motorway
Closed Nov-Etr
6 en suite (bth/shr) (2 fmly) Full central heating Open
parking available Child discount available 12yrs V meals
Last d 20.00hrs Languages spoken: English
ROOMS: s 180-200FF; d 230-300FF Reductions over 1 night
MEALS: Dinner 80-80FF
CARDS: Travellers cheques

CHENECHÉ Vienne

Château de Labarom (Prop: Eric Le Gallais)
86380
☎ 549512422 FAX 549514738
This 16th-century château is situated in the middle of a private
park of 180 hectares. The rooms are large and comfortable
and face south, and the château is furnished with old family
pieces. A large swimming pool is available. Many interesting
walks nearby. English spoken.
Near lake Forest area Near motorway
5 rms (3 bth/shr) (3 fmly) No smoking on premises Radio in
rooms Full central heating Open parking available Child
discount available 2yrs Languages spoken: English

CHERVES-RICHEMONT Charente

Logis de Boussac (Prop: François Mehaud)
16730
☎ 545831301 545832222 FAX 545832121
(take D731 from Cognac after 5km to L'Epine, turn left towards
Richemont, over 3 small bridges house on left)

Built in 1692, this residence is now protected as a historic
monument for its architectural interest. Situated in the middle
of a vineyard in the Cognac region, five kilometres from the
town centre. You may dine with your hosts for a fixed price,
finishing off your meal with a taste of Cognac! English
spoken.
Near river Forest area Near motorway
3 en suite (bth/shr) (1 fmly) Full central heating Open
parking available Covered parking available Child discount
available 12yrs Outdoor swimming pool Fishing Riding
Bicycle rental Canoeing Last d 12.00hrs Languages spoken:
English
ROOMS: (room only) d 350FF Special breaks: Wine & food
tasting breaks
MEALS: Continental breakfast 50FF Dinner 150FF
CARDS: Travellers cheques

CHERVEUX Deux-Sèvres

Château de Cherveux (Prop: F & M-T Redien)
79410
☎ 549750655 FAX 549750655
(from Niort take D743 then right onto D8 to Cherveux)
Bed and breakfast is available in this fifteenth century château, which you can explore during your stay. The guardroom is now used for guests. In good weather family meals are served with the proprietors (or separately, if you wish) in the courtyard. A little English spoken.
Near lake Near sea Near beach
4 rms (2 bth 1 shr) (2 fmly) Open parking available Covered parking available Child discount available Fishing Riding Languages spoken: English
ROOMS: s 200-250FF; d 250-300FF *

CONDÉON Charente

Le Bois de Mauré (Prop: M & Mme Testard)
16360
☎ 545785315
This old house was built in 1830. Ample French breakfasts are served and dinner is served at the family table, with your hosts. Specialities offered include dishes made with duck. There are swings in the garden. English spoken.
Near river
4 en suite (shr) Full central heating Open parking available Child discount available 10yrs Languages spoken: English
MEALS: Dinner 65FF*

COURCERAC Charente-Maritime

Le Bourg (Prop: M & Mme Moreau)
8 rue de Chez Mothe *17160*
☎ 546250007
Situated in a small village, bordered by trees and vineyards, this house offers kitchen, barbecue, linen available. For your relaxation: television, games room and table-tennis. Dinner available by reservation.
Near river Near lake Forest area
4 en suite (bth/shr) (1 fmly) No smoking on premises Full central heating Open parking available Child discount available
MEALS: Dinner fr 80FF*

DANGÉ-ST-ROMAIN Vienne

La Grenouillère (Prop: Noël Braguier)
17 rue de la Grenouillère *86220*
☎ 549864868 FAX 549864656
(from A10 exit at Châtellerault-Nord, take N10 to Dangé-St Romain. In town at 2nd set of lights follow signs for Chambres d'Hôtes. Over river, turn left at cross, under lime trees and into rue de Grenouillère)
This property is a 19th-century farmhouse, situated in tree-laden parkland. Guests are welcome to share the meals with the owners, Annie and Noël, on the patio during the good weather, or indoors when the weather is cold. Take a walk in the park, where carp and roach can be seen swimming in the water. A small boat is available should you wish to take a boat ride. Birdwatchers will be interested to see the abundance of birds in this area. The owners will be happy to give guidance on local attractions and places to visit. Futuroscope is close by. English spoken.

Near river Forest area Near motorway
4 en suite (bth/shr) (2 fmly) No smoking on premises TV in 1 bedroom Full central heating Open parking available Supervised Child discount available 10yrs Fishing Boule Badminton Volleyball Table tennis Last d 20.00hrs Languages spoken: English & Spanish
ROOMS: s 180-200FF; d 210-280FF Special breaks
MEALS: Dinner 90FF
CARDS: Travellers cheques

ECHILLAIS Charente-Maritime

Bed & Breakfast (Prop: Mme D Couraud)
5 rue du Champ Simon *17620*
☎ 546831160
The rooms of this house look out onto a garden filled with mature trees. A dining room, the garden and parking are available to guests. Communal living room with television and fireplace. Pierre Lotis House, the Corderie Royale, the banks of the Charante, Royan, Ile de Olèron and La Rochelle are all nearby.
Forest area
2 rms No smoking on premises Full central heating Open parking available No children
MEALS: Dinner 70FF*

ÉCOYEUX Charente-Maritime

Chez Quimand (Prop: M H Forget)
17770
☎ 546959255 FAX 546959255
(autoroute A10 exit 35 proceeding towards Saintes)
Distillery visits can be arranged by the proprietors of this guesthouse in Cognac, as can lessons in the cooking of the region. The room on the ground floor has been specially adapted for the handicapped. Evening meals are taken with the owners. All meals are cooked with farm produce.
Near sea Near beach Forest area Near motorway
4 en suite (bth/shr) (1 fmly) No smoking on premises Night porter Full central heating Open parking available Child discount available V meals Last d 20.00hrs
MEALS: Dinner 85FF*

FONTENILLE Charente

Les Des (Prop: B Jolley)
Le Morices *16230*
☎ 545203972
(N10 towards Angouleme exit at Mansle and take direction for Fontenille, just before arriving there turn left at Plechage)
Set in the middle of the countryside, where peace, calm and
cont'd

tranquility are assured, this old farm has been lovingly restored and offers superb views of the surrounding country. Private pool in garden. The house is near to the protected village of Tusson and only half-an-hour from Cognac and two hours from the coast. Guests may dine with the proprietors. English spoken.
Near river Forest area Near motorway
4 rms (1 shr) (1 fmly) No smoking on premises Full central heating Open parking available Child discount available 12yrs Outdoor swimming pool Languages spoken: English
MEALS: Dinner 65FF*

FOURAS Charente-Maritime

Le Clos des Courtineurs (Prop: Mme Lefebvre)
4 ter rue des Courtineurs, BP 47 *17450*
☎ 546840287 FAX 546840287
(24km from La Rochelle & 13km from Rochefort, leave N137 onto D937, Fouras 5km west)
In a quiet wooded area of the Fouras peninsula, with sandy beach just 300 metres away and the shore only 150 metres. Guest rooms are on the ground floor, in a separate wing from the owner's home, and open onto a large garden.
Near sea Near beach Forest area
Closed Oct-Apr
5 en suite (shr) No smoking in all bedrooms Open parking available Covered parking available Languages spoken: English
ROOMS: s 260FF; d 320FF
CARDS: Travellers cheques

JARNAC Charente

Maison Karine (Prop: M & Mme Legon)
Bois Faucon *16200*
☎ 545362626 FAX 545811093
(from Jarnac towards Les Metairies on D376 at crossroads follow sign for Hotel Karina)

Accommodation is provided in long, low buildings typical of the region and attractively arranged around a central swimming pool. Rooms of all sizes are available including suites and family rooms and some open directly onto the pool area. For wine lovers the region is full of interest, with Bordeaux and St Emilion just an hour away. Boating on the Charente River and off the coast at La Rochelle.
Closed 15 Dec-15 Jan
10 en suite (bth/shr) Some rooms in annexe (2 fmly) No smoking in 1 bedroom TV in all bedrooms Radio in rooms Full central heating Open parking available Child discount available 10yrs Outdoor swimming pool Tennis Boule Bicycle rental Last d 22.30hrs Languages spoken: English

ROOMS: (room only) d 290-450FF *
MEALS: Full breakfast 50FF Continental breakfast 30FF Lunch fr 75FF Dinner 75-100FF
CARDS: ●● ▆

JARNAC-CHAMPAGNE Charente-Maritime

Domaine des Tonneaux (Prop: Mme Violette Lassalle)
17520
☎ 546495099 FAX 546495733
The Domaine des Tonneaux is a working distillery and winery. Set in a beautiful, shady old building, which looks out onto a park. Guests are invited to dine with their hosts. Children welcome.
Forest area Near motorway
Closed Dec-Etr
3 en suite (bth/shr) Radio in rooms Full central heating Open parking available Supervised Child discount available 10yrs Boule Table tennis TV room
MEALS: Dinner fr 120FF*
CARDS: Travellers cheques

JAZENEUIL Vienne

Les Ruffinières (Prop: D Foucault)
86600
☎ 549535519 & 549534917
(autoroute from Paris exit Poitiers South, from south exit Lusignan)
Set in lovely countryside, this house looks down into the valley. There are many tourist attractions on offer in this area. Hostess Mme. Foucault specialises in two-day stays in which guests discover the culinary art of the Middle Ages and the gardens and churches of the area. English spoken.
Near river
Closed 16 Sep-14 Apr RS 1-15 Nov
6 rms (4 bth/shr) No smoking in 2 bedrooms Full central heating Open parking available Child discount available 6yrs Open terrace Covered terrace Languages spoken: English
MEALS: Dinner 100-125FF*

JOURNET Vienne

La Boulinière (Prop: Deborah Earls)
86290
☎ 549915588 FAX 549915588
(on the D727, 10kms from Montmorillon)

Ideally suited for touring the attractions of Vienne, this charming manor house is surrounded by 115 hectares of farmland. Beautiful park with swimming pool nearby. Families truly welcome. There are plenty of facilities for children to

enjoy, including our free babysitting service if Mum and Dad want some time on their own. Guests may dine with their hosts. English spoken.
Near river Near lake Forest area
6 en suite (bth/shr) (1 fmly) Full central heating Open parking available Covered parking available Child discount available Outdoor swimming pool Fishing Bicycle rental V meals Last d 20.00hrs Languages spoken: English & Italian
ROOMS: s 280FF; d 320FF * Reductions over 1 night
MEALS: Dinner fr 95FF*
CARDS: Travellers cheques

LANDRAIS Charente-Maritime

Bed & Breakfast (Prop: M Francois Caillon)
Les Granges *17290*
☎ 546277381 FAX 546278713
(at Surgeres take D939 in direction of La Rochelle after 5km turn left on D117 to Landrais)
Forest area
Closed 24 Dec-1 Jan
5 en suite (shr) (1 fmly) No smoking on premises Full central heating Open parking available Child discount available Boule Languages spoken: English
ROOMS: s 160FF; d 200FF
MEALS: Dinner 70FF
CARDS: ▧

LAVOUX Vienne

Logis du Château du Bois Dousset (Prop: Hilaire de Villoutreys)
86800
☎ 549442026 FAX 549442026
(from A10, Poitiers Nord exit, N10 towards Limoges, after 7km, left to Bignoux and follow signs to Bois Dousset)
Forest area
3 en suite (bth) (1 fmly) Full central heating Open parking available Languages spoken: English
ROOMS: s 280-300FF; d 350FF Reductions over 1 night
Special breaks

MARENNES Charente-Maritime

Bed & Breakfast (Prop: Jean & Jacqueline Ferchaud)
5 rue des Lilas, La Mesnardière *17320*
☎ 546854177
Jacqueline and Jean Ferchaud welcome you to their renovated town house which boasts a lawn and veranda, garden furniture, barbecue, sports equipment and swings. Two rooms available. The Marennes-Oléron basin is renowned for its oysters. Beach and swimming pool are all within close proximity to the house.
Near sea Forest area
Closed Oct
4 en suite (bth/shr) No smoking on premises Full central heating Open parking available Supervised

MIGRON Charente-Maritime

Logis des Bessons (Prop: J Philippe)
17770
☎ 546949116 FAX 546949822
Comfortable rooms furnished with antiques in the Charantais style. Several rooms have exposed beams. The family rooms will take up to three people plus a child of up to four years. Garden with lush shrubs and swimming pool. A little English spoken.

Near river Near lake Forest area Near motorway
5 rms (3 bth/shr) (1 fmly) Radio in rooms Open parking available Covered parking available Supervised Child discount available 3-4yrs Outdoor swimming pool Boule Bicycle rental Table tennis Languages spoken: English
ROOMS: s fr 190FF; d 250-270FF Special breaks: (7 nights for price of 6 nights)

MIREBEAU Vienne

Bed & Breakfast (Prop: Mme Jeannin)
19 rue Jacquard *86110*
☎ 549505406
Situated between Angers and Poitiers, this rustic property offers two guests rooms on the first floor, with comfortable beds. Extra beds can be made available for a small supplement. French breakfast is served in a restored stable. The property is situated in front of the local gendarmerie.
Near lake Forest area In town centre Near motorway
2 en suite (bth/shr) Full central heating Open parking available Covered parking available

MONTS-SUR-GUESNES Vienne

Domaine de Bourg-Ville (Prop: Pierre Claude Fouquenet)
86420
☎ 549228158 FAX 549228989
This traditional building, with visible original beams, guarantees a peaceful night's sleep. Dinner is taken on the patio, or, if the weather is bad, indoors, by candlelight. Communal living room with television. Some reductions are available. English spoken.
Near lake Forest area
5 en suite (shr) (2 fmly) No smoking in 2 bedrooms Full central heating Open parking available Supervised Child discount available 12yrs V meals Last d 16.00hrs Languages spoken: English
MEALS: Dinner 110FF*
CARDS: Travellers cheques

MORTHEMER Vienne

Bed & Breakfast (Prop: Mme Dupond)
Bourpeuil *86300*
☎ 549564882 FAX 549564882
Near river Near lake Near beach Forest area
4 en suite (bth/shr) (2 fmly) TV available Full central heating Open parking available Languages spoken: English & German

NEUVILLE-DE-POITOU Vienne

La Galerne (Prop: Claude Morin)
Chemin de Couture *86170*
☎ 549511407 FAX 549544782
Five rooms available in this modern house just outside of Neuville, where total peace and quiet is assured. A swimming pool and pond are in the garden. Good restaurants at reasonable prices close by. Some English spoken.
Near lake Forest area
Closed 16 Nov-14 Mar
5 en suite (shr) (4 fmly) No smoking on premises TV available Full central heating Open parking available Outdoor swimming pool Languages spoken: English
CARDS: Travellers cheques

NUEIL-SUR-ARGENT Deux-Sèvres

Ferme Auberge de Regueil (Prop: Serge Ganne)
79250
☎ 549654256 FAX 549656987
Rooms are available on the first floor of this family home
overlooking woodland. Evening meal available by prior
arrangement. Reductions for children of under ten years.
Visits to see the farm animals are possible for the children.
Fishing on-site.
Near river Near beach Forest area
2 en suite (shr) No smoking on premises Full central heating
Open parking available Child discount available 10yrs
Fishing V meals Last d 17.00hrs
MEALS: Lunch 70-150FF Dinner 70-150FF*
CARDS: ● ▦

POITIERS Vienne

Château de Vaumoret (Prop: Mme Odile Vaucamp)
rue du Breuil Mingot *86000*
☎ 549613211 FAX 549010454
(access by N10 or A10, take eastern ring road round Poitiers
and take exit to Montamise on the D3, then D18 on the right,
Vaumoret is in 2km)
Mme. Odile Vaucamp welcomes you to her seventeenth
century château, surrounded by a fifteen hectare park.
Futuroscope is ten kilometres away. Tennis, horse-riding, ice-
skating and swimming pools all within thirteen kilometres.
English spoken.
Forest area
15 Feb-1 Nov, and school hols.
3 en suite (bth) (1 fmly) TV in 1 bedroom Full central heating
Open parking available Covered parking available
Supervised Bicycle rental Tennis and stables are nearby.
Languages spoken: English
ROOMS: s 300-350FF; d 350-400FF Reductions over 1 night
CARDS: Travellers cheques

POUANT Vienne

Le Bois Goulu (Prop: Jean and Marie Picard)
86220
☎ 549225205
An avenue of lime trees leads to the house, which is covered
in Virginia creeper. Large garden where guests may relax
under the huge trees. Children under three stay free and there
are reductions for children up to twelve years old. English
spoken.
3 rms (2 shr) Full central heating Open parking available
Covered parking available Child discount available 12yrs
Languages spoken: English
CARDS: Travellers cheques

POUILLAC Charente-Maritime

La Thébaide (Prop: Denise and Pierre Billat)
17210
☎ 564046517 FAX 546048538
Denise and Pierre Billat offer peace, calm and comfort at their
home. The bedrooms are separate from the main house and
look out over a shaded park. Living room, library and open
fire. Close to Montendre, where there is a lake. Water sports,
fishing and pine-forests close by. A little English spoken.
Near lake Forest area Near motorway
Closed Oct

4 rms (2 shr) No smoking on premises Full central heating
Open parking available Child discount available 7yrs Last d
18.00hrs
MEALS: Dinner fr 100FF*
CARDS: Travellers cheques

PRESSAC Vienne

L'Epine (Prop: Mme Mary Bradshaw)
86460
☎ 549849777 FAX 549849777
(N147 to Fleuri, turn right onto D2 to Gençay. At Gençay onto
D741 signposted Confolens, continue on D741 through St-
Martin-L'Ars. L'Epine is just N of the village on left)
A spacious farmhouse, with well equipped bedrooms and
large gardens at the side and rear of the house. A swimming
pool is being installed for 1998.
Near river Near lake Near motorway
3 en suite (shr) (1 fmly) Open parking available Covered
parking available Child discount available Outdoor
swimming pool Tennis Riding Boule Mini-golf V meals
Languages spoken: English
ROOMS: s 150FF; d 250FF Reductions over 1 night
MEALS: Dinner fr 80FF

PRINCAY Vienne

Château de la Roche du Maine (Prop: M & Mme Neveu)
86420
☎ 549228409 FAX 548228957
(from Paris A10 towards Bordeaux, exit no 25, Ste Maure de
Touraine/Richelieu (D760 then D58) after Richelieu toward
Chatellerault (D749) in 2km turn right D22 towards Monts-sur-
Guesnes, then D46 signposted)

Built between 1520 and 1530 Chateau de la Roche du Maine
has not altered, an authentic Renaissance building registered
as a historical monument. It offers magnificent views over the
gardens and park. The rooms are furnished with antiques and
breakfast, and optional dinner, are served in the vaulted
'Guards Room' with the owners.
Forest area Near motorway
Closed 2 Nov-Mar
6 en suite (bth/shr) Full central heating Open parking
available Covered parking available Indoor swimming pool
(heated) Last d noon Languages spoken: English
ROOMS: d 480-990FF Reductions over 1 night
MEALS: Dinner 280FF
CARDS: ● ▦ ▥ Travellers cheques

ROCHEFOUCAULD, LA Charente

Château de La Rochefoucauld (Prop: de la Rochefoucauld)
16110
☎ 545620742 FAX 545635494
(in centre of La Rochefoucauld)
Near river Forest area In town centre
RS winter
2 en suite (shr) Open parking available Covered parking available Languages spoken: English, Italian & Spanish
ROOMS: d 1000FF

ROCHELLE, LA Charente-Maritime

Bed & Breakfast (Prop: Mme Iribe)
33 rue Thiers *17000*
☎ 546416223 FAX 546411076
(follow signs 'centre ville' to main square, keep to left of traffic lights in front of cathedral, directly across first on left and straight past the market to house)
Situated in a busy city/port, this 18th century town house is like an 'oasis of calm'. Beautifully furnished, the salon and library are open to guests, as is the little garden.
Near sea Near beach Forest area In town centre Near motorway
Closed February
6 en suite (bth/shr) (2 fmly) (2 with balcony) TV in 1 bedroom Full central heating Open parking available Supervised Child discount available 12yrs V meals Last d 21.00hrs Languages spoken: English & Spanish
ROOMS: s fr 480FF; d 480FF
MEALS: Dinner 180FF
CARDS: Travellers cheques

ROCHES-PRÉMARIE, LES Vienne

Château de Prémarie (Prop: de Boysson)
86340
☎ 549425001 FAX 549420763
Castle built in the 14th century, situated in a wooded park of 18 hectares, just 11 kilometres south of Poitiers. Before entering the castle's large square courtyard, you will pass through an impressive archway flanked by towers with battlements. Five guest rooms are available. English spoken.
Forest area Near motorway
Closed 12 Nov-Etr
5 en suite (bth/shr) TV available Full central heating Open parking available Child discount available 12yrs Outdoor swimming pool (heated) Tennis Open terrace
ROOMS: d 400-450FF
CARDS: Travellers cheques

ROIFFÉ Vienne

Château de la Roche Marteau (Prop: Mme Jacqueline Moreau)
86120
☎ 549987754 FAX 549989830
(entrance of park is on D147, 4km S of Fontevraud Abbey, towards Loudun)
An eleventh century medieval castle, with drawbridge, set in parkland. A warm welcome awaits you, with spacious, comfortable rooms, furnished with antiques. Hearty breakfasts are served in the lounges, or on the sheltered terraces, with panoramic views. Open all year. English spoken.
Near lake Forest area Near motorway

5 en suite (bth/shr) (3 fmly) Open parking available Supervised Languages spoken: English, German, Italian & Spanish
CARDS: Travellers cheques

RONCE-LES-BAINS Charente-Maritime

Le Maumusson (Prop: Bernard Médat)
22 av St Martin, rte des Plages *17390*
☎ 546363690 FAX 546365691
(A10 exit 35)
Near sea Near beach Forest area In town centre
Closed mid Sep-mid Apr
24 en suite (bth/shr) (4 fmly) Open parking available Child discount available 10yrs Boule Languages spoken: English & Spanish
ROOMS: (room only) d 260-300FF
MEALS: Full breakfast 36FF*
CARDS: ●● ▦ Travellers cheques

ROULLET-ST-ESTEPHE Charente

Logis de Romainville (Prop: Francine Quillett)
Romainville *16440*
☎ 545663256 FAX 545664689
(from Angoulême take N10 direction Bordeaux in 12km enter village Roullet take D42 towards Mouthiers in 2km turn right for Romainville)
The rooms on offer in this Charentais-style house are comfortable and quiet. A large living room and dining room open onto the flowery terrace. Swimming pool and summer house, plus barbecue for guests' use. Near to Angoulême, where jazz festivals and a rich history provide much to explore for visitors. English spoken.
Near river Forest area Near motorway
5 rms (1 bth 3 shr) (1 fmly) No smoking in all bedrooms Full central heating Open parking available Child discount available 6yrs Outdoor swimming pool Bicycle rental Open terrace Last d 20.00hrs Languages spoken: English & Italian
ROOMS: s 250FF; d 300FF
MEALS: Dinner 100FF

ST-ADJUTORY Charente

La Grénouille (Prop: M & Mme Casper)
16310
☎ 545620034 FAX 545630641
Two cottages, plus rooms available, in an area bordering the Dordogne. La Grenouille is an old restored farmhouse, which specialises in breeding Anglo-Arabian horses. The property is situated on the brow of a hill bordering a forest. Both cottages have a private garden and fully equipped kitchens. All guests have use of the private swimming pool, bikes, boules, badminton, swings and hammock. English spoken.
Near river Forest area Near motorway
2 en suite (shr) Some rooms in annexe TV in 1 bedroom Full central heating Open parking available Covered parking available Supervised Child discount available Outdoor swimming pool Fishing Boule Bicycle rental Open terrace Badminton Languages spoken: English, German & Italian
ROOMS: s 200FF; d 300FF Reductions over 1 night

Taking your mobile phone to France?
See page 11

ST-CYR-LA-LANDE Deux-Sèvres

La Marotte
7 r du Muguet *79100*
☎ 549677377
Near river Near lake Forest area
Closed 16 Sep-14 Jun
2 en suite (bth/shr) (1 fmly) No smoking on premises Full
central heating Open parking available Child discount
available 12yrs Table tennis Languages spoken: English
MEALS: Dinner 80-150FF*
CARDS: Travellers cheques

ST-GEORGES-DES-COTEAUX Charente-Maritime

Bed & Breakfast (Prop: M & Mme Trouve)
5 rue de l'Église *17810*
☎ 546909666 FAX 546929666
(A10 exit Saintes village of Saintonge Romane in 7km on D137)
Forest area Near motorway
Closed 11 Nov-Mar
4 en suite (shr) No smoking on premises Full central heating
Open parking available Child discount available Table tennis
Languages spoken: English
ROOMS: s 200FF; d 260FF

ST-JEAN-D'ANGELY Charente-Maritime

Domaine de Rennebourg (Prop: M & F Frappier)
St Denis-du-Pin *17400*
☎ 546321607 FAX 546597738
Built in the seventeenth century, this property is situated on
the edge of the Forest of Essouverts in one hectare of land.
Richly furnished, with a rustic flavour. Swimming pool. Dinner
is available. English spoken.
Forest area
7 rms (5 bth/shr) (1 fmly) TV in 1 bedroom Full central
heating Open parking available Child discount available
10yrs Outdoor swimming pool Boule Bicycle rental Covered
terrace Stables nearby, V meals Languages spoken: English
ROOMS: (room only) s fr 170FF; d 350FF Reductions over 1
night
MEALS: Continental breakfast 30FF Dinner fr 110FF&alc
CARDS: Travellers cheques

ST-JEAN-DE-LIVERSAY Charente-Maritime

Bed & Breakfast (Prop: Ronald & Hazel West)
18 rue du Courseau, Luche *17170*
☎ 546018657
(Take the N11 from La Rochelle in the direction of Niort, after
20km turn onto D109 towards St Jean de Liversay. After 4km
is the village of Luche. Turn left into rue de Courseau,
signposted "Santenay". The Chambre d'hôte is 200 metres on
left)
Comfortable bedrooms on the ground floor of a renovated
Charentaise house, with exposed stone walls. Home-cooked
meals are made from home-grown produce and served in the
garden.
4 en suite (shr) (1 fmly) No smoking on premises Full central
heating Open parking available Child discount available
12yrs Croquet snooker Languages spoken: English
ROOMS: s 180FF; d 220FF
MEALS: Dinner 70FF
CARDS: Travellers cheques

ST-LOUP-LAMAIRÉ Deux-Sèvres

Château de St-Loup (Prop: De Bartillat)
79600
☎ 549648173 549648276 FAX 549648206
Set in superb gardens, this impressive château, built in the
reign of Henry IV, offers four rooms, three with canopied
beds. The château features an exceptional orangery and is full
of historical interest. The gardens and house are open to the
public. Meals are available in the dining room, which dates
back to the seventeenth century, or in the large kitchen.
Near river Near lake Forest area In town centre
5 en suite (bth/shr) Full central heating Open parking
available

ST-SAVINIEN Charente-Maritime

Le Moulin de la Quine (Prop: J Elmes)
17350
☎ 546901931 FAX 546901931
(exit 24 from A10, go into St Jean d'Angely, turn right onto
D18 to St Savinien. At traffic lights, turn right along river,
under rail bridge, left onto D124 towards Bords. After 2km at
Le Pontdreau follow Chambre d'Hôte signs)
Old farm with mill in a quiet and relaxing environment, three
kilometres from the picturesque town of St. Savinine-sur-
Charente. The guest room, with its private entrance, looks out
onto a superb garden. Furnished and decorated in an English
style, the house is attractive inside and out. A warm welcome
awaits you in this peaceful setting. Dinner available at a fixed
price. English spoken.
Near river
2 en suite (bth/shr) (1 fmly) No smoking in all bedrooms Full
central heating Open parking available Supervised Croquet
lawn Last d ngement Languages spoken: English
ROOMS: s 180FF; d 260FF
MEALS: Dinner fr 85FF

ST-SIMON-DE-PELLOUAILLE Charente-Maritime

Château de La Tillade (Prop: M De Salvert)
17260
☎ 546900020 FAX 549600223
Situated in Cognac country, this white stone château is
reached through a line of lime trees, beside vineyards. Guests
take breakfast in the dining room and are welcome to join
their hosts, the Vicomte and Vicomtesse Michel de Salvert, for
dinner, by reservation. You will have use of a Louis XVI
lounge, with comfortable chairs and television. On-site you
will find horses and bikes. Ideal location for artists - courses
available. The château is close to a swimming pool, golf course
and beaches. English spoken.
Forest area Near motorway
3 en suite (bth/shr) Full central heating Open parking
available Child discount available Languages spoken: English
CARDS: ●● ▆ Travellers cheques

ST-SORNIN Charente-Maritime

La Caussoliere (Prop: A M Pinel-Peschardiere)
10 rue du Petit Moulin *17600*
☎ 546854462 FAX 546854462
(take Paris-Bordeaux autoroute exit Saintes & continue in the
direction of Marennes-Oleron cross Cadeuil & St Nadeau &
continue until St Sornin)
A superbly renovated house of character, situated in a small,
pretty village close to Marennes. Large swimming pool,

tennis, table-tennis and bicycles. A living room is reserved for the use of guests with television and library. Meals are available by reservation. English spoken.
Near river Near lake Forest area
3 en suite (bth/shr) No smoking on premises Full central heating Open parking available Supervised Outdoor swimming pool Tennis Boule Bicycle rental Table tennis Languages spoken: English, Moroccan & Spanish
ROOMS: s 280FF; d 350FF
MEALS: Lunch 80FF Dinner 120FF&alc
CARDS: Travellers cheques

ST-VARENT Deux-Sèvres

Le Château de Biard (Prop: Gilles Texier)
79330
☎ 549676240
An old farmhouse with a large courtyard is on offer at the Château de Biard. A living room is situated in the tower, plus an old kitchen with fridge and freezer for guests' use. Evening meals may be taken with your hosts.
Forest area Near motorway
3 en suite (shr) (1 fmly) No smoking on premises Full central heating Open parking available V meals Last d 15.00hrs
ROOMS: s 160FF; d 200FF
MEALS: Dinner fr 70FF

STE-SOULLÉ Charente-Maritime

Bed & Breakfast (Prop: M & Mme Gilbert)
3 bis rue de Nantes, Usseau *17220*
☎ 546375032 FAX 546375032
Rooms in a renovated grange, set near the main house. View from the rooms over a shaded park. Large swimming pool, tennis court, table-tennis and games for children on-site. Living room with television reserved for guests. Comfortable rooms, pleasant surroundings. Beach, fifteen kilometres. English spoken.
Near river Near sea Near beach Forest area Near motorway
11 rms (3 shr) (1 fmly) No smoking on premises Full central heating Open parking available Child discount available Outdoor swimming pool Tennis Riding Bicycle rental Table tennis Languages spoken: English
ROOMS: s 250FF; d 280FF
CARDS: Travellers cheques

SAULGÉ Vienne

Les Gats (Prop: Philippe Dudoit)
86500
☎ 549910610 FAX 549910610·
This farm property, set around a courtyard, is situated in the

Gartempe Valley, by the river, backing onto the village of Saulgé. Gite accommodation is also available within the complex. A family atmosphere awaits you, with table-tennis and boats on site and mini-golf and tennis nearby. There is a restaurant in the centre of the village. English spoken.
Near river Forest area
2 en suite (shr) Full central heating Open parking available Covered parking available Languages spoken: English & Spanish

SAVIGNÉ Vienne

Chez Benest (Prop: M & Mme Reid)
86400
☎ 549873985 FAX 549879246
Set just outside the lovely twelfth century market town of Civray, this renovated farmhouse stands in ten acres of paddocks and woods. All bedrooms have superb views over the countryside. Only the owls and toads disturb the peaceful evenings. The rooms are decorated in a mixture of rustic and antique style. Communal lounge with separate dining room, both with open fires and exposed beams. Dinners, by arrangement. English spoken. No children under ten years.
Near river Forest area Near motorway
3 en suite (bth/shr) No smoking on premises Open parking available No children 10yrs V meals Last d 20.00hrs
Languages spoken: English
MEALS: Dinner 95FF*

SECONDIGNY Deux-Sèvres

Bed & Breakfast (Prop: M Julliot)
16 rue de la Vendée *79130*
☎ 549637034
The town is surrounded by apple orchards, and in the centre you will find a swimming pool, fishing, forest, bikes, walks and a twelfth century church. Comfortable and attractive rooms are available on the second floor of this large country house. Restaurants close by.
Near river Near lake Forest area In town centre Near motorway
3 rms (1 shr) Full central heating Open parking available Supervised

SEGONZAC Charente

Chez Bilhouet (Prop: M & Mme Marcadier)
16130
☎ 545834350 FAX 545834321
The Marcadier family warmly welcome you to their home, set among the vineyards of Grande Champagne, 9 km from Cognac. Swimming pool and barbecue in the garden. Use of kitchen, games room and living room. Why not visit the distillery on site and learn about the production of cognac before trying the results?
Forest area
5 rms (2 bth 1 shr) (2 fmly) No smoking on premises Full central heating Open parking available Outdoor swimming pool

SEPVRET Deux-Sèvres

Bed & Breakfast (Prop: Mme Jézequel)
79120
☎ 549073373
Farm lodgings available, offering rooms furnished in typical
cont'd

rustic style, with living room and dining room available to guests. All are situated on the first floor, looking out onto a large garden. Meals available by reservation, farm produce used. English spoken.
Near river Forest area
6 en suite (bth/shr) (1 fmly) Full central heating Open parking available Supervised Child discount available
CARDS: ▄▄ Travellers cheques

SOUBRAN Charente-Maritime

Les Simons (Prop: E & B Louis-Joseph)
☎ 46497677 FAX 46492579
(exit Miⅼambeau from A10 & take D730 in direction of Montenohe until Soubran, on entering Bourg continue to La Poste then left in direction of Allas-Bocage)
Rooms available on a working farm. Courtyard and small enclosed garden with terrace, garden furniture and barbecue. Living room with library and kitchen available for the use of guests. Located close to Marambeau and the Gironde. Fifteen kilometres from Montendre, with its lake for fishing and bathing. Restaurant within one kilometre.
Forest area
3 rms Radio in rooms Full central heating Open parking available

SOYAUX Charente

Domaine de Montboulard (Prop: M Madigout-Blanchon)
16800
☎ 545920735
Rooms available on this fifteenth century farm which has been entirely restored. All rooms are non-smoking. Situated in the middle of a wooded park, with private swimming pool. Five rural gites also available within the complex. English spoken.
Forest area
5 en suite (shr) (1 fmly) No smoking in all bedrooms Open parking available Outdoor swimming pool Languages spoken: English

SUAUX Charente

Brassac (Prop: Paule Sauzet)
16260
☎ 545711261
Comfortable 18th century residence with library and television available to guests. Living room and kitchen for guests use. Swimming pool, fishing, golf and restaurants all within close proximity. Vintage car collectors particularly welcome. A welcoming drink is given to all guests.
Near river Forest area Near motorway
Closed mid Sep-mid Jun
2 en suite (bth/shr) (1 fmly) Radio in rooms Full central heating Open parking available Supervised Child discount available
CARDS: Travellers cheques

TERNAY Vienne

Château de Ternay (Prop: Marquis de Ternay)
86120
☎ 549009282 FAX 549229754
Magnificent château set in parkland surrounded by trees, with a beautiful fifteenth century Gothic chapel close by. A dry moat surrounds the château. Guests rooms available, each with canopied double beds and antique furniture. Group

bookings taken to taste the wines and goat cheeses available in the cellars of the château.
Forest area
Closed Nov-Apr
3 en suite (bth/shr) Full central heating Open parking available Covered parking available Outdoor swimming pool Languages spoken: English
ROOMS: d 500-600FF
MEALS: Dinner fr 250FF
CARDS: Travellers cheques

THOUARS Deux-Sèvres

Bed & Breakfast (Prop: Michel & Annette Holstein)
3 ave Victor-Leclerc *79100*
☎ 549961170
Annette and Michel Holstein welcome you to their home and look forward to helping you discover the region. Dining room and living room, with television, available for the use of guests. Close to the châteaux of the Loire. Fishing and other sporting activities available close by. English spoken.
Near river Forest area In town centre Near motorway
2 en suite (shr) (1 fmly) (1 with balcony) No smoking on premises Full central heating Open parking available Bicycle rental Sports centre nearby Languages spoken: English & German
ROOMS: s fr 170FF; d 220-410FF

TRIMOUILLE, LA Vienne

Bed & Breakfast (Prop: M & Mme Vouhé)
Toel *86290*
☎ 549916759 FAX 549915566
Near river Forest area
Closed end Sep & early Jan
6 en suite (bth/shr) (1 fmly) No smoking on premises Full central heating Open parking available Supervised Child discount available
MEALS: Lunch 80FF*
CARDS: Travellers cheques

TRIZAY Charente-Maritime

Bed & Breakfast (Prop: Roland Lopez)
Le Chize *17250*
☎ 546820956 FAX 546821667
Rooms available at this old farm which has recently been renovated. Fixed price or à la carte menu available. Tranquil, country environment. Stables on-site. Swimming, tennis and fishing within close proximity.
Near lake Near sea Near beach Forest area
1 Apr-30 Sept
5 en suite (bth/shr) (2 fmly) No smoking on premises Full central heating Open parking available Supervised Boule Bicycle rental Languages spoken: English
ROOMS: s 260FF; d 280FF
MEALS: Dinner 90FF

VALLANS Deux-Sèvres

Le Logis d'Antan (Prop: M Francis Guillot)
79270
☎ 549049150 FAX 549048675
(from A10 exit 33, follow signs to La Rochelle Mauze, after 4km turn left to Vallans)
A warm welcome awaits you at this renovated property. Spacious, well-appointed, comfortable rooms with living area

on offer. Very good dinners available, on request. Brochures and information on the region available to help you plan your visits. Barbecue in garden. Bikes available. English spoken. Near river Near lake Forest area Near motorway 6 en suite (bth/shr) (2 fmly) No smoking on premises TV in all bedrooms STV Full central heating Open parking available Covered parking available Supervised Child discount available 10 yrs Open terrace Barbecue V meals Last d 20.00hrs Languages spoken: English
ROOMS: d 300-350FF
MEALS: Dinner fr 119FF
CARDS: Travellers cheques

VERRIÈRES Charente

La Chambre (Prop: Monique & Henri Geffard)
16130
☎ 545830274 FAX 545860182
Monique and Henri Geffard offer you accommodation among the vineyards of their working farm. Fitted kitchen, dining room and lounge available for guests' use. Mountain bikes and children's bikes for hire, table-tennis and table-soccer available. Children up to three years stay free. Distillery visits can be arranged, with tastings of brandy and wine. Restaurants within three kilometres. English spoken.
Near river Near motorway 5 en suite (shr) (1 fmly) No smoking on premises Full central heating Open parking available Child discount available 3yrs Languages spoken: English
ROOMS: s 180FF; d 220FF
CARDS: ●● ▨▨ ▨▨ ▣ Travellers cheques

VICQ-SUR-GARTEMPE Vienne

La Serenne (Prop: Daniel Bellande)
86260
☎ 549863315
Set in open countryside, close to the village of Angles-sur-l'Anglin, rooms are offered in an old renovated grange. One room is accessible to the handicapped. All are non-smoking bedrooms. Breakfast and dinner served by arrangement at the family table. English spoken.
Near river Forest area
Closed 21 Dec-28 Feb 3 en suite (shr) (1 fmly) No smoking on premises Full central heating Open parking available Languages spoken: English & Italian
CARDS: Travellers cheques

VIVONNE Vienne

La Rochette (Prop: Colette Vincent)
86370
☎ 549435017
This farmhouse is set in quiet, isolated countryside. Four rooms are available, including two family rooms. Dinner is served in the large dining room by reservation only. Private swimming pool. English spoken.
Near river Forest area Near motorway 4 rms (3 bth/shr) (2 fmly) Full central heating Open parking available Child discount available Languages spoken: English
MEALS: Dinner fr 70FF*

VOUILLÉ Vienne

Bed & Breakfast (Prop: M & Mme Lecanuet)
3 rue de la Grande Maison *86190*
☎ 549519638 FAX 549544815
Pretty house with garden which opens out onto the Auxance canal. Take a small boat ride and enjoy the tranquillity of the waterways. Three restaurants are within close proximity of the property. English spoken.
Near river Near lake Forest area In town centre Near motorway 4 en suite (shr) (2 fmly) No smoking on premises Full central heating Open parking available River & canoe Languages spoken: English

VOUNEUIL-SUR-VIENNE Vienne

Les Hauts de Chabonne (Prop: M & Mme Antoine Penot)
86210
☎ 549852825 FAX 549855517
Rooms available in a house built at the end of the eighteenth century between a river and the nature reserve of Pinail. Three rooms are on the ground floor, with direct access into the garden; the other two are on the first floor and are ideal for a family. Futuroscope, golf and many other sporting activities are all within close proximity. Bikes and pétanque on-site. A little English spoken.
Near river Near lake Forest area 5 en suite (bth) (1 fmly) No smoking on premises Full central heating Open parking available Covered parking available

YVES Charente-Maritime

La Cabane des Fresnes (Prop: Dominique Nadeau)
Le Marouillet *17340*
☎ 546564131
Small, isolated farm in the middle of the Charentais region. Large lounge, with kitchen area for guests' use. Birdwatchers will enjoy the local nature reserve within three kilometres. Sailing, swimming and cycling within eight kilometres. Camping for 25 on-site. Farm produce available. Some English spoken.
Near sea
6 rms (2 shr) (2 fmly) Full central heating Open parking available Child discount available Languages spoken: English
CARDS: Travellers cheques

Limousin

Many visitors pass through Limousin on their way to the mountains or the coast, yet those who do not stop to explore are missing a region rich in history, architecture, beautiful countryside, and a proud creative and artistic heritage. From the Monédières Mountains and the sound of accordions, to the Plateau de Millevaches and the sound of Limousin cattle; from the peaceful quiet of villages like Mortemart among the Mont de Blond hills, to the bustling markets of the region's capital Limoges, home of some of the world's finest porcelain, Limousin has something to offer to anyone who wishes to glimpse a region rich in both history and culture close to the very heart of France.

(Top): Plates for sale in Limoges, a town which produces some of the world's finest porcelain.

(Bottom): One of the many tapestries produced over the centuries on the looms at Aubusson.

ESSENTIAL FACTS

DÉPARTEMENTS:	Corrèze, Creuse, Haute-Vienne.
PRINCIPAL TOWNS	Limoges, Gueret, Tulle, Aubusson, Ussel, Brive-la-Gaillarde, Rochechouart.
PLACES TO VISIT:	Limoges for porcelain; Aubusson for tapestries; Vassivière for its lake, and Contemporary Art Centre; Brive-la-Gaillarde for its distillery.
REGIONAL TOURIST OFFICE	27, bd de la Corderie, 87031 Limoges. Tel: 55 45 18 80. Fax: 55 45 18 18.
LOCAL GASTRONOMIC DELIGHTS	Côte de boeuf Limousin á la moelle at au vin de Cahors, which uses the deep purple Cahors wine. "Le produits du terroir" such as mushrooms, truffles, cepes, apples, walnuts, chestnuts, and bush fruit such as strawberries, blackberries and raspberries. Red cabbage with chestnuts, creamy potato pie, clafoutis (a form of cherry pie), and a variety of soups.
DRINKS	Fine brandies made of fruits such as cherries, plums and prunes have been produced here for over a century. The area also produces good beers due to the purity of the local water.
LOCAL CRAFTS WHAT TO BUY	Tapestry weaving, porcelain, enamel work. Gentiane (a herbal aperitif), liqueurs, sweetmeats, black pudding with chestnuts, dried mushrooms, madeleines, lace, haute couture fashion, porcelain, pâtè de foie gras.

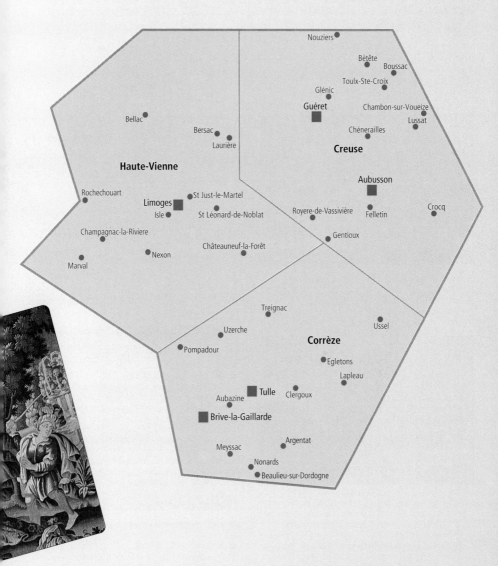

Nouziers

Bétête

Boussac

Toulx-Ste-Croix

Glénic

Chambon-sur-Voueize

Guéret

Lussat

Bellac

Chénerailles

Bersac

Creuse

Laurière

Haute-Vienne

Aubusson

Rochechouart

St Just-le-Martel

Royere-de-Vassivière

Crocq

Limoges

Felletin

Isle

St Léonard-de-Noblat

Champagnac-la-Riviere

Gentioux

Châteauneuf-la-Forêt

Marval

Nexon

Treignac

Ussel

Uzerche

Corrèze

Pompadour

Egletons

Lapleau

Tulle

Aubazine

Clergoux

Brive-la-Gaillarde

Argentat

Meyssac

Nonards

Beaulieu-sur-Dordogne

EVENTS & FESTIVALS:

May Chénerailles Horse Market; Beaulieu-sur Dordogne Stawberry Fair; Aubazine Holy Music & Heritage (concerts, readings, light shows);

Jun Glénic Craft Fair; Tours de Merle Light & Sound Show (Son et Lumière); Bellac Festival;

Jul Chénerailles Nocturnal Fantasy Son et Lumière; La Souterraine Arts Festival; Felletin She-lamb Fair; Egletons Medieval Pageant;

Jul/ Aug Le Dorat Light & Sound Show; Rilhac Images, Torches & Lights; Clergoux Music Festival at Château de Sédières; St-Léonard de Noblat Classical Music Summer Festival; Aubusson Classical Music Festival; Nexon Art running to Circus; St-Robert Summer Classical Music Festival; Chambon sur Voueize Son et Lumière at Robeyrie Lake; Tulle International Lace Festival (inc folk entertainment)

Jul/ Sep Annual Limoges Porcelain Exhibition

Aug Toulx-Ste-Croix Theatre Festival; Pays de Trois Lacs Three Lakes Music Festival; Plateau de Millevaches Summer Music Festival; TreignacTraditional Music Festival; Lapleau Festival de la Luzège (theatre); Felletin International Folklore Festival; Brive-la-

Gaillarde Orchestrades Universelles (40 youth orchestras); Crocq Horse Festival; Collonges la-Rouge Traditional Market; Nouziers Cider Festival; Pompadour National Stud Presentation of Arab Horses;

Sep Tulle "Les Nuits de Nacre" Accordian Festival;

Sep/Oct Limoges International French-language Festival (Theatre, workshops, exhibitions, music); St-Just-le-Martel International Cartoon Show

Oct Gueret Piano Festival; Limoges Butchers Guild Festival; Limoges Traditional & Gastronomic Festivals

Nov Limoges Jazz Festival

Dec Brive-la-Gaillarde Foie Gras Fair

ARGENTAT Corrèze

Au Pont de l'Hospital (Prop: M & Mme Mallows)
BP 38 *19400*
☎ 555289035 FAX 555282070
(from A20 (Vierzon-Toulouse) exit at Uzerche. Argentat-sur-Dordogne is on N120, follow blue sign posts to establishment)

Guest house owned by an English couple, situated on the banks of the Maronne River, 400 metres from the Dordogne River. Mallows is situated in a lovely rural area about 3 kilometres from the picturesque market town of Argentat-sur-Dordogne in the upper Dordogne valley. Enjoy a relaxed atmosphere, with many activities, such as canoeing, riding, trout fishing, golf and cycling plus of course the excellent food and wine of the region.
Near river Near lake Forest area Near motorway
RS Dec-Mar

11 rms (4 bth/shr) (4 fmly) Full central heating Open parking available Child discount available 12yrs Fishing Boule Open terrace Covered terrace Languages spoken: English & Spanish
ROOMS: (room only) s fr 120FF; d 140-180FF Reductions over 1 night

BEAULIEU-SUR-DORDOGNE Corrèze

Château d'Arnac (Prop: Gillian Webb)
Nonards *19120*
☎ 555915413 FAX 555915262
English owned turretted 12th century château, lovingly restored and retaining all its charm and character. Set beside a trout stream and lake and in 20 acres of parkland. In spring and autumn log fires are lit in all the rooms adding to the romantic atmosphere of the château. English spoken.
Near river Near lake Forest area Near motorway
5 en suite (bth/shr) Full central heating Open parking available Child discount available Fishing Boule Open terrace V meals Languages spoken: English
CARDS: ●● ▆▆ Travellers cheques

BERSAC Haute-Vienne

Château de Chambon (Prop: M & Mme Bersac)
87370
☎ 555714704 FAX 555715141
Set among gentle hills, the Château du Chambon welcomes guests to its ancient walls. The living rooms are furnished with antiques and Anbusson tapestries. You are offered home-cooked food made from fresh local produce. Fishing available in local waters. Ideal rambling area. English spoken.

Near river Near lake Near sea Forest area Near motorway
Closed Nov-Mar
4 en suite (bth/shr) (4 fmly) Full central heating Open
parking available Covered parking available Child discount
available Last d 20.00hrs

BÉTÊTE Creuse

Château de Moisse (Prop: M & Mme Deboutte)
23270
☎ 555808425 FAX 555808425
Near river Forest area
Closed Oct-May
4 en suite (bth/shr) (1 fmly) (2 with balcony) No smoking on
premises Open parking available No children 2yrs
Languages spoken: English & Dutch
CARDS: Travellers cheques

BOUSSAC Creuse

Bed & Breakfast (Prop: Françoise & Daniel Gros)
3 rue des Loges *23600*
☎ 555658009
(at junct off D916/D917)
A warm atmosphere awaits you in this 18th-century building
near to the Château de Boussac in the centre of France.
Breakfast can be served on the patio or in the library.
Children's games and table-tennis are available, together with
bikes for the guests. Ideal for ramblers. Five restaurants are all
within easy walking distance.
Near river Forest area
RS Oct & Jan
4 rms (3 bth/shr) (1 fmly) Full central heating Child discount
available 12yrs Open terrace Boules Table tennis

CHAMPAGNAC-LA-RIVIÈRE Haute-Vienne

Château de Brie
87150
☎ 555781752 FAX 555781402
Near lake Forest area
Closed Jan-Mar
4 en suite (bth/shr) Full central heating Open parking
available Child discount available 5yrs Languages spoken:
English

CHÂTEAUNEUF-LA-FORÊT Haute-Vienne

La Croix du Reh (Prop: M & Mme McLaughlin)
87130
☎ 555697537 FAX 555697538
(from Limoges take D979 towards Eymoutiers. At la Croix
Lattee take D15 to Chateauneuf-la-Forêt)
This beautiful seventeenth-century residence,set in a three
acre landscaped park, has been tastefully restored and is now
owned by a Scottish family, from whom a warm welcome and
delicious food are guaranteed. There is a lake with a beach,
fishing and tennis. Mountain bike hire at 500 metres.
Near river Near lake Near beach Forest area Near
motorway
4 en suite (bth/shr) (1 fmly) No smoking on premises Full
central heating Open parking available Child discount
available Boule Basketball Table tennis V meals Languages
spoken: English
ROOMS: s 200-260FF; d 280-350FF Reductions over 1 night
MEALS: Dinner fr 120FF*
CARDS: ⦿ 🏧 Carte Bleu Travellers cheques

GENTIOUX Creuse

La Commanderie (Prop: M Y Gomichon)
Pallier *23340*
☎ 555679173 FAX 555679173
(from Clermont-Ferrand take D941 to Aubusson. Then take
D982 to Felletin, then D992 to Gentioux.From here take D8 to
Pallier)
Built on the foundations of a commander's residence and the
home of royal notaries in the eighteenth century, this
historical building has many fine features that are a tribute to
the craftmanship of famous Gentoise stone cutters. There is a
medieval garden and a trout river. The bedrooms, each with
their own style, have antique furniture. In the village there is a
twelfth-century church.
Near river Forest area
Closed Jan-Mar RS Apr-May & Oct-Dec
4 en suite (bth/shr) No smoking on premises Full central
heating Open parking available Supervised Child discount
available 8yrs Fishing Last d 20.00hrs
ROOMS: s 245FF; d 290FF
MEALS: Dinner fr 95FF

ISLE Haute-Vienne

Bed & Breakfast (Prop: Edith Brunier)
Verthamont, Pic de l'Aiguille *87170*
☎ 555361289
(from Limoges take N21 towards PerigueuxAfter 9kms at 'Bas
Verthamont' follow road sign on right 'Chambres d'Hotes
600m'Take small road on right)
This is a contemporary house which enjoys a magnificent
panoramic view of the Vienne Valley. Your holiday will be
taken in this calm and peaceful area, situated in a wooded
park. Each room has its own terrace and independent
entrance. Close to the centre of Limoges. All meals are
prepared with organic produce. Guests have full use of the
swimming pool. English spoken.
Near river Forest area Near motorway
3 en suite (bth/shr) (1 fmly) (2 with balcony) No smoking on
premises TV in 2 bedrooms Full central heating Open
parking available Supervised Child discount available
Outdoor swimming pool Languages spoken: English &
German
ROOMS: d 220FF Reductions over 1 night
MEALS: Dinner fr 80FF

LAURIÈRE Haute-Vienne

La Bezassade (Prop: M & Mme Chanudet)
87370
☎ 555717807
Near river Near lake Forest area
Closed mid Sep-Jun
2 rms (1 shr) TV available Open parking available Supervised
Child discount available 4yrs Languages spoken: English &
Spanish

LUSSAT Creuse

Puy-Haut (Prop: M & Mme Ribbe)
23170
☎ 555821307
Nadine and Claude Ribbe welcome you to their home, built
between the fourteenth and seventeenth centuries, situated
between Guéret and Montluçon. Pleasant environment, amidst
cont'd

trees and country walks. Three bed & breakfast rooms available, one of which is a family room. Dinner available by prior reservation.
Closed Nov-Mar
3 en suite (bth) Full central heating Open parking available
MEALS: Dinner 95FF*
CARDS: Travellers cheques

MARVAL Haute-Vienne

Le Val du Goth (Prop: Mme Pez)
Le Vansanaud *87440*
☎ 555787665 FAX 555782379
A small Limousin farm surrounded by beautiful scenery. Claudine Pez will help you discover the porcelain of the area. François will be happy to tell you about raising horses. Fishing in the lake, a dive in the family swimming pool or a long walk will help you work off a large breakfast. English spoken.
Near lake
2 en suite (bth/shr) TV available Full central heating Open parking available Child discount available 12yrs Outdoor swimming pool Fishing Table tennis
MEALS: Dinner fr 85FF*
CARDS: Travellers cheques

MEYSSAC Corrèze

Manoir de Bellerade (Prop: Mme Jeanne Foussac-Lassale)
19500
☎ 555254142 FAX 558840751
(on the D38 between Collonges-la-Rouge and Meyssac)
Forest area
Closed Nov-Mar
4 en suite (bth/shr) (3 fmly) No smoking on premises TV available Full central heating Open parking available Covered parking available Supervised Child discount available 6yrs Languages spoken: English
MEALS: Dinner fr 120FF*
CARDS: Travellers cheques

NONARDS Corrèze

Le Marchoux (Prop: M & Mme Greenwood)
19120
☎ 555915273
(from Beaulieu-sur-Dordogne take D940 towards Tulle. After 5km turn left at garage Le Marchoux is 400m on the right)
The Greenwoods, your hosts, can provide two bedrooms in their lovingly restored 150 year old farmhouse, which nestles in the foothills of the Massif Central. Continental breakfast is served, usually at 8.30, but this is moveable. Dinner is available on request, to a previously agreed menu. Wine and coffee is included in the price. Meals are served in the family living/dining room.
Forest area
2 rms No smoking in all bedrooms Full central heating Open parking available Languages spoken: English
ROOMS: s 130FF; d 180FF
MEALS: Dinner 80FF

ROYÈRE-DE-VASSIVIÈRE Creuse

La Borderie (Prop: M Marc Deschamps)
St-Pierre Bellevue *23460*
☎ 555649651
Set in the heart of the forest, in a wild and unspoilt part of France, this old stone building offers accommodation for up to fifteen people. Evening meals available at a fixed price. Swings and barbecue available in the garden. English spoken.
Near river Forest area
6 rms (3 shr) (2 fmly) Full central heating Open parking available Child discount available 7yrs V meals Last d 20.00hrs Languages spoken: English
MEALS: Dinner fr 80FFalc*
CARDS: Travellers cheques

Taking your mobile phone to France? See page 11

HISTORY & CRAFTS IN LIMOUSIN

The First Home of the Franks

This region has long had significance in European history, and on almost every hillside medieval castles and villages can still be seen. The Romans felt Limoges to be so important that they granted the city its own senate and currency, as well as the first bridge in the area. This was also the region first settled by the Franks (after whom France is named) and has been the scene of a number of military engagements. Most notable of these was the siege of the Château Chabrol in Chalus, during which England's Richard the Lionheart was killed in 1199. Limousin escaped English rule during the 100 Years War, but since the rule of Charles VII began in 1429 the area has declined in historical importance, today being more valued for its agriculture, arts and crafts.

One of many tapestries produced by the looms of Aubusson, this depiction of a pastoral idyll is typical of Pre-Revolutionary art.

Arts and Crafts

On the north-western edge of the Massif Central are two towns which are famous for their creative output. Aubusson for its tapestries, and Limoges for its porcelain. The purest deposit of the raw material needed for this beautiful material - kaolin - was first discovered in Limousin in the mid-18th century and led to the creation of a worldwide trade in cups, vases, plates and other items. The ceramic and glass collections at the Musèe National Adrien Dubouchè are not to be missed.

Aubusson, huddled under the cliffs of the Creuse Valley, began tapestry production over five centuries ago with representations of rural scenes and fabulous animals, but now produces more modernistic work on low-warp looms in some fifteen workshops in the town, which not only weave the tapestries but also make the dyes they use to create such vibrant colours. The largest tapestry in the world - a 264 metre square picture of Christ which hangs in Coventry Cathedral - was woven in the nearby village of Felletin.

Auvergne

Auvergne's volcanic terrain offers some of the most wild and breath-taking scenery in France, which is best experienced in its two regional parks. Here, signposted walks designed for the whole family present excellent vantage points from which to view the winding rivers, cascading waterfalls and mountainous slopes. The spectacular gorges of the Haut-Allier are rich in wildlife, including peregrine falcons, red kites, owls and otters. There are water sports, hill walking and hang-gliding activities to challenge the robust and energetic, while the region's castles, Romanesque churches, village inns and spa towns, will inform and refresh those who prefer a gentler pace.

(top): The entombment of Christ is depicted in this late 15th-century tableau at a church in Salers.

(Bottom): The 11th-century chapel of St-Michel d'Aiguilhe tops an enormous dome of volcanic basalt at Le-Puy-en-Velay.

ESSENTIAL FACTS

DÉPARTEMENTS:	Allier, Cantal, Haute-Loire, Puy-de-Dôme
PRINCIPAL TOWNS	Moulins, Clermont-Ferrand, Aurillac, Vichy, Le Puy-en-Velay, Thiers, Montluçon, Issoire, Riom
PLACES TO VISIT:	Parc Régional des Volcans d'Auvergne with its array of old volcanic cones; Le Puy-en-Velay for its outstanding religious art and architecture; Tronçais Forest rich in wildlife, especially deer; the valley of the Dordogne
REGIONAL TOURIST OFFICE	43 av Julien, BP 395, 63011 Clermont-Ferand Tel: 04 73 29 49 49
LOCAL GASTRONOMIC DELIGHTS	Bleu d'Auvergne cheese and others — Auvergne has been called the cheeseboard of France; potée auvergnate, a stew of salt pork and vegetables, coq au vin; cassoulet; vichyssoise, cold leek and potato soup; cousinat, a stew of chestnuts, cream and fruit
DRINKS	Mineral water from the Vichy springs
LOCAL CRAFTS WHAT TO BUY	Honey, jams, cheese, liqueurs, Côtes d'Auvergne wines and many other regional specialities are available at the Village Auvergnat Centre

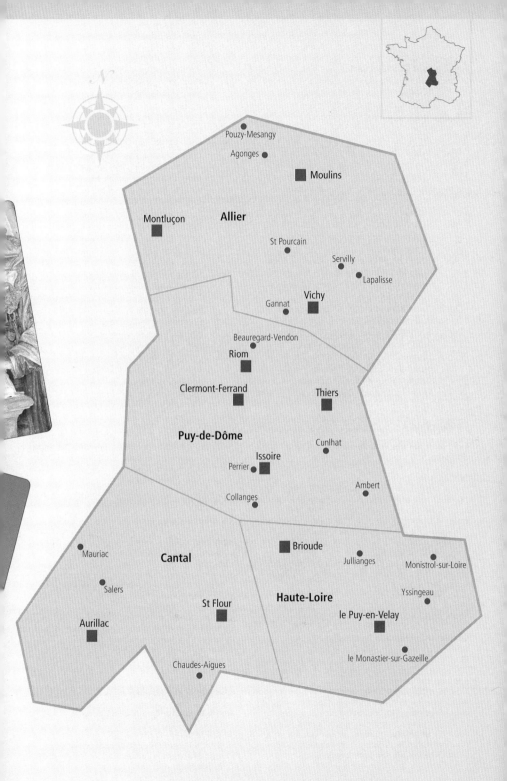

Pouzy-Mesangy

Agonges

Moulins

Montluçon

Allier

St Pourcain

Servilly

Lapalisse

Gannat

Vichy

Beauregard-Vendon

Riom

Clermont-Ferrand

Thiers

Puy-de-Dôme

Cunlhat

Perrier

Issoire

Ambert

Collanges

Mauriac

Cantal

Brioude

Jullianges

Monistrol-sur-Loire

Salers

Haute-Loire

Yssingeau

St Flour

le Puy-en-Velay

Aurillac

le Monastier-sur-Gazeille

Chaudes-Aigues

EVENTS & FESTIVALS

Jan Clermont-Ferrand International Short Film Festival; St-Bonnet-Le-Froid Monte Carlo Rally

Feb Superbesse motor racing on ice; Le Mont Dore Winter Jazz Festival; Aurillac, Palha Carnival;

Mar Massif Central Chamineige; Montluçon Carnival; Le Puy-En-Velay Street Music Carnival;

Apr Clermont-Ferrand International Video Meeting; Vichy Opera; Yzeure Dare to Dance Festival;

May Yzeure Children's Song Festival; Allanche Pasture Festival; Monistrol-Sur-Loire Springtime Reading;

Jun Riom International Piano Festival; St-Flour Medieval Festival; Chambon-Sur-Lac Hot Air Balloon Rally; Viellevie Cherry Festival; St-Flour Medieval Festival

Jul Ambert World Folk Festival; Yssingeaux Laughter Festival; Riom-ès-Montagnes International Festival of Civilian & Military Music, & Gentian Festival; Lapalisse Laser Nights; Salers Renaissance Festival; Souvigny Medieval Fair and Troubadours' Festival; Charbonnier-le-Mines, Val d'Allier Folk Festival; Le Puy-en-Velay Folk Festival; Issoire

Folklore Festival; Aurillac Horse Festival "Les Crins d'Or"; Hérisson Theatre Festival; Marcoles - strolling players perform in the streets;

Jul/ Aug Hérisson, Bourbonnais Music Festival (*medieval & chamber music*);

Aug Le Monastier-Sur-Gazeille Brass Music Festival; Champs-Sur-Tarentaine Rock Music Festival; Cunlat Harley Davidson Bike Rally; Le Monastier-sur-Gazeille Brass Music Festival, Murat Dance & Music Festival; Vic-sur-Cère, Carladez Festival (music & folklore); Saint-Germain l'Herm Arts Festival, Pierrefort Festival of Traditions; La Chaise-Dieu Classical Music Festival; Le Puy-en-Velay Marian Feast Day; Braize Donkey Fair; Chalvignac Cheese Fair; St-Pourçain-sur-Sioule Wine Festival

Sep Le Puy-En-Velay Renaissance Festival; Département Du Puy-De-Dôme Concerts & Theatre Festival; St-Martin Valmeroux Cheese Festival; St-Front Festival of The Wind

Oct Chaudes-Aigues Mountain & Adventure Festival; Mourjou Chestnut Fair; Clermont Ferrand Jazz Festival

Nov Le Puy-En-Velay Hot Air Balloon Rally; Monistrol-Sur-Loire Food and Wine Festival; Aurillac Story-telling Festival;

Dec Jaligny Turkey Fair

AGONGES Allier

Les Locateries des Fourches (Prop: M & Mme Schwartz)
03210
☎ 470439363
Chantal and Philippe Schwartz welcome you to their eighteenth century home. Situated in a medieval village which boasts many châteaux , this property is very close to the medieval Bourbon city of Souvigny. The spa town of Bourbon l'Archambauet is just five minutes away. The famous arboretum of Balaume is also within five minutes.
Near river Forest area Near motorway
7 en suite (bth/shr) Full central heating Open parking available Child discount available Open terrace V meals
Languages spoken: German
CARDS: ●● ▒▒ Travellers cheques

BEAUREGARD-VENDON Puy-de-Dôme

Chaptes (Prop: Elizabeth Beaujeard)
63460
☎ 473633562
(by motorway A71, exit Riom then take N144 in direction of Combronde/Montlucon after 10kms turn right onto D122)
Mme Elisabeth Beaujeard looks forward to welcoming guests to this family home dating from the eighteenth century. The fireplace and stone staircase lend charm to the property. Meals will only be served in the designated areas. Plenty to visit in the area: Roman churches, châteaux, ancient volcanoes. A must for ramblers. Facilities nearby include tennis, swimming and golf. English spoken.

Forest area Near motorway
RS Nov-Mar
3 en suite (bth/shr) No smoking on premises Full central heating Open parking available Child discount available
Languages spoken: English
ROOMS: s 250-270FF; d 300-350FF

COLLANGES Puy-de-Dôme

Château de Collanges (Prop: M & Mme Huillet)
63340
☎ 473964730 FAX 4739658721
(take exit 17 from A75 to St Germain-Lembron and proceed to Collanges)
A fifteenth century château in a wooded park. Evening meals by reservation. Games area, French billiards and boules on site. English spoken.
Forest area Near motorway
6 en suite (bth/shr) (1 fmly) Full central heating Open parking available Child discount available 3yrs Boule French billiards Last d 20.30hrs Languages spoken: English
ROOMS: s 300-400FF; d 350-500FF *
MEALS: Dinner fr 200FF
CARDS: Travellers cheques

CUNLHAT Puy-de-Dôme

Bed & Breakfast (Prop: Mme B Laroye)
rue du 8 Mai *63590*
☎ 473722087
(A72 exit at Thiers & take D906 towards Ambert. After Courpiere turn right to Cunlhat, D225. At church establisment is signposted)

Nineteenth century family house with large garden, situated in wooded parkland. Four rooms available, individually furnished with antiques. Dining room has a fireplace which is often lit. Regional cuisine, much appreciated by guests. Library dedicated to the Auverge region. English spoken.
Near lake Near beach Forest area
9 en suite (bth/shr) (2 with balcony) TV available Full central heating Open parking available Supervised Child discount available 3yrs Boule Languages spoken: English
ROOMS: s 210-250FF; d 260-330FF Reductions over 1 night
CARDS: Travellers cheques

JULLIANGES Haute-Loire

Domaine de la Valette (Prop: Michele & Louis Mejean)
43500
☎ 471032335
An ancient granite manor house, at the crossroads of the forests of Auvergne and Velay. A small park, rich with flowers, circles the house. A kitchen is available for guests' or a local grocer is happy to deliver meals. Reductions offered for children under five. Games in the park for children. Table-tennis and croquet available. English spoken.
Near river Near lake Forest area Near motorway
5 en suite (bth/shr) (2 fmly) (1 with balcony) No smoking on premises TV in 4 bedrooms Radio in rooms Full central heating Air conditioning in bedrooms Open parking available Covered parking available Supervised Child discount available 5yrs Table tennis Croquet Languages spoken: English, Italian & Spanish
ROOMS: s 310FF; d 380FF * Reductions over 1 night

LURCY-LÉVIS Allier

Domaine le Plaix (Prop: Claire Rauaz)
Pouzy Mesangy *03320*
☎ 470662406 FAX 470662582
(35km S of Nevers, take N7 for Moulins, exit at St-Pierre-le-Moutier. Go SW on D978a to Le Veurdre, left 1.5km on D13, right on D234, house signposted 3km on left)
Hidden between gentle hills and fields in the peace and tranquillity of the countryside, this sixteenth century building is a place to get back to nature. Fishing on site, River Bieudre borders the property. Bike rides, walks and pony rides all nearby. Some English spoken.
Near river Forest area
5 en suite (bth/shr) (3 fmly) No smoking in all bedrooms TV available Full central heating Open parking available Covered parking available Supervised Child discount available 10yrs Fishing Boule Open terrace Last d 18.00hrs
Languages spoken: English
ROOMS: s 190FF; d 220-250FF Reductions over 1 night
MEALS: Dinner fr 100FF
CARDS: Travellers cheques

PERRIER Puy-de-Dôme

Chemin de Siorac (Prop: M Paul Gebrillat)
63500
☎ 473891502 FAX 473550885
(A75 take exit 11 or 14 (Issoire Centre) then take direction to Champeix until you reach Perrier)
Paul Gebrillat and Mireille de Saint Aubin welcome you to their seventeenth century family home on the banks of the Couze Pavin. English spoken.
Near river Forest area Near motorway
2 en suite (bth) (1 fmly) Full central heating Open parking available Supervised Child discount available Open terrace
Languages spoken: English

SERVILLY Allier

Les Vieux Chênes (Prop: M & Mme Cotton)
03120
☎ 470990753 FAX 470993471
The proprietor, Elisabeth Cotton, welcomes you to this country house in a peaceful setting. The house is approached through a tree-lined path and is surrounded by parkland. Rooms are spacious and comfortable and are individually decorated. Evening meals available. ports hall and sauna. English spoken.
Near river Forest area Near motorway
6 en suite (bth/shr) (1 fmly) No smoking on premises Full central heating Child discount available 10yrs Languages spoken: English
MEALS: Lunch 80-300FF Dinner 80-300FF*

Rhône Alpes

Wonderfully situated at the meeting point of northern and southern Europe, and bordering Italy and Switzerland, the Rhône Alpes scenery is a spectacle of vivid contrasts: from snow-covered peaks and vast glaciers, to dense woodland and rich pastures. A paradise for outdoor leisure activities and sporting holidays. With 70 winter ski resorts, the Savoie is the largest ski area in the world, while the Ardèches is a veritable adventure playground of magnificent caves and gorges. And when the playing's done, relax with a glass of local wine. A Beaujolais, or Côte du Rhône, or Savoie - so many to choose from.

(Top): The impressive clock tower of the 17th-century church at Hauteluce dominates the village and surrounding countryside.

(Bottom): Among the outdoor pursuits offered in the region, canoeing is one of the most popular.

ESSENTIAL FACTS

DÉPARTEMENTS:	Ain, Ardèche, Drôme, Isère, Loire, Rhône, Haute-Savoie, Savoie
PRINCIPAL TOWNS	Lyon, St-Etienne Bourg-en-Bresse, Roanne, Villefranche-sur-Saône, Vienne, St-Chamond, Romans-sur-Isère, Valence, Montélimar, Grenoble, Chamonix, Annecy, Chambéry, Aix-les-Bains
PLACES TO VISIT:	The gorges of the Ardèche including the Grottes de St Marcel; the Roman buildings and Renaissance quarter in Lyon; Mont Blanc; the Parc National de la Vanoise; the Alpine region for skiers; the spa resorts of Aix-les-Bains, Evian and Thoron
REGIONAL TOURIST OFFICE	104 bis, route de Paris, 69260 Charbonnières-les-Bains. Tel: 72 59 21 59
LOCAL GASTRONOMIC DELIGHTS	Matelote, a fish stew made with red wine; chard, a green leaf vegetable served with well-seasoned white sauce; roast thrush; braised boar; nougat from Montélimar; various forms of raclette and fondue, including Savoyade made from three local cheeses; walnut from Grenoble; fruit tarts made from wild strawberries and blueberries
DRINKS	The Beaujolais region, where small villages prepare their world-famous wines; the green and yellow Chartreuse liqueur, originally produced by the monks at La Grand Chartreuse.
LOCAL CRAFTS WHAT TO BUY	Chocolate production at Pérouges; silks, clothes and textiles from St-Jorioz

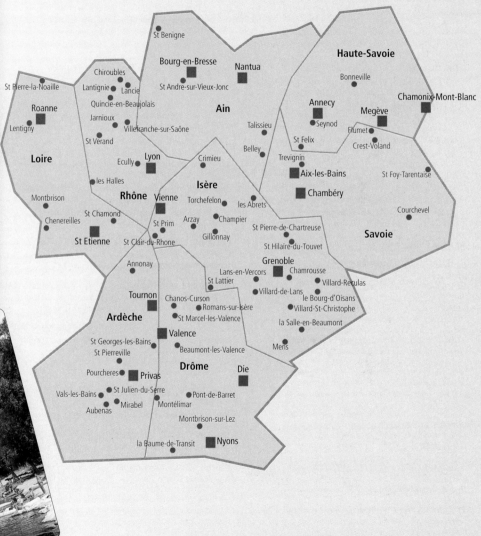

St Benigne

Bourg-en-Bresse

Nantua

Haute-Savoie

Bonneville

Chiroubles

St Pierre-la-Noaille

Lantignie Lancie

St Andre-sur-Vieux-Jonc

Chamonix-Mont-Blanc

Quincie-en-Beaujolais

Ain

Annecy

Megève

Roanne

Jarnioux

Seynod

Lentigny

Villefranche-sur-Saône

Talissieu

Flumet

Crest-Voland

St Verand

Belley

St Felix

St Foy-Tarentaise

Loire

Ecully **Lyon**

Crimieu

Trevignin

les Halles

Isère

Aix-les-Bains

Rhône Vienne

Torchefelon

Montbrison

St Chamond

Champier

les Abrets

Chambéry

Courchevel

Chenereilles

St Prim

Arzay

St Pierre-de-Chartreuse

Savoie

St Etienne

St Clair-du-Rhone

Gillonnay

St Hilaire-du-Touvet

Annonay

Grenoble

Lans-en-Vercors

Chamrousse

Tournon

St Lattier

Villard-Reculas

Chanos-Curson

Villard-de-Lans

le Bourg-d'Oisans

Ardèche

Romans-sur-Isère

Villard-St-Christophe

St Marcel-les-Valence

la Salle-en-Beaumont

St Georges-les-Bains

Valence

Mens

St Pierreville

Beaumont-les-Valence

Pourcheres

Drôme

Die

Vals-les-Bains

St Julien-de-Serre

Privas

Pont-de-Barret

Aubenas

Mirabel

Montélimar

Montbrison-sur-Lez

la Baume-de-Transit

Nyons

217

EVENTS & FESTIVALS

Jan Avoriaz Film Festival

Feb Chamonix 24-hour Ice Race; Lyon Art Fair

Mar St-Gervais-les-Bains Comedy & Theatre Festival; Grenoble Jazz Festival; Isère Festival of the Story; Chamrousse International Husky Sleigh Race; Meribel Red Ski Show (*son et lumière acrobatic skiing*); Flaine Snow Jazz Festival

Apr Bourg-d'Oisans International Mineral & Crystal Market ; Valloire International Chess Festival; Lyons International Fair

May Chamonix Festival of Science, Earth & Mankind; Condrieu Wine Festival; St-Etienne Music Festival

Jun International Chime & Bell Festivals at Annecy, Lyon, Miribel, St Genis Laval, St Nicholas, Aussois, Farnay, Taninges; Historical Reconstruction of the First Airship Flight at Annonay; Gex Bird Festival (*fairground, music, comic parade*); Annonay Street Art Festival

Jun/Jul Grenoble Theatre Festival; Jazz in Vienne; Son et Lumière at Val Grangent & St-Just-St Rambert

Jul St-Gervais Alpine Festival; Montélimar Miniature Art Festival; Albertville Military Music Festival; Buis-les-Baronnies Lime Blossom Fair; Olive Festivals at Nyons & Les

Vans; Saoû Picodon Cheese Festival; Les Aillons Bread Oven Festival; Tournon-sur-Rhône Musical Nights; Grignan Nocturnal Festival at the Château; Folklore Festivals at Bourg-St Maurice, Chambery & Voiron; Megève Jazz Contest; La Plagne Kite Festival; St-Antoine l'Abbaye Medieval Nights

Aug Tarentaise Baroque Music & Art Festival; Crest Acoustic Art Festival; Aix-les-Bains Steam Festival; Les Saises Lumberjack Competition; Coligny Traditional Fair; Ruoms Ardèche Vintners' Festival; Aix-les-Bains Flower Festival; La Rosière Shepherds' Festival at Col de Petit St Bernard; Châtel Alpine Festival

Sep Romans Brioche Festival; Charlieu Weaver Festival; Tain l'Hermitage Vintage Wine Festival;

Oct Montbrison Cheese Fair; Montbrison Folklore & Gastronomic Event; Lyons Pottery Festival "Foire aux Tupiniers"

Nov Grenoble Contemporary Music Festival; Villefranche-sur-Saône Official Launching of Beaujolais Nouveau Wine; Bourg-en-Bresse Flower Festival

Dec Autrans Snow, Ice & Adventure Film Festival; Lans-en-Vercors Festival of Children's Films; Val Thorens Motor Race on snow & ice

---

ABRETS, LES Isère

La Bruyère (Prop: M & Mme Chavalle)
38490
☎ 476320166 FAX 476320666
(from Lyon A43 Chimilin/Les Abrets exit towards Les Abrets and follow signs)
Large Dauphine house, set in the middle of a large shaded park with swimming pool. The property is situated in the heart of the countryside, surrounded by fields and forests. Gastronomic meals served. Your hosts will make you feel totally at home. English spoken.
Near river Near lake Forest area Near motorway
Closed 1st 2 wks Nov
6 en suite (bth) TV available Full central heating Open parking available Child discount available 12yrs Outdoor swimming pool Boule Open terrace Last d 20.00hrs
Languages spoken: English
MEALS: Dinner fr 200FF*
CARDS: ●● ▆▆

ARZAY Isère

Bed & Breakfast (Prop: M & Mme Virenque)
38260
☎ 474542155 FAX 474542474
Forest area
Closed Nov-Mar
3 rms (1 bth 1 shr) (1 fmly) Full central heating Open parking available Child discount available 12yrs Languages spoken: English

---

BAUME-DE-TRANSIT, LA Drôme

Domaine de Saint-Luc (Prop: L & E Cornillon)
26970
☎ 475981151 FAX 475981922
(from A7 exit at Bollène & take D994 towards Nyons. At Suze-la-Rousse Take D59 then D117 to la Baume-de-Transit)
Near river Forest area
5 en suite (bth/shr) (1 with balcony) Full central heating Open parking available V meals Languages spoken: English
ROOMS: s 300FF; d 360FF *
MEALS: Dinner fr 140FF
CARDS: Travellers cheques

BEAUMONT-LÈS-VALENCE Drôme

Bed & Breakfast (Prop: L de Chivre-Dumond)
Chambedeau *26760*
☎ 475597170 FAX 475597524
(from A7 exit at Valence Sud onto A49 towards Grenoble. Exit at J33 towards Beaumont, right onto D538. Approx 2kms after roundabout follow sign on right)
You are welcomed to this unique property, situated in a quiet area, that was a shepherd's hut built in the last century from the distinctive local round stones. There is a sitting room with TV and indoor games. Large breakfast are served. Your hostess has an extremely good knowledge of the region and will help you discover the best places to eat, the liveliest markets to visit, places to go and things to do. English spoken.
Near river Forest area Near motorway
3 en suite (shr) (1 with balcony) No smoking in all bedrooms

Open parking available Child discount available 5yrs
Languages spoken: English
ROOMS: s 180-220FF; d 200-260FF Reductions over 1 night
CARDS: Travellers cheques

BONNEVILLE Haute-Savoie

Les Gallinons (Prop: Mme Alice Rosset)
Ayze *74130*
☎ 450257858
(from A40 take exit for Bonneville, thenonto D19. Before
railway turn left for Ayze. In village turn left at school then
follow sign 'Chez Jeandets/Gallinous'. 200m)
This property is an alpine-style chalet situated within easy
access of the hills of the Haute Savoie, its interesting sites and
the many outdoor activities. You can admire the views from
one of the balconies, or relax in the private garden. There is a
warm and cosy atmosphere. A little English spoken.
Forest area
Closed 16 Sep-14 May RS Feb-Mar
4 rms (2 bth/shr) (2 with balcony) No smoking on premises
TV in 1 bedroom Full central heating Open parking available
Child discount available Languages spoken: Italian
ROOMS: s 190-270FF; d 250-300FF

BOURG-D'OISANS Isère

Les Petites Sources (Prop: Pauline Durdan)
Le Vert *38520*
☎ 476801392
Your hosts will be pleased to welcome you to their home next
to the Parc National des Ecrins. The interior design reflects the
traditional character of the house. Meals made from local
produce are available when requested in advance. Ski-ing is
available during the winter. Contact Mme Durdan to discuss
your requirements. English spoken.
Near river Near lake Forest area
Closed Oct-20 Dec & 20 Apr-20 May
6 en suite (bth/shr) (3 fmly) (4 with balcony) No smoking on
premises Full central heating Open parking available Child
discount available 13yrs Last d 21.00hrs Languages spoken:
English
ROOMS: s 190FF; d 240-280FF * Special breaks: winter
MEALS: Dinner fr 75FF*
CARDS: Travellers cheques

CHAMPIER Isère

Côteau des Bruyères (Prop: M & Mme Crepin)
38260
☎ 474544218
Very old, renovated farm which sits in one and a half acres of
land. The village is only one kilometre away. The mountains of
Chartreuse are clearly visible from the farm, and the calm
surroundings lend themselves to delightful walks. A telescope
may be used for star-gazing. Guests may dine with their hosts.
English spoken.
Near river Near lake Forest area Near motorway
4 en suite (bth/shr) (2 fmly) No smoking on premises Full
central heating Open parking available Child discount
available 10yrs Boule Open terrace Table tennis V meals
Languages spoken: English & Dutch
MEALS: Lunch fr 60FF Dinner fr 70FF*
CARDS: Travellers cheques

CHANOS-CURSON Drôme

Les Pichères
26600
☎ 475073272 FAX 475073065
The owners of this property welcome you to their home.
Family rooms available and children up to two years old stay
free. French breakfast served. English spoken.
Near motorway
Closed Oct-Etr
2 en suite (bth/shr) (2 fmly) No smoking on premises Full
central heating Open parking available Languages spoken:
English
CARDS: Travellers cheques

CHENEREILLES Loire

Les Vikings (Prop: M & Mme Roux)
42560
☎ 477757418
A Scandinavian-style cottage set amid pine trees in the
countryside beneath the Mounts of Forez in a quiet setting.
Two double rooms available plus living room for the use of
guests. Swings and table-tennis available in the garden.
Private swimming pool and sauna. English spoken.
Near river Forest area In town centre Near motorway
Closed Oct-Mar
2 en suite (shr) Radio in rooms Open parking available Child
discount available Outdoor swimming pool (heated) Sauna
Solarium Boule Open terrace Covered terrace
CARDS: Travellers cheques

CHIROUBLES Rhône

La Grosse Pierre (Prop: V & A Passot)
69115
☎ 474691217 FAX 474691352
(enter Fleurie/Villie Morgan D68 in direction of Chiroubles
D119 and follow signs to La Grosse Pierre)
Véronique and Alain Passot welcome you to their Beaujolais
home, situated in the middle of vineyards, just 500 metres
from Chiroubles. They offer you five comfortable rooms in a
calm and peaceful setting with panoramic view of the vines.
Breakfast is served in the dining room, or on the terrace in
fine weather. English spoken.
Forest area
5 en suite (shr) No smoking on premises Full central heating
Open parking available Covered parking available
Supervised Child discount available Outdoor swimming pool
Boule Languages spoken: English
ROOMS: s fr 280FF; d fr 300FF
CARDS: ●● ▆ Travellers cheques

CRÉMIEU Haute-Savoie

Les Heures Claires (Prop: Annie Huguet)
Chemin de Montradis *38460*
☎ 474907549
(from eastern Lyon take D517 to Cremieu)
A warm and friendly welcome is offered at this rustic house,
but booking is essential. An ideal place for those looking for
calm, greenery and comfort. Two comfortable, independent
rooms available, overlooking the park. Large French breakfast
served with home-made jams. Guests can pre-book an
evening meal. English spoken.

cont'd

2 en suite (shr) No smoking on premises Full central heating Open parking available Supervised No children Languages spoken: English & Spanish
ROOMS: d 300-320FF * Reductions over 1 night Special breaks

CREST-VOLAND Savoie

Bed & Breakfast (Prop: Mme Pascale Le Puil)
Le Saphir, Paravy 73590
☎ 479316958 FAX 479316958
(from Annecy take N508, then N212 towards Megeve. Then right onto D71 to Crest-Voland. From Office du Tourisme take road to Saisies. Before 'Mission 1940 cross', entrance at the top)
Set in a mountain chalet at an altitude of 1250 metres, with a superb view over the Aravis Mountain. Skiing in the winter time, with ski-lift fifty metres in front of the chalet. Evening meals available, served in the living room with your hosts and other guests. You will be welcomed with a bouquet of flowers. English spoken.
Near lake Forest area
3 en suite (shr) (2 fmly) No smoking on premises Full central heating Open parking available Child discount available 8yrs Languages spoken: English
ROOMS: s 175-195FF; d 245-285FF *
MEALS: Lunch 87FF Dinner 87FF
CARDS: Travellers cheques

ECULLY Rhône

St Columban Lodge (Prop: Annick & Michael Altuna)
7 rue du Hétre Pourpré 69130
☎ 478330557 FAX 472189080
A wonderful stopover on the outskirts of Lyon . The house is located in a private park. Excellent breakfasts served in the lounge or in the garden, depending on the weather. Guests are invited to eat with the hosts, although reservations must be made. Restaurants nearby. Eighteen hole golf five kilometres away with tennis courts in the local village. English spoken.
Near motorway
6 en suite (bth/shr) No smoking in all bedrooms TV available Full central heating Open parking available Supervised No children Open terrace Languages spoken: English & Spanish
CARDS: 💳 🏧 💳

FLUMET Savoie

La Cour (Prop: Beatrice Burnet-Merlin)
Les Seigneurs 73590
☎ 479317215
This residence offers two bed & breakfast rooms, one with a double and two single beds, the second, opposite the first, with a double bed. Large breakfast served. Swings and garden room available. Situated close to forest, lakes and rivers, near to the Swiss border. Twenty percent discount for children under ten years. Good skiing location. Open all year round. English spoken
Near river Near lake Forest area
2 en suite (shr) Full central heating Open parking available Supervised Child discount available 10yrs

GILLONNAY Isère

La Ferme des Collines (Prop: M Meyer)
Hameau Notre Dame 38260
☎ 474202793 FAX 474202793
Near lake Forest area
4 en suite (shr) Full central heating Open parking available

Covered parking available Supervised Child discount available 11yrs Bicycle rental Last d 17.00hrs Languages spoken: English & Italian
ROOMS: s 300FF; d 300FF
MEALS: Lunch 100-150FF Dinner 100-150FF
CARDS: Travellers cheques

HALLES, LES Rhône

Chateau de la Bonnetiere (Prop: Denise Roches)
69610
☎ 474266278 FAX 478379604
Nineteenth century house set in five hectares of parkland has a splendid romantic setting and much of the furniture is antique. Receptions, parties and weddings can all be catered for. Living room and library available. Tennis available on site. A little English spoken.
Forest area
Closed Nov-Apr
10 rms (4 shr) Open terrace Languages spoken: Italian

JARNIOUX Rhône

Château de Bois Franc (Prop: Robert Doat)
69640
☎ 474582091 FAX 474651003
This noble house enjoys panoramic views of neighbouring countryside. Trees and parkland can be enjoyed - many walks available. Continental breakfast served. Special discounts for visits of more than one night. English spoken.
Near motorway
2 en suite (bth/shr) Open parking available Child discount available Languages spoken: English & German
CARDS: Travellers cheques

LANCIE Rhône

Les Pasquiers (Prop: Jacques Gandilhon)
69220
☎ 474698633 FAX 474698657
(from A6 exit Macon-Sud, or Belleville on N6 to Nomanéche, Lancié is 3km along. In village take rd into Les Pasquiers, house is on square)
Near river Near motorway
3 en suite (bth/shr) (1 fmly) No smoking on premises TV in 1 bedroom Full central heating Open parking available Child discount available Outdoor swimming pool Tennis Boule Last d 20.00hrs Languages spoken: English & German
ROOMS: s 350FF; d 350FF
MEALS: Dinner 120FF

LANS-EN-VERCORS Isère

Le Renardière (Prop: M Rabot)
Les Blancs 38250
☎ 476951376
Situated in a small hamlet, in a peaceful environment, the two guest rooms in this attractive residence have a clear view and an independent access. Your hosts, Patrick and Christine, will be happy to help you discover the Vercors region, with its gastronomy, superb countryside and the flora and fauna of the largest nature reserve in France. Free for children under two years. English spoken.
Forest area
2 en suite (bth/shr) (1 fmly) (2 with balcony) Full central heating Open parking available Supervised Child discount available Languages spoken: English German & Spanish

LANTIGNIE Rhône

Domaine des Quarante Écus (Prop: Bernard Nesme)
Les Vergers *69430*
☎ 474048580 FAX 474692779
(exit Belleville from A6 in direction of Beaujeu, then D37 Pins
& onto D26 in direction of Julienas in 2km turn right)
In the heart of the Beaujolais region, in a wine-grower's
house, five guest rooms are offered on the first floor, with a
superb view of the vineyards. Wine-tasting of Beaujolais-
Villages available to those interested, in the cellars of the
property, with wines available to purchase from your host.
Swimming pool on-site. Plenty to see and do in the region.
Forest area
5 en suite (shr) (1 fmly) TV in 1 bedroom Full central heating
Open parking available Supervised Child discount available
12yrs Outdoor swimming pool Languages spoken: English

LA-SALLE-EN-BEAUMONT Isère

Villa a la Mitemps (Prop: Martine Grand)
Les Applauves *38350*
☎ 476304204 FAX 476304454
(on the N85 rte Napoleon between Grenoble and Gap)
Set on the route Napoleon (RN85), the proprietor of this
contemporary flower-decked villa, Martine Grand, offers her
visitors bedrooms with private facilities, a reading room and a
garden as well as covered parking. With views of the beautiful
mountain L'Obiou (2807m high), the Villa makes a useful
overnight-stop en route to further destinations.
Forest area Near motorway
4 en suite (shr) (2 fmly) Full central heating Open parking
available Covered parking available Child discount available
Boule
ROOMS: s fr 200FF; d fr 230FF

LENTIGNY Loire

Domaine de Champfleury (Prop: Maurice Gaume)
42155
☎ 477633143
(from Roanne take D53 in the direction Thiers/Clermont for
8km then take D18 to Lentigny approx 1km)
A collection of antiques can be found throughout this peaceful
turn-of-the-century house, which has tastefully furnished
bedrooms equipped with attractive bathrooms. The flower-
filled park has a private tennis court, seats and picnic tables. A
choice of restaurants can be found at Roanne, and outdoor
leisure activities are available nearby.
Near lake Forest area
Closed Nov-Mar
3 en suite (bth/shr) (1 fmly) No smoking on premises Full
central heating Open parking available Tennis Boule Bicycle
rental Badminton Table tennis Languages spoken: German
ROOMS: d 350FF Reductions over 1 night Special breaks

MENS Isère

Chez Pierrette
rue du Bourg *38710*
☎ 476346014 476348404
Near lake Forest area
Closed Jan-Feb
5 en suite (bth/shr) (1 fmly) No smoking on premises TV

available Full central heating Child discount available 12yrs
V meals Languages spoken: English
MEALS: Dinner fr 80FF*
CARDS: Travellers cheques

L'Engrangeou (Prop: Janic Grinberg)
pl de la Halle *38710*
☎ 476349448 & 476348563
(from Grenoble take N75 to Monestier then D34 to Mens, or
from Grenoble take N85 (rte Napoléon) to La Mure then D526
to Mens)
Bed & breakfast accommodation available in the home of
artist, Janic Grinberg, situated in the heart of the Mens region,
in a sixteenth century residence. Breakfast is served in the art
gallery. Three rooms with television on offer, with quality
decor. Your host can organise visits to art galleries and the
textile museum, or a tour by car of sites favoured by artists.
Open March to December. English spoken.
Near river Near lake Forest area In town centre Near
motorway
3 en suite (shr) No smoking on premises TV in all bedrooms
STV Full central heating Open parking available Child
discount available Riding Bicycle rental Languages spoken:
English
ROOMS: d 260FF Reductions over 1 night Special breaks

MIRABEL Ardèche

Le Mas des Vignes (Prop: M & Mme Meerloo)
La Prade *07170*
☎ 475942854
(off A7 at Montélimar N direction Le Teil-Aubenas. At
Lavilledieu turn right to Lussas, follow direction Mirabel, after
1km, immediately after bridge, take sharp right)
Alice and Robert Meerloo welcome you to their old Ardèche
house, nestled among fields and vineyards. Four rooms are
available, separate from the rest of the house. Patio, courtyard
and garden. Walks, bathing, mountain bikes, climbing and
canoeing close by. English spoken.
Near river Forest area Near motorway
Closed Oct-May
4 en suite (bth/shr) (1 with balcony) Full central heating
Open parking available Child discount available Languages
spoken: English, Dutch & German
ROOMS: d 300-350FF
CARDS: Travellers cheques

MONTBRISON-SUR-LEZ Drôme

Bed & Breakfast (Prop: M & Mme R Barjavel)
26770
☎ 475535404
Remy and Marie-Noëlle Barjavel welcome you to their three
rooms and two cottages, hidden in the middle of the vines.
The proprietors also run a wine-making business. The rooms
are very comfortable and a kitchenette can be used by guests.
Swimming pool in garden.
Forest area
3 en suite (bth/shr) (2 fmly) (2 with balcony) Full central
heating Open parking available Supervised Outdoor
swimming pool
ROOMS: s 170-190FF; d 190-210FF Reductions over 1 night

Taking your mobile phone to France?
See page 11

PONT-DE-BARRET Drôme

Les Tuillieres (Prop: S & H Jenny)
26160
☎ 475904391
This charming sixteenth century Provençal farmhouse is situated on a small hill surrounded by trees. Guest rooms, including three family rooms, are comfortable and well decorated. Continental breakfast and fixed price dinners served on the terrace or in the attractive dining room. Spacious living room with exposed beams, original stone walls, piano and open fire. Swimming pool, with shaded patio. English spoken.
Near river Forest area Near motorway
Closed Nov-14 Mar
6 en suite (bth/shr) (3 fmly) No smoking on premises Full central heating Open parking available No children 10yrs Child discount available 15yrs Outdoor swimming pool Boule V meals Last d 20.00hrs Languages spoken: English, German & Italian
MEALS: Dinner fr 135FF*
CARDS: Travellers cheques

POURCHÈRES Ardèche

Bed & Breakfast (Prop: Marcelle & Jean-Nicholas Goetz)
07000
☎ 475668199
This seventeenth century property is situated on the side of an extinct volcano and enjoys impressive views. Five guest rooms are offered by your hosts, Marcelle and Jean-Nicolas Goetz. Meals are available, with vegetarian options, using local produce. A warm country welcome awaits you. Reductions for children under five years. English spoken.
Forest area
5 en suite (bth/shr) No smoking on premises Full central heating Open parking available Supervised Child discount available 5yrs V meals Languages spoken: English & German

QUINCIÉ-EN-BEAUJOLAIS Rhône

Domaine de Romarand (Prop: Annie & Jean Berthelot)
69430
☎ 474043449 FAX 474043449
(from A6 exit Belleville-sur-Saone in the direction Beaujeu D37, before Beaujeu turn left to Quincie-en-Beaujolais D9 travel through village, before Grand Château turn right to Romarand)
Forest area Near motorway
3 en suite (shr) No smoking on premises Full central heating Open parking available Child discount available Outdoor swimming pool Languages spoken: English
ROOMS: s fr 250FF; d 280-300FF
MEALS: Dinner 100-120FF
CARDS: Travellers cheques

ST-ANDRÉ-SUR-VIEUX-JONC Ain

Château-de-Marmont (Prop: Guido-Alheritiere)
01960
☎ 474527974
Three bedrooms are available at this manor house dating back to the beginning of the nineteenth century, surrounded by a park bordered by a superb 18-hole golf course. Warm welcome assured by your hosts, who speak English. Breakfast served including eggs from the farm and home-made jams. Bicycles available. Guests can enjoy walks around the lakes.

Excellent restaurant with modest prices three kilometres away. Near lake Forest area
3 en suite (bth/shr) Full central heating Open parking available Covered parking available Supervised Child discount available Languages spoken: English Italian & Spanish

ST-BÉNIGNE Ain

Petites Varennes (Prop: Christine A Treal)
01190
☎ 385303198
Near river Forest area
5 rms (2 bth 1 shr) No smoking in all bedrooms Licensed Full central heating Open parking available Indoor swimming pool (heated) Open terrace Covered terrace Languages spoken: English

ST-CLAIR-DU-RHÔNE Isère

Les Prailles (Prop: Raymond Pasquarelli)
6 Chemin de Prailles *38370*
☎ 474872915
Pretty country house with swimming pool. Surrounded by one hectare of land, with terrace and floral garden leading to the river. Evening meals available on request prepared with great care by your hostess, Mme. Pasquarelli. Swimming pool and table-tennis in the garden. English spoken.
Near river Forest area
5 en suite (bth/shr) (4 fmly) No smoking on premises Full central heating Open parking available Child discount available Outdoor swimming pool V meals Languages spoken: English
MEALS: Dinner fr 100FFalc*

ST-FÉLIX Haute-Savoie

Les Bruyères (Prop: M B L Betts)
Mercy *74540*
☎ 450609653 FAX 450609465
Situated at the foot of the Alps, this restored nineteenth century Savoy farm offers accommodation surrounded by a landscaped park ablaze with flowers. Regional breakfasts are served and afternoon tea is offered on the terrace. Restaurants close by serve excellent cuisine. On-site facilities include tennis and croquet. Two of the most beautiful lakes in France are situated nearby: Lake du Bourget and Lake d'Annecy. English spoken.
Near river Near lake Near sea Near beach Forest area Near motorway
3 en suite (bth/shr) No smoking in all bedrooms TV available STV Full central heating Open parking available Covered parking available Supervised Child discount available 14yrs Tennis Croquet V meals Last d 20.30hrs Languages spoken: English
MEALS: Dinner 150FF*
CARDS: ●● ▇ Travellers cheques

ST-GEORGES-LES-BAINS Ardèche

St-Marcel-de-Crussol (Prop: Madame Biosse Duplan)
07800
☎ 475608177 FAX 475608632
Relax in this grand house in the heart of a two hectare park. The swimming pool can be used by the guests. All rooms are stylishly furnished with living area and television. Evening meals can be arranged between host and guest.

Near river Near lake Forest area Near motorway
2 en suite (bth) (1 fmly) TV available Full central heating
Open parking available Child discount available Languages
spoken: Spanish
MEALS: Dinner 100-150FF*

ST-HILAIRE-DU-TOUVET Isère

Les Hauts Granets (Prop: Nicole Raibon)
38660
☎ 476083056
Near lake Forest area
2 en suite (shr) TV available Full central heating Open
parking available Table Tennis Languages spoken: English

ST-JULIEN-DU-SERRE Ardèche

Le Moulinage (Prop: V Vandamme-Lefevre)
Le Chambon *07200*
☎ 475930509
(from Aubenas take N104 to St Privat, turn left opposite the
post office and take small road to St Julien-du-Serre. After
approx 1.5km cross small village called Le Chambon and then
take last road on right)
On the edge of a quiet river, an ancient silk-mill where
breakfast includes home cooked jams, flavoured bread and
cakes.
Near river Forest area Near motorway
1 en suite (shr) (1 fmly) No smoking on premises Full central
heating Open parking available Child discount available 2yrs
Riding Languages spoken: English
ROOMS: d fr 240FF Reductions over 1 night

ST-LATTIER Isère

Lièvre Amoureux (Prop: M Breda)
La Gare *38840*
☎ 476645067 FAX 476643121
Old hunting lodge, covered in ivy, situated in lovely
countryside at the foot of the marvellous site of Vercors. Rooms
are spacious: the quiet rooms are situated near to the swimming
pool and need to be booked early. Meals are served in the
charming dining room or on the pretty terrace in fine weather.
Forest area Near motorway
Closed Oct-24 Mar
12 rms (10 bth/shr) TV in 5 bedrooms Full central heating
Open parking available Outdoor swimming pool Open
terrace

ST-MARCEL-LES-VALENCE Drôme

La Pineraie (Prop: Marie Jeanne Katchikian)
Chemin Bel Air *26320*
☎ 475587225
(exit Valence Nord or Sud A7 then take A49/N532 & exit at St
Marcel-Les Valence)
This superb property, full of character, is hidden away in
parkland. All rooms benefit from an exceptional view of the
Vercors mountains, with direct access through a flower
garden via French doors. Decorated with taste, furnished with
antiques and carpets from the Orient, with stone-built
fireplaces, the house has an air of warmth and refinement.
Breakfast served in the garden in summer, by the fireplace in
winter, to include home-made pastries, jam and fruit from the
garden. English spoken.
Near river Near lake Near sea Near
beach Forest area Near motorway

3 rms (2 bth/shr) (2 with balcony) No smoking in 2 bedrooms
Full central heating Open parking available Supervised
Child discount available 12yrs Languages spoken: English,
Italian & Spanish
ROOMS: s 220-240FF; d 270-300FF Reductions over 1 night
Special breaks
CARDS: Travellers cheques

ST-PIERRE-DE-CHARTREUSE Isère

L'Arbi (Prop: M Baffert)
Les Egaux *38380*
☎ 476886086 FAX 476886922
This house lies in the heart of the Chartreuse. Two pretty
rooms are on the ground floor with independent access to the
terrace and lawn. The third is on the first floor. Close by are
walks in the forest and excursions in the Parc Naturel
Régional du Chartreuse.
Forest area
3 rms (2 bth/shr) (3 fmly) No smoking on premises TV in 2
bedrooms Full central heating Open parking available Child
discount available 12yrs
ROOMS: d 190-230FF
MEALS: Dinner 85FF*
CARDS: Travellers cheques

ST-PIERRE-LA-NOAILLE Loire

Domaine Château de Marchangy (Prop: Marie Colette
& Patrick Rufene)
42190
☎ 477699676 FAX 477607037
Huge property, partially covered in creeper, placed in the
grounds of an 18th-century château in the Roman Brionnais.
Panoramic view. Peace and quiet and comfortable rooms will
help you to relax whilst you discover this part of France.
Swimming pool. Guests may dine with the hosts. Organic
produce served. English spoken.
Near river Forest area
3 en suite (shr) (2 fmly) (1 with balcony) TV available Full
central heating Open parking available Child discount
available 12yrs Outdoor swimming pool Languages spoken:
English
MEALS: Dinner 60-130FFalc*
CARDS: Travellers cheques

ST-PIERREVILLE Ardèche

Le Moulinage Chabriol (Prop: E de Lang)
Chabriol Bas *07190*
☎ 475666208 FAX 475666599
(leave A7 at Loriol-exit (S of Valence), cross the Rhone
continue to la Voulte and St-Laurent-du-Pape, then take D120
direction St Fortunat till St-Sauveur-de-Montagut take D102
direction Albon stay on D102 approx 15km until blue sign
Chabriol)
An 18th century silk mill on the border of a river offers six
rooms with private facilities. The original stone walls, vault
ceilings and antique furnishings blend with the modern
construction materials. A kitchen is available to prepare salads
or sandwiches.
Near river Near lake Forest area Near motorway
6 en suite (shr) No smoking on premises Full central heating
Open parking available Fishing Boule Bicycle rental
Languages spoken: English, Dutch & German
ROOMS: d 280-330FF

ST-PRIM Isère

Bed & Breakfast (Prop: M & Mme Briot)
Chemin de Pré Margot *38370*
☎ 474564427 FAX 474563093
This property is situated ten kilometres from Vienne, opposite
Mont Pilat. Games machine and billiards available in air
conditioned room, furnished and decorated in an exotic style.
Air-conditioned dining room with views over the water. Two
gites available. English spoken.
Near lake Forest area
6 en suite (shr) No smoking on premises TV available Open
parking available Child discount available 10yrs Languages
spoken: English & German

ST-VERAND Haute-Savoie

Fondvielle (Prop: M & Mme Anning)
Lieu dit Taponas *69620*
☎ 474716264
(head south on A6 exit Villefranche-sur-Saone, follow D38
direction Roanne. In the village Fondvielle is signposted)

Tastefully decorated en suite rooms set in well-established
gardens, each with private terrace with lovely views
surrounded by vineyards. Self catering accommodation also
available.
Near lake Forest area Near motorway
6 rms (4 bth/shr) (2 fmly) Open parking available Child
discount available Boule Bicycle rental V meals Languages
spoken: English & Spanish
ROOMS: s fr 180FF; d 200-250FF
MEALS: Dinner fr 80FF
CARDS: Travellers cheques

STE-FOY-TARENTAISE Savoie

Yellow Stone Chalet (Prop: Nancy & Jean-Claude
Tabardel)
Bonconseil *73640*
☎ 479069606 FAX 479069605
(off D902, follow signs for Ste Foy winter sports station where
chalet is signposted)
This property can offer either guest rooms or an independent
chalet. Set high up in the Alps (1550 metres above sea level),
the chalet has access to the ski-lifts of the Bonconseil Station.
The snow in this area is amongst the best in France. "Ski-
safaris" available - thanks to the 600 kilometres of piste in this
area. A guide can be provided. Summer stays offer fabulous
walks. English spoken.
Near river Near lake Forest area
Closed 16 Sep-19 Dec & 22 Apr-14 Jun

5 en suite (bth/shr) (1 fmly) (2 with balcony) No smoking on
premises TV in all bedrooms Full central heating Open
parking available Covered parking available (charged)
Supervised Child discount available 12yrs Sauna Gym
Jacuzzi/spa Last d 20.00hrs Languages spoken: English
ROOMS: s 550-750FF; d 550-750FF
MEALS: Dinner fr 175FF
CARDS: ●● ▥ Travellers cheques

SEYNOD Haute-Savoie

Villa Dadounid (Prop: Maryse Roupioz)
32 rte de Pleins Champs *74600*
☎ 450467298 FAX 450467298
Maryse and her son, Eric, welcome you to their modern
house, with swimming pool, set in parkland. Each room has a
kitchenette. Breakfasts and dinners are served on a flowered
terrace and, if the weather permits, evening meals can be
taken by the swimming pool. Volleyball, table-tennis and
swings are available in the garden. Fishing and golf available
nearby. In the winter skiing is within ten kilometres.
Forest area Near motorway
Closed mid Sep-May
4 en suite (bth/shr) (3 with balcony) No smoking on premises
TV in 2 bedrooms Full central heating Open parking
available Child discount available 3yrs
MEALS: Lunch fr 100FF Dinner fr 100FF*

TALISSIEU Ain

Domaine de Château Froid (Prop: M Gilbert Pesenti)
01510
☎ 479873999 FAX 479874569
(leave A40 at Eloise exit, drive on N508 towards Frangy, then
D992 and D904 through Culoz, château is 5km along)
Built in 1625 by Carthusian monks on their vineyard estate,
this splendid residence has been restored by its present owner
and offers you calm and charm in a 27 acre park. The terrace
has a panoramic view of the vineyards. Beautifully appointed,
spacious rooms are available, with bedrooms in the turrets.
Use of library, billiard room, bicycles, tennis and swimming
pool. An opportunity to sample the regional food of Bugey.
English spoken.
Near river Near lake Forest area
Closed Jan-Mar
8 en suite (bth/shr) (2 fmly) TV available STV Full central
heating Open parking available Supervised Child discount
available 8yrs Outdoor swimming pool (heated) Tennis
Fishing Boule Bicycle rental Billiards Languages spoken:
English
ROOMS: s 550FF; d 600FF Reductions over 1 night
MEALS: Dinner fr 150FF*
CARDS: ●● ▥ Travellers cheques

TORCHEFELON Isère

Le Colombier (Prop: Nicole Rignoly)
La Taillat *38690*
☎ 474922928 FAX 474922733
Restored farm with comfortable guest rooms set in the middle
of fields. Your hostess looks forward to introducing you to her
passion: cooking. Horse and cart rides available, or if you
prefer you can see the area by bicycle. English spoken.
Near lake Near sea Forest area

5 en suite (bth/shr) No smoking in all bedrooms Radio in rooms Full central heating Open parking available Child discount available 7yrs Riding Open terrace V meals Languages spoken: English
MEALS: Lunch fr 90FF Dinner fr 90FF*
CARDS: ▨ ▣

TRÉVIGNIN Savoie

La Jument Verte (Prop: Chappaz)
pl de l'Église 73100
☎ 479614752 FAX 479354080
(from Aix les Bains D913 to Trevignin, then follow signs.) Several rooms available at this charming residence. Evening meal available at a fixed price. Tennis, squash, billiard table, boules, mini-golf, bicycles and riding centre on-site. Golf club nearby. Reduction for children under ten years. English spoken.
Near lake Near sea Forest area
7 en suite (shr) Full central heating Open parking available Child discount available 10yrs Outdoor swimming pool Tennis Pool table Boule Mini-golf Bicycle rental Open terrace Languages spoken: English
ROOMS: s fr 200FF; d fr 238FF Reductions over 1 night

VALS-LES-BAINS Ardèche

Domaine-de-Combelle (Prop: Caroline Mocquet)
Asperjoc 07600
☎ 475376277
(leave Vals-les-Bains, head for Awtraigues D578, after 1.5km, take the private bridge on left which is 0.2km after public bridge)
Combelle is a manor house built at the beginning of the 19th century. In a magnificent setting in the middle of a forest on the side of a hill with waterfall, lakes, fountains and ancient trees all around. Spacious rooms decorated in 19th-century style. Billiard room and library. A river runs at the foot of the house. English spoken.
Near river Forest area
4 en suite (bth/shr) Full central heating Open parking available Covered parking available Supervised Languages spoken: English
ROOMS: s 370-410FF; d 420-460FF Reductions over 1 night Special breaks

VILLARD-DE-LANS Isère

Le val Sainte Marie (Prop: Agnes Bon)
Bois Barbu 38250
☎ 476959280
Near river Forest area
3 en suite (shr) (1 fmly) No smoking on premises Open parking available Supervised Child discount available 5yrs Boule Table tennis Last d 16.00hrs Languages spoken: English
MEALS: Dinner fr 90FF*
CARDS: ▨

La Musardière (Prop: Odette & Marcel Haubert)
rte des Vieres 38250
☎ 476959777
Modern chalet-style house in sunny location, with garden. Peace and calm assured. One of the rooms on offer has a balcony which looks out onto mountains. Breakfast will be served either in the rustic dining room by the fire or outside on the terrace in the fine weather. Reductions for children.

Evening meal available, with 24 hours notice.
Near river Forest area
2 en suite (bth/shr) (1 with balcony) No smoking on premises Full central heating Open parking available
ROOMS: s 250FF; d 300FF
MEALS: Lunch fr 120FF*

Les 4 Vents (Prop: Jean Paul Uzel)
Bois Barbu 38250
☎ 476951068
This farm is located on the edge of a forest, in the midst of nature, where visitors can enjoy the panoramic view of the mountains. The proximity to the mountains and forest ensures super walks are possible. Guests are welcome to join the family at their evening meal. Fresh vegetables from the garden will be used. English spoken.
Near river Forest area
Closed 16 Sep-20 Dec & 16 Apr-14 Jun
5 en suite (shr) (4 fmly) (3 with balcony) No smoking on premises Full central heating Open parking available Covered parking available Child discount available 16yrs Last d 17.00hrs Languages spoken: English
MEALS: Dinner fr 75FF*
CARDS: Travellers cheques

VILLARD-RECULAS Isère

La Source (Prop: S. Wallace)
38114
☎ 476803032
(from Grenoble take road toward Briancon 6km before Bourg d'Oisans turn left for Villard-Reculas Vansany, 0z. Follow signsto Villard Reculas for 13km. Go down hill into village leave car in parking on rhs take first small lane right, then left)
This is an old stone grange overlooking the mountains. Villard Recules (altitude 1480 metres) is a satellite village in the ski area of Alpes d'Huez. The house has been renovated but has not lost any of its old-style charm. Living and dining room with vaulted ceiling, wood-burning stove and comfortable sofas. Visitors must take ski-insurance on booking. English spoken.
Forest area Near motorway
Closed mid April-mid Dec
5 rms (3 shr) (1 with balcony) Open parking available V meals Languages spoken: English
CARDS: Travellers cheques

VILLARD-ST-CHRISTOPHE Isère

Bed & Breakfast (Prop: Mme M Audinos)
38119
☎ 476830739
Accommodation available in this large country house. The rooms are situated on the first floor, with a large living room with fireplace, kitchen and library available to guests on the ground floor. Skiing possible in the winter. Children under three years stay free.
Near river Near lake Forest area
3 rms (1 shr) (1 fmly) No smoking on premises Full central heating Open parking available (charged) Child discount available 3yrs

Taking your mobile phone to France? See page 11

225

Aquitaine

Aquitaine is situated in the basin of the Garonne extending inland to the Dordogne, between the Atlantic and the Pyrénées. It is a region of huge variety, from mountains and valleys to vast surf-washed beaches and shady forests, as well as countless leisure and sporting opportunities. There are many reminders of the Renaissance and Middle Ages, particularly in the hills of Perigord, Agen and the Basque country which are dotted with castles, monuments and dwellings from prehistory. Towns such as Pau and Bordeaux are rich in medieval and classical heritage and contain many museums documenting the area's history. Festivals are excellent occasions to experience firsthand local traditions and sample the many gastronomic delights.

Two contrasting scenes of Aquitaine's rich heritage. (Top): The Lascaux II caves, which contain exact replicas of the prehistoric cave paintings which were discovered at the nearby village of Lascaux.

(Bottom): Two colourful characters at a fair in Bayonne, which has a strong Basque heritage.

ESSENTIAL FACTS

DÉPARTEMENTS:	Dordogne, Gironde, Landes, Lot-et-Garonne, Pyrénées-Atlantiques
PRINCIPAL TOWNS	Agen, Bayonne, Bergerac, Biarritz, Bordeaux, Dax, Mont-de-Marsan, Pau, Périgueux, Sarlat
PLACES TO VISIT:	Caves at Betharram-Ste Pé, Combarelles, Font-de-Gaume, Sare, Isturiz & Oxocelhaya; prehistoric sites in the Vézère valley; the cliffs at Vautours; narrow-gauge railways at Artouste Fabreges & La Rhune; St-Jean-Pied-de-Port, a 13th century town with Bishops' Prison; St-Jean-de-Luz including waxwork museum & Florenia floral valley; Kakouetta Gorge nr Ste-Engrâce.
REGIONAL TOURIST OFFICE	23 Parvis des Chartrons, 33074 Bordeaux. Tel 05 56017000 Fax 05 56017007. E.mail: Tourisme@cr-aquitaine.fr
LOCAL GASTRONOMIC DELIGHTS	goose or duck confit, foie gras, woodpigeon, wild boar, hare, trout, salmon, garbure - a rich, local stew, charcuterie, Bayonne ham, sauce béarnaise, poule au pot - a chicken casserole, Béarn Pastis - a cake not a drink, cheeses, Pyrénéen chocolates - with an ice-cool filling, lamprey, truffles.
DRINKS	Bordeaux wines from Bergerac, Medoc, Sauternes, St-Emilion, Graves; brandy from Armagnac; rosé from Béarn

Soulac-sur-Mer

Maubuisson

Gironde

BORDEAUX

Leogran Tabanac

Andernos-les-Bains

Beautiran

Arcachon

St Macaire

St Emilion

Ste Terre

St Quentin-de-Baron

Monsegur

Vendoire

St Paul-Lizonne Vertillac

Villars

Champagnac-de-Belair

la Chapelle-Gonaguet

Hautefort

Périgueux

Dordogne

Plazac

Eyzies

Bergerac

Sarlat-la-Canéda

Domme

Duras Villeréal

St Eutrope-de-Born

Marmande Laussou

Cancon Monflaquin

Bouglon

Grezet-Cavagnan Clairac Villeneuve-sur-Lot

St Antoine-de-Ficalba

Lot-et-Garonne

Agen

Landes

Mont-de-Marsan

Dax St Saver

St Lon-les-Mines Aire-sur-l'Adour

Port-de-Lanne

Geaune

St Jean de Luz Bayonne Arroses

Biarritz

Urrugne Salies-de-Béarn

Ciboure St Pee-sur-Nivelle

Lay-Lamidou Pau

Pyrénées-Atlantiques Oloron-Ste-Marie Bosdarros

Aramits Bruges

Montaut

227

EVENTS & FESTIVALS

Feb Bordeaux Antiques Fair; St Macaire Carnival; Bazas Traditional Promenade des Boeufs Gras

Mar Biarritz Carnival; Béarnais Carnival at Pau; Bayonne Ham Fair; Lacanau Windsurf Festival; St Emilion Concert & Wine Tasting

Apr Biarritz Musical Fair (classical); Bordeaux International Festival of Young Soloists; Ste Terre Fish Festival;

May Soulac-sur-Mer Theatre Festival; Thivier foie gras market

June Pau Festival; St-Sever International Folklore Festival; Aire sur l'Adour Feria; Bordeaux Wine Fair; St-Sever Feria; Mourenx Celebrations; St Emilion Vine Flowering Festivals; Montflaquin wine & cheese market;

July Terrasson Puppet Festival; Mont-de-Marsan Flamenco Festival; Oloron-Ste-Marie Jazz Festival; Biarritz International Folk Festival; Festival around Bergerac; Bayonne Jazz Festival; Capbreton Storytelling Festival; Perigord Noir Festival (Dordogne music); Montignac World Folklore Festival; Andernos les-Bains Jazz Festival; Sarlat Theatre Festival; St-Jean de Luz Tunafish Festival; Biarritz Surf Festival; Bayonne Medieval Fair; Orthez Fair & Cavalcade; Mont de Marsan Feria; Pau

Festival; St-Etienne de Baigorry Basque Game Festival; Son et Lumière at Bazas & Castillon la Bataille; Eymet Medieval Festival; La Junte de Roncal (*traditional Pyrenean celebrations*)

Aug Bayonne Festival; Biarritz Andalusian Feria; Oloron-Ste-Marie Pyrenean Folk Festival; Périgueux Mime Festival; Uzeste Art & Music festival; Marmande Song & Music Festival; Gujan-Mestras Oyster Fair; St Palais Basque Tug-of-War Festival; Arcachon Ocean Festival; Montfalquin Medieval Festival

Sep Dax Holy Art Festival; St-Sever Crossover Music Festival; Biarritz classical & modern dance festival; Oloron-Ste-Marie "La Garburade"; Eugénie-les-Bains Imperial Festival; Marathon of Médoc & Graves Châteaux; Salies de Béarn Salt Festival; Aramits Shepherds' Festival; Siros Song Festival (local dialect)

Oct St-Jean de Luz Country Choir Festival; Espelette Capsicum Pepper Festiva; Geaune Vintage Festival; Marcillac Vintage Festival

Nov Sarlat Film Festival; Hossegar European Kite Festival; Maubuisson Armistice Sailing Grand Prix

Dec Bazas Traditional Christmas Celebration; Monségur foie gras market

---

ARROSES Pyrénées-Atlantiques

Sauvemea (Prop: J Labat)
64350
☎ 559681601 FAX 559681608
A large farm, built in the grounds of a beautiful manor house. The farm overlooks countryside and a lake. Rooms are spacious, as are the bathrooms. Calm and comfort prevail. Home-cooked meals on request, with all food being prepared from farm produce. Horse-riding and swimming are on-site. English spoken.
Near lake Forest area
6 rms (4 bth 1 shr) (1 fmly) Full central heating Open parking available Outdoor swimming pool Fishing Riding Languages spoken: English & Spanish
CARDS: Travellers cheques

BEAUTIRAN Gironde

Château de Martignas (Prop: Catherine Vicard-Galea)
33640
☎ 556675241
Near river Forest area
2 en suite (bth) Full central heating Open parking available Child discount available Languages spoken: English, German, Japanese & Spanish
MEALS: Dinner 80FF*
CARDS: Travellers cheques

Taking your mobile phone to France?
See page 11

BOSDARROS Pyrénées-Atlantiques

Bed & Breakfast (Prop: Christianne Bordes)
Chemin de Labau, rte de Rebenacq *64290*
☎ 559217951 FAX 559216698
The family Bordes make a point of welcoming their guests warmly. The house is situated in the peaceful, attractive countryside. Games are available in the garden. Breakfasts have to be seen to be believed. English spoken.
Near river Forest area
5 en suite (bth/shr) No smoking on premises TV available STV Full central heating Open parking available No children 10yrs Child discount available Languages spoken: English & Spanish
CARDS: Travellers cheques

BRUGES Pyrénées-Atlantiques

Les Buissonets (Prop: Mme M Bourghelle)
64800
☎ 559710824
Restored eighteenth century house. The rustic interior and antique furniture give the place a comfortable atmosphere. Superb panoramic view of the mountains and three-hectare grounds will ensure you spend a relaxing holiday. Unwind on the patio in summer, or by the large fireplace in winter. English spoken.
Near river Forest area
6 en suite (shr) (2 fmly) No smoking on premises Full central heating Open parking available Covered parking available Supervised Child discount available 6yrs Languages spoken: English
CARDS: Travellers cheques

CANCON Lot-et-Garonne

Chanteclair (Prop: M & Mme Larribeau)
47290
☎ 553016334 FAX 553411344
To be found at the edge of a large wooded park. The house dates back to the nineteenth century and offers large and comfortable rooms. A swimming pool is situated in the park. The hosts welcome their guests to dine with them. English spoken.
4 en suite (shr) (1 fmly) TV available Full central heating Open parking available Child discount available 12yrs Outdoor swimming pool Pool table Boule Bicycle rental Open terrace Languages spoken: English
CARDS: Travellers cheques

CHAMPAGNAC-DE-BELAIR Dordogne

Château de la Borie-Saulinier
24530
☎ 553542299 FAX 553085378
(from D939 exit at Brantôme and take rue de chez Ravilles for 3.5kms)

The owners will welcome you as a friend in this castle built during the 14th-15th centuries and located in the heart of the Perigord near Brantome. Bedrooms offer comfort, privacy and calm.
Near river Forest area
Closed Dec-Etr
5 en suite (bth/shr) (1 fmly) TV in 3 bedrooms Full central heating Open parking available Outdoor swimming pool Languages spoken: English
ROOMS: s 390FF; d 450-480FF

CHAPELLE-GONAGUET, LA Dordogne

Les Brunies (Prop: M & Mme Monzies)
24360
☎ 553047983
(take direction of Angoulème exit Périgneux, then direction of Ribérac, Pas de l'Anglais on right look out for chambre d' hôte sign)
Near river Near lake Forest area Near motorway
2 en suite (bth/shr) Some rooms in annexe (2 fmly) TV in 1 bedroom Licensed Full central heating Open parking available Covered parking available Supervised Child discount available Outdoor swimming pool (heated) Fishing Languages spoken: English
ROOMS: d 250-200FF Reductions over 1 night
MEALS: Full breakfast 50FF Continental breakfast 30FF Dinner 80-150FF

CIBOURE Pyrénées-Atlantiques

Villa Erresinolettean (Prop: Henry Chardiet)
4 rue de la Tour Bordagain *64500*
☎ 559478788 FAX 559472741
This Basque residence offers three rooms. Panoramic views over the Bay of St Jean de Luz. Calm and tranquillity assured. Beach and golf in close proximity. Spain is within eleven kilometres. Private swimming pool and barbecue.
Near sea Near motorway
3 en suite (bth/shr) (2 fmly) (1 with balcony) TV in all bedrooms Full central heating Open parking available Child discount available 2yrs Outdoor swimming pool
ROOMS: s 280FF; d 420FF Reductions over 1 night
CARDS: Travellers cheques

CLAIRAC Lot-et-Garonne

Caussinat (Prop: M & Mme Massias)
47320
☎ 553842211
Aimé and Gisèle Massias welcome you to their 17th-century château, furnished with antiques, set in a shaded park, with swimming pool and barbecue. Just two kilometres from the village of Clairac. Dinners available at the family table. River fishing, canoeing, tennis and walks all close by.
Near river
Closed Nov-Feb
5 rms (1 bth 2 shr) (1 fmly) Full central heating Open parking available Child discount available 12yrs Outdoor swimming pool Boule Bicycle rental Table tennis Languages spoken: Spanish
MEALS: Dinner fr 80FF*

DOMME Dordogne

Le Jaonnet Chambres d'Hôtes (Prop: M & Mme Holleis)
Liaubou-Bas, Nabirat *24250*
☎ 553295929 FAX 553295929
(from Sarlat take D704 south. Cross Dordogne River, after 2kms turn right onto D50, after 50m turn left and follow signs for Plan d'eau, towards Nabirat. Take 2nd turn left after Plan d'eau)

Spacious, comfortable accommodation in the heart of Perigord. Shady garden and sun terrace. Dinners are served in the galleried salon or in the courtyard on fine evenings. Meals are prepared by your host, a professional chef. Special gourmet breaks are available. Ideal base for touring, walking and cycling. Pleasant sandy, lakeside beach providing safe bathing. Sporting pursuits are all within a short distance. English spoken.

cont'd

Near river Near lake Near beach Forest area
Closed mid Oct-mid Nov
5 rms (2 bth 1 shr) (2 fmly) (1 with balcony) No smoking on
premises Full central heating Open parking available
Supervised Child discount available 8yrs Tennis Fishing
Riding Boule Bicycle rental Badminton Canoeing River
swimming V meals Last d 18.00hrs Languages spoken:
English, German & Italian
ROOMS: (incl. dinner) s 295-330FF; d 460-520FF
CARDS: Travellers cheques

DURAS Lot-et-Garonne

Savary (Prop: C J J Schaepman)
Baleyssagues *47120*
☎ 553837782 FAX 553837782
(from Sainte Foy-la-Grande take D708 to Duras, then D134 to
Baleyssagues. After bridge, in 2kms at crossroad follow sign
on right for Savary)
A farmhouse dating back to the twelfth century, renovated in
country style and set in beautiful countryside among
vineyards and plum orchards. The guest dining room features
an impressive open fireplace and breakfast can be taken there.
Dinners on request. Comfortable guests' living room leading
to a terrace with swimming pool. Several golf courses nearby.
Dutch proprietors.
Near lake
Closed 2 Oct-14 Apr
5 en suite (shr) (2 fmly) No smoking on premises Licensed
Full central heating Open parking available Outdoor
swimming pool Open terrace Table tennis Languages
spoken: English, Dutch & German
ROOMS: (room only) s 265FF; d 295FF *

GREZET-CAVAGNAN Lot-et-Garonne

Château de Malvirade (Prop: Cuvillier)
47250
☎ 553206131 FAX 553892561
(exit A62 signed Marmande)
Spacious, light, individually furnished rooms are available at
this fifteenth century château. All rooms overlook the 23
hectare park which surrounds the house. Swimming pool on
site. A quiet environment in which to find out more about the
history of the château and the region. Meals available on
request. English spoken.
Near lake Forest area
Closed 16 Oct-Mar
(1 fmly) No smoking on premises Full central heating Open
parking available Covered parking available Supervised
Outdoor swimming pool Languages spoken: English &
Spanish
CARDS: Travellers cheques

Domaine de Montfleuri (Prop: Dominique Barron)
47250
☎ 553206130
(from Marmande take D933 south towards Casteljaloux. At Le
Clavier turn right for Bouglon. Montfleuri is approx 1 mile
beyond Bouglon on left)
This beautiful eighteenth century house is situated on the top
of a sunny hill. In this unspoilt area, guests are offered a
panoramic view which cannot fail to please. The hosts look
forward to welcoming you to their spacious home with
comfortable rooms. Large garden with Roman swimming
pool, orchard, badminton and table-tennis. Dinners available
on request. English spoken.

Forest area Near motorway
4 rms (1 shr) (2 fmly) No smoking on premises Full central
heating Open parking available Covered parking available
Child discount available Outdoor swimming pool Boule
Bicycle rental Table tennis, Badminton V meals Languages
spoken: English
ROOMS: s 250FF; d 280-350FF
MEALS:
CARDS: Travellers cheques

HAUTEFORT Dordogne

L'Enclos (Prop: D & R Ornsteen)
Pragelier Tourtoirac *24390*
☎ 553511140 FAX 553503721
(from Perigueux NE on D5 to Tourtoirac, right onto D67 in 1m
take left to Pragelier)
Well restored 250 year old stone cottages on historic country
estate surrounded by tranquil countryside, yet only minutes
from stores and restaurants. L'Enclos is a virtual village in
itself, including the village bakery and chapel, which are
among the seven cottages overlooking terraced gardens filled
with roses, flowers and shrubs. The Manor House and
cottages are built in typical regional style around an attractive
courtyard.
Near river Forest area Near motorway
Closed mid Oct-Apr
7 en suite (bth/shr) (2 fmly) No smoking in all bedrooms
Open parking available No children 13yrs Outdoor
swimming pool Bicycle hire & riding nearby Languages
spoken: English, Italian & Spanish
ROOMS: (room only) s 300-350FF
MEALS: Continental breakfast 40FF

LAUSSOU, LE Lot-et-Garonne

Le Soubéyrac (Prop: Claude Rocca)
47150
☎ 553365137 FAX 553363520
Guests here find themselves in a lovely family home
surrounded by flowers. This is a haven of serenity and calm.
Jacuzzi available, body-wraps and essential oils. Swimming
pool with jet-stream. Table-tennis, walks through the forests,
bikes, piano and golf. English spoken.
Near river Forest area
5 en suite (bth/shr) (1 fmly) TV available Radio in rooms Full
central heating Open parking available No children 12yrs
Outdoor swimming pool Tennis Fishing Bicycle rental Table
tennis Last d 20.00hrs Languages spoken: English
MEALS: Dinner fr 130FF*

LAY-LAMIDOU Pyrénées-Atlantiques

Bed & Breakfast (Prop: Mme M-F Desbonnet)
64190
☎ 559660044
(exit A64 Bayonne-Toulous for Artix and take direction for
Navarrenx. At Navarrenx take D2 then D27)
Near river Forest area Near motorway
2 en suite (bth/shr) No smoking on premises TV in 1
bedroom Radio in rooms Full central heating Open parking
available Supervised Child discount available 12yrs Bicycle
rental V meals Languages spoken: English & Spanish
ROOMS: d 250FF Special breaks
MEALS: Dinner fr 80FF
CARDS: Travellers cheques

LEOGNAN Gironde

Gravelande (Prop: Yolande Bonnet)
7 chemin du Bergey *33850*
☎ 556647204
(in Bordeaux on the ring road, take exit 18b towards Leognan. On the square, take the D214 towards Cestas, 4th turn on right and 1st gate on left)
Old master's house, situated in parkland in the heart of the famous vineyards of Graves de Pessac-Léognan, just twenty minutes from the centre of Bordeaux. A warm welcome is offered by your hostess, Yolande Bonnet, to her two attractive, comfortable family guest rooms. An extra bed is available, with a small supplement payable. Golf within ten kilometres. Reductions for children. English spoken.
Near motorway
Closed mid Oct-mid May
2 en suite (bth/shr) No smoking on premises TV in 1 bedroom Radio in rooms Full central heating Open parking available Supervised Child discount available 12yrs
Languages spoken: English
ROOMS: s 280FF; d 350FF Reductions over 1 night Special breaks
CARDS: Travellers cheques

MONFLANQUIN Lot-et-Garonne

Domaine de Roquefère (Prop: M & Mme Semelier)
47150
☎ 553364374
M and Mme Semelier welcome you to their large building by a twelfth century chapel in the heart of the country. Swimming pool, living room with open fire. Quiet and solitude is assured. Vast choice of home-made food for breakfast. English spoken.
Forest area
6 en suite (bth/shr) (1 fmly) Full central heating Open parking available Supervised Child discount available 12yrs
Outdoor swimming pool Last d 20.30hrs Languages spoken: English, Italian, Portugese & Spanish
MEALS: Dinner fr 135FF*
CARDS: Travellers cheques

Manoir du Soubeyrac (Prop: M & Mme Rocca)
Le Laussou *47150*
☎ 553365134
Near river Forest area Near motorway
8 en suite (bth/shr) (1 fmly) TV in all bedrooms Radio in rooms Direct dial from all bedrooms Licensed Night porter Full central heating Open parking available Supervised No children 15yrs Outdoor swimming pool Fishing Riding Solarium Boule Jacuzzi/spa Bicycle rental Open terrace Covered terrace Table tennis,piano Last d 20.00hrs
Languages spoken: English
MEALS: Dinner 130-200FF*
CARDS: Travellers cheques

MONSÉGUR Gironde

Grand Boucaud (Prop: M & Mme Levy)
4 l'Aubrade, Rimons *33580*
☎ 565718857 FAX 565718857
The house of Dominique and Patrick Levy is situated in a sixteenth century farmhouse, built in the "gavache" style. Evening meals a speciality, although guests are welcome to dine elsewhere. Dominique specialises in haute cuisine and regional cooking and enjoys discussing cooking with the guests. Vegetarian meals available. English spoken.

Near river Near lake Forest area
Closed Oct-Dec
2 en suite (bth/shr) (1 fmly) No smoking on premises
Licensed Full central heating Open parking available
Covered parking available Child discount available 10yrs
Fishing Riding Boule Bicycle rental Open terrace V meals
Last d 22.00hrs Languages spoken: English & German
ROOMS: s 270FF; d 320FF
MEALS: Dinner 110-195FF*
CARDS: Travellers cheques

MONTAUT Pyrénées-Atlantiques

Bed & Breakfast (Prop: Mme Toussaint)
39 rue de Lassun *64800*
☎ 559719804
Two rooms are available in this large white house. Dining room and living room for the guest's use. Gardens to rear of the house with many attractive plants and trees. Beautiful view over the countryside towards the hills. Many delightful walks possible in the areas, plus trout fishing. A spot for relaxation and unwinding. English spoken.
Near river Forest area Near motorway
Closed Sep-Apr
2 en suite (bth/shr) TV available Radio in rooms Full central heating Open parking available Languages spoken: English & German

NOAILLAC Gironde

La Tuilerie (Prop: M & Mme Antoine Labord)
33190
☎ 5567100551 FAX 5567100551
(from A62 take exit 4 "La Reole", after the toll turn left & cross the motorway bridge. Take 1st left after bridge and follow signs for 3km. From Bazas/La Reole take direction A62 or Bazas (D9), turn left to village of Noaillac & follow signs)
In the heart of the famous Bordeaux wine areas, this senstively restored farmhouse provides a warm, relaxed atmosphere by its Anglo-French owners. Evening meals are served by an open log fire prepared by the chef-proprietor and wine enthusiast.
Forest area Near motorway
5 en suite (bth/shr) (1 fmly) Full central heating Open parking available Child discount available Fishing Boule Bicycle rental V meals Languages spoken: English, German & Spanish
ROOMS: s 220FF; d 280FF
MEALS: Lunch fr 100FF Dinner fr 100FF

PLAZAC Dordogne

Les Tilleuls (Prop: Donald Hamilton)
le Bourg *24580*
☎ 553508065 FAX 553598969
(from Perigeux take N89 towards Brive. At Niversac take turning to the right on D710; at les Versannes turn left on the D6 towards Rouffignac, go through Rouffignac and turn left at roundabout to Plazac)
'Les Tilleuls' was formerly the summer home of the Bishop of Perigueux in the Middle Ages. It has been sympathetically restored to provide simple but comfortable guest accommodation.

cont'd

Near river Near lake Near sea Forest area Near motorway
5 rms (3 bth/shr) (1 fmly) (1 with balcony) Open parking
available Child discount available Tennis Fishing Riding
Languages spoken: English
ROOMS: s 150FF; d 200-275FF
MEALS: Dinner 95FF
CARDS: Travellers cheques

PORT-DE-LANNE Landes

Au Masson (Prop: M & Mme Duret)
rte du Port *40300*
☎ 558891457
The Duret family welcomes you to their calm, relaxing home,
set in a lush park. Many exotic plants can be found here,
including bamboo and banana trees. A pond in the park
attracts many animals – sheep, ponies, ducks and even some
wild animals come to drink from it. Fishermen are invited to
try for the roach which swim in the pond.
Near river Forest area Near motorway
5 en suite (bth/shr) Open parking available Child discount
available Open terrace

ST-ANTOINE-DE-FICALBA Lot-et-Garonne

Pechon (Prop: M & Mme de Laneuville)
47340
☎ 553417159 FAX 553417159
(on N21 between Agen and Villenuve-sur-Lot)
Eighteenth century house with a tower in which you will find
a comfortable guest room which opens onto a terrace looking
over a vast park with pretty trees. Large dining room and
living room with billiard table available to guests. Situated just
outside the village, with attractive views and an aura of calm.
Your hosts look forward to welcoming you.
Near lake Forest area Near motorway
Closed 16 Nov-14 Mar
1 en suite (shr) (1 with balcony) TV available STV Radio in
rooms Full central heating Open parking available
Supervised
CARDS: Travellers cheques

ST-EMILION Gironde

Château Millaud-Montlabert
33330
☎ 557247185 FAX 557246278
(D243 to Saint-Emilion then D245 in the direction Pomerol for
300 metres)
The architecture of the house is in the typical 18th-century
style of the Gironde. Set amongst vineyards, it has been
entirely renovated and offers bedrooms with private
bathroom, a lounge with open fire-place, day-room with
library, clothes-washing facilities as well as a fridge on the
first floor for guests' use. The garden has a shaded terrace and
visitors will be able to sample the house's own wine, a Grand-
Cru Saint-Emilion.
Closed 15 Jan-15 Feb
5 en suite (bth/shr) No smoking on premises TV in all
bedrooms Full central heating Open parking available
ROOMS: d 300-320FF Reductions over 1 night
CARDS: ▨

Taking your mobile phone to France?
See page 11

ST-EUTROPE-DE-BORN Lot-et-Garonne

Moulin de Labique (Prop: Helene Boulet)
47210
☎ 553016390 FAX 553017317

Eighteenth century country house surrounded by sixty acres
of pasture, wooded hills and well-stocked ponds and rivers.
Your hosts offer a friendly welcome and provide comfortable
rooms containing antique furniture, paintings and engravings.
In the restaurant you can enjoy regional dishes, made with
fresh farm produce. Swimming pool. English spoken.
Near river Near lake Forest area
Closed Jan-Feb & late Nov
5 en suite (bth/shr) (2 fmly) (2 with balcony) Full central
heating Open parking available Supervised Child discount
available 9yrs Outdoor swimming pool V meals Last d
21.30hrs Languages spoken: English
ROOMS: s 290FF; d 460FF
MEALS: Dinner 45-190FFalc*
CARDS: ●● ▨ Travellers cheques

ST-JEAN-DE-LUZ Pyrénées-Atlantiques

Untza Xoko (Prop: Marie Diane Colas)
Chemin Ithurbidea *64500*
☎ 559268452 FAX 559224732
Near river Near sea Near beach Forest area Near motorway
Closed Aug
2 en suite (shr) TV available Radio in rooms Full central
heating Open parking available Child discount available
16yrs Languages spoken: English & Spanish

ST-LON-LES-MINES Landes

Château du Monbet (Prop: M & Mme H de Lataillade)
40300
☎ 558578068 FAX 558578929
(exit St-Geours-de-Maremne off A10 & A63 or exit
Peyrehorade A64)
A tree-lined walk leads up to this seventeenth century château
surrounded by a vast park. Two double rooms and one suite
are available all year round, with continental breakfast
included in the price. Quiet and relaxing location, but close to
tennis, golf, and riding centre. There are numerous
restaurants nearby. English spoken.
Forest area
4 en suite (bth/shr) Full central heating Open parking
available Supervised Boule Languages spoken: English
ROOMS: s 250-550FF; d 300-600FF Reductions over 1 night
CARDS: Travellers cheques

ST-PAUL-LIZONNE Dordogne

La Vieille Maison (Prop: M Marc Leclercq)
St Paul-Lizonne *24320*
☎ 553916131
(South from Angouleme towards Riberac, North of Bergerac.
The hotel is in a village on the road from Riberac to St
Severin)
Very pretty building with panoramic terrace where breakfast,
lunch and dinner are served. Swimming at nearby Lake
Jamaye, which has pretty coves and fine sandy beaches. In
close proximity to the village with its charming Roman
church, golf course, tennis courts and bike hire. Dinner
combines international dishes with local fare. Home-made
soups and patés served. New open air swimming pool.
English spoken.
Near river Near lake Forest area
Closed Nov-Etr
12 en suite (bth/shr) (5 fmly) (4 with balcony) No smoking on
premises Full central heating Open parking available Child
discount available Outdoor swimming pool Tennis Fishing
Riding Boule Bicycle rental V meals Last d 22.00hrs
Languages spoken: English & Dutch
ROOMS: (room only) d 280-350FF Reductions over 1 night
MEALS: Lunch 45-75FF Dinner 65-175FF&alc*
CARDS: 💳 📷 💳 📷 Travellers cheques

ST-PÉE-SUR-NIVELLE Pyrénées-Atlantiques

Bidachuna (Prop: M Ormazabal)
rte Oihan Bidea *64310*
☎ 559545622 FAX 559473447
(from A63 at Bayonne take D3 to D'Arcangues then on to St
Pee-sur-Nivelle)
This nineteenth century country farm is situated at the edge of
a forest just six kilometres from the village. The rooms have
exposed beams and are decorated in Basque style. You will
enjoy exploring the Basque region from this base. Croquet
available. English spoken.
Near lake Forest area
3 en suite (bth/shr) No smoking on premises TV available
Full central heating Open parking available Croquet
Languages spoken: English & Spanish
CARDS: Travellers cheques

ST-QUENTIN-DE-BARON Gironde

Le Prieure (Prop: M & Mme de Castilho)
33750
☎ 557241675 FAX 557241380
(from Bordeaux take the D936 towards Bergerac, continue
straight through St Quentin de Baron look for K24 kilometre
marker, continue for 1km at K25 marker take rural road to the
right and follow round to left)
This twelfth century converted priory welcomes visitors who
will enjoy the beautiful setting, view and pool of this five acre
property. The atmosphere is informal and welcoming. A three
bedroom house also available. One hour from the beach.
Aromatherapy and natural healing offered. English spoken.
Near river Forest area Near motorway
5 rms (2 bth/shr) (1 fmly) (2 with balcony) No smoking on
premises Full central heating Open parking available
Outdoor swimming pool Boule Covered terrace Languages
spoken: English, Portuguese & Spanish

TABANAC Gironde

Château Sentout (Prop: M Gerald Peltier)
33550
☎ 556218577 FAX 556787095
(from Paris, exit A10 junct 1, just after junct 45 (direction
Bayonne/Toulouse) at junct 22 (direction Latresne/Cadillac)
follow D113 and D10 toward Cadillac after Baurech, take 1st
left follow blue signs 'Ch Sentout'. But, not as far as Tabanac)
Situated above the Garonne Valley, this magnificent 17th-
century château has been painstakingly restored to provide
five holiday houses offering accommodation of a very high
standard. The château is surrounded by forty acres of
grounds, so each house has its own garden area. All are
tastefully decorated and two rooms are also available in the
château. Superb swimming pool, table-tennis, badminton and
boules. Bicycles. Tennis nearby. Wine-tasting trips can be
arranged by your hosts.
Near river Near lake Forest area Near motorway
16 en suite (bth/shr) (6 fmly) TV available Open parking
available Outdoor swimming pool (heated) Tennis Fishing
Riding Boule Bicycle rental Badminton Table tennis
Languages spoken: English, German & Spanish
ROOMS: (room only) s 446FF; d 446FF Reductions over 1
night Special breaks
CARDS: 💳 💳 Travellers cheques

URRUGNE Pyrénées-Atlantiques

Château d'Urtubie
64122
☎ 559543115 FAX 559546251
Near sea Forest area Near motorway
6 rms (4 bth 1 shr) Full central heating Open parking
available Child discount available Languages spoken: English
& Spanish
CARDS: 📷 💳

VENDOIRE Dordogne

Le Bouchaud (Prop: M Andre Durieux)
24320
☎ 553910082
Pierrette and André Durieux are happy to welcome you to
their home and will enjoy telling you the history of the region.
Guest rooms are available on the ground floor, with a view
over the countryside. Peace and quiet assured. Dinner served
with hosts and other guests, featuring regional cuisine and
vegetables from the garden.
Near river Forest area
3 en suite (bth/shr) (1 fmly) Radio in rooms Full central
heating Open parking available Child discount available 7yrs
Fishing V meals
ROOMS: d fr 180FF *

VERTEILLAC Dordogne

La Bernerie (Prop: Tom & Patricia Carruthers)
Boureilles St-Sebastien *24320*
☎ 553915140 FAX 553910859
(at Angouleme head for Perigueux, after 200kms turn right. In
Verteillac opposite church, on sharp corner take right turn
D97, in 100m fork left to Bouteilles at cross roads turn left, in
village last house)

cont'd

Four bedrooms available, one of which is in a small cottage with self-contained kitchen, lounge and television. All have independent access plus terrace with garden furniture. Three/four days courses offered on the food and wine of Périgord, including wine with dinner and transport to different locations. Swimming pool and tennis court available. Fixed price dinner. English hosts. No children under sixteen.
Near river Near lake Forest area
Closed Nov-Apr
4 en suite (bth/shr) 1 rooms in annexe (3 with balcony) No smoking in 3 bedrooms Full central heating Open parking available Supervised No children 16yrs Outdoor swimming pool Boule Bicycle rental Languages spoken: English
ROOMS: s 300-350FF; d 400-450FF Reductions over 1 night
CARDS: Travellers cheques

VILLARS Dordogne

L'Enclos (Prop: M & Mme Rubbens)
Lavergne 24530
☎ 553548217 FAX 553548217
The Rubbens family look forward to welcoming guests to their home, which is a charming mill with four rooms, in the heart of the lush, green Périgord region. Heated swimming pool, with patio and tennis courts. Horse-riding, solarium, table-tennis, pétanque and bike hire nearby. English spoken.
Near river Near lake Forest area
Closed Oct-end Mar
4 en suite (bth/shr) Open parking available Outdoor swimming pool (heated) Tennis Solarium Bicycle rental Open terrace Table tennis Languages spoken: English, German & Spanish

VILLENEUVE-SUR-LOT Lot-et-Garonne

Domaine de Clavie Soubirous (Prop: M Marc Disgrens)
47300
☎ 553417430 FAX 553417750
Situated in an unspoilt area of Cévennes, in a small hamlet, this old renovated farmhouse overlooks the valley. Meals featuring local specialities can be arranged on request. In close proximity can be found river bathing, horse-riding, tennis, and a swimming pool. English spoken.
Near river Near lake Near sea Forest area In town centre
6 en suite (bth/shr) TV available Full central heating Open parking available Covered parking available Outdoor swimming pool V meals Languages spoken: English
MEALS: Dinner 165FF*

Les Huguets (Prop: M & Mme Edward Poppe)
47300
☎ 553704934 FAX 553704934
Near river Near lake Forest area Near motorway
5 en suite (bth/shr) (3 fmly) (1 with balcony) No smoking in all bedrooms TV available Full central heating Open parking available Covered parking available Child discount available 10yrs Outdoor swimming pool Tennis Riding Sauna Boule Bicycle rental Open terrace Last d 18.00hrs Languages spoken: English, Dutch & German
CARDS: Travellers cheques

VILLÉREAL Lot-et-Garonne

Colombie (Prop: M Pannetier)
Dévillac 47210
☎ 553366234 FAX 553360479
(on D272 between Monflanquin and Monpazier)
This property is owned by a pig farmer and has views of the castle of Biron. The rooms are situated in a stone house of great character. Individual access is available to each room, and there is a living room for the use of all guests. The garden can be used for picnics. Private swimming pool and also a sandpit for children. English spoken.
Forest area
2 en suite (shr) Full central heating Open parking available Child discount available Outdoor swimming pool Languages spoken: English
ROOMS: s 230-250FF; d 260-280FF
CARDS: Travellers cheques

AQUITAINE

The French Beret

The traditional French beret originated from Béarn and was part of the traditional costume of the Ossau Valley as early as the middle ages. Traditionally, the beret was worn from breakfast until bedtime and was even occasionally used as a purse. It was the mark of a man and a means of identifying him as a Béarnais. The door of the 13th-century church at Bellocq has a beret on it. Today the beret is worn by thousands,

Does the beret aid contemplation? Perhaps this citizen can provide the answer.

many having no idea of its origin, save that it came from France. Two local companies export the beret worldwide and it remains a local symbol as well as being a practical or fashionable hat for both men and women.

Périgord: a treasure trove of prehistoric sites

Périgord is home to a treasure trove of caves and sites and almost half the cave paintings found in France. Both the topography and climate of the Vézère valley in particular suited prehistoric man providing food and natural shelters in abundance. So it was here that much enterprise and development took place. The largest wall-painting representing aurochs known in Europe can be found at the caves of Lascaux as well as beautiful paintings of bulls and horses. The cave at Villars is home to a blue horse, whilst mammoths can be found on the ceiling of Rouffignac cave. The cave-dwelling fortress at the Roque St Christophe near Le Moustier is also worth a visit, as are wonderful caves full of stalagmites and stalactites at Les Eyzies and the chasm of Proumeyssac at Audrix.

Midi-Pyrénées

Midi-Pyrénées is a region of rich culture and natural beauty just waiting to be discovered. This is the place to enjoy some of the many colourful and traditional festivals which sometimes involve whole départements or just a village or town. Appreciate too the wonderful choice of music festivals staged throughout the year that offer something for every taste from local folk singing through to sacred music or jazz. Standing on the banks of the Garonne River, Toulouse is a lively city where the arts and modern technology live comfortably side by side amongst the characteristic squares and streets.

(Top): The beautiful village of Calvignac stands atop a vertical rock face above the river. The Tour de Gourdon has secret dungeons and a fine Renaissance gallery.

(Bottom): French bread - famous the world over for its freshness and flavour.

ESSENTIAL FACTS

DÉPARTEMENTS:	Ariège, Aveyron, Haute-Garonne, Gers, Lot, Tarn, Tarn-et-Garonne, Hautes-Pyrénées
PRINCIPAL TOWNS	Albi, Castres, Foix, Lourdes, Montauban, Tarbes, Toulouse, Millau
PLACES TO VISIT:	Archeological sites at La Graufenesque & Montmaurin; Beaulieu-en-Rouergue Abbey; Castles at Assier, Castelnau-Bretenoux & Gramont; Carmelite Chapel at Toulouse; boyhood home of Marshal Foch at Tarbes; Bagnères-de-Bigorre, a spa town since Roman times; the National Stud at Tarbes with their beautiful Anglo-Arabs; the pilgrimage town of Lourdes.
REGIONAL TOURIST OFFICE	54 boulevard de l'Embouchure, BP2166, 31022 Toulouse Tel 0561 13 55 55 Fax 05 61 47 1716
LOCAL GASTRONOMIC DELIGHTS	Cassoulet, a casserole of white haricot beans with a selection of fresh pork, smoked pork or garlic sausages, bacon, preserved goose or duck; foie gras, goose liver pâté; magret de canard; cabecou, small cheeses; croustades, small pies containing meat, game or poultry, often deep-fried.
DRINKS	Armagnac

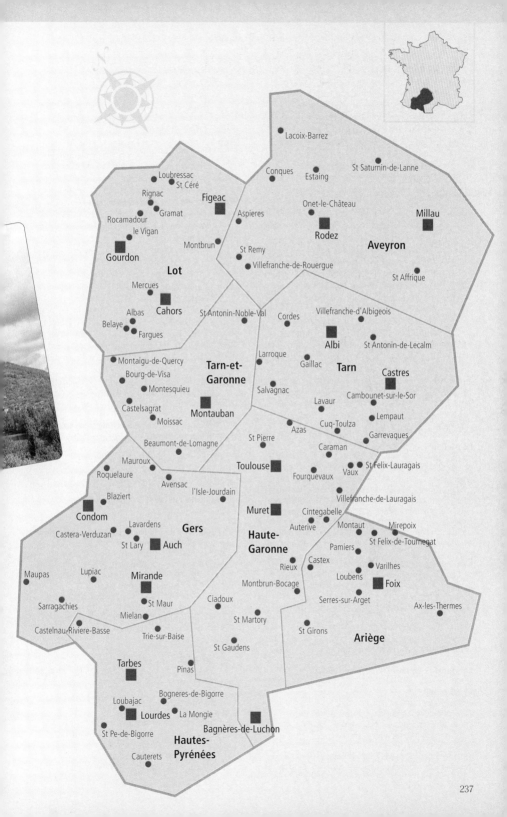

Lacoix-Barrez

Conques • Estaing • • St Saturnin-de-Lanne

Loubressac • St Céré
Rignac • Figeac
Gramat
Rocamadour • Aspieres
le Vigan • Onet-le-Château
Montbrun • Rodez
Gourdon • St Remy
Lot • Villefranche-de-Rouergue

Millau

Aveyron

St Affrique

Mercues
Albas • **Cahors**
Belaye
Fargues • St Antonin-Noble-Val • Cordes • Villefranche-d'Albigeois
Albi • St Antonin-de-Lecalm
Montaigu-de-Quercy • Larroque
Bourg-de-Visa • **Tarn-et-** Gaillac **Tarn**
Montesquieu • **Garonne** • Castres
Castelsagrat • Salvagnac • Cambounet-sur-le-Sor
Montauban • Lavaur • Lempaut
Moissac • Cuq-Toulza • Garrevaques
Beaumont-de-Lomagne • Azas •
Mauroux • St Pierre • Caraman
Roquelaure • **Toulouse** • St Felix-Lauragais
Avensac • Fourquevaux • Vaux
Blaziert • l'Isle-Jourdain • Villefranche-de-Lauragais
Condom • **Muret** • Cintegabelle
Lavardens • **Gers** • Auterive • Montaut • Mirepoix
Castera-Verduzan • **Haute-** • St Felix-de-Tournegat
St Lary • **Auch** • **Garonne** • Pamiers
Maupas • Lupiac • Rieux • Castex • Varilhes
Mirande • Montbrun-Bocage • Loubens • **Foix**
Sarragachies • St Maur • Ciadoux • Serres-sur-Arget • Ax-les-Thermes
Mielan • St Martory
Castelnau-Riviere-Basse • Trie-sur-Baise • St Gaudens • St Girons • **Ariège**
Tarbes • Pinas
Bogneres-de-Bigorre
Loubajac • **Lourdes** • La Mongie
St Pe-de-Bigorre • Bagnères-de-Luchon
Cauterets • **Hautes-** **Pyrénées**

EVENTS & FESTIVALS

Mar Lourdes International Festival of Sacred Music; Toulouse International Fair; St-Félix Lauragais Cocagne Traditional Fair;

Apr Albi Jazz Festival; Tarbes French Song Festival; Auterive Medieval Festival

May Toulouse International Children's Theatre Festival; Montauban French Song Festival; Festival at Condom; Haute-Garonne Département Poilus Rally for pre-1914 cars; Bourg St Bernard 'Pré de la Fadaise' Traditional Celebration

June Auch Classical Music Festival; Cahors Spring Festival; Villefranche-de-Rouergue European Festival Gramont Music Festival in the Castle; Vic Fezensac Whit Sunday Feria; Comminges Thermal Spa Rally for cycle-cars between 1914-1935; Toulouse Grand Férétra Festival

Jul Foix Medieval Pageant; Moissac Musical Evenings in the Abbey; Puylaurens Summer Festival; Saujac Light & Sound Show; St-Girons Folklore & Dance Festival; Germ-Louron Jazz Festival; St-Félix Lauragais Classical & Traditional Music Festival; Toulouse Summer Festival; Mirande Country Music Festival; Gourdon Summer Festival (classical & jazz); Jazz Festivals at Luz-St-Sauveur, Souillac & Montauban; Sylvanès

Sacred Music Festival; Castres Goya Festival Galvarnie Theatre Festival; Tarbres Equestria; Montréal-du-Gers Festival; St-Lizier Classical Music Festival; Cordes Festival of the Great Falconer; Lisle sur Tarn Wine Festival; Mirepoix Medieval Festival

Aug Moissac Musical Evenings in the Abbey; St Félix Lauragais Classical & Traditional Music Festival; Toulouse Summer Festival; Sylvanès Sacred Music Festival (*music, dance, theatre*); Gourdon Summer Festival (classical & jazz); Mirepoix International Puppet Festival; Capvern les Bains Latin American Festival; Assier Festival (theatre, music, attractions); Aveyron Département Folklore Festival; Vaour Comedy Festival; Fleurance Festival of the Heavens; Marciac Jazz Festival; Hauts-Pyrénées Département 'On the paths to Santiago de Compostela'; St-Paul Cap de Joux Historical Festival; Wine Festivals at Gaillac & Madiran; Trie sur- Baïse Pourcailhade (pig) Festival; Sauveterre-du-Rouergue Festival of Light; Peyrusse-le-Roc Medieval Festival;

Sep Toulouse Jacobin Piano Festival; Cordes Gastronomic Festival; Moissac Chasselas Grape Festival;

Oct Auch Festival of Contemporary Music & Dance; Toulouse Jazz Festival

---

ALBAS Lot

La Meline (Prop: N & E Vos)
rte de Sauzet D37 *46140*
☎ 565369725 FAX 565369725
(from Cahors take D911 towards Lot. In Castlefranc turn left onto D8 towards Albas, then take D37 towards Sauzet for 4km) Situated on a hillside in the Lot Valley, with beautiful views over forests and the Cahors vineyards, La Meline offers its guests a peaceful and relaxing stay. Cycling and walking tours, and visits to farms and the vineyards are added attractions.
Near river Forest area
Closed Oct-Mar
3 en suite (bth/shr) TV in all bedrooms STV Full central heating Open parking available Child discount available Boule Bicycle rental Last d 20.00hrs Languages spoken: English, Dutch & German
ROOMS: s 190FF; d 275FF
MEALS: Dinner 110FF
CARDS: Travellers cheques

ASPRIÈRES Aveyron

Le Mas de Clamouze (Prop: Serge Maurel)
12700
☎ 565638989
Idyllic spot for vacations. The Rouergue is a protected area and this farm will enable you to rediscover the simple pleasures of life. Evening meals available. English spoken.
Near river Forest area Near motorway
Closed Oct-Apr
5 en suite (shr) (3 fmly) Full central heating Open parking available Covered parking available Supervised No children

3yrs Child discount available 6yrs Languages spoken: English German & Italian
MEALS: Dinner 90FF*
CARDS: Travellers cheques

AUTERIVE Haute-Garonne

Les Murailles (Prop: M & Mme Tourniant)
rte de Grazac *31190*
☎ 561507698
Hélène and Philippe Tourniant are pleased to invite guests to the warm atmosphere of their terracotta grange. The furnishings are comfortable and the decoration is reminiscent of England. Here you can discover the cuisine of the Midi-Pyrénées, with fresh farm produce and simple but delicious cooking. A little English spoken.
Near river Near lake Forest area Near motorway
4 rms (3 shr) No smoking on premises Full central heating Open parking available Covered parking available Supervised Child discount available 7yrs Boule Table tennis Languages spoken: English
MEALS: Dinner 95-155FF*
CARDS: ⬤ 🟦 🟥 🔲 Travellers cheques

AVENSAC Gers

La Chavinière (Prop: T Morel)
32120
☎ 562650343 FAX 562650323
(on A62 Bordeaux/Toulouse motorway take exit 9 for Castelsarrasin in the direction of Auch, 10km after Beaumont de Lomagne on D928 turn right for Avensac)
Exquisite château dating back to the 18th-century, surrounded

by park and countryside. Guests are welcomed as friends in this family home. After a day riding or walking in the country, relax with your hosts over afternoon tea to discuss the history of the region. The art of dining and gourmet cuisine is a passion of the family Morel. Private swimming pool. Special themed weekend breaks by arrangement. English spoken.
Near river Near lake Forest area
Closed Nov-30 Apr
5 en suite (bth/shr) (2 fmly) No smoking on premises TV in 1 bedroom Radio in rooms Full central heating Open parking available Child discount available 10yrs Outdoor swimming pool Fishing Languages spoken: English & Spanish
ROOMS: (room only) d 350-750FF Reductions over 1 night
MEALS: Full breakfast 40FF Dinner 140FF
CARDS: ●● ▉▉ Travellers cheques

AZAS Haute-Garonne

En Tristan (Prop: Gerard & Chantal Zabé)
31380
☎ 561849488
(from Toulouse on the A68 exit 3 Montastruc, after Montastruc on N88 turn right towards Lavaur D30 in 4m turn left to Azas and follow signs)
This renovated farmhouse is set among fields approximately 2kms from the village, and on fine days you may have views of the Pyrénées. There are four large bedrooms all with private bathroom & wc, three double rooms, and one triple and a sitting area is available on the landing with books and stereo.
Near river Near lake Forest area Near motorway
4 en suite (bth/shr) (1 fmly) Full central heating Open parking available Covered parking available Child discount available 14yrs Boule Bicycle rental Last d 18.00hrs
Languages spoken: English
ROOMS: s 230FF; d 250FF
MEALS: Dinner fr 75FF
CARDS: Travellers cheques

BEAUMONT-DE-LOMAGNE Tarn-et-Garonne

L'Arbre d'Or (Prop: Tony Ellard)
16 rue Déspéyrous *82500*
☎ 563653234 FAX 563652985
(A62 Bordeaux/Toulouse, exit Castelsarrasin, Beaumont de Lomagne is on the D928 between Montauban/Auch)
Nestling in the beautiful Gascon countryside lies the ancient Bastide town of Beaumont de Lomagne, with a population of just 3,800. Elegant rooms are waiting for you at this superb seventeenth century house. Enjoy a relaxing stay in the tree-shaded garden, and sample the excellent Gascon cuisine at the family table. Confirm in advance if you wish to dine. Weekends catered for at special rates. English hosts.
Near river Near lake Forest area In town centre Near motorway
6 rms (5 bth/shr) (1 fmly) Radio in rooms Full central heating Open parking available Covered parking available (charged) Child discount available 10yrs V meals Last d 20.00hrs
Languages spoken: English
ROOMS: s 110-230FF; d 220-290FF Reductions over 1 night
MEALS: Dinner 100FF
CARDS: Travellers cheques

BELAYE Lot

Marliac (Prop: Veronique Stroobant)
46140
☎ 565369550
Near river Near lake Forest area

6 en suite (bth/shr) (2 fmly) No smoking in 1 bedroom Open parking available Child discount available 12yrs Outdoor swimming pool Table tennis Languages spoken: English, Dutch & Italian
MEALS: Dinner 100-120FF*
CARDS: Travellers cheques

BLAZIERT Gers

La Bajonne (Prop: Mme Ingrid D'Aloia)
32100
☎ 562682709
Four rooms are set apart from the owner's home but another room is in the main house, which is a restored building in the small hamlet of La Bajonne. The house is surrounded by a large garden, and many of the rooms are furnished with antiques. Swimming pool on site, Golf and tennis nearby. English spoken.
Forest area
4 en suite (bth/shr) Full central heating Open parking available Child discount available 12yrs Outdoor swimming pool Languages spoken: English, German & Italian

BOURG-DE-VISA Tarn-et-Garonne

Le Marquise (Prop: M & Mme Doi)
Brassac *82190*
☎ 563942516
Gilbert & Michèle Dio invite you to their farm, where all meals are cooked with fresh farm produce. The Dio family will help you rediscover the simple things in life: good traditional food, private fishing, fresh air and exercise. Tennis and golf nearby.
Near river Forest area
4 en suite (shr) Full central heating Open parking available Child discount available 10yrs
CARDS: Travellers cheques

CAMBOUNET-SUR-LE-SOR Tarn

Château de la Serre
81580
☎ 563717573 FAX 563717606
(situated 15km west of Castres via N126 & D4)

An impressive castle dating from 16th and 19th century, set in 270 acres of parkland, facing the Black Mountains. The castle is full of stunning historical features and furniture with bedrooms romantically decorated in genuine classic style.
Near river Near lake Forest area

cont'd

6 rms (3 bth) (2 fmly) Full central heating Open parking
available Child discount available 12yrs Outdoor swimming
pool Boule Languages spoken: English & Spanish
ROOMS: s 250-600FF
MEALS: Dinner 120-200FF

CARAMAN Haute-Garonne

Le Croisillat (Prop: Guerin)
Château du Croisillat *31460*
☎ 561831009 FAX 561833011
The Château de Croissillat, destroyed in the 16th century
during the Religious Wars, but since renovated, is a splendid
place to stay. Illuminated swimming pool set in the grounds.
Dining room, reception rooms, magnificent bedrooms.
English spoken.
Near river Near lake Near sea Forest area In town centre
Closed Nov-Mar
6 rms (3 bth 2 shr) (1 fmly) Open parking available Indoor
swimming pool Languages spoken: English
CARDS: Travellers cheques

CASTELNAU-RIVIÈRE-BASSE Hautes-Pyrénées

Châateau du Tail (Prop: Claude Bolac)
65700
☎ 562319375
(on the D935 Tarbes/Bordeaux.Village centre)
Claudie and Xavier welcome you to their home, where you
will be served a large continental breakfast. Private swimming
pool. Dinner available with your hosts. Reductions for
children under ten years old. English spoken.
Near river Near lake Forest area Near motorway
5 rms (4 bth/shr) (1 fmly) No smoking on premises Full
central heating Open parking available Covered parking
available Child discount available 10yrs Outdoor swimming
pool Boule Bicycle rental Table tennis Last d 20.00hrs
Languages spoken: English, German & Spanish
ROOMS: s fr 280FF; d fr 300FF
MEALS: Dinner fr 100FF

Flânerie (Prop: J L Guyot)
Hameau du Mazères *657003*
☎ 562319056 FAX 562319288
(from Maubourguet take D935 north.Turn right to Mazeres.
Flânerie is behind the church)
Situated in the Armagnac region is this large and welcoming
farm, where the bedrooms all have open fires. Your host,
Jean-Louis, has been accompanying ramblers on their walks
for twenty years. Riding, wine-tasting and many other
activities on offer in this peaceful area. English spoken.
Near river Near lake Forest area
3 en suite (bth/shr) (2 fmly) TV in 1 bedroom Full central
heating Open parking available Child discount available
12yrs Bicycle rental Boules Table tennis V meals Languages
spoken: English & German
ROOMS: d fr 250FF Reductions over 1 night Special breaks
MEALS: Dinner fr 85FF

CASTELSAGRAT Tarn-et-Garonne

Le Castel (Prop: Danielle Jonqua-Clement)
82400
☎ 563942055 FAX 563942055
(from Agen towards Puymirol and Bourg-de-Visa then
Moissac; from Castelsarrasin-Moissac towards Bourg-de-Visa;

from Valence d'Argen towards Cahors and after Lalande turn
left onto D46)
Danielle and Georges Clement have great pleasure in
welcoming you to their home at Castelsagrat. Originally, the
house was the hunting lodge of the Château of Plombis. In
1984, the restoration of this fine residence began, which
included the building of a gourmet restaurant. English
spoken.
3 en suite (bth/shr) (1 fmly) TV in 1 bedroom STV Open
parking available Covered parking available Child discount
available 13yrs Indoor swimming pool V meals Last d
18.00hrs Languages spoken: English
ROOMS: d 350-500FF Reductions over 1 night Special breaks
MEALS: Dinner fr 150FF

CASTERA-VERDUZAN Gers

Sonnard (Prop: M Guiraud)
32410
☎ 562681539 FAX 562681047
This restored Gascon farmhouse features a large open fire in
the dining room. Country air, wide-open spaces, and good
food all guarantee a relaxing holiday. English spoken.
Near river Near lake Near sea
6 en suite (bth/shr) (3 fmly) Full central heating Open
parking available Child discount available Languages
spoken: English & Italian
ROOMS: s 180FF; d 260FF Special breaks
MEALS: Lunch fr 70FF Dinner fr 100FF
CARDS: Travellers cheques

CASTEX Ariège

Manzac d'En Bas (Prop: Hopkins)
09350
☎ 561698525 FAX 561698525
(leave Daumazan in the direction of Foix & take D19 to Castex
and Lézat, after 2km turn right,after 600m turn left, Manzac
d'en Bas is 200m up the hill on the left)
This is a small bed & breakfast run by an English family in a
large house once used by a local landower. There is a
wonderful southern view over the Pyrénées. The house is set
in the midst of quiet, rolling countryside. Guests will breathe a
sigh of relaxation as they arrive for their holiday. Walking,
relaxation, pony-trekking, lakes, spas, golf, tennis and skiing
are all available in this area.
Near lake Forest area Near motorway
3 rms (1 shr) (2 fmly) Full central heating Open parking
available Child discount available Outdoor swimming pool
Languages spoken: English
ROOMS: s 140-150FF; d 180-200FF Reductions over 1 night
CARDS: Travellers cheques

CIADOUX Haute-Garonne

Le Manoir de la Rivière (Prop: Inge Roehrig)
31350
☎ 561881088 FAX 561881088
A romantic old manor house tucked away in woods beside a
stream, at the foot of the Pyrénées. Individually furnished,
spacious rooms. Continental breakfast served,and dinner
available by arrangement. Fishing, bike rides, riding, French
courses - on site. Possibility of golf, swimming, tennis, rafting,
canoeing, skiing. English spoken.

Near river Near lake Forest area Near motorway
4 rms (3 bth/shr) (1 with balcony) TV available STV Full
central heating Open parking available Covered parking
available Child discount available 12yrs Riding V meals
Languages spoken: English & German
ROOMS: s fr 280FF; d fr 260FF * Special breaks
MEALS: Dinner 80-100FF*

CINTEGABELLE Haute-Garonne

Serres d'en Bas (Prop: P & M J Deschamps-Chevrel)
rte de Nailloux *31550*
☎ 561084111 FAX 561084111
(Toulouse take direction of Foix on the N20)
Renovated farm, offering well-decorated rooms with views of
the Pyrénées. Convivial surroundings in which to spend a
relaxing holiday. Living room with fireplace. Dinner available.
Forest area
5 en suite (bth/shr) No smoking on premises Full central
heating Open parking available Child discount available
Outdoor swimming pool Tennis Table tennis V meals
Last d 20.00hrs Languages spoken: Spanish
ROOMS: s 230-250FF; d 230-250FF Reductions over 1 night
MEALS: Dinner 90-140FF

CORDES Tarn

Les Tuileries (Prop: Christian Rondel)
81170
☎ 563560593
(from Toulouse take N88 towards Albi. At Gaillac take D922 to
Cordes. In Cordes follow directions for parking(P1 & P2).
Approx 700m from car park)
This 200 year old property is situated in the heart of the
countryside at Cordes, with an exceptional view of the walled
town of Cathares. Rooms are quiet, comfortable and spacious.
Farm produce available at the dinner table, together with
other specialities of the house. Gastronomic menu on request.
Meals served in the garden in fine weather, in the shade of the
chestnut trees. Many leisure pursuits are available nearby.
English spoken.
Near river Forest area
5 en suite (shr) (2 fmly) Full central heating Open parking
available Covered parking available Supervised Child
discount available 12yrs Outdoor swimming pool Boule
Languages spoken: English
ROOMS: s 230FF; d 260FF
MEALS: Dinner 95FF
CARDS: Travellers cheques

ESTAING Aveyron

Bed & Breakfast (Prop: M A Alazard)
Cervel, rte de Vinnac *12190*
☎ 565650989 FAX 565650989
(from Rodez take D988 to Bozouls then D920 to Espalion.
From here continue on D920 to Estaing)
This ancient farm is situated on the side of a hill in the Lot
Valley. Guests are welcome to dine with the proprietors and
enjoy gourmet foods prepared with fresh farm and garden
produce. Living room reserved for guests, with open fire.
Library, piano, games, patio and T.V. French breakfast served.
Near river
Closed 15 Nov-1 Apr
4 en suite (shr) (2 fmly) No smoking on premises TV in all
bedrooms Full central heating Open parking available Child
discount available 10yrs Last d 19.30hrs
ROOMS: d 440FF Reductions over 1 night Special breaks
CARDS: Travellers cheques

FABAS Ariège

Estivades de Peyre (Prop: Rosina de Peira)
Peyré *09230*
☎ 561964016 FAX 561964236
(from Toulouse in the direction Tarbes, leave N117 at exit for
Cazère follow the D6 into Ste Croix-Volvestre from village turn
onto D35 Fabas in approx 4km)
Meals are taken with the family.
Forest area
12 rms (6 shr) No smoking on premises Open parking available
Child discount available 6yrs Outdoor swimming pool
ROOMS: s 160FF; d 250FF
MEALS: Lunch 95FF Dinner 95FF
CARDS: 💳

FARGUES Lot

Mondounet (Prop: Peter James Scott)
46800
☎ 565369632 FAX 565318489
(D656 towards Tournon, passing Villeseque, Sauzet and Bovila
take third turning left to Mondounet - signposted)
This charming seventeenth century farmhouse, built from
champagne coloured stone, overlooks a valley in a beautiful
setting. Lots of character, including the original fireplace and
oak beams. The lounge/dining room has views over the valley.
The garden terrace has a barbecue and garden furniture, and
there are also garden games and a heated salt-water
swimming pool. B&B and self-catering apartments available.
English hosts.
Near river Near lake Near beach Forest area
11 rms (9 bth/shr) (4 fmly) Full central heating Open parking
available Supervised Child discount available 10yrs Outdoor
swimming pool (heated) Fishing Boule Open terrace Table
tennis Badminton Languages spoken: English
ROOMS: s 140-190FF; d 250-300FF

FIGEAC Lot

Liffernet Grange (Prop: M & Mme Nielson de Lamothe)
46100
☎ 565346976 FAX 565500624
(from Figeac centre take N140 towards Rodez &
Decazeville.After 3kms turn left onto D2 to Montredon and
right on to D210 towards Lunan. Signposted from main road)
cont'd

Five miles from the pretty medieval town of Figeac is the country home of Anthony and Dominique Nielson. They have tastefully restored their large nineteenth-century barn to provide six spacious and comfortable en suite guest bedrooms. Antique furniture and oak floorboards complement the candlelit regional dinners that are accompanied by music. This is an ideal base for visiting the famous sites of Lot.
Near river Near lake Forest area Near motorway
Closed 1 Oct-31 Mar
6 en suite (bth/shr) (2 fmly) (1 with balcony) TV in all bedrooms Radio in rooms Open parking available Supervised No children 10yrs Outdoor swimming pool Tennis Fishing Riding Boule Bicycle rental Canoeing Kayaking Last d 20.30hrs Languages spoken: English, German & Spanish
ROOMS: s 250-300FF; d 350FF Special breaks: 'Stock a cellar' Wine Week
MEALS: Dinner 125FF
CARDS: ▨

FOURQUEVAUX Haute-Garonne

Château de Fourquevaux (Prop: .ierre Faux)
rue J-P Laurens *31450*
☎ 562717103 FAX 561272439
The Château de Fourquevaux is one of those buildings you dream of staying in. This sixteenth century château is surrounded by a large park. Orangery, large dining-rooms, regal bedrooms, living room, piano and library available for all sorts of occasions, including weddings! English spoken.
6 en suite (shr) Full central heating Open parking available Supervised Child discount available 10yrs Languages spoken: English & Spanish
CARDS: Travellers cheques

GAILLAC Tarn

Bed & Breakfast (Prop: Mme Lucile Pinon)
8 pl St-Michel *81600*
☎ 563576148 FAX 563410656
(from centre of Gaillac follow directions for Lavaur.House by river 'Le Tarn' as you leave the village)
Near river Forest area In town centre Near motorway
6 en suite (bth/shr) Full central heating Open parking available Supervised Child discount available 10yrs Languages spoken: English
ROOMS: s 220FF; d 240FF
CARDS: Travellers cheques

Mas de Sudre (Prop: Richmond Brown)
81600
☎ 563410132 FAX 563410132
(from Gaillac take D999 towards Montauban for 2kms to Ste-Cécile-d'Aves and turn right onto D18 towards Castelnau-de-Montmiral. Straight ahead for 2kms and left onto D4 towards Téoulet, straight ahead for 1.5kms and first left to house)
Near river Near lake Forest area Near motorway
5 en suite (bth/shr) 2 rooms in annexe Licensed Full central heating Open parking available Child discount available Outdoor swimming pool Bicycle rental Open terrace Last d 20.00hrs Languages spoken: English
CARDS: Travellers cheques

GARREVAQUES Tarn

Château de Garrevaques (Prop: Marie-Christine Combes)
81700
☎ 563750454 FAX 563702644
(from Revel city on D1 to Caramon, opposite police station onto D79 to Garrevaques. Cross the village, château at the end on the right)
The château was built in the 15th century and refurbished in the 19th century. Guests are welcomed by the fifteenth generation living in this castle. Attractive bedrooms with furniture of the period and today's modern comforts.
Near river Near lake Forest area Near motorway
8 en suite (bth/shr) Full central heating Open parking available Covered parking available Child discount available 12yrs Outdoor swimming pool Tennis Boule Open terrace V meals Languages spoken: English & Spanish
ROOMS: s 500FF; d 600FF Reductions over 1 night
MEALS: Lunch 100FF Dinner 150FF
CARDS: ▨ ▨ Travellers cheques

GRAMAT Lot

Le Gravier (Prop: Lydia & Patrice Ravet)
46500
☎ 565334188 FAX 565334188
(at Gramat take road to Figeac, just out of the village near Fina petrol stationturn at 1st road just before passing behind petrol station. House in 800m, signposted)
Typical farmhouse of the region only 1.5km from Gramat. Regional dishes are served at evening meals with most of the ingredients coming from the farm and garden.
5 en suite (shr) (2 fmly) No smoking on premises Full central heating Open parking available Child discount available 3yrs Boule Last d 20.00hrs Languages spoken: English & Italian
ROOMS: s 180FF; d 220-240FF
MEALS: Dinner 85FF

Moulin de Fresquet (Prop: M & Mme Ramelot)
46500
☎ 565387060 FAX 565387060
(at Gramat take N140 towards Figeac, then after 500 metres turn Left into a small lane that leads to Mill)
This charming, authentic water mill dates back to the seventeenth century and is situated in a three hectare park, with a private stretch of water running through it. The mill is decorated with tapestries, antique furniture, pictures and stained-glass windows. Exposed beams feature in each room. Five bed & breakfast rooms are offered by your hosts, M and Mme Ramelot. Dinner is served in the evening, comprising of five courses of traditional cuisine of the Quercy-Périgord region. A little English spoken.

Near river Forest area
Closed Nov-Mar
5 en suite (shr) No smoking in all bedrooms Open parking
available No children 5yrs Fishing Boule Open terrace
Covered terrace Languages spoken: English
Rooms: s 240FF; d 270-390FF
Meals: Dinner 110FF
Cards: Travellers cheques

LACROIX-BARREZ Aveyron

Vilherols (Prop: Laurens)
12600
☎ 565660824 FAX 565661998
Near river Near lake Forest area Near motorway
4 en suite (shr) (1 fmly) (1 with balcony) TV in 1 bedroom
Open parking available Child discount available Languages
spoken: English
Cards: Travellers cheques

LARRA Haute-Garonne

Château de Larra (Prop: Baronne de Carriere)
31330
☎ 561826251
Forest area
Closed 16 Nov-14 Apr
8 rms (4 bth/shr) Open parking available Supervised Child
discount available 7yrs Languages spoken: English
Meals: Dinner 120FF*

LARROQUE Tarn

Meilhouret (Prop: Christian Jouard)
81140
☎ 563331118
Near river Near lake Forest area
RS 15 Oct-Mar
2 en suite (bth/shr) No smoking in 1 bedroom Full central
heating Covered parking available Supervised Outdoor
swimming pool Languages spoken: English
Meals: Dinner 90FF*

LAVARDENS Gers

Mascara (Prop: Roger Hugon)
32360
☎ 562645217 FAX 562645833
4 en suite (bth/shr) (1 with balcony) Full central heating
Open parking available Covered parking available
Supervised Child discount available 9yrs Outdoor swimming
pool Languages spoken: English, German & Italian
Meals: Dinner 120-190FF*

LAVAUR Tarn

Le Cottage (Prop: Mme Y Ronjat-Valero)
Castex-Giroussens *81500*
☎ 563416372
Forest area
3 en suite (bth/shr) (1 fmly) No smoking on premises Radio
in rooms Full central heating Open parking available
Supervised Child discount available 7yrs Outdoor swimming
pool V meals Last d 19.00hrs Languages spoken: English &
Spain

LEMPAUT Tarn

Villa "Les Pins" (Prop: M & Mme Delbreil)
81700
☎ 563755101
(on the D12, leave N126 between Puylaurens/Soual or leave
D622 between Revel/Soual)
Magnificent views over the Black Mountains, set in a green
and lush area, This Italian-style villa was built at the turn of
the century and has since been lovingly restored. The rooms
are comfortable, the largest having a balcony. Breakfast and
dinner served on the patio. English spoken.
Near river Near lake Near sea Forest area
Closed 16 Oct-Apr
7 en suite (bth/shr) (1 fmly) (1 with balcony) Full central
heating Open parking available Child discount available
12yrs Fishing Boule Table tennis V meals Languages
spoken: English
Rooms: s 180-300FF; d 300-450FF
Meals: Dinner fr 130FFalc

LOUBAJAC Hautes-Pyrénées

Bed & Breakfast
28 rte de Bartres *65100*
☎ 562944417 FAX 562423858
Situated on a farm, in a rustic setting, six rooms are on offer in
a tranquil environment. Breakfasts and other meals are
prepared using farm produce. The farm is full of character and
has a splendid view of the Pyrénées. Lourdes is just four
kilometres away. Large garden with swings and slide.
Near river Near lake Forest area Near motorway
6 en suite (bth/shr) (4 fmly) (2 with balcony) Full central
heating Open parking available Child discount available 3yrs
Last d 20.00hrs
Meals: Dinner 70FF*
Cards: Travellers cheques

LOUBENS Ariège

Château de Loubens (Prop: Le Long)
09120
☎ 561053841 FAX 561053061

This château was built at the end of the Hundred Years War in
1450. During the French Revolution the château was restored,
and one of the stones on the roof of the tower doorway is
engraved with the date 1796. Lovely terrace with tables and
chairs in the six hectare garden. Dinners by reservation, with
superb varied menus. Rooms are spacious and full of
character. English spoken.
cont'd

Forest area
Closed Nov-Mar
3 en suite (bth/shr) No smoking on premises Full central
heating Open parking available Child discount available
10yrs Boule Badminton Croquet Languages spoken: English,
Portugese & Spanish
ROOMS: s 300FF; d 350FF
MEALS: Dinner 150FF

LOUBRESSAC Lot

Château de Gamot (Prop: M & Mme Belieres)
46130
☎ 565109203 FAX 565385850
This château has two turrets, one round and one square,
adding character to the property. The original round tower
has an attractive stairway, which dates back to the 15th or 16th
century. The square tower was added in the 17th century. The
house is surrounded by a beautiful park in the heart of the
Quercy region. Swimming pool: June to September.
Near river Forest area
Closed Oct-14 Apr
4 en suite (bth/shr) No smoking on premises Full central
heating Open parking available Outdoor swimming pool

LUPIAC Gers

Domaine de Hongrie (Prop: Jacqueline Gillet)
32290
☎ 562065958 FAX 562644193
This property is situated in Lupiac, a tiny village with just 350
inhabitants, and dates back to the 12th century. It may be
named for the Hungarian pilgrims for whom it was a stopover
point on route to St Jacques de Compostelle. Three
independently styled rooms available in a calm setting.
Dinners available by reservation only. English spoken.
Near lake Forest area
Closed Jan-Mar
3 en suite (bth/shr) Full central heating Open parking
available Child discount available 6yrs Languages spoken:
English
CARDS: ●● ▦

MAUPAS Gers

Le Pouy (Prop: M & Mme Ducasse)
32240
☎ 562090807 562096068
A renovated 17th-century building surrounded by eucalyptus
trees. Four guest rooms available. You are invited to try local
specialities at midday and in the evening. English spoken.
Near river Forest area
Closed 2 Nov-Mar
4 en suite (bth/shr) No smoking on premises Full central
heating Air conditioning in bedrooms Open parking
available Covered parking available Supervised Child
discount available 10yrs Outdoor swimming pool Play area
Last d 21.00hrs Languages spoken: English, German & Spanish

MAUROUX Gers

La Ferme d'Encarion (Prop: Lidy Van Wijk-Bentum)
32380
☎ 562663441 FAX 562663441
(5kms from St Clar. Follow signs for camping 'Les Roches'
between St Clar and Goudonville, from 'Les Roches' there are
signposts for Encarion)

A traditional stonebuilt farmhouse, in the rolling hills of the
Gers, a yet undiscovered area. 'Encarion' offers three newly
renovated luxury rooms with bathroom annexe. Surrounding
the property is a six hectare park, containing the remains of a
medieval hamlet, an ideal walking and birdwatching area.
Forest area
Closed Oct-14 Apr
3 en suite (bth/shr) Open parking available No children 4yrs
Child discount available 6yrs Outdoor swimming pool Boule
Languages spoken: English & German
ROOMS: d 200-240FF
MEALS: Dinner 100FF
CARDS: ●● ▦

La Ferme des Étoiles (Prop: M & Mme Monflier)
Le Cormeillon *32380*
☎ 562664683 FAX 562663296
(from the highway, exit number 8, direction Saint-Clar)

This old restored farm, situated in the country, offers five
guest rooms. Whether you come alone, with family, or with
friends, you will enjoy a taste of the charm and warmth of the
welcome. In a setting overlooking the Pyrénées, only the
sound of crickets, frogs and birds can be heard in this
peaceful environment. Famous astrophysicist, Hubert Reeves,
visits often and introduced the idea of encouraging visitors
who are keen on astronomy for specialist stays. Swimming
pool. English spoken.
Forest area Near motorway
Closed Dec-Mar
6 rms (5 bth/shr) (2 fmly) Full central heating Open parking
available Child discount available 12yrs Outdoor swimming
pool Library Languages spoken: English, German, Italian,
Portuguese & Spanish
ROOMS: s 160-195FF; d 220-260FF Special breaks
MEALS: Dinner 90-140FF

MERCUÈS Lot

Le Mas Azemar (Prop: Claude Patrolin)
46090
☎ 565309685 FAX 565309685
(Mercues is on the D911)
18th-century manor house with parks, outhouses and a
swimming pool. The house is situated at one end of the
Cahors vineyards. Meals can be taken with your hosts, who
use only local produce. While you're in the area, why not
sample the local Cahors 'vin noir'. English spoken.
Near river Forest area
6 en suite (bth/shr) Full central heating Open parking
available Supervised No children 6yrs Outdoor swimming
pool (heated) Languages spoken: English
ROOMS: d 360-430FF Reductions over 1 night
MEALS: Lunch 130-180FF
CARDS: Travellers cheques

MIÉLAN Gers

La Tannerie (Prop: B & C Bryson)
32170
☎ 562676262 FAX 562676262
(40km southwest of Auch on N21, in Miélan turn right after
the church)
Four spacious rooms are on offer in this 19th-century house,
situated on the top of a hill with a panoramic view of the
Pyrénées. Living room with television. La Tannerie is well
placed for visits up the Pyrénées (one hour), Lourdes (45
minutes) but particularly for the Gascogne region with its
attractive scenery and great cuisine. English spoken.
Near lake Forest area Near motorway
Closed Dec-Feb
4 en suite (bth) (1 fmly) Full central heating Open parking
available No children 5yrs Languages spoken: English &
Spanish
ROOMS: s 200FF; d 265-285FF

MILLAU Aveyron

Bed & Breakfast (Prop: M & Mme Decroix)
8 ave J-Cambetorte-Creissels *12100*
☎ 565612515
The villa of the Decroix family is situated on the outskirts of
Millau. Panoramic view and total quiet. The rooms all have
independent entrances which lead out into garden. The large
breakfast, which includes home-made cakes and jams, are
served in the garden. Olympic-sized swimming pool nearby
plus canoeing, fishing, walks, climbing and potholing. A little
English spoken.
Near river Forest area In town centre
Closed Oct-May
2 rms (1 shr) Open parking available Covered parking
available No children 2yrs Open terrace Covered terrace

MONTAIGU-DE-QUERCY Tarn-et-Garonne

Les Chênes de Ste-Croix (Prop: M & Mme Hunt)
82150
☎ 563953078 FAX 563953078
(5kms SE of Montaigu-de-Quercy on D2)
Your English hosts offer six rooms in a 250 year old stone
farmhouse, with shaded lawns, woodland and a swimming
pool. The house is set well back from the road, in a quiet
country area, but you will be within easy reach of a small
town, with market, restaurants and shops. Ten percent

reduction for one week and for children under ten.
Near lake
6 en suite (shr) 1 rooms in annexe (2 fmly) Full central
heating Open parking available Covered parking available
Child discount available 10yrs Outdoor swimming pool Boule
Bicycle rental Open terrace Languages spoken: English
ROOMS: s fr 175FF; d fr 230FF
MEALS: Dinner fr 70FF

MONTBRUN Lot

La Bastide de Caillac (Prop: M & Mme Jughon)
46160
☎ 565406529 FAX 565406961
(from Cajarc by the Lot Valley: D662, 7km Montbrun & 2km
Caillac, pass Restaurant la ferme de Montbrun. La Bastide is
150m along on left)
The Jughon home is typical of properties in the Quercy region
with outhouses and a south-facing aspect. It has been lovingly
restored by the current owners. Two rooms are available and
they offer comfort and solitude in a delightful part of the Lot
Valley. Large, heated swimming pool. Visitors are able to relax
here. A little English spoken.
Near river
2 en suite (shr) (2 with balcony) No smoking on premises TV
in 1 bedroom STV Full central heating Open parking
available Covered parking available No children Outdoor
swimming pool Languages spoken: English & Spanish
ROOMS: s 530-630FF; d 530-630FF Reductions over 1 night
MEALS: Lunch 100-120FF Dinner 100-120FF
CARDS: Travellers cheques

MONTBRUN-BOCAGE Haute-Garonne

Hameau de Pavé (Prop: Mme Josette Parinaud)
31310
☎ 561981125
(from Toulouse towards St Gaudens on N117 as far as
Carbonne, then left as far as Daumazan via Montesquieu-
Volvestre (D627 & D628). Turn right until Montbrun-Bocage
and farm further 5kms on right)
Near river Near lake Forest area
4 en suite (shr) (2 fmly) Full central heating Open parking
available Child discount available 10yrs
CARDS: Travellers cheques

MONTESQUIEU Tarn-et-Garonne

La Bayssé (Prop: M & Mme Delente)
82200
☎ 563045400
(at Moissac, take the D957 for Cohors - at the Laufol crossrds,
take D16 for Dufort-Locapelette and follow signs)
'La Baysee' is situated on the Santiago de Compostella
pilgrimage route, amidst vineyards and orchards. Each room
in this gabled house has a view of the pleasant and well-kept
garden where guests are invited to relax - deckchairs
provided! A gravel path leads the guests to individual front
doors. You may dine with your hosts by prior arrangement.
Near river Forest area Near motorway
4 en suite (bth/shr) No smoking in all bedrooms Full central
heating Open parking available Supervised Child discount
available Outdoor swimming pool Bicycle rental V meals
Languages spoken: English
cont'd

ROOMS: s 270FF; d 300-330FF Reductions over 1 night
Special breaks
MEALS: Dinner fr 110FF
CARDS: Travellers cheques

ONET-LE-CHÂTEAU Aveyron

Domaine de Vialatelle (Prop: Patrick & Anne David)
12850
☎ 565427656 FAX 565427656
(from Rodez D988 take direction of Aurillac in 2km turn right
for St-Mayme (D224) Vialatelle is on the left)

The David family invite you to an 18th-century hamlet, which
has been completely restored, set in the grounds of a ten
hectare park. The exposed stonework dates from the
Renaissance period. A range of activities is on offer in the
park: horse-riding, cycling, jogging, or there is a swimming
pool on site. English spoken.
Near river Forest area Near motorway
11 en suite (bth/shr) (4 fmly) TV in 6 bedrooms Full central
heating Open parking available Child discount available
10yrs Outdoor swimming pool Riding Boule Bicycle rental
V meals Last d 21.30hrs Languages spoken: English, Italian &
Spanish
ROOMS: s 235-360FF; d 265-420FF Reductions over 1 night
Special breaks
MEALS: Lunch 98-140FF Dinner 98-140FF&alc
CARDS: ● ▩ Travellers cheques

PINAS Hautes-Pyrénées

Domaine de Jean Pierre (Prop: Mme Marie Colombier)
24 route de Villeneuve *65300*
☎ 562981508 FAX 562981508
(5km East of Lanneluegaue on the N117. At Pinas church, take
the D158 for Villeneuve. The house is 800m up on the right-
follow signs)
Attractive 19th-century building, situated at the foot of the
Pyrénées on the plateau of Lannemezan. The rooms are quiet
and comfortable and look out over the wooded park. Antique
furniture in all the rooms. Living room, television, music,
piano and library for the use of guests. Breakfast is served on
the terrace in fine weather. English spoken.
Near river Forest area Near motorway
3 en suite (bth) (2 fmly) No smoking on premises Full central
heating Open parking available Supervised Languages
spoken: English & Spanish
ROOMS: s 210FF; d 250FF

RIGNAC Lot

Chambres d'Hôte à Darnis (Prop: Lillian Bell)
46500
☎ 565336684 FAX 565337131
(at Alvignac, take the D673 to Padirac. Just before the 'Grill de
Berger' turn right and follow the 'Chambre d'hôte' signs to
Pouch.)
Restored farmhouse set in a tiny hamlet only seven kilometres
from Rocamadour, one of the most famous pilgrimage
destinations in Christendom. Evening meals are served.
English hosts.
Near river Forest area Near motorway
3 en suite (bth/shr) (1 fmly) Child discount available 10yrs
Outdoor swimming pool Bicycle rental Tennis and boules
nearby Languages spoken: English
ROOMS: s 185FF; d 220-250FF Special breaks

ROQUELAURE Gers

En Boutan (Prop: Jeanne and Jean Dauzere)
32810
☎ 562655466 FAX 562655122
The proprietors' home is a large traditional house in the
Gasconne, situated in a park which spans several hectares and
which boasts many century-old oak trees. Traditional
breakfasts made from farm produce are served. Private lake,
leisure area, mini-golf, bikes, mopeds and billiards available
on-site. English spoken.
Forest area
Closed Nov-Etr
3 en suite (shr) (1 fmly) TV available Full central heating
Open parking available Covered parking available
Supervised Child discount available 10yrs Languages spoken:
English & Spanish
MEALS: Dinner 100FF&alc*

ST-ANTONIN-DE-LACALM Tarn

La Ginestarie (Prop: C H Teotski)
81120
☎ 563455346
(at Albi take direction for Réalmont-Castres and at Réalmont
direction for "Lac de La Bancalie", house signposted)
Chantal and Dragan Teotski welcome you to their restored
farm beside Lac Bancalié, in a region between mountains and
woods. They offer rooms which are spacious and comfortable.
You are invited to take meals at the family table. A large
central fireplace and wood panelling add to the charm of this
property. You will enjoy discovering the cheeses of this region.
Near river Near lake Near sea Near beach Forest area
3 en suite (bth/shr) (3 fmly) No smoking on premises Full
central heating Open parking available Supervised Child
discount available 8yrs V meals Last d 18.00hrs
MEALS: Dinner fr 85FF*
CARDS: Travellers cheques

ST-ANTONIN-NOBLE-VAL Tarn-et-Garonne

La Residence (Prop: Sean O'Shea)
rue Droite *82140*
☎ 563682160 FAX 563682160
(via A20 or N20 exit at Caussade take D929 towards
Septdonds, just before Septdonds take D5 towards St-
Antonin-Noble-Val, La Residence is in the centre of town
signposted)
Situated in the beautiful Aveyron Gorge in the centre of the

12th-century market town of St Antonin Noble Val. The property has been lovingly restored by its owners to create an atmosphere of luxury, style and relaxation making it an ideal location from which the whole family can enjoy this fascinating area of south west France.
Near river Forest area In town centre Near motorway
5 en suite (bth) (5 fmly) No smoking on premises Full central heating Open parking available Outdoor swimming pool (heated) Tennis Fishing Riding Boule Bicycle rental Last d 9pm Languages spoken: English
ROOMS: d 300-450FF Special breaks: fishing/painting/sport
MEALS: Dinner fr 120FF*
CARDS: Travellers cheques

ST-FÉLIX-DE-TOURNEGAT Ariège

Domaine de Montagnac (Prop: M & Mme Bertolino)
09500
☎ 561687275 FAX 561674484
Family home with a warm, friendly atmosphere in a traditional country house with home-made cooking. Swimming pool on-site. Wonderful views of the Pyrénées. English spoken.
Forest area
18 rms (4 bth 10 shr) Open parking available Child discount available 14yrs Outdoor swimming pool Riding Boule Bicycle rental Open terrace Languages spoken: English & Italian
MEALS: Lunch 90FF Dinner 100FF*
CARDS: Travellers cheques

ST-GIRONS Ariège

Le Relais d'Encaussé (Prop: H Kawczynski)
09200
☎ 561660580
(1km from St Girons, on the hill to Sauech.)
This 17th-century farmhouse is situated one kilometre from the village, in a tranquil location. Kitchen and dining room for guests use. Meals available by reservation at a fixed price, including drinks. Table-tennis. English spoken.
Forest area
5 rms (2 bth 2 shr) (1 fmly) Full central heating Open parking available Child discount available 10yrs Table tennis Billiards Last d 20.00hrs Languages spoken: English
ROOMS: s 115FF; d 230FF
MEALS: Full breakfast 25FF Dinner fr 80FF

ST-MARTORY Haute-Garonne

Domaine de Menaut (Prop: Mme Gabrielle Jander)
Auzas *31360*
☎ 561902151
This property is surrounded by park, in a forest area of some 90 hectares. All rooms, including the large lounge and dining room, have tiled floors. There is a terrace where meals can be served, which is shaded by oak trees. Good food on-site but many restaurants within five or six kilometres. Fishing, bathing, games, forest walks. English spoken.
Near river Near lake Near sea Near beach Forest area Near motorway
3 en suite (bth/shr) Supervised Languages spoken: English & German
CARDS: Travellers cheques

ST-MAUR Gers

Noailles (Prop: Louis et Marthe Sabathier)
32300
☎ 562675798
Accommodation on a farm raising capons and cattle in the Saint-Maur region. Dayroom with kitchenette, eating area and games area available to guests. Picnics a possibility on the terrace. Fishing on-site. Lakes, tennis courts and Gascon restaurants in close proximity. English spoken.
Near river Near lake Near sea Near beach Forest area Near motorway
Closed Jan-Apr
4 en suite (shr) (3 fmly) (2 with balcony) Open parking available Child discount available 12yrs Fishing Boule
ROOMS: d 220FF
CARDS: ● ▩

ST-PÉ-DE-BIGORRE Hautes-Pyrénées

Le Grand Cedre (Prop: M Christian Peters)
6 rue de Barry *65270*
☎ 562418204 FAX 562418585

18th-century manor house, situated just fifty metres from a twelfth century church in a leafy park with many trees. Evening meals available and served either in the dining room or outside, beneath the cedars. All rooms have their own exit onto the garden. Piano, guitars and organ available for the musically minded. Computer courses available. Swimming and tennis within 200 metres. English spoken.
Near river Near lake Forest area In town centre Near motorway
4 en suite (bth/shr) (1 fmly) (4 with balcony) TV in all bedrooms Full central heating Open parking available Child discount available Outdoor swimming pool Last d 19.00hrs Languages spoken: English, German, Italian & Spanish
ROOMS: d 300-320FF Reductions over 1 night
MEALS: Dinner 130-130FF

ST-PIERRE Haute-Garonne

Château de St-Martin (Prop: M Georges Maury)
31590
☎ 561357157 FAX 561747113
This magnificent 18th-century château is set in the midst of four hectares of parkland, only half an hour from Toulouse. Large reception rooms with antique furniture, and library with tapestries on the walls. Orangery which leads off from the courtyard. Children over fourteen only please, but reductions for them up to the age of eighteen. English spoken.

cont'd

Forest area
Closed Nov-Apr
Full central heating Open parking available No children
14yrs Child discount available 18yrs Languages spoken:
English & Spanish
CARDS: Travellers cheques

ST-RÉMY Aveyron

Mas de Jouas (Prop: Pierre Salvage)
Villefranche-de-Rouergue *12200*
☎ 565816472 FAX 565815070
Attractive residence offering six guest rooms. Steps lead down
from the terrace to the swimming pool and sun-loungers. Play
area for children. The property looks out onto a parkland,
fields and trees. Well-equipped kitchen for the guests.
Continental breakfast served. Meals can be taken on the
terrace, which is well-lit in the evenings. Children under three
go free. English spoken.
Near river Forest area Near motorway
Closed Oct-Apr
6 en suite (bth) (1 fmly) (3 with balcony) TV available STV
Full central heating Open parking available Child discount
available Languages spoken: English & Spanish

ST-SATURNIN-DE-LENNE Aveyron

Château St-Saturnin (Prop: Cliff & Victoria Lenton)
12560
☎ 565703600 FAX 565703619
Forest area
Closed 5 Jan-1 Apr
12 en suite (bth/shr) (2 with balcony) TV in all bedrooms
Licensed Full central heating Open parking available
Supervised Child discount available Outdoor swimming pool
(heated) Tennis Boule Bicycle rental Open terrace Covered
terrace Last q 20.30hrs Languages spoken: English
MEALS: Continental breakfast 35FF Dinner 175-200FF*
CARDS: ●● ▩ ▨

SALVAGNAC Tarn

Moulin de Trusse La Sauzière St Jean (Prop: Alain
Joly)
La Sauzière St-Jean *81630*
☎ 563405024 FAX 563335712
(from Toulouse take N20 for Montauban, then D8 as far as
Monclar de Quercy. Follow the signs for Moulin de Trusse)
Your hosts welcome you to their 18th-century home and hope
you will enjoy your stay in carefully restored stables next to
the house. Both buildings are close to a lake with weeping
willows along its bank. Dinner available at a fixed price.
English spoken.
Near river Near lake Forest area
Closed Nov-Etr
3 en suite (shr) Full central heating Open parking available
Supervised No children 10yrs Child discount available 18yrs
Fishing Languages spoken: English, German & Italian
MEALS: Dinner 100FF*
CARDS: Travellers cheques

SARRAGACHIES Gers

La Buscasse (Prop: M & Mme Abadie)
32400
☎ 562697607 FAX 562697917
The owners of this château extend a warm welcome to their

guests. This old house looks out over the Pyrénées, with a
large park nearby. Guests are invited to dine with their hosts -
all meals cooked from fresh farm produce. Reservations
needed. Tennis, swimming, canoeing, fishing, all close by.
English spoken.
Forest area
3 en suite (bth/shr) TV available Radio in rooms Full central
heating Open parking available Child discount available
Boule Bicycle rental Badminton Croquet V meals
Languages spoken: English
ROOMS: s 210FF; d 250FF
MEALS: Dinner 90FF
CARDS: Travellers cheques

SERRES-SUR-ARGET Ariège

Le Poulsieu (Prop: Jenny et Bob Brogneaux)
09000
☎ 561027772 FAX 561027772
(from Foix take D17 in the direction of Col de Marrous after
10km at La Mouline to the left then follow signs for chambre
d'hote)
This property is situated in open countryside surrounded by
woods with a superb view over the mountains. Continental
breakfast served and meals available in the evening by
reservation. Swimming pool, trout river, horses and mountain
walks on-site. Tennis within five kilometres. Medieval festivals
at nearby Foix during July and August. English spoken.
Near river Forest area
Closed 15 Nov-15 Mar
4 en suite (shr) (1 fmly) No smoking in all bedrooms Full
central heating Open parking available Supervised Child
discount available 8yrs Outdoor swimming pool Languages
spoken: English Dutch German & Spanish
ROOMS: s 180FF; d 220FF Special breaks
MEALS: Dinner fr 70FF
CARDS: Travellers cheques

TRIE-SUR-BAŒSE Hautes-Pyrénées

Jouandassou (Prop: M & Mme Collinson)
65220
☎ 562356443 FAX 562356613
(from town take D939 towards Auch/Mirande for 1km then
turn left at 'Chambre d'Hôtes' sign. Establishment first house
on left)
Calm, comfort and good hospitality are offered at this 18th-
century coaching inn in southern Gascony. Tastefully restored
by its Anglo-French owners, the rooms are individually
decorated to a high standard. Lounge/dining room available
to guests. Private swimming pool, table-tennis and mountain
bike rental in the grounds. Fishing in nearby lakes, with golf
within twenty minutes by car. Evening meals available
featuring regional specialities. English spoken.
Near river Near lake Forest area Near motorway
4 en suite (shr) No smoking in all bedrooms TV available Full
central heating Open parking available Supervised Child
discount available 12yrs Outdoor swimming pool Tennis
Boule Bicycle rental Table tennis Badminton Languages
spoken: English, German, Italian & Spanish
ROOMS: s 280FF; d 320FF
MEALS: Dinner 100FF
CARDS: Travellers cheques

VARILHES Ariège

Las Rives (Prop: M & Mme Baudeigne)
09120
☎ 561607342 FAX 561607876
Manor house set in the middle of a park. French breakfast
served. Leisure room and library, table-tennis, swimming pool
and games all ensure a pleasant stay. Non-smoking policy.
Free stays for children under two years. English spoken.
Near river Forest area
4 rms (3 shr) (1 fmly) No smoking on premises Open parking
available Supervised Child discount available 2 yrs Outdoor
swimming pool Tennis table tennis, park for children
Languages spoken: English & Spanish
CARDS: Travellers cheques

VAUX Haute-Garonne

Mazière de Sers (Prop: M & Mme de Kermel)
31540
☎ 561838777
From October to May the Lauragais region, an attractive part
of the Massif Central, at the foot of the Montagne Noir, is a
haven of peace and tranquillity. Your hosts welcome you to
this very old farm, full of character, which is situated in one
hectare of shaded parkland. Swimming pool and table-tennis
available to guests. Breakfast will be served in the dining
room or on the terrace.
Near river Near lake
2 en suite (bth/shr) TV available Radio in rooms Child
discount available 10yrs Outdoor swimming pool Open
terrace

VIGAN, LE Lot

Manoir La Barrière (Prop: Michel Auffret)
46300
☎ 565414073 FAX 565414020

Your hosts welcome you to this 13th-century manor house
which offers private external access to each room, decorated
and furnished with taste. Tennis, swimming, fishing, riding
and golf nearby. Dinners available on request. Situated in
parkland, in the heart of the Périgord-Quercy region.
Near river Near lake Forest area
Closed Nov-Etr
6 en suite (bth/shr) Open parking available Child discount
available 10yrs Outdoor swimming pool Fishing
ROOMS: s 300-350FF; d 350-400FF
MEALS: Dinner fr 150FF
CARDS: Travellers cheques

VILLEFRANCHE-D'ALBIGEOIS Tarn

La Barthe (Prop: Michele Wise)
81430
☎ 563559621 FAX 563559621
(from Albi take D999 to Millau. Keep going through
Villefranche d'Albigeois until you get to La Croix Blanche.
Turn left on D163, follow signs for Chambres d'Hotes.)
A peaceful stay in the heart of the Tarn region is offered by
your English hosts, Michael and Michele Wise. The
accommodation is set in the hills overlooking the River Tarn
and the valley. Part of a small farming community, the house is
about 150 years old. Mountain bikes available on loan. There is
a small swimming pool on site and walks, canoeing and
kayaking are all available nearby. Peace and quiet all year
round, where the guests can be as active or as lazy as they
wish. Telephone to check availability of rooms.
Forest area
3 rms (2 bth/shr) No smoking on premises Full central
heating Open parking available Covered parking available
Child discount available 7yrs Outdoor swimming pool Boule
Bicycle rental V meals Last d 15.00hrs Languages spoken:
English
ROOMS: s 180FF; d 210FF
MEALS: Dinner 60-90FF*
CARDS: Travellers cheques

VILLEFRANCHE-DE-LAURAGAIS Haute-Garonne

Château du Mauremont (Prop: M & Mme de Rigaud)
31290
☎ 561816438 FAX 561816438
12th to 13th-century château situated 25 kilometres from
Toulouse. On the first floor you are offered superb rooms
furnished with antiques. Each has an impressive view over the
Lauragais Plain and the Pyrénées. Ideal location for those who
enjoy walking. Living area available to guests. Very large
swimming pool on-site; tennis and riding one kilometre away.
Family breakfast served, incorporating home-made produce.
English spoken.
Near lake Forest area Near motorway
4 en suite (bth) (4 fmly) No smoking on premises Full central
heating Open parking available Child discount available 6yrs
Outdoor swimming pool Tennis Languages spoken: English
& Spanish

VILLEFRANCHE-DE-ROUERGUE Aveyron

Le Mas de Comte (Prop: Agnes Jayr)
Les Pesquies *12200*
☎ 565811648
The upper floor of this house is reserved for guests, and a
separate entrance is available which comes out into a
courtyard where the barbecue may be used. Kitchen and
living room for the use of guests. Children under five stay
free. Walks, fishing, canoeing, kayaking, cycling, swimming,
riding and tennis all within easy access. English spoken.
Near river Forest area
3 en suite (bth/shr) (1 fmly) Full central heating Open
parking available Child discount available 5yrs Barbecue
Languages spoken: English & German
ROOMS: s fr 200FF; d fr 250FF
CARDS: Travellers cheques

Languedoc-Roussillon

A bird's eye view of Languedoc-Roussillon would show a plain enclosed by a semicircle of mountains and a coastline that is half sand and half rock. The relatively simple geography hides diverse landscapes and as a result a rich variety of vistor locations. The gentle volcanic plains of Languedoc are thick with orchards whose gold-vermillion fruits fill the landscape. Further south, Roussillon is home to the breathtaking east range of the Pyrénées. The juxtaposition of French, Catalan and Spanish cultures creates a fascinating variety of traditions.

(Top): Legend has it that the mountain village of Castelbouc is haunted by a decadent noble in the shape of a giant billy goat!

(Bottom): Cattle-farming is popular throughout the Pyrénées regions.

ESSENTIAL FACTS

DÉPARTEMENTS:	Aude, Gard, Hérault, Lozère, Pyrénées-Roussillon
PRINCIPAL TOWNS	Perpignan, Beziers, Banyuls, Nimes, Carcassonne, Narbonne, Mende, Montpellier
PLACES TO VISIT:	Dolomite blocks at Aveyron, north of Montpellier; Bronze-age finds at Mende; underground river, grotto and swallow-hole just outside Meyrueis; the Fou canyon at Arles-sur-Tech.
REGIONAL TOURIST OFFICE	20 rue de la Republique, 34000 Montpellier. Tel: 67 58 05 10 Quai de Laittre-de-Tassigny, BO 540, 66005 Perpignan. Tel: 68 34 29 94
LOCAL GASTRONOMIC DELIGHTS	Snails served with a sauce aux noix: a Narbonne speciality made from crushed walnuts, ham, shallots and parsley; ollada: a Catalan soup made from pork, beans & vegetables; lou-kenkas: a spicy sausage; le suguet: a fish soup; chipirones guipuzcoanes: tiny squid stewed with onions, garlic and paprika; gâteau Basque: cake made with lemon & cherries.
DRINKS	Vin Collioure: a strong aromatic wine aged in oak barrels; Blanquette de Limoux: a sparkling white wine; the amber Rancio wines.
LOCAL CRAFTS WHAT TO BUY	Carved wood and cork ornaments, decorative ironwork, ceramics, espadrilles

Lozère

Mende
la Canourgue

St Ambroix Barjac
St Germain-de-Calberte   Potelieres   Venéjan
La Roque-sur-Ceze   Bagnols-sur-Cèze
Génerargues   Ales   Laudun
Alzon   le Vigan   Ribaute-les-Tavernes
    Uzès
St Mamert   Aramon

Gard

Beaucaire
Nîmes

Lodève   Villetelle
Hérault   St Clement-de-Riviere
Vailhauques
Lamalou-les-Bains   **Montpellier**
Riols   Roquebrun
Courniou

Béziers
Caunes-Minervois   Quarante   Villeneuve-les-Beziers
Montmaur   Pennautier   le Cap-d'Agde
Narbonne
Puicheric
Carcassonne
Peyrefitte-du-Razes   Gruissan
Limoux   Bouisse   Durban-Corbieres
Quillan   **Aude**

Perpignan
Pyrénées-   Castelnou
Roussillon   Alenya
Caixas
Font-Romeu   Banyuls-sur-Mer
Amélie-les-Bains-Palada
Arles-sur-Tech   Ceret

EVENTS AND FESTIVALS:

Jan -

Mar Limoux Traditional Carnival (every weekend)

Feb Arles-sur-Tech Bear Festival;

Mar Cap d'Agde Cerfvolantissimo;

Apr Gruissan Easter Monday Pilgrimage to Seamens' Cemetery; La Canourgue Bachelors' Festival; Nîmes Jazz Festival;

Jun Nîmes Whit Monday Feria; Uzès Garlic Fair; Amélie-les-Bains Mule Driver Festival; Venejan Musical evenings; Uzès Contemporary Dance Festival; Laudun Music at Lascours Castle; St Guilhem le Desert Music Season in Gellone Abbey (till mid-Aug); Montpellier Dance Festival;

July Bagnoles-sur-Ceze Blues Festival; Céret Feria; St Ambroix Volo Biou (flying beef) Legend Festival (traditional parade, theatre show); Beaucaire Summer Festival (inc Ste Madeleine's Fair, medieval procession); Cap d'Agde Sea Festival; Carcassonne Festival; Le Grau-du-Roi/Port-Camargue Jazz Festival; Ouveillan Fontcalvy Festival (music, street theatre); Béziers Classical Music Festival; Jazz in Junas; Lamalou-les-Bains Operetta Festival (to mid Aug); Béziers Orb Valley Music Festival (to mid Aug);

Aug Béziers Feria; Aigues-Mortes St Louis Festival (historical parade, street entertainment etc); Béziers Orb Valley Music Festival; Lamalou-les-Bains Operetta Festival; Villeveyrac Musical weeks at Valmagne Abbey; Amélie-les-Bains Folklore Festival

Sep Cap d'Agde Catamaran Sailing Trophy; Arles-sur Tech Medieval Festival; Mialet Protestant gathering

at Mas Soubeyran (1st Sun); Nîmes Grape Harvest Feria;

Nov Garons Salon des Santons (Christmas ornament fair)

The Wines of Roussillon

Vines were first planted in the region in the seventh and eighth centuries BC, thanks to the temporary colonisation of Greek sailors bringing cargoes of iron from Corinth. Vine growing here is essentially a family affair and almost every wine-producing village has its own co-operative. The saying is that the vine is the longest thread in the social fabric of the region.

The different soils and terrain of Roussillon's vineyards produce wine from Vins de Pays to Appellation Contrôlée. The latter reach their peak after two years and many are aged in wood to give greater character. Appellation Contrôlée wines include Collioure, Côtes du Roussillon, Côtes du Roussillon-Villages and Vins Doux Naturels.

There are many variations of Vin Doux Naturels. Both Banyuls and Rivesaltes are particularly good with melon and are often drunk as an aperitif or as a dessert wine, while Muscats de Rivesaltes has a particularly flowery bouquet. Rancio wines are amber in colour with a characteristic green tinge and it is said that they never leave the taster indifferent. You will either love them or hate them.

Coulliore produces warm, aromatic wines which go well with meat and game. Côtes du Roussillon can be either red, white or rosé, whilst Côtes du Roussillon-Villages are exclusively red. All are most enjoyable.

Whatever your preference in wine, you will find it here.

ALÉNYA Pyrénées-Orientales

Domaine de Mas Bazan (Prop: M & Mme Favier)
66200
☎ 468229826 FAX 468229737

The guest rooms are situated in a renovated Catalan 18th-century country house in a peaceful setting amidst peach trees and vines, and surrounded by palm trees and bamboo. Delicious home-made meals are available, with seafood being a speciality. Taste the wines prepared from grapes from the owners own vineyards. The property enjoys a games room, library and large private heated swimming pool. Children may ride the two ponies belonging to the owners. Golf is within three kilometres. The sea is also just three kilometres away. English spoken.
Near river Near lake Near sea Near beach Forest area
10 rms (6 bth/shr) (1 fmly) (4 with balcony) TV in 2 bedrooms Full central heating Open parking available Covered parking available Supervised Child discount available Outdoor swimming pool Boule Open terrace Languages spoken: English & Spanish
MEALS: Dinner fr 100FF*

ALZON Gard

Château du Mazel (Prop: Françoise Galliot)
rte du Villaret *30770*
☎ 467820633 FAX 467820637
(on the D999 between Nimes/Millau, 15km from le Vigan)
The Chateau du Mazel, a haven of peace and greenery and once the residence of the Bishops of Nîmes, is situated in the Cevennes at the gateway to the Averyon. Each of the spacious

bedrooms is decorated in its own individual style and boasts a harmonious blend of period and modern furniture.
Near river Forest area Near motorway
Closed Oct-Etr
6 en suite (bth/shr) (3 with balcony) Full central heating Open parking available Boule TV room,(tennis courts 500 metres) Last d 21.00hr Languages spoken: English
ROOMS: d 555-890FF Reductions over 1 night
MEALS: Lunch 115-165FF Dinner 115-165FF&alc*
CARDS: ▆ Travellers cheques

ARAMON Gard

Le Rocher Pointu (Prop: M & Mme Malek)
Plan de Dève *30390*
☎ 466574187 FAX 466570177
An old farmhouse situated near Provence and Avignon. Guests will relax in this oasis of calm where a large swimming pool and barbecue are available. Four rooms are on offer. Reductions for children up to two years old. English spoken.
Forest area
Closed Nov
4 en suite (bth/shr) No smoking on premises Child discount available 2yrs
CARDS: Travellers cheques

BARJAC Gard

Mas Escombelle (Prop: Isabelle Agapitos)
La Villette *30430*
☎ 466245477 FAX 466245477
(from Barjac in the direction of Vallon-Pont d'Arc)
This authentic 18th-century farm is situated outside the

Renaissance village of Barjac, near the Ardèche Gorge. The property has been lovingly restored and you will be welcomed into a friendly atmosphere. Private swimming pool with sun loungers. English spoken
Forest area
4 en suite (bth/shr) (2 fmly) Full central heating Open parking available Child discount available Outdoor swimming pool Languages spoken: English
ROOMS: s fr 250FF; d fr 280FF Reductions over 1 night
Special breaks: Sep-May weekend break
MEALS: Dinner fr 90FF*
CARDS: Travellers cheques

BOUISSE Aude

Domaine des Goudis (Prop: Michele & Michael Delattre)
11190
☎ 468700276 FAX 468700074
(from D54 at Arques take D54 then D70)
Renovated 18th-century stone houses situated on a hill which is the start of the two-hundred kilometre stretch of the Pyrénées. Swimming, rambling and table-tennis are on-site but if you wish you can help your hosts on the farm. Simple regional cuisine available, made with local farm produce. There is something for everyone with châteaux visits, boat rides up the Midi canal and visits to historical sites. English spoken.
Near river Near lake Forest area
Closed 4 Jan-26 Mar
6 en suite (bth/shr) (2 fmly) No smoking in all bedrooms Full central heating Open parking available Covered parking available Child discount available 12yrs Outdoor swimming pool (heated) Table tennis V meals Languages spoken: English & German
ROOMS: s 400FF; d 450FF
MEALS: Lunch 99FF Dinner 129FF
CARDS: ●● ▥ ▣ Travellers cheques

CAIXAS Pyrénées-Orientales

Mas Cammas (Prop: J Vissenaeken & A Vaes)
66300
☎ 468388227 FAX 468388367
(from A9 exit at Perpignan Sud and take D612 through Thuir to Llupia. Take D615 to Fourques, then D2 to Caixas.Continue on this road until sign for Mas Cammas)
Bed & breakfast accommodation available in a typically Catalan home, where an inventive menu is offered by your hosts, featuring produce of the Catalan vineyards. The warm welcome extended by your host, a comedian and producer, includes a visit to his workshop, where you will find some pleasant surprises. The property is situated at 500 metres altitude and has a panoramic view over the Roussillon plain. Swimming pool. English spoken.
Near river Forest area
Closed Jan & Dec
6 en suite (shr) Full central heating Open parking available Child discount available 8yrs Outdoor swimming pool Open terrace V meals Languages spoken: English & German
ROOMS: d 660-760FF *

Mas St-Jacques (Prop: Jane Richards & Ian Mayes)
66300
☎ 468388783 FAX 468388783
(from motorway A9 exit Perpignan-Sud towards Thuir. At the entrance to Thuir follow direction Llupia, driving for a further 5.5 km to Fourques. In Fourques take the D2 to Caixas, 11km,

then follow sign Mairie Eglise-Chambre d'Hotes)
This old Catalan country house, built between 150 and 200 years ago, is situated in the quiet valley of Caixas, surrounded by splendid countryside with the Mediterranean beyond. Bedrooms are light and airy, with French windows looking out to sea, with some views of the foothills of the Pyrénées. Two extra garden rooms are available in the summer, with own private terrace. Picnic lunches available. Dinner with local produce, accompanied by Roussillon wines. Your English hosts offer a warm welcome.
Forest area
5 en suite (bth/shr) (1 fmly) Open parking available Child discount available 8yrs Outdoor swimming pool Languages spoken: English & German
CARDS: Travellers cheques

CASTELNOU Pyrénées-Orientales

Domaine de Querubi (Prop: Francoise Nabet)
66300
☎ 468531908 FAX 468531896
Set in the heart of Catalonia, twenty kilometres from Spain. Françoise and Roland Nabet welcome you to their 12th-century home, where you will be served traditional southern fare. Special breaks available on request. English spoken.
Near river Near lake Forest area
6 en suite (bth/shr) (2 fmly) (1 with balcony) TV available STV Full central heating Open parking available Child discount available Last d 20.00hrs Languages spoken: English & Spanish
MEALS: Dinner fr 150FF*
CARDS: Travellers cheques

CAUNES-MINERVOIS Aude

L'Ancienne Boulangerie (Prop: Terry & Lois Link)
rue St Genes *11160*
☎ 468780132
(leave A61 at Carcassonne west exit, follow signs in direction Mazamet from first 4 rdbts at 5th rdbt follow D620 to Caunes-Minervois. In Caunes follow signs to chambre d'hote)

Located in the heart of a medieval village with a restored abbey, 23km north east of Carcassonne. This locality has all services, including two restaurants. Surrounding the village are vineyards and forested public land for hiking.
Near river Forest area
5 rms (3 shr) (2 fmly) Bicycle rental Riding, petanque & tennis in the village Languages spoken: English
ROOMS: s 150-200FF; d 200-300FF
CARDS: Travellers cheques

COURNIOU Hérault

Bed & Breakfast (Prop: M & Mme J L Lunes)
Hameau de Prouilhe *34220*
☎ 467972159 FAX 467972159
(from Beziers in direction of St Paul on N112)
Overnight stay with breakfast offered in this family farm in the mountains, at the heart of the Parc Naturel of the Haut-Languedoc. Shaded garden with hundred-year-old lime trees. Farm animals for children to visit. Two rooms available, with kitchen area for guests use. Plenty of walks. A little English spoken.
Forest area
Closed Oct-Mar
2 en suite (bth) Open parking available Boule Open terrace
CARDS: Travellers cheques

DURBAN-CORBIÈRES Aude

Château Haut-Gléon
Villeseque-des-Corbières *11360*
☎ 468488595 FAX 468484620
(exit from motorway in direction of Portel des Corbieres. 6.5km from Portel cross small bridge on left & climb 300m to Château)

This wine estate château has been entirely refurbished and is situated in lovely countryside at the heart of the Corbières.
Near river Forest area
Closed Jan-mid Feb
6 rms (1 bth 4 shr) No smoking on premises Open parking available Caves & Wine cellars Languages spoken: Spanish
ROOMS: (room only) s 250-350FF; d 250-350FF Reductions over 1 night
MEALS: Full breakfast 50FF Continental breakfast 30FF
CARDS: ● ▥

GÉNÉRARGUES Gard

Le Gamaos (Prop: Victor & Johanne Vivian)
Cammaou et Roucan *30140*
☎ 466619379
(from Anduze take D129 to Generargues. In Generargues turn left onto D50 in direction of Mialet for 2km. PassLe Roucan on right and then Les Trois Barbus Hotel on left. After approx 150mtrs on right is entrance to Le Gamaos)
Set in a clearing amongst Spanish chestnut trees, intermingled with acacia and wild cherry, a comfortable home offering good accommodation.

Near river Near sea Forest area Near motorway
8 rms (3 shr) (1 with balcony) Full central heating Outdoor swimming pool Last d 21.00hrs Languages spoken: English & Norwegian
ROOMS: s 240FF; d 250FF
MEALS: Dinner 85FF*
CARDS: Travellers cheques

LAUDUN Gard

Château de Lascours (Prop: Jean Louis Bastouil)
30290
☎ 466503961 FAX 466503008
(exit A9 at Roquemaure/Tavel)
Near river Near lake Forest area Near motorway
6 en suite (bth/shr) (1 fmly) (1 with balcony) TV in 1 bedroom Full central heating Open parking available Supervised Child discount available Outdoor swimming pool Fishing Sauna Solarium Boule Bicycle rental Open terrace
Languages spoken: English & Italian
ROOMS: s 400FF; d 500FF
CARDS: Travellers cheques

MONTMAUR Aude

"La Castagne" (Prop: Jacqueline Martin)
11320
☎ 468600040 FAX 468600040
(from the N113 between Villefranche-du-Lauragais and Avignonet take the D43 towards Revel 6km and follow signs)
This restored farmhouse with prize winning garden offers guests two comfortable bedrooms with views over beautiful countryside.
Near river Near lake Forest area Near motorway
Closed mid Oct-Mar
2 en suite (shr) (1 fmly) No smoking on premises Full central heating Open parking available Covered parking available Child discount available 7yrs Outdoor swimming pool Boule Languages spoken: English
ROOMS: d 280FF
MEALS: Dinner fr 100FF

NARBONNE Aude

Domaine de L'Estarac (Prop: Alexandre Van der Elst)
Prat de Cest *11100*
☎ 468415731
(from Narbonne take the N9 in the direction of Perpignon, after 8km arrive in Prat-de-Cest, after last house on your left turn left to chambre d'hote in 1km)
This Catalonian style house is situated in a protected maritime area. Rooms are large, sleeping 1-4 persons, and breakfast is served in the room or in the garden.
Near lake Near sea Near beach Forest area Near motorway
5 en suite (bth) Full central heating Open parking available Child discount available 4yrs Languages spoken: English & Dutch
ROOMS: s 150FF; d 200FF
CARDS: Travellers cheques

PENNAUTIER Aude

Château de Liet (Prop: M & Mme de Stoop)
11610
☎ 468715524 FAX 468470522
19th-century château set in fifteen hectares of parkland with good-sized swimming pool. Archery, table-tennis, walks,

riding, fishing, tennis, sailing and rafting all on-site or within twenty kilometres. Meals can be taken with your hosts, except on Sundays. English spoken.
Near river Forest area Near motorway
6 en suite (bth/shr) (3 fmly) (2 with balcony) Full central heating Open parking available Child discount available 12yrs Outdoor swimming pool Badminton Table tennis Last d 21.00hrs Languages spoken: English
ROOMS: s 200-300FF; d 250-330FF
MEALS: Dinner 140FF

PEYREFITTE-DU-RAZÈS Aude

Domaine de Couchet (Prop: Jean-Pierre Ropers)
11230
☎ 468695506
Renovated 18th-century house, set amongst open fields and five hectares of grounds, 420 metres above sea-level. Peace and quiet are assured. The hostess is also the cook and invites her guests to dine with her. Excellent spot from which to tour the châteaux of Cathare. A little English spoken.
Near river Near lake Forest area
4 rms (3 shr) TV available Radio in rooms Full central heating Open parking available Child discount available

POTELIÈRES Gard

Le Château (Prop: J & F De Tcherepakhine)
30500
☎ 466248092 FAX 466248243
A residence which dates back to the 15th century. Swimming pool on site, park, lake and river, plus many activities available. Courses in drawing and painting are on offer, as are French lessons. Trips arranged to tourist sites. English spoken.
Near river Near lake Forest area Near motorway
8 en suite (bth/shr) TV in 2 bedrooms Radio in rooms Full central heating Open parking available Covered parking available Supervised Child discount available 12yrs Outdoor swimming pool Languages spoken: English
CARDS: Travellers cheques

PUICHÉRIC Aude

Château de St-Aunay (Prop: M C Berge)
11700
☎ 468437220 FAX 468437672
Superb château set in a verdant location, with meals served on a terrace. Guest rooms are available, including four family rooms, taking a total of 25 guests. Simple but generous meals available by arrangement, featuring regional cuisine and offering the wine of the house. Calm, peaceful environment. Swimming pool and billiard room. English spoken.
Near river Near lake Near motorway
Closed 5 Oct-Mar
10 rms (9 shr) (4 fmly) (2 with balcony) Full central heating Open parking available Child discount available Outdoor swimming pool Pool table Bicycle rental Last d 18.30hrs Languages spoken: English
ROOMS: s 260FF; d 280FF
MEALS: Dinner 140FF
CARDS: Travellers cheques

QUARANTE Hérault

Château de Quarante (Prop: M & Mme N Neukirch)
24 av du Chateau de Quarante *34310*
☎ 467894041 FAX 467894041
(W of Beziers, take D11 which becomes the D5, drive 2 km and turn right onto D184. Cross Canal du Midi drive 4km, château at village entrance. N of Narbonne take D13 onto D36 for 20km, cross village to reach château on D184)

Near river Near sea Near beach Forest area Near motorway
Closed Jan-Mar
5 en suite (bth/shr) (3 with balcony) No smoking on premises Open parking available Child discount available Bicycle rental Languages spoken: English & German
ROOMS: s 425FF; d 525FF Reductions over 1 night
MEALS: Dinner 150FF

RIBAUTE-LES-TAVERNES Gard

Château de Ribaute (Prop: Chamski-Mandajors)
30720
☎ 466830166 FAX 466838693
Near river
6 en suite (bth/shr) Open parking available Supervised Child discount available 12yrs Outdoor swimming pool Golf Tennis Riding Boule Open terrace V meals Languages spoken: English
MEALS: Full breakfast 50FF Dinner 130-200FF*
CARDS: ● ▆

RIOLS Hérault

La Cerisaie (Prop: M R Weggelaar)
1 av de Bédarieux *34220*
☎ 467970387 FAX 467970388
(leave A9 at Béziers Ouest, head for Castures, Mazamet, St Pons on the N112. Approx 1km before St Pons, turn right towards Bédarieux, Riols La Cerisaie is on left hand side, just after passing the church)
Near river Forest area
6 en suite (bth/shr) Licensed Open parking available Supervised Child discount available Outdoor swimming pool Boule Bicycle rental Open terrace Tennis nearby Languages spoken: English, Dutch & German
ROOMS: s 305-385FF; d 340-420FF Reductions over 1 night Special breaks
CARDS: ● ▆

ROQUEBRUN Hérault

Les Mimosas (Prop: La Touche)
av des Orangers *34460*
☎ 467896136 FAX 467896136
(A9 to Beziers then D14 to Roquebrun)

Situated in the beautiful village of Roquebrun, on the banks of the river Orb, in the regional park of the Haut-Languedoc. Charming, renovated 19th-century manor house. The rooms are spacious, with excellent showers. Delicious evening meals and a sumptuous breakfast are served. English spoken.
Near river Near sea Near beach Forest area Near motorway 5 en suite (shr) (1 fmly) (1 with balcony) No smoking on premises Open parking available Covered parking available Child discount available 5yrs Tennis Fishing Riding Boule Mini-golf Bicycle rental Open terrace river bathing, walking, wine tasting Last d 8pm Languages spoken: English
ROOMS: s 310-340FF; d 325-360FF
MEALS: Dinner 125-145FF
CARDS: Travellers cheques

ROQUE-SUR-CÈZE Gard

La Tonnelle (Prop: Rigaud)
30200
☎ 466827937
Near river Forest area In town centre
6 en suite (shr) (3 fmly) Outdoor swimming pool Boule Open terrace

ST-CLÉMENT-DE-RIVIÈRE Hérault

Domaine de St-Clément (Prop: M & Mme Bernabé)
34980
☎ 467840529 FAX 467840796
Henri and Calista Bernabé welcome you to their old, white-stoned house, partially covered in creeper. There is a real Mediterranean feel to this comfortable, white-shuttered residence. Situated near Montpelier with a swimming pool. English spoken.
Near river Near lake Near sea Near beach Forest area
3 en suite (bth/shr) (2 fmly) Full central heating Open parking available Covered parking available Supervised Outdoor swimming pool Languages spoken: English

ST-GERMAIN-DE-CALBERTE Lozère

Le Pradel (Prop: M Jean Nicole Bechard)
48370
☎ 466459246
(from Florac take N106 (direction of Alès) at Col de Jalcreste take D984 to La Croix de Bourel then D54 and D13 to Le Pradel)
Forest area
3 en suite (shr) (2 fmly) No smoking on premises Full central heating Open parking available Child discount available 6yrs Bicycle rental Languages spoken: English & German
ROOMS: d 260FF
MEALS: Dinner fr 75FF
CARDS: Travellers cheques

ST-MAMERT Gard

La Mazade (Prop: Eliette Couston)
12 rue de la Mazade *30730*
☎ 466811756 FAX 466296260
(exit Nîmes Ouest in direction Le Vigau continue 10km turn right, St Mamert in 4km)
Spacious rooms, overlooking the garden or open countryside in this stone-built residence. Queen-sized bed available in one room. Dinner available by request. Your hosts will be pleased to advise you on festivals of music, theatre and dance, and places of interest.
5 rms (1 bth 3 shr) (2 fmly) No smoking in 2 bedrooms Full central heating Open parking available Supervised Child discount available
CARDS: Travellers cheques

VAILHAUQUES Hérault

Mas de la Coste (Prop: M & Mme Bottinelli-Faidherbe)
114 Chemin de la Fontaine
☎ 467844126
Rooms available in this friendly family home, all with television. Evening meal plus wine available for a fixed price. A little English spoken.
Near river Near sea Forest area Near motorway
4 en suite (shr) (3 fmly) (2 with balcony) No smoking in 2 bedrooms TV available Full central heating Open parking available Supervised Child discount available 10yrs
CARDS: Travellers cheques

VILLENEUVE-LÈS-BÉZIERS Hérault

Bed & Breakfast (Prop: Andrew & Jennifer-Jane Viner)
7 rue de la Fontaine *34420*
☎ 467398715 FAX 467398715
Along a peaceful road in Villeneuve, guests will find this 15th-century building which has been lovingly restored by your hosts, the Viner family. They will be happy to show you the staircase in the tower which dates back to the Middle Ages. Dinner available.
Near river In town centre Near motorway
4 en suite (bth/shr) (4 fmly) (2 with balcony) Full central heating V meals Languages spoken: English
ROOMS: d 260FF Reductions over 1 night
MEALS: Dinner 85FF

VILLETELLE Hérault

Bed & Breakfast (Prop: Daniel & Simone Barlaguet)
343 Chemin des Combes Noires *34400*
☎ 467868700 FAX 467868700
Four rooms and two suites are available, with independent access from the rest of the house. Evening meals are provided from Monday to Friday. Communal living room with fridge and laundry facilities. Swimming pool, tennis court, table-tennis and childrens games all on-site for guests. English spoken.
Near river Near sea
6 en suite (bth/shr) (6 with balcony) TV available Full central heating Open parking available Covered parking available Child discount available Outdoor swimming pool Tennis Boule Table tennis Last d 20.00hrs Languages spoken: English
MEALS: Lunch fr 100FF Dinner fr 100FF*
CARDS: Travellers cheques

Provence

Imagine peaceful Romanesque villages nestling in mountain folds, Gothic palaces perched on hilltops giving way to enchanting olive groves and vineyards, the heady aroma of lavender fields bathed in clear sunshine and you are halfway to discovering one of the most diverse and dramatic regions of France. If action is on the agenda, the snow-clad Alpes are made for sport of all kinds and if a spot of people-watching is needed, head for the glamorous resorts in the south with their sublime coastlines of sandy beaches, caves and rocky inlets waiting to be explored.

(Top): The mountain town of Séguret has a 12th-century church, a 15th-century fountain, and a ruined castle.

(Bottom) One of Provence's best known products is sweet-smelling lavender, which is used as a basic ingredient in most of France's world-famous perfumes.

ESSENTIAL FACTS

DÉPARTEMENTS:	Alpes-de-Haute-Provence, Bouches-du-Rhône, Hautes-Alpes, Var, Vaucluse
PRINCIPAL TOWNS	Arles, Avignon, Carpentras, Gap, Sisteron, Digne les Bains, Aix-en-Provence, Marseille, Toulon
PLACES TO VISIT:	The Carmague with its white horses; the Roman remains at Arles; the Popes' Palace at Avignon; Cezanne's studio at Aix-en-Provence; Les Ecrins, the National Nature Park in Hautes-Alpes.
REGIONAL TOURIST OFFICE	13 rue Roux de Brignoles, 13006 Marseille Tel: 91 13 84 13; 5 rue Capitaine de Bresson, 05000 Gap Tel: 92 53 62
LOCAL GASTRONOMIC DELIGHTS	Bouillabaisse, fish stew; calissons, small diamond shaped almond-paste biscuits; rascasse, spiny fish; salade Niçoise, tuna fish salad; daube, a casserole; poutargue, a roe paste; pissaladière, an onion tart; tapenade, an olive paste; local cheeses such as Brousse du Rove, Arles & Le Ventoux Tome, Champsaur & Le Queyras Tome.
DRINKS	Red wines such as Châteauneuf-du-Pape and Gigondas. The herbal aperitif from Forcalquier 'pastis', an aniseed-flavoured aperitif usually diluted with water; local spirits such as Vieux Marc de Provence, Elixir du Révérend Père Gaucher, Eau de vie de Poire, and Genepy des Alpes.
LOCAL CRAFTS WHAT TO BUY	Provencal fabrics, honey perfumed with lavender and rosemary, pottery and earthenware, olive oil, lavender products, ornamental 'santons', crystallised fruits.

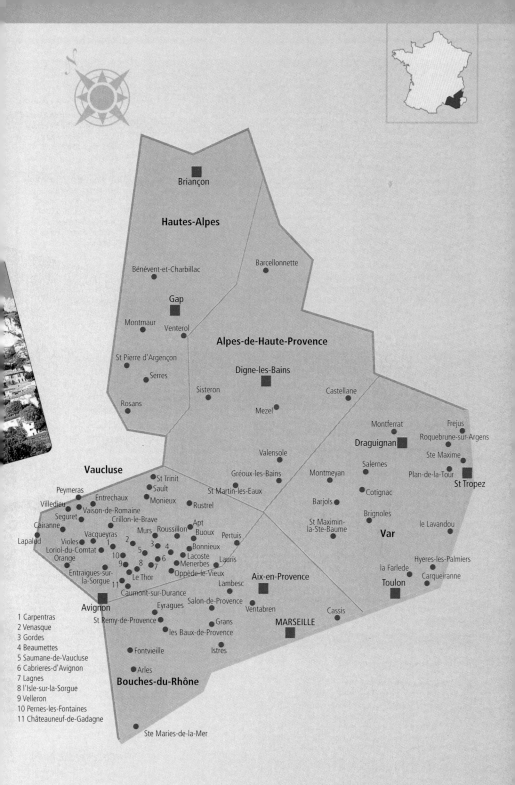

Briançon

Hautes-Alpes

Bénévent-et-Charbillac

Barcellonnette

Gap

Montmaur

Venterol

Alpes-de-Haute-Provence

St Pierre d'Argençon

Digne-les-Bains

Serres

Sisteron

Castellane

Rosans

Mezel

Montferrat

Frejus

Montmeyan

Roquebrune-sur-Argens

Valensole

Draguignan

Ste Maxime

Salernes

Vaucluse

St Trinit

Gréoux-les-Bains

Plan-de-la-Tour

St Tropez

Peymeras

Sault

St Martin-les-Eaux

Cotignac

Entrechaux

Monieux

Barjols

Villedieu

Vaison-de-Romaine

Rustrel

Brignoles

le Lavandou

Seguret

Crillon-le-Brave

Apt

St Maximin-

Var

Cairanne

Murs

Roussillon

Buoux

la-Ste-Baume

Lapalud

Vacqueyras

2

Pertuis

Violes

1

3

4

Bonnieux

Loriol-du-Comtat

5

Lacoste

Hyeres-les-Palmiers

Orange

10

9

8

6

Menerbes

Lauris

la Farlede

Carqueiranne

Entraigues-sur-

7

Oppède-le-Vieux

Aix-en-Provence

la-Sorgue

11

Le Thor

Lambesc

Toulon

Caumont-sur-Durance

Salon-de-Provence

Avignon

Eyragues

Ventabren

Cassis

St Remy-de-Provence

Grans

MARSEILLE

1 Carpentras

les Baux-de-Provence

2 Venasque

3 Gordes

Istres

4 Beaumettes

Fontvieille

5 Saumane-de-Vaucluse

6 Cabrieres-d'Avignon

Arles

7 Lagnes

8 l'Isle-sur-la-Sorgue

Bouches-du-Rhône

9 Velleron

10 Pernes-les-Fontaines

11 Châteauneuf-de-Gadagne

Ste Maries-de-la-Mer

EVENTS & FESTIVALS

Jan   Coudoux Wine Festival
Mar   Les Orres Comic Book Festival; Digne-les Bains Film Festival; Aix Wine Fair
Apr   Brignoles Agricultural Wine-Growing Fair & Exihibition
May   Les Mées Olive Tree Festival; Flower Shows at Tarascon & Sanary-sur-Mer; Stes-Maries-de-la-Mer Gypsy Pilgrimage with Procession of Ste-Sarah to the Sea
Jun   Cassis Fishermans Festival; Marseille Garlic Festival; Stes-Maries-de-la-Mer 'Jornadido Biou' (the day of the bull); Manosque Medieval Fair; Valréas Petit St Jean Night (since 1504); Le Val Holy Art Festival; Gréoux-les-Bains Craft Fairs; Trets Wine Festival; Wine Fairs at Gemenos & La Destrousse
Jul   Ferrassieres Lavender Festival; Jazz Festivals at Toulon, Chateau-Arnoux, St Raphael, Salon-de-Provence, Forcalquier, Ramatuelle; Martigues Venetian celebrations; Visan Wine & Harvest Festival; Stes-Maries-de-la-Mer Festival of the Virgin Mary; Châteauvallon Contemporary Dance Festival; Folklore Festival at Cavaillon, Marseille (Château Gombert); Arles International Photo Workshop & Exhibitions; Festivals at Avignon, Vaison-la-Romaine, Colmars-les-Alpes, Marseille, Carpentras; St-Etienne-les-Orgues Herb & Craft Fair
Aug   Frejus Grape Festival; Chateauneuf-du-Pain Medieval Festival of La Veraison; Monfort Wine Festival; Châteauneuf-du-Pape Medieval Celebration of Fruit Harvest; Draguignan 'Draguifollies' (jazz, rock, blues, street artists); Pont de Cervières 'Bacchu-ber' ancient sword dance parade; Castellane Craft Fair; Salon de Provence Chamber Music Festival (Chateau de l'Emperi); Brignoles Jazz Festival; Sault Notre Dame Fair & Lavender Festival; Forcalquier Provence Products Fair;
Sep   Peyruis Apple & Fruit Festival; Le Val Sausage Fair; Marseille International Fair; Allemagne-en-Provence Old Crafts Festival; Riez Honey & Lavender Fair; Plan-de-la-Tour Fortified Wine (Vin Cuit) Festival
Oct   Apt Wine Harvest Festival; Draguignan Jazz Festival; Stes-Maries-de-la-Mer Gypsy Festival & Pilgrimage
Nov   Marseille 'Santons' Fair; Aups Truffle Market; Avignon Naming of Côtes du Rhône Wine; Marseilles Christmas Ornaments Fair; Wine Fairs at Istres & Martiques
Dec   Istres Sheperds Festivals; Bandol Wine Festival, Seguret Yule Evening

---

AIX-EN-PROVENCE Bouches-du-Rhône

Bed & Breakfast (Prop: M & Mme Greyfie de Bellecombe)
43 av de Lattre-de-Tassigny, Quartier Varte Colline *13100*
☎ 442964283 & 442964185 FAX 442964193
The proprietors invite you to stay in their home, a farm in the historic region of Aix-en-Provence. Located in an old part of the town, the farm is in a quiet area, with large comfortable rooms. Children are welcome. Games room with billiards and table-tennis, library, use of bikes, plus private swimming pool. English spoken.
Forest area In town centre Near motorway
Closed Aug
1 en suite (bth/shr) TV available Full central heating Open parking available Child discount available 15yrs Outdoor swimming pool Boule Open terrace Languages spoken: English
CARDS: Travellers cheques

APT Vaucluse

Moulin du Lavon (Prop: Yves Nief)
84400
☎ 490743454 FAX 490742013
This charming eighteenth century farm is constructed from Luberon stone. Mireille and Yves Nief offer four attractive rooms, but there is also the possibility of self-catering accommodation in a cottage which will sleep up to sixteen people. You can join your hosts for dinner, cooked with the freshest farm produce. This is a paradise for ramblers and nature lovers. Private pool, piano and table-tennis.
Near river Near lake Forest area

10 rms (4 bth) (3 fmly) Full central heating Open parking available Child discount available 13yrs Outdoor swimming pool Boule Table tennis,Piano Last d 20.00hrs
ROOMS: s 60-190FF; d 120-224FF
MEALS: Dinner 80FF
CARDS: [■] Travellers cheques

BARJOLS Var

Séjours Decouverte et Nature (Prop: Michel Passebois)
St-Jaume *83670*
☎ 494771801 FAX 494771801
(from Barjols take D560 towards St Maxmin. After approx 1.7km take turning to right and follow signs 'Saint-Jaume'. After 500m,there is a red gate on left & farm entrance)
Here you can enjoy a holiday on a working farm with your hosts, Michel and Stéphanie Passebois. The farm was built on a Roman site during the 18th century and is surrounded by woods. Special weekends can be arranged to include dinner with your hosts, who will also make you a picnic for the next day. English spoken.
Near river Forest area
Closed Nov-Feb
6 en suite (shr) (2 fmly) Full central heating Open parking available Child discount available 10yrs Outdoor swimming pool Boule Open terrace Table tennis Languages spoken: English
ROOMS: s 305FF; d 410FF
MEALS: Dinner fr 115FF
CARDS: Travellers cheques

BEAUMETTES Vaucluse

Le Ralenti du Lierre (Prop: Marth Deneits)
Le Village *84220*
☎ 490723922
(on N100 between Apt/Coustellet)
17th-century house with swimming pool, gardens, a shaded
terrace and a small wood for your picnics. Five individual
rooms are available (all en-suite). One suite available in the old
wine-cellar. Large breakfast served. Three restaurants in
village. Walking, fishing, climbing, golf, tennis, riding and
canoeing nearby.
Near river Forest area
Closed Nov-Mar
5 en suite (bth/shr) (1 fmly) (1 with balcony) Full central
heating Open parking available No children

BÉNÉVENT-ET-CHARBILLAC Hautes-Alpes

Bed & Breakfast (Prop: M & Mme Gourdou-Pedrosa)
Le Cairn, Charbillac *05500*
☎ 492505487
Enjoy the beauty of the Alps in this restored house in the
heart of the Champsaur Valley. Bring your skis in the winter or
enjoy limitless walks in the summer. Climbing and other
alpine sports are available. Tennis, water-sports, horse-riding,
golf and bungee-jumping are all within minutes of the
property. English spoken.
Near river Near lake Forest area
4 en suite (shr) No smoking on premises Open parking
available Child discount available 12yrs Languages spoken:
English, Italian & Spanish

BONNIEUX Vaucluse

La Bouquière (Prop: Angel Escobar)
84480
☎ 490758717
(take D3 in direction of Apt in 2km signposted left)
Situated three and a half kilometres from the village of Bonnieux,
lost in a profusion of greenery in the heart of a regional
park, this old, restored farmhouse has a magnificent view over
the valley of Apt. Four comfortable rooms are available, each
with its own independent entrance and looking out onto the
garden. Open from March to November. English spoken.
Forest area
Closed Dec-Mar
4 en suite (bth/shr) Full central heating Open parking
available Languages spoken: English & Spanish
CARDS: Travellers cheques

BUOUX Vaucluse

Domaine de la Grande Bastide (Prop: Jean-Alain Cayla)
84480
☎ 490742910
(from A7 exit at Avignon Sud and take N100 to Apt. From Apt
take D113 south to Buoux.)
A 17th-century farm set in seventy hectares of beautiful
countryside, and in the middle of lavender fields. Five
spacious and comfortable rooms available. English spoken.
Near river Forest area
5 rms (4 shr) Full central heating Open parking available
Covered parking available Supervised Child discount
available 12yrs Boule Languages spoken: English & Spanish
ROOMS: s 200-300FF; d 250-350FF
CARDS: Travellers cheques

CABRIÈRES-D'AVIGNON Vaucluse

Bed & Breakfast (Prop: Jacquy Truc)
84220
☎ 490769703 FAX 490767467
(situated equidistant between Gordes/Fontaine de Vaucluse)
Comfortable rooms available in this attractive stone built
house, set in beautiful gardens. Guests have been returning to
this family home for the last ten years. Swimming pool with
sun-loungers.
Forest area
5 en suite (shr) (1 with balcony) No smoking on premises TV
available Full central heating Open parking available Child
discount available Outdoor swimming pool

CAIRANNE Vaucluse

Le Moulin Agapé (Prop: Denise Molla)
84290
☎ 490307704
(from N7 take D8 from Bollène or D13 from Orange, to
Cairanne)
Set in fifteen hectares of Orange countryside, between the
hills and rivers of Cairanne, which is renowned for its wine.
Patio, barbecue and swimming pool on-site. English spoken.
Near river Forest area Near motorway
7 rms (1 bth 5 shr) (3 fmly) No smoking on premises Full
central heating Open parking available Child discount
available 10yrs Outdoor swimming pool Boule Table tennis
Languages spoken: English
MEALS: Dinner fr 100FF*

CARPENTRAS Vaucluse

Bastide Ste-Agnes (Prop: Jacques Apotheloz)
rue de Caromb, Cheuin de le Fourtrose *84200*
☎ 490600301 FAX 490600253
(from Carpentras take D974 towards Mont-Ventoux/Bedoin
along the aqueduct. Then take the D13 towards Caromb, after
300m go left into the Chemin de la Fourtrose, house is 200m
on right)

Between Mont-Ventoux and Carpentras, in the heart of
Comtat Venaissain, this beautiful 19th-century guesthouse has
a peaceful atmosphere, particularly in the garden, where
typical Mediterranean plants and smells will greet you. A
swimming pool, boules and mountain bikes are on offer on
site. English spoken.
Near river Near lake Forest area
Closed 16 Nov-Feb

cont'd

6 rms (5 bth/shr) (2 fmly) (2 with balcony) TV in 2 bedrooms
Full central heating Open parking available Child discount
available 2-3yrs Outdoor swimming pool Boule Languages
spoken: English & German
ROOMS: s 360-420FF; d 400-700FF Reductions over 1 night
CARDS: Travellers cheques

CARQUEIRANNE Var

L'Aumonerie (Prop: P et D Menard)
620 av de Fontbrun *83320*
☎ 494585356
Situated in a beautiful villa, typical of Provençe, where all
rooms give a spectacular view onto the Mediterranean. A
garden filled with the dark, leafy trees of the region leads onto
a small private beach. The Ile de Porquerolles and St Tropez
are in close proximity to this southern property.
Near sea Forest area
3 en suite (bth/shr) Full central heating Open parking
available Child discount available 2yrs Boule Open terrace
ROOMS: s 300FF; d 400-450FF
CARDS: Travellers cheques

CAUMONT-SUR-DURANCE Vaucluse

Bed & Breakfast (Prop: Michelle & Bernard Lefebvre)
12 Chemin des Terres de Magues *84510*
☎ 490230749 FAX 490231427
(exit A7 at Avignon Sud follow signs Cavaillon. Over 2 bridges
& take D973 on left towards Caumont/le Thor. Through
Caumont, at lights turn left, then right after 150m towards le
Thor. Gite 0.5 mile on left)
Four rooms are available in a villa which is separate from the
main residence. Visitors will enjoy views of the forests from
the patio and the surrounding countryside. Garden room,
barbecue, bike-hire, all available on-site. Near to Luberon and
Avignon.
Forest area
8 rms (4 shr) No smoking in 2 bedrooms TV in 2 bedrooms
Full central heating Open parking available Child discount
available 10yrs Bicycle rental Last d 22.00hrs
ROOMS: d 210-280FF
MEALS: Dinner fr 120FF

CHÂTEAUNEUF-DE-GADAGNE Vaucluse

Bed & Breakfast (Prop: Colette Pabst)
211 Chemin de Bompas *84470*
☎ 490225302
The rooms are situated on one floor of a large, Provencal
house, and all have superb views of the plateaux of Vaucluse
and the Ventoux. The house is very light and welcoming, and
there are swings in the garden for the children. Reductions in
prices for children up to three years old. A little English
spoken.
Forest area
3 rms No smoking on premises Full central heating Open
parking available Covered parking available Child discount
available 3yrs Languages spoken: English

CRILLON-LE-BRAVE Vaucluse

Bed & Breakfast (Prop: Alaine Moine)
Chemin de la Sidoiné *84410*
☎ 490128096
(exit A7 at Orange in direction of Carpentras, at Carpentras
take direction for Bedoin)

A warm welcome is on offer here. All meals are taken together
with your hosts around a large friendly table. All rooms are
spacious and comfortable and overlook magnificent Provençal
countryside, with a view of Mount Ventoux and the very pretty
village of Crillon le Brave. Your hosts are happy to help you
discover Provence and have brochures and information
available. Pétanque and table-tennis on site. A little English
spoken.
Forest area
5 en suite (shr) (3 fmly) Full central heating Open parking
available Child discount available 8yrs Table tennis Petanque

Domaine la Condamine (Prop: Mme M J Eydoux)
84410
☎ 490624728 FAX 490624728
(exit A7 for Orange, take D950 for Carpentras, then D974 for
Bedoin. Take right turn onto D224)

Situated at the foot of Mount Ventoux, this 17th-century
property is set in fourteen hectares of vineyards. Five rooms
are available. Family meals on request, made in typical
Provençal style, using home-produced ingredients and virgin
olive oil accompanied by the wines of the house. Swimming
pool. Bikes available. English spoken.
Forest area
4 en suite (shr) (1 fmly) No smoking on premises TV in all
bedrooms STV Full central heating Open parking available
Covered parking available Supervised Outdoor swimming
pool Languages spoken: English, Italian & Spanish
ROOMS: s 260-270FF; d 300-320FF
CARDS: Travellers cheques

Moulin d'Antelon (Prop: M & Mme Ricquart)
84410
☎ 490627789 FAX 490624490
Near river Forest area
5 en suite (bth/shr) Full central heating Open parking
available Covered parking available Child discount available
8yrs
CARDS: Travellers cheques

ENTRAIGUES-SUR-LA-SORGUES Vaucluse

Domaine du Grand Causeran (Prop: Papapietro)
allée du Grand Causeran *84320*
☎ 490232909 FAX 490232907
In the heart of a park resplendent with lawns, flowers,
fountains and mature trees, this typical Provençal house offers
a family atmosphere. There are shops, tennis, eighteen hole
golf, riding centre and watersports available within a short
distance, or you could try hang-gliding at the airport nearby.
English spoken.

Near river Near motorway
5 rms (4 bth/shr) TV available Full central heating Open parking available Supervised No children 7yrs Outdoor swimming pool Boule Table tennis Croquet Languages spoken: English
MEALS: Lunch fr 130FF&alc Dinner fr 130FF&alc*
CARDS: Travellers cheques

Mas de 4 Chemins (Prop: M & Mme Martin)
19 Chemin des Tempines *84320*
☎ 490621439
This beautiful stone house on the road to Ventoux is just ten minutes from the ramparts of Avignon. Michel and Bernadette, your hosts, will be happy to offer advice about the many tourist attractions on offer. They offer home-cooked Mediterranean cuisine. A little English spoken.
Near river
Closed Nov-Etr
3 en suite (shr) No smoking on premises Full central heating Open parking available Child discount available
MEALS: Dinner fr 100FF*

L'Éscleriade (Prop: Vincent Gallo)
rte de St-Marcellin *84340*
☎ 490460132 FAX 490460371
Situated at the foot of the majestic Mont Ventoux and enjoying panoramic views, this house is on the Wine Route and offers a private swimming pool, French billiards and boules. Attractive walks in the nearby leafy park. English spoken.
Near river Near lake Forest area
Closed Nov-Feb
6 en suite (bth/shr) (1 fmly) (5 with balcony) TV available Direct-dial available Full central heating Open parking available Supervised Last d 19.30hrs Languages spoken: English & Italian
MEALS: Dinner 105FF*
CARDS: ●● ▆▆ Carte Bleue,Eurocard

Le Mas des Chats Qui Dorment (Prop: Robert & Christiane Poli)
Chemin des Prés *13630*
☎ 490941971 FAX 490941971
(from Avignon take D571 to Chateaurenard and on to Eyragues. In Eyragues from 'La Place' take the road with the pharmacy on your right, past 2 shops and after 1.5kms follow sign on left)
Three rooms in an 18th-century house, typically Provençal. Leafy garden backing onto countryside. Near the tourist sites of Provence. Breakfast can be taken in the garden. A little English spoken.
Forest area
Closed 16 Sep-31 Mar
3 rms (1 shr) (2 fmly) No smoking on premises Open parking available Child discount available 6yrs Open terrace Languages spoken: English Italian
ROOMS: s 200FF; d 280FF
CARDS: Travellers cheques

Bed & Breakfast (Prop: Maryse Lallier)
1417 rue de la Gare *83210*
☎ 494330179 FAX 494330179
Forest area
5 en suite (bth/shr) (1 fmly) (3 with balcony) No smoking on premises Full central heating Open parking available Child discount available Outdoor swimming pool Boule Table tennis Library TV room
MEALS: Dinner 86FF*

Bed & Breakfast (Prop: E & J Ricard-Damidot)
107 av Frederic Mistral *13990*
☎ 490547267 FAX 490546443
Two large rooms, comfortably furnished with antiques, are on offer at this property, set in a village location. Guests are invited to us the large living room, which has a TV and hi-fi and offers many comforts. English is spoken.
Forest area In town centre
Closed Nov-Etr
2 en suite (bth/shr) No smoking on premises Full central heating Covered parking available Supervised Child discount available Languages spoken: English
CARDS: Travellers cheques

Villa La Lebre (Prop: P Lawrence)
St-Pantaléon *84220*
☎ 490722074 FAX 490722074
(from Avignon take N100 towards Apt. At Coustellet take D2 for Gordes. After les Imberts take D207 & D148 to St Pantaleon. Pass church & stay on D104 for 50metres, take left onto small uphill road. 2nd drive on right)
1 en suite (bth/shr) Full central heating Open parking available Supervised Open terrace Languages spoken: English, German, Italian & Arabic
ROOMS: d 260FF Reductions over 1 night

Domaine de Bois Vert (Prop: J-P & V Richard)
Quartier Montauban *13450*
☎ 490558298 FAX 490558298
(from A7 exit at Salon Sud follow signs for Marseille. At Lancon-de-Provence turn right onto D19 for Grans. After 5kms turn right for establishment & turn right)
A haven of peace, this traditional residence with a swimming pool, is situated in grounds with oak and pine trees. The ground floor bedrooms are decorated in the colours of Provence and each has its own entrance. An ideal base from which to explore the writer Frederic Mistral's Provence and its traditions. English spoken.
Near river Forest area
3 en suite (bth/shr) (2 fmly) No smoking on premises Full central heating Open parking available Covered parking available Supervised Child discount available 12yrs Outdoor swimming pool Languages spoken: English
ROOMS: s 250FF; d 280-320FF

HYÈRES-LES-PALMIERS Var

Villa Li Rouvre (Prop: Jacqueline & Pierre Brunet)
Chemin de Beauvallon Haut *83400*
☎ 494354344
(A57 towards Hyeres/Nice. Then A570 towards Hyeres, at rdbt
(where rail station is indicated) take 4th exit/2nd exit at next
roundabout/ left at t-junc/1st right(Av.Victor)/2nd left(Ch
Maurettes)/2nd right/1stleft)

Two rooms are available in the extension of a Provençal villa.
Patio and swimming pool for guests' use. Panoramic view of
the stunning Provence countryside. Guests are invited to dine
with their hosts, although reservations must be made.
Near sea Forest area In town centre Near motorway
2 rms (1 bth/shr) (2 with balcony) Full central heating Open
parking available Child discount available 10yrs Outdoor
swimming pool Open terrace
ROOMS: d 350-550FF *
MEALS: Dinner fr 80FF*

ISLE-SUR-LA-SORGUE, L' Vaucluse

Domaine de la Fontaine (Prop: M & Mme Sundheimer)
920 Chemin du Bosquet *84800*
☎ 490380144 FAX 490385342
(from A7 exit at Avignon Sud. Take D25 to L'Isle-sur-la-Sorgue.
Take N100 towards Apt, on outskirts of village after Citroen
Station take 1st right then 1st left)

Situated in the Luberon Valley, near Avignon, is the Isle sur
Sorgue, a typical Provence village. This property is an old
Provençal house, where Irmi and Dominique Sundheimer
welcome you. Five comfortable, charming rooms available,
and a private swimming pool. The house is set in four hectares
of lush garden. Dine on the terrace in the romantic

atmosphere, under the shadow of the plane tree. A little
English spoken.
Near river Forest area
Closed 16 Jan-28 Feb
5 en suite (shr) (2 fmly) (1 with balcony) TV in all bedrooms
Full central heating Open parking available Outdoor
swimming pool Boule Last d 20.30hrs Languages spoken:
English & German
ROOMS: s 410-450FF; d 450-490FF *
MEALS: Dinner fr 130FF
CARDS: Travellers cheques

Domaines des Costières (Prop: Mme Josette Pecchi)
84800
☎ 490383919
(16 kms east of Avignon via N100)
Set amidst a twelve hectare estate, this renovated Provençal
building is unusual in that it is entirely marbled throughout. A
long tree-lined driveway leads up to the front courtyard,
which is shaded by an immense plane tree dating form 1730.
Mme Secchi, your hostess, is a talented cook who delights in
welcoming visitors to her home. Ideal for families. English
spoken.
Near river Forest area Near motorway
6 en suite (bth/shr) (2 fmly) No smoking on premises Full
central heating Open parking available Supervised Child
discount available 15yrs Open terrace Last d 17.30hrs
Languages spoken: English & Italian
MEALS: Dinner fr 130FF*
CARDS: Travellers cheques

La Meridienne (Prop: M & Mme G Tarayre)
Chemin de la Lone *84800*
☎ 490384026 FAX 490385846
Large, unusual house, set in the middle of the countryside,
with peace, calm and tranquillity assured. Each room has a
private patio and an entrance which is separate from the rest
of the house. Swimming pool for the use of guests. Enjoy the
delights of this island location.
Near river Forest area Near motorway
5 en suite (shr) (1 fmly) Open parking available Supervised
Outdoor swimming pool Languages spoken: English &
Spanish
CARDS: Travellers cheques

LACOSTE Vaucluse

Relais du Procureur (Prop: Antoine de Gebelin)
rue Basse *84480*
☎ 490758228 FAX 490758694
(from Avignon take N100 toward Apt, turn right at the village
of Lumieres following signs for Lacoste, once in the village
Relais du Procureur is well signed although the narrow streets
can be difficult to navigate in a large car)
Forest area Near motorway
RS Jan & Feb
7 en suite (bth/shr) TV available Full central heating Air
conditioning in bedrooms No children 7yrs Languages
spoken: English

LAGNES Vaucluse

L'Hacienda (Prop: Elayne Murphy)
Chemin des Ballardes *84800*
☎ 490382464
(from Isle sur la Sorgue, take Route d'Apt for approx 4km, at
sign on left 'Mas de Curebourg-Antiquaires, take the opposite

right turn, at crossrds turn left for approx 50m, at first electric pole on right, turn left, house on right at end of lane)
Near river Forest area
7 rms (5 shr) (2 fmly) Open parking available Child discount available Outdoor swimming pool Boule Open terrace
Languages spoken: English & Spanish
ROOMS: s 185FF; d 300FF Reductions over 1 night
MEALS: Dinner 90FF&alc
CARDS: Travellers cheques

Le Mas du Grand Jonquier (Prop: M & Mme Greck)
84800
☎ 49020901391 FAX 490209118
(exit autoroute Avignon Sud in the direction of Apt-Sisteron-Digne)
Forest area
6 en suite (shr) (1 fmly) (3 with balcony) TV in all bedrooms Full central heating Open parking available Child discount available 8yrs Outdoor swimming pool Boule Bicycle rental Last d 8pm Languages spoken: English, German, Italian & Spanish
ROOMS: d 450FF
MEALS: Dinner 130FF
CARDS: ●● ☵ Travellers cheques

La Pastorale (Prop: Elizabeth Negrel)
Les Gardiolles, rte de Fontaine de Vaucluse *84800*
☎ 490202518 FAX 490202186
Near river Forest area Near motorway
4 en suite (bth/shr) (3 fmly) Full central heating Open parking available Child discount available Boule Languages spoken: English & German
CARDS: Travellers cheques

LAMBESC Bouches-du-Rhône

Bed & Breakfast (Prop: Mme Jeanne Meunier)
Mas de Rabarin, Chemin des Fédons *13410*
☎ 442571489 FAX 442570367
Near river Forest area
1 en suite (shr) Radio in rooms Full central heating Open parking available Child discount available 10yrs Open terrace Covered terrace Languages spoken: English & Spanish
CARDS: Travellers cheques

LAPALUD Vaucluse

Le Bergerie les Iles (Prop: Simone Gabriel Guet)
84840
☎ 490403082 FAX 490402429
(leave A7 at Bollène, follow signs to Lapalud. At rdbt, go N towards Montéliuers, turning is about 500yds along rd)
Near lake Forest area
2 rms (1 shr) No smoking on premises Full central heating Open parking available Child discount available 10yrs Fishing Last d 17.00hrs Languages spoken: English, Spanish & Italian
ROOMS: s 180FF; d 240FF
MEALS: Dinner fr 90FF

LAURIS Vaucluse

Le Maison des Sources (Prop: Martin Collart)
Chemin des Fraysses *84360*
☎ 490082219 608330640 FAX 490082219
Near river Near lake Forest area Near motorway
4 en suite (bth/shr) (2 with balcony) Full central heating

Open parking available Table tennis
ROOMS: s 340-360FF; d 390-420FF
MEALS: Dinner 120FF

LORIOL-DU-COMTAT Vaucluse

Château Talaud (Prop: M & Mme H Deiters-Kommer)
84870
☎ 490657100 FAX 490657793
(A7 exit 23 Avignon North, after toll booth left D942 direction of Carpentras for 10km, exit D107 Loriol-du-Comtat/Monteux Est, after 1.8km châteaux on left at end long entrance)

A small fully restored castle dated 1732, located in its own vineyard just 15 minutes from the Cathedral city of Avignon. The atmosphere is one of calm and tranquility and the Dutch owners give their guests every consideration.
Near river Forest area Near motorway
Closed Jan-14 Mar
4 en suite (bth/shr) (2 fmly) No smoking on premises TV in all bedrooms STV Direct-dial available Full central heating Open parking available Covered parking available Child discount available 16yrs Outdoor swimming pool Boule Bicycle rental Languages spoken: English, Dutch, German & Russian
ROOMS: d 650-95FF Reductions over 1 night
MEALS: Dinner 100-250FF
CARDS: ●● ☵ Travellers cheques

Famille Guillermain (Prop: Claude & Josette Guillermain)
Le Deves *84870*
☎ 490657062
(on the D950 3km from Carpentras in the direction of Orange)
Six rooms available on a farm which has been completely restored, set in parkland. Dining room and fridge can be used by the guests. Situated in the centre of Provence, twenty kilometres from Avignon. Daughter-in-law speaks English. Garden furniture. Meals available in the evening, by request.
Near river Near lake Forest area Near motorway
6 en suite (bth/shr) Full central heating Open parking available Boule Languages spoken: English
ROOMS: s 180-200FF; d 210-230FF
MEALS: Dinner 65-70FF
CARDS: Travellers cheques

Taking your mobile phone to France?
See page 11

MÉNERBES Vaucluse

Mas du Magnolia (Prop: Monika Hauschild)
Quartier le Fort *84560*
☎ 490724800 FAX 490724800
(from the north: A7 exit Avignon in direction Apt-Digne on D22 then N100, after village of Coustellet and before Les Beaumettes turn right direction of Menerbes on D103 Mas du Magnolia 2km on left)
Situated in the heart of the National Park of the Luberon, with its many medieval villages, this beautiful mansion offers bed & breakfast in the traditional French way. Large pool, in garden full of old trees, roses, lavender, rosemary and a giant magnolia tree. Four non-smoking bedrooms available on the ground floor, with one studio for two adults and one or two children, which would be suitable for the handicapped. Swimming pool, pool-house, barbecue and boules in the garden. English spoken.
Near river Near sea Forest area In town centre Near motorway
Closed Jan & Feb
4 en suite (bth/shr) No smoking on premises Radio in rooms Full central heating Open parking available Supervised Outdoor swimming pool Sauna Boule Pool house Barbecue
Languages spoken: English, German, Greek, Italian & Spanish
CARDS: Eurocheques, FF Travellers cheques

MÉZEL Alpes-de-Haute-Provence

Domaine de Préfaissal (Prop: Georges Giraud)
04270
☎ 492355209
Near river Forest area Near motorway
3 en suite (shr) (1 with balcony) Full central heating Open parking available Covered parking available Supervised Child discount available Outdoor swimming pool Boule
Languages spoken: English & Spanish
MEALS: Dinner 85-150FF*
CARDS: Travellers cheques

MONIEUX Vaucluse

Le Moulin (Prop: M & Mme Picca)
84390
☎ 490640464
Michèle Picca offers five rooms on the second floor of an 18th-century house, situated at the foot of Mount Ventoux. Fields of lavender surround the property. Swimming pool and tennis court on-site. Two restaurants within two kilometres of the residence. Open from June to September. English spoken.
Near river Forest area
5 rms Full central heating Open parking available Supervised Child discount available Outdoor swimming pool Tennis Languages spoken: English
CARDS: Travellers cheques

MONTFERRAT Var

Le Chiffet
83131
☎ 494709277
Flat with independent access in a Provençal style villa, set in extensive grounds. A warm welcome is offered in this comfortable location with its magnificent view. Private swimming pool. Good food by reservation only. Seaside resorts of St Maxime and St Tropez nearby. Walking, fishing,

windsurfing, sand yachting and tennis nearby. A little English spoken.
Near river Forest area
Closed early Oct-19 Mar
2 rms (1 shr) Full central heating Open parking available Supervised No children 8yrs Outdoor swimming pool Tennis

MONTMAUR Hautes-Alpes

Château-de-Montmaur (Prop: M & Mme Laurens)
05400
☎ 492581142
(take D994 from Gap to Veynes and 4 kms before Veynes take D320 towards Devoluy. Chateau on edge of village after 2kms, visible from the road)
All guest rooms have been modernised but parts of the chateau date back to the 12th century. In the 14th century the main building was erected by the High Barons of Montmaur, who lived there until 1825. The rooms are in one of the wings of the château. Each room has independent access. Many restaurants within a fifteen mile radius. English spoken.
Near river Forest area
5 en suite (shr) Full central heating Open parking available Covered parking available Supervised

MONTMEYAN Var

Bed & Breakfast (Prop: M & Mme Gonfond)
rte de Quinson *83670*
☎ 494807803
This old country house is surrounded by greenery and offers three rooms, restored in 1993 in typical Provençal style, looking out onto a hundred-year-old lime tree. Panoramic view of the surrounding countryside. All rooms equipped with television. A little English spoken.
Forest area
3 en suite (shr) TV available Full central heating Open parking available Supervised Child discount available 10yrs

MURS Vaucluse

Les Hauts de Veroncle (Prop: Didier Del Corso)
84220
☎ 490726091 FAX 490726207
(from Gordes, travel in direction of Murs. After 6km follow sign for 'Chambre d'hôtes')
Large, stone house set in four hectares of land. Comfortable rooms with private entrances which lead out onto the garden. Absolute calm guaranteed. English spoken.
Near river Forest area
Closed 16 Nov-Feb
3 en suite (shr) (2 fmly) No smoking in 2 bedrooms TV in 1 bedroom Full central heating Open parking available Child discount available 14yrs Bicycle rental V meals Last d 19.30hrs Languages spoken: English & Italian
ROOMS: d 270-280FF
MEALS: Dinner 105-115FF
CARDS: Travellers cheques

OPPÈDE-LE-VIEUX Vaucluse

Le Petit Creuil (Prop: M Edmund Goudin)
84580
☎ 490768089 FAX 490769286
Come and stay in a peaceful country farmhouse in the heart of the Luberon region where the atmosphere is relaxed and guests will always receive a warm welcome. The rooms look

out over the countryside, providing a haven of peace and quiet, amongst the vineyards and cherry trees.
Forest area
1 May-15 Nov
6 en suite (bth/shr) TV available Full central heating Open parking available Outdoor swimming pool Boule Bicycle rental Table tennis
ROOMS: s 330-500FF; d 380-550FF

Le Village (Prop: Dominique Bal)
Le Vieux Village *84580*
☎ 490768908
This guesthouse is situated at the foot of the old medieval Château of Oppècle, dates from the 18th century, and is flanked by mountains. Situated at the centre of the major walking routes of France, this is a paradise for those who love nature. Breakfast will be served either in the bedroom or the dining-room.
Forest area Near motorway
5 en suite (bth/shr) Full central heating Tennis Boule Bicycle rental
ROOMS: s fr 230FF; d fr 280FF
CARDS: Travellers cheques

Domaine de la Petite Cheylude (Prop: M J Hak)
518 route de la Gasquin *84210*
☎ 490613724 FAX 490616700
(highhway A7, Avignon Nord/le Pantet, head towards Carpentras, follow 'Monteux Centre', at 3rd set lights turn right (D31), after 5km turn left towards Carpentras-D49, after 2km, 'Domaine' is on left hand side)
Set in woodland, this 17th-century house offers comfortable bedrooms plus a cottage. Living room with arched ceiling and kitchen available for guests use. Large swimming pool in grounds.
Near river Near lake Forest area Near motorway
5 en suite (shr) (1 fmly) Full central heating Open parking available Outdoor swimming pool Boule Bicycle rental Table tennis Languages spoken: English & German
ROOMS: s 240-280FF; d 280-400FF
CARDS: Travellers cheques

St-Barthélemy (Prop: Jacqueline Mangeard)
84210
☎ 490664779 FAX 490664779
Restored 18th-century Provençal house, set in a leafy park. Laundry facilities for long stays. Rooms are quiet, relaxing and comfortable, furnished in a welcoming Provencial style. Children stay free. English spoken.
Near river Forest area

5 en suite (bth/shr) Full central heating Open parking available Covered parking available Supervised Child discount available Tennis Fishing Boule Bicycle rental Badminton Table tennis Languages spoken: English
ROOMS: s 200FF; d 260FF

Bed & Breakfast (Prop: Gerard Bidault)
Campagne St-Loup, Quartier de Crozé *84120*
☎ 490790365
Situated on the banks of the Durance, at the foot of the Luberon Mountains. This is a place for horse lovers - all types of riding take place here. Beginners, improvers, pony-and cart lovers - all can be accommodated. Swimming and many other sporting and cultural activities on site.
Near river Forest area
4 en suite (bth/shr) (2 fmly) Radio in rooms Full central heating Open parking available Child discount available 12yrs
CARDS: Travellers cheques

Bed & Breakfast (Prop: Mme Chantal Vandame)
rte du Muy *83120*
☎ 494437169
(highway rd to le Muy, then head towards Sainte Maxime, at crossrds turn towards Plan-de-la-Tour, go through village, turn right)
Your hosts are eager to welcome you to their tree-shaded property. A swimming pool is available on-site. Reductions for children under ten years. Peace and quiet guaranteed. English spoken.
Near sea Forest area
2 rms (1 bth/shr) No smoking on premises Open parking available Child discount available 10yrs Outdoor swimming pool Languages spoken: English & Spanish
ROOMS: s 240-270FF; d 330FF Reductions over 1 night

Bed & Breakfast (Prop: Marie Françoise Rouston)
L'Oustaou des Oliviers *84110*
☎ 490464589 FAX 490464093
The Roustan residence is in the middle of the countryside, amidst vines and olive trees. This is a very quiet area: only the singing of the birds and the trickling of the stream disturbs the peace. Your breakfast will be served with home-made jam and honey. Comfortable rooms. English spoken.
Forest area
Closed 8 Jan-Feb
4 en suite (shr) No smoking on premises Full central heating Open parking available Boule
CARDS: Travellers cheques

Domaine le Puy du Maupas (Prop: M & Mme Sauvayre)
rte de Nyons *84110*
☎ 490464743 FAX 490464851
On a route de vin, this winery is set in a calm area at the foot of Mont Ventoux, near the town of Vaison-la-Romaine, where you will find a good Provençal market. Guests are invited to test the house wine!
Near lake Forest area

cont'd

5 en suite (bth/shr) No smoking in all bedrooms Full central heating Open parking available Child discount available Outdoor swimming pool Boule Table tennis Last d 19.30hrs
MEALS: Dinner fr 110FF*
CARDS: Travellers cheques

Le Saumalier (Prop: M Sauvayre)
84110
☎ 490464961 FAX 490464961
Michèle and Jean-Luc welcome you to their home where you can enjoy the indoor heated swimming pool. One of the rooms is situated in the tower and offers a panoramic view over the surrounding countryside. The other room looks directly over Mont Ventoux. Children under five have reduced room rates. Forest area
2 en suite (bth/shr) (1 fmly) No smoking on premises TV available Open parking available Covered parking available Child discount available 5yrs

ROQUEBRUNE-SUR-ARGENS Var

La Maurette (Prop: Daniel & Katrin Rapin)
83520
☎ 494454681 FAX 494454681
(leave N7 between Le Muy and Puget, take D7 towards Roquebrune-sur-Argens)
'La Maurette' stands alone dominating the top of a hillside in the heart of 13 hectares of grounds. A forest provides the backdrop for the property, the rooms open onto shaded terraces and a large swimming pool.
Near river Near lake Forest area Near motorway
Closed 21 Oct-14 Mar
11 en suite (bth/shr) TV in all bedrooms Full central heating Open parking available No children 8yrs Outdoor swimming pool Languages spoken: English & German
ROOMS: (room only) d 350-450FF Reductions over 1 night
CARDS: ● ■ Travellers cheques

ROSANS Hautes-Alpes

L'Ensoleillée (Prop: M & Mme D Pacaud)
Le Beal Noir *05150*
☎ 492666272 FAX 492666287
Near river Near lake Forest area
6 en suite (bth/shr) (2 fmly) (5 with balcony) TV available Open parking available Covered parking available
MEALS: Dinner fr 85FF*

ROUSSILLON Vaucluse

Mamaison (Prop: Jazz Summers)
Quartier Les Devens *84220*
☎ 490057417 FAX 490057463
An 18th-century farm, set in the heart of Luberon, restored and decorated by regional artists. Situated in the middle of three hectares of luxurious garden, with a large swimming pool. All food is cooked using produce grown in the garden or bought from local markets. Fish a speciality. English spoken.
Closed Nov-14 Mar
5 en suite (bth/shr) (2 fmly) Full central heating Open parking available Child discount available Outdoor swimming pool V meals Languages spoken: English & Italian
CARDS: ● ■

RUSTREL Vaucluse

La Forge (Prop: D & C Berger-Ceccaldi)
Notre Dame des Anges *84400*
☎ 490049222 FAX 490049522
(from Apt D22 in the direction of Rustrel, in 7.5km (2.5km before Rustrel) turn right for La Forge)
Situated in the Luberon park, the Colorado Provençal is a stunning area. The guesthouse was constructed in 1840 and became a listed building in 1989. The building was formerly part of a foundry. Studio for painting, ceramics and a darkroom. Wine cellars. English spoken.
Near river Near lake Forest area
Closed 16 Nov-14 Jan
3 en suite (bth/shr) (1 fmly) Full central heating Open parking available Covered parking available Outdoor swimming pool Boule Languages spoken: English
ROOMS: d 500FF
MEALS: Dinner 150FF
CARDS: Travellers cheques

ST-MARTIN-LES-EAUX Alpes-de-Haute-Provence

Domaine d'Aurouze (Prop: M D Masselot)
04870
☎ 492876651 FAX 492875635
Near river Near lake Forest area
Closed 21 Oct-19 Mar
5 en suite (bth/shr) (2 fmly) TV available STV Full central heating Open parking available Supervised Child discount available Outdoor swimming pool Solarium Gym Boule Jacuzzi/spa Open terrace Languages spoken: English German & Spanish

ST-PIERRE-D'ARGENÇON Hautes-Alpes

La Source (Prop: M & Mme Rene Leautier)
05140
☎ 492586781
House situated next to a source of mineral water, hence the name of the property. Guest rooms and living room. Games area in garden. English spoken.
Near river Forest area Near motorway
Closed Oct-Apr
5 rms (3 shr) Full central heating Open parking available Boule Languages spoken: English & Italian
ROOMS: d 180-210FF

ST-RÉMY-DE-PROVENCE Bouches-du-Rhône

Mas de Gros (Prop: Schneider Reboul)
rte du Lac *13210*
☎ 490924685 FAX 490924778
Your hosts, Dino and Teresa, offer four rooms in their home, set in the middle of a tree-filled park of two hectares, with attractive swimming pool. Positioned in the Provençal region, between the sea and the mountains, you will find peace and a warm welcome awaiting you. Guests have the use of a lounge, dining room, terrace, barbecue and games in the garden. Many leisure pursuits in close proximity.
Near lake Forest area
Closed Nov-Mar
6 en suite (bth/shr) 4 rooms in annexe (2 fmly) TV in 4 bedrooms Licensed Full central heating Open parking available Supervised Outdoor swimming pool Riding Boule Bicycle rental Last d 21.00hrs Languages spoken: English
CARDS: Travellers cheques

Mas de la Tour (Prop: Christian Blaser)
Chemin de Bigau *13210*
☎ 490926100 FAX 490926100
(exit A7 at Cavaillon and take D99 west to St Remy, before
entering town turn left on first street after the 'Centre Ville'
sign, Mas de la Tour is signposted)
Beautiful stone house, close to the centre of St Remy, offer
peace and tranquillity. The bedrooms are decorated with an
individual flavour, with antiques and collectors items. Separate
access from the vast garden. A haven of peace for travellers
without children. Swimming pool. Restaurants within five
minutes walk. Various sporting activities at St Remy. English
spoken.
Forest area In town centre Near motorway
Closed Nov-Mar
4 en suite (shr) TV available Full central heating Open
parking available Covered parking available Outdoor
swimming pool Languages spoken: English, German, Italian
& Spanish
CARDS: Travellers cheques

La Matabone (Prop: M & Mme Discacciati)
1614 rte de Vidauban *83510*
☎ 494676206 FAX 494676206
(A8 exit Le Luc N7 Vidauban)
Near river Near sea Forest area Near motorway
6 en suite (shr) (2 fmly) (5 with balcony) No smoking in 1
bedroom TV in all bedrooms Full central heating Open
parking available Child discount available 10 yrs Outdoor
swimming pool Boule Bicycle rental Open terrace
Languages spoken: Italian & Spanish
ROOMS: d 365-540FF
MEALS: Dinner fr 145FF

ST-TRINIT Vaucluse

Ferme Auberge Les Bayles (Prop: M Gerard Sanchez)
84390
☎ 490750091
Nine kilometres from Sault, two kilometres from the village of
St Trinit, this farmhouse faces the mountain of Ventoux.
Communal rooms are available, one with open fire, one with
reading area, plus television and video. Mountain bikes can be
hired. Covered swimming pool which can be used winter and
summer. Reductions for visits of more than three days.
Forest area
Closed Dec-Jan
5 en suite (shr) Full central heating Open parking available
Child discount available 10yrs Outdoor swimming pool
Languages spoken: Spanish

STE-MAXIME Var

Mas des Brugassières (Prop: Annick Engrand)
Plan-de-la-Tour *83120*
☎ 494437242 FAX 494430020
Near sea Forest area Near motorway
Closed 10 Oct-20 Mar
10 en suite (bth/shr) (3 with balcony) No smoking in 4
bedrooms Licensed Full central heating Open parking
available Child discount available Outdoor swimming pool
Tennis Solarium Boule Open terrace Table tennis
Languages spoken: English German & Italian
ROOMS: (room only) s 420-480FF; d 480-550FF
CARDS: ●● ▄▄

SALERNES Var

La Bastide Rose (Prop: Karel & Caroline Henny)
Quartier Haut-Gaudran *83690*
☎ 494706330 FAX 494707734

This pink farm dates back to the 18th century. In addition to
the twelve acres of vines, there are fruit trees, olive trees,
rabbits, goats and poultry on the property. You are invited to
dine at your hosts table at a fixed price. Separate building
available which can house family groups. It has a large
lounge, dining room with television and children's games.
Markets held in the local village on Wednesday and Sunday.
Near river Near lake Forest area
RS 15 Nov-30 Mar
4 en suite (bth/shr) (2 fmly) (4 with balcony) No smoking on
premises Radio in rooms Open parking available Child
discount available 12yrs Outdoor swimming pool Table
tennis Volleyball Languages spoken: English
ROOMS: s 200-300FF; d fr 300FF
MEALS: Dinner 100FF*
CARDS: Travellers cheques

SAUMANE-DE-VAUCLUSE Vaucluse

Bed & Breakfast (Prop: Robert Beaumet)
chemin de la Tapy *84800*
☎ 490203297
Close to the village of Saumane, this lovely house offers a
unique atmosphere of serenity and peace. A typical southern
house, in the countryside, with a spacious garden.
Near river Forest area
3 en suite (shr) (1 fmly) Full central heating Boule
ROOMS: d 230FF

SÉGURET Vaucluse

St-Jean (Prop: Gisele Augier)
84110
☎ 490469176
(exit A7 at Orange and head in the direction of Vaison la
Romaine N977 until you reach Seguret then take CD88 to
establishment)
Very pretty Provençal house situated in a large garden with
swimming pool. Television and telephone in each room. Living
room reserved for guests. Breakfasts include specialities of the
region. English spoken.
Near river Forest area

cont'd

3 en suite (shr) (2 fmly) (1 with balcony) TV available Full central heating Open parking available Outdoor swimming pool Languages spoken: English & Spanish

SERRES Hautes-Alpes

Bed & Breakfast (Prop: M & Mme Emile Moynier)
L'Alpillonne, Sigottier *05700*
☎ 492670898
Situated at Sigottier, at an altitude of 600 metres, this 18th-century property offers individually decorated and furnished rooms. The Moynier family have been in residence for five generations. Breakfasts served on the terrace. Swimming pool. Barbecue. Games for the children in the garden. Mme Moynier speaks English.
Near river Near sea Near beach Forest area
Closed mid Sep-mid Jan
3 en suite (bth/shr) (1 with balcony) Full central heating
Child discount available 10yrs Languages spoken: English
CARDS: ▄▄

THOR, LE Vaucluse

Mas des Gerbauts (Prop: Mme Doribi)
Qaurtier le Trentin *84250*
☎ 490338885
This accommodation is situated in a magnificent setting between Avignon and Carpentras. Marie-Claude Doridi offers a traditional Provençal cuisine and welcomes her guests to dine with her. All vegetables are fresh from the farm. Nearby the tourist attractions include the Grottos of Thouzon, the fountain at Vaucluse, Mont Ventoux, Avignon and Luberon.
Near river Forest area
Closed Oct-mid Apr
2 en suite (bth/shr) No smoking on premises Full central heating Open parking available
CARDS: Travellers cheques

VACQUEYRAS Vaucluse

Les Ramières (Prop: M & Mme Bruel)
84190
☎ 490658961
Built in the 17th century, this has been the home of the same family ever since. Set in the middle of vines, the little town of Vacqueyras is not far away. The house is typically Provençal, with views over the vineyards. The rooms have low ceilings and original beams. Swimming pool nearby.
Near river Forest area
Closed 16 Sep-Apr
5 en suite (shr) (1 fmly) Open parking available Covered parking available Supervised Outdoor swimming pool

VAISON-LA-ROMAINE Vaucluse

Château du Taulignan (Prop: M Remy Daillet)
St-Marcellin Les Vaison *84110*
☎ 490287116 FAX 490288763
(from Vaison la Romaine, head towards Carpentias, Mont Ventoux. Leave town and turn left at crossed sign for Vaison la Romaine, towards 'Chemin de Planchette', castle is signposted)
All the rooms in this impressive 15th-century château are independently accessible. M and Mme Remy Daillet are happy to welcome you to this historical building. Peace and calm

reign. Traditional breakfast available. There is a Roman chapel on-site and weddings and conferences are catered for. English spoken.
Near river Near sea Forest area
4 en suite (bth) No smoking on premises Full central heating Open parking available Supervised Outdoor swimming pool Boule Languages spoken: English, Spanish & Japanese
ROOMS: d fr 450FF Reductions over 1 night
CARDS: Travellers cheques

Les Cigales (Prop: Mme Claudette Horte)
Chemin des Abeilles *84110*
☎ 490360225
Near river Forest area Near motorway
Closed Oct-Mar
4 en suite (bth/shr) (2 fmly) Full central heating Open parking available Covered parking available Outdoor swimming pool Languages spoken: English
CARDS: ▄▄▄ Travellers cheques

Délesse
Quartier le Brusquet *84110*
☎ 490363838
Huge rooms available in this whitewashed building near the foot of the mountains. All rooms have access independent of the rest of the house. Covered terrace with fridge, overlooking the vines. Large swimming pool. Reductions for children under ten and for guests staying more than one night. English spoken.
Near lake Forest area Near motorway
2 rms (1 bth/shr) (2 fmly) (1 with balcony) No smoking on premises Full central heating Open parking available Child discount available 10yrs Outdoor swimming pool Languages spoken: English & German
CARDS: Travellers cheques

L'Évêché (Prop: M A Verdier)
BP 13 Ville Medievale *84110*
☎ 490361346 FAX 490363243
This former Bishop's Palace, in the medieval part of Vaison-la-Romaine, was built in the 17th century. Four rooms are on offer. Breakfast is served on the terrace, which offers a stunning view of Vaison-la-Romaine. Your hosts love having visitors and certainly enjoy sharing a glass or two of wine. English spoken.

Taking your mobile phone to France?
See page 11

Near river Forest area Near motorway
5 rms (1 bth 3 shr) Full central heating Child discount available Bicycle rental Covered terrace Languages spoken: English
ROOMS: s 330-400FF; d 380-420FF
CARDS: Travellers cheques

VELLERON Vaucluse

Villa Velleron (Prop: Wim Visser et Simone Sanders)
rue Roquette *84740*
☎ 490201231 FAX 490201034
(from A7 exit at 'Auignon Nord/Centre' then follow direction Carpentras until Monteux. Follow Monteux Centre. At lights follow signs for Velleron, in Velleron find post office, the house is opposite.)

This bed & breakfast property is situated in the centre of the small Provençal village of Velleron, set between Mont Ventoux and Lubéron. The house is an old mill, constructed on the ruins of an ancient Roman fortification. Six rooms are available, decorated with taste and individual style. In the enclosed garden, you will find peace and relaxation beside the swimming pool. Meals are served on the terrace, creating a romantic atmosphere in the evenings. English spoken.
Near river Forest area
Closed Nov-Etr weekend
6 en suite (bth/shr) (1 fmly) (2 with balcony) Full central heating Covered parking available (charged) Supervised No children 8yrs Outdoor swimming pool Boule Bicycle rental
Last d 20.00hrs Languages spoken: English, Dutch & German
ROOMS: d 500-590FF
MEALS: Dinner fr 150FF
CARDS: Travellers cheques

VENASQUE Vaucluse

La Maison aux Vilets Bleus (Prop: Martine Maret)
pl des Bouviers-Le Village *84210*
☎ 490660304 FAX 490661614
(near Carpentras by the D4)
The view from the breakfast room of this Provençal house is stunning. The mountains opposite the house are breathtaking. Martine Maret, your hostess, will provide meals in the evening, and typical Provençal cuisine is on offer. Vegetarians catered for, by reservation in advance. Special childrens menu available. English spoken.
Forest area In town centre Near motorway
Closed 1 Nov-14 Mar
5 en suite (bth/shr) TV available Full central heating Last d 19.30hrs Languages spoken: English
ROOMS: d 350-450FF
MEALS: Dinner fr 120FF
CARDS: Travellers cheques

Maison Provencale (Prop: M Gerard Ruel)
Le Village *84210*
☎ 490660284 FAX 490666132
Renovated Provençal house in a village location. Guest rooms available, one with kitchenette. Communal lounge with television. Panoramic terrace with summer flower garden. Possibility of group bookings for up to fifteen people.
Forest area In town centre
5 en suite (bth/shr) (1 fmly) Full central heating Open parking available Open terrace

VENTABREN Bouches-du-Rhône

Val Lourdes (Prop: Murielle Lesage)
rte de Berre *13122*
☎ 442287515 FAX 442289291
19th-century house, offering attractive, spacious guest rooms looking out onto a large ornamental pond. Extra bed available to allow for three person occupancy. Reductions in room rate after four nights. English spoken.
Near river Forest area Near motorway
2 en suite (shr) No smoking on premises TV available Radio in rooms Full central heating Open parking available Supervised Languages spoken: English & Spanish

VENTEROL Hautes-Alpes

La Meridienne (Prop: M Boyer)
Le Blanchet *05130*
☎ 492541851 FAX 492541851
Old renovated farm surrounded by orchards, with panoramic views. Guests are invited to dine with the family. The Sene-Porçon lake is only fifteen minutes away. Painting and reading are the hobbies of the proprietors in this pretty region of France. English spoken.
Near lake Forest area
7 rms (1 bth 5 shr) (6 fmly) No smoking in 1 bedroom TV available Full central heating Open parking available Supervised Child discount available 12yrs Fishing Riding Gym Boule Bicycle rental Open terrace Last d 21.00hrs Languages spoken: English
MEALS: Continental breakfast 20FF Lunch 65-80FF Dinner 65-80FF*
CARDS: Travellers cheques

VILLEDIEU Vaucluse

Château la Baude (Prop: Gerard Monin)
84110
☎ 490289518 FAX 490289105
This fortified farm is a place where guests are invited to feel at home with their hosts, the Monin family, with whom meals may be taken. A courtyard overlooks the swimming pool and jacuzzi, and a tennis court is available. Magnificent view over the hills and valleys of Provence. Living room, library, snooker and boules available. English spoken.
Near river Forest area
Closed Dec-Feb
6 en suite (bth/shr) (2 fmly) No smoking on premises TV in all bedrooms Full central heating Open parking available Supervised Child discount available 12yrs Outdoor swimming pool Tennis Boule Table tennis Languages spoken: English & Italian
ROOMS: s 450FF; d 520FF
MEALS: Dinner fr 135FF
CARDS: Travellers cheques

VIOLES Vaucluse

La Farigoulé (Prop: Augustine Cornaz)
Le Plan de Dieu *84150*
☎ 490709178
18th-century restored house, set in a vineyard, where peace and calm are assured. Barbecue available. Your hosts are happy to accompany you on walks through the surrounding area. Bikes can be hired for a modest rate. The little town of Violès is just one and a half kilometres away and is right in the midst of the wine-making area of France. Large breakfasts served.
Near river Forest area Near motorway
Closed Nov-Mar
5 en suite (shr) Full central heating Open parking available Supervised Boule Bicycle rental Open terrace Table tennis Languages spoken: German & Spanish
ROOMS: s 220-260FF; d fr 290FF
CARDS: ●● ⚏ ▣ Travellers cheques

PROVENCE

Wine

The wine-growing areas in Provence are the oldest in France. Vines and cultivation methods were brought here by the Phonecians more than 2,600 years ago. The excellent and richly-coloured wines produced are of lasting quality, each having its own very distinct character. A visit to these wine-producing areas should

One of the many roadside billboards advertising the produce of Provence vineyards.

include, if possible, one of the many festivals where you will experience the cultural and artistic traditions associated with wine-growing and be charmed by the warm welcome and friendly cheer of the locals who are justifiably proud of their produce and so willing to share it.

Lavender

This delicate amethyst blue plant has been described as the 'soul of Upper Provence, its coat-of-arms'. It is hard to imagine the landscape without the endless expanse of blue which stretches to the horizon and fills the peaceful villages and beauty spots with its fragrance. Lavender origins lie in Persia; it was brought to Provence in ancient times and is an integral part of Provençal culture. Lavender flourishes, blooming here for just a short time during mid-summer.

Harvest time brings with it a time for colourful celebration, of numerous festivals including displays of both modern and traditional methods of lavender distillation. The local tourist boards organise sight-seeing tours which usually include architectural places of interest.

A common sight in Provence, a purple blanket of lavender.

Côte D'Azur

Summer and winter here are positively packed with arts festivals, many of which are famous the world over. But if you take the time to experience the gentler pace of life in the villages perched on the hillside and leisurely drive along some of the breath-taking roads through forests, past Roman churches, Gothic palaces and breathe in the scent from fields of lavender or the rosemary and thyme growing wild, you will experience something very different to the pace of life in the smart towns of Cannes and Nice.

(Top): A typical Côte D'Azur countryside landscape

(Bottom): The village of Cotignac was built in the 17th and 18th centuries, although previous inhabitants lived in the caves and tunnels in the 80m-high cliff.

ESSENTIAL FACTS

DÉPARTEMENTS:	Alpes-Maritimes
PRINCIPAL TOWNS	Grasse, Cannes, Antibes, Nice
PLACES TO VISIT:	Cannes for the shopping; Grasse for the perfume museum and tours at the Molinard, Fragonard or Galimard Perfumeries (the latter two are also in Eze Village); Mercantour national nature park; Villa Ephrussi de Rothschild at St-Jean-de-Cap-Ferrat; Picasso Museum
REGIONAL TOURIST OFFICE	Palais des Festival, 06400 Cannes Tel 04 93 39 24 53 Fax 04 93 99 37 06; 55 Promenade des Anglais, BP 602 Nice 06011 Tel 04 93 37 78 78 Fax 04 93 86 01 06
LOCAL GASTRONOMIC DELIGHTS	bouillabaisse, a fish stew; aïoli, garlic-flavoured mayonnaise; calissons, small diamond shaped almond-paste biscuits; rascasse, a spiny fish; salade Niçoise, tuna fish salad; pissaladière, an onion tart from Nice; tapenade, an olive paste; ratatouille; pistou soup, a thick vegetable soup with basil and garlic; squid; bourride, fish soup; anchoïade, an anchovy mixture.
DRINKS	Pastis, an aniseed-flavoured aperitif usually diluted with water to make a long drink; sweet aperitif wines such as Muscat des Beaume de Venise and Rasteau; or try some of the Provençal spirits - Vieux Marc de Provence, Elixir du Révérend Père Gaucher, Eau de vie de Poire, Genepy des Alpes.
LOCAL CRAFTS WHAT TO BUY	soaps and perfume from Grasse, lavender honey, Provençal fabrics, herbs, olive oil, crystallised fruit

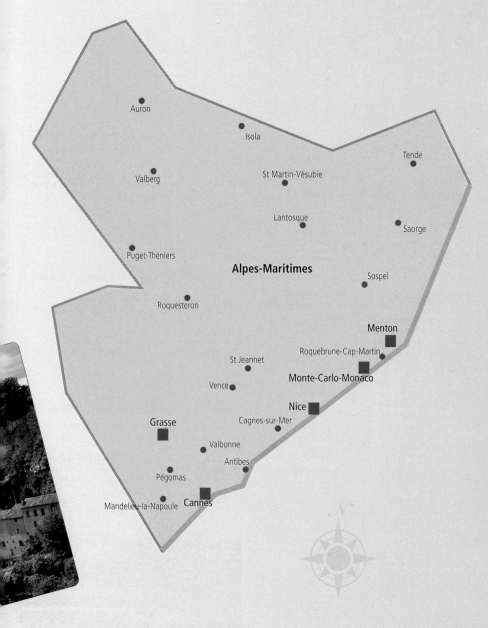

Auron

Isola

Tende

Valberg

St Martin-Vésubie

Lantosque

Saorge

Puget-Théniers

Alpes-Maritimes

Sospel

Roquesteron

Menton

Roquebrune-Cap-Martin

St Jeannet

Monte-Carlo-Monaco

Vence

Nice

Cagnes-sur-Mer

Grasse

Valbonne

Antibes

Pégomas

Mandelieu-la-Napoule

Cannes

EVENTS & FESTIVALS

Feb Cannes International Games Festival;
Antibes/Juan-les-Pins Jazz Festival; Menton
Lemon Festival; Nice Carnival; Cagnes-sur
Mer International Flower Exhibition;
Mandelieu-la-Napoule Mimosa Festival

Mar Antibes Golden Dove Magic Festival; Nice
International Fair; Antibes Antiques Show

Apr Antibes Antiques Show

May Antibes Bridge Festival; Cannes International
Film Festival; Cannes Contemporary Art
Market (*Palais de Festivals*); Cagnes-sur-Mer
Comic Book Festival; May Festivals at Nice,
Menton, Roquebrune; Grasse International
Flower Show; Monaco (Monte Carlo) Formula
One Grand Prix;

Jun Cannes International Festival of Actors'
Performances (*humour, theatre, music hall*);
Antibes International Young Soloist Festival

Jul Nice Jazz Festival; Antibes/Juan-les-Pins Jazz
Festival in the pine forest; Nice, Cimiez
Monastery Cloister Festival (chamber &
choral music); Menton Music Festival
(*chamber music, recitals*)

Aug Cagnes-sur-Mer Medieval Festival; Nice,
Menton Music Festival (*chamber music,
recitals*)

Oct Antibes World Festival of Underwater
Photography & Film;

Nov Antibes Maritime & Military Film Festival;
Cannes International Dance Festival

Lavender

This delicate amethyst blue plant has been described
as the 'soul of Upper Provence, its coat-of-arms'. It is
hard to imagine the landscape without the endless
expanse of blue which stretches to the horizon and
fills the peaceful villages and beauty spots with its
fragrance. Lavender origins lie in Persia; it was
brought to Provence in ancient times and is an
integral part of Provençal culture. The lavender
flourishes in the stony ground and the flowers bloom
for just a short time during mid-summer.

Harvest time brings with it a time for colourful
celebration, of numerous festivals including displays
of both modern and traditional methods of lavender
distillation. The local tourist boards organise many
sight-seeing tours taking in the region's architectural
gems during this interesting time.

ANTIBES Alpes-Maritimes

La Bastide du Bosquet (Prop: C & S Aussel)
14 chemin des Sables *06160*
☎ 493673229 FAX 493673229
(from town centre follow signs for Le Cap;at L'ilet crossroads
follow signs for Juan-Les-Pins Direct. No 14 is at top of
chemin des Sables)
This family home dates from the 17th century, and is situated
between Antibes and Juan les Pins, at the edge of the Cap
d'Antibes. The beaches are a mere five minutes away and the
centre of old Antibes is only a quarter of an hour walk along
the sea-front. The house faces south and offers peace and
relaxation. English spoken.
Near sea Near beach Forest area Near motorway
3 en suite (bth/shr) (1 fmly) Full central heating Open
parking available Child discount available 3yrs Languages
spoken: English & Finnish
ROOMS: d 420FF
CARDS: Travellers cheques

Villa "Panko" (Prop: M & Mme B Bourgade)
17 chemin du Parc Saramartel *06160*
☎ 493679249 FAX 493612932
(from Antibes follow signs for Cap d'Antibes. Take right into
'Chemin du Crouton', then 1st left into cul-de-sac.
Establishment at end)
Set amidst exquisite greenery and charming gardens, full of
flowers, this house is within a ten minute walk of white, sandy
beaches. The comfortable house has been recently decorated
in traditional, colourful Provançal-style furnishings with many
beautiful water colours adorning the walls. You are assured of
a warm welcome and your hosts can give you helpful advice

about the local area. Close to Picasso's Museum, Maeghts
Foundation, jazz and classical music festivals, the old city of
Antibes and gardens to visit.
Near sea Near beach Forest area
2 en suite (bth) (1 fmly) No smoking on premises Radio in
rooms Full central heating Open parking available Child
discount available 10yrs Languages spoken: English & Italian
ROOMS: s 400FF; d 420FF *
CARDS: Travellers cheques

LA COLLE-SUR-LOUP Alpes-Maritimes

Le Clos de St Paul (Prop: Beatrice Ronin Pillet)
71 ch de la Rouguière *06480*
☎ 493325681 FAX 493325681
(on A8 exit 47 Villeneuve-Loubet, then towards St Paul de
Vence. In la Colle/Loup turn right at lights. Towards la
Rouguiere. House on right in 2nd valley after old houses)

Just near St Paul de Vence, this Provençal-style house is situated in a quiet residential area and has comfortable rooms. Breakfast is served on the veranda by the large swimming pool. English spoken.
Near sea Forest area Near motorway
3 en suite (bth/shr) (1 fmly) (2 with balcony) No smoking on premises Open parking available Outdoor swimming pool Boule Table tennis Languages spoken: English & German
ROOMS: s 250-260FF; d 300-380FF Reductions over 1 night

PÉGOMAS Alpes-Maritimes

Les Bosquet (Prop: M & Mme Cattet)
74 Chemiq du Perissols 06580
☎ 492602120 FAX 492602149
Near river Near lake Forest area
Closed 15 Feb-2 Mar
16 en suite (bth/shr) Some rooms in annexe (7 with balcony) TV in all bedrooms Radio in rooms Full central heating Open parking available Covered parking available Supervised Outdoor swimming pool Tennis Boule Open terrace Languages spoken: English & Italian
CARDS: Travellers cheques

ST-JEANNET Alpes-Maritimes

Bed & Breakfast (Prop: M & Mme Benoit)
136 rue St-Claude 06640
☎ 493247630 FAX 493247877
(exit the A8 at St Laurent du Var in the direction of St Jeannet)

Comfortable, quiet and self-contained rooms, in a private house, looking out onto a south-facing garden, with a view over the bay of Nice and Antibes. Set at an altitude of 450 metres in a village perched at the foot of St Jeannet. Swimming pool with sun-loungers. The sea is twenty minutes away. English spoken.
Forest area Near motorway
Closed 2wks Aug
3 en suite (bth/shr) TV available Radio in rooms Full central heating Open parking available Supervised Child discount available Outdoor swimming pool Languages spoken: English & German
ROOMS: d 350-450FF

SOSPEL Alpes-Maritimes

Domaine du Parais (Prop: Matie Mayer)
Chemin du Paradis, La Vasta 06380
☎ 493041578
(exit Menton from A8 onto D2566 in direction of Sospel continue until La Mairie (townhall) then turn left in direction of Moulinet continue for nearly 2km then left to La Vasta. For 1300m, Domaine will be on the right after 2 camp sites and a ranch)
An imposing manor house set eighteen kilometres from Menton. An ideal spot for those wishing to discover the surrounding countryside. Fluent English spoken.
Forest area
4 en suite (shr) (1 fmly) Full central heating Open parking available Languages spoken: English & German
ROOMS: s 250-350FF; d 280-400FF
CARDS: Travellers cheques

VALBONNE Alpes-Maritimes

Le Cheneau (Prop: Christianne & Alain Ringenbach)
205 rte d'Antibes 06560
☎ 493121394 FAX 493129185
(from A8 exit Antibes take direction of Sophia Antipolis then Valbonne, continue on rte du Parc until the Bois Dore restaurant approx 100mtrs after a private lane leads to Le Cheneau)
Large Provence-style house on a shaded private quiet park, located near the old village of Valbonne. Bedrooms are well kept and sunny with self contained entrance. Beaches, harbours and Nice International airport are only 20 mins drive away.
Forest area
3 en suite (bth/shr) (2 fmly) No smoking on premises TV in 1 bedroom Full central heating Open parking available Covered parking available Child discount available 2yrs Languages spoken: English
ROOMS: s 280-380FF; d 320-420FF *
CARDS: Travellers cheques

SELECTED LIST OF HOTEL GROUPS OFFERING GOOD OVERNIGHT ACCOMMODATION:

Balladins, Bonsai, Clarines, Formule 1, Hotel Mister Bed, Marmotte, Nuits d'Hotel, Première Classe, Villages Hotel,

This quick reference list gives the locations (the town or city in capital letters, followed by the département name with the hotel telephone number below) of selected hotel groups in France which have competitively priced overnight accommodation of a good modern standard. A brief description of the style of hotel in each group is given at the beginning of each group's listing. Some hotel groups use the group name for each hotel and some groups have individual hotel names. Where there are two or more listings under a town heading it means there are two or more hotels in that town and telephone numbers

BALLADINS

This chain of hotel restaurants has locations across France, and all have ample parking. The bedrooms are modern and comfortable with en-suite showers and WC, direct dial telephone and colour television. The restaurants offer relaxed and pleasant surroundings in which to enjoy lunch or dinner and have an all-you-can-eat buffet or you can choose from a menu of regional dishes.

Major credit cards are accepted and accommodation can be booked on Balladins central reservation number - 05396666.

AIX-EN-PROVENCE Bouches-du-Rhône
Balladins 442272525
AMIENS Somme
Balladins 322539070
ANGERS Maine-et-Loire
Balladins 241370505
ANGOULEME Charente
Balladins 545692300
ARGENTEUIL Val-d'Oise
Balladins 239476767
ARLES Bouches-du-Rhône
Balladins 450371017
AUBAGNE Bouches-du-Rhône
Balladins 442320708
AVIGNON Vaucluse
Balladins 490868892
BAILLET-EN-FRANCE Val-d'Oise
Balladins 534698848
BEAUVAIS Oise
Balladins 344029666
BESANCON Doubs
Balladins 381515251
BLOIS Loir-et-Cher
Balladins 254426990
BORDEAUX Gironde
Balladins 556500817

BREST Finistère
Balladins 298406870
BRIVE-LA-GAILLARDE Corrèze
Balladins 555744040
BUCHELAY Yvelines
Balladins 534768383
CAEN Calvados
Balladins 231474000
CALAIS Pas-de-Calais
Balladins 321977273
CARCASSONNE Aude
Balladins 468723434
CERGY-PONTOise Val-d'Oise
Balladins 134240654
CHAMBERY Savoie
Balladins 479961122
CHANTILLY Oise
Balladins 344581312
CHARTRES Eure-et-Loir
Balladins 237302705
CHILLY-MAZARIN Essonne
Balladins 169204455
CLERMONT-FERRAND Pûy
Balladins 473918134
CRETEIL Val-de-Marne
Balladins 143392315
DUNKERQUE Nord
Balladins 328274669
EPONE Yvelines
Balladins 130903737
FREJUS Var
Balladins 494170250
GOUSSAINVILLE Val-d'Oise
Balladins 139883000
GRENOBLE Isère
Balladins 476758999
LE BLANC-MESNIL Seine-St-Denis
Balladins 248650619
LE BOURGET Seine-St-Denis
Balladins 148353318
LE MANS Sarthe
Balladins 243216027
LILLE Nord
Balladins 320540002
LILLE Nord
Balladins 320890077
LIMOGES Haute-Vienne
Balladins 555375533
LINAS-MONTLHERY Essonne
Balladins 164490000
LORIENT Morbihan
Balladins 297764641
LYON Rhône
Balladins 472045676
LYON Rhône
Balladins 478204222
MACON Saône-et-Loire
Balladins 385390926
MARSEILLE Bouches-du-Rhône
Balladins 442151414
MARSEILLE Bouches-du-Rhône
Balladins 491257575
MARTIGUES Bouches-du-Rhône
Balladins 442808951
MELUN Seine-et-Marne
Balladins 564103600
MERLINES Corrèze
Balladins 555944280

METZ Moselle
Balladins 387331956
MONTPELLIER Hérault
Balladins 467220922
MONTPELLIER Hérault
Balladins 467610130
MULHOUSE Haut-Rhin
Balladins 389617011
NANTES Loire-Atlantique
Balladins 240301212
NICE Alpes-Maritimes
Balladins 492598928
NICE Alpes-Maritimes
Balladins 493444101
NIMES Gard
Balladins 466382400
ORLEANS Loiret
Balladins 238737273
PARIS Paris
Balladins 144677575
PERPIGNAN Pyrénées-Orientales
Balladins 468855055
POISSY Yvelines
Balladins 139220050
POITIERS Vienne
Balladins 549415500
PONTAULT-COMBAULT Seine-et-
Marne Balladins 160294242
QUIMPER Finistère
Balladins 298595500
REIMS Marne
Balladins 326827210
RENNES Ille-et-Vilaine
Balladins 299416611
ROISSY-AEROPORT CH DE GAULLE
Val-d'Oise
Balladins 360036565
ROSNY-SOUS-BOIS Seine-St-Denis
Balladins 148942330
ROUEN Seine-Maritime
Balladins 232591819
RUNGIS Val-de-Marne
Balladins 549780145
SANTENAY Côte-d'Or
Balladins 143861516
SARCELLES Val-d'Oise
Balladins 139948080
SENS Yonne
Balladins 386952295
ST CYR-L'ECOLE Yvelines
Balladins 130585252
ST GENIS-POUILLY Ain
Balladins 450206512
ST OUEN-L'AUMONE Val-d'Oise
Balladins 134488484
STRASBOURG Bas-Rhin
Balladins 388769588
STRASBOURG Bas-Rhin
Balladins 388814499
TARBES Hautes-Pyrénées
Balladins 562511256
TORCY Seine-et-Marne
Balladins 160176309
TOULON Var
Balladins 494212707
TOULOUSE Haute-Garonne
Balladins 561392025

TOULOUSE AIRPORT
Haute-Garonne Balladins 561712707
TOURS Indre-et-Loire
Balladins 247289292
TOURS Indre-et-Loire
Balladins 247419797
VALENCE Drome
Balladins 475829297
VALENCIENNES Nord
Balladins 327295555
VERT-ST-DENIS Seine-et-Marne
Balladins 164416666

BONSAI GROUP

This group of roadside lodges offers three differing levels of good-value accommodation

Bonsai ESCALE offers en-suite bedrooms with toilet and shower which can sleep up to three persons. Colour television is provided and pay phones are available in reception. Breakfast is provided at a buffet bar in the lounge.

Bonsai ETAPE are one star hotels and have larger bedrooms with en-suite, toilet and shower and they also have colour television and direct dial telephones.
Bonsai RELAIS form the top of this range and are graded two or three star; some have a swimming pool. Well equipped bedrooms include en-suite facilities, colour television and direct dial telephones. They have restaurants with a range of fine cuisine and local dishes.

Central reservations can be made by telephoning 36637271.

AVIGNON Vaucluse Hotel Bonsai Etape
490273515
BELFORT Territoire-de-Belfort
Hotel Bonsai Escale 384540967
CERGY Val-d'Oise
Hotel Bonsai Escale 130732533
CHAMBRAY-LES-TOURS
Indre-et-Loire
Hotel Bonsai Escale 247289393
CHANTEPIE Ille-et-Vilaine
Hotel Bonsai Etape 299416566
CHILLY-MAZARIN Essonne
Hotel Bonsai Etape 164548991
L'UNION Haute-Garonne
Hotel Bonsai Etape 561099314
LUDRES Meurthe-et-Moselle
Hotel Bonsai Escale 383257466
MARSANNAY-LA-COTE Côte-d'Or
Hotel Bonsai Escale 380524400
MARTIGUES Bouches-du-Rhône
Hotel Bonsai Etape 442800808
METZ Moselle
Hotel Bonsai Escale 387751957
MOISSY-CRAMAYEL Seine-et-Marne
Hotel Bonsai Escale 564889134
MONDEVILLE Calvados
Hotel Bonsai Etape 231340003
MONTAGNAT Ain
Hotel Bonsai Escale 474226023

OLIVET Loiret
Hotel Bonsai Etape 238760304
PLERIN Côtes-d'Armor
Hotel Bonsai Relais 296792525
SEPTENES-LES-VALLONS Bouches-du-Rhône Hotel Bonsai Etape
391961723
ST EMILION Gironde
Hotel Bonsai Relais 557252507
TOURLAVILLE Manche
Hotel Bonsai Etape 233431860
VIENNE Isère
Hotel Bonsai Etape 474317460
VITROLLES Bouches-du-Rhône
Hotel Bonsai Etape 442751313

CLARINE

This group offers a range of hotel accommodation in locations throughout France, many in the town centres. A mix of traditional and modern is a feature, but they pride themselves on consisten quality and standard rates for accommodation. Most bedrooms have en-suite facilities and colour television, and many have private parking. In most you will find pleasant restaurants serving traditional and local specialities.

A central booking service is available by telephoning 0164624848.

ANNECY Haute-Savoie
Hotel du Nord (Centre) 450450878
(Clarine)
CAEN Calvados
Clarine 231783838
CAEN Calvados
Clarine 231958700
CARCASSONNE Aude
Clarine (La Cite) 468471631
CHALON-SUR-SAONE
Saône-et-Loire
Clarine (Centre) 385487043
DIJON Côte-d'Or
Clarine (Est-Mirande) 380316912
DIJON Côte-d'Or
Terminus Hotel 380435378 (Clarine)
EPINAL Vosges
Ariane Hotel(Centre) 329821074
(Clarine)
LE HAVRE Seine-Maritime
Clarine 235264949
LILLE Nord
Nord Hotel (Sud) (Clarine)
LIVRY-GARGAN Seine-St-Denis
Clarine 243854141
LYON Rhône
Les Relais Perrache 478371664
(Clarine)
MARSEILLE Bouches-du-Rhône
Hotel Castellane 564624848 (Clarine)
MARTIGUES Bouches-du-Rhône
Clarine 442818494
MEAUX Seine-et-Marne
Clarine 564330088
MELUN Seine-et-Marne
Clarine 564524141
NEVERS Nièvre
Clarine 386719500
NICE Alpes-Maritimes
Clarine 491877508

ORLY Val-de-Marne
Clarine 469383000
PARIS Paris
Clarine (Alésia) 145414145
PARIS Paris
Clarine (La Défense) 147882858
PARIS Paris
Hotel Lorette 142851881 (Clarine)
PARIS Paris
Hotel de Paris (Montmartre)
148741094 (Clarine)
PAU Pyrénées-Atlantiques
Hotel de Paris (Centre) 559825800
(Clarine)
ROUEN Seine-Maritime
Clarine (Nord) 235598000
ROUEN Seine-Maritime
Clarine (centre) 235152525
STRASBOURG Bas-Rhin
Clarine (Pont de l'Europe) 388601052
TORCY Seine-et-Marne
Clarine Marne-la-Vellée 564800232
TOULON Var Gardotel 494758225
TOULOUSE Haute-Garonne
Clarine(Centre) 561624292
TOURS Indre-et-Loire
Hotel le Royal (Centre) 247647178

FORMULE 1 GROUP

This major chain consists of modern, functional roadside lodges specifically designed for stopovers. Bedrooms have a double bed, single bunk bed and wash basin. Other facilities include colour television and alarm. Near to each room are showers and toilets, fitted with self-clean systems. Self-service buffet breakfast is provided in the bar-style restaurant. Visa, Mastercard, American Express and Eurocheque are accepted.

Central booking is available by telephoning 236685685.

ABBEVILLE Somme
Formule 1 322240750
AGEN Lot-et-Garonne
Formule 1 553983700
AIX-EN-PROVENCE Bouches-du-Rhône
Formule 1 442586303
ALBERTVILLE Savoie
Formule 1 479370076
ALBI TARN
Formule 1 563475927
ALENCON Orne
Formule 1 233286000
AMIENS Somme
Formule 1 322470304
ANGERS Maine-et-Loire
Formule 1 241602020
ANGERS Maine-et-Loire
Formule 1 241732990
ANGOULEME Charente
Formule 1 545691155
ANNECY Haute-Savoie
Formule 1 450271122
ANNEMASSE Haute-Savoie
Formule 1 450946799
ANTIBES Alpes-Maritimes
Formule 1 493652020
ARRAS Pas-de-Calais
Formule 1 321249484

AULNAY-SOUS-BOIS Seine-St-Denis
Formule 1 545912325
AULNAY-SOUS-BOIS Seine-St-Denis
Formule 1 248655050
AUXERRE Yonne
Formule 1 386532902
AVIGNON Vaucluse
Formule 1 490269351
AVIGNON Vaucluse
Formule 1 490329000
AVIGNON Vaucluse
Formule 1 490864855
AVRANCHES Manche
Formule 1 233582600
BAILLEUL Nord
Formule 1 328412626
BAYONNE Pyrénées-Atlantiques
Formule 1 559555751
BEAUVAIS Oise
Formule 1 344847084
BELFORT Territoire-de-Belfort
Formule 1 384216060
BELFORT Territoire-de-Belfort
Formule 1 384222610
BESANCON Doubs
Formule 1 381480925
BESANCON Doubs
Formule 1 381510444
BEUVRY Pas-de-Calais
Formule 1 321641919
BEYNOST Rhône
Formule 1 478552700
BEZIERS Hérault
Formule 1 467359080
BLOIS Loir-et-Cher
Formule 1 254424269
BLOIS Loir-et-Cher
Formule 1 254780185
BOLLENE Vaucluse
Formule 1 490301171
BORDEAUX Gironde
Formule 1 556287378
BORDEAUX Gironde
Formule 1 556317324
BORDEAUX Gironde
Formule 1 556328833
BORDEAUX Gironde
Formule 1 556348064
BORDEAUX Gironde
Formule 1 556375098
BORDEAUX Gironde
Formule 1 557800340
BOULOGNE-SUR-MER Pas-de-Calais
Formule 1 321312628
BOURG-DE-PEAGE Drome
Formule 1 475051727
BOURG-EN-BRESSE Ain
Formule 1 474450554
BOURGES Cher
Formule 1 248265454
BREST Finistère
Formule 1 298402727
BREST Finistère
Formule 1 298414142
BRETIGNY-SUR-ORGE Essonne
Formule 1 469806699
BRIE-COMTE-ROBERT Seine-et-Marne
Formule 1 360620577
BRIGNOLES Var
Formule 1 394694505
CAEN Calvados
Formule 1 231721050
CAEN Calvados
Formule 1 231751531
CAHORS LOT
Formule 1 565223422

CALAIS Pas-de-Calais
Formule 1 321826700
CAMBRAI Nord
Formule 1 327749922
CARCASSONNE Aude
Formule 1 468787374
CERGY-PONTOise Val-d'Oise
Formule 1 130732737
CHALON-SUR-SAONE Saône-et-Loire
Formule 1 385415131
CHALONS-EN-CHAMPAGNE Marne
Formule 1 326677777
CHAMBERY Savoie
Formule 1 479251266
CHAMBERY Savoie
Formule 1 479280093
CHAMBLY Oise
Formule 1 139372209
CHANTELOUP-LES-VIGNES Yvelines
Formule 1 239707277
CHARLEVILLE-MEZIERES Ardennes
Formule 1 324371232
CHARTRES Eure-et-Loir
Formule 1 237307076
CHASSE-SUR-Rhône Isère
Formule 1 478739111
CHATELLERAULT Vienne
Formule 1 549933748
CHAUMONT Haute-Marne
Formule 1 325321616
CHERBOURG Manche
Formule 1 233446262
CHILLY-MAZARIN Essonne
Formule 1 469098771
CHOLET Maine-et-Loire
Formule 1 241585252
CLERMONT-FERRAND Pûy-de-Dome
Formule 1 473923200
COLMAR Haut-Rhin
Formule 1 389410606
COMPIEGNE Oise
Formule 1 344900202
CONFLANS-STE-HONORINE Yvelines
Formule 1 239197242
CORBEIL-ESSONNE Essonne
Formule 1 564961818
CORBEIL-ESSONNES Essonne
Formule 1 469900636
COULOMMIERS Seine-et-Marne
Formule 1 564750180
CROSNE Essonne
Formule 1 469833131
DENAIN-VALENCIENNES Nord
Formule 1 327318702
DIEPPE Seine-Maritime
Formule 1 235401595
DIJON Côte-d'Or
Formule 1 380520852
DIJON Côte-d'Or
Formule 1 380744421
DINARD Ille-et-Vilaine
Formule 1 299882211
DOLE JURA
Formule 1 384792929
DOUAI Nord
Formule 1 327883131
DREUX Eure-et-Loir
Formule 1 237462841
DUNKERQUE Nord
Formule 1 328215156
ECUELLES Seine-et-Marne
Formule 1 564311666
ENGLOS Nord
Formule 1 320090848
EPINAL Vosges
Formule 1 329344422

EPINAY-SUR-ORGE Essonne
Formule 1 469343536
EPONE Yvelines
Formule 1 130900947
EVREUX Eure
Formule 1 232288000
EVRY Essonne
Formule 1 360780909
EVRY Essonne
Formule 1 564970220
FERNEY-VOLTAIRE Ain
Formule 1 450404684
FONTENAY-TRESIGNY Seine-et-Marne
Formule 1 564251548
FOUGERES Ille-et-Vilaine
Formule 1 299999741
FOUQUIERES-LES-BETHUNE Pas-de-Calais
Formule 1 321570740
FREJUS Var
Formule 1 494816161
GAP Hautes-Alpes
Formule 1 492535355
GOUSSAINVILLE Val-d'Oise
Formule 1 239889090
GRENOBLE Isère
Formule 1 476219548
GRENOBLE Isère
Formule 1 476425454
GRENOBLE Isère
Formule 1 476750101
GRIGNY Essonne
Formule 1 469431312
HYERES Var
Formule 1 494052764
ISSOIRE Pûy
Formule 1 473969137
LA ROCHE-SUR-YON Vendée
Formule 1 251626666
LA ROCHELLE Charente-Maritime
Formule 1 546569460
LAVAL Mayenne
Formule 1 243493838
LE HAVRE Seine-Maritime
Formule 1 235453183
LE LUC Var
Formule 1 491609600
LE MANS Sarthe
Formule 1 243216262
LE MANS Sarthe
Formule 1 243252215
LES MUREAUX Yvelines
Formule 1 534743656
LES ULIS Essonne
Formule 1 469829500
LESQUIN Nord
Formule 1 320604747
LIEVIN Pas-de-Calais
Formule 1 321441700
LIMOGES Haute-Vienne
Formule 1 555370237
LINAS Essonne
Formule 1 564498662
LORIENT Morbihan
Formule 1 297812525
LOUVIERS Eure
Formule 1 232598880
LYON Rhône
Formule 1 472390222
LYON Rhône
Formule 1 472480707
LYON Rhône
Formule 1 478005984
LYON Rhône
Formule 1 478029444

LYON Rhône
Formule 1 478042291
LYON Rhône
Formule 1 478207979
LYON Rhône
Formule 1 478358080
LYON Rhône
Formule 1 478480023
LYON Rhône
Formule 1 478791140
MACON Saône-et-Loire
Formule 1 385339216
MACON Saône-et-Loire
Formule 1 385375900
MAGNANVILLE Yvelines
Formule 1 534771156
MARNE-LA-VALLEE Seine-et-Marne
Formule 1 243041022
MARNE-LA-VALLEE Seine-et-Marne
Formule 1 564110580
MARNE-LA-VALLEE Seine-et-Marne
Formule 1 564110580
MARSEILLE Bouches-du-Rhône
Formule 1 442025522
MARSEILLE Bouches-du-Rhône
Formule 1 442320171
MARSEILLE Bouches-du-Rhône
Formule 1 442790610
MARSEILLE Bouches-du-Rhône
Formule 1 491272020
MARSEILLE Bouches-du-Rhône
Formule 1 491452874
MARSEILLE Bouches-du-Rhône
Formule 1 491960103
MARSEILLE Bouches-du-Rhône
Formule 1 491962442
MARTIGUES Bouches-du-Rhône
Formule 1 442421212
MAUBEUGE Nord
Formule 1 327644800
MAUREPAS Yvelines
Formule 1 130511010
MEAUX Seine-et-Marne
Formule 1 360042232
MEAUX Seine-et-Marne
Formule 1 360230866
MELUN Seine-et-Marne
Formule 1 360605275
MELUN Seine-et-Marne
Formule 1 564389210
MELUN Seine-et-Marne
Formule 1 564417222
MERLEBACH Moselle
Formule 1 387816944
MERY-SUR-Oise Val-d'Oise
Formule 1 534481100
METZ Moselle
Formule 1 387313661
METZ Moselle
Formule 1 387737302
METZ Moselle
Formule 1 387763481
MONS-EN-BARCEUL Nord
Formule 1 320334600
MONTAUBAN TARN-ET-Garonne
Formule 1 563914370
MONTCHANIN Saône-et-Loire
Formule 1 385788000
MONTELIMAR Drome
Formule 1 475631363
MONTLUCON Allier
Formule 1 470037707
MONTPELLIER Hérault
Formule 1 467474770
MONTPELLIER Hérault
Formule 1 467589898

MONTPELLIER Hérault
Formule 1 467873606
MOULINS Allier
Formule 1 470462424
MULHOUSE Haut-Rhin
Formule 1 389423055
MULHOUSE Haut-Rhin
Formule 1 389523000
MULHOUSE Haut-Rhin
Formule 1 389617410
NANCY Meurthe-et-Moselle
Formule 1 383227879
NANCY Meurthe-et-Moselle
Formule 1 383560808
NANCY Meurthe-et-Moselle
Formule 1 383951716
NANTES Loire-Atlantique
Formule 1 240507910
NANTES Loire-Atlantique
Formule 1 240509200
NANTES Loire-Atlantique
Formule 1 240636400
NANTES Loire-Atlantique
Formule 1 240651818
NARBONNE Aude
Formule 1 468416100
NEMOURS Seine-et-Marne
Formule 1 564291764
NEVERS Nièvre
Formule 1 386594060
NIMES Gard
Formule 1 466263800
NIMES Gard
Formule 1 466381405
NIORT Deux-Sèvres
Formule 1 549053400
ORANGE Vaucluse
Formule 1 490344477
ORLEANS Loiret
Formule 1 238764843
ORLEANS Loiret
Formule 1 238866161
PAU Pyrénées-Atlantiques
Formule 1 559844943
PERIGUEUX Dordogne
Formule 1 553086200
PERONNE Somme
Formule 1 322852522
PERPIGNAN Pyrénées-Orientales
Formule 1 468569600
PLAISIR Yvelines
Formule 1 130556265
POISSY Yvelines
Formule 1 239116534
POITIERS Vienne
Formule 1 549550707
POITIERS Vienne
Formule 1 549628102
PONTARLIER Doubs
Formule 1 381468440
PONTOISE Val-d'Oise
Formule 1 130319393
PROVINS Seine-et-Marne
Formule 1 164601777
QUIMPER Finistère
Formule 1 298958282
REIMS Marne
Formule 1 326040621
REMIREMONT Vosges
Formule 1 329324646
RENNES Ille-et-Vilaine
Formule 1 299149260
RENNES Ille-et-Vilaine
Formule 1 299231011
RENNES Ille-et-Vilaine
Formule 1 299518711

RENNES Ille-et-Vilaine
Formule 1 299537784
ROANNE Loire
Formule 1 477726754
ROISSY Seine-et-Marne
Formule 1 360037979
RONCQ Nord
Formule 1 320034610
ROUBAIX Nord
Formule 1 320735713
ROUEN Seine-Maritime
Formule 1 2355911
ROUEN Seine-Maritime
Formule 1 235655959
ROUEN Seine-Maritime
Formule 1 235798687
RUNGIS Val-de-Marne
Formule 1 545609879
SAINTES Charente-Maritime
Formule 1 546921448
SALON-DE-PROVENCE Bouches-du-Rhône
Formule 1 490536881
SARCELLES Val-d'Oise
Formule 1 239949292
SAVERNE Bas-Rhin
Formule 1 388718871
SAVIGNY-SUR-ORGE Essonne
Formule 1 469969988
SENLIS Oise
Formule 1 344541616
SENS Yonne
Formule 1 386656595
SETE Hérault
Formule 1 467480705
SOCHAUX Doubs
Formule 1 381320711
SOISSONS Aisne
Formule 1 450404684
ST BRIEUC Côtes-d'Armor
Formule 1 296614044
ST DENIS Seine-St-Denis
Formule 1 248274108
ST DIE Vosges
Formule 1 329551718
ST DIZIER Haute-Marne
Formule 1 325566363
ST ETIENNE Loire
Formule 1 477365566
ST ETIENNE Loire
Formule 1 477736245
ST ETIENNE Loire
Formule 1 477792143
ST JULIEN-EN-GENEVOIS Haute-Savoie
Formule 1 450047375
ST LO Manche
Formule 1 233720072
ST LOUIS Haut-Rhin
Formule 1 389676830
ST MALO Ille-et-Vilaine
Formule 1 299815710
ST NAZAIRE Loire-Atlantique
Formule 1 240458787
ST OMER Pas-de-Calais
Formule 1 321393915
ST POL-SUR-MER Nord
Formule 1 328646900
ST QUENTIN-FALLAVIER Isère
Formule 1 474955393
ST WITZ Val-d'Oise
Formule 1 534686848
STAINS Seine-St-Denis
Formule 1 248214444
STRASBOURG Bas-Rhin
Formule 1 388498383

STRASBOURG Bas-Rhin
Formule 1 388614746
STRASBOURG Bas-Rhin
Formule 1 388674021
STRASBOURG Bas-Rhin
Formule 1 3388818675
TARASCON Bouches-du-Rhône
Formule 1 490914041
TARBES Hautes-Pyrénées
Formule 1 562367070
THIONVILLE Moselle
Formule 1 382511616
THONON-LES-BAINS Haute-Savoie
Formule 1 450262211
TOULON Var
Formule 1 494064225
TOULON Var
Formule 1 494081414
TOULON Var
Formule 1 494130800
TOULOUSE Haute-Garonne
Formule 1 561350626
TOULOUSE Haute-Garonne
Formule 1 561409503
TOULOUSE Haute-Garonne
Formule 1 561514525
TOULOUSE Haute-Garonne
Formule 1 561750412
TOULOUSE AIRPORT Haute-Garonne
Formule 1 561300099
TOURCOING Nord
Formule 1 320252832
TOURS Indre-et-Loire
Formule 1 247511300
TRAPPES Yvelines
Formule 1 130690022
TROYES AUBE
Formule 1 325783223
USSAC Corrèze
Formule 1 555861111
VALENCE Drome
Formule 1 475836145
VANNES Morbihan
Formule 1 497631623
VERDUN MEUSE
Formule 1 329837676
VERNON Eure
Formule 1 232515008
VESOUL Haute-Saône
Formule 1 384752000
VIGNEUX Essonne
Formule 1 469426060
VILLEFRANCHE-SUR-Saône Rhône
Formule 1 474683157
VILLEMOMBLE Seine-St-Denis
Formule 1 549351010
VILLENEUVE-D'ASCQ Nord
Formule 1 320914899
VILLENEUVE-LE-ROI Val-de-Marne
Formule 1 545975252
VILLENEUVE-LOUBET Alpes-
Maritimes
Formule 1 493223222
VILLEPARISIS Seine-et-Marne
Formule 1 360211000
VILLEPINTE Seine-St-Denis
Formule 1 549380015
VITRY-SUR-SEINE Val-de-Marne
Formule 1 546807600

MARMOTTE HOTEL - RESTAURANTS

These economical and practical hotels are situated in locations on the outskirts of towns and cities throughout France.

The bedrooms offer well appointed en-suite facilities, colour television and direct dial telephones. They also have lounge facilities and a pleasant, relaxing restaurant which serves lunch and dinner as well as breakfast.

Visa cards are accepted for rooms and meals.

BELFORT Territoire-de-Belfort
Hotel Relais Marmotte 384220984
CHALLANS Vendée
Hotel Restaurant Marmotte
251687575
CHARTRES Eure-et-Loir
Hotel Restaurant Marmotte
237345802
CHATEAUBRIANT Loire-Atlantique
Hotel Restaurant Marmotte
240818283
CHATEAUDUN Eure-et-Loir
Hotel Restaurant Marmotte
237457878
CHOLET Maine-et-Loire
Hotel Restaurant Marmotte
241710520
GRANVILLE Manche
Hotel Restaurant Marmotte
233500505
ISSOUDUN Indre
Hotel Restaurant Marmotte
254030056
LA FLECHE Sarthe
Hotel Restaurant Marmotte
243947040
LANGRES Haute-Marne
Hotel Restaurant Marmotte
328575757
LAON Aisne
Hotel Restaurant Marmotte
323203637
LE POINCONNET Indre
Hotel Marmotte Chateauroux
254360909
REDON Ille-et-Vilaine
Hotel Restaurant Marmotte
299727171
ROCHEFORT Charente-Maritime
Hotel Restaurant Marmotte
546876565
SABLE-SUR-Sarthe Sarthe
Hotel Relais Marmotte 243953053
SEDAN Ardennes
Hotel Restaurant Marmotte
324294444
ST AUBIN-SUR-SCIE Seine-Maritime
Hotel Marmotte Dieppe 235843182
THEIX Morbihan
Hotel Marmotte Theix 297470660
VALFRAMBERT Orne
Hotel Marmotte Alençon 233274264
VIERZON Cher
Hotel Restaurant Marmotte
248719797
VILLEUAUDEUR Loiret
Hotel Marmotte Montargis 238982200

HOTEL MISTER BED

This group of roadside lodges offers practical, economical accommodation which is tailor-made for stopovers. Bedrooms have en-suite toilet and shower and sleep up to three persons.

Facilities include colour television and telephone. Ample parking is available for guests.

Mastercard and Visa credit cards are accepted.

ARQUES Pas-de-Calais
Hotel Mister Bed 321938120
BEUVRY Pas-de-Calais
Hotel Mister Bed 321659595
CHAMBRAY-LES-TOURS Indre-et-
Loire
Hotel Mister Bed 247282425
LE MANS Sarthe
Hotel Mister Bed 442241100
LE SUBDRAY Cher
Hotel Mister Bed 248265455
LONGWY Meurthe-et-Moselle
Hotel Mister Bed 382255066
MAUREPAS Yvelines
Hotel Mister Bed 130507883
MERVILLE Nord
Hotel Mister Bed 328496118
MONETEAU Yonne
Hotel Mister Bed 386405592
NANCY Meurthe-et-Moselle
Hotel Mister Bed 383980333
NEMOURS Seine-et-Marne
Hotel Mister Bed 564780632
NOYELLES-GODAULT Pas-de-Calais
Hotel Mister Bed 321207776
OSTWALD Bas-Rhin
Hotel Mister Med 388667784
RANG-DU-FLIERS Pas-de-Calais
Hotel Mister Bed 546143800
STE-SAVINE AUBE
Hotel Mister Bed 325719975
TIGERY Essonne
Hotel Mister Bed 469130003
TINQUEUX Marne
Hotel Mister Bed 326041220

NUIT D'HOTEL

This chain of roadside lodges operates across France and offers comfortable, economical accommodation in pleasant modern surroundings. Bedrooms sleep up to three and have remote control television, toilet and wash basin and self-cleaning showers are located on each floor. Some hotels also have full en-suite facilities. The dining room offers continental breakfast.

Major credit cards are accepted.

ALBERTVILLE Savoie
Nuit d'Hotel 479314550
ANGERS Maine-et-Loire
Nuit d'Hotel 241699999
ANNECY Haute-Savoie
Nuit d'Hotel 450225697
ARLES Bouches-du-Rhône
Nuit d'Hotel 490966633
AVIGNON Vaucluse
Nuit d'Hotel 491312400
BORDEAUX Gironde
Nuit d'Hotel 556749988
BOURG-EN-BRESSE Ain
Nuit d'Hotel 474451135
BREST Finistère
Nuit d'Hotel 298473102

BRIVE-LA-GAILLARDE Corrèze
Nuit d'Hotel 555880800
CAEN Calvados
Nuit d'Hotel 231824546
CERGY Val-d'Oise
Nuit d'Hotel 534241212
CHALONS-SUR-MARNE Marne
Nuit d'Hotel 326211616
CHATELLERAULT Vienne
Nuit d'Hotel 549930439
COIGNIERES Yvelines
Nuit d'Hotel 534611991
DUNKERQUE Nord
Nuit d'Hotel 328213606
ESMANS Seine-et-Marne
Nuit d'Hotel Montereau 564702299
GRENOBLE Isère
Nuit d'Hotel 476500001
GRIGNY Essonne
Nuit d'Hotel 469060101
JOUY-AUX-ARCHES Moselle
Nuit d'Hotel 387383127
LA QUEUE-EN-BRIE Val-de-Marne
Nuit d'Hotel 545940808
LA ROCHELLE Charente-Maritime
Nuit d'Hotel du Rochelle Aytre
546441822
LES ULIS Essonne
Nuit d'Hotel 545940808
LILLE Nord
Nuit d'Hotel 320921212
LIMOGES Haute-Vienne
Nuit d'Hotel 555351530
LYON Rhône
Nuit d'Hotel 474270440
LYON Rhône Nuit d'Hotel 478983232
MACON Saône-et-Loire
Nuit d'Hotel 385299797
MARSEILLE Bouches-du-Rhône
Nuit d'Hotel 442791010
MARSEILLE Bouches-du-Rhône
Nuit d'Hotel 491960063
METZ Moselle
Nuit d'Hotel 387711718
MONTPELLIER Hérault
Nuit d'Hotel 467474646
MULHOUSE Haut-Rhin
Nuit d'Hotel 389598430
NANCY Meurthe-et-Moselle
Nuit d'Hotel 383261040
NANTES Loire-Atlantique
Nuit d'Hotels Nantes 240639717
NIORT Deux-Sèvres
Nuit d'Hotel 549331950
NOYELLES-GODAULT Pas-de-Calais
Nuit d'Hotel 321757515
ORLEANS Loiret
Nuit d'Hotel 238696666
ORLEANS Loiret
Nuit d'Hotel 238740666
PAU Pyrénées-Atlantiques
Nuit d'Hotel 559920880
PERPIGNAN Pyrénées-Orientales
Nuit d'Hotel 468569090
QUIMPER Finistère
Nuit d'Hotel 298101255
REIMS Marne Nuit d'Hotel 326361136
ROUEN Seine-Maritime
Nuit d'Hotel 235922211
ST BRIEUC Côtes-d'Armor
Nuit d'Hotel 296781737
ST GENIS-POUILLY Ain
Nuit d'Hotel 450206767
ST QUENTIN Aisne
Nuit d'Hotel 323089797
STRASBOURG Bas-Rhin
Nuit d'Hotel 388671516

TOUL Meurthe-et-Moselle
Nuit d'Hotel 383643737
TOULON Var Nuit d'Hotel 494090809
TOULOUSE Haute-Garonne
Nuit d'Hotel 494090909
VALENCE Drome
Nuit d'Hotel 475573600

HOTEL PREMIERE CLASSE

A nation-wide group of economical, practical stopover hotels, conveniently located close to autoroutes. Ample parking is available for guests and the modern bedrooms have a double bed (some have twins) and a bunk bed. All have en-suite toilet and shower and colour television, and there are rooms for disabled people in each hotel. There are self-service breakfast facilities and also vending machines offering hot and cold beverages and toiletries. Automatic payment by credit card is available.

Central Reservation number is 64624955.

AGEN Lot-et-Garonne
Première Classe Sud 553682386
AIX-EN-PROVENCE
Bouches-du-Rhône
Première Classe 442242525
AMIENS Somme
Première Classe 322461212
ANGERS Maine-et-Loire
Première Classe 241481717
ANGOULEME Charente
Première Classe 545697913
ARLES Bouches-du-Rhône
Première Classe 490939311
AUXERRE Yonne
Première Classe 386406777
AVALLON Yonne
Première Classe 386330233
AVIGNON Vaucluse
Première Classe (Nord) 490311188
BAYONNE Pyrénées-Atlantiques
Première Classe (Nord) 559559570
BEAUVAIS Oise
Première Classe 344025713
BELLEGARDE-SUR-
VALSERINE Ain
Première Classe 450566253
BESANCON Doubs
Première Classe 381885750
BETHUNE Pas-de-Calais
Première Classe 321569848
BEZIERS Hérault
Première Classe 467359010
BIARRITZ Pyrénées-Atlantiques
Première Classe 559439191
BLOIS Loir-et-Cher
Première Classe 254568078
BOLLENE Vaucluse
Première Classe 490400510
BORDEAUX Gironde
Première Classe 556376844
BORDEAUX Gironde
Première Classe (Nord) 254748928
BORDEAUX Gironde
Première Classe (Ouest) 556160038

BORDEAUX Gironde
Première Classe (Sud) 556367242
BORDEAUX Gironde
Première Classe (Sud) 556368303
BOURGES Cher
Première Classe 248208952
BREST Finistère
Première Classe 298417120
BRIVE-LA-GAILLARDE Corrèze
Première Classe 555861331
CAEN Calvados
Première Classe 231848784
CAMBRAI Nord
Première Classe 327831528
CARCASSONNE Aude
Première Classe 468256364
CHALONS-EN-CHAMPAGNE Marne
Première Classe 326674218
CHAMBERY Savoie
Première Classe 479260288
CHARLEVILLE-MEZIERES Ardennes
Première Classe 324377878
CHASSE-SUR-Rhône Isère
Première Classe 472240402
CHATELLERAULT Vienne
Première Classe 549214832
CLERMONT-FERRAND Pûy-de-Dome
Première Classe 473270113
COMPIEGNE Oise
Première Classe 344901911
CREIL Oise Première Classe 344745617
DIJON Côte-d'Or
Première Classe 380701700
DIJON Côte-d'Or
Première Classe (Sud) 380587474
DOUAI Nord
Première Classe 327875858
DREUX Eure-et-Loir
Première Classe 237644247
DUNKERQUE Nord
Première Classe 328616304
DUNKERQUE Nord
Première Classe 328649074
EPINAL Vosges
Première Classe 329340734
EVREUX Eure
Première Classe 232311739
FREYMING-MERLEBACH Moselle
Première Classe 387813535
GRENOBLE Isère
Première Classe 476354444
GRENOBLE Isère
Première Classe 476548080
GUERET Creuse
Première Classe 555411635
LA ROCHE-SUR-YON Vendée
Première Classe 251479020
LA ROCHELLE LLE Nord
Première Classe 320611164
LILLE Nord
Première Classe 320967208
LIMOGES Haute-Vienne
Première Classe 555355732
LOURDES Hautes-Pyrénées
Première Classe 562420442
LYON Rhône
Première Classe 472489552
LYON Rhône
Première Classe 472570303
LYON Rhône
Première Classe 478265720
MARSEILLE Bouches-du-Rhône
Première Classe 442899883
MARSEILLE Bouches-du-Rhône
Première Classe 491440044
MEAUX Seine-et-Marne
Première Classe 360230139

MELUN Seine-et-Marne
Première Classe 360230139
METZ Moselle
Première Classe 387383757
MONTAUBAN TARN-ET-Garonne
Première Classe 563230001
MONTELIMAR Drome
Première Classe 475900092
MONTLUCON Allier
Première Classe 470288787
MONTPELLIER Hérault
Première Classe 467581080
MONTPELLIER Hérault
Première Classe 467699836
MULHOUSE Haut-Rhin
Première Classe 389604717
NANCY Meurthe-et-Moselle
Première Classe 383332831
NANTES Loire-Atlantique
Première Classe 240752649
NANTES Loire-Atlantique
Première Classe 251790169
NIMES Gard
Première Classe 466296600
NIORT Deux-Sèvres
Première Classe 549082243
NOYELLES-GODAULT Pas-de-Calais
Première Classe 321751212
ORANGE Vaucluse
Première Classe 490346550
ORLEANS Loiret
Première Classe 238638300
ORLEANS Loiret
Première Classe 238732323
PARIS (Ouest - Trappes) Paris
Première Classe 33066625
PARIS (Ouest - Plaisir)
Première Classe 330681721
PARIS (Nord - Chaumontel) Première
Classe 534099191
PARIS (Nord-St Brice-sous-Foret)
Première Classe 534381280
PARIS (Ouest - St Cyr)
Première Classe 534600546
PARIS (Nord - St-Ouen-L'Aumone)
Première Classe 534649200
PARIS (Nord-Ouest Conflans-Ste
Honorine) Première Classe 534901600
PARIS (Nord - Herblay) Première
Classe 239311616
PARIS (Nord - Goussainville)
Première Classe 239928720
PARIS (Sud - Villeneuve-St-Georges)
Première Classe 243864085
PARIS (Est - Noisy-le-Grand)
Première Classe 545922455
PARIS (Est - Boissy-St-Leger)
Première Classe 545980753
PARIS (Nord - Villepinte)
Première Classe 248603941
PARIS (Nord - Le Blanc Mesnil)
Première Classe 248653746
PARIS (Est - Chelles) Première Classe
360089656
PARIS(Est - Torcy) Première Classe
360173019
PARIS (Est - St-Thibault-des-Vignes)
Première Classe 360350134
PARIS (Est - Fontenay-Trésigny)
Première Classe 564426384
PARIS (Est - Mouroux) Paris
Première Classe 564751470
PARIS (Sud - Courtaboeuf)
Première Classe 469311300
PARIS (Sud - Epinay-sur-Indre)
Première Classe 469342577

PARIS (Sud - Fleury Mérogis)
Première Classe 469460741
PERIGUEUX Dordogne
Première Classe 553071755
PERPIGNAN Pyrénées-Orientales
Première Classe 468542221
POITIERS Vienne
Première Classe 549522921
QUIMPER Finistère
Première Classe 298647980
REIMS Marne
Première Classe 326366001
REIMS Marne
Première Classe 326821836
RENNES Ille-et-Vilaine
Première Classe 299311764
RENNES Ille-et-Vilaine
Première Classe 299837110
ROANNE Loire
Première Classe 477709239
RODEZ Aveyron
Première Classe 565781820
ROUEN Seine-Maritime
Première Classe 235641520
ROUEN Seine-Maritime
Première Classe 235665959
SAINTES Charente-Maritime
Première Classe 546933822
SALON-DE-PROVENCE Bouches-du-
Rhône
Première Classe 490530835
SETE Hérault
Première Classe 467432674
SOCHAUX Doubs
Première Classe 381322424
SOISSONS Aisne
Première Classe 323739100
ST BRIEUC-TREGUEUX Côtes-
d'Armor Première Classe 296620710
ST ETIENNE-VILLARS Loire
Première Classe 477926476
ST MALO Ille-et-Vilaine
Première Classe 299818386
ST NAZAIRE Loire-Atlantique
Première Classe 240458000
ST QUENTIN Aisne
Première Classe 323642440
TARBES Hautes-Pyrénées
Première Classe 562512418
TOULON Var
Première Classe 494060706
TOULOUSE Haute-Garonne
Première Classe 561130693
TOULOUSE Haute-Garonne
Première Classe 561711514
TOULOUSE Haute-Garonne
Première Classe 561724505
TOURCOING Nord
Première Classe 320701332
TOURS Indre-et-Loire
Première Classe 247290202
TOURS Indre-et-Loire
Première Classe 247678788
TOURS Indre-et-Loire
Première Classe 247719575
TROYES AUBE
Première Classe 325493370
VALENCIENNES Nord
Première Classe 327211120
VALENCIENNES Nord
Première Classe 327330637
VANNES Morbihan
Première Classe 297454947
VICHY Allier
Première Classe 470599540

VIERZON Cher
Première Classe 248757074

VILLAGES HOTEL

This company operates modern roadside lodges offering economical
accommodation, close to major
autoroutes. Bedrooms are simple but
practical and are brightly decorated.
They have one double bed, a single
bunk bed, toilet and shower en-suite
and colour television. Buffet-style
snacks are available in the reception
area and ample parking is provided.

ARGONAY Haute-Savoie
Villages Hotel Annecy 450273002
BEAUNE Côte-d'Or
Villages Hotel Beaune 380241450
BOURGES Cher
Villages Hotel Bourges 248203280
DIJON Côte-d'Or
Villages Hotel Dijon Nord 380732900
EVRY Essonne
Villages Hotel Evry Cedex 469110110
ILLZACH Haut-Rhin
Villages Hotel Mulhouse 389615444
JOUY-AUX-ARCHES Moselle
Villages Hotel Metz Sud 387384500
LAXOU Meurthe-et-Moselle
Villages Hotel Nancy (Laxou)
383962324
LE COUDRAY Eure-et-Loir
Villages Hotel Chartres 237911100
LIMOGES Haute-Vienne Villages Hotel
Limoges Nord 555359210
MARSANNAY-LA-COTE Côte-d'Or
Villages Hotel Dijon Sud 380588175
MAUREPAS Yvelines
Villages Hotel Maurepas 30629900
NOISY-LE-GRAND Seine-St-Denis
Villages Hotel (Noisy le Grand)
243030003
ORANGE Vaucluse
Villages Hotel Orange 490110366
OSTWALD Bas-Rhin Villages Hotel
Strasbourg Sud 388663938
ROQUEBRUNE-SUR-ARGENS Var
Villages Hotel Roquebrune Sur
Argens 494454500
ST BONNET-DE-MURE Rhône
Villages Hotel Lyon Est 478407475
ST CONTEST Calvados
Villages Hotel Caen 231730033
ST JEAN-DE-VEDAS Hérault
Villages Hotel Montpellier 467479250
ST MICHEL-SUR-ORGE Essonne
Villages Hotel St Michel Sur Orge
469809051
ST PARRES-AUX-TERTRES AUBE
Villages Hotel Troyes 325805561
ST SATURNIN Sarthe
Villages Hotel le Mans Nord
243252428
TOURS Indre-et-Loire
Villages Hotel Tours Nord 247880030
VENDENHEIM Bas-Rhin
Villages Hotel Strasbourg Nord
388204477
VILLEPINTE Seine-St-Denis
Villages Hotel Villepinte 549639811
WINTZENHEIM Haut-Rhin
Villages Hotel Colmar 389808023

INDEX

Please note that not all locations may appear on the maps but the map reference will give you a guide to the nearest large town.